The New Unconscious

Oxford Series in Social Cognition and Social Neuroscience

Series Editor

Ran R. Hassin

The New Unconscious

Ran R. Hassin, James S. Uleman, and John A. Bargh

THE NEW UNCONSCIOUS

Edited by
Ran R. Hassin
James S. Uleman
John A. Bargh

UNIVERSITY PRESS

OXFORD
UNIVERSITY PRESS

Oxford University Press, Inc., publishes works that further
Oxford University's objective of excellence
in research, scholarship, and education.

Oxford New York
Auckland Cape Town Dar es Salaam Hong Kong Karachi
Kuala Lumpur Madrid Melbourne Mexico City Nairobi
New Delhi Shanghai Taipei Toronto

With offices in
Argentina Austria Brazil Chile Czech Republic France Greece
Guatemala Hungary Italy Japan Poland Portugal Singapore
South Korea Switzerland Thailand Turkey Ukraine Vietnam

First published in 2005 by Oxford University Press, Inc.
198 Madison Avenue, New York, New York 10016

www.oup.com

First issued as an Oxford University Press paperback, 2007

Library of Congress Cataloging-in-Publication Data
The new unconscious / edited by Ran R. Hassin, James S. Uleman,
and John A. Bargh.
p. cm — (Oxford series in social cognition and social
neuroscience)
Includes bibliographical references and index.
ISBN 978-0-19-514995-1; 978-0-19-530769-6 (pbk.)

1. Subconsciousness. I. Hassin, Ran R. II. Uleman, James S. III.
Bargh, John A. IV. Series.
BF315 .N47 2004
154.2—dc22
2003021368

9 8 7 6 5 4 3

Printed in the United States of America
on acid-free paper

Contents

Contributors

Henk Aarts
Heidelberglaan 1
Utrecht 3584 CS
The Netherlands
H.Aarts@fss.uu.nl

Nalini Ambady
Department of Psychology
Tufts University
490 Boston Avenue
Medford, MA 02155
Nalini.Ambady@tufts.edu

Susan M. Andersen
Department of Psychology
New York University
6 Washington Place, Ste. 468
New York, NY 10003
sma1@nyu.edu

Janet Wilde Astington
Department of Human Development and Applied Psychology
OISE/University of Toronto
252 Bloor Street West
Toronto, ON Canada M5S 1V6
jwastington@oise.utoronto.ca

Jodie A. Baird
Department of Human Development and Applied Psychology
OISE/University of Toronto
252 Bloor Street West
Toronto, ON Canada M5S 1V6
jodie.baird@villanova.edu

John A. Bargh
Department of Psychology
Yale University
Box 208205
New Haven, CT 06520–8205
john.bargh@nyu.edu

Ute C. Bayer
Fachgruppe Psychologie
Universität Konstanz
Postfach 5560
78434 Konstanz
bayer@soz.psychologie.uni-konstanz.de

Steven L. Blader
Management Department
Stern School of Business
40 West 4th Street, Room 7–18
New York University
New York, NY 10012
sblader@stern.nyu.edu

Tanya L. Chartrand
Fuqua School of Business
Box 90120
Duke University
134 Towerview Drive, Room A304
Durham, NC 27708
Tanya.chartrand@duke.edu

Y. Susan Choi
Department of Psychology
Harvard University
1418 William James Hall
33 Kirkland Street
Cambridge, MA 02138
choi@wjh.harvard.edu

Ap Dijksterhuis
Social Psychology Program
University of Amsterdam
Roetersstraat 15
1018 WB Amsterdam
The Netherlands
a.j.dijksterhuis@uva.nl

Ayelet Fishbach
The University of Chicago
Graduate School of Business
1101 East 58th Street
Chicago, IL 60637
ayelet.fishbach@gsb.uchicago.edu

Adam D. Galinsky
Kellogg Graduate School of Management
Northwestern University
Evanston, IL 60208
agalinsky@kellogg.nwu.edu

Dedre Gentner
Department of Psychology
Northwestern University
2029 Sheridan Road
Evanston, IL 60208
gentner@northwestern.edu

Jack Glaser
Goldman School of Public Policy
University of California, Berkeley
2607 Hearst Avenue
Berkeley, CA 94720–7320
glaserj@socrates.berkeley.edu

Noah S. Glassman
Department of Psychology
New York University
6 Washington Place, Room 484
New York, NY 10003
noah@psych.nyu.edu

Peter M. Gollwitzer
Department of Psychology
New York University
6 Washington Place, Room 781
New York, NY 10003
peter.gollwitzer@nyu.edu

Heather M. Gray
Department of Psychology
Harvard University
33 Kirkland Street
Cambridge, MA 02138
hgray@wjh.harvard.edu

Ran R. Hassin
Psychology Department
The Hebrew University
Mount Scopus, Jerusalem
Israel, 91905
ran.hassin@huji.ac.il

E. Tory Higgins
Department of Psychology
401-D Schermerhorn Hall
Columbia University
New York, NY 10027
tory@psych.columbia.edu

Larry L. Jacoby
Department of Psychology
Washington University
Campus Box 1125
St. Louis, MO 63130–4899
lljacoby@artsci.wustl.edu

John F. Kihlstrom
Department of Psychology, MC 1650
Tolman Hall 3210
University of California, Berkeley
Berkeley, CA 94720–1650
kihlstrm@socrates.berkeley.edu

Jessica L. Lakin
Department of Psychology
Drew University
36 Madison Avenue
Madison, NJ 07940
jlakin@drew.edu

Alan J. Lambert
Department of Psychology
Washington University
Campus Box 1125
St. Louis, MO 63130–4899
alambert@artsci.wustl.edu

Angeline S. Lillard
Department of Psychology
Gilmer Hall, P.O. Box 400400
University of Virginia
Charlottesville, VA 22904–4400
Lillard@Virginia.edu

William W. Maddux
Department of Psychology
The Ohio State University
1885 Neil Avenue
Columbus, OH 43210
maddux.4@osu.edu

Bertram F. Malle
Department of Psychology and Institute of Cognitive and Decision Sciences
University of Oregon
Eugene, OR 97403–1227
bfmalle@darkwing.uoregon.edu

Arthur B. Markman
Department of Psychology
University of Texas at Austin
5.218 Seay Building
Austin, TX 78712
markman@psy.utexas.edu

Kathleen C. McCulloch
Department of Psychology
New York University
6 Washington Place
New York, NY 10003
km413@nyu.edu

B. Keith Payne
Department of Psychology
1885 Neil Avenue Mall
Columbus, OH 43210
payne.265@osu.edu

Elizabeth A. Phelps
Department of Psychology
New York University
6 Washington Place, Room 863
New York, NY 10003
liz.phelps@nyu.edu

Inga Reznik
Psycho-Oncology Fellow
Memorial Sloan-Kettering Cancer Center
1275 York Avenue
New York, NY 10021

Neal J. Roese
Department of Psychology
University of Illinois
Champaign, IL 61820
roese@uiuc.edu

Lawrence J. Sanna
Department of Psychology
University of North Carolina
Chapel Hill, NC 27599–3270
sanna@unc.edu

Lori Skibbe
Department of Psychology
Gilmer Hall, P.O. Box 400400
University of Virginia
Charlottesville, VA 22904–4400
les4f@virginia.edu

Pamela K. Smith
Department of Psychology
New York University
6 Washington Place
New York, NY 10003
pks208@nyu.edu

Alexander Todorov
Department of Psychology
Green Hall
Princeton University
Princeton, NJ 08544
atodorov@Princeton.edu

Yaacov Trope
Department of Psychology
New York University
6 Washington Place, 7th floor
New York, NY 10003
yaacov.trope@nyu.edu

James S. Uleman
Department of Psychology
New York University
6 Washington Place, Room 753
New York, NY 10003
jim.uleman@nyu.edu

Daniel M. Wegner
Department of Psychology
Harvard University
1470 William James Hall
33 Kirkland Street
Cambridge, MA 02138
wegner@wjh.harvard.edu

The New Unconscious

Introduction: Becoming Aware of the New Unconscious

James S. Uleman

Over the past decade or two, a new picture of unconscious processes has emerged from a variety of disciplines that are broadly part of cognitive science. Unconscious processes seem to be capable of doing many things that were, not so long ago, thought of as requiring mental resources and conscious processes. These range from complex information processing through behavior to goal pursuit and self-regulation. Much has changed since Kihlstrom's (1987) description of the "cognitive unconscious." This collection of chapters provides a sampling of some of the most important developments at the heart of this new picture.

The Context

The ancient unconscious in Western thought might be traced as far back as the fifth century BCE in Greece, if we define the unconscious as internal qualities of mind that affect conscious thought and behavior, without being conscious themselves. Hippocrates proposed (and Galen elaborated on) four basic temperaments—sanguine, melancholic, choleric, and phlegmatic—that are based on bodily humors and shape behavior in conjunction with rational (conscious) thought. This same division into unconscious, biologically based influences and conscious, mental influences is echoed in Kant's thought over two millennia later. He distinguished temperament from moral character, with only the latter enabling people to consciously control themselves and be morally accountable to others.

The details of the unconscious mind changed as metaphors for the mind changed over these two millennia, but it was almost always present. Plato's innate "ideas" are present at birth (and his "ideal forms" are eternal), but experience and education are required to make them available to any individual. Aristotle viewed the mind as part of the soul, with the properties of each dependent on the body's condition. His view of people as basically rational, curious, and social left plenty of room for experience to shape habits and dispositions that operated without conscious awareness. In the fourth and fifth centuries CE, Augustine elaborated the concepts of free will, conscience, and individual responsibility to control urges and impulses that arise from our lesser natures. At the beginning of the Renaissance, Descartes developed a psychology based on the influence of an immaterial will and eternal soul on the reflexes and animal spirits that controlled the body. This famous dualism was reinforced by his conviction that what animated the hydraulically operated moving figures in the French Royal Gardens could not be the same substance that animated people. But the nature of this substance and how it moved the body was obscure, even mysterious, and thus not even open to naturalistic study. In some sense, Descartes's unconscious was spiritual.

Whatever frameworks have been used, thoughtful observers of human behavior have almost always found it necessary to distinguish between internal influences that are hidden and must be inferred (fate, temperament, soul, character) and those they believe are transparent, experienced directly, or open to introspection (see Robinson, 1995).

Assumptions about the relative importance of conscious and unconscious influences have varied greatly with the times, and even within the same era. At the end of the nineteenth and beginning of the twentieth centuries, while Wundt and Titchener were building a psychology of what is conscious by training participants in introspection, Freud was building a psychology of what is unconscious. Many of Freud's ideas had already been expressed artistically in the literature and drama of the nineteenth century, and he regarded Dostoyevsky as the greatest psychologist of that century. Freud's great contribution was to gather, elaborate, systemize, and refine these ideas, in an attempt to build a scientific approach to unconscious processes. In doing so, he put the unconscious on the intellectual and cultural map, and gave the term itself currency.

The psychoanalytic unconscious is, to most laypeople and those in the arts and humanities, the only unconscious. It has many more characteristics (besides operating outside of awareness) than can be reviewed here. It includes the id (the innate and inherently antisocial sexual and aggressive drives that blindly seek expression and satisfaction) and most of the superego (the conscience and ego ideals) and ego (processes that deal with reality, such as perception and motor control, and defense mechanisms that mediate conflicts between reality, id, and superego). The primary metaphor is a hydraulic system with various fluids (drives, energy) seeking discharge (pleasure) and being channeled or blocked by defenses and sublimations. It is extremely complex because it includes many interacting processes that are not easily isolated from each other, and that both conflict with and accommodate each other. The conflicts are dramatic and the stakes are high, but the outcomes of these struggles are quite unpredictable. Thus the psychoanalytic unconscious is widely acknowledged to be a failure as a scientific theory because evidence of its major components cannot be observed, measured precisely, or manipulated easily. The theory's complexity renders it largely unfalsifiable. The unfalsifiability of the theory as a whole has not prevented investigators from adapting its ideas to make them more empirically tractable (e.g., chapter 16, this volume; Pennebaker, 1990) or finding support for aspects of the theory in contemporary research (e.g., Erdelyi, 1985). But it does not provide an influential framework for understanding unconscious processes in academic or scientific circles (see Westen, 1998, for a dissenting view).

The "behavioral unconscious" may sound like an oxymoron because behaviorism treated conscious experience as epiphenomena, saw "the mind" as a dangerous fiction, and said nothing explicitly about unconscious processes. Nevertheless, the organism's history of reinforcement and other behaviorally relevant experiences is stored within, and might be called the behavioral unconscious. That history is the key to predicting behavior. Behaviorism avoided the problems of introspection's unreliability and psychoanalysis's complexity and empirical intractability by avoiding analyses of internal processes altogether and treating the mind in some ways as a black box. Behavior and its consequences (e.g., reinforcements) served to make stimulus-response connections inside the box, in much the way that telephone operators made connections on a manual switchboard. The high-water mark of behaviorism's attempt to account for complex behavior is probably Skinner's (1957) book *Verbal Behavior*. Chomsky's (1959) incisive critique made the limitations of behaviorism clear to most, and it is no longer regarded as adequate for explaining most complex human behavior.

The cognitive unconscious was first described by Kihlstrom (1987), and the title of this volume pays homage to his influential essay. In it, he describes the ways in which the computer as metaphor formed the basis for increasingly complex conceptions of human mental processes. In early models, the unconscious referred to preattentive perceptual processes and latent memory traces, so that complex higher mental processes depended on awareness for their operation. Unlike the psychoanalytic unconscious, it has no innate drives that seek gratification without regard to constraints of reality and society. In fact it is rather cold, apparently rational, and amotivational, compared to the heat and irrationality of psychoanalytic drives and conflicts. In later models, complex processing did not require awareness of the information that was transformed, so much more complex unconscious cognitive processing occurs. To illustrate all this, Kihlstrom reviewed research on automatic processes, subliminal perception, implicit memory, and hypnosis. He concluded that "conscious awareness . . . is not necessary for complex psychological functioning" (p. 1450). That is, the cognitive revolution in psychology and the development of cognitive science across disciplines (including anthropology, computer science, linguistics, and philosophy) had discovered a great deal about complex unconscious mental phenomena and provided rigorous methods for studying them.

The Contents

So what is new about the new unconscious? It is still basically cognitive, firmly embedded in cognitive science and historically beholden to the computer as a metaphor. The computer metaphor legitimized complex theories about unobservable processes while apparently avoiding the sins of anthropomorphizing and using homunculi as causes. But as Glaser and Kihlstrom note in chapter 7, the new unconscious is much more concerned with affect, motivation, and even control and metacognition than was the old cognitive unconscious. Goals, motives, and self-regulation are prominent, without the conflict and drama of the psychoanalytic unconscious. And the new unconscious includes the causes of the phenomenal experience of having intentions and free will, of attributing these to oneself and others. It thus assumes and includes the determinants of free will (see chapter 1 and chapters 9 through 11 on theory of mind). In fact, the list of psychological processes carried out in the new unconscious is so extensive that it raises two questions: What, if anything, cannot be done without awareness? What is consciousness for? (see chapter 2).

The other new thing is the multitude of methods used to study this plethora of processes. The chapters in this volume only sample that range, from neuroscience to cognitive and social lab experiments to naturalistic developmental observations (on theory of mind) to field experiments (on self-regulation). Although this book describes its fair share of reaction time studies (including my own), no set of methods is supreme, and converging operations are preferred.

As editors, we solicited chapters from many of the best researchers in this field. Four of them turned us down because of other commitments. We did not ask others whom we might have asked, because we wanted to limit the book's size. So these chapters provide a representative rather than exhaustive sampling of cutting-edge research and theory on the new unconscious.

Fundamental Questions

An important class of unconscious processes is those that are automatic. Automatic processes contrast with controlled processes, which typically require attention and awareness. Wegner (chapter 1) raises a basic question that is implicit in decades of research on "controlled" processes, but seldom confronted: Who controls the controlled processes? He reviews the reasons why homunculi have no place in scientific theories and makes it clear that the question of control is unscientific if it presupposes an autonomous who. Then he turns to an easier question: Why does it feel as though we're doing things? His answer rests on three principles: (1) the priority principle, that intentions precede actions; (2) a principle that intentions and actions are consistent with each other; and (3) the exclusivity principle, that there exist no other obvious causes of action besides intentions. He describes several ingenious studies that support these ideas by demonstrating conditions that create an illusion of free will, that is, an illusion that intentions control actions. He then moves on to argue that the very conditions associated with "controlled" processes are the conditions described by these principles. That is, the characteristics of what we call controlled processes are just the conditions that promote inferences that our will or intentions cause behavior. Our sense of agency is an inference, not incorrigible direct evidence that intentions cause actions.

The mounting evidence that the new unconscious can account for so many complex, "higher" mental processes raises the fundamental question of what consciousness is for. Is it an epiphenomenon, as the behaviorists would have it? Does it have a function? Bargh (chapter 2) reviews evidence from several areas of psychology, all demonstrating that people can perform complex, flexible, goal-oriented behavior nonconsciously. Neuropsychology studies of patients with frontal lobe damage show this in one way, and priming research from social psychology with normal college students shows it in another. Wegner's research (chapter 1) shows how much the feeling of intentional control can be illusory. Cognitive neuroscience suggests that separate pathways are involved in controlling goal-directed behavior and knowing about it. The relevance of recent views of working memory as at least partially unconscious (see chapter 8), evidence from hypnosis, and developmental research on the acquisition of behavioral concepts is also described. What is consciousness for, if so much complex behavior can occur nonconsciously? Bargh proposes that one function of consciousness is to flexibly select behaviors that can be performed automatically, so they then can occur without conscious attention.

Basic Mechanisms

Classifying mental processes as unconscious involves fundamentally psychological—indeed phenomenological—criteria. Yet understanding how they function requires many levels of analysis. The tools and findings of neuroscience have much to contribute to this effort, as Phelps (chapter 3) illustrates.

It would be impossible to summarize the contributions of neuroscience to our understanding of the new unconscious in a single chapter, given the explosive growth and rapid developments in this field. Instead, Phelps illustrates the kinds of complex interactions that are likely to exist in many domains, by focusing on the role of the amygdala in the experience and consequences of fear—interactions among unconditioned fear stimuli, conscious expectations, memory systems, perception, and physiological fear responses. This work helps explain why, for example, long-term memory for emotional experiences is generally better than for neutral experiences, and how the preconscious perceptual analysis of emotional stimuli regulates attention and conscious emotional experience. As chapter 3 makes clear, (social) psychologists and (social) neuroscientists may gain a lot by exchanging ideas, methodologies, and data. We communicate more than we used to, but much less than we should. I do hope that future books in the series that this book initiates, the Oxford Series in Social Cognition and Social Neuroscience, will help bring (social) cognition and (social) neuroscience closer together.

Subliminal perception was one of the areas Kihlstrom (1987) cited in support of his cognitive unconscious. Dijksterhuis, Aarts, and Smith (chapter 4) present an updated and critical review of research on subliminal perception and subliminal persuasion. Given the widespread "knowledge" and strong opinions about these phenomena, they find surprisingly little solid research on these topics. After discussing why so many people (both laypeople and scientists) have such strong opinions, they examine the evidence. They find substantial research demonstrating that subliminal stimuli can change attitudes, consumer behavior, and health-related behavior—under the right conditions. Just what those conditions are, or might be, is an important focus of their chapter and of their recommendations for future research.

Similarity detection is fundamental and ubiquitous, has many consequences, and usually occurs unconsciously. Markman and Gentner (chapter 5) describe three models of what similarity may mean, focusing on their structure-mapping model as the best account of decades of research. They show how it accounts for the role of similarity in allocating attention among objects and features, how similar patterns in events and objects are detected, how repeated comparisons can change the bases of comparison, and how these processes operate in infants and children. Unintentional similarity detection also shapes adults' choices between items, as in economic decision making; unconscious selection of metaphors in analogical reasoning; choices of comparison others that then shape the outcome of social comparison processes; and retrieval of significant others whose similarity to strangers affects our impressions of them (chapter 16).

Conscious thoughts are not limited to what occurred, but often include what might have been. Roese, Sanna, and Galinsky (chapter 6) examine counterfactual thinking—the thoughts about what might have been that put actual events into a larger perspective. While people sometimes generate counterfactuals intentionally, more often they spring to mind unbidden. The authors' two-stage model describes both what activates counterfactual thinking (primarily negative affect) and what determines its content. Chapter 6 goes on to describe the ways in which goals and counterfactuals are intimately related to each other. With performance goals, counterfactual mental simulations can aid planning and improve performance. Their precise form (e.g., additive vs. subtractive) is affected by whether a person's dominant regulatory focus is promotion (gain oriented) or prevention (loss oriented; see chapter 18), and this affects analyses of causality. Affect goals (e.g., mood repair, mood maintenance, and self-protection) affect both the automaticity and content of counterfactuals. In addition, entertaining counterfactuals creates a mind-set in which people are more likely to consider alternatives. Other determinants and consequences of counterfactuals are discussed.

Glaser and Kihlstrom (chapter 7) note how complex the "cognitive unconscious" has become since Kihlstrom (1987) first used that term. Then it was conceived of largely in terms of cognitive processes. Since then, affect, motives, and goal-directed behavior have been added to our conception of what unconscious processes are possible. Glaser and Kihlstrom add to this list, arguing that unconscious processes possess multiple levels of "awareness" and that unconscious metacognition is possible. In support of these ideas, they describe their work on reverse priming, in which "automatic correction for automatic evaluation" seems to occur. Contrary to the usual findings on automatic evaluation, participants in their priming studies show the fastest reactions when primes are extreme in valence and prime and target are of opposite valence. This suggests the operation of unconscious monitoring and overcorrection of unconsciously anticipated biases. Research from other labs shows similar results, as does evidence from research on automatically controlling stereotypes.

Working memory is traditionally thought of as the mental blackboard or workspace where flexible, conscious planning and control of action take place. Early conceptions of working memory were relatively undifferentiated, but recent conceptions paint a more complex picture. Hassin (chapter 8) modifies this picture even further, making the case that working memory can operate unconsciously, flexibly controlling cognitions and behavior without conscious awareness. He supports his argument with evidence from a series of studies that provide direct evidence of the operation of implicit working memory. In addition, he reviews other research on nonconscious goal pursuit to buttress his case (see chapter 2). This gives rise to the apparently oxymoronic idea of nonconscious control. If control is nonconscious, in what sense can it be control? Hassin distinguishes two meanings of control that are usually confounded, thereby resolving this apparent paradox. This allows him to suggest a new trichotomy for controlled processes.

Intention and Theory of Mind

If free will is an illusion, as Wegner (2002) suggests, what produces it and what functions might it serve? Why do we have such a powerful feeling that we, and other people, are doing things intentionally? Wegner (chapter 1) identifies a set of conditions for this illusion. But other important questions remain. Do other species have this illusion? Do all people have it? How does it develop? One set of answers (and controversies) is suggested by research on theory of mind (ToM). People's theory of (their own and others') mind includes conceptions of free will and intentions, as well as desires, beliefs, and a host of other mental states and processes. It provides a basic theoretical framework within which person perception, communication, and social interaction take place. Yet like the rules of the language we speak, it seems to operate largely outside of awareness and be opaque to introspection.

Malle (chapter 9) gives a broad introduction to ToM, describing the ways it functions as an unconscious conceptual framework that enables and is presupposed by a host of other conscious and unconscious processes. In this sense, it provides the conceptual foundation of social cognition. Like syntax, it includes classifications and relationships among (mental) elements that we use unconsciously and that most people cannot make explicit. Its importance is most apparent when it is absent (as in autism) or not fully developed (as among children). He argues that one of the most important ways it classifies behavior is into the intentional and the unintentional. This distinction, along with the distinction between observable and unobservable (e.g., mental) events, allows him to predict differences in patterns of attention and kinds of explanation shown by actors and by observers. He describes four kinds of explanations that adults give for their own and others' behaviors, based on a fully developed but implicit ToM: causes, reasons, causal history of reasons, and enabling factors. Then he outlines the cognitive, motivational, and social conditions that govern the use of these kinds of explanations.

The concept of intentions and the difference between intentional and unintentional behavior is central to adults' ToM (as Malle notes in chapter 9). Baird and Astington (chapter 10) focus on the concept of intention—its place in adults' ToM; how it differs from the concepts of desire and action; and how it develops in infants and toddlers. Of course, the conceptual foundations of children's early understanding of intention are implicit, inferred by observers from children's actions and reactions in natural play and laboratory situations. By the time children are 3 years old, their language includes explicit reference to intentional states. But this early explicit conception of intention is not well differentiated from the concept of desire. Baird and Astington (chapter 10) describe the ways that language development and communicative interactions each contribute to the differentiation of desire from intention, so that by 5 years of age, children's conception of intention approaches that of adults. Language development seems to be critical to these changes.

People's remarkable ability to anticipate others' behavior is based in large part on their ability to accurately infer their states of mind. Most people have the capacity to develop a ToM that they can use to understand others. Lillard and Skibbe (chapter 11) tackle the fundamental question of where this capacity comes from. Some have argued that it is based on innate concepts, represented in a mental module that evolutionary pressures selected for because it confers significant advantages in a species as social as ours. Lillard and Skibbe pose two challenges to a strong modularity view of ToM, with its assumption of encapsulated cognitive processes. The first is the great cultural diversity in how people conceive of others' mental life and the causes of their behavior. The second is evidence that spontaneous explanations of behavior and spontaneous trait inferences (see chapter 14)—both products of the automatic operation of ToM—vary with cultural and social class background. They argue that there is little room for this kind of variation in a strongly modular view of ToM and discuss how these two opposing views of the origins of ToM might be reconciled.

Perceiving and Engaging Others

Not all research on perceiving others makes reference to theory of mind. In fact, it is remarkably absent from most research on person perception, and is not even mentioned in the latest authoritative handbook chapter on the topic (Gilbert, 1998). Such integrations await future development (but see chapter 11; Malle & Hodges, in press). However, there is already a rich and exciting frontier of research on unconscious process involved in perceiving others, which is sampled next.

A remarkable amount of information is communicated to others nonverbally, without either party being aware of expressing (encoding) or interpreting (decoding) it. Choi, Gray, and Ambady (chapter 12) summarize the growing body of research on the unintended communication of personal characteristics such as emotions, beliefs and expectations, information about social relations, and personality traits. What kinds of information get communicated in this way? How accurate are the impressions based on these processes? How automatic are these processes, and how much could be controlled? What functions might these processes serve? Choi et al. describe the methods that they and others have used to study these questions and outline the remarkable answers that this research suggests.

Chartrand, Maddux, and Lakin (chapter 13) summarize what is known about nonconscious mimicry of others' behaviors. Mimicry of others' speech, facial expressions, other behavior, and even emotion and mood has long been noted. What is new is the mounting evidence that mimicry often occurs not only without awareness, but also without cognitive mediation. That is, there is now good evidence of a direct perception-behavior link, which these authors describe. What adaptive functions might mimicry serve, in our species' evolution and in our current social life? What facilitates and what inhibits nonconscious mimicry? Can conscious goals promote nonconscious mimicry? These are the kinds of questions to which Chartrand et al. seek answers, based on the latest research from their own and others' laboratories.

Uleman, Blader, and Todorov (chapter 14) describe a program of research on "implicit impressions"—unconscious impressions of others based on long-forgotten episodes. People may not be able to verbalize implicit impressions or even realize they have them, but implicit impressions nevertheless affect explicit impressions and behaviors toward others. Andersen's research on social cognitive transference (see chapter 16) shows the power of preexisting implicit impressions. Uleman et al. show that new implicit impressions can be created in the laboratory, and that they have automatic, unconscious effects on the subsequent formation of explicit impressions. They describe a new application of Jacoby's process dissociation procedure (PDP; see chapter 15) which shows that both implicit and explicit memory of others affects subsequent explicit impressions. This work provides new perspectives on the sources of errors and biases and ways of reducing them in our perceptions of others.

Payne, Jacoby, and Lambert (chapter 15) develop the idea that implicit attitudes, including stereotypes, consist of biases in category accessibility. Thus they produce errors in how we respond to people and objects, but only when conditions preclude the use of objective information that would produce accurate responses. In this accessibility view of stereotypes and attitudes, stereotyped perceptions occur when controlled processes fail, not when stereotype inhibition fails. Implicit attitudes contrast not with explicit attitudes, but with "the ability to respond in a manner consistent with one's goal," that is, with having cognitive control in situations where accurate perception is possible. They make a strong case for using the PDP to estimate effects of both implicit attitudes and controlled processes within the same task, because performance on many tasks is determined both by automatic (implicit) and controlled processes. Their accessibility model fits their PDP data better than an inhibition model, suggesting that more stereotyping under conditions that lower control—such as making speeded decisions like those of the police officers in the Amadou Diallo case, or forming impressions of others in public—is due directly to the failure of controlled processes, rather than to failing to inhibit or correct the influence of stereotypes.

Andersen, Reznik, and Glassman (chapter 16) summarize an extensive research program that documents how representations of significant others unconsciously influence our responses to strangers. In this research, participants describe significant others (SOs) in one session. Then later, in an ostensibly unrelated session, they encounter a stranger who has some of the features of one of their SOs. Results show that this partial resemblance automatically activates the SO representation, which affects impressions of and emotional reactions to the stranger, all without the participants' awareness. In addition, representations of the self that are associated with the SO also become activated, including in some cases self-regulatory processes that were developed in interaction with threatening SOs. These demonstrations all suggest that "the self is fundamentally interpersonal and relational, providing all people with a repertoire of relational selves grounded in the web of their important interpersonal relationships." And these relational selves can and usually do operate outside of awareness.

Self-Regulation

Self-regulation would seem to be one of the last bastions of conscious self-determination and autonomous agency. But both its failures and successes provide many demonstrations of the operation of the new unconscious. Research reviewed here shows successful strategies for turning goals into unconscious procedures that operate almost automatically when appropriate conditions arise. It shows how unconscious chronic orientations affect decision making and the evaluation of outcomes. And it suggests other arenas of self-regulation where unconscious processes may be shown to operate in future research.

How might consciousness function to make relatively novel, intentional behaviors occur more automatically (as Bargh suggests it does in chapter 2)? Gollwitzer, Bayer, and McCulloch (chapter 17) outline a theory of "implementation intentions" that provides at least one answer. Implementation intentions are situation-specific plans of the form, "If I encounter X, I will do Y." Forming such plans effectively turns over control of behavior initiation to the environment, making the appropriate performance of the behavior later much more likely, and making it less dependent on consciously monitoring situations and renewing behavior intentions. Gollwitzer et al. review remarkable evidence which shows that simply forming implementation intentions makes detection of goal-relevant situations more likely, and initiation of goal-relevant behavior more rapid in those situations, for as long as the goal is important. A great variety of both wanted and unwanted behavior can thus be controlled more effectively. And self-regulation through implementation intentions seems to have few of the drawbacks associated with more arduous therapies.

Higgins (chapter 18) describes two motivational orientations (usually unconscious), how they affect a remarkable variety of decision processes outside of awareness, and how they affect the evaluation of outcomes. The promotion regulatory focus involves emphasizing positive outcomes (both gaining them and avoiding their absence) and is characterized by eagerness in goal pursuit. The prevention focus emphasizes negative outcomes (avoiding them and seeking their absence) and is characterized by vigilance in goal pursuit. Strategies emphasizing eagerness and vigilance each have their advantages and disadvantages. Decision makers are typically unaware of the unintended trade-offs they produce. They affect not only hits and false alarm rates (in signal detection terms), but also creativity, counterfactual thinking (see chapter 6), and how expectancies and values interact. They also lead to value transfer, in which outcomes arrived at through strategies that match the decision maker's orientation (promotion or prevention) are valued more highly. Higgins provocatively questions whether or not these unconscious motivational effects are irrational, and what "rationality" might mean in various contexts.

Trope and Fishbach (chapter 19) pose the question of what self-regulatory strategies people use to protect their long-term goals from being thwarted by short-term temptations. They outline and describe empirical support for a theory that addresses this question, counteractive control theory. Counteractive self-control occurs when people do something, usually consciously, to counteract the effects of temptations to act in ways they would rather avoid. Strategies include imposing penalties for acting badly (e.g., eating fattening foods), giving oneself a bonus for acting well, or reevaluating outcomes. The evidence supports a model in which temptations detract from long-term goal attainment directly but indirectly promote it by instigating counteractive control processes. Counteractive control is goal dependent and almost invariably proportional to the strength of short-term temptations. Current evidence indicates that some (or perhaps all) of the processes of counteractive control can be made automatic.

The Coda

Our view of the new unconscious is partial, developing, "seen through a glass darkly." But like some of the other views of human nature reviewed at the beginning, it may have the potential to revolutionize our understanding of ourselves and change our social institutions, once it is more fully articulated. Some of its features challenge common sense and suggest ways that either common sense will have to be revised, or explicitly and intentionally part company with scientific theory. Folk theories and scientific theories often diverge. But when the object of the theory is our own nature, the stakes are higher. It is not yet clear, for example, whether the new unconscious must challenge our fundamental notions of free will and social responsibility, of merit and blame, and of the self and religious beliefs. Perhaps the drama it seems to lack at the moment, compared to the psychoanalytic unconscious, will be found in how it impacts our culture and institutions in the future. But that's a different book and set of concerns. Until then, there is plenty of research to do.

References

Chomsky, N. (1959). A review of Skinner's *Verbal Behavior. Language, 35*, 26–58.

Erdelyi, M. H. (1985). *Psychoanalysis: Freud's cognitive psychology.* New York: W. H. Freeman.

Gilbert, D. T. (1998). Ordinary personology. In D. T. Gilbert, S. T. Fiske, & G. Lindzey (Eds.), *The handbook of social psychology* (4th ed., Vol. 2, pp. 89–150). New York: McGraw Hill.

Kihlstrom, J. F. (1987). The cognitive unconscious. *Science, 237*, 1445–1452.

Malle, B. F., & Hodges, S. D. (Eds.). (in press). *Other minds.* New York: Guilford.

Pennebaker, J. W. (1990). *Opening up: The healing power of expressing emotions.* New York: Guilford.

Robinson, D. N. (1995). *An intellectual history of psychology* (3rd ed.). Madison: University of Wisconsin Press.

Skinner, B. F. (1957). *Verbal behavior.* New York: Appleton-Century-Crofts.

Wegner, D. M. (2002). *The illusion of conscious will.* Cambridge, MA: MIT Press.

Westen, D. (1998). The scientific legacy of Sigmund Freud: Toward a psychodynamically informed psychological science. *Psychological Bulletin, 124*, 333–371.

PART I

FUNDAMENTAL QUESTIONS

1

Who Is the Controller of Controlled Processes?

Daniel M. Wegner

We are the robots,
We are the robots.
We're functioning automatic,
And we are dancing mechanic.

—"The Robots," Kraftwerk (1978)

Are we the robots? This question surfaces often in current psychological research, as various kinds of robot parts—automatic actions, mental mechanisms, even neural circuits—keep appearing in our explanations of human behavior. Automatic processes seem responsible for a wide range of the things we do, a fact that may leave us feeling, if not fully robotic, at least a bit nonhuman. The complement of the automatic process in contemporary psychology, of course, is the controlled process (Atkinson & Shiffrin, 1968; Bargh, 1984; Posner & Snyder, 1975; Shiffrin & Schnieder, 1977), and it is in theories of controlled processes that vestiges of our humanity reappear. Controlled processes are viewed as conscious, effortful, and intentional, and as drawing on more sources of information than automatic processes. With this power of conscious will, controlled processes seem to bring the civilized quality back to psychological explanation that automatic processes leave out. Yet by reintroducing this touch of humanity, the notion of a controlled process also brings us within glimpsing range of a fatal theoretical error—the idea that there is a controller.

This chapter begins by examining why the notion of a controller is a problem. As we shall see, theories of controlled processes often imply that the person (or some other inner agent such as "consciousness" or "the will" or "the self") is a legitimate possible cause of the person's observed thought or behavior. This supposition undermines the possibility of a scientific theory of psychology by creating an explanatory entity that cannot itself be explained. The task, then, is to examine how controlled processes might work if they are not the acts of such an agent. What happens if indeed there is no controller? The chapter's conclusion, if you prefer reading from back to front, is this: The operation of controlled mental processes is part of the mental mechanism that gives rise to a sense of conscious will and the agent self in the person. Controlled processes do not start with a controller—in other words, they result in one.

The Homunculus Problem

In the film *Manhattan*, Woody Allen searches at one point for the right word to describe his romantic rival. He finally ends up calling him "this little . . . homunculus." He is referring to the rival's stature, in the sense that a homunculus is a little person, a dwarf or manikin. In the sciences of the mind, however, the term is pejorative in quite a different sense. It stands for an absurd explanation—an inner executive agent who "does" the person's actions. Freud's theory of id, ego, and superego, for instance, has often been criticized as a homunculus-based explanatory system in which the person's behavior is explained by reference to an inner agent (in this case, a committee of them) that is responsible for the person's actions. Whenever we explain a behavior by saying that some personlike agent inside the person simply caused it, we have imagined a homunculus and have thereby committed a classic error of psychological explanation.

The issue here, of course, is that a homunculus must itself be explained. The path of explanation implied by the homunculus idea is to reapply the same trick and suggest that another smaller homunculus might be lurking inside the first. This path leads to the specter of an infinite regress of homunculi, nested like Russian dolls, that quickly descends into absurdity. Another way to explain a homunculus is simply to say that it has free will and can determine its own behavior. This means the homunculus causes things merely by deciding, without any prior causes leading to these decisions, and thus renders it an explanatory entity of the first order. Such an explanatory entity may explain lots of things, but nothing explains it. This is the same kind of explanation as saying that God has caused an event. A first-order explanation is a stopper that trumps any other explanation, but that still may not explain anything at all in a predictive sense. Just as we cannot tell what God is going to do, we cannot predict what a free-willing homunculus is likely to do either. There cannot be a science of this.

Most psychologists and philosophers are well aware of the homunculus problem (e.g., Baars, 1997; Dennett, 1978), and it has been generally avoided in contemporary theorizing, with one noteworthy exception. The notions of controlled and automatic processes carry with them the implicit assumption of a kind of homunculus. Now it is true, of course, that most current cognitive and social cognitive research focuses specifically on the automatic side of this dichotomy, so much so that there seems to be progressively less room for the "little person in the head" (e.g., Bargh, 1997; Bargh & Chartrand, 1999; but see Bargh & Ferguson, 2000). But why should there be any room at all? The steady march of automaticity findings is only interesting and understandable because it occurs in the context of its complement, the controlled process. And the controller of controlled processes all too often resembles that inexplicable mini-me, the homunculus.

The homunculus in controlled processing is usually implicit rather than explicit. No theorist has actually said "and therefore, the little person in the head is responsible for the nonautomatic processes we have observed." Baumeister (2000, p. 25) has come very close to this by saying "the self is the controller of controlled processes," and it is not clear what this could mean other than that there is a homunculus to be found controlling things.[1] However, this is a rare expression of what is usually an unspoken assumption, a background belief that controlled processes are somehow more person-like than automatic processes, representing the work of a human agent rather than that of some kind of mechanism. Controlled processes are often seen as conscious, moral, responsible, subtle, wise, reflective, and willful, not because they are described as such in so many words, but rather because they are what is left when we subtract the automatic processes. Everyone knows, after all, that automatic processes may be unconscious, unintentional, primal, and simple-minded—as well as impulsive, selfish, and prejudiced to boot.

The human and the robot inside each person have traditionally been characterized as two different personalities in the person. This was a popular line of theory in early psychology, exemplified by commentators such as Sidis (1898), who described what he called the "subliminal self." This unconscious netherself carries out automatic behaviors (such as those suggested by hypnotists) and performs simple-minded actions. Contrasted with this, of course, is the conscious self, capable of all of the fine and intelligent thoughts and actions that any human or homunculus could desire. The subliminal self was robotic and in its simplicity did not need to be viewed as having a mind. In more contemporary discussions, the automatic or unconscious self continues to be appreciated as little smarter than a bar code reader (e.g., Greenwald, 1992), while the conscious self is still accorded full status as a human agent. These comparisons of automatic processes with the processes of the conscious self leave us marveling at the wonders of which the conscious self is capable. They do not, however, explain the conscious self.

Unfortunately, psychology's continued dependence on some version of a conscious self makes it suspect as a science. In the halls of science, controlled processes are haunted by the controller. They seem to have lower status as scientific explanations than automatic processes because there is a ghost in their machine. Automatic processes are seen as more scientifically authentic, reflecting the true nature of humans rather than their conscious and strategic affectations. So, we grimly but readily accept evidence indicating that automatic processes express racial prejudices (e.g., Banaji & Dasgupta, 1998; Devine, 1989) and render careless judgments (Gilbert, 1989). We accept as well that automatic processes prompt blind mimicry of others' behaviors (e.g., Bargh, Chen, & Burrows, 1996; Dijksterhuis & van Knippenberg, 1998), and we readily assent, too, that automatic processes are devilishly difficult to overcome (Macrae, Bodenhausen, Milne, & Jetten, 1994; Wegner, 1994). Automatic processes seem robotic and deeply "causal." Controlled processes, for their part, seem less than genuine, reflecting unpredictable human choices rather than scientifically respectable causes.

The temptation to imagine a controller seems to be fueled by our deep appreciation of the idea of mind. Early in life, we develop the tendency to understand events that are attributable to minds, and to distinguish them from events that are caused by mechanical processes. The studies of Heider and Simmel (1944), for example, highlighted our extraordinarily compelling inclination to perceive even cartoon geometrical figures as causal agents. The tendency for people to anthropomorphize physical objects and events is a further expression of this natural proclivity (e.g., Guthrie, 1993), and contemporary research on the development of theory of mind in animals and humans suggests that this faculty for mind perception is a strong guiding force in perception more generally (e.g., Carey, 1996).

Our readiness to perceive minds behind events is enhanced further by the experiences we have of our own minds—particularly, the experience of causal agency. We each have extensive experience with the sense that we control our actions, from finger wags to the grandest gestures, and these many instances add up to the convincing intuition that we are controllers who cause our actions. Regardless of whether this feeling that we are doing things is a valid indicator of control, it is this feeling that we tend to equate with the idea of control and that gives us the further intuition that there is always an agent behind the processes that control human thought and action. For controlled processes to reach their full scientific utility, though, they need to be understood apart from any notion of a controller. Controlled processes can indeed be understood as mechanistic processes—for example, as in the cybernetic and dynamical processes posited in control theories (e.g., Bargh & Ferguson, 2000; Carver & Scheier, 1998; Miller, Galanter, & Pribram, 1960; O'Reilly, Braver, & Cohen, 1999; Vallacher & Wegner, 1985; Wegner & Bargh, 1998). These approaches examine the nature of controlled processes without positing a controller. This is the way it needs to be for progress in the explanation of human psychology. The agent self cannot be a real entity that causes actions, but only a virtual entity, an apparent mental causer.

The controller, in this light, is a personal construction that blends into a scientific illusion. The sense we each have that we are agents who cause our actions is constructed and installed on an act-by-act basis each time we experience causing our action. This experience is available to us primarily during the operation of controlled processes. The personal experience of agency is not a good foundation for a science of mind, however, and we must be careful as scientists to appreciate the basis of this feeling rather than to incorporate the feeling in our theories. To free controlled processes of the controller, it is important to examine how it is that people come to see themselves as controllers. We need to explore the genesis of the experience of conscious will.

Apparent Mental Causation

Why does it feel as though we are doing things? The experience of consciously willing our actions seems to arise primarily when we believe our thoughts have caused our actions. This happens when we have thoughts that occur just before the actions, when these thoughts are consistent with the actions, and when other potential causes of the actions are not present. A theory of apparent mental causation (Wegner, 2002; Wegner & Wheatley, 1999) suggests that these principles of priority, consistency, and exclusivity govern the inferences people make about the causal influence of their thoughts on their actions, and thus underlie the experience of doing things on purpose. In essence, the theory suggests that we experience ourselves as agents who cause our actions when our minds provide us with previews of the actions that turn out to be accurate when we observe the actions that ensue.

Consider some examples to illustrate these principles. If you think of standing up and walking to the window, and then find yourself doing this, the appearance of the thought in mind appropriately prior to the action would support your inference that your thought caused your action. Imagine, however, finding that you had walked to the window without any preview. Having the thought appear only after the action was complete would undermine your experience of will. For that matter, an experience of will would also be subverted if the thought appeared long before the action and then was lost to consciousness by the time you walked to the window. Again, it would not feel as if you had done it, and you might then wonder how you got there. The experience of involuntariness in hypnosis and in automatisms such as Ouija board spelling, water dowsing, and automatic writing can be traced to anomalies of priority (Wegner, 2002). In each case, actions occur without thoughts of them occurring just beforehand, and as a result the actions are experienced as unwilled. The priority principle suggests that the thought must appear in a timely way just before the action for the action to be experienced as voluntary, so departures from this sequence lead to experiences of involuntariness.

In a study of this principle, Wegner and Wheatley (1999) presented people with thoughts (e.g., a tape-recorded mention of the word *swan*) relevant to their action (moving an onscreen cursor to select a picture of a swan). The movement the participants performed was actually not their own, as they shared the computer mouse with an experimental confederate who gently forced the action without the participants' knowledge. (In yet other trials, the effect of the thought on the participant's own action was found to be nil when the action was not forced.) Nevertheless, when the relevant thought was provided either 1 or 5 seconds before the action, participants reported feeling that they acted intentionally in making the movement. This experience of will followed the priority principle. This was clear because on other trials, thoughts of the swan were prompted 30 seconds before the forced action or 1 second afterward—and these prompts did not yield an inflated experience of will. Even when the thought of the action is wholly external—appearing as in this case over headphones—its timely appearance before the action leads to an enhanced experience of apparent mental causation.

The second key to apparent mental causation is the consistency principle, which describes the semantic connectedness of the thought and the action. Thoughts that are relevant to the action and consistent with it promote a greater experience of mental causation than thoughts that are not relevant or consistent. So, for example, having the thought of eating a salad (and only this thought) just before you find yourself ordering a plate of fries is likely to make the ordering of the fries feel foreign and unwilled (Where did these come from?). Thinking of fries and then ordering fries, in contrast, will prompt an experience of will. As another example, consider what happens when people with schizophrenia experience hearing voices. Although there is good evidence that these voices are self-produced, the typical response to such auditory hallucinations is to report that the voice belongs to someone else. Hoffman (1986) has suggested that the inconsistency of the utterance with the person's prior thoughts leads to the inference that the utterance was not consciously willed—and so to the delusion that others' voices are speaking "in one's head." Ordinarily, we know our actions in advance of their performance and experience the authorship of action because of the consistency of this preview with the action.

In a laboratory test of the consistency principle, Wegner, Sparrow, and Winerman (2004) arranged for each of several undergraduate participants to observe their mirror reflection as another person behind them, hidden from view, extended arms forward on each side of them. The person behind the participant then followed instructions delivered over headphones for a series of hand movements. This circumstance reproduced a standard pantomime sometimes called Helping Hands in which the other person's hands look, at least in the mirror, as though they belong to the participant. This appearance did not lead participants to feel that they were controlling the hands if they only saw the hand movements. When participants could hear the instructions that the hand helper followed as the movements were occurring, though, they reported an enhanced feeling that they could control the other's hands.

In another experiment on hand control, this effect was again found. In addition, the experience of willing the other's movements was found to be accompanied by an empathic sensation of the other's hands. Participants for this second study watched as one of the hands snapped a rubber band on the wrist of the other, once before the sequence of hand movements and once again afterward. All participants showed a skin conductance response (SCR) to the first snap—a surge in hand sweating that lasted for several seconds after the snap. The participants who had heard previews of the hand movements consistent with the hands' actions showed a sizeable SCR to the second rubber band snap as well. In contrast, those with no previews, or who heard previews that were inconsistent with the action, showed a reduced SCR to the snap that was made after the movements. The experience of controlling the hand movements seems to induce a sort of emotional ownership of the hands. Although SCR dissipated after the movements in participants who did not hear previews, it was sustained in the consistent preview condition. The consistency of thought with action, in sum, can create a sense that one is controlling someone else's hands and, furthermore, can yield a physiological entrainment that responds to apparent sensations in those hands. It makes sense in this light that consistency between thought and action might be a powerful source of the experience of conscious will we feel for our own actions as well.

The third principle of apparent mental causation is exclusivity, the perception that the link between one's thought and action is free of other potential causes of the action. This principle explains why one feels little voluntariness for an action that was apparently caused by someone else. Perceptions of outside agency can undermine the experience of will in a variety of circumstances, but the most common case is obedience to the instructions given by another. Milgram (1974) suggested in this regard that the experience of obedience introduces "agentic shift"—a feeling that agency has been transferred away from oneself. More exotic instances of this effect occur in trance channeling, spirit possession, and glossolalia or "speaking in tongues," when an imagined agent (such as a spirit, entity, or even the Holy Spirit) is understood to be influencing one's actions, and so produces a decrement in the experience of conscious will (Wegner, 2002).

A further example of the operation of exclusivity is the phenomenon of facilitated communication (FC), which was introduced as a manual technique for helping autistic and other communication-impaired individuals to communicate without speaking. A facilitator would hold the client's finger above a letter board or keyboard, ostensibly to brace and support the client's pointing or key-pressing movements, but not to produce them. Clients who had never spoken in their lives were sometimes found to produce lengthy typed expressions this way, at a level of detail and grammatical precision that was miraculous. Studies of FC soon discovered, however, that when separate questions were addressed (over headphones) to the facilitator and the client, those heard only by the facilitator were the ones being answered. Facilitators commonly expressed no sense at all that they were producing the communications, and instead they attributed the messages to their clients. Their strong belief that FC would work, along with the conviction that the client was indeed a competent agent whose communications merely needed to be facilitated, led to a breakdown in their experience of conscious will for their own actions (Twachtman-Cullen, 1997; Wegner, Fuller, & Sparrow, 2003). Without a perception that one's own thought is the exclusive cause of one's action, it is possible to lose authorship entirely and attribute it even to an unlikely outside agent.

Another example of the exclusivity principle at work is provided in studies of the subliminal priming of agents (Dijksterhuis, Preston, Wegner, & Aarts, 2004). Participants in these experiments were asked to react to letter strings on a computer screen by judging them to be words or not—and to do this as quickly as possible in a race with the computer. On each trial in this lexical decision task, the screen showing the letters went blank either when the person pressed the response button, or automatically at a short interval (about 400–650 ms) after the presentation. This made it unclear whether the person had answered correctly and turned off the display or whether the computer did it, and on each trial the person was asked to guess who did it. In addition, however, and without participants' prior knowledge, the word *I* or *me* or some other word was very briefly presented on each trial. This presentation lasted only 17 ms, and was both preceded and followed by random letter masks—such that participants reported no awareness of these presentations.

The subliminal presentations influenced judgments of authorship. On trials with the subliminal priming of a first-person singular pronoun, participants more often judged that they had beaten the computer. They were influenced by the unconscious priming of self to attribute an ambiguous action to their own will. In a related study, participants were subliminally primed on some trials with the thought of an agent that was not the self—God. Among those participants who professed a personal belief in God, this prime reduced the causal attribution of the action to self. Apparently, the decision of whether self is the cause of an action is heavily influenced by the unconscious accessibility of self versus nonself agents. This suggests that the exclusivity of conscious thought as a cause of action can be influenced even by the unconscious accessibility of possible agents outside the self.

The theory of apparent mental causation, in sum, rests on the notion that our experience of conscious will is normally a construction. When the right timing, content, and context link our thought and our action, this construction yields a feeling of authorship of the action. It seems that we did it. However, this feeling is an inference we draw from the juxtaposition of our thought and action, not a direct perception of causal agency. Thus, the feeling can be wrong. Although the experience of will can become the basis of our guilt and our pride, and can signal to us whether we feel responsible for action in the moral sense as well, it is merely an estimate of the causal influence of our thoughts on our actions, not a direct readout of such influence. Apparent mental causation nevertheless is the basis of our feeling that we are controllers.

From Controlled Processes to an Agent

The feeling of conscious will that occurs with any given action is likely to be influenced by the psychological process responsible for that action. If the process allows access to information indicating that thoughts occurred with appropriate levels of priority, consistency, and exclusivity, the action will be experienced as willed, whereas in other cases it will not. So, for instance, psychological processes that create snoring when we are asleep might yield a particularly impoverished array of information and/or computational ability regarding will—and so fail to create an experience that we are snoring on purpose. The information in this case fails to establish conscious will because, in sleep, we do not even have conscious thoughts that can be assessed for their relative priority, consistency, and exclusivity, nor are we likely to be doing much computation.

This observation suggests that variability in the experience of conscious will may be attributable to variations in the availability of the essential sources of information for the computation of apparent mental causation, as well as the availability of mental resources. Such availability could flow from the very processes creating action. Certain processes, then, allow the experience of will, while others do not. In particular, the operation of will may be inferred to the degree that there are available (1) conscious thoughts, (2) observable actions, and (3) time and attention to infer a causal link between them. In each of these respects—conscious thinking, action monitoring, and attention deployment—controlled processes are more likely to support an inference of conscious will than are automatic processes. This line of reasoning suggests how it is that controlled processes can create the experience of a controller.[2]

Consider first the role of conscious thinking. If a person has no conscious thoughts prior to an action, apparent mental causation cannot be inferred. The idea that controlled processes are conscious maps onto this criterion directly. Indeed, it is difficult to imagine a controlled process that ensues without some kind of conscious preview, so much so that it is common to find the term *conscious* substituting for *controlled* and compared with *automatic* in the research literature (e.g., Bargh, 1994; Wegner & Bargh, 1998). If controlled processes involve conscious thought, while automatic processes need not do so, then it is primarily through controlled processes that a controller might be inferred. The same reasoning applies when we consider the intentionality of the controlled process. In emphasizing that controlled processes are intentional, Bargh (1994) and most other commentators allow that the intention may cause the action (and by this suggestion, they breathe a bit of life into the controller). Bargh and Ferguson (2000) and Wegner and Bargh (1998) have recognized this problem and have suggested that concepts of control and intention need to be defined without reference to a controlling agent. The apparent mental causation perspective that follows from this view suggests that the intention is important not as a cause, but because it is a conscious preview of the action that is often consistent with the action that is subsequently observed. The intent that precedes or accompanies a controlled process thus serves as a basis for an experience of will and enables the inference of a controller.

The second feature of controlled processes that allows us to infer an agent is the fact that they involve action monitoring. Automatic processes, of course, are generally understood as unmonitored or even ballistic—processes that once started cannot be stopped or even guided. The outputs of automatic processes may thus never be known to the person. Controlled processes, in contrast, typically involve a feedback loop, a comparison between what was intended and what actually happened. This comparison requires that the person know at some level, sometimes consciously, what action has indeed occurred. And it is this conscious monitoring of the completed action that is necessary for the inference of apparent mental causation. One can only feel will for actions one knows one has performed. This means that many of the automatic actions observed in psychological laboratories cannot give rise to any inference of mental causation. Unless participants in a study specifically know that they are walking more slowly, for example (see Bargh et al., 1996), they will not be able to infer that they consciously willed doing this. When automatic processes do happen to announce their resulting actions and thoughts to consciousness, they may then be eligible to give rise to a sense of agency. But controlled processes do this every time.

The third feature of controlled processes that supports the inference of agency is the degree of attention deployment they allow. Controlled processes are typically marked by slowness and thoroughness, as the attention devoted to them makes them both resource draining and methodical. Consider their slowness first. Time to think is particularly useful when causal inferences need to be made regarding one's own thought and action, and automatic processes are not likely to provide this time. Automatic processes can yield results, often in milliseconds, whereas controlled processes may take days—and at a minimum seem to require several hundred milliseconds. Responding to a green light by punching the accelerator, for instance, can occur almost before we are conscious that the light is green. In a study in which participants were tracking by hand an unexpectedly moving target, for example, the change in their hand trajectory toward the target's movement happened as early as 100 ms following the target jump. However, the vocal signal by which they reported their consciousness of the jump (in this case, saying "Pah") did not occur on average until more than 300 ms later (Castiello, Paulignan, & Jeannerod, 1991). The sheer speed of automatic processes leaves inferences of agency in the dust.

The thoroughness of controlled processes is related to their use of attention deployment as well. A conscious half hour meandering through all the possible responses one might make to an insult, for example, is likely to produce a far more thorough, studied, and balanced response than is a quick, automatic retort. The thoroughness of controlled processes allows them to review and integrate a far wider range of information on the way to their output than is the case for automatic processes. It makes sense, then, that the reasoning involved in examining priority, consistency, and exclusivity for an action is more likely to be developed through controlled processes than through automatic processes.

Because automatic actions do not support inferences of agency during the action, it turns out that many of our most fluid, expert, and admirable actions are ones we do not experience consciously willing. Should we write a particularly beautiful piece of prose, there is often a distinct sense that it happened to us rather than that we did it. Scientists and mathematicians similarly claim that their creative discoveries seemed just to pop into their heads (e.g., Koestler, 1989). This loss of the sense of authorship in skilled action occurs widely in sports as well, such that calling a player "unconscious" turns out to be a major compliment. Admittedly, most people are quite willing to take credit for skilled actions after the fact, as few writers, scientists, or sports stars turn down their paychecks. But the intriguing aspect of automatic actions is that they do not feel willed as they unfold. Because appropriate previews do not seem to come to mind to allow the inference of conscious will, the authors of skilled actions often report feeling like spectators who happen to have particularly good seats to view the action.

Feelings of conscious will are most likely, in this view, for actions that we traditionally understand as involving "willpower." When our thoughts about an action appear very prominently before the action occurs—such as when we ponder in depth our plan to resist that drink or smoke or extra muffin—we then experience an unusual surge of the feeling of will. The exercise of self-control creates an apt circumstance for this feeling because it specifically involves an intense preview period just before the action (of resistance). When we succumb to some automatic or habitual indulgence, in contrast, we seldom think much about it; and so we experience little sense of willing the indulgent act. Automatic indulgences tend to occur when we have thought of the action long in advance of its occurrence (such as when we premeditate dropping by the bar on the way home just in case some friends are drinking), or when we think of the action as it occurs (such as when we're putting the drink to our lips). The optimal time for thought that contributes to feelings of will is a few moments before the action, and this is when our thoughts of moderation, when effective, can yield great waves of will and resultant self-congratulation.

These observations suggest that we feel conscious will as we perform our actions primarily in the case of actions that are caused by controlled processes. These processes allow us the conscious thoughts, self-observed actions, and time and attention necessary to draw causal inferences about how our minds seem to be involved in producing our behaviors. In drawing these inferences, we accumulate the picture of a virtual agent, a mind that is apparently guiding the action. Although this mind is a deeply important construction, allowing us to understand, organize, and remember the variety of things we find ourselves doing, it is a construction nonetheless and must be understood as an experience of agency derived from the perception of thoughts and actions—not as a direct perception of an agent.

Virtual Agency

The creation of our sense of agency is critically important for a variety of personal and social processes, even if this perceived agent is not a cause of action. The experience of conscious will is fundamentally important because it provides a marker of our authorship—what might be called an authorship emotion. In the words of T. H. Huxley (1910, p. 218), "Volition . . . is an emotion indicative of physical changes, not a cause of such changes." Each surge of will we sense in the operation of controlled processes provides a bodily reminder of what we think we have done. In this sense, the function of will is to identify our actions with a feeling, allowing us to sense in a very basic way what we are likely to have done, and to distinguish such things from those caused by events in the world or by other people or agents. Like the somatic marker function of emotion (Damasio, 1994), the experience of conscious will anchors our actions to us in a way that transcends rational thought.

Conscious will is a cognitive feeling, like confusion or the feeling of knowing (see Clore, 1992). Although it does not have an associated facial expression, it shares with the basic emotions an experiential component—we do not just deduce that we did an action, we feel that we did it. We resonate with what we do, whereas we only notice what otherwise happens or what others have done—so we can keep track of our own contributions, remembering them and organizing them into a coherent picture of our own identity as agents. By this reasoning, conscious will can be understood as part of an intuitive accounting system that allows us to deserve things. We must know what we have done if we are going to claim that our actions have earned us anything (or have prevented us from deserving something nasty). Our sense of what we have achieved, and our ideas, too, of what we are responsible for in moral domains, may arise because we gain a deep apprehension of our likely causal role in the experience of will.

The creation of personal action authorship must thus be attributable to controlled processes. This means that automatic processes regularly fail to create an agent self, the sense that there is an "I" who did the action. Automatic processes seem to emanate from an unperceived center, a seemingly robotic source that does not experience its own likely complicity in action causation. Automatic processes can occur and leave us like zombies, often not knowing our actions in advance or afterward, and also without the mental resources to compute our complicity. Automatic processes leave us in the dark that we are authors at all. In promoting an experience of will, in turn, controlled processes allow us to experience the subjective causation of the controlled action, and so open the door to the experience of personal emotions such as pride and disappointment in achievement domains, not to mention moral emotions such as guilt and elevation in moral domains (cf. Uleman, 1989).

Because controlled processes give rise to the sense of authorship, they open up the possibility that thoughts of authorship can influence subsequent action. Controlled processes leave a residue of memories of past authorship, and give rise as well to anticipations of future authorship. It is in this sense that many theorists have spoken of the self as a kind of narrator, creating a life story (e.g., Dennett, 1992). Controlled processes can take authorship issues into account because authorship has been created by other controlled processes in the past and can be anticipated to arise from controlled processes in the future. The experiences of authorship that enter into action this way are not direct perceptions of an agent, it should be remembered, but rather are estimates of the role of one's own thoughts in action that are produced by the system that infers apparent mental causation. Far from a simple homunculus that "does things," then, the self can be understood as a system that arises from the experience of authorship, and is developed over time by a set of controlled processes that manage memories and anticipations of authorship experiences. We become agents by experiencing what we do, and this experience then informs the processes that determine what we will do next.

Yes, this line of thinking does seem a bit cumbersome when we compare it to the naive simplicity of homunculus talk. To be accurate, we must speak of apparent mental causation, or of virtual agency, rather than of intention or of a controller. But the labor we expend to keep the controller out of our theorizing may well repay us with new insights into phenomena that were impenetrable given only the notion that there is a little person in the head. Profound mysteries in the psychology of self and identity might become a bit less mysterious. We might begin to appreciate, for example, how there could ever be multiple little people (as in multiple personality disorder) or how there could be replacement little people (as in spirit possession or channeling) or even how each person's own sense of the little person inside (as in the development of the agent self) might become open to more effective explanation. On the fringes of our current understanding lie many phenomena that have not been tractable because the assumption of a real controller makes them seem quite out of the question. These phenomena do seem to exist, and our further thinking about the nature of control, automaticity, and the self can be informed by them. All we need to do is assume, for sake of argument, that we are the robots.

Real Mental Causation

In focusing on the topic of apparent mental causation, this chapter has tiptoed quietly around the big sleeping problem of real mental causation. Questions of whether thought actually does cause action, for example, have been left in peace, and the issue of the role of consciousness in the causation of action has been ignored as well. This is because the focus of this theory is the experience of conscious will, not the operation of the will. According to this theory, the experience of will is based on interpreting one's thought as causing one's action. The experience of will comes and goes in accord with principles governing that interpretive mechanism, then, and not in accord with any actual causal link between thought and action. This theory is mute on whether thought does cause action.

Most theories of behavior causation have gotten this all confused. Questions of how thought or consciousness might cause action have been muddled together with questions of the person's experience of such causation, and in this snarl nothing seems particularly clear. In large part, this seems to have happened because the feeling of free will is so deeply powerful and impressive. All too often, we take as gospel truth our personal intuition that our conscious thoughts cause our actions ("See, I'm moving my finger!"), and we assume that this experience is a direct pipeline to the truth of the matter.

But imagine for a minute that we are robots. Imagine that our actions arise from a complicated set of mechanisms. Imagine, too, that these excellent mechanisms also give rise to thoughts about what we will do that preview our actions quite reliably. In other words, all the trappings are present to allow us to experience apparent mental causation. If we were robots, would our reports of willed actions (e.g., "I raised my finger") be understood as infallible indicators of the actual causal sequence underlying our actions? If someone had installed a will-interpretation mechanism that used our thoughts of actions and our actions to infer our authorship (e.g., "Thought of finger raising occurred 800 ms before finger went up"), would the output of that mechanism be considered a direct readout of how the action had been produced?

Far from it. The robot analysis team down at the factory would take this output as one piece of evidence, but would want to have tests and sensors and gauges in every sprocket to discern whether this potential causal path was indeed the right one. In this sense, reports of apparent mental causation from humans and robots alike should be taken as estimates of the underlying mechanism at best—and certainly not as readouts of the causal mechanism underlying actions. The way the mind seems to its owner is the owner's best guess at its method of operation, not a revealed truth.

Notes

1. The "self" in Baumeister's theory is more a repository of prior causal influences than it is a homunculus or uncaused cause. So I am probably picking on him unfairly in singling out this statement. Still, such talk of a controller certainly prompts images of a little person.

2. A note on definition is helpful here. Attempts to define automatic and controlled processes have pointed to several features that seem to distinguish them. Bargh (1994) suggested that the processes tend to differ in their susceptibility to consciousness, ability to be intended, efficiency, and susceptibility to inhibition. Automatic processes do not usually have all of these features—they are not simultaneously unconscious, unintended, efficient, and unstoppable—and instead seem to be defined as having at least one of the features. Controlled processes, on the other hand, regularly do seem to share all the complementary features—they are conscious, intended, inefficient, and stoppable. Wegner and Bargh (1998) suggested this asymmetry reveals that controlled processes are the defining end of this dimension, from which automatic processes are noted for their departure.

References

Atkinson, R. C., & Shiffrin, R. M. (1968). Human memory: A proposed system and its control processes. In K. W. Spence & J. T. Spence (Eds.), *The psychology of learning and motivation* (Vol. 2, pp. 89–195). New York: Academic Press.

Baars, B. J. (1997). *In the theater of consciousness.* New York: Oxford University Press.

Banaji, M. R., & Dasgupta, N. (1998). The consciousness of social beliefs: A program of research on stereotyping and prejudice. In V. Y. Yzerbyt, B. Dardenne, & G. Lories (Eds.), *Metacognition: Cognitive and social dimensions* (pp. 157–170). Thousand Oaks, CA: Sage.

Bargh, J. A. (1984). Automatic and conscious processing of social information. In R. S. Wyer Jr. & T. K. Srull (Eds.), *Handbook of social cognition* (Vol. 3, pp. 1–43). Hillsdale, NJ: Erlbaum.

Bargh, J. A. (1994). The four horsemen of automaticity: Awareness, intention, efficiency, and control. In R. S. Wyer Jr. & T. K. Srull (Eds.), *Handbook of social cognition* (2nd ed., Vol. 1, pp. 1–40). Hillsdale, NJ: Erlbaum.

Bargh, J. A. (1997). The automaticity of everyday life. In R. S. Wyer, Jr. (Ed.), *The automaticity of everyday life: Advances in social cognition* (Vol. 10, pp. 1–61). Mahway, NJ: Erlbaum.

Bargh, J. A., & Chartrand, T. L. (1999). The unbearable automaticity of being. *American Psychologist, 54*, 462–479.

Bargh, J. A., Chen, M., & Burrows, L. (1996). Automaticity of social behavior: Direct effects of trait construct and stereotype activation on action. *Journal of Personality and Social Psychology, 71*, 230–244.

Bargh, J. A., & Ferguson, M. J. (2000). Beyond behaviorism: On the automaticity of higher mental processes. *Psychological Bulletin, 126*, 925–945.

Baumeister, R. F. (2000). Ego depletion and the self's executive function. In A. Tesser, R. B. Felson, & J. M. Suls (Eds.), *Psychological perspectives on self and identity* (pp. 9–33). Washington, DC: American Psychological Association.

Carey, S. (1996). Cognitive domains as modes of thought. In D. R. Olson & N. Torrance (Eds.), *Modes of thought: Explorations in culture and cognition* (pp. 187–215). New York: Cambridge University Press.

Carver, C. S., & Scheier, M. F. (1998). *On the self-regulation of behavior.* New York: Cambridge University Press.

Castiello, U., Paulignan, Y., & Jeannerod, M. (1991). Temporal dissociation of motor responses and subjective awareness: A study in normal subjects. *Brain, 114*, 2639–2655.

Clore, G. (1992). Cognitive phenomenology: Feelings and the construction of judgment. In L. L. Martin (Ed.), *The construction of social judgments* (pp. 133–163). Hillsdale, NJ: Erlbaum.

Damasio, A. R. (1994). *Descartes' error: Emotion, reason, and the human brain.* New York: Avon.

Dennett, D. C. (1978). Toward a cognitive theory of consciousness. In D. C. Dennett (Ed.), *Brainstorms* (pp. 149–173). Cambridge, MA: Bradford Books/MIT Press.

Dennett, D. C. (1992). The self as a center of narrative gravity. In F. Kessel, P. Cole, & D. Johnson (Eds.), *Self and consciousness: Multiple perspectives* (pp. 103–115). Hillsdale, NJ: Erlbaum.

Devine, P. G. (1989). Stereotypes and prejudice: Their automatic and controlled components. *Journal of Personality and Social Psychology, 56*, 680–690.

Dijksterhuis, A., & van Knippenberg, A. (1998). The relation between perception and behavior or how to win a game of Trivial Pursuit. *Journal of Personality and Social Psychology, 74*, 865–877.

Dijksterhuis, A., Preston, J., Wegner, D. M., & Aarts, H. (2004). *Effects of subliminal priming of natural and supernatural agents on judgments of authorship.* Manuscript submitted for publication.

Gilbert, D. T. (1989). Thinking lightly about others: Automatic components of the social inference process. In J. S. Uleman & J. A. Bargh (Eds.), *Unintended thought* (pp. 189–211). New York: Guilford.

Greenwald, A. G. (1992). New Look 3: Unconscious cognition reclaimed. *American Psychologist, 47*, 766–779.

Guthrie, S. E. (1993). *Faces in the clouds: A new theory of religion.* New York: Oxford University Press.

Heider, F., & Simmel, M. (1944). An experimental study of apparent behavior. *American Journal of Psychology, 57*, 243–259.

Hoffman, R. E. (1986). Verbal hallucinations and language production processes in schizophrenia. *Behavioral and Brain Sciences, 9*, 503–548.

Huxley, T. H. (1910). *Methods and results.* New York: Appleton Co.

Koestler, A. (1989). *The act of creation.* London: Arkana/Penguin.

Macrae, C. N., Bodenhausen, G. V., Milne, A. B., & Jetten, J. (1994). Out of mind but back in sight: Stereotypes on the rebound. *Journal of Personality and Social Psychology, 67*, 808–817.

Milgram, S. (1974). *Obedience to authority.* New York: Harper and Row.

Miller, G. A., Galanter, E., & Pribram, K. H. (1960). *Plans and the structure of behavior.* New York: Holt, Rinehart, and Winston.

O'Reilly, R. C., Braver, T. S., & Cohen, J. D. (1999). A biologically-based computational model of working memory. In A. Miyake & P. Shah (Eds.), *Models of working memory: Mechanisms of active maintenance and executive control* (pp. 102–134). New York: Cambridge University Press.

Posner, M. I., & Snyder, C. R. R. (1975). Attention and cognitive control. In R. L. Solso (Ed.), *Information processing and cognition* (pp. 55–85). Hillsdale, NJ: Erlbaum.

Shiffrin, R. M., & Schneider, W. (1977). Controlled and automatic human information processing II. Perceptual learning, automatic attending, and a general theory. *Psychological Review, 84*, 127–190.

Sidis, B. (1898). *The psychology of suggestion.* New York: D. Appleton and Co.

Twachtman-Cullen, D. (1997). *A passion to believe: Autism and the facilitated communication phenomenon.* Boulder, CO: Westview.

Uleman, J. S. (1989). A framework for thinking intentionally about unintended thought. In J. S. Uleman & J. A. Bargh (Eds.), *Unintended thought* (pp. 425–449). New York: Guilford.

Vallacher, R. R., & Wegner, D. M. (1985). *A theory of action identification.* Hillsdale, NJ: Erlbaum.

Wegner, D. M. (1994). Ironic processes of mental control. *Psychological Review, 101*, 34–52.

Wegner, D. M. (2002). *The illusion of conscious will.* Cambridge, MA: MIT Press.

Wegner, D. M., & Bargh, J. A. (1998). Control and automaticity in social life. In D. Gilbert, S. T. Fiske, & G. Lindzey (Eds.), *Handbook of social psychology* (4th ed., pp. 446–496). Boston: McGraw-Hill.

Wegner, D. M., Fuller, V. A., & Sparrow, B. (2003). Clever hands: Uncontrolled intelligence in facilitated communication. *Journal of Personality and Social Psychology, 85*, 5–19.

Wegner, D. M., Sparrow, B., & Winerman, L. (2004). Vicarious agency: Experiencing control over the movements of others. *Journal of Personality and Social Psychology, 86*, 838–848.

Wegner, D. M., & Wheatley, T. (1999). Apparent mental causation: Sources of the experience of will. *American Psychologist, 54*, 480–491.

2

Bypassing the Will: Toward Demystifying the Nonconscious Control of Social Behavior

John A. Bargh

Paris, 1986: Doctor Lhermitte accompanies two patients of his to various locations around the city. Both of them had suffered a stroke, which had damaged portions of their prefrontal cortex, areas critical for the planning and control of action. First, in his office, the woman gives Dr. Lhermitte a physical exam using the available equipment and utensils. Later, after they spend a half hour in the professor's apartment, he escorts the two of them out to the balcony, casually mentions the word *museum*, and leads them back inside. Their behavior becomes suddenly different: they scrutinize with great interest the paintings and posters on the wall, as well as the common objects on the tables, as if each was an actual work of art. Next, the man enters the bedroom, sees the bed, undresses, and gets into it. Soon he is asleep. Across these and several other situations, neither patient is able to notice or remark on anything unusual or strange about their behavior.

New York, 1996: University students take part in an experiment on the effects of behavior-concept priming. As part of an ostensible language test, participants are presented with many words. For some participants, words synonymous with rudeness are included in this test; for others, words synonymous with politeness are included instead. After finishing this language test, all participants are sent down the hall, where they encounter a staged situation in which it is possible to act either rudely or politely. Although participants show no awareness of the possible influence of the language test, their subsequent behavior in the staged situation is a function of the type of words presented in that test.

People are often unaware of the reasons and causes of their own behavior. In fact, recent experimental evidence points to a deep and fundamental dissociation between conscious awareness and the mental processes responsible for one's behavior; many of the wellsprings of behavior appear to be opaque to conscious access. That research has proceeded somewhat independently in social psychology (e.g., Dijksterhuis & Bargh, 2001; Wilson, 2002), cognitive psychology (e.g., Knuf, Aschersleber, & Prinz, 2001; Prinz, 1997), and neuropsychology (e.g., Frith, Blakemore, & Wolpert, 2000; Jeannerod, 1999), but all three lines of research have reached the same general conclusions despite the quite different methodologies and guiding theoretical perspectives employed.

This consensus has emerged in part because of the remarkable resemblance between the behavior of patients with some forms of frontal lobe damage and (normal) participants in contemporary priming studies in social psychology. In both cases, the individual's behavior is being "controlled" by external stimuli, not by his or her own consciously accessible intentions or acts of will. Both sets of evidence demonstrate that action tendencies can be activated and triggered independently and in the absence of the individual's conscious choice or awareness of those causal triggers. In the examples that opened this chapter, for Lhermitte's (1986) patients as well as our undergraduate experimental participants (Bargh, Chen, & Burrows, 1996), individuals were not aware of the actual causes of their behavior.

In this chapter, I compare and contrast lines of research relevant to the nonconscious control of individual social behavior—that is, behavior induced to occur by environmental factors and not by the individual's conscious awareness and intentions. Such factors include, but are not limited to, the presence, features, and behavior of another person or persons (such as interaction partners). These are the environmental triggers of the behavior, which then occurs without the necessity of the individual forming a conscious intention to behave that way, or even knowing, while acting, what the true purpose of the behavior is (see Bargh & Chartrand, 1999). My main purpose is to help demystify these phenomena by showing how several very different lines of research are all converging on the same conclusions regarding the degree of conscious access to the operation and control of one's own higher mental processes. Another purpose is to demystify the seeming power over psychological and behavioral processes wielded by some simple words—namely those that are synonymous with behavioral and motivational concepts such as *rude* and *achieve*.

These lines of relevant research come from social psychology as well as cognitive neuroscience, cognitive psychology, developmental psychology, and the study of hypnosis. Yet they converge on the same story: that, at best, we have imperfect conscious access to the basic brain/mind processes that help govern our own behavior, broadly defined (i.e., from the motoric to the social and motivational levels). This harmony between the growing evidence of nonconscious influences on social behavior and higher mental processes (e.g.,

Bargh & Ferguson, 2000; Wilson, 2002) on the one hand, and the neuropsychological evidence from both imaging and patient research concerning executive functioning, working memory, and the control of action on the other (e.g., Baddeley, 2001; Fourneret & Jeannerod, 1998; Frith et al., 2000), is reciprocally strengthening of the conclusions of both lines of research.

Of course, there are key important differences between these two areas of research as well. For example, the fact that our undergraduate experimental participants could be induced by subtle priming manipulations to behave in one way or another does not mean they largely lack the ability to act autonomously, as Lhermitte's patients did. The damage to those patients' prefrontal cortices greatly reduced their ability to behave in any way except those afforded through external, perceptual means. Yet the priming and the patient studies do complement and support each other in demonstrating the same two principles: that an individual's behavior can be directly caused by the current environment, without the necessity of an act of conscious choice or will; and that this behavior can and will unfold without the person being aware of its external determinant.

Social Psychology's Magical Mystery Tour

Two streams of research in social psychology have converged on the idea that complex social behavior tendencies can be triggered and enacted nonconsciously. One line of research focuses on ideomotor action or the perception-behavior link—the finding that mental content activated in the course of perceiving one's social environment automatically creates behavioral tendencies (Prinz, 1997). Thus, for example, one tends to mimic, without realizing it, the posture and physical gestures of one's interaction partners (Chartrand & Bargh, 1999).

This "chameleon effect" has been found to extend even to the automatic activation of abstract, schematic representations of people and groups (such as social stereotypes) in the course of social perception (see Dijksterhuis & Bargh, 2001). For example, subtly activating (priming) the professor stereotype in a prior context causes people to score higher on a knowledge quiz, and priming the elderly stereotype makes college students not only walk more slowly but have poorer incidental memory as well (both effects consistent with the content of that stereotype). Similarly, activating the African American stereotype (which includes the trait of hostility) through subliminal presentation of faces of young Black men causes young White participants to react with greater hostility to a request by the experimenter.

Thus, the passive activation of behavior (trait) concepts through priming manipulations increases the person's tendency to behave in line with that concept, as long as such behavior is possible in the subsequent situation. It is the tendency or predisposition to behave in a certain way that is created, but the situation must be appropriate or applicable (Higgins, 1996) for that behavior to be performed.

The second stream of research has shown that social and interpersonal goals can also be activated through external means (as in priming manipulations), with the individual then pursuing that goal in the subsequent situation without consciously choosing or intending to do so or even being aware even of the purpose of his or her behavior (Bargh, 1990; Bargh, Gollwitzer, Lee-Chai, Barndollar, & Troetschel, 2001). Again, all that is needed is for words or pictures closely related in meaning to the goal concept to be presented in an offhand and unobtrusive manner so that the person is not and does not become aware of the potential influence or effect those goal-related stimuli might have on his or her behavior (Bargh, 1992). For example, even though subliminally presented primes related to cooperation did cause participants to cooperate on a task more than did the nonprimed control group, participants' subsequent ratings of how much they had wanted and tried to cooperate during the task were uncorrelated with their actual degree of cooperative behavior. Yet the same items administered to participants who had been explicitly (i.e., consciously) instructed to cooperate did significantly correlate with their actual degree of cooperation (Bargh et al., 2001, Experiment 2).

Alternatively, words related to achievement and high performance might be embedded along with other, goal-irrelevant words in a puzzle, or words related to cooperation might be presented subliminally in the course of an ostensible reaction time task. Just as with single types of behavior such as politeness or intelligence, presenting goal-related stimuli in this fashion causes the goal to become active and then operate to guide behavior toward that goal over an extended period of time. People primed with achievement-related stimuli perform at higher levels on subsequent tasks than do control groups; those primed with cooperation-related stimuli cooperate more in a commons-dilemma game; and those primed with evaluation-related stimuli form impressions of other people while those in a control group do not (see review in Chartrand & Bargh, 2002).

Such effects are unlikely to be restricted to the laboratory environment; for example, merely thinking about the significant other people in our lives (something we all do quite often) causes the goals we pursue when with them to become active and to then guide our behavior without our choosing or knowing it, even when those individuals are not physically present (Fitzsimons & Bargh, 2003). And the nonconscious ideomotor effect of perception on action becomes a matter of widespread social importance when applied to the mass exposure of people to violent behavior on television or in movies (see Hurley, 2002).

For many years now, social psychologists have been busily documenting all of the complex, higher mental processes that are capable of occurring nonconsciously. Yet we still know little of how these effects occur, how they develop, and why so much in the way of complex, higher mental processes should take place outside of conscious awareness and control. Without some consideration of these issues, automatic behavior, judgment, and goal pursuit will continue to seem somewhat magical and mysterious to many people.[1]

Two aspects of these phenomena seem particularly magical. One is the profound dissociation between these varied psychological and behavioral responses to one's environment, on the one hand, and one's intentions and awareness of them on the other. People are behaving, interacting, and pursuing goals, all apparently without meaning to or knowing they are doing so. How is this possible? The second mysterious feature of these effects is that the same verbal or pictorial stimuli produce all of them. All it takes, it seems, is to activate the relevant concept in some manner—achievement or rudeness or cooperation or slowness, and so on—then, its activation and effect immediately spread and project to evaluations and approach-avoidance tendencies, to putting motivations and goals into play, and to creating traitlike behavior tendencies in the current situation. What accounts for this remarkable power of concepts?

Demystifying the Nonconscious Control of Higher Mental Processes

The Illusion of Conscious Control

One reason why these effects seem magical is our fundamental belief in our own free will, which is derived in large part from our subjective experience of possessing it. We (on occasion) experience making a choice or forming an intention, and then enacting the decision or behavior, and take this as incontrovertible evidence that the intention caused the outcome. Whether or not it does, the subjective experience of will alone is insufficient, and even flawed, evidence of the existence of free will. As Hume (1748) first noted, we can observe antecedents, and we can observe consequences, but we cannot directly observe causal connections between events; that is, causation is always an inference and never something directly observable.

Wegner (2002) has applied this principle to the subjective experience of free will, arguing that it is logically impossible for us to have introspective access to the causal connection between determining forces and influences, and their behavioral consequences. More than that, he has furnished empirical demonstrations that our experience of willing is rooted in a causal attribution process that can be experimentally manipulated to produce false experiences of will.

Wegner and Wheatley (1999) reported studies in which participants used a computer mouse to move a cursor around a computer screen filled with pictures of objects, doing so along with another participant (actually a confederate of the experimenters) so that the two of them jointly determined the cursor's location. While they were doing this, the names of the different objects were spoken to them one at a time over headphones. Unknown to the actual participant, the confederate was given instructions over his or her headphones from time to time to cause the screen cursor to point to a given object. By manipulating whether the name of the moved-to object had or had not been presented to the participant just (i.e., a second or two) before the cursor landed on it (as opposed to earlier, or after the cursor had landed on it), so that the "thought" about that object had been in the participant's consciousness just prior to the cursor's movement to it, the experimenters were able to manipulate the participant's attributions of personal responsibility and control over the cursor's movement. In these experiments, therefore, beliefs about personal agency could be induced by manipulations of the key factors presumed to underlie feelings of will, according to the authors' attributional model—even though those factors had not, in fact, been causal in the cursor's movement.

Such findings demonstrate that people do not and cannot have direct access to acts of causal intention and choice. Kenneth Bowers (1984) had anticipated this finding when he pointed out that it is "the purpose of psychological research to enhance our comprehension and understanding of causal influences operating on thought and action. Notice, however, that such research would be totally redundant if the causal connections linking thought and behavior to its determinants were directly and automatically self-evident to introspection" (p. 250).

Within (especially social) psychology, a further reason for the widely held belief in a free, undetermined will is the contrast often made between automatic (nonconscious, implicit) and controlled (conscious, explicit) cognitive processes in the many dual-process models of social (and nonsocial) psychological phenomena (see Chaiken & Trope, 1999). Here, automatic processes are seen as determined, mechanistic, and externally (environmentally) triggered, while controlled processes are largely seen as their antithesis, leading to an implicit understanding of them as internally instigated and somehow undetermined and without mechanism. But it is another logical error to consider only automatic processes as caused and having underlying mechanisms, while controlled processes (somehow) do not, and are thus "free" (see Bargh & Ferguson, 2000). Regardless, this implicit belief in the uncaused, almost metaphysical nature of conscious or controlled mental processes has existed in psychology for some time. Indeed, it was the main reason for their rejection as psychological phenomena by behaviorism, an irony noted many years ago by Donald Campbell (1969):

> The stubborn certainty I find in my experimental psychologist [behaviorist] friends on this point bespeaks not only a naïve realism . . . but also a mentalistic dualism. They tend to forget that thinking, decision making, or rational inference is carried out by brain tissue fully as much as are automatic reactions. They tend to think of them instead as purely mental. (pp. 64–65)

Neuropsychological Mechanisms of Nonconscious Control

Thus far I have argued for the existence of sophisticated nonconscious monitoring and control systems that can guide behavior over extended periods of time in a changing environment, in pursuit of desired goals. Recent neuropsychological evidence, reviewed in this section, is consistent with these claims, as well as with the core proposition that conscious intention and behavioral (motor) systems are fundamentally dissociated in the brain. In other words, the evidence shows that much if not most of the workings of the motor systems that guide action are opaque to conscious access (see Prinz, 2003). This helps greatly to demystify the notion of nonconscious social behavior, because such a dissociation between motoric behavior and conscious awareness is now emerging as a basic structural feature of the human brain.

The brain structure that has emerged as the primary locus of automatic, nonconsciously controlled motor programs is the cerebellum, and specifically the neocerebellum (Thach, 1996). With frequent and consistent experience of the same behaviors in the same environmental context, this brain structure links the representations of those specific behavioral contexts with the relevant premotor, lower level movement generators. In this way, complex behavior can be mapped onto specific environmental features and contexts and so be guided automatically by informational input by the environment (i.e., bypassing the need for conscious control and guidance). Critically, cerebellar output extends even to the main planning area of the brain, the prefrontal cortex, providing a plausible neurological basis for the operation of automatic, nonconscious action plans (e.g., Bargh & Gollwitzer, 1994). As Thach (1996) concludes from his review of research on the role and function of the cerebellum, "[it] may be involved in combining these cellular elements, so that, through practice, an experiential context can automatically evoke an action plan" (p. 428).

Evidence from the study of brain evolution also points to an important role for the (neo)cerebellum in the deliberate acquisition of new skills (see Donald, 2001, pp. 191–197). A major advance in human cognitive capacity and capability was the connection between the prefrontal cortex and the neocerebellum, which increased in size by a factor of five. This expanded pathway enables nonconscious control over higher executive mental processes, because it connects the main cerebellar receiving areas in the brain stem with the frontal tertiary cortex (two levels of analysis removed from direct sensation). This part of the cortex receives inputs only from secondary analysis areas of the brain (which take input only from other mental representations and not from sensory organs), and thus is entirely buffered from direct sensory areas. "The fact that these pathways are connected to high level cognitive regions places the cerebellum in a strategic location. . . . The overwhelming size of this connection to the prefrontal areas suggests an important executive role, probably in the generation of automated programs of executive control" (Donald, 2001, pp. 196–197). Hence, there appears to be a sound anatomical basis for the notion of nonconscious guidance of higher mental processes, such as interpersonal behavior and sophisticated goal pursuit.

Dissociations Between Mental Systems for "Knowing" versus "Doing"

Several lines of cognitive neuroscience research support the idea of a dissociation between conscious awareness and intention, on the one hand, and the operation of complex motor and goal representations on the other (Prinz, 2003). One major area of such research focuses on the distinct and separate visual input pathways devoted to perception versus action.

Separate Visual Input Pathways The first such evidence came from a study of patients with lesions in specific brain regions (Goodale, Milner, Jakobsen, & Carey, 1991). Those with lesions in the parietal lobe region could identify an object but not reach for it correctly based on its spatial orientation (such as a book in a horizontal versus vertical position), whereas those with lesions in the ventral-visual system could not recognize or identify the item but were nonetheless able to reach for it correctly when asked in a casual manner to take it from the experimenter. In other words, the latter group showed appropriate action toward an object in the absence of conscious awareness or knowledge of its presence.

Decety and Grèzes (1999) and Norman (2002) concluded from this and related evidence that two separate cortical visual pathways are activated during the perception of human movement: a dorsal one for action tendencies based on that information, and a ventral one used for understanding and recognition of it. The dorsal system operates mainly outside of conscious awareness, while the workings of the ventral system are normally accessible to consciousness. Jeannerod (2003) has similarly argued that there exist two different representations of the same object, one "pragmatic" and the other "semantic." The former are actional, used for interacting with the object; the latter are for knowing about and identifying the object.

Thus the dorsal stream (or activated pragmatic representation) could drive behavior in response to environmental stimuli in the absence of conscious awareness or understanding of that external information. It could, in principle, support a nonconscious basis for action that is primed or driven by the current or recent behavioral informational input from others—in other words, be a neurological basis for the chameleon effect of nonconscious imitation of the behavior of one's interaction partners (Chartrand & Bargh, 1999). Moreover, the discovery of "mirror neurons," first in macaque monkeys (Rizzolatti & Arbib, 1998) and now in humans (Buccino et al., 2001)—in which simply watching mouth, hand, and foot movements activates the same functionally specific regions of the premotor cortex as when performing those same movements oneself—is further compelling evidence for a direct connection between visual information and action control (see also Woody & Sadler, 1998).

Taken together, these findings implicate the parietal cortex as a potential candidate for the location of (social) priming effects. Recall that Goodale et al. (1991) had concluded from their patients that those with lesions in the parietal lobe region could identify an object but not reach for it correctly, but those with intact parietal lobes but lesions in the ventral-visual system could reach for it correctly even though they could not recognize or identify it. Lhermitte's patients had intact parietal cortices that enabled them to act, but solely upon the behavioral suggestions afforded by the environmental situations or objects (i.e., primes).

Lack of Conscious Access to Operating Behavior Procedures Related to this existence of a visual input pathway directly connected to the action system and relatively inaccessible to conscious awareness is that there is also minimal if any conscious access to any operating motor system (see review in Frith et al., 2000). This research is showing, to a startling degree, just how unaware we are of how we move and make movements in space. Again, this evidence is consistent with the proposition that our behavior can be outside of conscious guidance and control.

A person cannot possibly think about and be consciously aware of all of the individual muscle actions in compound and sequential movements—there are too many of them and they are too fast (see, e.g., Thach, 1996). Therefore they can occur only through some process that is automatic and subconscious. Empirical support for this conclusion comes from a study by Fourneret and Jeannerod (1998). Participants attempted to trace a line displayed on a computer monitor, but with their drawing hand hidden from them by a mirror. Thus they were not able to see how their hand actually moved in order to reproduce the drawing; they had to refer to a graphical representation of that movement on a computer monitor in front of them. However, unknown to the participants, substantial bias had been programmed into the translation of their actual movement into that which was displayed on the screen, so that the displayed line did not actually move in the same direction as had their drawing hand. Despite this, all participants felt and reported great confidence that their hand had indeed moved in the direction shown on the screen. This could only have occurred if normal participants have little or no direct conscious access to their actual hand movements.

Dissociations Between Intention and Action Within Working Memory

Under the original concept of working memory as a unitary short-term store, or that portion of long-term memory that was currently in conscious awareness (e.g., Atkinson & Shiffrin, 1968), the idea of nonconscious operation of working memory structures was incoherent at best. If working memory was a single mental "organ" that held both the current goal and purpose, along with the relevant environmental information on which that goal was acting, then one should always be aware of the intention or goal that is currently residing in active, working memory. There cannot be dissociations within the operations of the same mental structure.

Yet such dissociations do in fact exist between conscious intention and behavior, even complex social behavior as exhibited by Lhermitte's patients, and it is these dissociations that are most relevant to understanding the mechanisms underlying nonconscious social behavior and goal pursuit. Such complex behavior, which is continually responsive to ongoing environmental events and coordinated with the behavior of others, has to involve the operation of the brain structures that support working memory—namely the frontal and prefrontal cortex. But if working memory contents are accessible to conscious awareness (cf. chapter 8, this volume), how can such dissociations exist?

The answer to this apparent paradox, of course, is that working memory is not a single unitary structure. This idea was originally proposed by Baddeley and Hitch (1974; see also Baddeley, 1986), who envisaged a system comprising multiple components, not just for the temporary storage of information (the phonological loop and visuospatial scratchpad) but also for the direction and allocation of limited attention (the "central executive"). In a parallel development, psychiatrists working with patients with frontal lobe damage—the frontal lobes being brain structures underlying the executive control functions of working memory (Baddeley, 1986)—were noting how the behavioral changes associated with frontal lobe damage were exceedingly complex and variable, depending on the exact locations of the damage (Mesulam, 1986, p. 320). This too was consistent with the notion that executive control was not a single resource but rather comprised of several distinct specialized functions, located in different parts of the frontal and prefrontal cortex.

If so, then at least in theory it becomes possible that there are dissociations between consciously held intentions on the one hand and the goal-driven operation of working memory structures on the other. This is what is manifested in Lhermitte's (1986) syndrome; as he called it, "an excessive control of behavior by external stimuli at the expense of behavioral autonomy" (p. 342). Postmortem analyses of his patients showed inferior prefrontal lesions in the same location of the brain. These had produced excessive behavioral dependency on the environment (which he termed environmental dependency syndrome or EDS)—the imitation of others' gestures and behaviors without control; also utilization of tools and props to behave in the way they suggested or afforded. Lhermitte concluded that "EDS is a loss of autonomy: for the patient, the social and physical environments issue the order to use them, even though the patient himself or herself has neither the idea nor the intention to do so" (p. 341).

How exactly did damage to the inferior prefrontal regions of the brain result in this loss of autonomy, of one's behavior being so strongly controlled by the environment? This is a critical question for present purposes because, as noted at the outset of this chapter, there are striking similarities between the behavior of Lhermitte's patients and that of "primed" normal college students in this regard. Lhermitte (1986) reasoned that EDS is due to the "liberation of parietal lobe activity, which is no longer submitted to the inhibitory effect of the frontal lobe. . . . The frontal lobe systems that control the parietal sensorimotor systems have been known for a long time. The hypothesis that these systems link the individual to the environment is logical" (p. 342). Subsequent research in cognitive neuroscience has largely supported Lhermitte's deductions. Frith et al. (2000) concluded from their review of this research that intended movements are normally represented in the prefrontal and premotor cortex, but the representations actually used to guide action are in the parietal cortex. In other words, intentions and the motor representations used to guide behavior are apparently held in anatomically separate, distinct parts of the brain. This makes it possible for some patients to no longer be able to link their intentions to their actions if there is impairment in the location where intended movements are represented, but no impairment in the location where action systems actually operate.

The finding that within working memory, representations of one's intentions (accessible to conscious awareness) are stored in a different location and structure from the representations used to guide action (not accessible) is of paramount importance to an understanding of the mechanisms underlying priming effects in social psychology. If intentions and corresponding action plans were stored in the same location (or if there were conscious access to all of the operations of working memory; see chapter 8), so that awareness of one's intention was solely a matter of conscious access to the currently operative goal or behavior program, then it would be difficult to see how nonconscious control over social behavior could be possible. This finding alone—a dissociation within working memory itself between conscious intention and action—has the potential to remove much of the mystery behind the nonconscious activation and guidance of complex social behavior and goal pursuit. The storage of current intentions in brain locations that are anatomically separate from their associated and currently operating action programs would appear to be nothing less than the neural basis for nonconscious goal pursuit and other forms of unintended behavior.

Similarities of Priming and Hypnosis

The classic phenomenon demonstrating a dissociation between conscious will and behavior is hypnosis. Here too, the phenomenon has long been seen as magical and mysterious, and in fact was often featured in carnival and county fair magic shows, in which subjects were somehow induced to do bizarre and even superhuman acts. But hypnosis is also used today as an alternative to anesthesia, such that the patient feels no pain although undergoing a normally quite painful procedure. In reviewing the hypnosis literature up to that point, Sarbin and Coe (1972) remarked on how the many behaviors induced by hypnotic means violate our expectations of the normal limits of human behavior, which we normally think of as being under our own control:

> [This] aspect of the hypnotic situation creates surprise and puzzlement. *How can we account for the apparent magnitude of response to such a benign stimulus?* How can only a verbal request bring about so dramatic a change as analgesia to the surgeon's scalpel? . . . The tendency is to interpret these exaggerated responses as being almost magical. (p. 17, italics in original)

The various modern theories of hypnosis, such as those of Hilgard (1986), Woody and Bowers (1994), and Kihlstrom (e.g., 1998) are dissociation theories of one sort or another; Hilgard and Kihlstrom propose that the person does not experience the control of his or her own behavior, while Woody and Bowers argued that hypnosis may alter not just the self-perception of the control of one's behavior but the actual nature of that control (dissociated control theory). In this theory, highly hypnotizable people's subsystems of control may be relatively directly or automatically accessed, without being governed by higher level executive control as much as they normally would.

There are obvious parallels between hypnotic and priming phenomena, and the neuropsychological research reviewed above supports the notion of dissociated will or control in hypnosis as well as in priming effects. In both cases, the will is apparently controlled from outside, by external forces. However, there are also important differences between hypnosis and priming phenomena. For one thing, only 15% or so of people are so deeply hypnotizable that they will carry out posthypnotic suggestions in which their behavior is not guided by their own conscious intention (Kihlstrom, 1998), whereas research that has demonstrated the priming of goals or social behavior involved randomly selected (normal) participants. The reason for this difference may lie in the participants' relative degrees of knowledge of the potential influence of the hypnotic suggestion versus the prime: in the former situation, one is certainly aware of the intent of the hypnotist to make one behave in a certain way, but in the priming situation one is not. The latter thus enables a more passive influence of the environment; it also allows a cleaner dissociation between awareness of what one is doing or trying to do, and one's actual actions. Nevertheless, given the obvious similarities between hypnosis and social priming phenomena, it would be interesting to explore further the potential common mechanisms underlying them. (For instance, do people who are more easily and deeply hypnotized also show stronger priming effects?)

Demystifying the Power of Concepts

One other "magical" issue needs to be addressed. How is it, in the goal and behavior priming research, that the same verbal or pictorial stimuli can produce such a variety of effects? In an automatic evaluation study (see Bargh, Chaiken, Raymond, & Hymes, 1996; Duckworth, Bargh, Garcia, & Chaiken, 2002), the prime "achieve," for example, immediately activates the concept "good" with spreading, unintended consequences for subsequent concept accessibility (see Ferguson & Bargh, 2002). The same word as a priming stimulus in an impression formation task causes the participant to view the target person as more achieving in nature. If the dependent variable is changed instead to a measure of the participant's own behavior, he or she shows higher performance on that task and also manifests the classic qualities of motivational states such as persistence and returning to finish an uncompleted task (Bargh et al., 2001). How can the mere activation of the identical concept, through presenting synonyms of it in an unobtrusive, offhand manner, produce such strong effects on such a variety of psychological dependent measures? What is the nature of this power of activated concepts over our judgments and behavior?

The Acquisition of Behavioral Concepts in Young Children

To answer this question, we must turn to how concepts develop in young children in the first place. According to the influential research and theories of Vygotsky (1934/1962) and Luria (1961), learning a concept involves invoking it, linking it with the performance procedure and external information for which it stands. This is Vygotsky's "outside-inside" principle: Symbolic thought first represents external action, and only later becomes internal speech (i.e., thought; see Bruner, 1961; Donald, 2001, p. 250). Vygotsky argued that concepts and functions exist for the child first in the social or interpersonal sphere and only later are internalized as intrapsychic concepts (see Wertsch, 1985, p. 64).

Thus, according to this framework, the child learns behavioral concepts initially by having them paired by the caretaker with the observable, external features of those behaviors. In this way, the early learning of behavior concepts is linked to the perceptual features of that behavior, to what it means to behave in that certain way. The strong associations formed in early development between the perceptual features of a type of social behavior and the behavior concept itself is likely a major contributor to the spontaneous behavior-to-trait inference effect documented by Uleman and his colleagues (e.g., chapter 14, this volume).

But social behavior and goal-priming research reverses this effect, by presenting synonyms of the concept under scrutiny and assessing whether the participant then behaves in that manner. Thus not only must concepts be learned by the young child in terms of their external observable features ("That is a polite boy"; "That was a mean thing to say"), but they also must be strongly associated with the behavioral procedures or action systems used to behave in that same way oneself. This was, in fact, another important part of the theory. According to Luria (1961, p. 17), it is through these behavior concepts that the parent or caretaker controls the very young child's behavior, naming objects and giving orders and instructions using behavior concepts. It is through the use of words that he or she steers the child's behavior. In this way, the behavior concept becomes strongly—and directly—associated with the mental representation of how to behave that way.

Note also that at this young age there is not a matter of choice or personal selection of the behavior. The child is not given an option; the behavior word is understood as an imperative and obligatory act to be performed. Luria (1961, p. 52) called this the "impellant or initiating function of speech." Thus the linkage, in early learning, of the concept with the behavioral procedure does not include an intervening choice point or act of will—rather, the child is told what to do. It is only well after this imperative nature of word-to-behavior associations is established that the child later learns to formulate his or her own wishes and intentions. But the original, early learning of the behavior concept is as an imperative, choiceless relation.

So in a very real sense, according to this developmental framework, the original and earliest learning of a behavioral concept is without free will or choice. This may help to explain how mere presentation of these concepts later in life, in hypnosis as well as in social behavior priming experiments, has such an imperative effect on the participant's behavior.

Cognitive Neuroscience Evidence: The Verb-Behavior Link

As with the other proposed dissociations between intention and action, cognitive neuroscience research findings are consistent with an automatic, nonconscious connection between behavioral concept representations and their corresponding motor representations. Perani et al. (1999) showed that merely hearing action verbs activates implicit motor representations, as well as working memory structures such as the dorsolateral prefrontal cortex, the anterior cingulate, and premotor and parietal cortices, all of which are needed to carry out that behavior in an uncertain environment. Jeannerod (1999) showed that this link works in the other direction as well: observation of a meaningful action activated the same brain area (Brodman 45) as did the generation of action verbs or the retrieval of verbs from memory. Grèzes and Decety (2001, p. 12) concluded from a review of the verb-motor program research that "motor programs can be seen as part of the meaning of verbal items that represent action."

Baddeley (2001) also highlighted the potential importance of verbal means of controlling action in an update of his model of working memory. In that model, the "phonological loop" is the working memory component corresponding to the temporary storage of verbal material (and thus may well be the component involved in verbal priming effects on behavior). Baddeley, Chincotta, and Adlam (2001) found that when the normal operation of the phonological loop in experimental participants is interfered with through articulatory suppression instructions, in which participants repeat out loud some task-irrelevant information in order to prevent or interfere with overt or covert rehearsal processes, working memory performance (such as the ability to switch between two tasks) suffered, as did performance on tests of executive functioning (such as the Wisconsin Card Sorting task). The authors concluded that their "results offer strong evidence for the verbal control of action . . . [and] the neglected but important role of the verbal control of executive processes" (pp. 655–656).

Implications for the Purpose of Consciousness

> There is a baffling problem about what consciousness is for. It is equally baffling, moreover, that the function of consciousness should remain so baffling. It seems extraordinary that despite the pervasiveness and familiarity of consciousness in our lives, we are uncertain in what way (if at all) it is actually indispensable to us. (Frankfurt, 1988, p. 162)

> What is consciousness for, if perfectly unconscious, indeed subjectless, information processing is in principle capable of achieving all the ends for which conscious minds were supposed to exist? (Dennett, 1981, p. 13)

I have argued here that conscious acts of will are not necessary determinants of social judgment and behavior; neither are conscious processes necessary for the selection of complex goals to pursue, or for the guidance of those goals to completion. Goals and motivations can be triggered by the environment, without conscious choice or intention, then operate and run to completion entirely nonconsciously, guiding complex behavior in interaction with a changing and unpredictable environment, and producing outcomes identical to those that occur when the person is aware of having that goal (see review in Chartrand & Bargh, 2002). But this is not to say that consciousness does not exist or is merely an epiphenomenon. It just means that if all of these things can be accomplished without conscious choice or guidance, then the purpose of consciousness (i.e., why it evolved) probably lies elsewhere.

In an important (if indirect) way, then, research on nonconscious forms of social cognition, motivation, and behavior speaks to the question of what consciousness is for, by eliminating some of the more plausible and widely held candidates. If we are capable of doing something effectively through nonconscious means, that something would likely not be the primary function for which we evolved consciousness.

For example, the fact that automatic goal pursuit involves monitoring the (perceived) environment and guidance or control over extended time periods of one's responses to it (e.g., Bargh et al., 2001) suggests that consciousness is not necessary for online monitoring and control, as is widely held by contemporary models of metacognition (e.g., Nelson, 1996; Paris, 2001). Of course, one can be meta-aware of one's perceptions, thoughts, and actions (monitoring) and also be aware of guiding those thoughts and actions toward a goal (control), but if this guidance can also occur without conscious awareness and intent, then these capabilities do not distinguish conscious from nonconscious processes. Thus online monitoring and control does not seem to be a viable candidate for the reason why we evolved consciousness.

But there is a second potential function and benefit of metacognitive awareness—of being aware at an abstract level, all at the same time, of what is going on in the current environment, along with one's current thoughts, purposes, actions, and their effects. This higher level, abstract domain of awareness enables the coordination and integration of all the various mental states and activities "to get them working together in the complex and sophisticated ways necessary to achieve complex and sophisticated ends" (Armstrong, 1981, p. 65; see also Johnson & Reeder, 1997). Just as active attention is necessary for object recognition and perceptual binding (integration of features into a single percept), as many experts have argued (see Donald, 2001, p. 182), metacognitive consciousness is the workplace where one can assemble and combine the various components of complex perceptual-motor skills. This ability has given humans a tremendous advantage over other animals, because "whereas most other species depend on their built-in demons to do their mental work for them, *we can build our own demons*" (Donald, 2001, p. 8, italics in original). With remarkable prescience, Neisser (1963) had similarly speculated that the ability to develop and carry out many complex processes in parallel outside of the "main line" of conscious thought was the special advantage that human cognition had over that of other animals:

> It is worth noting that, anatomically, the human cerebrum appears to be the sort of diffuse system in which multiple processes would be at home. In this respect it differs from the nervous system of lower animals. Our hypothesis thus leads us to the radical suggestion that the critical difference between the thinking of humans and of lower animals lies not in the existence of consciousness but in the capacity for complex processes outside of it. (p. 10)

In a very real sense, then, the purpose of consciousness—why it evolved—may be for the assemblage of complex nonconscious skills. In harmony with the general plasticity of human brain development, people have the capability of building ever more complex automatic "demons" that fit their own idiosyncratic environment, needs, and purposes. As William James (1890) argued, consciousness drops out of those processes where it is no longer needed, freeing itself for where it is. A major reason why it is adaptive for consciousness to be deployed only when needed is its limited-capacity nature, as shown best by findings of the dramatic "ego-depleting" consequences of even minimal conscious choice and regulatory processes (e.g., Baumeister, Bratslavsky, Muraven, & Tice, 1998).

Intriguingly, then, one of the primary objectives of conscious processing may be to eliminate the need for itself in the future by making learned skills as automatic as possible. It would be ironic indeed if, given the current juxtaposition of automatic and conscious mental processes in the field of psychology, the evolved purpose of consciousness turns out to be the creation of ever more complex nonconscious processes.

Conclusion

Action tendencies can be activated and put into motion without the need for the individual's conscious intervention; even complex social behavior can unfold without an act of will or awareness of its sources. Evidence from a wide variety of domains of psychological inquiry is consistent with this proposition. Behavioral evidence from patients with frontal lobe lesions, behavior and goal-priming studies in social psychology, the dissociated behavior of deeply hypnotized subjects, findings from the study of human brain evolution, cognitive neuroscience studies of the structure and function of the frontal lobes as well as the separate actional and semantic visual pathways, cognitive psychological research on the components of working memory and on the degree of conscious access to motoric behavior—all of these converge on the conclusion that complex behavior and other higher mental processes can proceed independently of the conscious will. Indeed, the brain evolution and neuropsychological evidence suggests that the human brain is designed for such independence.

These are tentative conclusions at this point, because cognitive neuroscience research is still in its infancy, and the cognitive psychological study of the underlying mechanisms of behavior and goal-priming effects in social psychology is perhaps in early childhood. But the two literatures clearly speak to each other. Indeed, Posner and DiGirolamo (2000) drew the more general and encompassing conclusion that the information-processing and the neurophysiological levels of analysis have achieved a level of mutual support greater than previously imagined. In opening their review, they remark on "how closely linked the hardware of the brain is to the performance of cognitive and emotional tasks, and the importance of environment and self-regulation to the operations of the human brain" (p. 874). The case of nonconscious social behavior reviewed in this chapter serves as an excellent example of that linkage: the neuropsychological evidence giving greater plausibility to the priming phenomena, and the priming phenomena demonstrating how deeply the neuropsychological phenomena affect the daily life of human beings.

Acknowledgments Preparation of this chapter was supported in part by a Guggenheim Fellowship, a Fellowship at the Center for Advanced Study in the Behavioral Sciences, and by the U.S. National Institute for Mental Health (Grant MH60767). I am grateful to Alan Baddeley, Roy Baumeister, Jerome Bruner, Jean Decety, Peter Gollwitzer, Ran Hassin, Denis Phillips, Lee Ross, Jim Uleman, and Dan Wegner for feedback, comments, and suggestions; thanks also to Melissa Ferguson, Grainne Fitzsimons, Ravit Levy, K. C. McCulloch, Ezequiel Morsella, and Pamela Smith for comments on an earlier version of the manuscript.

Note

1. In fact, early on, Thorndike (1913, p. 105) did attack the ideomotor action principle as "magical thinking," and his criticism effectively stifled scientific research on ideomotor action for the next 60 years (see Knuf et al., 2001, p. 780).

References

Armstrong, D. M. (1981). *The nature of mind, and other essays.* Ithaca, NY: Cornell University Press.

Atkinson, R. C., & Shiffrin, R. M. (1968). Human memory: A proposed system and its control processes. In K. W. Spence & J. T. Spence (Eds.), *The psychology of learning and motivation: Advances in research and theory* (Vol. 2, pp. 89–195). New York: Academic Press.

Baddeley, A. D. (1986). *Working memory.* New York: Oxford University Press.

Baddeley, A. D. (2001). Is working memory still working? *American Psychologist, 56,* 849–864.

Baddeley, A. D., Chincotta, D., & Adlam, A. (2001). Working memory and the control of action: Evidence from task switching. *Journal of Experimental Psychology: General, 130,* 641–657.

Baddeley, A. D., & Hitch, G. J. (1994). Developments in the concept of working memory. *Neuropsychology, 8,* 485–493.

Bargh, J. A. (1990). Auto-motives: Preconscious determinants of social interaction. In E. T. Higgins & R. M. Sorrentino (Eds.), *Handbook of motivation and cognition* (Vol. 2, pp. 93–130). New York: Guilford.

Bargh, J. A. (1992). Why subliminality does not matter to social psychology: Awareness of the stimulus versus awareness of its influence. In R. F. Bornstein & T. S. Pittman (Eds.), *Perception without awareness* (pp. 236–255). New York: Guilford.

Bargh, J. A., Chaiken, S., Raymond, P., & Hymes, C. (1996). The automatic evaluation effect: Unconditional automatic attitude activation with a pronunciation task. *Journal of Experimental Social Psychology, 32,* 185–210.

Bargh, J. A., & Chartrand, T. (1999). The unbearable automaticity of being. *American Psychologist, 54,* 462–479.

Bargh, J. A., Chen, M., & Burrows, L. (1996). Automaticity of social behavior: Direct effects of trait construct and stereotype priming on action. *Journal of Personality and Social Psychology, 71,* 230–244.

Bargh, J. A., & Ferguson, M. L. (2000). Beyond behaviorism: On the automaticity of higher mental processes. *Psychological Bulletin, 126,* 925–945.

Bargh, J. A., & Gollwitzer, P. M. (1994). Environmental control over goal-directed action. *Nebraska Symposium on Motivation, 41,* 71–124.

Bargh, J. A., Gollwitzer, P. M., Lee-Chai, A. Y., Barndollar, K., & Troetschel, R. (2001). The automated will: Nonconscious activation and pursuit of behavioral goals. *Journal of Personality and Social Psychology, 81,* 1014–1027.

Baumeister, R. F., Bratslavsky, E., Muraven, M., & Tice, D. M. (1998). Ego-depletion: Is the active self a limited resource? *Journal of Personality and Social Psychology, 74,* 1252–1265.

Bowers, K. S. (1984). On being unconsciously influenced and informed. In K. S. Bowers & D. Meichenbaum (Eds.), *The unconscious reconsidered* (pp. 227–272). Hillsdale, NJ: Erlbaum.

Bruner, J. S. (1961). Introduction. In A. R. Luria, *The role of speech in the regulation of normal and abnormal behavior*. New York: Macmillan.

Buccino, G., Binkofski, F., Fink, G. R., Fadiga, L, Fogassi, L, Gallese, V., Seitz, R. J., Zilles, K., Rizzolatti, G., & Freund, H.-J. (2001). Action observation activates premotor and parietal areas in somatotopic manner: An fMRI study. *European Journal of Neuroscience, 13*, 400–404.

Campbell, D. T. (1969). A phenomenology of the other one. In T. Mischel (Ed.), *Human action: Conceptual and empirical issues* (pp. 61–69). New York: Academic Press.

Chaiken, S., & Trope, Y. (Eds.). (1999). *Dual process theories in social psychology*. New York: Guilford.

Chartrand, T. L., & Bargh, J. A. (1999). The chameleon effect: The perception-behavior link and social interaction. *Journal of Personality and Social Psychology, 76*, 893–910.

Chartrand, T. L, & Bargh, J. A. (2002). Nonconscious motivations: Their activation, operation, and consequences. In A. Tesser, D. A. Stapel, & J. V. Wood (Eds.), *Self and motivation: Emerging psychological perspectives* (pp. 13–41). Washington, DC: American Psychological Association.

Decety, J., & Grèzes, J. (1999). Neural mechanisms subserving the perception of human actions. *Trends in Cognitive Sciences, 3*, 172–178.

Dennett, D. C. (1981). Introduction. In D. R. Hofstadter & D. C. Dennett (Eds.), *The mind's I* (pp. 1–13). New York: Basic Books.

Dijksterhuis, A., & Bargh, J. A. (2001). The perception-behavior expressway: Automatic effects of social perception on social behavior. In M. P. Zanna (Ed.), *Advances in experimental social psychology* (Vol. 33, pp. 1–40). San Diego: Academic Press.

Donald, M. (2001). *A mind so rare*. New York: Norton.

Duckworth, K. L., Bargh, J. A., Garcia, M., & Chaiken, S. (2002). The automatic evaluation of novel stimuli. *Psychological Science, 13*, 513–519.

Ferguson, M. J., & Bargh, J. A. (2002). Sensitivity and flexibility: Exploring the knowledge function of automatic attitudes. In L. F. Barrett & P. Salovey (Eds.), *The wisdom of feelings: Processes underlying emotional intelligence*. New York: Guilford.

Fitzsimons, G. M., & Bargh, J. A. (2003). Thinking of you: Nonconscious pursuit of interpersonal goals associated with relationship partners. *Journal of Personality and Social Psychology, 83*, 148–164.

Fourneret, P., & Jeannerod, M. (1998). Limited conscious monitoring of motor performance in normal subjects. *Neuropsychologia, 36*, 1133–1140.

Frankfurt, H. G. (1988). *The importance of what we care about*. New York: Cambridge University Press.

Frith, C. D., Blakemore, S.-J., & Wolpert, D. M. (2000). Abnormalities in the awareness and control of action. *Philosophical Transactions of the Royal Society of London, 355*, 1771–1788.

Goodale, M. A., Milner, A. D., Jakobsen, L. S., & Carey, D. P. (1991). Perceiving the world and grasping it: A neurological dissociation. *Nature, 349*, 154–156.

Grèzes, J., & Decety, J. (2001). Functional anatomy of execution, mental simulation, observation, and verb generation of actions: A meta-analysis. *Human Brain Mapping, 12*, 1–19.

Higgins, E. T. (1996). Knowledge activation: Accessibility, applicability, and sa-

lience. In E. T. Higgins & A. T. Kruglanski (Eds.), *Social psychology: Handbook of basic principles* (pp. 133–168). New York: Guilford.
Hilgard, E. R. (1986). *Divided consciousness: Multiple controls in human thought and action*. New York: Wiley.
Hume, D. (1748). *An enquiry concerning human understanding*. London: A. Millar.
Hurley, S. (2002). *Imitation, media violence, and freedom of speech*. Unpublished manuscript, Oxford University, Oxford, UK.
James, W. (1890). *Principles of psychology*. New York: Holt.
Jeannerod, M. (1999). To act or not to act: Perspectives on the representation of actions. *Quarterly Journal of Experimental Psychology, 52A*, 1–29.
Jeannerod, M. (2003). Consciousness of action and self-consciousness: A cognitive neuroscience approach. In J. Roessler & N. Eilan (Eds.), *Agency and self-awareness: Issues in philosophy and psychology*. New York: Oxford University Press.
Johnson, M. K., & Reeder, J. A. (1997). Consciousness and meta-processing. In J. D. Cohen & J. W. Schooler (Eds.), *Scientific approaches to consciousness* (pp. 261–293). Hillsdale, NJ: Erlbaum.
Kihlstrom, J. F. (1998). Dissociations and dissociation theory in hypnosis: Comment on Kirsch and Lynn (1998). *Psychological Bulletin, 123*, 186–191.
Knuf, L., Aschersleben, G., & Prinz, W. (2001). An analysis of ideomotor action. *Journal of Experimental Psychology: General, 130*, 779–798.
Lhermitte, F. (1986). Human anatomy and the frontal lobes. Part II: Patient behavior in complex and social situations: The "environmental dependency syndrome." *Annals of Neurology, 19*, 335–343.
Luria, A. R. (1961). *The role of speech in the regulation of normal and abnormal behavior*. New York: Macmillan.
Mesulam, M.-M. (1986). Frontal cortex and behavior. *Annals of Neurology, 19*, 320–325.
Neisser, U. (1963). The multiplicity of thought. *British Journal of Psychology, 54*, 1–14.
Nelson, T. O. (1996). Consciousness and metacognition. *American Psychologist, 51*, 102–116.
Norman, J. (2002). Two visual systems and two theories of perception: An attempt to reconcile the constructivist and ecological approaches. *Behavioral and Brain Sciences, 24*, 73–96.
Paris, S. G. (2001). When is metacognition helpful, debilitating, or benign? In P. Chambres, M. Izaute, & P.-J. Marescaux (Eds.), *Metacognition: Process, function, and use* (pp. 157–178). Dordrecht, Netherlands: Kluwer.
Perani, D., Cappa, S. F., Schnur, T., Tettamanti, M., Collina, S., Rosa, M. M., & Fazio, F. (1999). The neural correlates of verb and noun processing: A PET study. *Brain, 122*, 2337–2344.
Posner, M. I., & DiGirolamo, G. (2000). Cognitive neuroscience: Origins and promise. *Psychological Bulletin, 126*, 873–889.
Prinz, W. (1997). Perception and action planning. *European Journal of Cognitive Psychology, 9*, 129–154.
Prinz, W. (2003). How do we know about our own actions? In S. Maasen, W. Prinz, & G. Roth (Eds.), *Voluntary action: Brains, minds, and sociality* (pp. 21–33). New York: Oxford University Press.
Rizzolatti, G., & Arbib, M. A. (1998). Language within our grasp. *Trends in Neuroscience, 21*, 188–194.

Sarbin, T. R., & Coe, W. C. (1972). *Hypnosis: A social psychological analysis of influence communication*. New York: Holt, Rinehart and Winston.
Thach, W. T. (1996). On the specific role of the cerebellum in motor learning and cognition: Clues from PET activation and lesion studies in man. *Behavioral and Brain Sciences, 19*, 411–431.
Thorndike, E. L. (1913). Ideo-motor action. *Psychological Review, 20*, 91–106.
Vygotsky, L. S. (1962). *Thought and language* (E. Hanfmann & G. Vakar, Trans.). Cambridge, MA: MIT Press. (Original work published 1934)
Wegner, D. M. (2002). *The illusion of conscious will*. Cambridge, MA: MIT Press.
Wegner, D. M., & Wheatley, T. (1999). Apparent mental causation: Sources of the experience of will. *American Psychologist, 54*, 480–492.
Wertsch, J. V. (1985). *Vygotsky and the social formation of mind*. Cambridge, MA: Harvard University Press.
Wilson, T. D. (2002). *Strangers to ourselves*. Cambridge, MA: Harvard University Press.
Woody, E. Z., & Bowers, K. (1994). A frontal assault on dissociated control. In S. J. Lynn & J. W. Rhue (Eds.), *Dissociation: Clinical and theoretical perspectives* (pp. 52–79). New York: Guilford.
Woody, E., & Sadler, P. (1998). On reintegrating dissociated theories: Comment on Kirsch and Lynn (1998). *Psychological Bulletin, 123*, 192–197.

PART II

Basic Mechanisms

3

The Interaction of Emotion and Cognition: The Relation Between the Human Amygdala and Cognitive Awareness

Elizabeth A. Phelps

Over the last few decades, psychological theories on the relation between cognition and emotion have been shaped by evidence from neuroscience techniques. In particular, the debate of whether or not emotion occurs in the absence of cognitive awareness has been influenced by studies of a subcortical brain structure, the amygdala, that is more or less specialized for emotional processing (Aggleton, 1992). In nonhuman animals, the amygdala has been shown to elicit learned emotional responses in the absence of cortical inputs (Romanski & LeDoux, 1992), which strongly suggests that cognitive awareness may not be a mediating factor. Although several psychological studies have provided evidence that emotion may operate independently of cognitive awareness (e.g., Zajonc, 1980), the convergence of support from neuroscience has added another layer to the debate about the relation between cognitive awareness and emotion.

However, the neuroscience studies with nonhuman animals, while suggestive, do not directly address the relationship between emotion, the amygdala, and cognitive awareness. For obvious reasons, awareness cannot be easily assessed in species other than humans. In this chapter, I discuss what is known about the human amygdala and its relation to cognitive awareness and emotion. I begin by briefly reviewing what has been learned about the amygdala from studies with nonhuman animals. I then outline how the human amygdala/emotion system can operate independently of cognitive awareness. Finally, I explore the ways in which the amygdala interacts with awareness, highlighting both the influence of awareness on the amygdala and the role of the amygdala in modulating cognitive awareness.

The Amygdala: Insights From Research From Nonhuman Animals

The amygdala is a small, almond-shaped structure in the medial temporal lobes that sits adjacent to the hippocampus. Its potential role in emotional processing first became apparent in studies with monkeys in which the medial temporal lobe was damaged (Kluver & Bucy, 1939). These monkeys were described as suffering from "psychic blindness," also known as Kluver-Bucy syndrome. Monkeys with Kluver-Bucy syndrome displayed abnormal emotional responses, such as approaching and exploring stimuli they would normally avoid and fear (e.g., snakes). Although the description of Kluver-Bucy syndrome was important in emphasizing a role for the medial temporal lobe in emotional processing, it was not until 20 years later that Weiskrantz (1956) was able to show that it was damage to the amygdala specifically that resulted in altered emotional behavior.

More recent research with nonhuman animals has emphasized the amygdala's role in emotional learning and memory. Work by Davis (1992), Kapp, Pascoe, and Bixler (1984), and LeDoux (1992) has shown that while the amygdala is not critical to express an emotional reaction to stimuli that are inherently aversive, it is critical for learned fear responses. The primary paradigm used in these studies is fear conditioning, in which a neutral stimulus comes to acquire aversive properties by virtue of being paired with an aversive event. For instance, if a rat is presented a tone, it may show an orienting response at first, but little else. However, if during the presentations of the tone the rat receives a footshock on a few occasions, when the tone is presented later the rat may freeze or show changes in heart rate, which are normal fear reactions for the rat. By being paired with the shock, the tone is no longer neutral. Instead, it represents a potential aversive consequence and elicits a conditioned fear response. These studies have shown the amygdala is critical for both the acquisition and expression of conditioned fear responses (LeDoux, 1996).

Investigations into the neural systems of fear conditioning have mapped the pathways for learning from stimulus input to response output. One finding that has emerged from this research is that information about the identity of a stimulus can reach the amygdala by more than one pathway. Romanski and LeDoux (1992) have shown that there are separate cortical and subcortical pathways to convey perceptual information to the amygdala. If one pathway is damaged, the other is sufficient to signal the presence of a conditioned stimulus and elicit a conditioned response. It has been suggested that these dual pathways may be adaptive (LeDoux, 1996). The amygdala responds to stimuli in the environment that represent potential threat. The amygdala then sends signals to other brain regions and the autonomic nervous system, preparing the animal to respond quickly. The subcortical pathway to the amygdala can provide only a crude estimation of the perceptual details of the stimulus, but it is very fast. The cortical pathway allows the stimulus to be fully processed, but it is somewhat slower. This crude, fast subcortical pathway may prepare the animal to respond more quickly if, when the stimulus is fully processed and identified by the cortical pathway, the threat turns out to be real.

Although the amygdala is critical for fear conditioning, it also plays a broader, noncritical role in other types of learning and memory. The amygdala can modulate the function of other memory systems, particularly the hippocampal memory system necessary for declarative or episodic memory. McGaugh, Introini-Collision, Cahill, Munsoo, and Liang (1992) have shown that when an animal is aroused, the storage of hippocampal-dependent memory is enhanced. This enhanced storage with arousal depends on the amygdala. The amygdala modulates storage by altering consolidation. Consolidation is a process that occurs after initial encoding by which a memory becomes more or less "set"or permanent. McGaugh (2000) has suggested that perhaps one adaptive function of this slow consolidation process is to allow the neurohormonal changes that occur with emotion to alter memory. In this way, events that elicit emotional reactions, and thus may be more important for survival, are remembered better than nonemotional events. This secondary role of modulating the consolidation of hippocampal-dependent memories with mild arousal is another way the amygdala can influence emotional memory.

The research on the role of the amygdala in nonhuman animals has laid the groundwork for investigations in humans. It is impossible to investigate neural systems in humans with the specificity of research with nonhuman animals. However, to the extent that we obtain similar results with similar paradigms in humans, we can assume that we are tapping into the same basic neural processes across species. Fear conditioning has been shown to be a primary means of emotional learning across a range of species, including humans (LeDoux, 1996). An investigation into the role of the human amygdala in fear conditioning can serve as basis for understanding the relation between the amygdala, emotional learning, and cognitive awareness.

The Amygdala and Fear Conditioning in Humans: Evidence for the Independence of Emotional Learning and Cognitive Awareness

Fear-conditioning procedures are essentially the same across species. A typical paradigm in humans involves presenting a neutral stimulus, such as a blue square, and pairing it with an aversive stimulus, such as a mild shock to the wrist. The shock elicits physiological responses consistent with an aversive emotional stimulus. For instance, autonomic nervous system arousal occurs as part of a fear response, one measure of which would be an increase in the skin conductance response (SCR), an indicator of the mild sweating that occurs with arousal. After a few trials of pairing the blue square and shock, the blue square begins to elicit an SCR when presented alone. This conditioned response indicates that the previously neutral blue square has acquired aversive properties.

Fear-conditioning paradigms, like the one just described, were conducted with normal subjects while examining brain activity using functional magnetic resonance imaging (fMRI). These studies reported activation of the amygdala during fear conditioning in response to the conditioned stimulus (Buchel, Morris, Dolan, & Friston, 1998; LaBar, Gatenby, Gore, LeDoux, & Phelps, 1998). In one study, the strength of the conditioned response was correlated with the magnitude of amygdala activation (LaBar et al., 1998). When this paradigm was conducted on patients suffering from amygdala damage, they failed to acquire a conditioned response to the neutral, conditioned stimulus even after several pairings with the aversive stimulus (Bechara et al., 1995; LaBar, LeDoux, Spencer, & Phelps, 1995). They failed to acquire this conditioned response in spite of a normal fear response to the stimulus that was inherently aversive (e.g., shock). These results provide support for the conclusion that the amygdala in humans, as in other species, is necessary for the acquisition and expression of a conditioned response.

However, when conducting the studies with patients suffering from amygdala damage it became apparent that even though these patients failed to show a physiological indicator of a conditioned response, they had a very good cognitive understanding of the fear-conditioning paradigm. They could verbally report the events of the procedure and the relationship between the neutral stimulus and the aversive event, including the fact that the neutral stimulus came to predict the aversive event. An example of this is patient SP, who suffers from bilateral damage to the amygdala but has little other significant brain injury. She was shown an example of her lack of an SCR to a blue square that had been paired with shock along with the data from a normal control subject (Phelps, 2002). When asked what she thought of her lack of a normal conditioned SCR to the blue square, she made the following comment:

> I knew that there was an anticipation that blue square, at some particular point in time, would bring on one of the volt shocks. But even though I knew that, and I knew that from the very beginning, except for the very first one when I was surprised, that was my reaction—I knew it was going to happen. So I learned from the very beginning that it was going to happen: blue-shock. And it happened. I turned out to be right. (p. 559)

It is clear that SP was aware of the relationship between the blue square and shock. To SP, the blue square predicted an aversive event and thus was no longer neutral, even though she failed to express this learning through an implicit physiological response.

Bechara and colleagues (1995) conducted a similar study in another patient with bilateral amygdala damage, along with patients with hippocampal damage that suffered from amnesia. Like SP, the patient with a damaged amygdala was able to report the relationship between the neutral and aversive events but failed to demonstrate any physiological evidence of a learned conditioned response. The patients with hippocampal damage showed the opposite pattern of results. These patients demonstrated normal conditioned responses as measured by SCR. However, they had no conscious recollection of the fear-conditioning paradigm and could not verbally report the relationship between the neutral and aversive events.

The hippocampal memory system is necessary for forming lasting representations of the relations between the multiple cues that make up the learning context or episode (Cohen & Eichenbaum, 1993). In humans, the impairment following hippocampal damage, called anterograde amnesia, results in a deficit in the ability to explicitly or consciously remember events (Squire, 1986). When undergoing fear conditioning, the amygdala and hippocampal memory systems are acting simultaneously, but are independent. The amygdala forms a link between the automatic physiological responses that occur with an emotional reaction and the neutral conditioned stimulus. This link underlies the conditioned response that is expressed automatically and implicitly. The hippocampus encodes the relations between the many events that make up the fear-conditioning procedures, allowing for the conscious recollection and cognitive understanding of the fear-conditioning paradigm. In normal human subjects, both types of learning are available and can be expressed. Damage to the amygdala only impairs the learned implicit physiological emotional response, but leaves cognitive awareness intact.

It is interesting to note that humans with amygdala damage do not display the type of impaired emotional responses apparent in monkeys suffering from Kluver-Bucy syndrome (Anderson & Phelps, 2002). This may be because in humans the conscious recollection and understanding of the relationship between stimuli and their potential aversive consequences is sufficient to guide action in most circumstances. Unlike other animals, humans may not need to rely on physiological indicators when choosing what types of stimuli or situations to approach or avoid. Although there may be circumstances in which our learned physiological responses are important in guiding normal behavior (Damasio, 1999), in most circumstances patients with amygdala damage are able to function fairly well without this type of learned response.

The studies examining the role of the human amygdala in fear conditioning raise an issue that was not apparent in research with nonhuman animals. As in other animals, the amygdala in humans is critical for the acquisition and physiological expression of a conditioned response. However, the amygdala is not necessary for a cognitive awareness and understanding of the episode of fear conditioning. This dissociation between automatic emotional response and conscious recollection and awareness indicates that the amygdala and some emotional responses can operate independently of cognitive awareness. For the rest of this chapter, I focus on how these two independent factors can influence each other.

The Influence of Cognitive Awareness on the Amygdala/Emotion System: Instructed Fear

Learning with the fear-conditioning paradigm requires that subjects have direct experience with an aversive event in conjunction with a neutral event. Awareness of the relation between the neutral and aversive events occurs only after they have been paired, usually a few times. However, there are other means by which humans can learn that a neutral stimulus represents a potential aversive outcome. Humans can learn through verbal instruction. For example, you might fear a neighborhood dog because the dog once bit you. However, you might also fear a neighborhood dog because your neighbor mentioned in conversation that it is a mean dog that might bite you. In the second scenario, there is no direct experience with the dog and an aversive event; rather, there is an awareness and understanding of the aversive properties of the dog. When simply being told that the dog is unfriendly and could be dangerous, it is unlikely you would experience an emotional response. However, if you were to encounter the dog, you would likely have an emotional reaction.

This learning without direct experience relies on instruction and verbal communication. In humans, this type of learning is common. In many circumstances, we do not have to experience aversive events to learn which stimuli or situations to avoid because we have been warned. As mentioned earlier, the acquisition of knowledge about the relation between events that is available for conscious recollection and awareness depends on the hippocampus. Patients with amygdala damage who did not have extensive additional hippocampal damage are able to acquire and recollect this cognitive understanding of the emotional properties of stimuli learned through instruction. The question remains, however, whether having a cognitive awareness of the emotional properties of a stimulus, without direct experience, will influence or involve the amygdala.

The role of the amygdala in learning through instruction was assessed using a paradigm called "instructed fear" (Phelps et al., 2001). As in the fear-conditioning paradigm described previously, a blue square was paired with shock. However, instead of the subjects actually experiencing the blue square and shock together, they were simply told that they might receive a shock to the wrist when the blue square was presented. None of the subjects in this study actually received a shock, although all of the subjects indicated that they believed the instructions and thought they would receive a shock at some time when the blue square was presented. When SCR was assessed, all of the subjects showed increased arousal to the blue square, consistent with a mild fear response that might occur when one is anticipating a shock to the wrist. This study was conducted while amygdala responses were being assessed using fMRI. There was an increase of activation of the amygdala during the presentation of the blue square that was verbally linked to a potential shock. Across subjects, the magnitude of this amygdala activation was correlated with the magnitude of the SCR response to the blue square. These results suggest that the amygdala may respond when there is an awareness and understanding of the emotional properties of a stimulus in the absence of any direct experience.

As mentioned previously, patients with amygdala damage who have a relatively intact hippocampus can acquire a representation of the emotional properties of stimuli through instruction and can consciously recollect this knowledge when asked. However, do these patients show normal physiological responses to these types of stimuli? To address this question, patients with amygdala damage participated in the instructed fear procedure (Funayama, Grillon, Davis, & Phelps, 2001). After instruction, all of the patients had acquired a cognitive awareness and understanding of the aversive properties of the blue square (i.e., indicating the possibility of a shock) and verbally reported this knowledge to the experimenter. However, in spite of this cognitive awareness, the patients failed to demonstrate a normal physiological indicator of fear in response to the blue square. In other words, even though the patients explicitly knew that the blue square indicated a potential shock, their physical responses did not demonstrate this knowledge. These results, when combined with the fMRI results, indicate that the amygdala is involved when there is a cognitive awareness of the aversive properties of events acquired without direct aversive experience, and that the amygdala's role in this situation is to modulate some physiological indicators of this learned emotional response.

These studies demonstrate that cognitive awareness can influence the amygdala. They are important because they extend the amygdala's role in emotional learning beyond fear conditioning, to the expression of fears that are imagined and anticipated but never actually experienced. Unlike fear conditioning, the amygdala does not play a role in the acquisition of fear learning with instruction. However, its role in the modulation of the physiological expression of the learned emotional response appears to be similar in the two paradigms. Even though the amygdala can operate independently of conscious knowledge and awareness, this type of cognitive awareness interacts with the amygdala to produce normal emotional reactions in certain circumstances.

The Influence of the Amygdala/Emotion System on Cognitive Awareness

The Modulation of Long-Term Conscious Recollection

In the earlier review of research on the role of the amygdala in nonhuman animals, it was mentioned that the amygdala has a secondary role in emotional memory, specifically the modulation of the storage of hippocampal-dependent memories with arousal (McGaugh, 2000). In humans, hippocampal-dependent memories are the types of representations that are available for explicit or conscious recollection, and are what we refer to most often when we use the term *memory* in everyday speech. At the time an event occurs, we are usually aware of a great deal of what is happening. However, over time we forget. After even a week, it may difficult to recollect a number of events that occurred. For instance, most of us cannot remember what we ate for lunch a week ago, even though we were certainly aware of it at the time. With the passage of time, we can only consciously recollect a portion of the events that have occurred in our lives, even though we were fully aware of them at the time they occurred. To the extent that the amygdala modulates the retention or consolidation of hippocampal-dependent memories, it influences the events that are available for long-term conscious recollection. This is one way in which the amygdala may influence cognitive awareness.

Several studies with humans have examined the amygdala's role in the modulation of hippocampal-dependent memories with arousal. These studies asked subjects to recall or recognize emotional stimuli that elicit an arousal response.. One of the first studies examining this question used positron emission tomography (PET) to examine the relation between recall for neutral and arousing film clips and glucose metabolism in the amygdala while subjects viewed these films (Cahill et al., 1996). This study found that subjects who had greater glucose metabolism in the amygdala at the time of initial viewing of the arousing film clips showed better recall of these film clips 2 weeks later. There was no relationship between amygdala glucose metabolism and later recall for the neutral film clips. Another PET study (Cahill,

Babinsky, Markowitsch, & McGaugh, 1995) and a later fMRI study (Canili, Zhao, Brewer, Gabrieli, & Cahill, 2000; Hamann, Ely, Grafton, & Kilts, 1999) confirmed these results. In the fMRI study, the correlation was within subjects. Subjects were more likely to later recollect a highly emotional slide if that slide elicited amygdala activation when it was first encountered. These brain imaging studies indicate that for emotional stimuli, the amygdala response during encoding can partially predict long-term retention.

Studies examining patients with amygdala damage confirm a role for the amygdala in the ability to consciously recollect arousing events over time. In one of the first studies of this type (Cahill et al., 1995), normal control subjects and patients with amygdala damage were shown a slide show with a narrative. In one version of this slide show, the slides in the middle of the show depicted an arousing, negative event (i.e., a boy is hit by a car and his legs are severed and reattached). Control subjects and patients rated the slides from the middle portion as equally arousing and more arousing than slides from the rest of the show. When asked to recognize details from the slides several days later, normal control subjects recollected the arousing slides better than the neutral slides. Patients with amygdala damage did not show a significant advantage for the arousing slides, indicating a deficit in the enhancement of hippocampal-dependent memories with arousal.

The findings with nonhuman animals examining the role of the amygdala in the modulation of the hippocampus suggest that the amygdala modulates the consolidation of memories with arousal. As mentioned earlier, consolidation is a process that occurs over time by which memories become more or less permanent. If arousal is modulating consolidation, then the effect of arousal should emerge over time. In other words, if recollection is assessed immediately after learning, when consolidation processes have not yet had time occur, any effect of emotion could not be due to the modulation of consolidation. The effect of consolidation can only be observed if recollection occurs after a delay, when there has been sufficient time for consolidation processes. The effect of arousal on consolidation should be reflected in recollection over time, specifically in the rate of forgetting. A number of psychological studies suggest that arousal slows the rate of forgetting, resulting in greater retention of memories of emotional events (e.g., Kleinsmith & Kaplan, 1963). In an effort to determine if the amygdala is modulating the rate of forgetting for arousing events, LaBar and Phelps (1998) examined forgetting curves for the recall of arousing and nonarousing words in normal control subjects and patients with amygdala damage. The forgetting rates for control subjects were consistent with previous studies. Over time, they forgot fewer of the arousing words than the neutral words. For patients with amygdala damage, however, there was no difference in the rate of forgetting for arousing and neutral words. The patients forgot an equal number of the arousing and neutral words. These results are consistent with animal models, suggesting that the amygdala modulates the consolidation or storage of hippocampal-dependent memories with arousal.

In general, emotional events are consciously recollected over time better than neutral events. When we look back upon our lives, the memories that seem to last are those of emotional or significant events. One mechanism (of many) by which memories for emotional events is enhanced is the amygdala's modulation of the hippocampal consolidation with arousal (Phelps et al., 1998). To the extent that the amygdala is altering our ability to consciously recollect information, it is exerting an influence on our cognitive awareness for the events of our lives.

The Modulation of Perceptual Encoding

Another mechanism by which the amygdala and emotion may influence cognition is modulating which information in the environment reaches awareness. At any given time, we are bombarded with sensory input. Only a portion of this input is available for cognitive awareness. With attention, we can select a subset of information in the environment for awareness and further cognitive processing. However, our attentional resources and the amount of information we can keep in mind at any one time are limited (see Lachman, Butterfield, & Lachman, 1979). Early research on attentional selection demonstrated that meaningful and important information may be more likely to break through our limited attentional resources and reach awareness (Moray, 1959). A number of other psychological studies have confirmed that attention and awareness may be influenced by the emotional content of a stimulus (Niedenthal & Kitayama, 1994).

If emotional stimuli are more likely to reach awareness, then information about the emotional significance of a stimulus must be processed prior to awareness in some way. A number of researchers (e.g., Bargh & Chartrand, 1999; Ohman & Mineka, 2001) have suggested that the emotional qualities of a stimulus may be processed more automatically (i.e., without requiring elaborative cognitive processing) than the nonemotional qualities. For instance, in a classic study, Murphy and Zajonc (1993) demonstrated that an emotional face presented so briefly it is impossible to detect or identify can influence the rating of a neutral stimulus presented immediately afterward. This automaticity of emotional processing suggests that emotion information is available at the earliest stages of stimulus processing.

The amygdala has been shown to respond to the emotional significance of stimuli automatically, prior to cognitive awareness. A number of fMRI studies have shown amygdala activation to the presentation of faces with fearful expressions (e.g., Breiter et al., 1996). In an effort to determine if this amygdala response to fear faces is automatic, Whalen and colleagues (1998) presented these faces so quickly that subjects were unaware of their presentation. They found that the amygdala response to faces presented subliminally was as robust as the response to faces that were presented with awareness. In other words, the amygdala's response to the emotional quality of the fearful face stimulus appears to be automatic, not requiring awareness, identification, or additional cognitive processing (see also Morris, Ohman, & Dolan, 1998).

The psychological studies on emotion and awareness indicate that the emotional quality of a stimulus can be processed automatically, without cognitive awareness, and that this automatic processing of emotion can influence attention and awareness. The cognitive neuroscience research suggests that the amygdala can detect the emotional properties of a stimulus prior to explicit identification and awareness. The question remains whether this automatic detection of emotion by the amygdala has a role in the modulation of awareness for emotional events.

The amygdala's role in modulating awareness for emotional events was examined using a paradigm called the attentional blink (Chun & Potter, 1995; Raymond, Shapiro, & Arnell, 1992). In this paradigm, subjects are presented a series of around 15 items very quickly, about one every 100 ms. At this presentation rate, subjects are aware that something is being presented, but the items go by so quickly that they are unable to identify any of them. To make the task easier, subjects are told that they do not need to identify all of the items, but that they should concentrate on identifying only two of the items, called Target 1 (T1) and Target 2 (T2). These items can be distinguished from the "ignore" items by some salient characteristic; for instance, they may be printed in green ink instead of black ink. When subjects have to identify only 2 of the 15 items, they are successful most of the time. However, the success rate for reporting T2 items drops off significantly if T2 is presented soon after T1. For instance, if T1 is the second item presented (of 15 total) and T2 is the ninth item, then subjects are likely to report both items. However, if T1 is the second item and T2 is the fourth item, subjects are likely to miss T2 and will not be able to identify it. A short lag (one to three intervening items) between T1 and T2 impairs the ability to identify and report T2. It is as if noticing and encoding T1 creates a brief refractory period during which it is difficult to notice and encode a second item. In other words, it is as if attention "blinked."

Using this standard paradigm, Anderson and Phelps (2001) manipulated the emotional salience of T2. The stimuli they used were arousing words and nonarousing neutral words. With neutral words, they found the standard attentional blink effect. That is, subjects had difficulty reporting T2 when it came soon after T1. However, when T2 was an arousing word, they found that the blink effect was diminished. In other words, subjects were more likely to report a T2 word presented at a short lag if it was arousing rather than neutral. The ability to report the T1 words was unaffected by emotion. This enhanced ability to identify an arousing T2 word during the blink period suggests that when attentional resources are limited, emotional stimuli are more likely to reach cognitive awareness than neutral stimuli.

To determine if the amygdala is playing a role in the emotional modulation of the attentional blink effect, this paradigm was conducted on patients with amygdala damage and normal control subjects (Anderson & Phelps, 2001). The normal control subjects showed the pattern described above. That is, the blink effect was diminished for the arousing words, suggesting enhanced perceptual encoding and awareness for emotional stimuli. The patients with amygdala damage failed to show any difference in their ability to report arousing and neutral T2 words. For both types of words, patients showed a significant and equal deficit in the ability to report the T2 word when it was presented in a short lag position following the T1 word. Patients with amygdala lesions failed to show the emotional modulation of the attentional blink effect. These results suggest that the amygdala not only recognizes the emotional significance of an event early in stimulus processing, but that this early processing will then alter later perceptual encoding.

The amygdala has reciprocal connections with a number of sensory cortical regions (Amaral, Price, Pitkanen, & Carmichael, 1992). For instance, early visual cortical areas project to the amygdala, and the amygdala projects back to these regions. A study with nonhuman animals recording from neurons in both the amygdala and visual cortex indicated that the amygdala response to an emotional stimulus is correlated with a change in the baseline firing rate of neurons in the visual cortex (Kapp, Wilson, Pascoe, Supple, & Whalen, 1990). In other words, when the amygdala responds to an emotional event, the visual cortex shows enhanced neural processing as well. An fMRI study in humans has also shown a correlation between amygdala activation to an emotional stimulus and visual cortex activation to the same stimulus (Morris, Friston, et al., 1998). These results imply that early in visual processing the amygdala may receive information about a stimulus, and if the amygdala responds to this stimulus, it may then modulate later visual processing. This type of feedback mechanism, where the amygdala receives information about the emotional salience of a stimulus early in perceptual processing and in turn modulates later perceptual processing, may underlie the enhanced perceptual encoding for emotional stimuli observed with the attentional blink.

The results with the attentional blink paradigm (Anderson & Phelps, 2001) demonstrate that the amygdala modulates the enhanced perceptual encoding of emotional stimuli. Altering the information that may break through limited attentional resources to reach cognitive awareness is another mechanism by which the amygdala influences cognition. In situations where attentional resources are challenged, the automaticity of processing for emotional stimuli ensures that this information is more likely to get our full attention.

Conclusion

This chapter has explored the relation between emotion and cognition by examining the interaction of the amygdala and cognitive awareness. The amygdala and cognitive awareness can operate independently. The amygdala is necessary for the acquisition and physiological expression of fear conditioning, which does not require awareness. A cognitive awareness and understanding of the episode of fear conditioning is acquired and expressed independently of the amygdala and the conditioned response.

However, these two independent factors, the amygdala and cognitive awareness, also interact in subtle but important ways. Cognitive awareness can influence the amygdala. Having an awareness and understanding of the emotional properties of an event does not require the amygdala, but such knowledge will alter amygdala processing, which in turn modulates some physiological expressions of emotion. The amygdala also influences cognitive awareness in a few ways. First, the amygdala alters our ability over time to consciously recollect events that are emotional and important. Second, the amygdala can modulate perception and attention by increasing the likelihood that emotional information in the environment will break through to cognitive awareness.

The interactions between the amygdala and cognitive awareness suggest a complex picture of the relation between cognition and emotion. It no longer seems fruitful to debate whether cognition and emotion are independent or interdependent. Research on the neural systems of emotion and cognition suggest that they are both. By combining research and theories from psychological, cognitive neuroscience, and neuroscience approaches, we can begin to achieve a more complete understanding of the relationship between emotion and cognitive awareness.

References

Aggleton, J. P. (Ed.). (1992). *The amygdala: Neurobiological aspects of emotion, memory and mental dysfunction.* New York: Wiley-Liss.

Amaral, D. G., Price, J. L., Pitkanen, A., & Carmichael, S. T. (1992). In J. P. Aggleton (Ed.), *The amygdala* (p. 1–66). New York: Wiley-Liss.

Anderson, A. K., & Phelps, E. A. (2001). Lesions of the human amygdala impair enhanced perception of emotionally salient events. *Nature, 411*, 305–309.

Anderson, A. K., & Phelps, E. A. (2002). Is the amygdala critical for the subjective experience of emotion? Evidence of intact dispositional affect in patients with amygdala lesions. *Journal of Cognitive Neuroscience, 14*, 1–12.

Bargh, J. A., & Chartrand, L. (1999). The unbearable automacity of being. *American Psychologist, 54*, 462–479.

Bechara, A., Tranel, D., Damasio, H., Adolphs, R., Rockland, C., & Damasio, A.,R. (1995). Double dissociation of conditioning and declarative knowledge relative to the amygdala and hippocampus in humans. *Science, 269*, 1115–1118.

Breiter, H. C., Etcoff, H. L., Whalan, P. J., Kennedy, W. A., Rauch, S. L., Buckner, R. L., Strauss, M. M., Hyman, S., & Rosen, B. (1996). Response and habituation of the human amygdala during visual processing of facial expression. *Neuron, 17*, 875–887.

Buchel, C., Morris, J., Dolan, R. J., & Friston, K. (1998). Brain systems mediating aversive conditioning: An event-related fMRI study. *Neuron, 20*, 947–957.

Cahill, L., Babinsky, R., Markowitsch, H. J., & McGaugh, J. L. (1995). The amygdala and emotional memory. *Science, 377*, 295–296.

Cahill, L., Haier, R. J., Fallon, J., Alkire, M. T., Tang, C., Keator, D., Wu, J. & McGaugh, J. L. (1996). Amygdala activity at encoding correlated with long-term, free recall of emotional information. *Proceedings of the National Academy of Sciences, 93*, 8016–8021.

Canili, T., Zhao, Z., Brewer, J., Gabrieli, J. D., & Cahill, L. (2000). Event-related activation in the human amygdala associates with later memory for individual emotional experience. *Journal of Neuroscience, 20*, RC99.

Chun, M. M., & Potter, M. C. (1995). A two-stage model for multiple target detection in rapid serial visual presentation. *Journal of Experimental Psychology: Human Perception Performance, 21*, 109–127.

Cohen, N. J., & Eichenbaum, H. (1993). *Memory, amnesia, and the hippocampal system*. Cambridge, MA: MIT Press.

Damasio, A. R. (1999). *The feeling of what happens: Body and emotion in the making of consciousness*. New York: Harcourt Brace and Company.

Davis, M. (1992). The role of the amygdala in conditioned fear. In J. P. Aggleton (Ed.), *The amygdala: Neurobiological aspects of emotion, memory and mental dysfunction* (pp. 255–306). New York: Wiley-Liss.

Funayama, E. S., Grillon, C. G., Davis, M., & Phelps, E. A. (2001). A double dissociation in the affective modulation of startle in humans: Effects of unilateral temporal lobectomy. *Journal of Cognitive Neuroscience, 13*, 721–729.

Hamann, S. B., Ely, T. D., Grafton, S. T., & Kilts, C. D. (1999). Amygdala activity related to enhanced memory for pleasant and aversive stimuli. *Nature Neuroscience, 2*, 289–293.

Kapp, B. S., Pascoe, J. P., & Bixler, M. A. (1984). The amygdala: A neuroanatomical systems approach to its contributions to aversive conditioning. In N. Butters & L. R. Squire (Eds.), *Neuropsychology of memory* (pp. 473–488). New York: Guilford.

Kapp, B. S., Wilson, A., Pascoe, J. P., Supple, W., & Whalen, P. J. (1990). In M. Gabriel & J. Moore (Eds.), *Neurocomputation and Learning: Foundations of Adaptive Networks* (pp. 53–90). Cambridge, MA: MIT Press.

Kleinsmith, L. J., & Kaplan, S. (1963). Paired-associate learning as a function of arousal and interpolated interval. *Journal of Experimental Psychology, 65*, 190–193.

Kluver, H., & Bucy, P. C. (1939). Preliminary analysis of functions of the temporal lobes in monkeys. *Archives of Neurology and Psychiatry Chicago, 42*, 979–1000.

LaBar, K. S., Gatenby, C., Gore, J. C., LeDoux, J. E., & Phelps, E. A. (1998). Human amygdala activation during conditioned fear acquisition and extinction: A mixed-trial fMRI study. *Neuron, 20*, 937–945.

LaBar, K. S., LeDoux, J. E., Spencer, D. D., & Phelps, E. A. (1995). Impaired fear conditioning following unilateral temporal lobectomy in humans. *Journal of Neuroscience, 15*, 6846–6855.

LaBar, K. S., & Phelps, E. A. (1998). Role of the human amygdala in arousal mediated memory consolidation. *Psychological Science, 9*, 490–493.

Lachman, R., Butterfield, E. C., & Lachman, J. L. (1979). *Cognitive psychology and information processing: An introduction*. Hillsdale, NJ: Erlbaum.

LeDoux, J. E. (1992). Emotion and the amygdala. In J. P. Aggleton (Ed.), *The amygdala: Neurobiological aspects of emotion, memory, and mental dysfunction* (pp. 339–351). New York: Wiley-Liss.

LeDoux, J. E. (1996). *The emotional brain: The mysterious underpinnings of emotional life*. New York: Simon and Schuster.

McGaugh, J. L. (2000). Memory—a century of consolidation. *Science, 287*, 248–251.

McGaugh, J. L., Introini-Collision, I. B., Cahill, L., Munsoo, K., & Liang, K. C. (1992). Involvement of the amygdala in neuromodulatory influences on memory storage. In J. P. Aggleton (Ed.), *The amygdala: Neurobiological aspects of emotion, memory, and mental dysfunction* (pp. 431–451). New York: Wiley-Liss.

Moray, N. (1959). Attention and dichotic listening: Affective cues and the influence of instructions. *Quarterly Journal of Experimental Psychology, 11*, 56–60.

Morris, J. S., Friston, K. J., Buchel, C., Frith, C. D., Young, A. W., Calder, A. J., & Dolan, R. J. (1998) A neuromodulatory role for the human amygdala in processing emotional facial expressions. *Brain, 121*, 47–57.

Morris, J. S., Ohman, A., & Dolan, R. J. (1998). Conscious and unconscious emotional learning in the amygdala. *Nature, 393*, 467–470.

Murphy, S. T., & Zajonc, R. B. (1993). Affect, cognition, awareness: Affective priming with optimal and suboptimal stimulus exposures. *Journal of Personality and Social Psychology, 64*, 723–739.

Niedenthal, P. M., & Kitayama, S. (1994). *The heart's eye: Emotional influences in perception and attention*. San Diego: Academic Press.

Ohman, A., & Mineka, S. (2001). Fears, phobias, and preparedness: Toward an evolved module of fear and fear learning. *Psychological Review, 108*, 483–522.

Phelps, E. A. (2002). The cognitive neuroscience of emotion. In M. S. Gazzaniga, R. B. Ivry, & G. R. Mangun (Eds.), *Cognitive neuroscience: The biology of mind* (2nd ed., pp. 537–576). New York: Norton.

Phelps, E. A., LaBar, D. S., Anderson, A. K., O'Conner, K. J., Fulbright, R. L., & Spencer, D. S. (1998). Specifying the contributions of the human amygdala to emotional memory: A case study. *Neurocase, 4*, 527–540.

Phelps, E. A., O'Conner, K. J., Gatenby, J. C., Grillon, C., Gore, J. C., & Davis, M. (2001). Activation of the human amygdala to a cognitive representation of fear. *Nature Neuroscience, 4*, 437–441.

Raymond, J. E., Shapiro, K. L., & Arnell, K. M. (1992). Temporary suppression of visual processing in an RSVP task: An attentional blink? *Journal of Experimental Psychology: Human Perception Performance, 18*, 849–860.

Romanski, L. M., & LeDoux, J. E. (1992). Bilateral destruction of neocortical and perirhinal projection targets of the acoustic thalamus does not disrupt auditory fear conditioning. *Neuroscience Letters, 142*, 228–232.

Squire, L. R. (1986). Mechanisms of memory. *Science, 232*, 1612–1619.

Weiskrantz, L. (1956). Behavioral changes associated with ablation of the amygdaloid complex in monkeys. *Journal of Comparative Physiological Psychology, 49*, 381–391.

Whalen, P. J., Rauch, S. L., Etcoff, N. L., McInerney, S. C., Lee, M. B., & Jenike, M. A. (1998). Masked presentations of emotional facial expressions modulate amygdala activity without explicit knowledge. *Journal of Neuroscience, 18*, 411–418.

Zajonc, R. B. (1980). Feeling and thinking: Preferences need no inferences. *American Psychologist, 35*, 151–175.

4

The Power of the Subliminal: On Subliminal Persuasion and Other Potential Applications

Ap Dijksterhuis, Henk Aarts, and Pamela K. Smith

> In a word, is not the subliminal self superior to the conscious self?
>
> —Henri Poincaré

In the past century, a few hundred articles have been published about subliminal perception and applications such as subliminal persuasion (see Dixon, 1971, 1981). This number suggests a mature field of research, in which, as in any mature field, researchers agree on a number of well-documented findings and argue over more recent contributions. However, in the field of subliminal perception and persuasion, scientists agree that the field is controversial and argue over everything else. Despite numerous findings demonstrating effects of subliminal perception, some people still maintain that the phenomenon itself does not even exist. Holender (1986), for instance, drew the conclusion that subliminal perception had never been reliably demonstrated, which led Dixon (who reviewed the field twice in 1971 and 1981) to comment that

> the most interesting phenomenon to which Holender's paper draws attention is the extraordinary antipathy some people still have towards the idea that we might be influenced by things of which we are unaware. Would it be putting it too strongly to say it reminds one of the skepticism of "flat earth theorists" when confronted with the alarming theory that the world is round? (Dixon, 1986, p. 30; see also Merikle & Reingold, 1992)

The empirical study of subliminal perception started over a hundred years ago.[1] Peirce and Jastrow (1884) showed that participants (actually Peirce and Jastrow themselves) could discriminate between two objects on the basis of their weights even when the difference in weight was so small that it could not be detected consciously. After choosing between objects, they indicated their confidence on a scale from 0 to 3, with a higher score representing more confidence. On almost all trials, they chose zero. However, they chose the correct object on more than 60% of the occasions. Although he minor differences in weight may have escaped consciousness, unconscious processes dealt with them with reasonable accuracy. In addition, they obtained comparable data with pressures that differed slightly in intensity and surfaces that differed slightly in brightness.

Other pioneering work was done by Sidis (1898; described in Merikle & Reingold, 1992, p. 58) and by Pötzl (1917/1960). In Sidis's work, subjects were shown cards containing a single digit or letter, but these cards were so far away that the subject "saw nothing but a dim, blurred spot or dot" (Sidis, 1898, p. 170). In fact, "the subjects often complained that they could not see anything at all; that even the black, blurred, dim spot often disappeared from their field of vision" (p. 171). However, when Sidis asked the subjects to name the character on the card, their responses were correct more often than would be expected on the basis of pure random guessing, even though many subjects stated "that they might as well shut their eyes and guess" (p. 171).

Finally, Pötzl (1917/1960) investigated the consequences of subliminal perception on imagery during dreams. He showed participants various pictures for very short durations (10 ms) and predicted that although these pictures could not reach conscious awareness, they would remain active subconsciously long enough to be able to present themselves in dreams. According to Pötzl, some of the images recurred in the dreams of the experimental participants.

In the first half of the twentieth century, others replicated and extended the aforementioned early studies (see Adams, 1957, for a review). On the basis of these findings, one may be excused for not grasping why the study of subliminal perception is so controversial. After all, the field appears to have had a promising start. When a few people report interesting results and when a few others replicate and extend these results, one would normally conclude that a healthy new field has been born.

In our view, there are two (interacting) reasons for the unusual development of the field of subliminal perception. First of all, the idea that our behavior—or our functioning in general—is driven by unconscious perception makes many people uncomfortable. As Nørretranders (1998, p. 158) pointed out, "the notion that human behavior can be influenced by perceptions which do not lead to consciousness but merely remain in the organism has always been associated with considerable fear." The second reason is James Vicary and the notion of subliminal persuasion. Subliminal persuasion refers to the subliminal presentation of stimuli by people (e.g., advertisers) who intentionally try to influence our behavior. Vicary claimed in 1957 that he increased the sales of popcorn and cola after subliminally flashing "Eat Popcorn" and "Drink Coke" in a New Jersey cinema. This caused a stir both inside and outside the scientific community. A few years later, Vicary admitted that his (nonreliable) results did not warrant strong conclusions and that there was no evidence at all for subliminal persuasion, but the damage had already been done. The number of researchers seriously working on the topic decreased dramatically for at least the next 20 years. Moreover, the few experimental psychologists that did publish on subliminal phenomena were far from supportive. Some indicated that the chance that subliminal persuasion could ever work was extremely remote (Moore, 1982) or worse, that the whole idea was just a myth and that we should stop investigating it altogether (Pratkanis, 1992; see also Packard, 1978).

But is it a myth? Should we stop? In this chapter, we argue that we should not stop and that subliminal persuasion and other applications of subliminal stimulation should be investigated, not ignored. The remainder of this chapter is divided into four parts. First, we discuss our definition of subliminal perception. We also present arguments for why it is impossible, or at least difficult, to maintain that all (important) behavior should be the result of conscious thought. In the second part, examples of basic effects of subliminal stimulation are used to demonstrate what subliminal stimulation can do. Third, a crude theoretical basis for the effects of subliminal persuasion and other applications is provided, relying largely on social cognition research. In the fourth and most important part, we discuss research relevant for the practical, commercial, or political use of subliminal stimulation. A distinction is made between (a) the manipulation of attitudes by subliminal evaluative conditioning, (b) the influence of subliminal messages on consumer behavior, and (c) the influence of subliminal messages on health. With these empirical results, we hope to show that applications of subliminal stimulation are worthy of space on the scientific agenda. In our concluding section, we discuss three arguments in favor of the study of subliminal perception.

Definition Issues

A Note on Thresholds

Both the content and the tone of many publications on subliminal phenomena have been affected by the fear and antipathy they elicit. One example, important for the present purposes, is the effort to define subliminal perception out of existence (Eriksen, 1960; Holender, 1986).

The definition of subliminal perception was a topic of hot debate in the mid-1980s (Cheesman & Merikle, 1984, 1986; Fowler, 1986; Holender, 1986; Wolford, 1986; see also Kihlstrom, Barnhardt, & Tataryn, 1992). The discussion was based on the concepts of objective and subjective thresholds (e.g., Cheesman & Merikle, 1984). An objective threshold has to be passed for a stimulus to be sensed, that is, to enter the appropriate sensory system. A subjective threshold is one that has to be passed for a stimulus to enter conscious awareness. If the objective threshold is not passed, perception does not occur. If the objective threshold is passed but the subjective is not, subliminal perception occurs. If the subjective is passed as well, conscious perception occurs.

Holender (1986) argued that researchers could not rely on the subjective threshold as a measure of conscious perception. Instead, Holender said that only an objective threshold could be a dependable defining criterion. He argued that when there is some demonstrable sensory effect of a stimulus—that is, if the objective threshold is reached—it can never be guaranteed that people did not also become conscious of the stimulus. Imagine sitting in front of a computer screen on which a word is briefly shown. It goes so fast that you only see a flash. You do not know which word it was. According to Holender, if you cannot verbally report a stimulus, this does not necessarily mean that it did not reach consciousness. Maybe it reached consciousness half a second ago and you forgot. It should be clear that this sole reliance on the objective threshold proposed by Holender "effectively rules the phenomenon of subliminal perception out of existence," as noted by Kihlstrom and colleagues (1992, p. 20).

Most researchers disagreed with Holender (1986). He imposed a criterion that ignores an essential aspect of consciousness: awareness. A definition of consciousness must appeal to the notion of awareness, not just to some psychophysiological definition of detection. As Paap (1986, p. 45) in his comment on Holender noted, "it simply does not make sense to say that the thermostat in my house is conscious of New Mexico's hot days and cool evenings." Nørretranders (1998; see also Jaynes, 1976; Libet, 1985) argued convincingly that consciousness should be treated as a primary phenomenon. What is in consciousness is in consciousness; what is not is not. If one wants to know what is in consciousness, one should ask consciousness itself. Or, as Nørretranders (1998, p. 226) puts it, "conciousness is a primary phenomenon, which the experimenter has no right to argue with."

So subliminal perception is perception that passes the objective threshold (i.e., it is discriminated by the senses) but fails to pass the subjective threshold (i.e., it fails to reach conscious awareness and cannot be reported verbally). But can we determine this subjective threshold? Not really, or at least not in an absolute sense. There is no fixed subjective threshold that works for all people under all circumstances. The idea of a fixed threshold has been superseded as a consequence of insights from signal detection theory (see e.g., Greenwald, Draine, & Abrams, 1996). Whether a briefly presented stimulus does reach conscious awareness or not depends on stable individual differences, on current goals and needs, and on various contextual effects.

Some have argued that as there is no such thing as a fixed subjective threshold, we should abandon the term *subliminal* (*limen* means threshold in Latin) altogether (e.g., Kihlstrom et al., 1992), and instead use terms such as *implicit* or *unconscious perception* instead. We chose to use *subliminal* because it is the term most often used to describe these phenomena (see also Greenwald et al., 1996). Implicit or unconscious perception refers to perception that does not reach conscious awareness, but these terms do not distinguish between the various reasons why the information did not enter consciousness. A perceived stimulus may not enter consciousness because it is presented very briefly. However, a perceived stimulus also may not enter consciousness because little attention is paid to it; with a bit more attention the stimulus could have entered consciousness. For instance, while driving a car people "see" many billboards, although the information on these billboards never reaches conscious awareness, simply because people do not pay attention to them. With more attention, the information on the billboards would enter consciousness. This is implicit perception or unconscious perception. However, subliminal perception is generally used to refer to stimuli that are presented in such a way that they cannot reach conscious awareness, even if attention is directed to them. This, then, is also the definition we adopt for this chapter.[2]

Do We Really Want Consciousness to Be in Charge?

Researchers who investigate subliminal perception (or even unconscious psychology in general) have always met with some resistance. Many people simply want to believe that subliminal perception does not exist. Others, forced to admit there is something to it after hearing about one or more convincing demonstrations, downplay its importance. This is rooted in the fear that "we" (our consciousness) are not in control of our behavior, and in the belief that conscious thought should mediate everything we do, at least when our behavior and the decisions we make become more important. But should we really hold onto that belief? Do we really always want conscious thought to produce, or at least mediate, our behavior?

First of all, and strictly speaking, conscious thought does not exist. Thought, when defined as producing meaningful associative constructions, happens unconsciously (Jaynes, 1976). One may be aware of some of the elements of a thought process or one may be aware of a product of a thought process, but one is not aware of thought itself. Watt (1905; see also Jaynes, 1976; Nisbett & Wilson, 1977) demonstrated the inaccessibility of thought to consciousness. In his experiment, participants were presented with nouns (e.g., oak) and were asked to come up with a particular association as quickly as they could. Sometimes, participants were required to associate the noun with a superordinate word (oak-tree), while on other occasions they were to name a part (oak-acorn) or a subordinate (oak-beam). The idea was that conscious thinking could be divided into four stages: the instructions (e.g., superordinate), the presentation of the noun (e.g., oak), the search for an appropriate association, and the uttered reply (e.g., tree). Participants were asked to introspect on all four stages separately, to assess the contribution of consciousness during each stage. Of course, the third stage (searching for an association) is the stage during which the actual thinking takes place and hence, it is during this stage that one would have expected conscious thought. This stage, however, was introspectively blank: participants could not report anything. The instruction in combination with the presentation of the noun automatically started the thinking process. And this thinking occurred outside of conscious awareness. Importantly, this is true for all thought, not just an elementary experiment on word association, and for important creative processes as well. Thinking about an article we want to write is an unconscious affair. We read and talk, but only to acquire the necessary materials for our unconscious mechanisms to chew on. We are consciously aware of some of the products of thought that sometimes intrude into consciousness ("I have to use the article by Watt to get this message across!"), but not of the thinking—or chewing—itself.

Frankly, we think we should be happy that thought is unconscious. Nørretranders (1998) summarizes results from the 1950s and 1960s, when a number of people were interested in human processing capacity. Their research was devoted to the processing capacity of consciousness and of the senses. The processing capacity of the senses can be seen as our total processing capacity. In order to compare different forms of information (e.g., tactile versus visual versus auditory), information was measured in bits. As it turned out, our senses can handle about 11 million bits per second (Zimmermann, 1989; see Nørretranders, 1998, for a detailed analysis). This whopping number is largely the result of our sophisticated visual system, which can handle about 10 million bits per second. The processing capacity of consciousness pales in comparison. The exact number of bits consciousness can process depends on the task. When we read silently, we process about a maximum of 45 bits per second (a few words); when we read aloud, it drops to 30. When we calculate (e.g., when we multiply two numbers), we can handle only 12 bits per second. Compared to our total capacity, these numbers are incredibly small. If we conclude that our consciousness can process 50 bits per second (which is optimistic; see Küpfmüller, 1962; Nørretranders, 1998), our total capacity is 200,000 times as high as the capacity of consciousness. In other words, consciousness can only deal with a very small percentage of all incoming information. All the rest is processed without awareness. Let's be grateful that unconscious mechanisms help out whenever there is a real job to be done, such as thinking.

The enormous processing capacity of the unconscious is very important. One of the authors of this chapter recently bought an apartment. Between the moment he first entered the building to explore it and the moment he made a bid, all of about 10 minutes passed (it was a two-bedroom apartment, so exploring it didn't take long). Intuitively, one may say that this is a very poor way of deciding. Granted, if the decision to buy this apartment was based solely on conscious processes, it would have been very poor indeed. Consciousness cannot accomplish much within 10 minutes, as we have seen. However, the decision was based on a sense that "this place just feels very good; let's do it" (and obviously on a few things that were known beforehand, such as the location of the building and the quality of its foundations). Many people take days or weeks to decide to buy a home, but the real decision is often made in a matter of minutes. The remaining time is used to make such an important decision feel less scary and maybe to rule out a few potential risks. The reason we can make such a decision fast is that within 10 minutes, unconscious perception and unconscious thought can process (about) 6.6 billion bits. This sense of "it feels good; let's do it" (see also Damasio, 1994), then, could well be based on an enormous amount of information. One could defend that from a normative perspective (more than 6 billion bits!), it isn't a poor way of deciding.[3]

Do we really want to depend primarily on consciousness? We should appreciate unconscious perception. Without it, we would not be able to accomplish much at all. If we assume, on the basis of the previous paragraph, that it takes the processing of roughly 6.6 billion bits to decide to buy a house, consciousness alone would need 4 years to make such a decision.

Importantly, if we accept that unconscious perceptual processes have a paramount influence on human functioning, then we also should accept that subliminal perception may have far-reaching consequences. We cannot agree that many things are perceived and processed unconsciously and at the same time rule out the possibility that subliminal exposure to stimuli can affect us.

The Strings We Can Pull

As alluded to above, for many years the question of whether subliminal perception did exist was a topic of hot debate. More recently, however, evidence for subliminal perception has accumulated. As a result, the controversy has shifted more and more toward the question of what exactly can be elicited by exposure to subliminal stimuli. Does subliminal perception only have relatively "innocent" and brief semantic effects, or can it affect more important matters such as our emotional life or our overt behavior? In concrete terms, if we subliminally flash the word *steak*, what are the consequences? Does it prime the associated word *cow*? Does it cause changes in affect so that vegetarians have a strong negative reaction and hungry nonvegetarians have a strong positive reaction? Does it affect behavior? Are we getting hungry? In sum, exactly which strings can we pull subliminally?

In this section, we point at some evidence of the known consequences of subliminal stimulation. For now, we restrict ourselves to effects on nonapplied domains, and we discuss one or two examples from each domain. We differentiate between (a) neurological correlates, (b) evaluative and affective effects, (c) semantic effects, (d) effects on social judgments, and (e) effects on overt behavior.

Neurological Correlates

Libet, Alberts, Wright, and Feinstein (1967) were presumably the first to provide physiological evidence for subliminal perception. In their experiments, they stimulated the skin of their participants so subtly participants could not consciously report it. Concurrently measured evoked potentials, however, showed changes in the electrical field around the brain. Although their measurements were crude, they did provide unequivocal evidence for brain activity as a result of perception that escaped conscious awareness. Later, Dehaene et al. (1998) and Whalen et al. (1998) also reported evidence of neurological effects of subliminal stimulation.

Evaluative and Affective Effects

In 1968, Zajonc launched the idea of mere exposure: the more we are exposed to a stimulus, the more we like it. Kunst-Wilson and Zajonc (1980) first demonstrated that even subliminal exposure to a stimulus enhances one's attitude toward this stimulus. In their experiment, participants were presented with 10 polygons, each five times for only 1 ms. Afterward, participants were presented with pairs of polygons, consisting of an "old" (e.g., previously presented) and a "new" polygon. For each pair, participants had to indicate which one they thought was previously presented to them and which one they liked most. Participants more often preferred the previously presented polygon to the new one, without being able to say which polygon had been presented. This subliminal mere exposure effect has been replicated a number of times since (see Bornstein, 1992, for a review).[4]

Basic Semantic Effects

Debner and Jacoby (1994) obtained evidence for semantic subliminal processing with a particularly convincing paradigm. In their experiments, they presented five-letter words (e.g., *scalp*) on the computer screen subliminally. After a word had appeared, participants were presented with a word stem with three letters of a word (e.g., *sca-*). Participants were requested to generate a five-letter word to complete the presented word stem. In some conditions, participants were urged not to choose the word that had just been presented. Relative to a control condition in which the same word stem was presented without earlier exposure to an applicable subliminal word, people who were asked not to use the subliminally presented word used it more often. With this task, evidence was obtained for the semantic processing of a word while at the same time ensuring that this word was not consciously perceived (see also Marcel, 1983; Merikle, Joordens, & Stolz, 1995).

Social Judgments

Bargh and Pietromonaco (1982) showed that subliminally activated trait constructs affect the impression we form of others. Participants in their experiments were presented with flashes (actually words) on different locations on the screen and were asked to identify the location of each flash. Depending on the experimental condition, either 0%, 20%, or 80% of the words were associated with the trait construct of hostility. After completing this task, participants were presented with a brief description of a stimulus person who behaved in an ambiguously hostile way. The impression participants formed of this stimulus person was influenced by their subliminal exposure to the words: the more hostile words presented earlier, the more negative the impression of the stimulus person became. Importantly, recognition memory for the flashed words did not exceed chance level. In later work, these findings were replicated for subliminally activated social stereotypes (Devine, 1989; Lepore & Brown, 1997).

Behavior

Research has demonstrated that activated trait constructs and social stereotypes not only affect judgments about others, but also affect participants' own overt behavior. Activated traits and stereotypes bring behavior in line with the particular trait or stereotype (Bargh, Chen, & Burrows, 1996; Dijksterhuis & van Knippenberg, 1998; see Dijksterhuis & Bargh, 2001, for a review). Bargh and colleagues (1996, Experiment 3) found enhanced hostility among participants for whom the stereotype of African Americans was activated subliminally. In their experiment, participants performed a very laborious computer task. During this task, some participants were subliminally presented with photographs of male African Americans while others were subliminally presented with photographs of White males. After participants had been performing the task for a while, the computer program beeped, an error message appeared, and participants were told that they had to start all over again. The participants were videotaped during the experiment and the dependent variable was the level of hostility participants displayed upon hearing that they had to redo the task. The experimenter (who was blind to conditions) and several independent coders rated the reaction of the participants primed with African American faces as more hostile than the reaction of the participants primed with White faces. Later, these effects were replicated and extended in other research (Chen & Bargh, 1997; Dijksterhuis, Aarts, Bargh, & van Knippenberg, 2000; Dijksterhuis & Corneille, 2001).

It should be clear from these many experiments that subliminal perception does much more than bring about small semantic effects. Subliminal perception can elicit affective responses, and it can influence both social judgments and overt behavior.

Mental Representations Are Crucial

Some may find the effects described in the previous section surprising. This surprise stems largely from the fact that these effects were elicited by subliminal stimulation. If effects such as the ones described above were the result of some form of a supraliminal (i.e., conscious) manipulation, they would be much less surprising. But is that justified?

The surprise is based on the implicit assumption that our brain makes a distinction between supraliminal and subliminal priming episodes. That is, it is based on the idea that our brain cares whether something is primed with conscious mediation or without conscious mediation. We would like to argue, however, that 99 out of 100 times the brain does not care at all whether something is primed subliminally or supraliminally. "We" (i.e., humans) do, as shown by the strong reactions evoked by the possibility of effects of subliminally presented stimuli on behavior, but our brains do not. If the mental representation of *hostile* or *woman* is activated, certain psychological consequences follow, irrespective of whether activation of the word was the result of subliminal or supraliminal perception. Therefore, if supraliminal activation of a stimulus has a particular effect, subliminal activation of the same stimulus should have the same effect (for similar reasoning, see Bargh, 1989, 1992). In sum, it is the activation of a mental representation that is crucial for launching other psychological processes. The way this representation was activated (subliminal versus supraliminal) is not important.

In the realm of social cognition, there is much support for the claim that activation of mental representations is crucial regardless of the way they were activated. A number of phenomena that were first demonstrated with supraliminal presentation techniques were later replicated with subliminal techniques. Higgins, Rholes, and Jones (1977; see Srull & Wyer, 1979, 1980, for other early demonstrations) showed that supraliminal exposure to trait terms influences impressions we form of others. The previously discussed experiment by Bargh and Pietromonaco (1982) later demonstrated that this effect could be evoked by subliminal activation of a trait construct as well. Dovidio, Evans, and Tyler (1986) found that supraliminal activation of a social category ("elderly") led to enhanced accessibility of associated stereotypes ("slow" or "forgetful"). A few years later, Devine (1989) extended these effects by showing that subliminal category activation led to stereotype activation as well. After Fazio, Sanbonmatsu, Powell, and Kardes (1986) demonstrated that supraliminal words were automatically evaluated, Greenwald and colleagues (Greenwald, Klinger, & Liu, 1989; Greenwald, Klinger, & Shuh, 1995) obtained evidence for the automatic evaluation of subliminally presented stimuli. Bargh, Dijksterhuis, and colleagues (e.g., Bargh et al., 1996; Dijksterhuis & van Knippenberg, 1998; Dijksterhuis, Spears, et al., 1998; see Dijksterhuis & Bargh, 2001, for a review) found evidence that both subliminally and supraliminally activated traits and stereotypes affect overt behavior. They even compared supraliminal and subliminal activation while using the same stereotype and the same behavioral measure. Dijksterhuis, Bargh, and Miedema (2000) demonstrated that having participants answer questions about elderly people for a few minutes made participants forgetful, whereas Dijksterhuis, Aarts, et al. (2000) showed that subliminally flashing words related to the stereotype of the elderly reduced memory performance in the same way.

In all these cases, activation of a mental representation drove the effects, irrespective of whether this representation was activated supraliminally or subliminally. We concede, however, that there are a few exceptions in which awareness is crucial (see Bargh, 1992). Importantly, stimuli we are consciously aware of can elicit control strategies—often aimed at counteracting the influence of the stimulus—that will not be evoked when stimuli are perceived without awareness. What is critical in such cases is that people are aware of how a stimulus may influence their judgments or behavior. If people are not aware of such influence, or if people do not know how a stimulus might influence them, these control processes are not used (see Bargh, 1989, 1992). Still, under some conditions, conscious awareness of a stimulus does elicit processes aimed at controlling the influence of this stimulus. When "sensitive" material is activated—such as racial stereotypes—participants may be motivated to suppress the influence of the activated stereotypes (e.g., Monteith, Devine, & Sherman, 1998).

Notwithstanding a few diverging cases, we believe that in the vast majority of cases supraliminal exposure and subliminal exposure have the same effects. This, then, has important consequences for subliminal persuasion and other applications of subliminal presentation techniques.

Using and Abusing Subliminal Stimulation

In this section, we discuss applications of subliminal stimulation. Our aim is to give an objective account of the possibilities and impossibilities of intentionally influencing people's behavior with subliminal presentation techniques. Old evidence is discussed and some recent evidence is presented. Furthermore, based on our assumption that activation of mental representations is crucial (often) irrespective of the way they are activated, we occasionally extrapolate from findings obtained with supraliminal presentation techniques.

We differentiate between three different applications. First, people have attempted to change attitudes through evaluative conditioning techniques. Such methods have been used to change attitudes toward both people and objects. Second, rather than affecting behavior through changing their attitudes, people have tried to directly influence consumer behavior. Third, people have tried to design devices that convey subliminal messages aimed at affecting people's health.

Changing Attitudes

In September 2000, U.S. presidential candidate George W. Bush was accused of employing dubious campaigning techniques. One of the television ads Bush broadcast during his campaign used near-subliminal evaluative conditioning techniques. In this ad, the face of his Democratic opponent Al Gore appeared, while pieces of the words *bureaucrats* and *democrats* were flashed on the screen repeatedly. At one point, the face of Al Gore appeared on the screen, while simultaneously the word *RATS* was presented. The word appeared in the center of the screen, covering the entire screen, for one thirtieth of a second. Since it could be consciously detected by paying very close attention, presentation of the word was not subliminal (or, as Bush would have it, "subliminable" [Bruni, 2000]). Still, it was presented so briefly that it presumably escaped conscious detection among the vast majority of viewers.

For scientists, the interesting question is whether such a technique works. Can we pair a person with a subliminally presented (pretending that Bush's people had done a proper job) extremely negative word and change people's attitude toward this person? Can such a technique even influence actual voting behavior? Or can people's attitudes toward a product be enhanced by pairing presentation of this product with a subliminally presented positive stimulus? Will people actually buy it?

Razran (1940) was the first to use evaluative conditioning techniques to influence attitudes. He reasoned that by pairing presentation of an object (from now on referred to as CS, or its plural, CSi) with presentation of a negatively or positively valenced stimulus (US, USi), this object would eventually acquire the same negative or positive experienced valence. Razran's method was simultaneously crude and ecologically appealing. Participants were presented with slogans and had to indicate whether they agreed with each slogan or not. Some participants were presented with the statements while they enjoyed a free lunch, while others were presented with the slogans while inhaling unpleasant odors. When Razran measured agreement with the statements on a later occasion, participants agreed more with the statements if they were first presented during lunch than if they were first presented while participants inhaled the odors.

Later, Staats, Staats, and colleagues (Staats & Staats, 1957, 1958; Staats, Staats, & Crawford, 1962) investigated evaluative conditioning under more controlled circumstances. They paired words (sometimes nonsense words) with various valenced stimuli, ranging from positive or negative words to electric shocks or annoying sounds. Attitudes toward the words were consistently affected by their evaluative conditioning techniques: words paired with positive stimuli were rated as more positive, whereas words paired with negative stimuli were rated as more negative. Staats and Staats also proposed that the effect was not dependent on participants being consciously aware of the contingency between paired stimuli (CS-US).

But is that true? Though the phenomenon of evaluative conditioning itself has been demonstrated numerous times (see De Houwer, Thomas, & Baeyens, 2001, for a review), the question of contingency awareness is still a topic of debate. While most maintain that contingency awareness is not necessary (De Houwer, Hendrickx, & Baeyens, 1997; Hammerl & Grabitz, 1993; Krosnick, Betz, Jussim, & Lynn, 1992; Olson & Fazio, 2001), others are still not convinced (Davey, 1993; Field, 2000). For the present purposes, however, we can go one step further: Is it possible to demonstrate evaluative conditioning with subliminally presented positive or negative USi? If this is true, the contingency awareness question is solved, as one cannot be aware of a contingency between a CS and a US without being first aware of the existence of a US.

Indeed, there is evidence for subliminal evaluative conditioning. Krosnick and colleagues (1992) presented their participants with nine slides of a target person engaging in routine daily activities. These slides were preceded by slides of positive or negative events (e.g., a child with a Mickey Mouse doll versus a bloody shark) presented for 13 ms. Later, participants were asked to assess their evaluation of the target person. A target person paired with positive stimuli was evaluated more positively in general and was rated as having a nicer personality than a target person paired with negative stimuli. These findings were replicated in a second experiment. Other researchers have also found evidence for subliminal evaluative conditioning (De Houwer, Baeyens, & Eelen, 1994; De Houwer et al., 1997; Murphy, Monahan, & Zajonc, 1995; Murphy & Zajonc, 1993; Niedenthal, 1990).

In light of all the evidence, we may safely conclude that attitudes can be changed (or formed) by subliminal evaluative conditioning. This does not imply, of course, that commercial or political use of subliminal evaluative conditioning will have any success. Most potential applications of subliminal evaluative conditioning differ from published research in two ways. First, Al Gore, McDonald's, or Coca-Cola are stimuli people are already familiar with. Second, people already have existing positive or negative attitudes toward such stimuli. In other words, the stimuli of import for applied purposes are not neutral (at least not for the vast majority of people). While the role of familiarity has received some attention in past research, as far as we know prior attitudes have never been taken into account. In fact, most published research on evaluative conditioning has used only neutral stimuli as CSi. One may expect that people with neutral and/or weak attitudes are easier to influence than people with strong and/or extreme attitudes, but this matter awaits scrutiny.

The potential moderating role of familiarity has been investigated in the supraliminal evaluative conditioning domain. Shimp, Stuart, and Engle (1991; see also Stuart, Shimp, & Engle, 1987) used both well-known brands (Coca-Cola and Pepsi) and new brands in their evaluative conditioning research. In their experiments, they paired these brand names with pleasant and unpleasant pictures. The attitudinal effects of evaluative conditioning were more pronounced for unfamiliar than for familiar stimuli, but even attitudes toward familiar stimuli were influenced. Cacioppo, Marshall-Goodell, Tassinary, and Petty (1992) obtained similar findings, again with supraliminal evaluative conditioning. They presented people with both words (i.e., familiar stimuli) and nonwords (i.e., unfamiliar stimuli) paired with mild electric shocks. Whereas the attitudes toward nonwords were affected to a greater extent than attitudes toward words, attitudes toward words were affected as well. In sum, there is some converging evidence for the moderating effect of familiarity: attitudes toward familiar stimuli can be changed with evaluative conditioning, but attitude change is more pronounced when stimuli are novel.

For practical applications, important parameters of evaluative conditioning are the relation between frequency of CS-US pairing and the size of the effect, as well as the decay function of these effects. After all, advertisers need to know whether only couch potatoes who watch hours of television (and thus television advertisements) will be affected by their subliminal messages, and if these effects will dissipate before their viewers ever step inside a store (or into a voting booth). The Bush campaign showed their almost-subliminal ad about 4,000 times (Berke, 2000). Intuitively, it makes sense to opt for a high frequency of CS-US pairings, but this idea is only partly supported by research findings. Comparing conditions of 1, 3, 10, and 20 supraliminally presented pairings, Stuart and colleagues (1987) concluded that higher frequencies led to greater effects, but also that the effect of frequency was weak.

Finally, Baeyens and colleagues (Baeyens, Crombez, van den Bergh, & Eelen, 1988; Baeyens, Eelen, Crombez, & van den Bergh, 1992) also compared different frequencies of supraliminally presented CS-US pairings and found that up to at least 10 pairings, higher frequencies led to greater effects. Beyond this point, however, they suggest that there may actually be an inverse relation between frequency and effect size. In sum, one may—with some care—conclude that for low frequencies there seems to be a weak but positive relation between frequency and effect size, while the relation for higher frequencies is unclear at this point.

The relevant findings concerning the decay or extinction of evaluative conditioning effects are quite spectacular. Baeyens and colleagues (1988) supraliminally paired neutral faces with liked or disliked faces and showed that attitudes toward the neutral faces paired with liked pictures were more positive than attitudes toward neutral faces paired with disliked stimuli. Two months later, when participants evaluated the same conditioned pictures again, there was no sign of decay: the difference in liking between the neutral faces paired with liked pictures and the neutral faces paired with disliked pictures was still highly significant. Levey and Martin (1975) reported even more impressive findings: their effects of evaluative conditioning were still reliable after 18 months.

Can we conclude, on the basis of the current evidence, that subliminal evaluative conditioning can have effects when it is applied for political or commercial reasons? It is true that subliminal evaluative conditioning has been shown to work. It is also true that effects of evaluative conditioning do not decay quickly. Finally, both familiar and unfamiliar targets can be conditioned, although attitudes toward the latter are easier to manipulate. Hence, though we do not yet know whether prior attitudes (and the strength and extremity of these attitudes) moderate effects of evaluative conditioning, it is possible that advertisers or politicians could subliminally shape or change our attitudes toward a new toothpaste, McDonald's, or Al Gore.

An important disclaimer is that evaluative conditioning affects attitudes but not necessarily behavior. Someone may be able to subliminally influence our attitude toward a new toothpaste or even toward Al Gore, but that does not yet imply that they also affect what toothpaste we buy or which presidential candidate we vote for. The factors that influence the relation between attitudes and behavior are too numerous to discuss here, but some assumptions can be made regarding the relation between attitudes influenced by evaluative conditioning and actual behavior. Cacioppo and colleagues (1992) reasoned that attitudes based on evaluative conditioning could determine less rational and impulsive behavior, while they could not (or could hardly) affect more deliberate, intention-driven behavior. This idea is supported by other contributions in the attitude literature. Evaluative conditioning creates attitudes that can be activated automatically upon perception of the attitude object (Olson & Fazio, 2001). According to Fazio's (1990; see also Fazio et al., 1986) MODE model, attitudes that are automatically activated upon perception of the attitude object affect overt behavior in the absence of more motivated and elaborate issue-relevant thinking and have far smaller effects when people engage in significant deliberation. Roughly speaking, the more we think about a behavior, the less influence prior evaluative conditioning should have on this behavior. Hence, with subliminal evaluative conditioning it may well be possible to exert some influence over the toothpaste people buy. However, it is likely to be much harder to influence a house purchase, at least for people who deliberate about such things. As for a decision such as a vote for a presidential candidate, it seems highly doubtful that evaluative conditioning could exert much influence. Given the current evidence, though, it is premature to give definite answers or to rule out any possibilities.

Changing Consumer Behavior

The single most controversial area within the domain of subliminal psychological processes is "subliminal persuasion": the direct influence of consumer behavior by subliminal directives. As alluded to before, this idea can be traced to a newspaper publication about James Vicary, who claimed that he had greatly increased the sales of popcorn and cola in a New Jersey cinema by subliminally flashing "Eat Popcorn" and "Drink Coke" during a movie. This newspaper article caused a tremendous stir: Moore (1982), who published a very insightful review of the area, quotes *The Nation* as stating that it is "the most alarming and outrageous discovery since Mr. Gatling invented his gun" (p. 206). Although Vicary later admitted he never found any evidence for subliminally influencing behavior, the majority of people outside academia believe in the potential power of subliminal messages. This is partly because Vicary's original claim was noticed by many, while his later "erratum" was noted by very few (Pratkanis, 1992). Another reason for this belief's persistence is that people have made grandiose yet largely unsubstantiated claims about both the effectiveness and pervasiveness of subliminal persuasion (e.g., Key, 1989), whereas the skeptics have published their work in scientific articles that are obviously less accessible to people outside the scientific community. Still, many people believe in the power of subliminal persuasion: Rogers and Smith (1993) found that 75% of Americans had heard of subliminal persuasion and of these 75%, another 75% believed it worked (see Zanot, Pincus, & Lamp, 1983, for comparable figures).

Can we, on the basis of the current scientific evidence, draw any conclusions regarding the effectiveness of subliminal persuasion techniques? Despite quite a number of publications, this is surprisingly difficult. To explain why the popular belief in subliminal persuasion is strong, Pratkanis (1992) characterized the study of subliminal persuasion as a form of "cargo cult" science (see Feynman, 1985). A cargo cult science "has all the trappings of science—the illusion of objectivity, the appearance of careful study, and the motions of an experiment—but lacks one important ingredient: skepticism" (Pratkanis, 1992, p. 264). This is without doubt true: Many claims have been made on the basis of the flimsiest of evidence (e.g., Key, 1989). However, to objectively assess whether subliminal persuasion can work, one has to deal with a second problem: the science devoted to showing that subliminal persuasion does not work can just as well be characterized as a cargo cult science. Because many scientists simply do not want subliminal persuasion to work, rather unusual practices can be witnessed in the literature. It may be the only area in psychology where greater value and credibility are attached to null results than to actual significant results, and where it is so easy to publish noneffects. Furthermore, effects that are obtained are often downplayed by the authors themselves because they did not want to find them (e.g., Trappey, 1996). In addition, scientists often advise their colleagues not to investigate the topic (see, e.g., Packard, 1978; Pratkanis, 1992) and many have used rather extreme and often suggestive language in their publications (see also the first paragraph of this chapter). Pratkanis (1992) said, "Of course, as with anything scientific, it may be that someday, somehow, someone will develop a subliminal technique that may work, just as someday a chemist may find a way to transmute lead into gold" (p. 269).

But let us return to the important question. Can it work? Should we buy lead futures? If we want to assess whether subliminal persuasion could ever work, it may be useful to differentiate between three distinct psychological processes that may be influenced. First, can we make people hungry or thirsty by subliminal messages? That is, can we alter people's basic physiological needs or the subjective experience of these needs? Second, can we change people's behavior itself? Can we make them drink or eat more? Finally, can we affect people's choices? Given that people want to drink, can we get them to choose one brand over another through subliminal messages? We discuss these issues in three sections.

Thirst and Hunger One way to subliminally influence people's behavior is to make them hungry or thirsty. Byrne (1959) was the first to test this idea. In his experiment, he flashed the word *beef* repeatedly (140 times) during a 16-minute movie. Importantly, Byrne (1959) ensured that people were not aware of the subliminally presented word. Compared to a control group, subliminal presentation of the word had no semantic effects and no effect on people's preference for a beef sandwich over alternatives, but it did affect subjective ratings of hunger.

A few years later, Spence (1964; see also Spence & Ehrenberg, 1964) replicated Byrne's (1959) findings. He presented participants with words on a screen. Between these words, Spence (1964) subliminally flashed the word *cheese*. After exposure to these words, participants were asked whether their hunger had increased, decreased, or remained the same as it was before the experiment. Of his 35 participants, 24 reported increased hunger, 9 reported decreased hunger, and 2 reported no change, a reliable effect. One may object here that experimenter demands are looming large, but this effect occurred only after 30 stimulus exposures and not after 5 stimulus exposures. An alternative explanation in terms of demand characteristics would have to explain why demands did not exert an effect in a condition that differed only in frequency of exposure.

Hawkins (1970) flashed either *Coke* or *Drink Coke* for 2.7 ms intervals during the presentation of unrelated supraliminal material. In a third, control group, participants were subliminally exposed to nonsense syllables. As expected, subjective thirst ratings were higher for both experimental groups than for the control group. Although the difference between the *Drink Coke* and the control group did not reach conventional levels of significance ($p < .06$), the difference between the *Coke* and the control condition was significant ($p < .022$).

One common objection is that there have been a few known failures to replicate these experiments (see e.g., Moore, 1982). Although this is important, these three experiments are themselves replications of the same phenomenon: Subliminally flashing words designating food or drinks can increase subjective hunger or thirst. Hence, simply concluding that subliminal manipulations of hunger or thirst cannot work is premature. However, the relation between subjectively felt needs such as hunger or thirst and actual consumer behavior is complex and presumably rather weak. As Moore (1982, p. 42) concluded, "even if the results are taken at face value, their relevance to advertising is minimal."

Drinking and Eating A second question is whether we can subliminally elicit drinking or eating behavior. Earlier work has already shown that subliminally activated personality traits or stereotypes can affect overt behavior (see Dijksterhuis & Bargh, 2001, for a review). Importantly, the effects of activated stereotypes and traits on overt behavior are mediated by the activation of behavior representations. For instance, activation of the stereotype of professors or the trait intelligence leads to activation of behavior representations such as "concentrate" or "think," which in turn affect actual performance on an intellectual task. Given that behavior is influenced by activation of behavior representations such as "think," one can hypothesize that the same can be expected from activation of a representation of, for instance, "drink."

We (Dijksterhuis, Wegner, & Aarts, 2001) tested this idea. Participants performed a standard lexical decision task. In total, participants were presented with 20 letter strings, either random letter strings or mundane, short words (e.g., *door*, *bike*). However, prior to the presentation of the words, other, subliminal words were flashed. In one condition, we flashed the word *drink*, in another condition we flashed the word *cola*, and in the control condition, we presented a four-letter random letter string. These words were flashed for 15 ms and were immediately masked by the target word. Importantly, when asked, none of the participants reported seeing anything prior to the target words. After participants finished the lexical decision task, the experimenter, who was blind to condition, announced the second task would be rather long and said, "I am going to have a drink. Do you want a drink as well? We have cola and mineral water." Participants who indicated they wanted a drink (the majority) were given the appropriate can. They then read text from the computer screen before the experimenter said the experiment was over. Both people in the drink prime condition ($M = 80$ cc) and people in the cola prime condition ($M = 96$ cc) drank more than people in the control condition ($M = 33$ cc). At the same time, however, the cola prime did not affect participants' choice of beverage.

Strahan, Spencer, and Zanna (2002) also obtained evidence for subliminally influencing drinking behavior. Participants in their experiment were asked not to eat or drink anything for 3 hours before the experimental session to make sure participants would arrive at the lab thirsty. Subsequently, participants were asked to taste cookies. Afterward, some participants were given a glass of water, allegedly to cleanse their palate. Hence, some participants were kept thirsty, whereas others were allowed to quench their thirst. Participants were then subliminally primed. In one condition, participants were subliminally presented with words associated with thirst (e.g., *thirst*, *dry*), whereas in the control condition they were presented with words unrelated to thirst. After this task, participants performed another taste test. They were asked to evaluate two beverages and were told they could drink as much as they wanted. Participants who had been presented with the thirst-related words drank significantly more than the control participants.

One may argue that advertisers are interested not so much in how much people drink but instead in what people drink. However, more drinking in general implies that people will also drink more of a particular drink. After all, in bars guests are often given salty food (such as peanuts) for free to get them to drink more. This is beneficial for both the owner of the bar and the manufacturer of a particular drink. Finally, it should also be noted that the size of both effects discussed here is considerable.

Choice The third question is whether one can influence the consumer choices people make via subliminal messages. Can we get people to choose Coca-Cola over Pepsi? A substantial literature in the advertising and marketing domain is devoted to this question. In his review of this domain, Trappey (1996) listed previous narrative reviews. Out of nine earlier reviews (some covering more than choice behavior), five concluded that subliminal messages could affect behavior, whereas four concluded that there was no evidence for such effects. Based on his own meta-analytic review, he concluded that subliminal messages do have an effect on choice. However, he seemed to regret this, as he spent the better part of his discussion downplaying the importance of the effect. The combined effect size he reported is indeed small ($r = .06$), and Trappey said that it "falls between the effect of aspirin on heart attacks and the relationship between alcohol abuse and a tour of duty in Vietnam" (p. 527) and later concluded that it "is negligible" (p. 528).

But is this effect really that small? An r of .06 means that if without treatment 50 out of 100 people choose a certain product, after treatment 53 people would do so. Psychologically such an effect is small, but advertisers may have a different opinion. For multinational corporations, such a small effect corresponds—in theory at least—to millions of dollars. Moreover, one might wonder if supraliminal advertising techniques might perform better. Actually, a closer look reveals that it is very surprising that Trappey found an effect at all. In 17 out of the 23 experiments in the meta-analysis, the subliminal message was only presented once. It is a well-known fact that more frequent presentation of a message leads to greater psychological effects (e.g., Dijksterhuis & van Knippenberg, 1998; Higgins, Bargh & Lombardi, 1985; Marcel, 1983; Srull & Wyer, 1979, 1980).

Strahan and colleagues (2002) showed that subliminally influencing choices may work better in combination with supraliminal information among people who already have a relevant need. They invited thirsty participants to the laboratory. Some participants were presented with subliminally presented words related to thirst or with control words. Subsequently, participants were offered two drinks, Super Quencher and Power Pro. Super Quencher was advertised as the best thirst-quencing beverage on the market, while Power Pro was not so advertised. Interestingly, participants who had not been presented with the thirst-related words indicated no preference, despite the fact that they were thirsty, whereas participants who had been presented with the thirst-related words had a clear preference for Super Quencher. In other words, if one is already thirsty, a relevant advertisement can be more "convincing" if it is accompanied by subliminal messages. Importantly, Strahan and colleagues replicated this effect a number of times.

Now where do all these results leave us? It seems to be possible to subliminally influence people's self-reported thirst or hunger. It seems to be possible to subliminally affect the amount people consume. Finally, it may be possible to subliminally affect choices. On the one hand, it is certainly premature to claim that subliminal advertising does work and that we should seriously think about guarding ourselves against it. On the other hand, the evidence is definitely strong enough to say that commercial applications of subliminal stimulation can, in principle, work, and that we should not treat them as a myth unworthy of investigation. Instead, we should study applications of subliminal stimulation to come to an objective appreciation of exactly what is, and what is not, possible. The least we should conclude is that the possibility that one or another form of subliminal advertising will be shown to have an effect is much greater than the possibility that people will learn to turn lead into gold. And if not, it really is time to buy a lot of lead.

Improving Health

Various companies have abused the popular belief in the power of subliminal phenomena by marketing subliminal self-help devices. For instance, customers can buy audiotapes in which subliminal messages are hidden. Supposedly, by processing subliminal messages such as "I feel fantastic this morning" or "Let's stay away from the pizza in the refrigerator today," people will feel better or lose weight.

During the 1980s, self-help audiotapes were so popular in the United States that various scientists were prompted to test their effectiveness. For example, Greenwald, Spangenberg, Pratkanis, and Eskenazi (1991) tested the effects of two tapes, one designed to improve memory and the other designed to improve self-esteem. Greenwald and colleagues switched some of the labels on the tapes before handing them to their participants. The participants listened to the tapes each day for a 1-month period, and both before and after this period, self-esteem and memory performance were assessed. The results were clear: All that was found was a placebo effect. The labels on the tapes had an effect, but the subliminal messages on the tapes did not. At about the same time, various other researchers tested self-help tapes (e.g., Russell, Rowe, & Smouse, 1991) and reached the same conclusion: Subliminal self-help messages do not have any effect at all.[5]

Does this mean that physical or mental health cannot benefit from the processing of subliminal stimuli? That conclusion is premature, because these experiments all investigated auditory subliminal perception. Visual subliminal perception may be generally more effective than auditory subliminal perception. Both Mayer and Merkelbach (1999) and Theus (1994) have remarked that the probability that subliminal stimuli are cognitively processed is much higher for visual than for auditory stimuli. This may be partly caused by the difference between the human processing capacity for visual versus auditory stimuli.

Recently, various companies have advertised self-help devices that use visual subliminal stimuli. When connected to a VCR, such a device presents subliminal messages on a TV screen. Customers may lose weight, reduce stress, and improve self-esteem while they watch the Superbowl or *Oprah*. We do not know whether these devices have been scientifically tested. Though visual subliminal stimulation is more likely to be effective than auditory stimulation, we should not yet be optimistic. One device (made by a company called Motivision) presents subliminal messages that are rather long (20–40 letters). Greenwald (1992; see also Abrams & Greenwald, 2000; but see Silverman, 1976) has already showed that subliminally presenting anything more than a single word is a hazardous affair, whereas short sentences are unlikely to have any effect at all. Assuming that people can pick up bits and pieces of a sentence, the subliminal presentation of a sentence such as "Do not eat much" can have various consequences. Unfortunately, the probability that it urges people to eat more (when only "eat" or "eat much" are perceived) is higher than the probability that it urges people to eat less (for which the entire sentence is needed).

But what if we subliminally present single words? Recently, Dijksterhuis (2001) started to test the idea that subliminal exposure to stimuli related to relaxation may affect cardiovascular activity. It has often been demonstrated that consciously thinking or imagining relaxation can have a profound impact on autonomic processes such as heart rate (Jones & Johnson, 1980; Lucini et al., 1997), respiration rate (Jones & Johnson, 1980), and skin resistance (Himle, 1973). In our view, the critical mediator causing these changes in autonomic functioning is not the conscious imagination but rather the activation of the mental representation of relaxation. In our experiment, participants were asked to watch a computer screen during three 1-minute task periods. These periods were separated by 1-minute breaks. During the second task period, participants were subliminally presented with either the word *rest* or *relax* every 3 s. The words remained on the screen for only 15 ms and were both premasked and postmasked by random letter strings. The first and third task periods, during which only the pre- and postmasks appeared, were used as controls. Heart rate was measured throughout these three task periods. Heart rate was indeed significantly lower ($M = 70.3$ bpm) during the experimental 1-minute period relative to the two control periods ($M = 72.1$ bpm). Subliminal stimulation, then, indeed affects cardiovascular activity. At about the same time, Hull, Slone, and Matthews (2001) obtained comparable results in two different experiments. They subliminally presented participants (17 ms) with words such as *angry* or *relax*. Immediately afterward, systolic and diastolic blood pressure was lower for the participants presented with the word *relax* than for participants presented with the word *angry*.

Of course, these findings should not be taken as evidence that we can now design self-help devices to reduce stress. The effects obtained in the cited studies decay quickly and the effects are small in size. Still, they are enough reason to take the idea seriously and to continue to investigate effects of subliminal stimulation on health.

Conclusion: Three Good Reasons for Investigating Subliminal Phenomena

In closing, we would like to give three good reasons for taking the domain seriously and for doing scientific research on subliminal phenomena. The first reason regards the potential beneficial use of subliminal stimulation. Self-help tapes have been proven to be ineffective, but it seems worthwhile to continue to study other possibilities. The studies demonstrating that heart rate and blood pressure can be temporarily decreased by subliminal stimulation provide enough evidence to give the idea of subliminal stimulation to promote health another chance.

The second reason regards the abuse of subliminal stimulation. The idea of subliminal influence has met with strong aversion. People do not want to be subliminally steered toward buying "toothpaste X" and certainly not toward voting for a particular political candidate. Nobody wants to pay $200 for some ineffective health-improving device. However, we should be aware that subliminal techniques are applied and sold, and we can act to decrease or maybe even stop this abuse. One way would be legislation. Another way would be to objectively inform society about the effectiveness or ineffectiveness of certain techniques. Importantly, whatever we choose, it is necessary to first come to know what is possible and what is not.

The third reason is purely scientific. If, in a certain area, a few findings have been documented and a few articles have been published, this usually leads more people to investigate these findings. Researchers abandon a domain for a limited number of reasons: They know everything they want to know; they conclude it does not lead to something substantial; or they simply stop being fascinated by a certain topic. None of these reasons is relevant to the application of subliminal stimulation. We do not know much yet; we cannot say that it does not lead to something; and many people are fascinated by findings such as the ones presented in this chapter. Instead, the reason that so little research has been done is emotional. Vicary and others (e.g., Key, 1989) have influenced popular beliefs about subliminal research based on shoddy research. In reaction, the vast majority of the psychological community has claimed that subliminal persuasion cannot work and that we should remove it from the agenda. This, however, is simply unscientific. If, as scientists, we base our statements on things other than sound research, science itself will become superfluous.

Acknowledgments The authors would like to thank Tony Greenwald and the editors for very helpful comments on an earlier draft.

Notes

1. Kihlstrom, Barnhardt, and Tataryn (1992) point out that the Peirce and Jastrow studies were not just the first experiments on subliminal perception, but also the first American psychological experiments: These were the first studies conducted at Hopkins, the first psychological laboratory in America.

2. We concede that we cannot guarantee that all experiments cited in this chapter do indeed fit this definition. An awareness check is needed to rule out the possibility that participants could perceive stimuli consciously. While most authors report such a check, a few (mainly in older articles) do not.

3. Of course, at any point in time it is not the case that our total processing capacity is aimed at one "target" (such as judging an apartment). But even if one assumes that only a small part of the overall processing capacity was devoted to judging the apartment, it is likely that far more relevant information was dealt with unconsciously than consciously.

4. Although subliminally presented words can be classified on the basis of their valence, Abrams and Greenwald (2000) demonstrated that under some circumstances subliminal perception leads to processing only word parts. For instance, repeated exposure to the negative words *smut* and *bile* leads to a negative evaluation of the subliminally presented word *smile*. In other words, rather than processing *smile* as a whole, participants processed the word parts *sm* and *ile* that were both evaluated negatively due to earlier exposure to *smut* and *bile*. These results should not be taken as evidence that people can only process word parts subliminally, as such a conclusion is at odds with much other research. Rather, these results show that under some circumstances word parts are given more weight during processing of subliminal stimuli than entire words.

5. At about the same time, religious fanatics accused the rock band Judas Priest of hiding subliminal messages (actually, backward messages) in their music that supposedly caused the suicide of a 10-year-old boy. As one might expect, people cannot make sense of backward speech. Begg, Needham, and Bookbinder (1993; see also Vokey & Read, 1985) have shown that people cannot differentiate between backward nursery rhymes, Christian messages, Satanic messages, or pornography.

This should not be taken as evidence that subliminal self-help tapes cannot have an effect. The tapes that were tested were designed for commercial use by people who did not quite know what they were doing (other than trying to make money). They certainly knew much less about subliminal influence than most, if not all, of the people cited in this chapter.

References

Abrams, R. L., & Greenwald, A. G. (2000). Parts outweigh the whole (word) in unconscious analysis of meaning. *Psychological Science, 11*, 118–124.

Adams, J. K. (1957). Laboratory studies of behavior without awareness. *Psychology Bulletin, 54*, 383–405.

Baeyens, F., Crombez, G., van den Bergh, O., & Eelen, P. (1988). Once in contact always in contact: Evaluative conditioning is resistant to extinction. *Advances in Behavior Research and Therapy, 10*, 179–199.

Baeyens, F., Eelen, P., Crombez, G., & van den Bergh, O. (1992). Human evaluative conditioning: Acquisition trials, presentation schedule, evaluative style and contingency awareness. *Behaviour Research and Therapy, 30*, 133–142.

Bargh, J. A. (1989). Conditional automaticity: Varieties of automatic influence in social perception and cognition. In J. S. Uleman & J. A. Bargh (Eds.), *Unintended thought* (pp. 3–51). New York: Guilford.

Bargh, J. A. (1992). Being unaware of a stimulus versus unaware of its interpretation: Why subliminality per se does not matter to social psychology. In R. Bornstein & T. Pittman (Eds.), *Perception without awareness* (pp. 236–255). New York: Guilford.

Bargh, J. A., Chen, M., & Burrows, L. (1996). The automaticity of social behavior: Direct effects of trait concept and stereotype activation on action. *Journal of Personality and Social Psychology, 71*, 230–244.

Bargh, J. A., & Pietromonaco, P. (1982). Automatic information processing and social perception: The influence of trait information presented outside of conscious awareness on impression formation. *Journal of Personality and Social Psychology, 43*, 437–449.

Begg, I. M., Needham, D. R., & Bookbinder, M. (1993). Do backward messages unconsciously affect listeners? No. *Canadian Journal of Experimental Psychology, 47*, 1–14.

Berke, R. L. (2000, September 12). Democrats see, and smell, rats in G.O.P. ad. *New York Times*, p. 1.

Bornstein, R. F. (1992). Subliminal mere exposure effects. In R. F. Bornstein & T. S. Pittman (Eds.), *Perception without awareness: Cognitive, clinical and social perspectives* (pp. 191–210). New York: Guilford.

Bruni, F. (2000, September 13). Bush says rats reference in ad was unintentional. *New York Times*, p. 19.

Byrne, D. (1959). The effect of a subliminal food stimulus on verbal response. *Journal of Applied Psychology, 43*, 249–252.

Cacioppo, J. T., Marshall-Goodell, B. S., Tassinary, L. G., & Petty, R. E. (1992). Rudimentary determinants of attitudes: Classical conditioning is more effective when prior knowledge about the attitude stimulus is low than high. *Journal of Experimental Social Psychology, 28*, 207–233.

Cheesman, J., & Merikle, P. M. (1984). Priming with and without awareness. *Perception and Psychophysics, 36*, 387–395.

Cheesman, J., & Merikle, P. M. (1986). Distinguishing conscious from unconscious perceptual processes. *Canadian Journal of Psychology, 40*, 343–367.

Chen, M., & Bargh, J. A. (1997). Nonconscious behavioral confirmation processes: The self-fulfilling nature of automatically activated stereotypes. *Journal of Experimental Social Psychology, 33*, 541–560.

Damasio, A. R. (1994). *Descartes' error: Emotion, reason and the human brain.* New York: Avon Books.

Davey, G. C. L. (1993). Defining the important theoretical questions to ask about evaluative conditioning: A reply to Martin and Levey. *Behaviour Research and Therapy, 32*, 307–310.

Debner, J. A., & Jacoby, L. L. (1994). Unconscious perception: Attention, awareness, and control. *Journal of Experimental Psychology: Learning, Memory and Cognition, 20*, 304–317.

Dehaene, S., Naccache, L., Le Clec'H, G., Keochlin, E., Mueller, M., Dehaene-Lambertz, G., van de Moortele, P., & Le Bihan, D. (1998). Imaging unconscious semantic priming. *Nature, 395*, 597–600.

De Houwer, J., Baeyens, F., & Eelen, P. (1994). Verbal conditioning with undetected US presentations. *Behavior Research and Therapy, 32*, 629–633.

De Houwer, J., Hendrickx, H., & Baeyens, F. (1997). Evaluative learning with "subliminally" presented stimuli. *Consciousness and Cognition, 6*, 87–107.

De Houwer, J., Thomas, S., & Baeyens, F. (2001). Associative learning of likes and dislikes: A review of 25 years of research on human evaluative conditioning. *Psychological Bulletin, 127*, 853–869.

Devine, P. G. (1989). Stereotypes and prejudice: Their automatic and controlled components. *Journal of Personality and Social Psychology, 56*, 5–18.

Dijksterhuis, A. (2001). Unconscious relaxation: The influence of subliminal priming on heart rate. Unpublished manuscript, University of Amsterdam.

Dijksterhuis, A., Aarts, H., Bargh, J. A., & van Knippenberg, A. (2000). On the relation between associative strength and automatic behavior. *Journal of Experimental Social Psychology, 36*, 531–544.

Dijksterhuis, A., & Bargh, J. A. (2001). The perception-behavior expressway: The automatic effects of social perception on social behavior. In M. P. Zanna (Ed.), *Advances in experimental social psychology* (Vol. 33, pp. 1–40). San Diego, CA: Academic Press.

Dijksterhuis, A., Bargh, J. A., & Miedema, J. (2000). Of men and mackerels: Attention and automatic behavior. In H. Bless & J. P. Forgas (Eds.), *Subjective experience in social cognition and behavior* (pp. 36–51). Philadelphia: Psychology Press.

Dijksterhuis, A., & Corneille, O. (2001). On the relation between stereotype activation and intellectual performance. Unpublished manuscript, University of Amsterdam.

Dijksterhuis, A., Spears, R., Postmes, T., Stapel, D. A., Koomen, W., van Knippenberg, A., & Scheepers, D. (1998). Seeing one thing and doing another: Contrast effects in automatic behavior. *Journal of Personality and Social Psychology, 75*, 862–871.

Dijksterhuis, A., & van Knippenberg, A. (1998). The relation between perception and behavior or how to win a game of Trivial Pursuit. *Journal of Personality and Social Psychology, 74*, 865–877.

Dijksterhuis, A., Wegner, D. M., & Aarts, H. (2001). Unpublished data set.

Dixon, N. F. (1971). *Subliminal perception*. New York: McGraw-Hill.

Dixon, N. F. (1981). *Preconscious processing*. New York: Wiley.

Dixon, N. F. (1986). On private events and brain events. *Behavioral and Brain Sciences, 9*, 29–30.

Dovidio, J. F., Evans, N., & Tyler, R. B. (1986). Racial stereotypes: The contents of their cognitive representations. *Journal of Experimental Social Psychology, 22*, 22–37.

Eriksen, C. W. (1960). Discrimination and learning without awareness: A methodological survey and evaluation. *Psychological Review, 67*, 279–300.

Fazio, R. H. (1990). Multiple processes by which attitudes guide behavior: The MODE model as an integrative framework. In M. P. Zanna (Ed.), *Advances in*

Experimental Social Psychology (Vol. 23, pp. 75–109). New York: Academic Press.

Fazio, R. H., Sanbonmatsu, D. M., Powell, M. C., & Kardes, F. R. (1986). On the automatic activation of attitudes. *Journal of Personality and Social Psychology, 50*, 229–238.

Feynman, R. P. (1985). *Surely you're joking, Mr. Feynman*. New York: Bantam Books.

Field, A. P. (2000). I like it, but I'm not sure why: Can evaluative conditioning occur without conscious awareness? *Consciousness and Cognition, 9*, 13–36.

Fowler, C. (1986). An operational definition of conscious awareness must be responsible to subjective experience. *Behavioral and Brain Sciences, 9*, 33–35.

Greenwald, A. G. (1992). New Look 3: Unconscious cognition reclaimed. *American Psychologist, 47*, 766–779.

Greenwald, A. G., Draine, S., & Abrams, R. (1996). Three cognitive markers of unconscious semantic activation. *Science, 273*, 1699–1702.

Greenwald, A. G., Klinger, M. R., & Liu, T. J. (1989). Unconscious processing of dichoptically masked words. *Memory and Cognition, 17*, 35–47.

Greenwald, A. G., Klinger, M. R., & Schuh, E. S. (1995). Activation by marginally perceptible ("subliminal") stimuli: Dissociation of unconscious from conscious cognition. *Journal of Experimental Psychology: General, 124*, 22–42.

Greenwald, A. G., Spangenberg, E. R., Pratkanis, A. R., & Eskenazi, J. (1991). Double-blind tests of subliminal self-help audiotapes. *Psychological Science, 2*, 119–122.

Hammerl, M., & Grabitz, H. J. (1993). Human evaluative conditioning: Order of stimulus presentation. *Integrative Physiological and Behavioral Science, 28*, 191–194.

Hawkins, D. (1970). The effects of subliminal stimulation on drive level and brand preference. *Journal of Marketing Research, 8*, 322–326.

Higgins, E. T., Bargh, J. A., & Lombardi, W. (1985). Nature of priming effects on categorization. *Journal of Experimental Psychology: Learning, Memory, and Cognition, 11*, 59–69.

Higgins, E. T., Rholes, W. S., & Jones, C. R. (1977). Category accessibility and impression formation. *Journal of Experimental Social Psychology, 13*, 141–154.

Himle, D. P. (1973). Effects of instructions upon an autonomic response: An analogue of systematic desensitization. *Psychological Reports, 32*, 767–773.

Holender, D. (1986). Semantic activation without conscious identification in dichotic listening, parafoveal vision, and visual masking: A survey and appraisal. *Behavioral and Brain Sciences, 9*, 1–66.

Hull, J. G., Slone, L. B., & Matthews, A. R. (2001, February). *The non-consciousness of self-consciousness*. Poster presented at the second annual Society for Personality and Social Psychology Conference, San Antonio, TX.

Jaynes, J. (1976). *The origin of consciousness in the breakdown of the bicameral mind*. Boston: Houghton Mifflin.

Jones, G. E., & Johnson, H. J. (1980). Heart rate and somatic concomitants of mental imagery. *Psychophysiology, 17*, 339–347.

Key, W. B. (1989). *The age of manipulation*. New York: Holt.

Kihlstrom, J. F., Barnhardt, T. M., & Tataryn, D. J. (1992). Implicit perception. In R. F. Bornstein & T. S. Pittman (Eds.), *Perception without awareness: Cognitive, clinical and social perspectives* (pp. 17–54). New York: Guilford.

Krosnick, J. A., Betz, A. L., Jussim, L. J., & Lynn, A. R. (1992). Subliminal conditioning of attitudes. *Personality and Social Psychology Bulletin, 18*, 152–162.

Kunst-Wilson, W., & Zajonc, R. (1980). Affective discrimination of stimuli that cannot be recognized. *Science, 207*, 557–558.

Küpfmüller, K. (1962). Nachrichtenverarbeitung im Menschen. In K. Steinbuch (Ed.), *Taschenbuch der Nachrichtenverarbeitung* (pp. 1481–1501). Berlin: Springer.

Lepore, L., & Brown, R. (1997). Category and stereotype activation: Is prejudice inevitable? *Journal of Personality and Social Psychology, 72*, 275–287.

Levey, A. B., & Martin, I. (1975). Classical conditioning of human "evaluative" responses. *Behavior Research and Therapy, 13*, 221–226.

Libet, B. (1985). Unconscious cerebral initiative and the role of conscious will in voluntary action. *Behavioral and Brain Sciences, 8*, 529–566.

Libet, B., Alberts, W. W., Wright, E. W., & Feinstein, B. (1967). Responses of human somatosensory cortex to stimuli below threshold for conscious sensation. *Science, 158*, 1597–1600.

Lucini, D., Covacci, G., Milani, R., Mela, G. S., Malliani, A., & Pagani, M. (1997). A controlled study of effects of mental relaxation on autonomic excitatory responses in healthy subjects. *Psychosomatic Medicine, 59*, 541–552.

Marcel, A. J. (1983). Conscious and unconscious perception: An approach to the relations between phenomenal experience and perceptual processes. *Cognitive Psychology, 15*, 238–300.

Mayer, B., & Merkelbach, H. (1999). Unconscious processes, subliminal stimulation, and anxiety. *Clinical Psychology Review, 19*, 571–590.

Merikle, P. M., Joordens, S., & Stolz, J. A. (1995). Measuring the relative magnitude of unconscious influences. *Consciousness and Cognition, 4*, 422–439.

Merikle, P. M., & Reingold, E. M. (1992). Measuring unconscious perceptual processes. In R. F. Bornstein & T. S. Pittman (Eds.), *Perception without awareness: Cognitive, clinical and social perspectives* (pp. 55–80). New York: Guilford.

Monteith, M. J., Devine, P. G., & Sherman, J. W. (1998). Suppression as a stereotype control strategy. *Personality and Social Psychology Review, 2*, 63–82.

Moore, T. E. (1982). Subliminal advertising: What you see is what you get. *Journal of Marketing, 46*, 38–47.

Murphy, S., Monahan, J., & Zajonc, R. B. (1995). Additivity of nonconscious affect: Combined effects of priming and exposure. *Journal of Personality and Social Psychology, 69*, 589–602.

Murphy, S., & Zajonc, R. B. (1993). Affect, cognition, and awareness: Affective priming with optimal and suboptimal stimulus exposures. *Journal of Personality and Social Psychology, 64*, 723–739.

Niedenthal, P. M. (1990). Implicit perception of affective information. *Journal of Experimental Social Psychology, 26*, 505–527.

Nisbett, R., & Wilson, D. T. (1977). Telling more than we can know: Verbal reports on mental processes. *Psychological Review, 84*, 231–259.

Nørretranders, T. (1998). *The user illusion: Cutting consciousness down to size.* New York: Viking.

Olson, M. A., & Fazio, R. H. (2001). Implicit attitude formation through classical conditioning. *Psychological Science, 12*, 413–417.

Paap, K. R. (1986). The pilfering of awareness and guilt by association. *Behavioral and Brain Sciences, 9*, 45–46.

Packard, V. (1978). *The people shapers.* London: MacDonald and Jane's.

Peirce, C. S., & Jastrow, J. (1884). On small differences in sensation. *Memoirs of the National Academy of Science, 3*, 75–83.

Pötzl, O. (1960). The relationship between experimentally induced dream images and indirect vision (J. Wolff, D. Rapoport, & S. Annin, Trans.). *Psychological Issues, 3*(7), 41–120. (Original work published 1917)

Pratkanis, A. R. (1992). The cargo-cult science of subliminal persuasion. *Skeptical Inquirer, 16*, 260–272.

Razran, G. H. S. (1940). Conditioned response changes in rating and appraising sociopolitical slogans. *Psychological Bulletin, 37*, 481.

Rogers, M., & Smith, K. H. (1993, March/April). Public perceptions of subliminal advertising: Why practitioners shouldn't ignore the issue. *Journal of Advertising Research*, pp. 10–18.

Russell, T. G., Rowe, W., & Smouse, A. D. (1991). Subliminal self-help tapes and academic achievement: An evaluation. *Journal of Counseling and Development, 69*, 359–362.

Shimp, T. A., Stuart, E. W., & Engle, R. W. (1991). A program of classical conditioning experiments testing variations in the conditioned stimulus and context. *Journal of Consumer Research, 18*, 1–12.

Sidis, B. (1898). *The psychology of suggestion.* New York: D. Appleton.

Silverman, L. H. (1976). Psychoanalytic theory: The reports of my death are greatly exaggerated. *American Psychologist, 31*, 621–637.

Spence, D. P. (1964). Effects of a continuously flashing subliminal verbal food stimulus on subjective hunger ratings. *Psychological Reports, 15*, 993–994.

Spence, D. P., & Ehrenberg, B. (1964). Effects of oral deprivation on responses to subliminal and supraliminal verbal food stimuli. *Journal of Abnormal and Social Psychology, 69*, 10–18.

Srull, T. K., & Wyer, R. S., Jr. (1979). The role of category accessibility in the interpretation of information about persons: Some determinants and implications. *Journal of Personality and Social Psychology, 37*, 1660–1672.

Srull, T. K., & Wyer, R. S., Jr. (1980). Category accessibility and social perception: Some implications for the study of person memory and interpersonal judgments. *Journal of Personality and Social Psychology, 38*, 841–856.

Staats, A. W., & Staats, C. K. (1958). Attitudes established by classical conditioning. *Journal of Abnormal and Social Psychology, 57*, 37–40.

Staats, A. W., Staats, C. K., & Crawford, H. L. (1962). First order conditioning of meaning and the parallel condititioning of a GSR. *Journal of General Psychology, 67*, 159–162.

Staats, C. K., & Staats, A. W. (1957). Meaning established by classical conditioning. *Journal of Experimental Psychology, 54*, 74–80.

Strahan, E. J., Spencer, S. J., & Zanna, M. P. (2002). Subliminal priming and persuasion: Striking while the iron is hot. *Journal of Experimental Social Psychology, 38*, 556–568.

Stuart, E. W., Shimp, T. A., & Engle, R. W. (1987). Classical conditioning of consumer attitudes: Four experiments in an advertising context. *Journal of Consumer Research, 14*, 334–349.

Theus, K. T. (1994). Subliminal advertising and the psychology of processing unconscious stimuli: A review of research. *Psychology and Marketing, 11*, 271–290.

Trappey, C. (1996). A meta-analysis of consumer choice and subliminal advertising. *Psychology and Marketing, 13*, 517–530.

Vokey, J. R., & Read, J. D. (1985). Subliminal messages: Between the devil and the media. *American Psychologist, 40*, 1231–1239.

Watt, H. J. (1905). Experimentelle beitrage zur einer theorie des denkens. *Archiv für Geschichte der Psychologie, 4*, 289–436.

Whalen, P. J., Rauch, S. L., Etcoff, N. L., McInerney, S. C., Lee, M. B., & Jenike, M. A. (1998). Masked presentations of emotional facial expressions modulate amygdala activity without explicit knowledge. *Journal of Neuroscience, 18*, 411–418.

Wolford, G. (1986). A review of the literature with and without awareness. *Behavioral and Brain Sciences, 9*, 49–50.

Zajonc, R. B. (1968). Attitudinal effects of mere exposure. *Journal of Personality and Social Psychology, 9*, 1–27.

Zanot, E. J., Pincus, J. D., & Lamp, E. J. (1983). Public perceptions of subliminal advertising. *Journal of Advertising, 12*, 37–45.

Zimmermann, M. (1989). The nervous system in the context of information theory. In R. F. Schmidt & G. Thews (Eds.), *Human physiology* (pp. 166–173). Berlin: Springer.

5

Nonintentional Similarity Processing

Arthur B. Markman and Dedre Gentner

Similarity in Cognitive Processing

Similarity is a compelling part of everyday experience. In the visual world, objects that are similar in shape or color may seem to leap to our attention. In conceptual processing, we have an immediate sense of whether a pair of concepts is similar. The prominence of similarity in conscious experience has made it an important explanatory construct in psychological theories. New problems are assumed to be solved on the basis of their similarity to known problems (e.g., Reed, Ernst, & Banerji, 1974; Ross, 1987). Objects are assumed to be classified on the basis of their similarity to some stored category representation (e.g., Medin & Schaffer, 1978; Reed, 1972). Predictions of new features of an item may be based on what other similar items have those features (e.g., Blok & Gentner, 2000; Heit & Rubinstein, 1994; Osherson, Smith, Wilkie, Lopez, & Shafir, 1990; Sloman, 1993).

Yet despite extensive work on mechanisms of similarity, there has been very little discussion of why and how similarity is important in cognitive processing beyond the general recognition that similarity often provides a good basis for generalization (Shepard, 1987). In this chapter, we consider the role of similarity in the cognitive architecture and the relationship of similarity to automatic processing. We suggest that some types of similarity are determined automatically. When the cognitive system recognizes similarities, they influence cognitive processing, even when the person does not intend processing to be affected by similarities. To support this claim, we first outline three approaches to similarity. Then, we examine how similarity can influence both low-level processes like attention and memory retrieval and higher cognitive processes like analogical reasoning and decision making. Next, we explore a number of examples in which cognitive processing is influenced by the presence of similarities in a stimulus set. Finally, we broaden the discussion to include similarities in more deliberate cognitive processes.

Three Approaches to Similarity

Representation and Similarity

When a person makes a similarity comparison, the result is typically both a judgment of similarity and also some awareness of the commonalities and differences of the pair compared. A model of similarity must account for both of these outputs. How it does so is bound up with proposals about mental representation. Similarity processing involves the comparison of two representations. Thus the selection of a formalism for representation in a model of similarity influences not only the complexity and computational resources required but also the nature of the output.

In this section, we start by discussing similarity models that assume spatial representations. These models are fairly simple in both their output and their processing requirements. Then, we turn to more complex featural and structural models of representation and the comparison processes that operate over them. In the next section, we examine the implications of these models for the cognitive architecture.

The spatial view of similarity is embodied in multidimensional scaling models of similarity, as well as in distributed connectionist models and high-dimensional semantic space models (e.g., Gärdenfors, 2000; see Gentner & Markman, 1995; Markman, 1999; Medin, Goldstone, & Gentner, 1993, for discussion). According to spatial models, concepts are represented as points or vectors in a semantic space (e.g., Shepard, 1962). Calculating similarity involves finding the distance between points or vectors using some metric. These models have the important advantage that finding distance in a space is a computationally simple calculation. Thus, similarity comparisons do not require significant processing resources. However, spatial models have two major disadvantages as psychological models. First, the comparison process gives rise only to a distance between concepts. This scalar value can be used to model similarity judgments, but there is no way to access the specific commonalities and differences that form the basis of the similarity judgment. Second, similarity in a space is influenced only by the differences between concepts, not by their similarities. Adding dimensions to the space along which two concepts are the same will not increase similarity, but adding dimensions on which two concepts differ will decrease similarity (Tversky, 1977). Thus, spatial representations cannot capture Tversky's (1977) finding that the same pair (e.g., U.S.A./Canada) can be both more similar to and more different from each other than another pair (e.g., Venezuela/Bolivia).

While spatial models of similarity have been used to model many similarity phenomena (see Shoben, 1983, for a review), the above limitations, along with others catalogued by Tversky (1977), make spatial models problematic as a general theory of similarity (but see Krumhansl, 1978; Nosofsky, 1986, for attempts to address some of the shortcomings of spatial models). Spatial models yield only a scalar measure of similarity, and only differences influence the calculation of similarity. Thus, they fail to capture the fact that people are able to access the commonalities and differences of pairs in addition to rating their similarity; and similarity judgments are, if anything, more influenced by the pair's commonalities than by its differences (Markman & Gentner, 1993b; Tversky, 1977).

In response to these shortcomings, Tversky (1977) proposed a featural approach to similarity called the contrast model. According to the contrast model, concepts are represented by sets of features. Pairs of feature sets can be compared using elementary set operations. Features in the intersection of the sets are commonalities of a pair, and features not in the intersection are differences. Rated similarity increases with the commonalities of a pair and decreases with the differences. Thus, this model is able to calculate a scalar rating of similarity that is influenced by both commonalities and differences, but it also permits access to the particular commonalities and differences of a pair. As in spatial models, the calculation of similarity in featural models is computationally inexpensive, as each feature in the representation of one item simply needs to be matched against the set of features representing the other item.

A third approach to similarity was developed to account for phenomena that demonstrate the importance of relations in similarity (Gentner, 1983; Gentner & Markman, 1997; Markman & Gentner, 1993b; Goldstone, Medin, & Gentner, 1991). For example, figure 5.1(a) depicts two simple geometric configurations. These configurations could be viewed as being similar because there is a circle and a square in each or because there is one figure above another in each. On a featural representation like the one in figure 5.1(b), it is not clear how to match up the features in the two lists. Indeed, the first seven features in each feature list are the same; they are simply listed in a different order. When the intersection of these feature sets is taken as in Tversky's (1977) contrast model, the features are matched without regard to the way they are ordered. While it might be possible to add configural features such as square-above-circle to this list in order to account for the way objects are attached to relations, the number of configural features required as new relations are added quickly becomes unwieldy (Foss & Harwood, 1975; Markman & Gentner, 2000).

Structured representations, like the ones in the graphs in figure 5.1(c), are useful for dealing with relations. These representations consist of entities, attributes, and relations. Entities such as Square 1 stand for the objects in a

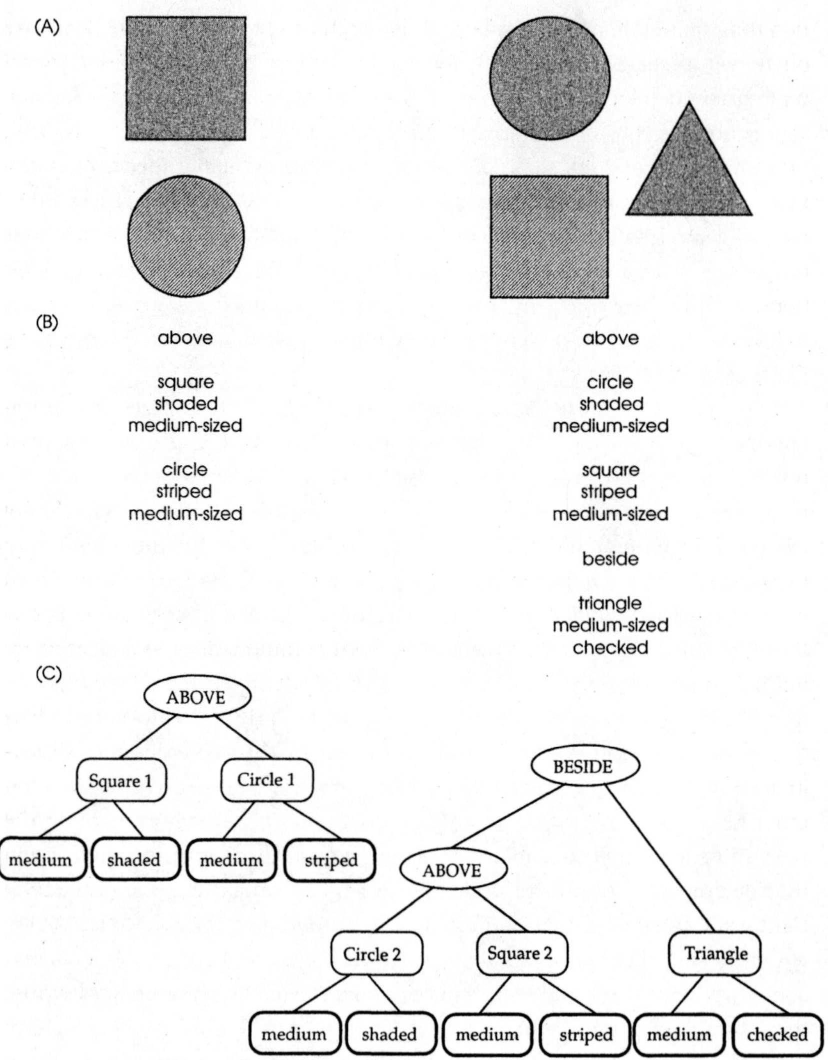

Figure 5.1 (a) A geometric configuration used as an example of information that is available in similarity comparisons; (b) a simple feature list describing these configurations; (c) a graph of structured representations that describe the configurations. The ovals in the graph are relations; the bold rectangles are attributes; and the light rectangles are entities.

domain. Attributes [e.g., shaded(x)] represent descriptive properties (e.g., the property of being shaded). Attributes take one argument (in this case, x), which binds the attribute to a particular object. For example, shaded (Square 1) means that Square 1 is shaded. Relations like above(x,y) are representational elements that relate two or more arguments. The arguments to a relation may be objects, attributes, or other relations—that is, relations that take other relations as arguments. Higher-order relations are particularly important, because they often capture system-level connections within a domain such as causal and functional relations and implications.

Comparing pairs of relational representations like the ones depicted in figure 5.1(c) involves a process of structural alignment—part of the structure-mapping process that is proposed as the basis of analogical comparisons (Falkenhainer, Forbus, & Gentner, 1989; Keane, Ledgeway, & Duff, 1994; Gentner, 1983, 1989; Gentner & Markman, 1997). On this view, the comparison process seeks a structurally consistent match between two domains. First, the comparison process finds identical attributes and relations in each domain. For example, there are above(x,y) relations in the two representations shown in figure 5.1(c). Potential matches are examined to ensure that they are structurally consistent.

Structural consistency comprises the constraints of parallel connectivity and one-to-one mapping. Parallel connectivity says that if an attribute or relation in each domain is placed in correspondence, then their arguments must also match. For example, if the above(x,y) relations are placed in correspondence, then the first arguments to that relation (i.e., the things on top) must be matched, as must the second arguments (i.e., the things on the bottom). One-to-one mapping requires that each element in one representation match to at most one element in the other. Thus, if the square in the left-hand configuration is matched to the circle on the right because both are on top, then the square on the left cannot also be matched to the square on the right because of their similarity in shape. In cases such as the configuration in figure 5.1(a) in which there is some ambiguity about how the objects should be placed in correspondence, the structural alignment process may yield more than one structurally consistent match (Markman & Gentner, 1993b). The structural alignment process has been implemented in a number of computational models using both symbolic (Falkenhainer et al., 1989; Keane et al., 1994) and connectionist (Holyoak & Thagard, 1989; Hummel & Holyoak, 1997) architectures.

The structure-mapping model is much more intensive computationally than spatial or featural models. The calculation of parallel connectivity requires checking each correspondence among relations to ensure that the arguments of those relations also match. In addition, enforcing one-to-one mapping may require a number of comparisons among potential matches.[1] The benefit of this increased complexity is that structural alignment provides a more adequate model of similarity than the prior models.

First, the model's assessment of degree of similarity matches the human phenomena. For example, rated similarity tends to increase with the number of commonalities of a pair and to decrease with the number of differences (Markman & Gentner, 1993a). Furthermore, subjective similarity tends to be higher when people focus on relational commonalities than when they focus on object-attribute commonalities (Gentner, Rattermann, & Forbus, 1993; Markman & Gentner, 1993b). This is especially true if the relations form a system governed by common higher order relations (Clement & Gentner, 1991; Gentner et al., 1993).

Second, the structure-mapping model provides an account of directionality in similarity that fits human data. Bowdle and Gentner (1997) found that people preferred to see comparisons in the direction from a well-structured, systematic situation to a less well-structured situation. For example, people's knowledge about a familiar domain is usually better structured than is their knowledge about an unfamiliar domain, which leads to an asymmetry in a comparison, so that people prefer the comparison "scanners are copiers" to the reverse.

Third, structure mapping predicts inferences that follow from a comparison (Clement & Gentner, 1991; Gentner & Markman, 1997). People spontaneously project new information that is connected to the common structure, but which is not yet present in the target.

Fourth, this account of similarity makes novel predictions about the types of commonalities and differences that emerge from comparisons. As in featural models, commonalities are matching elements. For example, the left and right representations in figure 5.1(c) might be seen as similar, because there is an above(x,y) relation in each. Unlike other models, structure mapping predicts two kinds of differences that emerge from comparisons. First, elements connected to the common structure may participate in the perception of differences. For example, seeing that one figure is above another in each representation leads to noticing that there is a square on the top in one configuration and a circle on the top in the other. Differences like this that are noticed because of the way the representations were matched are called alignable differences (Markman & Gentner, 1993a). Second, alignable differences can be contrasted with nonalignable differences, which are aspects of one representation that are not connected to the common structure and have no correspondence in the other. For example, the triangle in the right-hand configuration is not part of the above relation and has no correspondence in the other configuration, and thus is a nonalignable difference.

The distinction between alignable and nonalignable differences goes beyond what is predicted by featural models. For example, Tversky's (1977) contrast model assumes that the commonalities and differences that emerge from comparisons are independent. The structural alignment approach predicts that alignable differences are fundamentally related to commonalities, though nonalignable differences are not.

Considerable evidence has been gathered to support the distinction between alignable and nonalignable differences. This evidence suggests both that alignable differences are related to commonalities and that alignable differences tend to be favored over nonalignable differences in comparisons. Two lines of evidence support the relationship between commonalities and differences. First, pairs for which people can list many commonalities are also those for which they can list many alignable differences. Second, alignable differences tend to be conceptually related to commonalities, but nonalignable differences do not (Gentner & Gunn, 2001; Markman & Gentner, 1993a, 1996).

Also, a number of demonstrations have shown that alignable differences are more focal (or salient) than nonalignable differences in comparisons. For example, in free property listing tasks, more alignable differences tend to be listed than nonalignable differences (Markman & Gentner, 1993a). People find it easier to list a difference for similar pairs (which have many alignable differences) than for dissimilar pairs (which have few alignable differences; Gentner & Gunn, 2001; Gentner & Markman, 1994). Further, carrying out a similarity comparison renders differences more available. Finally, following a similarity comparison of a pair of pictures, an object that was an alignable difference serves as a better retrieval cue than does an object that was a nonalignable difference (Markman & Gentner, 1997; Stilwell & Markman, 2001).

Types of Similarity and Their Use

This review of similarity models reveals two critical dimensions along which models differ. First is the expressive power of the models. Spatial models provide a scalar measure of similarity that is influenced by the similarities or the differences of a pair, but not both. Featural models provide a measure of similarity that is influenced by both commonalities and differences and that can output independent sets of common and distinctive features. Only the structure-mapping model captures both commonalities and differences, as well as the more precise (and psychologically important) distinction between alignable and nonalignable differences. The model also captures the relation between alignable differences and the commonalities of a pair. Further, it is the only one of the three approaches that provides an account of which inferences will be drawn from a comparison.

The second dimension along which models of similarity can be evaluated is computational complexity. The expressive power of structural alignment comes at a computational cost. Ensuring that matching relations in two domains also have matching arguments and that the entire correspondence obeys the constraint of one-to-one mapping is a complex process. In contrast, comparing two points in a multidimensional space and finding correspondences within a set of features are both fairly simple processes to carry out. Thus, the greater complexity of structural alignment requires more time and effort than do the simpler spatial and featural processing models.

It is typical when evaluating research to pick one model as the best one. We want to take a different tack here. As we discuss below, different similarity processes make different tradeoffs with respect to complexity and expressive power. We suggest that there are two modes of similarity processing (Forbus, Gentner, & Law, 1995; Gentner et al., 1993). The first—the one we have discussed so far—is based on structural alignment, provides slower, more effortful judgments, and also yields access to the commonalities and differences (particularly the alignable differences) of a pair. This process is useful in cognitive processes that can be carried out over a period of many seconds (as opposed to milliseconds) or those which involve a small number of comparisons that require access to commonalities and differences. The second is based on the principles embodied in the spatial and featural views, and provides fast judgments of the degree of similarity of a pair, but does not take the structure of the representations into account. This fast process is most useful when judgments are required quickly or when many similarity comparisons must be made in parallel, as when accessing long-term memory.

One piece of evidence in favor of this dichotomy comes from research on analogical reminding. Much research suggests that remindings show much less influence of structure than do analogy comparisons. In one study, Gentner and colleagues (1993) asked people to read a set of stories. For example, one story was about a hawk that gives feathers to a hunter to use in his arrows in exchange for the hunter's agreement not to shoot the hawk. A week later, the same people read new stories and were asked to recall any stories from the previous week that were similar to the new story. When given new stories that involved similar characters (e.g., an eagle), people were likely to recall the original story. This reminding happened even when the new story had a very different plot from the original. In contrast, when given a story with different characters (e.g., countries) and an analogically similar plot (e.g., one country gives computers to the other to guide its missiles in exchange for an agreement not to shoot the missiles at them), people were unlikely to recall the original story. This finding suggests that retrieval—which requires making a comparison of the cue against the contents of memory—uses a computationally simple form of similarity (see Holyoak & Koh, 1987; Reeves & Weisberg, 1994; Ross, 1989; Wharton, Holyoak, Downing, Lange, & Wickens, 1991, for related studies).

Although structure was not important for retrieving analogs in the study by Gentner et al. (1993), it was important in people's judgments of similarity when they were given the same pairs of stories to compare. When people were shown pairs of stories together, the highest similarity ratings were given to stories that shared the same plot, even if they had different characters. In contrast, stories with similar characters and a different plot were judged as much less similar. In fact, the pattern of rated similarity was the reverse of that of memory reminding. Thus, when people were making only a single comparison (with no time pressure), their judgments strongly relied on structural overlap, but retrieval from memory showed little effect of common structure.

This distinction between types of similarities led Forbus and Gentner to hypothesize that the initial retrieval stage in similarity-based remindings are a cheap parallel search for possible matches. This hypothesis is embodied in computational models of analogy and analogical reminding (Forbus et al., 1995; Thagard, Holyoak, Nelson, & Gochfeld, 1990). For example, in Forbus and colleagues' (1995) MAC/FAC (many are called/few are chosen) model, analogical retrieval begins with a parallel sweep to find items in memory that share similar representational elements without regard to the structure of the representations. Once a small candidate set of remindings is found, a second stage makes a structural comparison between the cue and the items retrieved in the first pass. The best structural matches to the cue are retained and explained.

Similarity and Metacognition

Here we propose to extend the notion of fast and efficient similarity estimation processes. A computationally simple form of similarity that calculates the degree of similarity could operate all the time searching for similarities among items in the environment as well as between items in the environment and background knowledge. This process could serve as the basis of metacognitive judgments of where to spend processing effort. That is, a pair that has some initial overlap is likely to yield a better return on processing effort than is a pair that has little overlap.

This proposal would explain why the feeling of similarity is so accessible. Similarity theorists have rarely considered why people are able to make judgments of similarity so easily, or why similarity is such a compelling part of conscious experience. The view we outline here suggests that the initial assessment of similarity is used as a guide for the allocation of attentional resources (see Markman, 2001, for a related discussion). It provides a reliable guide for further processing. On this account, much of the process of accessing and computing similarity comparisons may not be consciously accessible; indeed, unconscious outputs may drive further cognitive processing. It should be clear that explicit similarity judgments and numerical ratings (like those often collected in the lab) may not reflect the range of ways in which similarity processes can influence cognition and behavior.

Another instance of rough, nonstructural similarity processing may occur early in processing a comparison. Even when a comparison is explicitly presented—removing the need for a reminding from long-term-memory—the early stages of similarity and analogy processing appear local and unstructured. This is captured in the structure-mapping engine (SME, described in the section "Similarity and Comparisons in Development") by an initial stage that creates a multitude of local matches, with no regard for structural consistency; overall structural consistency emerges later in processing (Falkenhainer et al., 1989; Forbus et al., 1995).

Findings with metaphors underscore the idea of an initial rapid similarity process followed by a slower, more detailed process. An early study by Glucksberg, Gildea, and Bookin (1982) asked people to judge whether sentences were literally true or false in a timed task. Some of the literally false sentences were metaphors (e.g., "Some jobs are jails"). People were slower to reject these metaphoric sentences than to reject false sentences that had no interesting semantic overlap (e.g., "Some dogs are birds"), indicating that metaphoric processing begins before literal processing is complete. Wolff and Gentner (2000) further found that people were equally slow to reject reversed metaphors (e.g., "Some jails are jobs"). There are three salient points here. First, the fact that the interference effects are independent of the order of the terms suggests that the initial stages of metaphor processing are symmetric. Second, metaphoric interference is far greater for high-similarity metaphors like "Some soldiers are pawns" than for low-similarity metaphors like "Some senators are pawns," regardless of whether the metaphors occur in forward or reversed order. Third, these interference effects occur early in processing; by 1,100–1,200 ms, the metaphors are detected as (literally) false and rejected. These results are consistent with an early, rapid symmetrical similarity process.

Wolff and Gentner (2000) also verified that the metaphors were directional when processed to completion. This is a crucial point because metaphors are known to be strongly directional: for example, people greatly prefer "Some jobs are jails" to "Some jails are jobs" (Ortony, 1979). Further, according to the structure-mapping model, the initial alignment process is followed by directional projection of inferences. Thus, metaphoric directionality should emerge if people are allowed to complete the comprehension process. Consistent with this prediction, when new subjects were given the same metaphors as in the prior studies and asked to indicate whether the metaphor was comprehensible, they showed strong directional preferences: 75% of the forward metaphors were judged comprehensible, compared to 37% of the reversed metaphors. Further, forward metaphors were comprehended more quickly than reversed metaphors ($M = 1{,}644$ ms for forward, $M = 1{,}778$ ms for reversed). Also, as predicted, high-similarity metaphors were more likely to be judged comprehensible than low-similarity metaphors. In sum, the results indicate that early processing of metaphors, as tapped in the interference effect, is symmetrical; but when full processing is allowed, there is a strong directional advantage for forward metaphors. Overall, the pattern fits the structure-mapping claim of initially symmetrical processing followed by later directional projection of inferences.

Carrying these findings to the next logical step, Wolff and Gentner (2004) gave subjects a task in which they received sentences like the above—including forward or reversed metaphors, literal similarity statements, and anomalous sentences that were clearly false—and had to say whether they were comprehensible before a deadline passed. As expected, at long deadlines (1,800 ms), the forward metaphors were rated as comprehensible far more often than the reversed. However, at short deadlines (1,200 ms), the forward and reversed metaphors were indistinguishable. Importantly, both are more comprehensible than the anomalous sentences at fast deadlines, indicating that they have attracted some early processing attention.

These results fit with our conjecture that an early rapid similarity assessment is used to guide the allocation of processing resources. Here the early similarity comparison process identifies sentences that share semantic overlap—both the forward and reversed metaphors. As indicated by the results of the full-comprehension studies, once such a semantically overlapping sentence is identified, a more elaborate process of structural alignment and inference projection takes place, such that some of these initially promising sentences will be accepted and others rejected.

Research on sentence verification is also consistent with this proposal. For example, Smith, Shoben, and Rips (1974) examined the speed with which people could verify sentences like "A dog is an animal." Of particular interest to them was the finding that people were very fast to respond to false sentences like "A dog is a bird," but slower to respond to false sentences like "A bat is a bird." They suggested that people are using the initial similarity of bat and bird as a guide to processing. In contrast, the absence of similarity between dog and bird is a reliable indication that dogs are not birds.

In the results so far, we have focused on cases in which the detection of similarity leads to the allocation of more attentional resources. However, there are cases in which the effect of similarity is to allocate fewer resources. We will return to this point when we consider infant habituation studies in the next section.

Although the feeling of similarity may be consciously accessible, the basis of this judgment may not be consciously accessible. One way to see this point is that associations between words increase people's similarity ratings for a pair, even though these associations do not increase the number of commonalities of a pair (Bassok & Medin, 1997; Gentner & Brem, 1999; Wisniewski & Bassok, 1999). For example, coffee and milk are rated as more similar than coffee and lemonade, even though they do not share more properties, because of their strong co-occurrence association.

This observation could be taken to suggest that similarity and relatedness are psychologically intertwined, or that they are simply two different aspects of the same process. However, Gentner and Brem (1999) suggest that it is sometimes difficult to tell the difference between two different "cognitive sensations": the sense of similarity that results from comparing items and discovering commonalities, and the sense of associative linkage that results from retrieving a stored association.[2] Indeed, one could ask whether similarity and association result from the same process (e.g., Bassok & Medin, 1997; Sloman, 1996). One piece of evidence that there are different underlying processes despite this confusion, is that there are two patterns of results over the same materials. When asked to choose which is most similar to a dart, some people choose a bull's-eye as more similar than a javelin. However, if people are given a word extension task—for example, they are told that darts are called "blickets" in a certain language—they virtually always extend the new term to the similar item (javelin) and never to the associate (Gentner & Brem, 1999). Thus, even though the cognitive sensations engendered by comparison activity and by retrieval of associations may be difficult to distinguish explicitly, the processes may have separate courses and separate implicit outcomes.

From the perspective of this chapter, if we postulate a set of early signals used to guide the allocation of attentional resources, then it makes sense to include associative retrieval as well as a sense of similarity in this set, because associations are another good indication that additional processing would be fruitful. The early sense of "something interesting happening" may be difficult to distinguish (or perhaps even identical) for finding a stored association and computing a new similarity.

The presence of a metacognitive process that makes use of the output of similarity judgments to guide future processing has important implications for cognitive processing. One that we explore in the rest of this chapter is that the presence of similarities among items will influence cognitive processes that operate on those items. Thus, the nonintentional perception of similarities between items that occurs during the normal course of processing will have unintended effects on the output of other cognitive processes.

Nonintentional Similarity

In this section, we explore the implications of using similarity processing—whether or not it is explicitly coded as similarity—to allocate attentional resources. We begin with a discussion of information that infants and children are able to extract from repeated presentations of a similar pattern. Then we turn to research on adults that demonstrates that people process information differently when items are similar than when they are dissimilar. This work comes from studies of conceptual combination, decision making, and person perception. Finally, we broaden the discussion to consider some influences of similarity that occur when people are induced to make comparisons during processing.

Similarity and Comparisons in Development

It is generally assumed that infants' cognitive processing is less strategic than that of adults. Thus, influences of similarities on the cognitive abilities of infants can be viewed as evidence that nonintentional similarity affects the output of cognitive processes. We begin by describing some influences of similarity on infant cognition and then turn to data from older children.

Many studies of infant cognition make use of the habituation paradigm. Habituation studies with infants rely on the observation that repeated presentations of a set of items eventually lead to a decrease in attention (e.g., Baillargeon, Spelke, & Wasserman, 1985; Eimas, 1971). The general technique is to expose the infant to an event and then repeat the event until the infant's looking time to the event decreases. In this case, similarity leads to a reduced allocation of resources; intuitively, infants act as though they are bored. At this point, test events are given. If the infant's looking time remains the same, then the experimenter infers that this event is treated by the infant as similar to the one seen previously. If the infant's looking time increases (i.e., they dishabituate), then the experimenter infers that the current event is seen by the infant as different from the habituation event.

In these studies, the stimuli need not be identical on each trial. For example, when 7-month-old infants are presented with a series of pictures of members of a particular category (e.g., cats), their looking time will decrease over trials (e.g., Cohen & Younger, 1983). Thus, in this case, the assessment of similarity is being used to suggest that additional resources need not be expended. Often these studies include a test phase in which a new item is presented. If infants look longer at a test trial than they did at trials at the end of the habituation phase, this is interpreted as evidence that they noticed a difference between the test trial and the habituation trials. What is important for the present purposes, however, is that a feeling of similarity can be used to drive the allocation of resources.

In one set of studies, Baillargeon (1991) examined infants' ability to reason about the properties of a hidden object. First, subjects in the study were habituated to an event in which a screen that was initially flat on a table rotated backward through a 180° arc. After habituation, a box was placed on the table in front of the subject, and then the screen was again rotated. In the possible event condition, the screen rotated back until it reached the angle at which it touched the top of the box and stopped. In the impossible event condition, the screen rotated back so that it would have passed through the top 50% or the top 80% of the box's height. When given this task alone, 6.5-month-old infants dishabituated to the 80% violation, but not the 50% violation, and 4.5-month-old infants remained habituated to both of these impossible events.

A subsequent experiment demonstrated the importance of similarity to this type of physical reasoning. During the test event, two boxes of the same height were used. One was in the path of the screen and the other was not, so that the second box would always be visible to the infant. Furthermore, the perceptual similarity of the two boxes was varied, so that they were identical, similar, or dissimilar. When the boxes were identical, both 4.5- and 6.5-month-old infants dishabituated to the 50% violations. When the boxes were highly similar but not identical (i.e., same size and shape but different color), the 6.5-month-olds, but not the 4.5-month-olds, dishabituated to the 50% violation. Finally, neither group of infants reliably dishabituated to this violation when the boxes were dissimilar. This finding suggests that infants would spontaneously use the visible box as a kind of standard to help them calibrate the height of the occluded box only when there was considerable perceptual similarity (even though the relevant comparison involved only the height dimension). The younger the infant, the greater the degree of perceptual similarity required to align the standard with the box when occluded.

Other findings suggest that infants may be able to use similarities in a set of stimuli to generate representations of relational information in stimuli. As one demonstration of this point, Marcus, Vijayan, Bandi Rao, and Vishton (1999) played 7-month-old infants a sequence of novel three-syllable utterances. These training utterances followed one of two patterns, either ABA (e.g., ga ti ga) or ABB (e.g., ga ti ti). During the test, the infants heard examples of the same pattern they had heard during training or examples of a different pattern. Importantly, the test utterances used a new set of syllables different from those in the training utterances (e.g., wo fe wo or wo fe fe). In this work, the dependent measure was the infant's looking time at a light flashing over a speaker from which the syllables were played. Infants looked reliably longer at the source when the utterances violated the abstract pattern heard during training than when the new utterances followed the training pattern, suggesting that they were dishabituating to the new pattern. A similar result was obtained by Gomez and Gerken (1999) with 12-month-olds using a more complex artificial grammar.[3]

A model of the influence of repeated comparisons on this task was developed by Gentner, Kuehne, and Forbus (2004; Kuehne, Gentner, & Forbus, 2000). This model made use of the SEQL architecture, a model of category learning by abstraction over exemplars that uses the SME (Falkenhainer et al., 1989) to carry out its similarity computation and to derive its abstractions (Skorstad, Gentner, & Medin, 1988). Briefly, SME is a computational model that takes as input structured representations of the two items being compared. For example, the relation that the first and third syllables in an utterance are the same might be represented as SAME (wo1, wo3). The output of SME is a set of correspondences between the items that satisfies the constraints on analogy described above (e.g., structural consistency and systematicity). SEQL extends this model by making repeated comparisons. Each comparison yields a set of commonalities, which are retained and used in comparison with the next input item. Over time, the abstraction comes to contain the relational commonalities that reoccur across the items in the input. Importantly, these comparisons are made automatically and are not under strategic control, making this process appropriate for modeling infant habituation.

In the domain of utterances, repeated comparisons among utterances with a common relational structure allow the model to abstract away the relational commonalities from a set of items, leaving few if any surface (i.e., phonological) properties. When the model is given the same sequence of input utterances (with each syllable represented with 12 phonetic features) as the infant and tested on the same test patterns, it finds the new patterns markedly less similar to its abstraction than the old ones.

There are two types of similarities that infants are likely to use to create relational representations of the novel utterances. First, each utterance contains some similar elements (i.e., the first and last syllables in the ABA utterances and the repeated syllables in the ABB utterances). These repetitions are a form of internal regularity that may be salient for infants as it is for adults (Ferguson, 1994; Kubovy, 1995; Leyton, 1992). In addition, because utterances following the same pattern are repeated, infants may compare across patterns in the manner described above to notice relational similarities.

The idea that repeated comparisons can facilitate children's ability to represent more abstract relational systems can also be seen in a study with preschool children done by Kotovsky and Gentner (1996). In this study, 4-year-old children were given a similarity choice task in which they were shown a standard and were asked to determine which of two comparison figures showed the same abstract pattern. The standard and comparison figures were configurations of three geometric shapes in a line. The shapes in a configuration were the same except for one dimension: size or darkness of color. In the standard, the configuration either had the pattern ABA (symmetry) or ABC (monotonic change). One comparison figure had a configuration with the same abstract relation either along the same dimension or along a different dimension than the standard. The other configuration had the same three shapes in an arbitrary pattern (e.g., ABB on a symmetry trial or ACB on a monotonic change trial). Children chose whichever alternative they felt was most similar to the standard; they were given no feedback beyond general encouragement.

The 4-year-olds were reliably above chance at this task on trials where the standard and comparison figures varied along the same dimension (e.g., all varied in size or all varied in darkness) and when the polarity of the relation was the same (e.g., when little-big-little was matched to little-big-little), but not when the polarity was reversed (e.g., little-big-little to big-little-big). These children were also unable to perform cross-dimensional matches, where the standard varied along a different dimension than the comparison figures (e.g., dark-light-dark vs. big-little-big). Thus, 4-year-olds required substantial perceptual similarity to support the abstract match.

Kotovsky and Gentner (1996) suggested that repeated simple comparisons might lead to abstracting structural regularities that would enable children to learn to do the more difficult cross-dimensional matches. To test this possibility, the comparisons were given in a blocked fashion. First, a block of within-dimension trials was given. Within this block, children first saw configurations that varied only in size (which they tended to find easy) and then configurations that varied only in color (which they tended to find more difficult). Only after this block were they given cross-dimensional trials that involved changes in both size and color. Children who responded correctly to the initial within-dimension trials were able to perform the cross-dimensional matches reliably as well.

In order to rule out a simple practice effect, a second group was initially given the same number of within-dimension trials as the above group, but they saw only triads involving the size dimension. These children performed well on within-dimension trials but were not able to do the cross-dimension trials successfully. This result suggests that repeated within-dimension comparisons support the creation of more abstract relational representations that were then useful in performing the cross-dimensional matches. Obviously, this study involved comparisons that were part of the experimental task rather than spontaneous comparisons, but these findings are consistent with the Marcus et al. (1999) data described above.

The idea that comparisons promote the recognition of abstract relational similarities received additional support from research by Gentner and Namy (1999; Namy & Gentner, 2002) on word learning in 4-year-olds. They examined how children would extend a novel noun that they heard. For one group of children, the noun was applied to a single object (e.g., the experimenter pointed to a picture of a bicycle and said, "This is a dax"). For a second group, the same procedure was followed for a tricycle as standard. A third group was shown both standards (which were always from the same taxonomic category) and invited to compare them; for example, the experimenter pointed first to a bicycle and then to a tricycle and said, "This is a dax, and this is a dax too. Can you see why they're both daxes?" The children were then shown two test objects. One test object was perceptually similar to the standard(s) but belonged to a different category (e.g., eyeglasses). The second test object was not perceptually similar to the standard(s), but belonged to the same taxonomic category (e.g., a skateboard). The children were asked which of these alternatives should be given the same label as the standard (e.g., "Can you show me another dax?").

When given either of the two standards by themselves, children tended to select the perceptual match (the eyeglasses). When shown both standards together, children chose the taxonomic match, despite preferring the perceptual match for either of the standards presented singly. That is, carrying out a comparison enabled children to override compelling perceptual commonalities in favor of deeper conceptual ones. This outcome provides critical evidence that carrying out a structural alignment facilitates attention to common functional and causal relations over common perceptual features. Thus, when children are invited to compare a pair of objects, they are much more likely to focus on more abstract properties like those that form the basis of taxonomic categorization.

These results show that engaging in a comparison process can actually shift the basis for categorization from perceptual properties to conceptual relations. This is because, as predicted by structure-mapping theory, comparison leads to alignment of common relational structure, thereby promoting the relations' salience. This relational focus is most dramatic in a far analogy, where there are few object commonalities; but common relations are promoted to some degree even in close similarity comparisons. Because relations (even core relations such as internal causal or function relations) tend to be less accessible than object features, this alignment process will render relational commonalities more obvious in the pair than in either of the separate exemplars. In other words, the relations stand to gain more from this alignment process than do more obvious object properties.

In this section, we have reviewed findings that assess the influence of similarity and comparison on cognitive processing in infants and young children. The presence of compelling similarities in the environment supports complex reasoning. These comparisons also enable children to extract more abstract commonalities of items than they would be able to find when considering a single object. Furthermore, these effects occur spontaneously, but they can also be observed when the task calls for a more explicit comparison. In the next section, we turn to a parallel set of phenomena in research with adults.

Changes in Adults' Processing With Similarity

Cognitive processing in adults is typically more strategic than that of children. There are many instances in which the particular strategy that people adopt is influenced by whether the items being processed are similar. We suggest that this effect occurs because similarity affects the way processing resources are allocated. To demonstrate this point, we begin with some results from studies of conceptual combination. Then we turn to research on decision making. We end with a discussion of research on person perception. In all of these cases, the influences of similarity are likely to be unintentional, because the goal of the task does not require attention to similarity.

Conceptual Combination Conceptual combination is the study of the way people interpret complex noun phrases such as adjective-noun combinations like "the brown apple" and noun-noun combinations like "the turkey apple." In the present discussion, we focus only on noun-noun combinations, which have been the subject of extensive research (Costello & Keane, 2000; Gagne, 2000; Gerrig & Murphy, 1992; Murphy, 1988; Wisniewski & Gentner, 1991; Wisniewski & Love, 1998).

In a noun-noun combination like "goose horse," the first noun typically modifies the second, and so the first noun is called the modifier, and the second is called the head. Studies of conceptual combination suggest that there are three dominant strategies that people adopt when interpreting novel noun-noun phrases. The first, called property mapping, involves carrying over a property from the modifier to the head. For example, a goose horse could be interpreted as a horse with a long neck, in which case the property "long neck" is carried from goose to horse. The second strategy, called relational combination,[4] involves positing a relationship between the two nouns. For example, a goose horse could be interpreted as a horse that lives near geese. Finally, some noun-noun combinations are hybrids, which involve combining the two concepts on a massive scale. Often, the definition given by a subject simply specifies that the resulting combination is a mix of the two concepts. For example, a goose horse could be interpreted as a mixture of goose and horse. This definition specifies that the referent is such a complete combination of the concepts that the individual components could not be separated out.

An important observation is that the relative frequency of different kinds of combinations changes as a function of the similarity of the constituents of the noun phrase (Markman & Wisniewski, 1997; Wisniewski, 1996; Wisniewski & Gentner, 1991). In general, the more similar the pair, the more likely that it will be given a property mapping interpretation. For extremely similar pairs, hybrid interpretations also become common. One explanation for this phenomenon is that it is easier to align the representations of similar pairs than of dissimilar pairs. This alignment highlights an alignable difference of a pair (e.g., that geese have longer necks than do horses) which can be carried over from the modifier to the head noun in property definitions. When a pair is very similar, their representations are highly alignable, which makes combining the concepts into a hybrid more attractive. Dissimilar pairs are less likely to be spontaneously aligned, and hence give rise to fewer property mapping definitions.

As support for this account, Wisniewski and Markman (1993) had people interpret conceptual combinations of noun phrases for which other subjects had listed commonalities and differences. They found that the properties carried over in property mapping definitions were much more likely to be alignable differences of a pair than to be nonalignable differences. This phenomenon demonstrates clearly how similarity can affect cognitive processing in indirect ways.

Decision Making Decision-making situations are ones in which people have an unsatisfied goal and at least two different courses of action (where one of those courses of action may be to do nothing or to defer the choice). Decision making is particularly interesting to look at from the perspective of nonintentional similarity because people use many different strategies for making choices (Payne, Bettman, & Johnson, 1993). Thus, it is easy to look at how people's strategies shift with the similarity of the options. In addition, at some level all choices require some form of comparison. Economic models predict that options are evaluated abstractly for their goodness or utility and that only these utilities are compared. However, often choice strategies involve comparison of one or more of the more specific attributes of the options (Medin, Goldstone, & Markman, 1995). We make two general points in this section. First, increasing the similarity of the options increases the degree to which people compare specific attributes of those options when making a choice. Second, when people compare the options, they tend to focus on the alignable differences of the options rather than on the nonalignable differences.

As one demonstration that similarity of options affects the way people make choices, Johnson (1984) asked people to make choices between options that were comparable (e.g., two toasters) or noncomparable (e.g., a toaster and a smoke alarm) at the level of their specific features. For comparable choice sets, people describing their choice process mentioned specific attributes of the options. For example, when choosing between toasters, they might mention the number of slots or the number of heat settings. In contrast, when choosing between noncomparable choice sets, people tended to use abstract attributes such as utility. For example, when deciding between a toaster and a smoke alarm, the choice involved which item they needed more. Specific attributes of the products did not enter into the choice. This finding suggests that when the options are comparable, people spontaneously access the commonalities and differences of the options. In contrast, when the options are difficult to compare, other strategies are brought to bear to make the choice.

Ease of comparison also influences the attributes people use to make choices. In a simple demonstration of this point, Tversky and Kahneman (1986) gave people choices between the pairs of gambles shown in table 5.1. In these gambles, people would be paid an amount that depended on the color of a marble drawn from a basket. Some people chose between A and B, and others chose between C and D. Gamble A is clearly better than Gamble B, because the green marble has a higher payoff and the blue one a lower loss for Gamble A than for Gamble B. Consistent with this analysis, everyone in the group given this pair of gambles selected gamble A. Gambles C and D are equivalent to A and B. Gamble C is created from Gamble A by merging the green marble into the set of red marbles. Gamble D is created from Gamble B by merging the blue marble into the set of yellow marbles. Despite the fact that Gamble C is strictly better than Gamble D in the same way A is better than B, 58% of the people given the choice between Gambles C and D chose D. This choice is based on the fact that a comparison of the outcomes of C and D makes salient the loss of $10 versus the gain of $30 associated with the green marble. Thus, people appear to be focusing on the attributes that are easy to compare rather than calculating the expected value of the gamble, which is a more general measure of a gamble's goodness.

From the standpoint of structural alignment, strategies that involve property comparisons are particularly interesting, because decisions must focus on the differences among options. Some research has explored whether people spontaneously use alignable differences among options rather than nonalignable differences. In a classic set of studies, Slovic and MacPhillamy (1974) found that people making judgments about which of a pair of students would have a higher grade point average were more likely to make use of scores on a test that both had taken (i.e., an alignable difference) than scores on a test that only one of them had taken (i.e., a nonalignable difference). More gener-

Table 5.1 Choice Options From Tversky and Kahneman (1986)

	Marble Color				
Option	White	Red	Green	Blue	Yellow
A					
Percentage	90	6	1	1	2
Outcome	$0	Win $45	Win $45	Lose $10	Lose $15
B					
Percentage	90	6	1	1	2
Outcome	$0	Win $45	Win $30	Lose $15	Lose $15
C					
Percentage	90	7	1		2
Outcome	$0	Win $45	Lose $10		Lose $15
D					
Percentage	90	6	1		3
Outcome	$0	Win $45	Win $30		Lose $15

ally, it has been observed that people tend to discount dimensions for which one option has a missing value relative to dimensions for which all options have a value (Markman & Medin, 1995; Ross & Creyer, 1992; Sanbonmatsu, Kardes, & Herr, 1992).

In one set of studies, Zhang and Markman (1998) looked specifically at the use of alignable and nonalignable differences in choice. A series of three novel brands of microwave popcorn were introduced across two experimental sessions. In the first session, subjects were exposed to a description of one brand of popcorn that included 10 attributes. In the second session, the initial brand was shown again followed by descriptions of two other brands that also included 10 attributes. Across the set, four of the attributes were commonalities of all of the brands. Three of the attributes were alignable differences. Finally, three of the attributes were nonalignable differences. People were better able to recall the alignable differences than the nonalignable differences. In addition, the alignable differences had a bigger impact on people's preferences than did the nonalignable differences. This finding suggests that people spontaneously compared the attributes of the new brands to the attributes of the brand learned first in the course of forming their preferences (but see Zhang & Markman, 2001, for a discussion of boundary conditions on the use of alignable differences).

Two central conclusions can be drawn from this research on decision making. First, the ease with which options can be compared affects what kind of information is available for choice processing. When the options can be compared easily, then their attributes are used to make a decision. When the options cannot be compared easily, choice strategies that involve more abstract evaluations of the options are brought to bear. Second, when the choice sets are comparable, the alignable differences among options are often more important to people's decisions than are nonalignable differences. These effects occur despite the fact that there is no explicit direction to compare the attributes of the options. Comparisons occur as a by-product jointly considering the two alternatives, and strongly influence choice processing.

Situation Perception and Person Perception One influence of comparisons that we have not yet addressed involves the way that known information influences the way that new items are represented. People spontaneously make comparisons between background knowledge and new situations that affect how those situations are perceived. The background knowledge that gets used may be general schemas or it may involve specific instances. In this section, we start with influences of reminding in the physical arena. Then we move to effects of comparisons on person perception.

Comparisons of new situations to known situations are common in cognitive processing. This has been explored in some detail in research on analogy and metaphor. Analogies and metaphors are often used to help people structure their knowledge about a new domain by carrying over the relations from a known domain. In one extended analysis, Gentner and Gentner (1983) examined the way people reasoned about the flow of electricity based on whether they conceptualized it as being like the flow of water or like the movement of a crowd. Some aspects of electricity are reasonably easy to conceptualize using either analogy. For example, both analogies help people to differentiate current from voltage. However, these analogies are not equally good at explaining all aspects of electricity. For example, in the moving-crowd model it is much easier to reason about resistors than about batteries. In contrast, the flowing-water model is more transparent for batteries than for resistors. As would be predicted by this analysis, when asked to reason about circuits with combinations of components in series or in parallel, people who held the moving-crowd model were relatively better at reasoning about combinations of resistors than about combinations of batteries, and the reverse was true for people with the flowing-water model.

The application of analogical systems also occurs in real life, sometimes with little explicit awareness. For example, Kempton (1986) studied the use of analogies in people's naive theories of home heat control. A thermostat can be conceptualized as being like a switch or as being like an accelerator. The switch model (which is the correct one) suggests that when the temperature in a room cools to a certain point, a switch goes on and the heater starts. The heater continues operating until the temperature exceeds the set point, at which time the heater shuts off and the cycle continues. The accelerator model says that the amount of heat produced by the heater is proportional to the difference between the current temperature and the set point, just as pressing down the accelerator of a car further increases the amount of gas that reaches the engine and hence the speed of the engine. People who hold this incorrect model tend to change their thermostats more times each day and tend to use more energy to heat their homes.

As a further example, historians have examined the influence of analogies such as the domino theory on political decisions (Glad & Taber, 1990). Before the United Nations intervened in the Korean War, the political situation was often framed using an analogy of a line of falling dominos, where the fall of a single domino causes the entire line to collapse. In this analogy, Communism was an external force pressing on the governments of countries. If one government fell, then many others would follow soon after. As a consequence of this analogy, the Communist insurgency in Korea was viewed as coming from the outside, and thus the United Nations could intervene. Had this same conflict been viewed as a civil war, the United Nations would not have been able to get involved.

To complete this discussion, it is important to recognize that mappings between domains can become conventionalized. For example, Lakoff and Johnson (1980) discuss a number of metaphorical systems in English in which a domain is described in terms initially used by a second domain (e.g., "He was boiling mad"). We suggest that such systems develop through a process in which repeated comparisons lead to progressive abstraction of metaphorical meanings (much as in the sequential categorization models discussed earlier). This conventionalization process results in the existence of alternative meanings for words that once were active metaphors (Gentner & Wolff, 1997). For example, the verb *boil* now has a metaphorical meaning—"to become emotionally agitated [like a boiling liquid]"—as well as its literal meaning.

There are also more global metaphoric systems. For example, Gentner, Imai, and Boroditsky (2002; Gentner, 2001) showed that space-time metaphors are comprehended in terms of two different global systems of mappings, rather than on an individual lexical basis. In particular, there are two main spatial metaphors for time. In one, an individual moves through time (e.g., "We are approaching Christmas"). In the other, time moves toward the individual (e.g., "Christmas is approaching") Gentner et al. (2002) showed that people process a sequence of temporal sentences faster if the sentences remain in the same space-time metaphor; there appears to be a processing cost for a shift from one of these metaphor systems to the other.

Further, Boroditsky (2000) demonstrated that the mapping is asymmetrical: people conceptualize time in terms of space. In one study, people were primed with pictures of individuals moving past objects or of objects moving on a conveyor belt past people. Then, they were given the sentence "Wednesday's meeting has been moved forward two days," and were asked to state on what day the meeting would occur (McGlone & Harding, 1998).

If space-time priming occurs, the two spatial situations should prime different interpretations of the temporal sentence. A person moving past a set of objects should prime the ego-moving metaphor system. In contrast, objects moving past a person should prime the time-moving metaphor. Consistent with these predictions, people in the moving-person condition considered that moving the meeting forward changed it to Friday, whereas people in the moving-object condition considered that the meeting was moved to Monday. Furthermore, the reverse priming could not be obtained. That is, using different metaphors for time did not influence people's reasoning about space.

The use of background knowledge is also important for forming impressions about people. Theories of social comparison (e.g., Festinger, 1954; Goethals & Darley, 1977) have acknowledged the diagnostic advantages of comparisons with standards who are similar in critical ways. Similarity is important in social comparison processes in at least two ways. First, there is considerable evidence that perceived similarity influences the selection of a standard. Second, the psychological consequences of social comparisons for self-evaluation, affect, and behavior also depend critically on the perceived similarity to the standard (e.g., Brown, Novick, Lord, & Richards, 1992; Catrambone, Beike, & Niedenthal, 1996; Gilbert, Giesler, & Morris, 1995; Lockwood & Kunda, 1997; Mussweiler, 2003). Mussweiler and Gentner (2004) found evidence that social comparisons involve a process of structural alignment and mapping. Selection of a standard was sensitive not merely to surface commonalities between the self and the social comparison standard (e.g., being good at sports), but also to higher order relational structures (e.g., caring enough about mastery in some arena—whether sports or music—to sacrifice greatly to achieve it). Further, consistent with the framework already presented, making a social comparison appears to render the common information more accessible.

Social comparison is also an important influence on first impressions. When we meet a new individual, we typically have a limited set of interactions with him or her. Nonetheless, we are quickly able to form impressions about this person's characteristics and to determine whether this person is someone we want to get to know better. An intriguing set of findings by Andersen and colleagues (Andersen & Cole, 1990; Chen & Andersen, 1999; Chen, Andersen, & Hinkley, 1999) suggests that similarities between new people and particular known individuals affect how the new person is perceived. As a demonstration of this point, subjects in experiments are asked to describe the characteristics of a significant other such as their mother. The same subjects are asked to participate in an unrelated study at another time. They are given descriptions of new people, some of whom have characteristics in common with the significant others they described. People are more likely to attribute other characteristics of their significant other to the new person than are control subjects who did not have this significant other. This finding suggests that similarities of a new person to known individuals have a strong influence on the way the new person is represented (see chapter 16).

To summarize, comparisons between new situations and background knowledge have an important influence on the way people represent and reason about the new situation. These comparisons often happen spontaneously. The point of having background knowledge is to enable a reasoner to recognize a familiar situation and to apply previous strategies to new cases. Initially, the relationship between a new domain and existing knowledge must involve an active comparison between domains. Eventually, however, if a mapping between domains is important enough to reoccur, it may be stored and become part of the background for the domain.

Conclusion

In this chapter, we have examined a number of influences of similarity on cognitive processing. These effects often occur spontaneously in cognitive processing, though some of the experiments we described involved tasks in which people were directed to make comparisons. We discussed four central influences of similarity on cognitive processing. First, comparisons may help people to see more abstract commonalities between situations than they would be able to find if only one domain were explored in isolation. We demonstrated this point with a number of developmental studies involving infants and young children. Second, the presence of similarities between items can influence cognitive processing by making specific properties of the items readily available. In particular, comparable pairs promote access to the commonalities and differences of items, which can then influence processing. Third, the presence of some similarities among items can be used as a signal that additional processing resources should be devoted to exploring a pair. This metacognitive aspect of similarity is evident in demonstrations that similarities influence looking time in infants and response times in adults. The similarity processes that give rise to these metacognitive judgments also appear to incorporate other information such as associations between terms that may signal that additional processing would be useful. Finally, new situations are spontaneously compared to previous experiences. These comparisons facilitate the representation of the new domain. Comparisons that are made frequently may become stored concepts.

Another important aspect of similarity is the distinction between the full structural alignment process and cheaper kinds of similarity processing. We suggested, first, that a quick, cheap similarity process is used to generate reminders from long-term memory, and, second, that early in any similarity comparison the processing is a kind of free-for-all of local matches. When the process of comparison is carried further, however, it results in the alignment of the representational structures of the two items. These comparisons promote noticing the commonalities and alignable differences of pairs, which can then be used in a variety of cognitive processes such as decision making, reasoning, problem solving, and person perception.

We suggest that these similarity processes are always active. In particular, the comparison process that influences metacognitive judgments need not be under conscious control, and need not yield products that are consciously accessible. Thus, the presence of similarities among items may have unintended influences on higher level cognitive processes, because attentional resources may be allocated on the basis of nonintentional similarity comparisons.

Acknowledgments This research was supported by NSF Grant SBR-9905013 to the first author and by ONR Grant N00014–92-J-1098, NSF Grant SBR-9511757, and NSF-LIS Grant SBR-9720313 to the second author. The authors thank Miriam Bassok, Eric Dietrich, Ryan Gossen, Brad Love, Hunt Stilwell, and Ed Wisniewski for helpful comments on this research. The authors thank Jason Kidd for an MVP-caliber season. The authors also thank Ran Hassin, Jim Uleman, and John Bargh for their patience and their excellent comments.

Notes

1. Formally, the process of finding the maximal match between two predicate structures is a variant of the problem of matching two arbitrary directed acyclic graphs. This problem is known to be in the class of NP-complete problems, meaning that the effort required to perform the computation is some exponential function of the size of the representations (see Falkenhainer et al., 1989, for more discussion).

2. There are, of course, cases of stored similarity links—such as *horse* and *zebra*—that may be retrieved from memory like other stored associations. What we are contrasting here is newly computed similarities versus stored associations.

3. Interestingly, the looking-time measure used in the study by Gomez and Gerken (1999) showed the opposite pattern from that found by Marcus et al. (1999). Infants in this study looked reliably longer at new strings that followed the training grammar than at strings that did not follow the training grammar. The source of this difference is not clear. One possibility is that the materials used by Gomez and Gerken were more complex than those used by Marcus et al., which could lead to a preference for familiar strings (Cohen, 2001).

4. This terminology is unfortunate, because "relational" combinations actually involve associative relations rather than relational commonalities.

References

Andersen, S. M., & Cole, S. W. (1990). "Do I know you?": The role of significant others in general social perception. *Journal of Personality and Social Psychology, 59*(3), 384–399.

Baillargeon, R. (1991). Reasoning about the height and location of a hidden object in 4.5- and 6.5-month-old infants. *Cognition, 38*(1), 13–42.

Baillargeon, R., Spelke, E. S., & Wasserman, S. (1985). Object permanence in 5-month old infants. *Cognition, 20*, 191–208.

Bassok, M., & Medin, D. L. (1997). Birds of a feather flock together: Similarity judgments with semantically rich stimuli. *Journal of Memory and Language, 36*(3), 311–336.

Blok, S. V., & Gentner, D. (2000). *Reasoning from shared structure: Proceedings of the 22nd meeting of the Cognitive Science Society.* Philadelphia: Erlbaum.

Boroditsky, L. (2000). Metaphoric structuring: Understanding time through spatial metaphors. *Cognition, 75*(1), 1–28.

Bowdle, B. F., & Gentner, D. (1997). Informativity and asymmetry in comparisons. *Cognitive Psychology, 34*, 244–286.

Brown, J. D., Novick, N. J., Lord, K. A., & Richards, J. M. (1992). When Gulliver travels: Social context, psychological closeness, and self-appraisals. *Journal of Personality and Social Psychology, 62*(5), 717–727.

Catrambone, R., Beike, D., & Niedenthal, P. (1996). Is the self-concept a habitual referent in judgments of similarity? *Psychological Science, 7*(3), 158–163.

Chen, S., & Andersen, S. M. (1999). Relationships from the past in the present: Significant-other representations and transference in interpersonal life. In M. P. Zanna (Ed.), *Advances in experimental social psychology* (Vol. 31, pp. 123–190). San Diego, CA: Academic Press.

Chen, S., Andersen, S. M., & Hinkley, K. (1999). Triggering transference: Examining the role of applicability in the activation and use of significant-other representations in social perception. *Social Cognition, 17*(3), 332–365.

Clement, C. A., & Gentner, D. (1991). Systematicity as a selection constraint in analogical mapping. *Cognitive Science, 15*, 89–132.

Cohen, L. B. (2001). *Uses and misuses of habituation: A theoretical and methodological analysis.* Paper presented at the annual meeting of the Society for Research on Child Development, Minneapolis, MN.

Cohen, L. B., & Younger, B. A. (1983). Perceptual categorization in the infant. In E. Scholnick (Ed.), *New trends in conceptual representation* (pp. 197–220). Hillsdale, NJ: Erlbaum.

Costello, F. J., & Keane, M. T. (2000). Efficient creativity: Constraint guided conceptual combination. *Cognitive Science, 24*(2), 299–349.

Eimas, P. D. (1971). Speech perception in infants. *Science, 171*, 303–306.

Falkenhainer, B., Forbus, K. D., & Gentner, D. (1989). The structure-mapping engine: Algorithm and examples. *Artificial Intelligence, 41*(1), 1–63.

Ferguson, R. W. (1994). MAGI: Analogy-based encoding using regularity and symmetry. In A. Ram & K. Eiselt (Eds.), *The proceedings of the sixteenth annual conference of the Cognitive Science Society* (pp. 283–287). Atlanta, GA: Erlbaum.

Festinger, L. (1954). A theory of social comparison processes. *Human Relations, 7*, 117–140.

Forbus, K. D., Gentner, D., & Law, K. (1995). MAC/FAC: A model of similarity-based retrieval. *Cognitive Science, 19*(2), 141–205.

Foss, D. J., & Harwood, D. A. (1975). Memory for sentences: Implications for human associative memory. *Journal of Verbal Learning and Verbal Behavior, 14*, 1–16.

Gagne, C. L. (2000). Relation-based combinations versus property-based combinations: A test of the CARIN theory and the dual-process theory of conceptual combination. *Journal of Memory and Language, 42*, 365–389.

Gärdenfors, P. (2000). *Conceptual spaces: The geometry of thought.* Cambridge, MA: MIT Press.

Gentner, D. (1983). Structure-mapping: A theoretical framework for analogy. *Cognitive Science, 7*, 155–170.

Gentner, D. (1989). The mechanisms of analogical learning. In S. Vosnindou & A. Ortony (Eds.), *Similarity and analogical reasoning* (pp. 199–241). New York: Cambridge University Press.

Gentner, D. (2001). Spatial metaphors in temporal reasoning. In M. Gattis (Ed.), *Spatial schemes in abstract thought* (pp. 203–222). Cambridge, MA: MIT Press.

Gentner, D., & Brem, S. K. (1999). *Is snow really like a shovel? Distinguishing similarity from thematic relatedness.* In M. Hahn & S. C. Storess (Eds.), *Proceedings of the twenty-first annual conference of the Cognitive Science Society* (pp. 179–184). Vancouver, BC, Canada: Erlbaum.

Gentner, D., & Gentner, D. R. (1983). Flowing water or teeming crowds: Mental models of electricity. In D. Gentner & A. L. Stevens (Eds.), *Mental models* (pp. 99–130). Hillsdale, NJ: Erlbaum.

Gentner, D., & Gunn, V. (2001). Structural alignment facilitates the noticing of differences. *Memory and Cognition, 29*(4), 565–577.

Gentner, D., Imai, M., & Boroditsky, L. (2002). As time goes by: Evidence for two systems in processing space-time metaphors. *Language and Cognitive Processes, 17*, 537–565.

Gentner, D., Kuehne, S. E., & Forbus, K. D. (2004). *Modeling infant learning as an analogical abstraction.* Manuscript in preparation.
Gentner, D., & Markman, A. B. (1994). Structural alignment in comparison: No difference without similarity. *Psychological Science, 5*(3), 152–158.
Gentner, D., & Markman, A. B. (1995). Analogy-based reasoning. In M. Arbib (Ed.), *The handbook of brain theory and neural networks* (pp. 91–93). Cambridge, MA: MIT Press.
Gentner, D., & Markman, A. B. (1997). Structural alignment in analogy and similarity. *American Psychologist, 52*(1), 45–56.
Gentner, D., & Namy, L. L. (1999). Comparison in the development of categories. *Cognitive Development, 14*(4), 487–513.
Gentner, D., & Wolff, P. (1997). Alignment in the processing of metaphor. *Journal of Memory and Language, 37*, 331–355.
Gentner, D., Rattermann, M. J., & Forbus, K. D. (1993). The roles of similarity in transfer: Separating retrievability from inferential soundness. *Cognitive Psychology, 25*(4), 524–575.
Gerrig, R. J., & Murphy, G. L. (1992). Contextual influences on the comprehension of complex concepts. *Language and Cognitive Processes, 7*, 205–230.
Gilbert, D. T., Giesler, R. B., & Morris, K. A. (1995). When comparisons arise. *Journal of Personality and Social Psychology, 69*(2), 227–236.
Glad, B., & Taber, C. S. (1990). Images, learning, and the decision to use force: The domino theory of the United States. In B. Glad (Ed.), *Psychological dimensions of war* (pp. 56–82). Newbury Park, CA: Sage.
Glucksberg, S., Gildea, P., & Bookin, H. B. (1982). On understanding nonliteral speech: Can people ignore metaphors? *Journal of Verbal Learning and Verbal Behavior, 21*(1), 85–98.
Goethals, G. R., & Darley, J. M. (1977). Social comparison theory: An attributional approach. In J. M. Suls & R. L. Miller (Eds.), *Social comparison processes: Theoretical and empirical perspectives* (pp. 259–278). Washington, DC: Hemisphere.
Goldstone, R. L., Medin, D. L., & Gentner, D. (1991). Relational similarity and the non-independence of features in similarity judgments. *Cognitive Psychology, 23*, 222–262.
Gomez, R. L., & Gerken, L. (1999). Artificial grammar learning by 1-year-olds leads to specific and abstract knowledge. *Cognition, 70*(2), 109–135.
Heit, E., & Rubinstein, J. (1994). Similarity and property effects in inductive reasoning. *Journal of Experimental Psychology: Learning, Memory, and Cognition, 20*(2), 411–422.
Holyoak, K. J., & Koh, K. (1987). Surface and structural similarity in analogical transfer. *Memory and Cognition, 15*(4), 332–340.
Holyoak, K. J., & Thagard, P. (1989). Analogical mapping by constraint satisfaction. *Cognitive Science, 13*(3), 295–355.
Hummel, J. E., & Holyoak, K. J. (1997). Distributed representations of structure: A theory of analogical access and mapping. *Psychological Review, 104*(3), 427–466.
Johnson, M. (1984). Consumer choice strategies for comparing noncomparable alternatives. *Journal of Consumer Research, 11*, 741–753.
Keane, M. T., Ledgeway, T., & Duff, S. (1994). Constraints on analogical mapping: A comparison of three models. *Cognitive Science, 18*, 387–438.
Kempton, W. (1986). Two theories of home heat control. *Cognitive Science, 10*(1), 75–90.

Kotovsky, L., & Gentner, D. (1996). Comparison and categorization in the development of relational similarity. *Child Development, 67*, 2797–2822.

Krumhansl, C. L. (1978). Concerning the applicability of geometric models to similarity data: The interrelationship between similarity and spatial density. *Psychological Review, 85*(5), 445–463.

Kubovy, M. (1995). Symmetry and similarity: The phenomenology of decorative patterns. In C. Cacciari (Ed.), *Similarity in language, thought and perception* (pp. 41–66). Brussels: Brepols.

Kuehne, S. E., Gentner, D., & Forbus, K. D. (2000). Modeling infant learning via symbolic structural alignment. In L. Gleitman & A. K. Joshi (Eds.), *The proceedings of the 22nd annual conference of the Cognitive Science Society* (pp. 286–291). Philadelphia: Erlbaum.

Lakoff, G., & Johnson, M. (1980). *Metaphors we live by*. Chicago: University of Chicago Press.

Leyton, M. (1992). *Symmetry, causality, mind*. Cambridge, MA: MIT Press.

Lockwood, P., & Kunda, Z. (1997). Superstars and me: Predicting the impact of role models on the self. *Journal of Personality and Social Psychology, 73*, 91–103.

Marcus, G. F., Vijayan, S., Bandi Rao, S., & Vishton, P. M. (1999). Rule learning by seven-month-old infants. *Science, 283*, 77–80.

Markman, A. B. (1999). *Knowledge representation*. Mahwah, NJ: Erlbaum.

Markman, A. B. (2001). Structural alignment, similarity, and the internal structure of category representations. In U. Hahn & M. Ramscar (Eds.), *Similarity and categorization* (pp. 109–130). Oxford, UK: Oxford University Press.

Markman, A. B., & Gentner, D. (1993a). Splitting the differences: A structural alignment view of similarity. *Journal of Memory and Language, 32*(4), 517–535.

Markman, A. B., & Gentner, D. (1993b). Structural alignment during similarity comparisons. *Cognitive Psychology, 25*(4), 431–467.

Markman, A. B., & Gentner, D. (1996). Commonalities and differences in similarity comparisons. *Memory and Cognition, 24*(2), 235–249.

Markman, A. B., & Gentner, D. (1997). The effects of alignability on memory. *Psychological Science, 8*(5), 363–367.

Markman, A. B., & Gentner, D. (2000). Structure mapping in the comparison process. *American Journal of Psychology, 113*(4), 501–538.

Markman, A. B., & Medin, D. L. (1995). Similarity and alignment in choice. *Organizational Behavior and Human Decision Processes, 63*(2), 117–130.

Markman, A. B., & Wisniewski, E. J. (1997). Similar and different: The differentiation of basic level categories. *Journal of Experimental Psychology: Learning, Memory, and Cognition, 23*(1), 54–70.

McGlone, M. S., & Harding, J. L. (1998). Back (or forward?) to the future: The role of perspective in temporal language comprehension. *Journal of Experimental Psychology: Learning, Memory, and Cognition, 24*(5), 1211–1223.

Medin, D. L., Goldstone, R. L., & Gentner, D. (1993). Respects for similarity. *Psychological Review, 100*, 254–278.

Medin, D. L., Goldstone, R. L., & Markman, A. B. (1995). Comparison and choice: Relations between similarity processing and decision processing. *Psychonomic Bulletin and Review, 2*(1), 1–19.

Medin, D. L., & Schaffer, M. M. (1978). Context theory of classification. *Psychological Review, 85*(3), 207–238.

Murphy, G. L. (1988). Comprehending complex concepts. *Cognitive Science, 12*, 529–562.

Mussweiler, T. (2001). Focus of comparison as a determinant of assimilation versus contrast in social comparison. *Personality and Social Psychology Bulletin, 27*, 38–47.

Mussweiler, T. (2003). Comparison processes in social judgment: Mechanisms and consequences. *Psychological Review, 110*, 472–489.

Mussweiler, T., & Gentner, D. (2004). *On apples and oranges: Structure mapping in social comparison.* Manuscript in preparation.

Namy, L. L., & Gentner, D. (2002). Making a silk purse out of two sow's ears: Young children's use of comparison in category learning. *Journal of Experimental Psychology: General, 131*(1), 5–15.

Nosofsky, R. M. (1986). Attention, similarity and the identification-categorization relationship. *Journal of Experimental Psychology: General, 115*(1), 39–57.

Ortony, A. (1979). Beyond literal similarity. *Psychological Review, 86*, 161–180.

Osherson, D. N., Smith, E. E., Wilkie, O., Lopez, A., & Shafir, E. (1990). Category based induction. *Psychological Review, 97*(2), 185–200.

Payne, J. W., Bettman, J. R., & Johnson, E. J. (1993). *The adaptive decision maker.* New York: Cambridge University Press.

Reed, S. K. (1972). Pattern recognition and categorization. *Cognitive Psychology, 3*, 382–407.

Reed, S. K., Ernst, G. W., & Banerji, R. (1974). The role of analogy in transfer between similar problem states. *Cognitive Psychology, 6*, 436–450.

Reeves, L. M., & Weisberg, R. W. (1994). The role of content and abstract information in analogical transfer. *Psychological Bulletin, 115*(3), 381–400.

Ross, B. H. (1987). This is like that: The use of earlier problems and the separation of similarity effects. *Journal of Experimental Psychology: Learning, Memory and Cognition, 13*(4), 629–639.

Ross, B. H. (1989). Distinguishing types of superficial similarities: Different effects on the access and use of earlier examples. *Journal of Experimental Psychology: Learning, Memory and Cognition, 15*(3), 456–468.

Ross, W. T., & Creyer, E. H. (1992). Making inferences about missing information: The effects of existing information. *Journal of Consumer Research, 19*, 14–25.

Sanbonmatsu, D. M., Kardes, F. R., & Herr, P. M. (1992). The role of prior knowledge and missing information in multiattribute evaluation. *Organizational Behavior and Human Decision Processes, 51*, 76–91.

Shepard, R. N. (1962). The analysis of proximities: Multidimensional scaling with an unknown distance function, I. *Psychometrika, 27*(2), 125–140.

Shepard, R. N. (1987). Toward a universal law of generalization for psychological science. *Science, 237*, 1317–1323.

Shoben, E. J. (1983). Applications of multidimensional scaling in cognitive psychology. *Applied Psychological Measurement, 7*(4), 473–490.

Skorstad, J., Gentner, D., & Medin, D. L. (1988). Abstraction processes during concept learning: A structural view. In *The proceedings of the 10th annual conference of the Cognitive Science Society*. Montreal: Erlbaum.

Sloman, S. A. (1993). Feature-based induction. *Cognitive Psychology, 25*(2), 231–280.

Sloman, S. A. (1996). The empirical case for two systems of reasoning. *Psychological Bulletin, 119*(1), 3–22.

Slovic, P., & MacPhillamy, D. (1974). Dimensional commensurability and cue utilization in comparative judgment. *Organizational Behavior and Human Performance, 11*, 172–194.

Smith, E. E., Shoben, E. J., & Rips, L. J. (1974). Structure and process in semantic memory: A featural model for semantic decisions. *Psychological Review, 81*, 214–241.

Stilwell, C. H., & Markman, A. B. (2001). *The fate of irrelevant information in analogical mapping.* Paper presented at the 23rd annual meeting of the Cognitive Science Society, Edinburgh, Scotland.

Thagard, P., Holyoak, K. J., Nelson, G., & Gochfeld, D. (1990). Analog retrieval by constraint satisfaction. *Artificial Intelligence, 46*, 259–310.

Tversky, A. (1977). Features of similarity. *Psychological Review, 84*(4), 327–352.

Tversky, A., & Kahneman, D. (1986). Rational choice and the framing of decisions. *Journal of Business, 59*(4), S251–S278.

Wharton, C. M., Holyoak, K. J., Downing, P. E., Lange, T. E., & Wickens, T. D. (1991). Retrieval competition in memory for analogies. In *The proceedings of the thirteenth annual meeting of the Cognitive Science Society* (pp. 528–533). Chicago: Erlbaum.

Wisniewski, E. J. (1996). Construal and similarity in conceptual combination. *Journal of Memory and Language, 35*(3), 434–453.

Wisniewski, E. J., & Bassok, M. (1999). What makes a man similar to a tie? Stimulus compatibility with comparison and integration. *Cognitive Psychology, 39*, 208–238.

Wisniewski, E. J., & Gentner, D. (1991). On the combinatorial semantics of noun pairs: Minor and major adjustments to meaning. In G. B. Simpson (Ed.), *Understanding word and sentence* (pp. 241–284). Amsterdam: Elsevier.

Wisniewski, E. J., & Love, B. C. (1998). Relations versus properties in conceptual combination. *Journal of Memory and Language, 38*, 177–202.

Wisniewski, E. J., & Markman, A. B. (1993). The role of structural alignment in conceptual combination. In *The proceedings of the fifteenth annual conference of the Cognitive Science Society* (pp. 1083–1086). Boulder, CO: Erlbaum.

Wolff, P., & Gentner, D. (2000). Evidence for role-neutral initial processing of metaphors. *Journal of Experimental Psychology: Learning, Memory, and Cognition, 26*(2), 512–528.

Wolff, P., & Gentner, D. (2004). *Structure-mapping in metaphor: Evidence for a multistage model of metaphor processing.* Manuscript in preparation.

Zhang, S., & Markman, A. B. (1998). Overcoming the early entrant advantage: The role of alignable and nonalignable differences. *Journal of Marketing Research, 35*, 413–426.

Zhang, S., & Markman, A. B. (2001). Processing product-unique features: Alignment and involvement in preference construction. *Journal of Consumer Psychology, 11*(1), 13–27.

6

The Mechanics of Imagination: Automaticity and Control in Counterfactual Thinking

Neal J. Roese, Lawrence J. Sanna, and Adam D. Galinsky

> Imagination [is] a blind but indispensable function of the soul, without which we should have no cognition whatever, but of the working of which we are seldom conscious.
>
> —Immanuel Kant, *Critique of Pure Reason*[1]

Counterfactuals are thoughts of what might have been. They are mental representations of alternatives to past occurrences, features, and states. As such, they are imaginative constructions fabricated from stored representations, typically embracing a blend of traces from both episodic and semantic memory. For example, "If only she had remembered her umbrella, she would have stayed dry" is a counterfactual rooted to (and directly evoked by) an episodic memory involving a recent occurrence in which an acquaintance became drenched by a summer downpour. This counterfactual is constructed via alteration (or mutation) of one discrete element of the factual episode (e.g., presence versus absence of umbrella), but this mutation draws upon semantic memory's abstract generalizations about the world (e.g., umbrellas are water repellent and thus can protect from moisture). Like many judgments, counterfactual thinking can be both automatic, in that its unconscious activation may follow from the simple recognition of particular outcomes, or intentional and controlled, in that it may be deliberately recruited, sculpted, or suppressed in response to ongoing goals.

Counterfactuals often take the form of "if-then" conditional propositions in which "if" corresponds to an action and "then" refers to a goal, such as "if only she had practiced harder, then she would have passed the audition."

Counterfactuals provide a basic context by which factual events may be benchmarked (McGill & Tenbrunsel, 2000). As such, they influence emotions such as satisfaction (Medvec, Madey, & Gilovich, 1995) and inferences such as causation and likelihood (Roese, 1997; Spellman & Mandel, 1999), which in turn influence global impressions of self and others (Miller, Visser, & Staub, 2001). Counterfactuals may be stored and subsequently retrieved, but far more commonly counterfactuals are constructed online in light of specific evoking outcomes (Kahneman & Miller, 1986). Thus, counterfactual activation typically refers not to heightened accessibility of stored representations but to the initiation of a constructive process of mental simulation that produces novel representations. Counterfactual speculations are potentially limitless, but though they may conjure the bizarre and the fantastic, everyday counterfactual thinking is often mundane. Counterfactuals preserve the integrity of the world as we know it, altering but one or two specific features and simulating the immediate results against a backdrop that is essentially the same as actuality.

Hofstadter (1979) argued that counterfactuals are an essential ingredient for consciousness and intelligence; hence, any artificial intelligence device would require some subroutine that produces such thoughts in order to calibrate the meaning of episodic representations. This conception, echoed subsequently by Kahneman and Miller (1986), positioned counterfactual generation as a heuristic process that was automatic, efficient, and effortless. At the same time, however, the richly detailed hypothetical suppositions of storytellers (e.g., Philip K. Dick's 1962 novel, *The Man in the High Castle*, imagines a 1960s America that had been defeated in World War II and was thus partitioned into a Nazi German East Coast and an Imperial Japanese West Coast) as well as everyday social perceivers (e.g., if my sister had been accepted into medical school to become a pediatrician, then she would now be very useful in helping to diagnose my daughter's mysterious cough) suggest rather more effortful and elaborative counterfactual constructions. The seminal chapter by Kahneman and Tversky (1982) was itself ambivalent on this score, in that their discussion of a simulation heuristic reflected both automatic, effortless processing and also elaborative processing of complex inferences of likelihood and causality (cf. Kahneman, 1995).

Current dual-processing conceptions (Chaiken & Trope, 1999) can well account for many previous findings in the counterfactual literature. A somewhat facile summary would thus be that the process of mental simulation is automatic, but more detailed, speculative counterfactual musings can also be deployed effortfully to achieve specific conscious goals, given sufficient time or processing capacity. Beyond this summary lurks a variety of more complicated yet informative subpatterns that form the core of the present chapter. The theme is that goal perceptions offer a unifying conception of a variety of counterfactual processing effects, both automatic and controlled. Following a brief overview of two theories of the determinants of counterfactual thinking, three sections follow. The first focuses on performance goals and counterfactual activation. The second focuses on affect goals and counterfactual activation. And the third focuses on the activation by counterfactuals of mind-sets that reflect higher order goal-based cognitions. We conclude by discussing implications and drawing connections to related recent research.

Theoretical Background

Norm Theory

Kahneman and Miller's (1986) norm theory was the first and remains the most influential theoretical depiction of counterfactual thinking. This work was broader than a simple exposition of counterfactual thinking, however, presenting a general model of exemplar-based concept activation with counterfactually mediated judgments presented as a particularly interesting but by no means singular consequence. Two of the theory's assertions are particularly relevant to the present discussion.

First, reactions to particular events are influenced not only by previously stored expectancies, but also by "postcomputed" norms. Norm theory posited that events activate semantically related exemplars from episodic memory that combine collectively to create the norm. Unlike the global anchors specified by such earlier models as adaptation level theory (Helson, 1964), norms are specific and vary as a function of the features of their evoking outcomes (McGill, 1993). Thus, counterfactuals can produce effects independently of expectancies (Medvec et al., 1995). For example, consider two individuals en route to an airport, both having identical expectancies that they will depart successfully on their assigned flights (Kahneman & Tversky, 1982). Both expectancies are disconfirmed in that both individuals are stuck in traffic and miss their flights. For one, however, the flight had been delayed and thus had been missed by a mere 5 minutes. For the other, the flight had departed on schedule and thus had been missed by a full 30 minutes. Most observers assume that the first individual would be much more regretful than the second. For this person, a counterfactual is more easily constructed: it is easier to imagine having shaved off 5 than 30 minutes of travel time (e.g., by driving faster, ignoring amber traffic lights, etc.). Kahneman and Tversky argued that although both the expectancies and objective situation of each man are identical (both expect to depart on time and both arrive too late to do so), the relative availability of counterfactual representations differs and thus accounts for diverging affective responses (see also Miller, Turnbull, & McFarland, 1990; Sanna & Turley-Ames, 2000).

Second, a principle of norm asymmetry governs counterfactual construction. Counterfactual representations are much more likely to embrace antecedents that seize upon an unusual, exceptional, or abnormal event and to return it to its normal state than vice versa. An automobile accident victim, for example, will likely generate "if only" thoughts aimed at mentally undoing the accident. A victim who had been driving an atypical route at his typical time of day would wish that he had stuck to his typical route, but another victim who had been driving along her typical route but at an atypical time of day would instead wish that she had driven at the more typical time (Kahneman & Tversky, 1982). In this way, counterfactuals recapitulate norms.

But more generally, this principle suggests an interesting twist on the process of category activation, in which priming is defined as the effect of activation of one representation on the activation of a semantically related one. Semantic relation is usually defined with regard to alignment between salient features of each representation (Higgins, 1996). In norm theory, priming may also be understood with regard to the placement of a construct along a dimension of normality, such that extreme category members prime representations of other category members that are positioned closer to the central tendency (or norm) of the category, but not vice versa. Plantains may remind one of bananas, but bananas rarely bring plantains to mind. Macintosh computer users frequently complain about PCs, but PC users rarely speak of Macs. Canadians define their national identity in contrast to Americans, but Americans scarcely realize Canada exists. The extreme primes the normal, but the normal does not prime the extreme. As these examples make clear, extremity/normality may embody a variety of specific dimensions, including numerosity, frequency of occurrence, or depth of knowledge.

Although this principle bears some resemblance to the asymmetry in the direction of comparison of relational (e.g., similarity, difference) judgments that occurs when the objects of comparison differ in their extremity versus normality (e.g., Medin, Goldstone, & Gentner, 1993; Tversky, 1977), the underlying mechanisms differ markedly. When a perceiver sees greater similarity between Canada and the United States than between the United States and Canada (i.e., a direction of comparison effect), for example, differential salience of unique versus shared features drives the effect. Thus, when the more prominent object is privileged by being the subject (rather than object) of comparison (as when comparing the United States to Canada), its relatively greater amount of unique features assume prominence and thereby weaken perceptions of similarity (Gati & Tversky, 1984). By contrast, the norm theory account centers not on features within objects but rather on the relative standing of objects with regard to a distribution. Intriguingly, however, norm theory can indeed supply an independent explanation for direction of comparison asymmetry effects when norms surrounding grammatical construction are considered. Specifically, in English and other languages, convention demands that the more normal category member be placed second (or last) in comparative statements (e.g., "llamas are smaller than horses"; but not "horses are larger than llamas"). Violation of this linguistic norm (within statements or questions presented to subjects) raises eyebrows, demands further consideration, and results in more moderate relational judgments (Roese, Sherman, & Hur, 1998). In general, however, the applicability of the norm theory principle of asymmetrical priming of category members, depending on their position within a distribution, has many applications yet to be articulated. Some potential examples include the manner in which minority groups establish self-identity with regard to the majority (McGuire, McGuire, Child, & Fujioka, 1978), the hostility that extremist groups direct toward slightly less extreme (i.e., more moderate) groups (White & Langer, 1999), and the greater effort and attention that subordinates direct to leaders than leaders direct to subordinates (Goodwin, Gubin, Fiske, & Yzerbyt, 2000).

Norm theory asserts that recognition of an atypical antecedent activates construction of a counterfactual structured around the more typical form of that antecedent. Importantly, norm theory construes norm activation and thus counterfactual activation as purely automatic, akin to a perceptual orienting response (Kahneman, 1995). Research that has specified counterfactual operations in terms of mental models similarly views counterfactual processing as a rapid, low-level operation (Byrne, 1997; Byrne, Segura, Culhane, Tasso, & Berrocal, 2000; Quelhas & Byrne, 2000). And evidence suggests that counterfactual judgments are automatic in the sense of efficiency, in that cognitive load does not interfere with counterfactual inferences during encoding of focal information but does interfere with subsequent attempts to correct or suppress the inappropriate application of counterfactual inferences to judgments of victim blame and compensation (Goldinger, Kleider, Asuma, & Beike, 2003).

The Two-Stage Model

The two-stage model (Roese, 1997; Roese & Olson, 1995a, 1997) was designed to address the observation that most everyday counterfactual thoughts are not content- or valence-neutral but focus mainly on failure to achieve a desired goal.[2] When people think about what might have been, they think of personally meaningful desires that have gone unmet, such as missed educational opportunities or lost loves (Gilovich & Medvec, 1995; Landman & Manis, 1992). Counterfactuals that are upward (i.e., specifying how outcomes might have been better) rather than downward (i.e., specifying how outcomes might have been worse) appear to be the default under many conditions, suggesting that counterfactuals typically recapitulate goals rather than norms. Thus, the two-stage model repositions counterfactual thinking in relation to motivation and performance goals rather than perceptions of base rates and typicality.

A key feature of the model was the separation of the determinants of counterfactual thinking into two stages, those influencing mere activation and those influencing content. Failure and unmet goals in general, and the resulting negative affect in particular, activate counterfactual thinking. Normality, on the other hand, dictates the content of counterfactuals once the constructive process is initiated (Roese, 1997; Roese & Hur, 1997; Roese & Olson, 1997). That is, once an accident or heartbreak prompts an individual to think about what might have been, unusual features such as out-of-character behaviors will assume a central position within the counterfactual, with the counterfactual antecedent specifying in-character behaviors that ought to have been performed. If nothing out of the ordinary preceded the negative evoking outcome, counterfactuals will still be constructed, driven by the desire to avoid (mentally rather than actually) the negative outcome (Davis & Lehman, 1995). In one experiment, for example, participants were given false feedback (success vs. failure) regarding their performance on a computer-presented anagram task (Roese & Hur, 1997, Experiment 2). Participants recorded more counterfactuals in a thought-listing task following failure than following success feedback. Negative affect but not expectancies or norm violations mediated this effect. Norms, however, indeed guided the content of counterfactuals so generated. That negative affect activates counterfactual thinking was framed in terms of a functional perspective in which counterfactuals furnish useful inferences for subsequent performance enhancement (Roese, 1994, 2001). Thus, in the same way that negative affect mobilizes problem-solving cognition generally (Taylor, 1991), in part because negative affect is informative with regard to goal blockage (Schwarz, 1990), counterfactual thinking is also activated automatically by negative affect.

In the two-stage model, negative affect (as opposed to norm violation) is the principal engine driving counterfactual thinking, and this was the primary divergence between it and norm theory. Evidence in support of this contention came from studies that either independently manipulated both affect and norms or simultaneously examined self-reported perceptions of both in regression analyses of counterfactual activation (Roese & Hur, 1997; Roese & Olson, 1997). However, several experiments have suggested that norm violation may activate counterfactual thinking independently of affect (Galinsky & Moskowitz, 2000; Goldinger et al., 2003; Roese & Olson, 1996, Experiment 3). Although further work is needed to resolve the discrepancy across these studies, one obvious candidate for resolution is the central role of goal perceptions. Both affect and norm violation can inform goal inferences, which are central to counterfactual thinking in a number of ways. This is the theme of the remainder of this chapter.

Summary

Two theoretical depictions of counterfactual thinking, norm theory and the two-stage model, both focus on the determinants of counterfactual thinking. The two-stage model partitions determinants into those influencing activation versus those influencing content, with negative affect positioned as the key variable influencing the activation stage. The theme of this chapter is that goals are a crucial component of counterfactual thinking. Accordingly, the three remaining sections each embody this theme. The first two focus on counterfactual activation, examining the roles of performance goals and affect goals, respectively. The third section explores the goal-based consequences of counterfactuals within the context of mind-set priming.

Performance Goals and Counterfactual Activation

William James (1890) argued that the fundamental goal of cognition is to produce behavior. Perhaps the most basic description of counterfactual thinking is that it is a class of cognitions that bridges affect, goal perception, and action tendencies. In this section we explore performance goals, which center on achievement of particular outcomes, such as winning a basketball game, finding a spouse, or earning a living wage. Although affect is both a cause and consequence of such goals, it is not integral. By contrast, affect goals, explored in the subsequent section, are those in which a particular affective result, such as effective coping, satisfaction, or simply feeling good, is the goal itself. Such a distinction has proven useful in various literatures, most notably those of coping (Lazarus & Folkman, 1984) and social comparison (Suls & Wheeler, 2000).

Preparatory Causal Inferences

Counterfactual thinking may suggest particular causal insights regarding actions and desired outcomes. If a young man fails to impress a young woman to whom he is attracted, he may ponder actions that might have won her heart: if only he had showered her with gifts such as flowers and candies, if only he had been more charmingly amusing, if only he had been more persistent or less pushy. Such conditional thoughts, as long as they are aimed at the past, are appropriately termed counterfactual, in that they clearly did not occur ("If I had done X, I might have gotten Y"). But the same hypothetical actions may also form the basis for prefactual thoughts, which are causal conditionals aimed at possible future actions (Sanna, 1996, 2000). The young man may speculate that if he deploys flowers, candies, and humor in his next attempt, he may well attain romantic fulfillment. Such prefactuals, also structured as action-oriented conditional propositions ("If I do X, I may get Y"), may form the basis of intentions, which may then propel behavior. Roese (1994) manipulated counterfactual thinking and showed that, in the context of academic achievement (Experiment 2) and a laboratory anagram task (Experiment 3), such thoughts heightened intentions to perform, and the actual performance of, specific success-facilitating behaviors. Longitudinal research by Nasco and Marsh (1999) confirmed that the relation between counterfactuals (regarding an exam grade) and subsequent academic achievement (improvement on a subsequent exam) were mediated by self-reported perceptions of contingency between actions (studying) and outcomes (succeeding). In general, expectancy-based mental simulation that focuses on specific plans and processes enhances achievement (Olson, Roese, & Zanna, 1996; Pham & Taylor, 1999; Taylor & Pham, 1996). Thus, counterfactuals, though directed at the past, can provide causal information that may supply a roadmap for future action: Counterfactuals are prescriptive.

Direction of Comparison

As derived from the social comparison literature (cf. Folger & Kass, 2000; Kruglanski & Mayseless, 1990; Olson, Buhrmann, & Roese, 2000; Taylor & Lobel, 1989; Wood, 1989), the distinction between upward counterfactuals (e.g., "If Jean had gotten that new job, her income would have doubled") and downward counterfactuals (e.g., "If Jean had lost her current job, her income would have vanished") has been indispensable to the counterfactual literature. Precisely the same logic applies to prefactual thinking: An upward prefactual is a contrast between an expected trajectory and some better future prospect (e.g., "Jason is not currently projected to win, but if he can woo local investors, he might just win the nomination"), whereas a downward prefactual is a contrast between an expected outcome and a worse future prospect (e.g., "Jason is not currently projected to win, but if he is caught in a sex scandal, his share of the popular vote will be even worse than expected"). Direction of comparison is a description that applies equally well to any pairwise evaluative contrast, including counterfactual comparisons (comparing factual self to alternative self), social comparisons (comparing self to others), temporal comparisons (comparing current self to past or future self), and prefactual comparison (comparing expected future self to alternative future self).[3] In all cases, an affective contrast effect seems to be the default outcome: Upward contrasts produce relatively more negative affect and downward contrasts produce more positive affect (cf. Smith, 2000). But affect aside, in previous research in both counterfactual thinking and social comparison, upward comparisons have been viewed as the most useful with regard to achieving performance goals because such thoughts specify improvement to, rather than preservation of, the status quo (Aspinwall & Taylor, 1993; Huguet, Dumas, Monteil, & Genestoux, 2001; Roese & Olson, 1995a; Taylor & Lobel, 1989). We consider the interplay between counterfactuals and prefactuals in the subsequent section on affect goals.

Regulatory Focus

As discussed in the section on the two-stage model, negative affect evokes upward counterfactuals. But negative affect, and negative outcomes in general, may be differentiated on the basis of regulatory goals (Roese, Hur, & Pennington, 1999), permitting the observation of diverging patterns of activation. In research by Higgins (e.g., 1997) and colleagues, promotion focus was defined as cognitive emphasis on acquisition of positive goals; that is, a concern with advancement, accomplishment, and realization of positive end states. A prevention focus, by contrast, centers on preservation of an absence of unwanted occurrences; that is, a concern with security, protection, and maintenance of the status quo. Promotion failure versus prevention failure evoke qualitatively different affective experiences: dejection and agitation, respectively (Higgins, Shah, & Friedman, 1997). If, as Schwarz and Clore (1996) argued, different kinds of negative affect provide qualitatively different informational insights into goal blockage, then confronting different problems that evoke dejection versus agitation might activate different types of counterfactual thoughts. A preliminary experiment indicated that overall counterfactual activation did not vary as a function of promotion or prevention failure (Pennington & Roese, 2003). Rather, these two types of failure dictated the structural form of counterfactuals: either additions or subtractions.

This research was initiated by a puzzle in the counterfactual literature, namely conflicting reports as to whether individuals typically wish that they had performed some hypothetical past action (an additive counterfactual) or wish that they had not performed some factual action (a subtractive counterfactual). Thus, an additive counterfactual might be "If only Sarah had bought the study guide, she would have performed better on the exam," whereas a subtractive counterfactual might be "If only Jack had not been drunk during the exam, he might have performed much better." Initial research by Kahneman and Tversky (1982) supported the latter as the default, whereas various other findings indicated the reverse (e.g., Roese & Olson, 1993).[4] Gilovich and Medvec (1995) demonstrated that temporal perspective moderates the relative frequency of these counterfactual subtypes, with subtractions dominating retrospections of recent events and additions dominating retrospections of long past events. However, as many conflicting research findings centered on the short term, Roese et al. (1999) argued that regulatory focus better accounted for the discrepancy. Specifically, additive counterfactuals seemed most prevalent in experiments involving missed opportunities or failed attempts, as in the case of academic (Roese & Olson, 1993) or athletic failure (Grieve, Houston, Dupuis, & Eddy, 1999) (i.e., "absence of a positive" or promotion failure). By contrast, subtractive counterfactuals seemed most prominent in experiments focusing on sudden accidents or attacks, such as automobile mishaps (Kahneman & Tversky, 1982) and sexual assaults (Catellani & Milesi, 2001) (i.e., "presence of a negative" or prevention failure). In an experiment that presented (on a within-subject basis) descriptions of situations that were examples of such promotion and prevention failures, participants indeed responded with more frequent additive versus subtractive counterfactuals, respectively (Roese et al., 1999, Experiment 1). Thus, ongoing regulatory goals determine the specific form of spontaneously generated counterfactuals.

The distinction between dejection and agitation was important as a determinant but not as a consequence of counterfactual activation (Roese et al., 1999). That is, although manipulations of counterfactual thinking produced no differential effects on ratings of dejection versus agitation (Experiment 2), the manipulation of dejection versus agitation activated additive versus subtractive counterfactuals, respectively (Experiment 3). To the extent that dejection and agitation send differential signals regarding promotion failure versus prevention failure, they might differentially activate those counterfactual subtypes best suited to effectively achieve those performance goals. Indeed, Experiment 2 suggested that additive counterfactuals tend to express causal sufficiency, whereas subtractive counterfactuals tend to express causal necessity (as indicated by subjects' categorizations of their own counterfactuals generated in response to recalled personal experiences). Sufficiency is more effective for reaching promotion goals, because one need specify only one action that, in and of itself, will facilitate goal attainment. By contrast, understanding necessity would not be as useful, because such causes may not be enough, in and of themselves, to bring about that desired goal. On the other hand, an understanding of necessity is more parsimonious for reaching prevention goals. With necessity information, the required avenue by which a negative outcome occurs may be eliminated, thereby effectively preventing the outcome's occurrence. An understanding of sufficiency would not be as useful in this case, because removing one sufficient cause cannot preclude the operation of other causes that are themselves sufficient to bring about that same undesired outcome. The following example clarifies these points.

If one has the promotion goal of getting to the zoo, one may terminate the search after locating causal sufficiency (e.g., finding correct directions to the zoo): One may then walk, cycle, or drive using those roads, and no further causal search for additional roads is needed. Necessity information, on the other hand, does not guarantee achievement of the promotion goal. It may be necessary to travel east in order to reach the zoo from downtown, for example, but traveling east alone does not guarantee arrival at the zoo, thus demanding further search for the correct sequence of roads still needed to attain the goal. Achieving a prevention goal is quite different, as in the goal of preventing oneself from being injured in a bicycle accident. Locating and ruling out one cause sufficient to produce a bicycle accident (e.g., skidding on wet roads, which may be prevented by never cycling during rainy weather) certainly does not preclude the operation of myriad other factors sufficient to induce bicycle accidents (e.g., even when riding in dry weather, drunk drivers, malevolent skateboarders, or sudden gusts of wind can similarly cause accidents). Consideration of causal sufficiency within the context of prevention focus demands an exhaustive search for all possible factors sufficient to produce the undesired outcome. But consideration of a cause necessary to produce an unwanted outcome permits the termination of the causal search after identification of just one such factor. If it is necessary to mount a bicycle in the first place to get into a bicycle accident, for example, one may very easily and effectively prevent the occurrence of bicycle accidents by never going near a bicycle. Thus, sufficiency information more effectively services promotion goals, whereas necessity information more effectively services prevention goals.

If counterfactuals are usually goal related, one implication is that such thoughts themselves can evoke a particular regulatory focus. In other words, generating a meaningful counterfactual about one's own actions (e.g., "I should have locked my car") may temporarily bring to mind a variety of inferences regarding higher order goals (e.g., "I need to protect myself from theft"). That is, counterfactual thinking can prime goal-oriented modes of processing. Indeed, the experimental induction of additive versus subtractive counterfactuals heightened promotion versus prevention focus, respectively (as indicated by importance ratings of a variety of everyday life goals; Roese et al., 1999, Experiment 2).

Summary

This section reviewed research on the activation of counterfactual thinking by negative affect, and the linkage of this effect to achievement of performance goals. Further, different kinds of negative affect (dejection versus agitation) are associated with different kinds of goals (promotion versus prevention), and these goals differentially evoke counterfactuals of varying structures (additive versus subtractive), which in turn have varying causal implications (sufficiency versus necessity). The additional finding that counterfactuals can stimulate general goal states is perhaps just one manifestation of the more general tendency for counterfactual thinking to prime a mind-set that produces effects independent of the particular counterfactual content.

This concept of mind-set priming forms the basis of the final section of the chapter. In the next section, however, we expand on the contention that goals determine counterfactual activation by considering recent theoretical work on affect goals.

Affect Goals and Counterfactual Activation

That counterfactuals influence affect was a core feature of the seminal work by Kahneman and Tversky (1982) and the literature it spawned (e.g., Davis & Lehman, 1995; Gleicher et al., 1990; Landman, 1987; Miller & McFarland, 1986; Niedenthal, Tangney, & Gavanski, 1994; Zeelenberg et al., 1998). Affect goals, considered in this section, represent the strategic generation of counterfactuals to bring about desired affective states (see Sedikides & Strube, 1997, for review). Sanna (2000) postulated a framework by which automatic versus controlled activation of counterfactual (and also prefactual) thoughts are linked to affect goals. In this section, we present a revised theoretical framework of affect goals that extends prior work while suggesting several directions for future research.

Contrast Effects

Because evaluative comparisons can produce affective contrast effects, such comparisons may be strategically generated to yield a desired emotional outcome. After skinning her knee, a novice bicyclist might console herself by noting that it could have been worse: She might have fractured a limb. Although counterfactual assimilation effects may sometimes occur (e.g., anxiety produced by vividly imagining a cycling accident that might have occurred; e.g., Markman & McMullen, 2003), contrast effects appear to be the default. Thus, one may generate downward counterfactuals strategically to make oneself feel better (discussed in previous works as the affective function of counterfactuals; e.g., Roese, 1994). Research has indeed shown that counterfactual direction influences emotion. For example, manipulation of counterfactual direction (by way of encouragement to consider how a recent exam performance might have been better or worse) produced corresponding shifts in self-reported affect (Roese, 1994). Downward counterfactuals made participants feel better, both relative to upward counterfactual consideration and relative to a no-counterfactual control condition (Experiments 1 and 2). Similarly, Olympic silver medalists feel bad because their most salient counterfactual is that they nearly won the gold (an upward comparison), whereas bronze medallists feel much better because their most salient counterfactual is that they might have gone home with no medal at all (a downward comparison; Medvec et al., 1995).

Subtypes of Affect Goals: A New Framework

Across various literatures in social psychology, three affect goals have been distinguished: mood repair, mood maintenance, and self-protection, each of which may relate uniquely to counterfactual and prefactual thinking (Sanna, 2000; Sanna, Chang, & Meier, 2001). Mood repair refers to strategies designed to improve mood after a negative event has depressed it. Mood maintenance reflects the tendency for people to enjoy and thus attempt to preserve good moods. Self-protection is a strategy designed to prepare for future threat by cognitively minimizing its potential impact. In the sections that follow, we present a revised theoretical framework that grounds these three motives to two underlying dimensions, temporal focus and outcome valence. Of course, the axiomatic assumption underlying all such theorizing is that of hedonic regulation: people prefer to feel good rather than bad.

By temporal focus, we distinguish between affect goals that are reactive and those which are proactive (Aspinwall & Taylor, 1997). In the case of a reactive strategy, a particular outcome has already occurred and cognitive resources are mobilized to confront its aftermath. One may have just had a car accident or just seen a superb film, and the resulting negative and positive emotions, respectively, impact subsequent affect regulation. By contrast, a proactive strategy is based on forecasting events that have yet to occur and acting in accordance with their expected emotional consequences (see Gilbert, Pinel, Wilson, Blumberg, & Wheatley, 1998, for examination of biases that accrue from affective forecasting). One may expect to lose money on the stock market or to move to California, and cognitions will change as a function of the expected negative and positive emotional repercussions of these events. Further, by outcome valence, we mean the traditional distinction between events of positive or negative emotional implication, coupled to the traditional assumption that individuals are motivated to approach positive and avoid negative affect. Combining these two dimensions yields a 2 × 2 framework in which the three affect goals described by Sanna (2000) are firmly ensconced (see table 6.1). The fourth affect goal of free fantasy (proactive/positive), previously articulated in separate theoretical work (Oettingen, 1996; Oettingen, Pak, & Schnetter, 2001), is implied by our framework, constituting an intriguing direction for future integrative research. To summarize, the four goals are as follows.

Reactive/Positive In response to a positive outcome, individuals behave in a manner that preserves the positive affect deriving from the outcome. The traditional term for this pattern is mood maintenance. For example, people in happy moods are particular likely to select activities on the basis of whether they will facilitate versus ruin their currently pleasant frame of mind (Wegener & Petty, 1994; Wegener, Petty, & Smith, 1995). With regard to counter-

Table 6.1 The 2 × 2 Framework of Affect Goals Rooted in Underlying Dimensions of Temporal Focus and Outcome Valence

	Reactive	Proactive
Positive outcome	Standard term: Mood maintenance Automatic comparison: Downward Strategic comparison: Downward Result: Match Outcome: Automatic processing	Standard term: Free fantasy Automatic comparison: Downward Strategic comparison: Upward Result: Mismatch Outcome: Controlled processing
Negative outcome	Standard term: Mood repair Automatic comparison: Upward Strategic comparison: Downward Result: Mismatch Outcome: Controlled processing	Standard term: Self-protection Automatic comparison: Upward Strategic comparison: Upward Result: Match Outcome: Automatic processing

factuals, an example of mood maintenance is the observation that people in happy (rather than sad) moods generate relatively greater numbers of downward counterfactuals and report enjoyment in doing so (Sanna, Meier, & Wegner, 2001).

Reactive/Negative In response to a negative outcome, individuals behave in a manner that improves upon their current negative affect. The traditional term for this pattern is mood repair. For example, individuals engage in a variety of activities, from outgroup denigration (Fein & Spencer, 1997) to prosocial acts (Schaller & Cialdini, 1990) to make themselves feel better in response to a negative experience. Downward counterfactuals are generated following negative outcomes relatively rarely, but goal-related moderators, such as perceived control (Roese & Olson, 1995b) and self-esteem (Sanna, Turley-Ames, & Meier, 1999) predict their appearance.

Proactive/Positive With regard to the prospect of a positive outcome, individuals might actively envision it and thus vicariously enjoy it. Such "free fantasies" are certainly linked to performance goals, but of interest here is their power to "seduce a person to enjoy the desired future in the here and now" (Oettingen et al., 2001, p. 737). Evidence that people "indulge" themselves in such positive fantasies comes from research on goal setting (Oettingen et al., 2001); one example is buying a lottery ticket and enjoying fleeting thoughts of yachts and feasts should one hold the winning number (Landman & Petty, 2000).

Proactive/Negative In anticipation of the prospect of a negative outcome, individuals might attempt to mitigate the impact of potential negative affect by "bracing for the loss" (Shepperd, Findley-Klein, Kwavnick, Walker, & Perez, 2000; Shepperd, Ouellette, & Fernandez, 1996). That is, active anticipation renders an outcome more predictable and thus more psychologically manageable. Defensive pessimism is an example of a strategy that provides not only motivational benefits (individuals may strive harder to avoid the salient negative prospect) but also affective benefits (great predictability reduces the sting of negative outcomes should they actually occur; Norem & Cantor, 1986; Sanna, 1998). Self-handicapping (e.g., Berglas & Jones, 1978), in which individuals intentionally emplace obstacles in their path and thus guarantee failure, is a conceptually similar tactic of threat management. Our present focus is on the manner in which individuals generate upward prefactuals, which clarify strategies that may generally aid performance, and thus similarly help individuals to brace for failure (Sanna, 1999; Sanna & Meier, 2000).

This 2×2 framework formalizes predictions as to when counterfactual thinking will be automatic versus controlled. It does so by specifying unique effects with regard to automaticity that occur within each of the four cells as a function of the interplay between three principles.

The first principle is that temporal focus dictates strategic (or motivated) direction of comparison: to produce and/or maintain positive affect, reactive versus proactive strategies favor downward versus upward comparisons, respectively. Specifically, affective contrast effects underlie reactive but not proactive affect regulation. Thus, downward counterfactuals are more likely for both reactive/positive (mood maintenance) and reactive/negative (mood repair) affect goals, because for both the contrast-effect–induced positive affect is the strategic goal. By contrast, upward contrasts are more likely for both proactive/positive (free fantasy) and proactive/negative (mood-protection). In the former case, fantasy and daydreams may be marked more by assimilation than contrast effects (cf. Markman & McMullen, 2003; Oettingen et al., 2001; Taylor & Lobel, 1989), and thus the upward prefactual (imagining a better car, employer, or house than is normatively expected) produces positive affect as one languorously elaborates the fantasy. In the latter case of bracing for loss, considering upward alternatives ("If only I had more study time, I might be able to do better than expected on tomorrow's exam") involves heightened negative affect, but is compensated by consideration of causal explanatory details that render the outcome more predictable, more manageable, and hence less threatening because the possibility of failure was dealt with beforehand.

The second principle is that outcome valence dictates the automatic (as opposed to strategic) direction of comparison: positive and negative outcomes tend to evoke downward and upward comparisons, respectively. This pattern was observed when participants were directly probed for counterfactual thoughts (Roese & Olson, 1995b) and when they verbalized freely in response to gambling outcomes (Markman, Gavanski, Sherman, & McMullen, 1993). Response time evidence also supports this contention: Sanna et al. (1999) reported that response latencies were briefest for upward (rather than downward) counterfactual statements following negative affect induction, and for downward (rather than upward) counterfactual statements following positive affect induction. However, open-ended dependent measures indicate that downward counterfactuals are generated spontaneously only rarely (Roese & Olson, 1997), a point to which we return in the general discussion. Even so, anecdotal reports of individuals cheering themselves or others up via thoughts of how things might have been worse ("Look on the bright side: You could have been killed, or worse!") suggest the need for actuarial assessments of the frequency with which various counterfactual subtypes are generated across life domains.

The third principle, and the key to the pattern of predictions summarized in table 6.1, is that the degree of match between the strategic and the automatic determines the amount of subsequent controlled processing (Sanna, 2000; Sanna, Chang, & Meier, 2001). A match requires no further processing and remains automatic, whereas a mismatch evokes remedial controlled processing that provides a direction of comparison that achieves the strategic goal. Thus, the framework predicts relatively rapid, automatic processing in the case of reactive/positive and proactive/negative affect goals. In the former case, downward counterfactuals are most likely to come to mind automatically, and they are also most desirable in terms of their affective consequences; hence no further controlled processing is required beyond that which is activated automatically. In the latter case, upward prefactuals are most likely to come to mind automatically, and they too are most desirable in their affective consequences, and so, again, no further controlled processing is required.

We therefore expect more effortful attempts at affect regulation in the case of both reactive/negative and proactive/positive affect goals, in that these represent mismatches between strategic and automatic thought processes. In the former case, the automatically generated counterfactual is upward (which facilitates achievement of performance goals), whereas the strategically preferred counterfactual (which facilitates affective regulation) is downward, and thus controlled processing would be required to override the automatic to produce a more favorable affective state. In the latter case, downward prefactuals are generated automatically, whereas upward fantasies are the preferred target for affect regulation, and so again controlled processing is invoked to override and replace downward with upward prefactuals. This framework thus provides, within the context of affect regulation, a clear menu of predictions as to when counterfactual activation may be automatic versus controlled.

Experimental Evidence

Two lines of evidence provide initial support for the framework of four affect goals presented here (see Sanna, 2000; Sanna, Chang, & Meier, 2001, for more discussion of consistency vs. inconsistency). First, Sanna et al. (1999, Experiments 3 and 4) manipulated mood (positive versus negative) and measured response latencies to counterfactual statements among individuals high and low in self-esteem. The assumption behind this research was that individuals with high (rather than low) self-esteem show a greater tendency to engage in mood-repair activity. Thus, by creating a reactive situation, such individuals might be expected to automatically activate upward counterfactuals, but then to expend relatively greater effort to replace these with positive mood-enhancing downward counterfactuals. Results indicated that individuals with high (rather than low) self-esteem indeed generated more downward counterfactual thoughts in response to negative mood and subsequently felt better after doing so. This interpretation is consistent with other research indicating that mood repair is itself an effortful process (e.g., Erber & Erber, 1994), but it also goes even further to suggest why mood repair may be effortful. Unfortunately, no other affect goals were tested by Sanna et al. (1999).

A second line of evidence examined three of the four affect goals described here. Sanna, Chang, et al. (2001, Experiment 3) manipulated success versus failure feedback to subjects following completion of a word-association task. Next, subjects made timed agree/disagree judgments about a series of upward or downward counterfactual statements. Further, half of the participants responded to the counterfactual statements while under time pressure, a manipulation designed to illuminate their initial, automatic reactions (Smith & DeCoster, 2000). While responding to the counterfactual statements, participants were asked to consider one of four strategies. Of these four, one was a performance goal and so is not considered further in this section; the other three goals corresponded to cells in table 6.1. In the mood-maintenance condition (reactive/positive), participants considered "whether such a thought would help keep your mood at its current level. That is, think about whether having such thoughts would help to maintain your mood." In the mood-repair (reactive/negative) condition, participants considered "whether such a thought would help you to feel better. That is, think about whether having such thoughts would help you to improve your mood." Finally, in the self-protection condition (proactive/negative), participants considered "whether such a thought would help you in case you did poorly in the future. That is, consider whether having such thoughts would help to protect your mood."

After failure, and with no time pressure, quick responses occurred for upward counterfactuals when self-protection goals were made salient, but slow responses occurred for downward counterfactuals when mood repair was salient. After success and with no time pressure, quick responses occurred for downward counterfactuals when mood maintenance was salient. These findings correspond to the predicted pattern of automatic versus controlled outcomes in table 6.1. Similar reactions were also obtained with regard to directly manipulated moods and with individual differences in motives (Sanna, Chang, et al., 2001, Experiments 1 and 2). When under time pressure, however, participants were quick to agree with upward counterfactuals after failure and downward counterfactuals after success, irrespective of the strategic goal made salient. Thus, upward comparisons after failure and downward after success represents people's first, and perhaps most automatic, responses under these conditions. This pattern is also consistent with our prior discussion that contrast effects may be a general default response. When time and effort permit, however, individuals modify their counterfactual responses so as to achieve particular affective goals.

Summary

Four affect goals were considered based on the two underlying dimensions of temporal focus and outcome valence. With regard to affect regulation, two such goals produce relatively automatic activation of counterfactuals, whereas the other two produce more controlled activation of counterfactuals. Three of these four goals have received some attention, but our framework suggests a number of untested implications that may guide future research. First, research has yet to explore the prediction implied by our framework that free fantasies are a controlled process. Second, because negative as opposed to positive affect generally produces stronger effects (Baumeister, Bratslavsky, Finkenauer, & Vohs, 2001; Ito, Larsen, Smith, & Cacioppo, 1998), we expect that effects depicted in the lower half of table 6.1 will be more powerful than those in the upper half. Indeed, one might argue that the relative paucity of downward counterfactuals spontaneously generated in research by Roese and Olson (1997) is an example of the weakness of effects in the positive/reactive cell, and that the lack of integrative discussion of positive/proactive goals by Sanna (2000) and others (e.g., Sedikides & Strube, 1997) reflects the relative rarity of this type of affect regulation as well. Third, the relation between affect goals and regulatory focus requires further specification; even now, however, it seems clear that mood maintenance and free fantasy are examples of promotion focus, whereas mood repair and self-protection are examples of prevention focus.

Mind-Set Priming

The previous sections centered on the activation of counterfactuals by goals; we turn now to the activation of goals by counterfactuals. Mind-set priming refers to the activation of higher order goal states by way of prior use of mental procedures related to the goal (Bargh & Chartrand, 2000). For example, comparative assessment of competing strategies versus implementation of a single selected strategy influences unrelated judgments that reflect the continued operation of those deliberative versus implemental mind-sets (Gollwitzer, Heckhausen, & Steller, 1990; see also Chen, Shechter, & Chaiken, 1996). Two lines of research suggest that counterfactual thinking can have similar mind-set priming effects, in that engaging in counterfactual thinking (a form of mental simulation) in one context might increase the tendency to use mental simulation (e.g., to consider alternatives) in an unrelated context. In the first line of research, counterfactual thinking was shown to influence unrelated impression formation; in the second, counterfactual thinking influenced unrelated problem solving.

Mind-Set Priming and Person Perception

If it is the mere process, as opposed to semantic content, of counterfactual thinking that activates a mind-set marked by heightened consideration of alternatives, then such effects should occur irrespective of the content or direction of comparison of the initial counterfactual inference. To test this, Galinsky, Moskowitz, and Skurnik (2000) employed the standard "unrelated studies" paradigm, in which primes are incidentally presented in a Study 1 and impressions are assessed in a separate unrelated Study 2. In the priming task, participants read a scenario designed to ignite spontaneous counterfactual thinking (a protagonist either wins or misses out on a contest prize awarded on the basis of seat assignment at a rock concert; the protagonist either did or did not switch her seat from the winning seat or to the winning seat). Participants then completed the "Donald" impression formation task, with ratings centering on applicable (reckless-adventurous) versus nonapplicable (aloof-independent) trait ascriptions. Priming effects occurred for the former but not the latter: Prior counterfactual activation made Donald appear more reckless to participants; no such effects occurred on judgments of aloofness-independence.

Mind-set priming effects were thus limited to applicable judgments. In this particular experiment, recklessness but not aloofness was deemed applicable because the former trait could be more effectively illuminated and elaborated using mental simulation processes, particularly those involving likelihood assessment. In the case of recklessness, the trait itself invites speculation on the calamitous consequences that might follow from irresponsible behavior in various situations. Moreover, if one is forced to interact with a reckless person, assessment of the various potential dangers to oneself would be extremely useful. By contrast, aloofness does not imply the same proliferation of varied problematic consequences across different situations, and so mental simulation would be less useful for elaborating the implications of the trait. Further, these mind-set priming effects were not contingent on the counterfactual prime's valence or direction (i.e., upward or downward), indicating that it was the process of thinking counterfactually and not the content of the counterfactuals per se that was responsible for the priming effects. Finally, whether participants rated the emotions of the prime scenario character had no reliable effects on impressions, suggesting that the mind-set priming effects were not dependent on drawing attention to the counterfactual emotions (e.g., regret, joy) implied by the scenarios.

Mind-Set Priming and Problem Solving

Priming influences not only simple judgments, but more complicated inferences and behavior (Bargh, Chen, & Burrow, 1996; Dijksterhuis & Bargh, 2001; Dijksterhuis & van Knippenberg, 1998). In the second line of research on mind-set priming, Galinsky and Moskowitz (2000) examined problem-solving effects in three tasks: the Duncker candle problem, the Wason card selection task, and a trait hypothesis-testing task.

The Duncker candle problem is an ideal vehicle to investigate counterfactual mind-set priming because solutions to the problem are facilitated by divergent thinking, that is, consideration of alternatives (Glucksberg & Weisberg, 1966; Higgins & Chaires, 1980). In this task, participants are shown a small candle, a full book of matches, and a box filled with thumbtacks. Their instructions are to affix the candle to a cardboard wall such that the candle burns properly and drips no wax on the floor below. The correct solution requires the realization that the box may function as platform as well as container: It may be tacked to a wall to support the candle. Participants tend to focus on the typical, singular function of the box as container. But counterfactuals primed in the same manner as the previous research resulted in dramatic improvement in solution rate (56%) relative to those in the no-prime control condition (6%; Galinsky & Moskowitz, 2000, Experiment 1). In this way, a tendency to consider alternatives may have subsequent performance benefits for relatively more complex tasks.

Counterfactual mind-set activation did not increase attention to all alternatives but only to relevant, even if converse, ones. In another experiment, counterfactual primes attenuated the confirmation bias in trait hypothesis testing by increasing the selection of questions designed to elicit hypothesis-disconfirming answers, but without increasing the selection of neutral questions. Thus, counterfactual activation in an unrelated context increased the subsequent attention to an alternative and converse hypothesis (Galinsky & Moskowitz, 2000, Experiment 3).

Counterfactual primes are neutral with regard to content and hence performance: They can both aid and hinder problem solving. In the Wason card selection task, success decreases if too many hypotheses are entertained. In the standard version of the task, participants are shown four cards, each bearing an alphanumeric character (e.g., E, K, 4, 7). Participants learn the rule that "if a card has a vowel on one side, then it has an even number on the other side" and are instructed to select only those cards that must be turned over to verify the rule. Logically, the only two cards that must be selected are the E and 7 cards, because they each may yield falsifying information. An error of commission occurs if the 4 card is turned: it provides no relevant information because the conditional is not bidirectional (i.e., an error termed "affirming the consequent"). An error of omission occurs when one fails to turn over the 7 card, which could provide falsifying information. Counterfactual primes reduced success at the Wason task in that participants were more likely to make errors of commission, relative to control participants (Galinsky & Moskowitz, 2000, Experiment 2). This finding reinforces work by Byrne and Tasso (1999), who found that heightened accessibility of alternatives that result from counterfactual conditionals results in fallacious conditional reasoning (e.g., affirming the consequent). However, in the Byrne and Tasso research, the counterfactual premise, affirmations of the consequent, and correct falsifications were embedded in the same task. By contrast, Galinsky and Moskowitz separated the counterfactuals from the falsifying task and found that counterfactual primes decreased the rate of solution through the simultaneous selection of the correct falsifying card and incorrect affirmations of the consequent. As in the trait hypothesis-testing experiment, counterfactual primes did not increase the selection of the irrelevant card. Across Galinsky and Moskowitz's three experimental tasks, the priming effects were that participants were only more likely to consider alternatives that were relevant, even if in a contradictory way, to the original hypothesis or function. As in the Galinsky et al. (2000) experiments, direction of the counterfactual primes did not moderate the effects on the problem-solving tasks. In general, priming effects reflect the impact of incidental exposure on what we think, whereas mind-set priming illustrates the additional impact of priming on how we think.

Summary

This section addressed the broader issue of how counterfactuals relate to goal execution, even for goals unrelated to the counterfactual activation. A counterfactual mind-set makes individuals more likely to consider alternatives, a tendency that can have a variety of consequences for social perception and problem solving. In the final section, we summarize the ideas in this chapter, explore a few new ideas, and consider directions for future research.

General Discussion

We have discussed two types of goals, performance and affect, as determinants of counterfactual activation, then reviewed evidence for counterfactuals as mind-set primes. In addition, we have presented a revised framework for classifying affect goals on the basis of underlying dimensions of temporal focus and outcome valence. As discussed next, research supporting these ideas clarifies and updates our understanding of the mechanics of imagination, but also ignites new questions deserving further research.

Downward Counterfactuals

A focal controversy centers on the two-stage model's assertion that upward counterfactuals and their power to serve performance goals represent the automatic default, whereas downward counterfactuals are constructed only rarely and effortfully. Our discussion of affect goals updates this contention by asserting that both upward and downward counterfactuals may be the automatic default or the controlled override, depending on the nature of the outcome and the affect goal that is currently active. Nevertheless, questions of the relative frequency of downward counterfactuals remain unresolved, and more deeply reflect the issue of the overall frequency of motives aimed at performance versus affect regulation. Available evidence is equivocal. On one hand, upward counterfactuals are spontaneously mentioned (in response to open-ended thought listings) after failure but not success, with downward counterfactuals appearing infrequently (Roese & Hur, 1997; Roese & Olson, 1997). However, this research has been limited to assessments within achievement domains, and it may be argued that such domains by definition inspire greater attention to performance than affect goals. On the other hand, success (Galinsky & Moskowitz, 2000; Markman et al., 1993) or good moods (Sanna et al., 1999; Sanna, Meier, et al., 2001) can evoke spontaneous downward counterfactual thinking, but because these latter demonstrations were also largely rooted in achievement, variation in judgment domain cannot account for the disparity in findings. One possible resolution rests on the regulatory focus perspective (Higgins, 1997): Prevention rather than promotion goals evoke more frequent downward counterfactuals. But even in research examining this connection (again conducted within achievement domains), relatively few examples of downward counterfactuals are observed (Hur, 2000).

A more satisfying resolution is that measurement strategy (i.e., whether counterfactuals are measured using open-ended thought listings or direct solicitations) explains some of these discrepant findings. Generally speaking, absence of counterfactuals following success is observed with the former strategy (e.g., Roese & Hur, 1997), and prevalence of downward counterfactuals following success is observed with the latter strategy (e.g., Grieve et al., 1999; Roese & Olson, 1993, 1995b, 1997; Sanna, Meier, & Turley-Ames, 1998; Sanna & Turley, 1996; Sanna et al., 1999).[5] But contrary to this pattern, Markman et al. (1993) found substantial downward counterfactual thinking in response to an open-ended, oral "think aloud" measure. Further, Medvec et al. (1995) found that bronze-medal winners spontaneously consider downward counterfactuals (e.g., "At least I got a medal") and Medvec and Savitsky (1997) showed that downward counterfactuals may be spontaneously considered when people barely surpass a threshold to obtain a desired outcome (e.g., "I almost didn't make the grade"). Moreover, these downward counterfactuals may themselves have motivational implications (McMullen & Markman, 2000): For example, recognition that investment decisions might have resulted in substantial losses constituted a wake-up call that prompted subsequent preventive behavior. Finally, the repeated observation of stronger effects involving negative valence than those of positive valence (Baumeister et al., 2001) suggests that any effects of positive valence will be weaker, even if measurable, than those of negative valence. It is clear, however, that at present we can offer no single resolution to these discrepant findings. Thus, questions of the frequency of downward counterfactual thinking, and the relative frequency with which performance versus affect goals dominate everyday cognition, remain open to further inquiry.

Rhetorical Goals

Although this chapter focuses on performance and affect goals, research has elaborated on other goals, such as those embracing persuasion and rhetoric. Counterfactuals can be persuasive, in that they can dramatize and illuminate arguments in a particularly vivid manner. The speculation of what life in North America might be like under Nazi rule had the Germans won World War II is far more interesting, arousing, and dramatic than a semantically similar "actualist" account of the causal determinants and aftermath of the outcome of that war. Scholarly examinations of historical events that are explicitly counterfactual (e.g., Cowley, 2000; Tetlock & Belkin, 1996) benefit from this vividness, as do the plethora of popular novels that are collectively termed "alternate history" (see http://www.uchronia.net for bibliography). Roese and Olson (1995a) argued that counterfactuals could be rhetorically illuminating when they draw contrasts that selectively highlight specific attributes (e.g., downward historical counterfactuals can make salient positive aspects of contemporary American life, such as civil liberties, whereas upward counterfactuals make shortcomings more salient, such as uneven health care availability). Tetlock (1998) showed that individuals strategically generate counterfactuals to preserve their beliefs. For example, conservative political theorists selectively argued that the 1991 Soviet coup attempt "almost" succeeded, which would have perpetuated the cold war in a manner compatible with their anti-Soviet belief system. Tetlock, Kristel, Elson, Green, and Lerner (2000) further demonstrated that individuals defend against the threat embodied by "heretical counterfactuals" with metaphorical "moral cleansing" or heightened declarations of moralistic belief. In one study, fundamentalist Christians reacted with disgust and moral outrage to suggestions that the sequence of events in Christ's life and mission might have been altered by accidental circumstance, for example, "if Jesus had given in to one of the devil's temptations during his fast of 40 days and nights in the wilderness" (p. 864). These varied research projects converge on the conclusion that counterfactuals may be employed in the service of effortful rhetorical goals, designed either to defend one's own beliefs or to proselytize others.

Counterfactual Automaticity Reconsidered

Some provisional conclusions regarding the automaticity of counterfactual thinking are rooted in Bargh's (1994) "four horsemen" framework. The view inherent in the two-stage model (Roese & Olson, 1997) is that counterfactual thinking is typically automatic in the postconscious sense, meaning that it is contingently evoked by recognition of negative valence associated with a target outcome. The present review suggests that this view is overly limited, and that counterfactual thinking also operates via goal-dependent automaticity, in that efficient problem solving, performance enhancement, and affective coping may develop from intentional, deliberative thought that over repeated experience becomes automated (Kahneman, 1995). The pervasiveness of counterfactual thinking stems from its functionality with regard to goal-directed behavior, and it is a mind-set that persists over time to affect unrelated judgments because it is a well-learned functional strategy for comprehending the world. The issue of awareness is less interesting with respect to counterfactual automaticity, in that individuals are nearly always conscious of the evoking outcome and usually of the production of counterfactual thoughts. More to the point, we suspect that individuals are often well aware of the connection between the two. Thus, when a gambler kicks herself for not having made a different bet, she will likely admit (and regard it as obvious) that this regret is contingent on the loss just suffered. Nevertheless, future research might employ a sequential priming paradigm to investigate whether counterfactuals can be subliminally primed (e.g., with extreme negative words presented parafoveally for brief intervals). Such a research program might inform us as to whether it is possible for counterfactuals to be activated without awareness of the evoking circumstance, but we assume that even if such effects can occur, they do so only rarely in everyday life. However, counterfactual activation can have unintended consequences that occur without awareness. In the Galinsky et al. (2000) experiments, none of the participants reported that the prime scenarios impacted their subsequent performance. Although the generation of counterfactual thoughts is almost conscious, individuals are perhaps rarely aware that counterfactuals, once activated, may affect their later judgments.

Counterfactuals may be generated with or without intention, and this marks the heart of the distinction between automatic versus controlled processes that we have discussed. Counterfactual thinking may be efficient, in that cognitive load apparently interferes with corrections for impact of counterfactual inferences but not with the inferences themselves (Goldinger et al., 2003). One suggestion noted here is that upward but not downward counterfactuals are efficient, as the latter but not the former are disrupted by cognitive load, at least under negative event conditions (Sanna et al., 1999). Furthermore, upward counterfactuals that are additive versus subtractive do not vary in efficiency, as cognitive load produced neither interruption nor variation in the frequency with which these two upward counterfactual subtypes are generated (Roese & Hur, 1998). Finally, counterfactuals are controllable (i.e., suppressable) once activated, and indeed those that are activated automatically may constitute the launchpad for further elaborative processing (Sanna et al., 1999; Sanna, Chang, et al., 2001). In our discussion of affect goals, we argued that a mismatch (as opposed to a match) between the direction of the counterfactual that is automatically generated versus the direction of the counterfactual that best fulfills a particular affect goal results in the initiation of more controlled processing. The result of that controlled processing, as discussed in this chapter, is a counterfactual that aids in affect. This, of course, does not preclude the possibility of controlled processing resulting from mismatches involving other goals, such as those involving performance (Sanna, Chang, et al., 2001).

Conclusion

When Hofstadter (1979) argued that any artificial intelligence capable of consciousness must necessarily rest on the capacity to generate counterfactuals, he hinted at the manner in which our essential understanding of reality, our science and our art, our very mental existence, emerge from the ability to draw comparisons from mentally constructed benchmarks. Counterfactual thinking, seen in this light, becomes a lynchpin of human consciousness. A central theme of the last century, extending from Einstein to postmodernism to the psychology of injustice, is that all is relative.[6] In purely psychological terms, one might argue that all judgment is relative, each occurring with respect to referents, be they representations of concrete objects or implicit summaries of prior frequency. If this is so, then a key function of brains is to constantly retrieve and construct representations that act as benchmarks for the online evaluation of currently active percepts. Many benchmarks might be recruited implicitly, but only a fraction may emerge into conscious thought. Counterfactuals are more than standards of comparison; they are full-blown mental scenarios of often striking vividness. Counterfactuals may be the conscious tip of a vast iceberg of competing judgmental standards that are collectively essential for basic comprehension and imaginative insight.

Acknowledgments Preparation of this chapter was supported in part by National Institute of Mental Health Grant MH55578 awarded to N. J. Roese and a Junior Faculty Development Award from the University of North Carolina at Chapel Hill to L. J. Sanna.

Notes

1. This quotation is taken slightly out of context. The focus of the assertion is synthesis, which is then characterized as "the mere operation of the imagination" (Kant, 1781/1990, p. 60).

2. Gamblers betting on football outcomes were vastly more likely to imagine how a bet might have gone differently following a loss than a win (Gilovich, 1983, Experiment 1). To our knowledge, this is the first demonstration that counterfactual activation is valence dependent.

3. Olson et al. (2000) argued that counterfactuals and social comparisons are related more deeply than previously assumed. They argued that "the typical effect of an upward social comparison—negative affect—is mediated by a counterfactual construction in which the self is transplanted into the shoes of the comparison target: 'That could have been me!'" (p. 393). Evidence for this mediating relation has yet to appear.

4. See Pennington and Roese (2003) for a full review of relevant studies.

5. Experiments reported by both Roese and Olson (1997) and Sanna and Turley (1996) included a direct manipulation of counterfactual assessment format that revealed this pattern.

6. Johnson (2001) argued that relativism, in all its myriad forms, was the signature intellectual development of the twentieth century.

References

Aspinwall, L. G., & Taylor, S. E. (1993). Effects of social comparison direction, threat, and self-esteem on affect, self-evaluation, and expected success. *Journal of Personality and Social Psychology, 64*, 708–722.

Aspinwall, L. G., & Taylor, S. E. (1997). A stitch in time: Self-regulation and proactive coping. *Psychological Bulletin, 121*, 417–436.

Bargh, J. (1994). The four horsemen of automaticity: Awareness, intention, efficiency, and control in social cognition. In R. S. Wyer, Jr., & T. K. Srull (Eds.), *Handbook of social cognition* (Vol. 1, 2nd ed., pp. 1–40). Hillsdale, NJ: Erlbaum.

Bargh, J. A., & Chartrand, T. L. (2000). The mind in the middle: A practical guide to priming and automaticity research. In H. Reis & C. Judd (Eds.), *Handbook of research methods in social psychology* (pp. 253–285). New York: Cambridge University Press.

Bargh, J. A., Chen, M., & Burrow, L. (1996). Automaticity of social behavior: Direct effects of trait construct and stereotype activation on action. *Journal of Personality and Social Psychology, 71*, 230–244.

Baumeister, R. F., Bratslavsky, E., Finkenauer, E., & Vohs, K. D. (2001). Bad is stronger than good. *Review of General Psychology, 5*, 323–370.

Berglas, S., & Jones, E. E. (1978). Drug choice as a self-handicapping strategy in response to noncontingent success. *Journal of Personality and Social Psychology, 36*, 405–417.

Byrne, R. M. J. (1997). Cognitive processes in counterfactual thinking about what might have been. In D. L. Medin (Ed.), *The psychology of learning and motivation: Advances in research and theory* (Vol. 37, pp. 105–154). San Diego, CA: Academic Press.

Byrne, R. M. J., Segura, S., Culhane, R., Tasso, A., & Berrocal, P. (2000). The temporality effect in counterfactual thinking about what might have been. *Memory and Cognition, 28*, 264–281.

Byrne, R. M. J., & Tasso, A. (1999). Deductive reasoning with factual, possible, and counterfactual conditionals. *Memory and Cognition, 27*, 726–740.

Catellani, P., & Milesi, P. (2001). Counterfactuals and roles: Mock victims' and perpetrators' accounts of judicial cases. *European Journal of Social Psychology, 31*, 247–264.

Chaiken, S., & Trope, Y. (Eds.). (1999). *Dual-process theories in social psychology*. New York: Guilford.

Chen, S., Shechter, D., & Chaiken, S. (1996). Getting at the truth or getting along: Accuracy- and impression-motivated heuristic and systematic processing. *Journal of Personality and Social Psychology, 71*, 262–275.

Cowley, R. (Ed.). (2000). *What if?: The world's foremost military historians imagine what might have been*. New York: G. P. Putnam's Sons.

Davis, C. G., & Lehman, D. R. (1995). Counterfactual thinking and coping with traumatic life events. In N. J. Roese & J. M. Olson (Eds.), *What might have been: The social psychology of counterfactual thinking* (pp. 353–374). Mahwah, NJ: Erlbaum.

Dijksterhuis, A., & Bargh, J. A. (2001). The perception-behavior expressway: Automatic effects of social perception on social behavior. In M. P. Zanna (Ed.), *Advances in experimental social psychology* (Vol. 33, pp. 1–40). New York: Academic Press.

Dijksterhuis, A., & van Knippenberg, A. (1998). The relation between perception and behavior, or how to win a game of Trivial Pursuit. *Journal of Personality and Social Psychology, 74*, 865–877.

Erber, R., & Erber, M. W. (1994). Beyond mood and social judgment: Mood incongruent recall and mood regulation. *European Journal of Social Psychology, 24*, 79–88.

Fein, S., & Spencer, S. J. (1997). Prejudice as self-image maintenance: Affirming

the self through derogating others. *Journal of Personality and Social Psychology, 73*, 31–44.
Folger, R., & Kass, E. E. (2000). Social comparison and fairness: A counterfactual simulations perspective. In J. Suls & L. Wheeler (Eds.), *Handbook of social comparison: Theory and research* (pp. 423–441). New York: Plenum.
Galinsky, A. D., & Moskowitz, G. B. (2000). Counterfactuals as behavioral primes: Priming the simulation heuristic and consideration of alternatives. *Journal of Experimental Social Psychology, 36*, 257–383.
Galinsky, A. D., Moskowitz, G. B., & Skurnik, I. (2000). Counterfactuals as self-generated primes: The effect of prior counterfactual activation on person perception judgments. *Social Cognition, 18*, 252–280.
Gati, I., & Tversky, A. (1984). Weighting common and distinctive features in perceptual and conceptual judgments. *Cognitive Psychology, 16*, 341–370.
Gilbert, D. T., Pinel, E. C., Wilson, T. D., Blumberg, S. J., & Wheatley, T. P. (1998). Immune neglect: A source of durability bias in affective forecasting. *Journal of Personality and Social Psychology, 59*, 617–638.
Gilovich, T. (1983). Biased evaluation and persistence in gambling. *Journal of Personality and Social Psychology, 44*, 1110–1126.
Gilovich, T., & Medvec, V. H. (1995). The experience of regret: What, when, and why. *Psychological Review, 102*, 379–395.
Gleicher, F., Kost, K. A., Baker, S. M., Strathman, A. J., Richman, S. A., & Sherman, S. J. (1990). The role of counterfactual thinking in judgments of affect. *Personality and Social Psychology Bulletin, 16*, 284–295.
Glucksberg, S., & Weisberg, W. R. (1966). Verbal behavior and problem solving: Effects of labeling in a functional fixedness problem. *Journal of Experimental Psychology, 71*, 659–664.
Goldinger, S. D., Kleider, H. M., Asuma, T., & Beike, D. (2003). "Blaming the victim" under memory load. *Psychological Science, 14*, 81–85.
Gollwitzer, P. M., Heckhausen, H., & Steller, B. (1990). Deliberative versus implemental mind-sets: Cognitive tuning toward congruous thoughts and information. *Journal of Personality and Social Psychology, 59*, 1119–1127.
Goodwin, S. A., Gubin, S., Fiske, S. T., & Yzerbyt, V. (2000). Power biases impression formation processes: Stereotyping subordinates by default and by design. *Group Processes and Intergroup Relations, 3*, 227–256.
Grieve, F. G., Houston, D. A., Dupuis, S. E., & Eddy, D. (1999). Counterfactual production and achievement orientation in competitive athletic settings. *Journal of Applied Social Psychology, 29*, 2177–2202.
Helson, H. (1964). *Adaptation-level theory*. New York: Harper and Row.
Higgins, E. T. (1996). Knowledge activation: Accessibility, applicability, and salience. In E. T. Higgins & A. W. Kruglanski (Eds.), *Social psychology: Handbook of basic principles* (pp. 133–168). New York: Guilford.
Higgins, E. T. (1997). Beyond pleasure and pain. *American Psychologist, 52*, 1280–1300.
Higgins, E. T., & Chaires, W. M. (1980). Accessibility of interrelational constructs: Implications for stimulus encoding and creativity. *Journal of Experimental Social Psychology, 16*, 348–361.
Higgins, E. T., Shah, J., & Friedman, R. (1997). Emotional responses to goal attainment: Strength of regulatory focus as moderator. *Journal of Personality and Social Psychology, 72*, 515–525.

Hofstadter, D. R. (1979). *Gödel, Escher, Bach: An eternal golden braid.* New York: Vintage Books.

Huguet, P., Dumas, F., Monteil, F. M., & Genestoux, N. (2001). Social comparison choices in the classroom: Further evidence for students' upward comparison tendency and its beneficial impact on performance. *European Journal of Social Psychology, 31*, 557–578.

Hur, T. (2000). *Counterfactual thinking and regulatory focus: Upward versus downward counterfactuals and promotion versus prevention.* Unpublished doctoral dissertation, Northwestern University.

Ito, T. A., Larsen, J. T., Smith, N. K., & Cacioppo, J. T. (1998). Negative information weighs more heavily on the brain: The negativity bias in evaluative categorization. *Journal of Personality and Social Psychology, 75*, 887–900.

James, W. (1890). *The principles of psychology.* New York: Henry Holt.

Johnson, P. (2001). *Modern times: The world from the twenties to the nineties.* New York: Perennial Classics.

Kahneman, D. (1995). Varieties of counterfactual thinking. In N. J. Roese & J. M. Olson (Eds.), *What might have been: The social psychology of counterfactual thinking* (pp. 375–396). Mahwah, NJ: Erlbaum.

Kahneman, D., & Miller, D. T. (1986). Norm theory: Comparing reality to its alternatives. *Psychological Review, 93*, 136–153.

Kahneman, D., & Tversky, A. (1982). The simulation heuristic. In D. Kahneman, P. Slovic, & A. Tversky (Eds.), *Judgment under uncertainty: Heuristics and biases* (pp. 201–208). New York: Cambridge University Press.

Kant, I. (1990). *Critique of pure reason* (J. M. D. Meiklejohn, Trans.). Amherst, NY: Prometheus Books. (Original work published 1781)

Kruglanski, A. W., & Mayseless, O. (1990). Classic and current social comparison research: Expanding the perspective. *Psychological Bulletin, 108*, 195–208.

Landman, J. (1987). Regret and elation following action and inaction: Affective responses to positive versus negative outcomes. *Personality and Social Psychology Bulletin, 13*, 524–536.

Landman, J., & Manis, J. D. (1992). What might have been: Counterfactual thought concerning personal decisions. *British Journal of Psychology, 83*, 473–477.

Landman, J., & Petty, R. (2000). "It could have been you": How states exploit counterfactual thought to market lotteries. *Psychology and Marketing, 17*, 299–321.

Lazarus, R. S., & Folkman, S. (1984). *Stress, appraisal, and coping.* New York: Springer-Verlag.

Markman, K. D., Gavanski, I., Sherman, S. J., & McMullen, M. N. (1993). The mental simulation of better and worse possible worlds. *Journal of Experimental Social Psychology, 29*, 87–109.

Markman, K. D., & McMullen, M. N. (2003). A reflection and evaluation model of comparative thinking. *Personality and Social Psychology Review, 7*, 244–267.

McGill, A. L. (1993). Selection of a causal background: Role of expectation versus feature mutability. *Journal of Personality and Social Psychology, 64*, 701–707.

McGill, A. L., & Tenbrunsel, A. E. (2000). Mutability and propensity in causal selection. *Journal of Personality and Social Psychology, 79*, 677–689.

McGuire, W. J., McGuire, C. V., Child, P., & Fujioka, T. (1978). Salience of ethnicity in the spontaneous self-concept as a function of one's ethnic distinctiveness in the social environment. *Journal of Personality and Social Psychology, 36*, 511–520.

McMullen, M. N., & Markman, K. D. (2000). Downward counterfactuals and motivation: The wake-up call and the pangloss effect. *Personality and Social Psychology Bulletin, 26*, 575–584.

Medin, D. L., Goldstone, R. L., & Gentner, D. (1993). Respects for similarity. *Psychological Review, 100*, 254–278.

Medvec, V. H., Madey, S. F., & Gilovich, T. (1995). When less is more: Counterfactual thinking and satisfaction among Olympic athletes. *Journal of Personality and Social Psychology, 69*, 603–610.

Medvec, V. H., & Savitsky, K. (1997). When doing better means feeling worse: The effects of categorical cutoff points on counterfactual thinking and satisfaction. *Journal of Personality and Social Psychology, 72*, 1284–1296.

Miller, D. T., & McFarland, C. (1986). Counterfactual thinking and victim compensation: A test of norm theory. *Personality and Social Psychology Bulletin, 12*, 513–519.

Miller, D. T., Turnbull, W., & McFarland, C. (1990). Counterfactual thinking and social perception: Thinking about what might have been. In M. P. Zanna (Ed.), *Advances in experimental social psychology* (Vol. 23, pp. 305–331). New York: Academic Press.

Miller, D. T., Visser, P. S., & Staub, B. D. (2001). *The impact of surveillance on perceptions of honesty: The counterfactual correspondence bias.* Manuscript submitted for publication.

Nasco, S. A., & Marsh, K. L. (1999). Gaining control through counterfactual thinking. *Personality and Social Psychology Bulletin, 25*, 556–568.

Niedenthal, P. M., Tangney, J. P., & Gavanski, I. (1994). "If only I weren't" versus "If only I hadn't": Distinguishing shame and guilt in counterfactual thinking. *Journal of Personality and Social Psychology, 67*, 585–595.

Norem, J. K., & Cantor, N. (1986). Defensive pessimism: "Harnessing" anxiety as motivation. *Journal of Personality and Social Psychology, 51*, 1208–1217.

Oettingen, G. (1996). Positive fantasy and motivation. In P. M. Gollwitzer & J. A. Bargh (Eds.), *The psychology of action: Linking cognition and motivation to behavior* (pp. 236–259). New York: Guilford.

Oettingen, G., Pak, H., & Schnetter, K. (2001). Self-regulation and goal-setting: Turning free fantasies about the future into binding goals. *Journal of Personality and Social Psychology, 80*, 736–753.

Olson, J. M., Buhrmann, O., & Roese, N. J. (2000). Comparing comparisons: An integrative perspective on social comparison and counterfactual thinking. In J. Suls & L. Wheeler (Eds.), *Handbook of social comparison: Theory and research* (pp. 379–398). New York: Plenum.

Olson, J. M., Roese, N. J., & Zanna, M. P. (1996). Expectancies. In E. T. Higgins & A. W. Kruglanski (Eds.), *Social psychology: Handbook of basic principles* (pp. 211–238). New York: Guilford.

Pennington, G. L., & Roese, N. J. (2003). Regulatory focus and mental simulation. In S. Spencer, S. Fein, M. P. Zanna, & J. M. Olson (Eds.), *Motivated social perception: The ninth Ontario symposium* (pp. 277–298). Mahwah, NJ: Erlbaum.

Pham, L. B., & Taylor, S. E. (1999). From thought to action: Effects of process- versus outcome-based mental simulations on performance. *Personality and Social Psychology Bulletin, 25*, 250–260.

Quelhas, A. C., & Byrne, R. M. J. (2000). Counterfactual conditionals: Reasoning latencies. In J. Madruga, N. Carriedo, & M. J. Gonzalez-Labra (Eds.), *Mental models in reasoning* (pp. 315–326). Madrid: UNED.

Roese, N. J. (1994). The functional basis of counterfactual thinking. *Journal of Personality and Social Psychology, 66*, 805–818.

Roese, N. J. (1997). Counterfactual thinking. *Psychological Bulletin, 121*, 133–148.

Roese, N. J. (2001). The crossroads of affect and cognition: Counterfactuals as compensatory cognitions. In G. Moskowitz (Ed.), *Cognitive social psychology: The Princeton symposium on the legacy and future of social cognition* (pp. 307–316). Mahwah, NJ: Erlbaum.

Roese, N. J., & Hur, T. (1997). Affective determinants of counterfactual thinking. *Social Cognition, 15*, 274–290.

Roese, N. J., & Hur, T. (1998). *Cognitive load and generation of additive versus subtractive counterfactuals.* Unpublished raw data.

Roese, N. J., Hur, T., & Pennington, G. L. (1999). Counterfactual thinking and regulatory focus: Implications for action versus inaction and sufficiency versus necessity. *Journal of Personality and Social Psychology, 77*, 1109–1120.

Roese, N. J., & Olson, J. M. (1993). The structure of counterfactual thought. *Personality and Social Psychology Bulletin, 19*, 312–319.

Roese, N. J., & Olson, J. M. (1995a). Functions of counterfactual thinking. In N. J. Roese & J. M. Olson (Eds.), *What might have been: The social psychology of counterfactual thinking* (pp. 169–197). Mahwah, NJ: Erlbaum.

Roese, N. J., & Olson, J. M. (1995b). Outcome controllability and counterfactual thinking. *Personality and Social Psychology Bulletin, 6*, 620–628.

Roese, N. J., & Olson, J. M. (1996). Counterfactuals, causal attributions, and the hindsight bias: A conceptual integration. *Journal of Experimental Social Psychology, 32*, 197–227.

Roese, N. J., & Olson, J. M. (1997). Counterfactual thinking: The intersection of affect and function. In M. P. Zanna (Ed.), *Advances in experimental social psychology* (Vol. 29, pp. 1–59). San Diego, CA: Academic Press.

Roese, N. J., Sherman, J. W., & Hur, T. (1998). Direction of comparison asymmetries in relational judgment: The role of linguistic norms. *Social Cognition, 16*, 353–362.

Sanna, L. J. (1996). Defensive pessimism, optimism, and simulating alternatives: Some ups and downs of prefactual and counterfactual thinking. *Journal of Personality and Social Psychology, 71*, 1020–1036.

Sanna, L. J. (1998). Defensive pessimism and optimism: The bitter-sweet influence of mood on performance and prefactual and counterfactual thinking. *Cognition and Emotion, 12*, 635–665.

Sanna, L. J. (1999). Mental simulations, affect, and subjective confidence: Timing is everything. *Psychological Science, 10*, 339–345.

Sanna, L. J. (2000). Mental simulation, affect, and personality: A conceptual framework. *Current Directions in Psychological Science, 9*, 168–173.

Sanna, L. J., Chang, E. C., & Meier, S. (2001). Counterfactual thinking and self-motives. *Personality and Social Psychology Bulletin, 27*, 1023–1034.

Sanna, L. J., & Meier, S. (2000). Looking for clouds in a silver lining: Self-esteem, mental simulations, and temporal confidence changes. *Journal of Research in Personality, 34*, 236–251.

Sanna, L. J., Meier, S., & Turley-Ames, K. J. (1998). Mood, self-esteem, and counterfactuals: Externally attributed moods limit self-enhancement strategies. *Social Cognition, 16*, 267–286.

Sanna, L. J., Meier, S., & Wegner, E. C. (2001). Counterfactuals and motivation:

Mood as input to affective enjoyment and preparation. *British Journal of Social Psychology, 40*, 235–256.

Sanna, L. J., & Turley, K. J. (1996). Antecedents to spontaneous counterfactual thinking: Effects of expectancy violation and outcome valence. *Personality and Social Psychology Bulletin, 22*, 906–919.

Sanna, L. J., & Turley-Ames, K. J. (2000). Counterfactual intensity. *European Journal of Social Psychology, 30*, 273–296.

Sanna, L. J., Turley-Ames, K. J., & Meier, S. (1999). Mood, self-esteem, and simulated alternatives: Thought-provoking affective influences on counterfactual direction. *Journal of Personality and Social Psychology, 76*, 543–558.

Schaller, M., & Cialdini, R. B. (1990). Happiness, sadness, and helping: A motivational integration. In E. T. Higgins & R. M. Sorrentino (Eds.), *Handbook of motivation and cognition: Foundations of social behavior* (Vol. 2, pp. 265–296). New York: Guilford.

Schwarz, N. (1990). Feelings as information: Informational and motivational functions of affective states. In E. T. Higgins & R. M. Sorrentino (Eds.), *Handbook of motivation and cognition: Foundations of social behavior* (Vol. 2, pp. 527–561). New York: Guilford.

Schwarz, N., & Clore, G. L. (1996). Feelings as phenomenal experiences. In E. T. Higgins & A. W. Kruglanski (Eds.), *Social psychology: Handbook of basic principles* (pp. 433–465). New York: Guilford.

Sedikides, C., & Strube, M. J. (1997). Self-evaluation: To thine own self be good, to thine own self be sure, to thine own self be true, and to thine own self be better. In M. P. Zanna (Ed.), *Advances in experimental social psychology* (Vol. 29, pp. 209–269). San Diego, CA: Academic Press.

Shepperd, J. A., Findley-Klein, C., Kwavnick, K. D., Walker, D., & Perez, S. (2000). Bracing for loss. *Journal of Personality and Social Psychology, 78*, 620–634.

Shepperd, J. A., Ouellette, J. A., & Fernandez, J. K. (1996). Abandoning unrealistic optimism: Performance estimates and the temporal proximity of self-relevant feedback. *Journal of Personality and Social Psychology, 70*, 844–855.

Smith, E. R., & DeCoster, J. (2000). Dual-process models in social and cognitive psychology: Conceptual integration and links to underlying memory systems. *Personality and Social Psychology Review, 4*, 108–131.

Smith, R. H. (2000). Assimilative and contrastive emotional reactions to upward and downward social comparisons. In J. Suls & L. Wheeler (Eds.), *Handbook of social comparison: Theory and research* (pp. 173–200). New York: Plenum.

Spellman, B. A., & Mandel, D. R. (1999. When possibility informs reality: Counterfactual thinking as a cue to causality. *Current Directions in Psychological Science, 8*, 120–123.

Suls, J., & Wheeler, L. (Eds.). (2000). *Handbook of social comparison: Theory and research.* New York: Plenum.

Taylor, S. E. (1991). Asymmetrical effects of positive and negative events: The mobilization-minimization hypothesis. *Psychological Bulletin, 110*, 67–85.

Taylor, S. E., & Lobel, M. (1989). Social comparison activity under threat: Downward evaluation and upward contact. *Psychological Review, 96*, 569–575.

Taylor, S. E., & Pham, L. B. (1996). Mental simulation, motivation, and action. In P. M. Gollwitzer & J. A. Bargh (Eds.), *The psychology of action: Linking cognition and motivation to behavior* (pp. 219–235). New York: Guilford.

Tetlock, P. E. (1998). Close-call counterfactuals and belief system defense: I was not almost wrong but I was almost right. *Journal of Personality and Social Psychology, 75*, 639–652.

Tetlock, P. E., & Belkin, A. (Eds.). (1996). *Counterfactual thought experiments in world politics: Logical, methodological, and psychological perspectives.* Princeton, NJ: Princeton University Press.

Tetlock, P. E., Kristel, O. V., Elson, S. B., Green, M. C., & Lerner, J. S. (2000). The psychology of the unthinkable: Taboo trade-offs, forbidden base rates, and heretical counterfactuals. *Journal of Personality and Social Psychology, 78*, 853–870.

Tversky, A. (1977). Features of similarity. *Psychological Review, 84*, 327–352.

Wegener, D. T., & Petty, R. E. (1994). Mood management across affective states: The hedonic contingency hypothesis. *Journal of Personality and Social Psychology, 66*, 1034–1048.

Wegener, D. T., Petty, R. E., & Smith, S. M. (1995). Positive mood can increase or decrease message scrutiny: The hedonic contingency view of mood and message processing. *Journal of Personality and Social Psychology, 69*, 5–15.

White, J. B., & Langer, E. J. (1999). Horizontal hostility: Relations between similar minority groups. *Journal of Social Issues, 55*, 537–559.

Wood, J. V. (1989). Theory and research concerning social comparisons of personal attributes. *Psychological Bulletin, 106*, 231–248.

Zeelenberg, M., van Dijk, W. W., van der Pligt, J., Manstead, A. S. R., van Empelen, P., & Reinderman, D. (1998). Emotional reactions to the outcomes of decision: The role of counterfactual thought in the experience of regret and disappointment. *Organizational Behavior and Human Decision Processes, 75*, 117–141.

7

Compensatory Automaticity: Unconscious Volition Is Not an Oxymoron

Jack Glaser and John F. Kihlstrom

After nearly three decades of research on automaticity and construct activation, it is increasingly clear that much of human mental life operates without awareness or intent. In the literature of cognitive psychology, automatic processes are held to be inevitably evoked by the presence of a relevant environmental stimulus; once triggered, their execution proceeds rapidly, effortlessly, and incorrigibly to completion, leaving no traces accessible to conscious recollection. The concept of automaticity, long central in cognitive psychology (e.g., Schneider & Shiffrin, 1977), has come to occupy an important place in social psychology as well (e.g., Bargh, 1994, 1997; Kihlstrom, 1996, 1999; Wegner & Bargh, 1998). At the same time, some of the features canonically attributed to automaticity have been called into question (e.g., Logan, 1997; Shiffrin, 1997), and newer research reveals that automatic responses, while unintended, may not be inevitable (e.g., Glaser, 2003; Glaser & Banaji, 1999; Moskowitz, 2001; Moskowitz, Gollwitzer, Wasel, & Schaal, 1999). It appears that unconscious vigilance for bias can lead to corrective processes that also operate without conscious awareness or intent. Given these developments, we contend that the unconscious, in addition to being a passive categorizer, evaluator, and semantic processor, has processing goals (e.g., accuracy, egalitarianism) of its own, can be vigilant for threats to the attainment of these goals, and will proactively compensate for such threats. One might call this "compensatory automaticity"; strategic yet nonconscious compensations for unintended thoughts, feelings, or behaviors. For some, this will pose a paradox because automaticity has been equated with lack of control or intent. We believe, however, that it is important at this stage to move beyond that conflation and to entertain the possibility that intention operates at multiple levels of consciousness. There can be nonconscious intentions (e.g., goals) that, when the potential for their imminent frustration becomes evident, automatic compensatory processes will promote and protect. All of this can operate outside of conscious awareness and control, thereby rendering the unconscious relatively "complete," although not, of course, the entirety of mental life.

The Unconscious and the Triarchic Mind

Arguments that the unconscious is complex and wide ranging have been made compellingly, and with increasing empirical support, for several decades. It is probably not a coincidence that the person who wrote definitively about the mental trilogy of affect, cognition, and conation (Hilgard, 1980) also conducted groundbreaking work on the complexity of the unconscious, even arguing that the unconscious is comprised of multiple levels of awareness (Hilgard, 1977). Hilgard's (1977) research revealed that percepts not available to conscious recollection could nevertheless guide a person in a nonconscious, hypnotic state. Most important to the present thesis, Hilgard provided evidence of "divided consciousness" and specifically the concept of the *hidden observer*, wherein a hypnotized subject was able to perceive and respond to auditory instruction even while otherwise "deaf" by hypnotic suggestion and accordingly nonresponsive to startling noises.

Partly inspired by Hilgard's (1977) insights, Kihlstrom (1987) made the case that the cognitive unconscious was expansive and sophisticated. At the time that Kihlstrom first argued that a modern, cognitive conception of the unconscious was likely to be wide ranging, evidence was concentrated on the cognitive component of the mind, with ample demonstrations of implicit memory and automatic cognition (e.g., Neely, 1977; Schacter, 1987; Schneider & Shiffrin, 1977; Shiffrin & Schneider, 1977). Unconscious affect and motivation were, for the most part, theoretical constructs with smatterings of empirical support. But the early trickle of research on unconscious affect (e.g., Kunst-Wilson & Zajonc, 1980; Zajonc, 1980), gave way to a steady flow in the late 1980s with Fazio's (Fazio, Sanbonmatsu, Powell, & Kardes, 1986) demonstration that evaluative responses can occur automatically, and Bargh's (Bargh, Chaiken, Govender, & Pratto, 1992; Bargh, Chaiken, Raymond, & Hymes, 1996) extension that this automatic evaluation was a highly general phenomenon. Greenwald (Greenwald, Draine, & Abrams, 1996; Greenwald, Klinger, & Liu, 1989) as well as Niedenthal (1990) and Murphy and Zajonc (1993) made a convincing case for unconscious affective responses, demonstrating that they occurred even for stimuli that were subliminal and therefore not consciously perceived (see Kihlstrom, Mulvaney, Tobias, & Tobis, 2000, for a review).

In recent years, unconscious goals and motives have also appeared on the radar screen (e.g., McClelland, Koestner, & Weinberger, 1989). Bargh and his colleagues (e.g., Bargh, 1996, 1997; Bargh & Barndollar, 1996; Bargh & Chartrand, 1999; Bargh & Ferguson, 2000; Chartrand & Bargh, 1996), in particular, have brought their research to bear to make the compelling argument that all major mental processes, including motivation (see also Gollwitzer, 1999), can operate automatically. Most recently, Bargh, Gollwitzer, Lee-Chai, Barndollar, and Trötschel (2001) have demonstrated that nonconscious goal pursuits possess properties similar to those deemed fundamental to conscious motivation, specifically, vigorous action toward goal satisfaction, persistence, and resumption after disruption. Although to date less comprehensive than the research on unconscious cognition and affect, their work strongly indicates that goals and behaviors can also be activated automatically and will be pursued nonconsciously.

If, as theorists (e.g., Bargh, 1997; Hilgard, 1977; Kihlstrom, 1987, 1999) have suggested for decades, nonconscious mental life is sophisticated and comprehensive, we must entertain the possibility that in addition to the trilogy of affect, cognition, and conation being represented there, another critical aspect of human psychology, self-awareness and metacognition, may also reside outside of consciousness. The very terms *self-awareness* and *metacognition*, raised in the context of the unconscious, will likely raise consternation among those who, for good reason, equate awareness with consciousness. The very absence of a term like *awareness* or *introspection* in the lexicon of the study of the unconscious is a testament to the prevalence of the belief that nonconscious processes operate outside any monitoring capability. Hilgard (1977) questioned this rigidity with his concept of the hidden observer, but to date the idea is still counterintuitive, and we are left to ponder the oxymoronic nature of the proposition. Nevertheless, evidence for the apparent automatic control, or attempts at control, of automatic processes (e.g., Glaser, 2003; Glaser & Banaji, 1999; Moskowitz, 2001; Moskowitz et al., 1999), leads us to theorize that people are capable of nonconscious vigilance for nonconscious bias and further of automatic compensatory processes that are triggered outside of conscious awareness or control. Evidence for this comes from developments in the priming literature, specifically with regard to assimilation and contrast in construct activation and stereotype suppression effects. These findings are discussed as they relate to compensatory automaticity and unconscious volition.

The Role of Awareness in Construct Activation and Inhibition

Research on construct activation (Higgins, 1996; Higgins, Rholes, & Jones, 1977) has been guided to some extent by the assumption that unconscious/automatic processes lead to assimilation effects while more deliberate processes, such as correction, lead to contrast. Lombardi, Higgins, and Bargh (1987), for example, reported that subjects were likely to judge an ambiguous target person in a manner consistent with a construct (e.g., "stubborn" or "persistent") that was made accessible (an assimilation effect), if the priming event presenting the construct was not explicitly remembered. If, on the other hand, the priming event was remembered at all, the target person was judged in a manner inconsistent with the construct (a contrast effect). Lombardi et al. attributed this difference to distinctions between automatic and controlled processing—automatic processes accounting for assimilation, and controlled processes engendering contrast.

Support for the role of awareness and deliberation in determining assimilation versus contrast also comes from a study by Martin, Seta, and Crelia (1990). Theorizing that contrast effects result from an overgeneralization in attempts to counteract the biasing influence of priming stimuli (Martin, 1986), Martin et al. hypothesized that this would be most likely to occur when one has the cognitive resources to make such an adjustment, but not when such resources are depleted (a limitation to which automatic processes are, by the way, immune). Accordingly, they found that distracted subjects showed assimilation toward primed concepts, while those who were not distracted showed contrast. Martin et al. corroborated this finding by reporting similar effects for subjects who were low and high in need for cognition, respectively. Similarly, Newman and Uleman (1990) found that contrast effects occurred when primes were blatant, and Strack, Schwarz, Bless, Kübler, and Wänke (1993) reported that subjects who were reminded of a priming procedure showed contrast effects, whereas those who were not reminded exhibited assimilation.

It appears from the research described that the salience of the prime, to the extent that salience is related to awareness, may determine whether priming is assimilative or contrastive. One determinant of salience is extremity. Indeed, Herr, Sherman, and Fazio (1983; see also Herr, 1986), studied the effects of extremely large or small (and, in another experiment, ferocious and meek) animal primes on judgments of the size (or ferocity) of target animals. They found that extreme primes yielded contrastive judgments, whereas moderate primes led to assimilative judgments of an ambiguous target. Taken together, the results of such experiments suggest that as the priming stimulus, or at least its potential to influence the judgment of the target, becomes more salient, and therefore more accessible to conscious awareness, contrast effects in judgments are more likely to result.

The effect of prime salience on assimilation and contrast effects may be moderated by the motivation to be accurate, which, not surprisingly, influences how judgments are made (Neuberg & Fiske, 1987). In fact, in one of their experiments, Martin et al. (1990) found that subjects who believed that their judgments would be averaged with those of others made assimilative responses, whereas those who believed that their judgments would be evaluated individually exhibited contrast effects, most likely attempting to compensate, but regrettably overcompensating, for the biasing effect of the prime. This result suggests, consistent with other research on accountability and accuracy (e.g., Lerner & Tetlock, 1999), that anticipated accountability motivated subjects to be vigilant and adjust for the biasing influence of the primes. Other studies have more directly manipulated accuracy motivation, finding that it attenuates assimilation effects (Ford & Kruglanski, 1995; Thompson, Roman, Moskowitz, Chaiken, & Bargh, 1994). Stapel, Koomen, and Zeelenberg (1998) have drawn upon such findings to make the case that accuracy motivation leads to more careful processing of the target, thereby attenuating assimilation effects, but that a correction strategy is required to bring about contrast effects. Of most relevance to the present thesis, Stapel, Martin, and Schwarz (1998) have shown that the corrections that engender contrast effects are made spontaneously when biasing information is blatant, but not when it is subtle. Such corrections would almost certainly be dependent on an accuracy goal (in the absence of such a goal, why would one correct for biasing information?).

Correction has also been posited as a determinant of both contrast and assimilation effects by Petty and Wegener (1993; Wegener & Petty, 1995), who provide evidence that people's lay theories about assimilation and contrast predict the direction of their corrections for the potential biasing effects of contextual stimuli. Specifically, in Petty and Wegener's studies, subjects who expected assimilation effects corrected away from the direction of the contextual information (i.e., the priming stimulus) while those who expected contrast effects corrected toward the contextual information. These findings convey the complexity of perceivers' strategies when they attempt to mitigate the effects of judgmental biases.

In sum, a substantial body of research indicates that while contextual information can bias a response to supposedly unrelated stimuli, at times the result shows a contrastive pattern. It appears that contrast effects occur especially when the perceiver is aware of the potential biasing influence of the prime, perhaps as a result of its salience, and/or when the perceiver has the cognitive resources and motivation to recognize or remember the prime. It also appears to be the case that, while assimilation effects occur spontaneously, contrast effects are more likely the result of an active correction. To date, studies of contrast effects have been restricted to conditions under which judgments are relatively controlled and deliberate (e.g., rating a target stimulus on a scale). Perhaps this is the case because of the assumption that contrast effects result from deliberate processes (e.g., Lombardi et al., 1987; Wilson & Brekke, 1994). Given that assumption, one would expect to see only assimilation effects in automatic processing. However, the results of recent research provide clear evidence, apparently the first, of what might be called contrast effects under conditions where controlled processing is precluded, thus suggesting an automatic correction process. The evidence for automatic correction calls into question prevailing conceptions of unconscious processes as passive and reactive, and therefore warrants further examination.

Reverse Priming: Automatic Correction for Automatic Evaluation

Fazio et al. (1986) first demonstrated automatic evaluation (aka automatic attitude activation, affective priming) using a semantic priming procedure in which research subjects categorized target adjectives as being positive or negative. The presentation of each target was preceded by the presentation of another word (a prime) that was either positive or negative (evaluatively neutral nonword letter strings were also used as primes). Responses were faster when the prime and target in a given pair were evaluatively congruent. This necessarily indicated that the primes had been evaluated too. Prior research on automaticity had shown that when the time from the onset of the prime to the onset of the target, otherwise known as the stimulus onset asynchrony (SOA), was brief (e.g., under 500 ms), the effects of controlled processes on priming effects could be precluded (Neely, 1977). Fazio et al. (1986), employing a 300 ms SOA, made a strong case that the evaluations of the primes were automatic and unintended. Furthermore, comparisons with response times when the prime was "neutral" revealed that subjects were evaluating both the positive and negative primes, which were having facilitative and inhibitory effects on responses to evaluatively congruent and incongruent targets, respectively. Bargh and colleagues (1992) expanded on this finding, demonstrating that automatic evaluation is a very general phenomenon that occurs even for objects toward which attitudes are weak. Further, Bargh et al. (1996) employed more subtle techniques, including the mere pronunciation, rather than evaluative categorization, of the targets, to make a compelling case that automatic evaluation occurs very spontaneously and relatively unconditionally (see also Hermans, de Houwer, & Eelens, 1994). In the absence of cues that the experiment was about evaluating the stimuli, and the consequent elimination of corresponding demand characteristics, Bargh et al. (1996) obtained robust automatic evaluation effects (i.e., faster pronunciation of targets preceded by evaluatively congruent primes) for both weak and strong attitude objects.

Inspired by the effectiveness of the Bargh et al. (1996) procedure, Glaser and Banaji (1999) set out to adapt the paradigm to measure implicit race prejudice unobtrusively. Researchers had previously employed similar procedures to measure racial bias (e.g., Dovidio, Evans, & Tyler, 1986; Fazio, Jackson, Dunton, & Williams, 1995), but such procedures, involving judgments about the valence or category of the target, while effectively nonreactive, were relatively obtrusive. With the use of a pronunciation, rather than an evaluation or a categorization task, subjects would be unlikely to presume the procedure was designed to assess their racial attitudes. Glaser and Banaji (1999) expanded the stimulus categories beyond those of Bargh et al. (1996) to include words and names that are stereotypically associated with African American and European American culture (e.g., basketball, homeboy, Cosby; and golf, hippies, Letterman). In addition, they used a list of extremely positive and negative but race-neutral words (e.g., kindness, puppy, accident, tumor) termed "generic" stimuli, and another set of race-neutral positive and negative words that were all related to food (e.g., fudge, soup, beets, meatloaf).[1] Pairing these categories of words in all possible types of combinations allowed for a test for automatic evaluation (race-neutral primes with race-neutral targets), race categorization (race primes with race targets), and race prejudice (race-neutral primes with race targets, or vice versa), and further enhanced the unobtrusiveness of the measure by lending the appearance of true arbitrariness. These multiple possible outcomes within one paradigm also promised to bolster the internal validity of the findings. For example, if race-neutral (i.e., generic or food) primes and targets produced automatic evaluation effects (e.g., faster responding to positive-positive and negative-negative prime-target pairs), and race primes and targets produced race categorization effects (e.g., faster responding to Black-Black and White-White pairings) that would support the interpretation of an interaction of race-neutral primes with race targets (e.g., faster responding to negative-Black and positive-White than to negative-White and positive-Black prime-target pairings) as reflecting prejudice (i.e., an association between evaluations and groups).

Indeed, all three types of unconscious association were evident with both types of race-neutral stimuli (generic and food), and the effects tended to be large. However, when the generic words served as primes, the results were counterintuitive and perplexing. The effects were in the opposite direction of what had been predicted and of what had been obtained on trials where the food words served as primes. Specifically, on trials where the generic words served as primes, subjects were faster to respond to evaluatively incongruent targets than to the congruent targets. Similarly, regarding the test for automatic prejudice, with the food primes subjects were faster to pronounce Black-associated and White-associated targets when preceded by negative and positive primes, respectively, indicating the predicted pro-White or anti-Black bias. However, as with the automatic evaluation effect, the opposite was true for generic primes, giving the impression of an anti-White/pro-Black bias that might have been interpreted as such had it not been for the similar pattern of results observed with the race-neutral stimuli in the automatic evaluation analysis.

Glaser and Banaji (1999) dubbed the effect "reverse priming" because the priming effect was the reverse of what one would expect. Importantly, these reverse priming effects were very large and highly statistically significant. Furthermore, careful inspection of the data revealed that virtually all subjects showed this pattern, and that the pattern of results was very consistent across trials, with subjects showing reverse priming with generic primes, and normal priming with food primes in the early, middle, and late phases of the task. The inferential statistical tests were, accordingly, very conclusive. Consequently, despite having predicted otherwise, Glaser and Banaji were not inclined to dismiss the finding as random.

Clearly, something interesting was happening in the automatic evaluation evidenced in this study, as a function of the type of prime. What was it about the food and generic words that led to such dramatically different patterns? One thing that was evident immediately was that the food and the generic words differed in evaluative extremity. Because food words are unlikely to be extremely negative (anything that is extremely aversive is probably not edible, or at least not considered a food), and because the negative and positive words were selected to be balanced on evaluative extremity, the food words tended to be only mildly valenced (averaging –1.0 for negative and +1.03 for positive food words on an 11-point evaluation scale from –5 to +5). In contrast, the generic words, selected to be unambiguously positive or negative, were fairly extreme in valence (–3.7 and +3.85). Evaluative extremity seemed a likely candidate for the critical difference between the food and generic words. Indeed, subsequent, post hoc analyses revealed that the most extremely valenced subset of the generic primes showed an even more exaggerated reverse priming effect, while the least extreme of them (still considerably more extreme than the food primes) showed a flat line—no priming effect at all.

The post hoc analyses were suggestive, but a priori replication was required to isolate prime extremity as a determinant of reverse priming. Accordingly, Glaser and Banaji replicated this experiment selecting new race-neutral stimuli that varied only in evaluative extremity, to replace the generic and food words. The results (see figure 7.1) matched those of the first experiment almost precisely, with mild (instead of food) primes leading to normal effects and extreme (instead of generic) primes yielding reversed effects (Glaser & Banaji, 1999, Experiments 2 and 3).

Nevertheless, the reverse priming effect was counterintuitive, and so Glaser and Banaji (1999) sought to identify other conditions that gave rise to it.

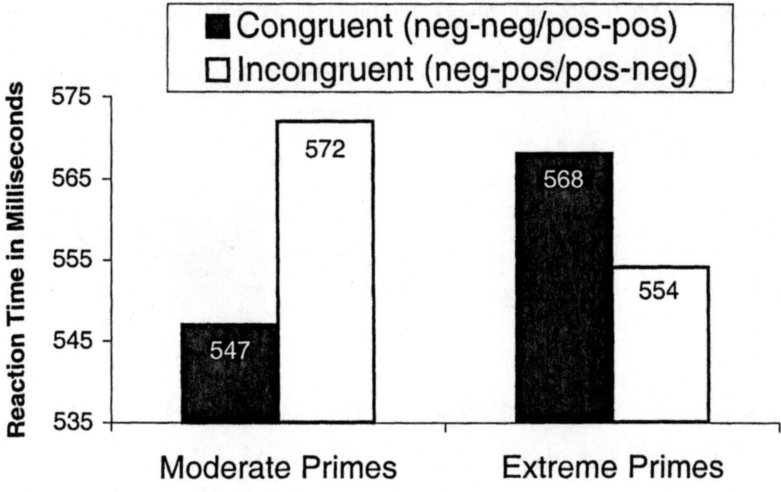

Figure 7.1 Automatic evaluation by prime extremity in Glaser and Banaji (1999), Experiment 3 (with racial stimuli present, but not in the trials represented by these data). Neg = negative; pos = positive.

Most prominently, it seemed possible that the presence of the racial stimuli in the procedure caused subjects to react in an unusual, perhaps acutely self-conscious manner, even on trials where there were no racial stimuli, when prime and target were race neutral, as with the data presented in figure 7.1. A series of three experiments (Glaser & Banaji, 1999, Experiments 4, 5, and 6) excluded racial stimuli from the procedure and also tested the effects of procedural variables, such as stimulus presentation durations and the presence of an orienting stimulus prior to each prime, in an effort to rule out obscure procedural variants as explanations for reverse priming. While replications of the experiment without any racial stimuli revealed that the racial stimuli did make a difference, it was not with regard to reverse priming. As figure 7.2 illustrates, whereas with racial stimuli present (see figure 7.1) normal priming was evident with mild primes and reverse priming with extreme primes, in the absence of racial stimuli, there was no longer any priming effect with the mild primes, but with the extreme primes the reverse priming effect was still evident. We can only speculate at this stage, but it seems plausible that the presence of the racial stimuli served to enhance the salience of the evaluative aspect of the stimuli, thereby enabling even mild primes to activate an associated attitude. Importantly, though, reverse priming (i.e., priming in the opposite direction of that predicted given the valence of the prime) persisted, as before, when the primes were evaluatively extreme, across various samples, stimulus sets, and procedures.

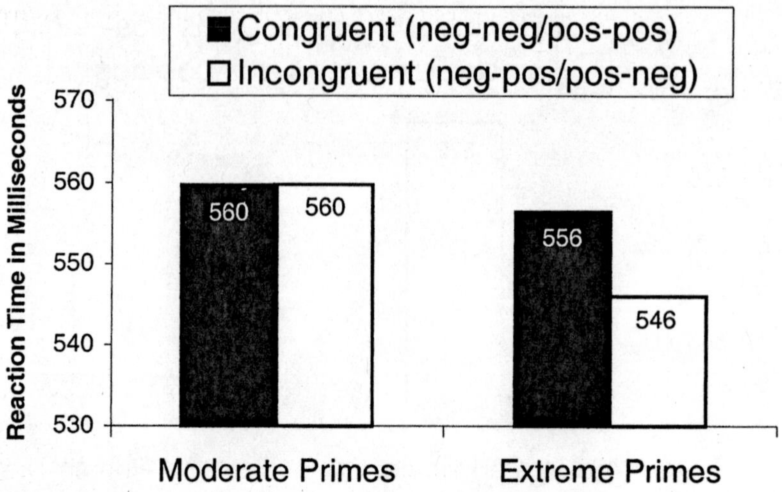

Figure 7.2 Automatic evaluation by prime extremity in Glaser and Banaji (1999), Experiment 4 (with no racial stimuli present in the experiment). Neg = negative; pos = positive.

Automatic Correction for Unintended Bias

We propose that the observed reverse priming effects reflect a correction that is instigated by the perceived potential of the peripheral prime to bias the response to the intended target. The task is to pronounce the target word correctly. In an orthographically deep (i.e., nonphonetic) language like English, this very likely involves processing the target's meaning, which includes, perhaps centrally, its evaluative valence (i.e., whether it is good or bad) (Osgood, Suci, & Tannenbaum, 1957; Tesser & Martin, 1996). When an extraneous stimulus (the prime) that is particularly obtrusive (by virtue of its evaluative extremity) appears, the perceiver is all the more likely to recognize its potential to bias the response (i.e., the identification of meaning and resultant correct pronunciation) to the intended target of judgment. If the strategy employed were simply to disregard or actively inhibit the prime, we would see no priming effect at all. However, the consistently obtained reverse priming effects indicate that an unconscious, but tactical correction is taking place in order to neutralize the threat to the accuracy of the intended response. As is the case with more deliberate judgments (e.g., Lombardi et al., 1987; Martin et al., 1990; Stapel et al., 1998), the compensatory process is excessive; an overcompensation. As a result, the extreme primes end up activating the evaluative associations that are opposite to that of their intrinsic meaning and consequently facilitate responses to words of opposite valence, and perhaps inhibit responses to words of the same valence.

Previous findings implicate accuracy motivation as a mediator of correction effects (e.g., Ford & Kruglanski, 1995; Martin et al., 1990; Stapel et al., 1998). The contribution of the reverse priming findings is the suggestion that accuracy motivation, manifested in an attempt to avoid bias, can operate automatically and outside of conscious awareness.

Correction or Comparison?

The effect of prime extremity, yielding reverse priming, is reminiscent of the findings of Herr et al. (1983), wherein extreme primes led to contrast effects. Such contrast effects are typically attributed to comparison-contrast, wherein the judgment of the target is contrasted away from a presumably irrelevant prime or comparison standard (Sherif & Hovland, 1961), and this could be the case with Herr et al. (1983) as well. Thoughts of extremely large (small) animals may have made target animals of an ambiguous size seem small (large) by comparison. Such an explanation is not, however, likely for Glaser and Banaji's (1999) reverse priming results, for several reasons. First, we must consider that the dependent variable was reaction time to pronounce the target word, not a qualitative judgment (e.g., evaluative rating, or size or weight estimation) of the target as employed in typical studies of comparison-contrast. In order for comparison-contrast to explain the reverse priming results in a reaction time paradigm, we would have to allow that, after seeing an extreme prime, the subject judges the target in the opposite direction of the prime (via comparison, e.g., "Compared to a tumor, war isn't such a bad thing"), and then the automatic activation process has to start all over (with the newly contrasted target), yielding differential activation. In other words, in a two-stage priming process, the prime and target would both be perceived, and then the judgment of the target would have to be radically adjusted for its comparative relation to the prime, such that it is now perceived to have the opposite valence of what it normatively has. Subsequent to that adjustment, the response to the newly adjusted (in terms of evaluation) target would be either facilitated or inhibited by the prime. Not only is this explanation awkward and unparsimonious, it also predicts that all targets, or at least all mildly valenced targets, would be contrasted by extreme primes (those that are similar and different in valence alike). This would yield relatively slow responses to all targets following extreme primes, not just those targets of similar valence to the prime. In all the Glaser and Banaji (1999) experiments, priming with extreme primes was characterized by slower responses to evaluatively congruent (e.g., positive-positive and negative-negative) prime-target pairs.

Perhaps more profoundly, the comparison-contrast explanation fits poorly in this context because the reverse priming effects, while limited to trials with evaluatively extreme primes, were obtained for trials with evaluatively extreme as well as moderate targets. The primes and targets were drawn from the same pool of words (although the same word was never presented with itself as prime and target in the same or even a proximal trial). It is unlikely that the comparison of extreme targets to equally extreme primes would yield comparison contrast, since, by virtue of their equality, there is no basis for contrasting one with the other.

Finally, another comparison with Herr et al.'s (1983) findings is illuminating. They found assimilation effects only when the targets were ambiguous (i.e., fictitious animals). When targets were unambiguous (real animals), contrast effects occurred with moderate and extreme primes alike. If the comparison-contrast explanation typically applied to Herr et al.'s results applies to the reverse priming findings, we would expect to see contrast effects when the prime is moderate and the target is extreme (i.e., unambiguous). Again, this is not the case, and correction is therefore a more plausible explanation. In fact, it is difficult to envision how comparison-contrast could explain any priming effect with a reaction-time-dependent variable. It is for this reason that we have been careful to adhere to the term *reverse priming* and to endorse a correction explanation, so as to avoid confusion with comparison-contrast. While there are some striking parallels to research on assimilation and contrast, and specifically comparison-contrast (e.g., the Herr et al. findings), the relation appears to be more one of analogy than similarity. For the reasons stated above, the cause of the reversal of the priming effect appears to lie in the response to the prime alone, not the comparison of the prime and target. While reverse priming results in what may look like a contrast effect, because the hypothesized underlying mechanism, correction, is distinct from comparison, we are careful not to call this a contrast effect, lest it be confused with the more commonplace comparison-contrast effects.

Unconscious Volition?

If the reverse priming effects do represent an automatic correction, they provide evidence for a complex, sophisticated, and even volitional unconscious. Not only are subjects spontaneously correcting for an unwanted bias, they are doing so in the context of having no conscious awareness of the potential for bias. Because of the unobtrusiveness of the procedure (e.g., due to the use of the pronunciation task and the generic, nonsensitive—i.e., not race-related—nature of the stimuli), subjects do not even know that they are evaluating the targets, let alone the primes, or that they might respond faster when the prime and target are evaluatively congruent. Discussions with subjects during debriefing confirmed this lack of awareness.

The goal to pronounce the target accurately may well be a deliberate one, given that the experiment instructions demand as much. The goal to evaluate the target, however, and any intention to correct for threats to such a goal, would almost certainly have to be unconscious, because participants are unaware and unlikely to infer that evaluative priming is the subject of the experiment. Furthermore, the use of short SOAs (150 and 300 ms), coupled with relatively short mean response times (approximately 550 ms), make it almost certain that latencies to respond to the targets as a function of their relation to the primes reflect automatic processes that are, therefore, not subject to conscious control (e.g., Neely, 1977). Given these conditions, the likelihood is very low that the correction derives from any deliberate process. Additionally, the accuracy motivation itself is not a sufficient cause of reverse priming; rather, a sense that accuracy might be threatened must also be present, and this may derive from a chronic unconscious vigilance for bias.[2]

There is further evidence in the Glaser and Banaji (1999) data that the vigilance necessary to trigger the accuracy-motivated correction is nonconscious. First of all, the pattern (normal priming for mild primes and reverse priming for extreme primes) obtains throughout the procedure, in the earliest, middle, and latest trials of the experiment. Therefore, it does not appear to result from a developing strategy arising from aroused suspicion on the part of subjects. More important, the effect obtained for a remarkably high number of subjects (virtually all) in the earliest experiments (those including racial stimuli) despite the fact that only a handful, during debriefing, guessed that prime and target congruence would affect response time (and no subjects surmised that evaluative congruence mattered). Past research has demonstrated convincingly that evaluation can occur spontaneously, unintentionally, and without awareness (e.g., Bargh et al., 1992, 1996; Fazio et al., 1986; Greenwald et al., 1989, 1996; see Fazio, 2001; Klauer, 1998, for reviews). The reverse priming effects appear to indicate that on some nonconscious level we know—we are "aware," if you will—that we evaluate extraneous, potentially distracting or biasing stimuli, and we will consequently attempt to correct accordingly.

The Prevalence of Reverse Priming

If reverse priming is restricted to the specific conditions of the Glaser and Banaji (1999) research, even with its many procedural variances and differing stimulus sets across experiments, then its generality and, consequently, importance is debatable. However, reverse priming effects reported by others suggest that the phenomenon is not altogether rare and that it is not limited to specific conditions such as pronunciation tasks.

Hermans (1996, as described in Banse, 2001) obtained reverse priming results in an automatic evaluation experiment using an evaluative judgment task. More recently, Banse (2001) found reverse priming with an evaluation task with subliminal face and name primes, but not when the primes were supraliminal. Although at this stage the discrepancy in Banse's findings with regard to the perceptibility of the primes is inexplicable, the fact that reverse priming occurred with subliminal primes, which subjects could not consciously perceive, makes an even stronger case that the compensatory processes, if that is what they are, transpire outside of conscious awareness or control.

Another study may shed light on the issue of underlying mechanisms for reverse priming. Hypothesizing that people with high anxiety may be more likely to elaborate affective stimuli (Mogg & Marden, 1990), which, in turn, would lead to reverse priming among high- but not low-anxiety subjects, Maier, Berner, and Pekrun (2003) adopted the Glaser and Banaji (1999) procedure (as in the later experiments, excluding racial stimuli), and segmented their sample into low-, moderate-, and high-anxiety subjects. Consistent with Glaser and Banaji's (1999) findings, moderate primes yielded no priming effects. However, with extreme primes, subject anxiety moderated the priming effect qualitatively. Low- and moderate-anxiety subjects showed normal priming effects, while high-anxiety subjects showed reverse priming. In addition to providing a replication of reverse priming and offering a moderating variable, this finding could be interpreted as evidence that reverse priming reflects a vigilance for biasing information and an accuracy-motivated correction, which may be higher among highly anxious people.

Perhaps of greatest relevance to the issue of automatic correction, Wentura (2000) has found that, with subliminal priming and an evaluation task, when the speed of the response is emphasized in the instructions to subjects, normal priming effects are obtained. When accuracy is emphasized, however, reverse priming results. Wentura offers a different explanation than automatic correction. Drawing on Milliken, Joordens, Merikle, and Seiffert's (1998) application of selective attention to negative priming,[3] Wentura argues that accuracy motivation will lead subjects to try to discriminate between stimuli, thereby leading to slower responding when prime and target are congruent, presumably because discrimination is harder when they are similar. Such an explanation would not likely apply to the Glaser and Banaji (1999) findings because only prime, and not target, extremity determined reverse priming. If incongruence effects resulted merely from difficulty in discriminating between prime and target, and even if one argued that such difficulty would occur only when stimuli are clearly valenced (as with extreme words), Wentura's explanation would predict target extremity to play at least as large a role as prime extremity. That Wentura's discrimination explanation probably does not apply to the Glaser and Banaji findings is not as important as the fact that this explanation, like that of automatic correction, requires unconscious vigilance for biasing information, considering that Wentura's primes were presented subliminally.

Like Wentura, Glaser (2003) has directly tested the role of accuracy motivation in reverse priming. In an effort to reconcile the findings of Glaser and Banaji (1999) with those of Bargh et al. (1996) wherein, despite very similar procedures, no reverse priming was evidenced, Glaser (2003) replicated one of the Bargh et al. (1996) experiments, with identical word stimuli and highly similar procedures. Hypothesizing that accuracy motivation was a necessary condition for the corrective processes that yield reverse priming, Glaser (2003) manipulated between subjects the presence of an accuracy-enhancing instruction. Specifically, in earlier research in which reverse priming effects were consistently obtained with extreme primes (e.g., Glaser & Banaji, 1999), experiments had included in the instructions to subjects a directive which stated that trials on which they made errors would be repeated later, and indicated explicitly that it was therefore in the subjects' interests to respond accurately. Such an instruction could serve to boost the drive to be accurate, lest subjects have to endure a longer procedure. In the more recent experiment (Glaser, 2003), this instruction was given to only one group of subjects, while the others were given no such warning. The results indicate that the instruction was influential. Specifically, those who did not receive the instruction showed a pattern of results more consistent with that of Bargh et al. (1996), with normal priming for extreme primes.[4] More important, for the subjects who were given the accuracy-enhancing instructions, no priming effect was obtained with extreme primes. Interestingly, in this instruction condition (with the accuracy imperative), a reliable priming effect was obtained with moderate primes, suggesting that the accuracy instructions were sufficient to bolster attention to the stimuli enough to strengthen priming with even weakly valenced primes, but perhaps also sufficient to instigate some degree of correction with the extreme primes, but not as much as in previous experiments where overcorrection (and hence reverse priming) was evident. The presence of the priming effect with moderate primes in this condition is important in ruling out the possibility that the accuracy instructions simply prevented priming of any sort, a possibility that was nevertheless unlikely given that such instructions have been used in previous experiments (Glaser & Banaji, 1999) that repeatedly obtained both normal and reverse priming with similar procedures.

The absence of a reverse priming effect with strong accuracy instructions is not entirely compelling evidence for an accuracy-mediated correction account. However, in the presence of a normal priming effect with moderate primes, the absence of any effect with extreme primes, with which reverse priming effects have been repeatedly obtained in the past, suggests that some degree of reverse priming is occurring when accurate responding is encouraged. Consistent with this, Wentura (2000) entertained the possibility, and we agree, that a null result in an automatic evaluation experiment, "might reflect a heterogeneous distribution of some subjects showing a congruence effect and some showing an incongruence effect" (p. 4). In other words, reverse priming, and the unconscious vigilance for biasing information that gives rise to it, may be relatively common but masked by individual differences within an experiment wherein normal and reverse priming effects may cancel each other out. Similarly, null results in automatic evaluation studies may result from the use of priming stimuli that straddle the evaluative extremity continuum enough to engender competing, and self-canceling, normal and reverse priming responses, as may be the case in Glaser and Banaji's (1999) post hoc analyses of the least extreme of their extreme primes, which showed no priming effect at all. This is not to say that all or even most null results in affective priming experiments are confounded by reverse priming; this would be an unfalsifiable and reckless assertion. Rather, it simply seems likely that, because until recently reverse priming was undiscovered, it may be more prevalent than one would think.

Glaser and Banaji (1999) suggested that, because of the counterintuitive nature of reverse priming effects and the likelihood that they will confound predictions, many such findings may never have been published and allowed to see the proverbial light of day. In fact, as Glaser and Banaji noted, a quick survey of the published research on nonconscious priming reveals more than a few unexpected, and often unexplained, contrast effects (e.g., Banaji, Hardin, & Rothman, 1993; De Houwer, Hendrickx, & Baeyens, 1997; Eimer & Schlaghecken, 1999; Murphy & Zajonc, 1993) that may reflect unconscious compensatory mechanisms and at least raise the question of the prevalence of such findings, published or not.

Controlling Automatic Stereotypes

Another literature promises to shed further light on the issue of unconscious correction for unintended thoughts and biases. In recent years, acknowledging that exposure to cultural stereotypes is virtually inevitable (Devine, 1989; but see Lepore & Brown, 1997, 1999), social psychologists have sought to identify conditions under which the automatic activation and application of such stereotypes can be derailed. Although most conceptions of automatic processes hold that they are beyond deliberate control (e.g., Bargh, 1994; Schneider & Shiffrin, 1977; Shiffrin & Schneider, 1977), there have been compelling arguments allowing for some measure of control (e.g., Logan, 1989). With regard to controlling automatic stereotypes, initial findings indicate that, while stereotype suppression is difficult and perhaps even counterproductive (e.g., Macrae, Bodenhausen, Milne, & Jetten, 1994; Macrae, Bodenhausen, Milne, & Wheeler, 1996; Wegner, 1994), under some circumstances people appear capable of moderating the effects of automatic stereotype activation (see Monteith, Sherman, & Devine, 1998; and Blair, 2002, for reviews). Research has now documented that people who are highly motivated to control prejudice can dampen the explicit expression of automatically activated biases (e.g., Fazio et al., 1995), perhaps with the subsequent activation of egalitarian "replacement thoughts" (Monteith, 1993), and this has been demonstrated even when measuring the automatic activation of the stereotypes, as in a semantic priming paradigm (Blair & Banaji, 1996). Similarly, Kawakami, Dovidio, Moll, Hermsen, and Russin (2000) have shown that following considerable counterstereotype training, subjects will show less automatic stereotype activation. This concept of competing impulses is also expressed in Wilson, Lindsey, and Schooler's (2000) model of dual attitudes, where the concept of automatic override (p. 106) holds that explicit attitudes may trump implicit ones. However, promising as these stereotype elimination effects are, they require a somewhat deliberate strategy and/or the complete relearning of automatic associations, which cannot be readily equated with unconscious volition and control.

The question of whether the automatic activation of stereotypes can be prevented or intercepted due to nonconscious motivations has only recently been addressed. Moskowitz et al. (1999; see also Moskowitz, 2001) demonstrated that people with high egalitarian (e.g., antiprejudice) goals exhibit less automatic activation of stereotypes even though they have the same knowledge of these stereotypes as do those with lower egalitarian motives, who showed greater automatic activation of stereotypes. Having identified an indirect measure of chronic egalitarian goals, Moskowitz et al. (1999) submitted subjects who scored high and low in egalitarianism to a procedure with striking similarities to that employed by Glaser and Banaji (1999) and Glaser (2003); an automatic gender stereotyping test employing a semantic priming paradigm with a 200 ms SOA (the time from onset of the prime to the onset of the target stimulus) and latency to pronounce the target word as the dependent variable. Photographs of men and women were used as primes, while attributes stereotypical of men and women, as well as gender-irrelevant words, were presented as targets. The use of the short SOA as well as the relatively ambiguous pronunciation task served a function similar to that intended by Glaser and Banaji (1999); to ensure that differential response times as a function of prime-target gender stereotype match reflected automatic activation of gender stereotypes by the mere perception of the primes, and not an intentional response. Predicting that chronic egalitarian goals would serve to obstruct even the automatic activation of gender stereotypes, Moskowitz et al. (1999) indeed found that subjects who scored high on their indirect measure of chronic egalitarianism exhibited no automatic gender stereotyping. Importantly, those who had scored low in chronic egalitarianism did exhibit automatic gender stereotype activation in this experiment.

In order to demonstrate more directly that those high in chronic egalitarianism actively, albeit nonconsciously, inhibited the automatic activation of stereotypes, Moskowitz et al. (1999) followed up this experiment with a negative priming experiment wherein participants were presented with two primes simultaneously; one that was supposed to be ignored but that varied in its female stereotype relevance. Target words, which were again to be pronounced, were also either stereotype relevant or not, and they were either the same word as the prime that was to be ignored or not. Moskowitz et al. found again that only those subjects who were low in chronic egalitarianism exhibited automatic stereotype activation. In contrast, those who had scored high in chronic egalitarianism were actually slower to respond to feminine-stereotypical target words following female distractor primes than following gender-irrelevant primes, indicating that they were effectively inhibiting, or perhaps correcting for, the stereotypical content that might have been activated by these primes. Moskowitz et al. concluded that egalitarians, while sharing knowledge of cultural stereotypes, are able to counteract the automatic activation of those stereotypes without conscious intent.

We are very sympathetic to Moskowitz et al.'s view, similar to that expressed by Glaser and Banaji (1999), that volition, in the form of vigilance for unintended bias, can occur outside of consciousness: "Despite the fact that the English language vernacular equates intent with conscious and effortful forms of pursuing a desired end state, volition can be exerted preconsciously. A passive process like stereotype activation could be controlled by goal pursuit, which could be activated as passively as stereotype activation" (Moskowitz et al., 1999, p. 169).

Although the Moskowitz et al. findings make a strong case for unconscious volition and compensation for unwanted thoughts, the reverse priming in automatic evaluation effects (Glaser & Banaji, 1999) add some value to the argument because, in the absence of group-relevant information (e.g., faces, names, stereotypes), motivations to avoid bias are unlikely to originate consciously. In other words, the Moskowitz et al. findings illustrate compellingly that chronic goals will motivate the suppression of an automatic response, but it is not yet entirely clear that such goals would be activated without the conscious recognition that something about bias was being measured. In fact, Wasel and Gollwitzer (1997) found, using a similar paradigm, that high egalitarians inhibited automatic stereotype activation only when primes were supraliminal (i.e., consciously perceptible), but when primes were presented subliminally, even high egalitarians failed to inhibit automatic stereotyping, suggesting that at least the potential for bias may need to reach consciousness for inhibition or correction to occur. On the other hand, reverse priming in automatic evaluation with a highly nonreactive pronunciation task, especially in experiments excluding racial stimuli (Glaser & Banaji, 1999, Experiments 4–6), holds considerably less chance that the correction is related to a consciously activated goal. Furthermore, Banse's (2001) finding of reverse priming with subliminal primes indicates that conscious awareness of the potential for bias is not necessary. Finally, the demonstrated moderating role of accuracy instructions (Glaser, 2003; Wentura, 2000) and trait anxiety (Maier et al., 2003) strongly suggest that reverse priming reflects a motivated, specifically accuracy-motivated, corrective response. Even though in the Glaser and Banaji (1999) studies and for some subjects in Glaser (2003), accuracy is explicitly encouraged in the instructions, such exhortations are likely to only indirectly influence the nonconscious accuracy motivation that we posit gives rise to reverse priming. Subjects are typically unaware that evaluation is being measured, and consequently any motivation to correct for bias in a judgment that one does not even know is being made, let alone that the potential for bias exists, must itself have nonconscious bases. With reverse priming, therefore, we have a full representation of the evaluative process, including the evaluative response itself, the goal to evaluate accurately, and the corrective measures to ensure accuracy, all operating under the proverbial hood—nonconsciously.

Conclusion

Evidence from studies of automatic affect (e.g., Glaser & Banaji, 1999) and cognition (e.g., Moskowitz et al., 1999) suggests that, in addition to the ability to process the meaning of, categorize, and evaluate perceived stimuli automatically, the human mind is capable of maintaining unconscious vigilance over its own automatic processes. This suggests a volitional nature of the unconscious, an idea that to many may seem self-contradictory. In the construct activation literature so central to social cognitive theory and research, the unconscious has been credited with (or blamed for, as the case may be) simplistic, assimilative influences on judgments, while the compensatory efforts necessary to obtain contrast effects have been ascribed strictly to deliberate, conscious processes (e.g., Wilson & Brekke, 1994). However, when observed in responses that most likely reflect automatic processes, "contrast" effects stemming from correction (e.g., Glaser & Banaji, 1999) indicate that people can unconsciously monitor and correct for bias in judgments, just as they might consciously.

That goals can operate at the unconscious level, and subsequently influence explicit judgments and behaviors, is now well demonstrated (e.g.,

Bargh & Barndollar, 1996; Bargh et al., 2001; Chartrand & Bargh, 1996). Evidence that corrective processes can occur even when a person is unaware that she is making a judgment, as in the case of a priming procedure with a nonreactive response task (i.e., the pronunciation task), and especially considering that accuracy motivation moderates such automatic compensatory effects (Glaser, 2003; Wentura, 2000), however, implicates unconscious, metacognitive processing goals. Similarly, demonstrations of the effects of chronic ideological goals (e.g., egalitarianism) on suppressing automatic, and therefore previously presumed uncontrollable, responses (Moskowitz et al., 1999) bolster the thesis of unconscious volition. Building on the trend to allow for a full spectrum of mental life (i.e., affect, cognition, and motivation) in the unconscious (Bargh, 1996, 1997; Kihlstrom, 1987, 1999), we go a step further to suggest that the unconscious is indeed capable of holding such metacognitive processing goals (e.g., accuracy) which it will pursue through self-monitoring, and that it will, under some conditions, compensate for anticipated threats to the attainment of those goals. This thesis, and the findings supporting it, represents a departure from traditional conceptions of the unconscious as passive and reactive, suggesting an unconscious that is, paradoxically, "aware."

Acknowledgments Production of this chapter was supported by a National Research Service Award Postdoctoral Fellowship from the National Institute of Mental Health, Grant MH12195 to the first author and Grant MH35856 to the second author, as well as institutional support from the Institute of Personality and Social Research at the University of California, Berkeley. We are grateful to Molly Parker Tapias for incisive comments and Miranda Chiu and Brian Penrod for assistance with the research.

Notes

1. The food words were included because of an interest in a possible "disgust" component of racial bias.
2. This concept of unconscious vigilance should be distinguished from Pratto and John's (1991) theory of "automatic vigilance," which holds that people are chronically vigilant for negative information.
3. "Negative priming" is an inhibitory effect wherein responses are slower to targets that served as primes in preceding trials (May, Kane, & Hasher, 1995). It is distinct from what we are calling reverse priming, which appears to be a within-trial phenomenon.
4. Inconsistent with Bargh et al. (1996), no priming effect was obtained with moderately valenced primes in the low-accuracy instruction condition, suggesting that attitude strength may under some conditions moderate attitude activation (e.g., Fazio et al., 1986).

References

Banaji, M. R., Hardin, C. D., & Rothman, A. J. (1993). Implicit stereotyping in person judgment. *Journal of Personality and Social Psychology, 65*, 272–281.

Banse, R. (2001). Affective priming with liked and disliked persons: Prime visibility determines congruency and incongruency effects. *Cognition and Emotion, 15*, 501–520.

Bargh, J. A. (1994). The four horsemen of automaticity: Awareness, intention, efficiency, and control in social cognition. In R. S. Wyer, Jr., & T. K. Srull (Eds.), *Handbook of social cognition: Vol. 1. Basic processes* (2nd ed., pp. 1–40). Hillsdale, NJ: Erlbaum.

Bargh, J. A. (1996). Principles of automaticity. In E. T. Higgins & A. W. Kruglanski (Eds.), *Social psychology: Handbook of basic principles* (pp. 169–183). New York: Guilford.

Bargh, J. A. (1997). The automaticity of everyday life. In R. Wyer (Ed.), *Advances in social cognition* (Vol. 10, pp. 1–61). Mahwah, NJ: Erlbaum.

Bargh, J. A., & Barndollar, K. (1996). Automaticity in action: The unconscious as repository of chronic goals and motives. In P. M. Gollwitzer & J. A. Bargh (Eds.), *The psychology of action* (pp. 457–481). New York: Guilford.

Bargh, J. A., Chaiken, S., Govender, R., & Pratto, F. (1992). The generality of the automatic attitude activation effect. *Journal of Personality and Social Psychology, 62*, 893–912.

Bargh, J. A., Chaiken, S., Raymond, P., & Hymes, C. (1996). The automatic evaluation effect: Unconditional automatic attitude activation with a pronunciation task. *Journal of Experimental Social Psychology, 32*, 104–128.

Bargh, J. A., & Chartrand, T. L. (1999). The unbearable automaticity of being. *American Psychologist, 54*, 462–479.

Bargh, J. A., & Ferguson, M. J. (2000). Beyond behaviorism: On the automaticity of higher mental processes. *Psychological Bulletin, 126*, 925–945.

Bargh, J. A., Gollwitzer, P. M., Lee-Chai, A., Barndollar, K., & Trötschel, R. (2001). The automated will: Nonconscious activation and pursuit of behavioral goals. *Journal of Personality and Social Psychology, 81*, 1014–1027.

Blair, I. V. (2002). The malleability of automatic stereotypes and prejudice. *Personality and Social Psychology Review, 6*, 242–261.

Blair, I. V., & Banaji, M. R. (1996). Automatic and controlling processes in stereotype priming. *Journal of Personality and Social Psychology, 70*, 1142–1163.

Chartrand, T. L., & Bargh, J. A. (1996). Automatic activation of impression formation and memorization goals: Nonconscious goal priming reproduces effects of explicit task instructions. *Journal of Personality and Social Psychology, 71*, 464–478.

De Houwer, J., Hendrickx, H., & Baeyens, F. (1997). Evaluative learning with "subliminally" presented stimuli. *Consciousness and Cognition, 6*, 87–107.

Devine, P. G. (1989). Stereotypes and prejudice: Their automatic and controlled components. *Journal of Personality and Social Psychology, 56*, 5–18.

Dovidio, J. F., Evans, N., & Tyler, R. B. (1986). Racial stereotypes: The contents of their cognitive representations. *Journal of Experimental Social Psychology, 22*, 22–37.

Eimer, M., & Schlaghecken, F. (1998). Effects of masked stimuli on motor activation: Behavioral and electrophysiological evidence. *Journal of Experimental Psychology: Human Perception and Performance, 24*, 1737–1747.

Fazio, R. H. (2001). On the automatic activation of associated evaluations: An overview. *Cognition and Emotion, 15*, 115–141.

Fazio, R. H., Jackson, J. R., Dunton, B. C., & Williams, C. J. (1995). Variability in automatic activation as an unobtrusive measure of racial attitudes: A bona fide pipeline? *Journal of Personality and Social Psychology, 69*, 1013–1027.

Fazio, R. H., Sanbonmatsu, D. M., Powell, M. C., & Kardes, F. R. (1986). On the automatic activation of attitudes. *Journal of Personality and Social Psychology, 50*, 229–238.

Ford, T. E., & Kruglanski, A. W. (1995). Effects of epistemic motivations on the use of accessible constructs in social judgment. *Personality and Social Psychology Bulletin, 21*, 950–962.

Glaser, J. (2003). Reverse priming: Implications for the (un)conditionality of automatic evaluation. In J. Musch & K. C. Klauer (Eds.), *The psychology of evaluation: Affective processes in cognition and emotion* (pp. 87–108). Mahwah, NJ: Erlbaum.

Glaser, J., & Banaji, M. R. (1999). When fair is foul and foul is fair: Reverse priming in automatic evaluation. *Journal of Personality and Social Psychology, 77*, 669–687.

Gollwitzer, P. M. (1999). Implementation intentions. *American Psychologist, 54*, 493–503.

Greenwald, A. G., Draine, S. C., & Abrams, R. L. (1996). Three cognitive markers of unconscious semantic activation. *Science, 273*, 1699–1702.

Greenwald, A. G., Klinger, M. R., & Liu, T. J. (1989). Unconscious processing of dichoptically masked words. *Memory and Cognition, 17*, 35–47.

Hermans, D. (1996). *Automatic stimulus evaluation: An experimental analysis of the preconditions for evaluative stimulus discrimination using an affective priming paradigm.* Unpublished doctoral dissertation, University of Leuven, Belgium.

Hermans, D., De Houwer, J., & Eelen, P. (1994). The affective priming effect: Automatic activation of evaluative information in memory. *Cognition and Emotion, 8*, 515–533.

Herr, P. M. (1986). Consequences of priming: Judgment and behavior. *Journal of Personality and Social Psychology, 51*, 1106–1115.

Herr, P. M., Sherman, S. J., & Fazio, R. H. (1983). On the consequences of priming: Assimilation and contrast effects. *Journal of Experimental Social Psychology, 19*, 323–340.

Higgins, E. T. (1996). Knowledge activation: Accessibility, applicability, and salience. In E. T. Higgins & A. W. Kruglanski (Eds.), *Social psychology: Handbook of basic principles* (pp. 133–168). New York: Guilford.

Higgins, E. T., Rholes, W. S., & Jones, C. R. (1977). Category accessibility and impression formation. *Journal of Experimental Social Psychology, 13*, 141–154.

Hilgard, E. R. (1977). *Divided consciousness.* New York: John Wiley.

Hilgard, E. R. (1980). The trilogy of mind: Cognition, affection, and conation. *Journal of the History of the Behavioral Sciences, 16*, 107–117.

Kawakami, K., Dovidio, J. F., Moll, J., Hermsen, S., & Russin, A. (2000). Just say no (to stereotyping): Effects of training in the negation of stereotypic associations on stereotype activation. *Journal of Personality and Social Psychology, 78*, 871–888.

Kihlstrom, J. F. (1987). The cognitive unconscious. *Science, 237*, 1445–1452.

Kihlstrom, J. F. (1996). Unconscious processes in social interaction. In S. Hameroff, W. W. Kaszniak, & A. C. Scott (Eds.), *Toward a science of consciousness: The first Tucson discussions and debates* (pp. 93–104). Cambridge, MA: MIT Press.

Kihlstrom, J. F. (1999). The psychological unconscious. In L. A. Pervin & O. John (Eds.), *Handbook of personality: Theory and research* (2nd ed., pp. 424–442). New York: Guilford.

Kihlstrom, J. F., Mulvaney, S., Tobias, B. A., & Tobis, I. P. (2000). The emotional unconscious. In E. Eich, J. F. Kihlstrom, G. H. Bower, J. P. Forgas, & P. M. Niedenthal (Eds.), *Cognition and emotion* (pp. 30–86). New York: Oxford University Press.

Klauer, K. C. (1998). Affective priming. In W. Stroebe & M. Hewstone (Eds.), *European review of social psychology* (pp. 67–103). New York: John Wiley and Sons.

Kunst-Wilson, W. R., & Zajonc, R. B. (1980). Affective discrimination of stimuli that cannot be recognized. *Science, 207*, 557–558.

Lepore, L., & Brown, R. (1997). Category and stereotype activation: Is prejudice inevitable? *Journal of Personality and Social Psychology, 72*, 275–287.

Lepore, L., & Brown, R. (1999). Exploring automatic stereotype activation: A challenge to the inevitability of prejudice. In D. Abrams & M. A. Hogg (Eds.), *Social identity and social cognition* (pp. 141–163). Malden, MA: Blackwell.

Lerner, J. S., & Tetlock, P. E. (1999). Accounting for the effects of accountability. *Psychological Bulletin, 125*, 255–275.

Logan, G. D. (1989). Automaticity and cognitive control. In J. S. Uleman & J. A. Bargh (Eds.), *Unintended thought* (pp. 52–74). New York: Guilford.

Logan, G. D. (1997). The automaticity of academic life: Unconscious applications of an implicit theory. In R. S. Wyer (Ed.), *Advances in social cognition* (Vol. 10, pp. 157–179). Mahwah, NJ: Erlbaum.

Lombardi, W. J., Higgins, E. T., & Bargh, J. A. (1987). The role of consciousness in priming effects on categorization: Assimilation versus contrast as a function of awareness of the priming task. *Personality and Social Psychology Bulletin, 13*, 411–429.

Macrae, C. N., Bodenhausen, G. V., Milne, A. B., & Jetten, J. (1994). Out of mind but back in sight: Stereotypes on the rebound. *Journal of Personality and Social Psychology, 67*, 808–817.

Macrae, C. N., Bodenhausen, G. V., Milne, A. B., & Wheeler, V. (1996). On resisting the temptation for simplification: Counterintentional effects of stereotype suppression on social memory. *Social Cognition, 14*, 1–20.

Maier, M. A., Berner, M. P., & Pekrun, R. (2003). Directionality of affective priming: Effects of trait anxiety and activation level. *Experimental Psychology, 50*, 116–123.

Martin, L. L. (1986). Set/reset: Use and disuse of concepts in impression formation. *Journal of Personality and Social Psychology, 51*, 493–504.

Martin, L. L., Seta, J. J., & Crelia, R. A. (1990). Assimilation and contrast as a function of people's willingness and ability to expend effort on forming an impression. *Journal of Personality and Social Psychology, 59*, 27–37.

May, C. P., Kane, M. J., & Hasher, L. (1995). Determinants of negative priming. *Psychological Bulletin, 118*, 35–54.

McClelland, D. C., Koestner, R., & Weinberger, J. (1989). How do self-attributed and implicit motives differ? *Psychological Review, 96*, 690–702.

Milliken, B., Joordens, S., Merikle, P. M., & Seiffert, A. E. (1998). Selective attention: A reevaluation of the implications of negative priming. *Psychological Review, 105*, 203–229.

Mogg, K., & Marden, B. (1990). Processing of emotional information in anxious subjects. *British Journal of Clinical Psychology, 29*, 227–229.

Monteith, M. J. (1993). Self-regulation of prejudiced responses: Implications for progress in prejudice reduction efforts. *Journal of Personality and Social Psychology, 65*, 469–485.

Monteith, M. J., Sherman, J. W., & Devine, P. G. (1998). Suppression as a stereotype control strategy. *Personality and Social Psychology Review, 2*, 63–82.

Moskowitz, G. B. (2001). Preconscious control and ompensatory cognition. In G. B. Moskowitz (Ed.), *Cognitive social psychology: The Princeton symposium on the legacy and future of social cognition* (pp. 334–358). Mahwah, NJ: Erlbaum.

Moskowitz, G. B., Gollwitzer, P. M., Wasel, W., & Schaal, B. (1999). Preconscious control of stereotype activation through chronic egalitarian goals. *Journal of Personality and Social Psychology, 77*, 167–184.

Murphy, S. T., & Zajonc, R. B. (1993). Affect, cognition, and awareness: Affective priming with optimal and suboptimal stimulus exposures. *Journal of Personality and Social Psychology, 64*, 723–739.

Neely, J. H. (1977). Semantic priming and retrieval from lexical memory: Roles of inhibitionless spreading activation and limited-capacity attention. *Journal of Experimental Psychology: General, 106*, 225–254.

Neuberg, S. L., & Fiske, S. T. (1987). Motivational influences on impression formation: Outcome dependency, accuracy-driven attention and individuating processes. *Journal of Personality and Social Psychology, 53*, 431–444.

Newman, L. S., & Uleman, J. S. (1990). Assimilation and contrast effects in spontaneous trait inference. *Personality and Social Psychology Bulletin, 16*, 224–240.

Niedenthal, P. M. (1990). Implicit perception of affective information. *Journal of Experimental Social Psychology, 26*, 505–527.

Osgood, C. E., Suci, G. J., & Tannenbaum, P. H. (1957). *The measurement of meaning.* Urbana: University of Illinois Press.

Petty, R. E., & Wegener, D. T. (1993). Flexible correction processes in social judgment: Correcting for context-induced contrast. *Journal of Experimental Social Psychology, 29*, 137–165.

Pratto, F., & John, O. P. (1991). Automatic vigilance: The attention-grabbing power of negative social information. *Journal of Personality and Social Psychology, 61*, 380–391.

Schacter, D. L. (1987). Implicit memory: History and current status. *Journal of Experimental Psychology: Learning, Memory, and Cognition, 13*, 501–518.

Schneider, W., & Shiffrin, R. M. (1977). Controlled and automatic human information processing: I. Detection, search and attention. *Psychological Review, 84*, 1–66.

Sherif, M., & Hovland, C. I. (1961). *Social judgment: Assimilation and contrast effects in communication and attitude change.* New Haven, CT: Yale University Press.

Shiffrin, R. M. (1997). Attention, automatism, and consciousness. In J. D. Cohen & J. W. Schooler (Eds.), *Scientific approaches to consciousness* (pp. 49–64). Hillsdale, NJ: Erlbaum.

Shiffrin, R. M., & Schneider, W. (1977). Controlled and automatic human information processing: II. Perceptual learning, automatic attending and a general theory. *Psychological Review, 84*, 127–190.

Stapel, D. A., Koomen, W., & Zeelenberg, M. (1998). The impact of accuracy motivation on interpretation, comparison, and correction processes: Accuracy × knowledge accessibility effects. *Journal of Personality and Social Psychology, 74*, 878–893.

Stapel, D. A., Martin, L. L., & Schwarz, N. (1998). The smell of bias: What instigates correction processes in social judgments? *Personality and Social Psychology Bulletin, 24*, 797–806.

Strack, F., Schwarz, N., Bless, H., Kübler, A., & Wänke, M. (1993). Awareness of the influence as a determinant of assimilation versus contrast. *European Journal of Social Psychology, 23*, 53–62.

Tesser, A., & Martin, L. (1996). The psychology of evaluation. In E. T. Higgins & A. W. Kruglanski (Eds.), *Social psychology: Handbook of basic principles* (pp. 400–432). New York: Guilford.

Thompson, E. P., Roman, R. J., Moskowitz, G. B., Chaiken, S., & Bargh, J. A. (1994). Accuracy motivation attenuates covert priming: The systematic reprocessing of social information. *Journal of Personality and Social Psychology, 66*, 474–489.

Wasel, W., & Gollwitzer, P. M. (1997). Willful control of "automatic" stereotype activation: The role of subliminally vs. supraliminally presented stimuli. *Sprache und Kognition, 16*, 198–210.

Wegener, D. T., & Petty, R. E. (1995). Flexible correction processes in social judgment: The role of naive theories in corrections for perceived bias. *Journal of Personality and Social Psychology, 68*, 36–51.

Wegner, D. M. (1994). Ironic processes in mental control. *Psychological Review, 101*, 34–52.

Wegner, D. M., & Bargh, J. A. (1998). Control and automaticity in social life. In D. T. Gilbert, S. T. Fiske, & G. Lindzey (Eds.), *Handbook of social psychology* (Vol. 2, 4th ed., pp. 446–496). Boston: McGraw-Hill.

Wentura, D. (2000). *Masked priming in the evaluation task: A switch from positive to negative priming due to speed-accuracy instructions.* Unpublished manuscript, University of Münster, Germany.

Wilson, T. D., & Brekke, N. (1994). Mental contamination and mental correction: Unwanted influences on judgments and evaluations. *Psychological Bulletin, 116*, 117–142.

Wilson, T. D., Lindsey, S., & Schooler, T. Y. (2000). A model of dual attitudes. *Psychological Review, 107*, 101–126.

Zajonc, R. B. (1980). Feeling and thinking: Preferences need no inferences. *American Psychologist, 35*(2), 151–175.

8

Nonconscious Control and Implicit Working Memory

Ran R. Hassin

A question that is raised by almost every chapter in this book, in one guise or another, concerns the types of processes that can occur nonconsciously versus those that cannot. The evidence, regrettably, is mixed. On the one hand, there is no doubt that the unconscious can carry out some complex computations more efficiently than the most powerful computer available to date. For example, it transforms activation patterns on the retina into meaningful pictures of the world, and patterns of sound waves into meaningful sentences. Similarly, the unconscious earns our admiration because it coordinates our physical and mental processes in a seemingly effortless way, thus allowing us, for example, to drive, listen to NPR, bless the driver in the car in front of us, and talk to our mothers-in-law on the cell phone, all at the same time and at least somewhat successfully.

On the other hand, other evidence suggests that our admiration might be a little premature, and that there are many straightforward computations that the unconscious cannot carry out. Examples include simple things such as ignoring irrelevant visual information when judging the length of lines (thus creating visual illusions such as the Müller-Lyer), sufficiently incorporating evidence about the current situation into our explanations of human behavior (Gilbert, Pelham, & Krull, 1988; Trope, 1986), and properly using available information in our judgments and decisions (Tversky & Kahneman, 1974).

The empirical examination of the capacities and capabilities of the cognitive unconscious creates an ongoing debate, partly because each new piece of evidence may carry far-reaching implications for our understanding of consciousness, or, more generally, for our views on what is it like to be human.

Adding to this discourse, the current chapter tackles the question by empirically and conceptually examining working memory (WM) and controlled processes, which—unlike their longtime companions, the automatic processes—are exclusively associated with conscious processing.

Automatic cognitive processes are internal automatons that help us navigate a multifaceted and complex environment by slicing it into easily digestible bites. They may be unintentional, nonconscious, ballistic, and effortless, and can thus free our very-limited-capacity consciousness from many burdens. Although traditionally such automatons were thought to have a very limited range, research in the last quarter century indicates that their scope is much wider than we used to think: Not only can people automatically understand language and perceive visual scenes, they can also evaluate objects as good and bad, form impressions of other individuals, and make use of stereotypes and other categorical information while thinking of other people.

Controlled processes are usually thought of as the counterpart of automatic processes. They are intentional, conscious, and effortful, and hence allow more comprehensive information processing, one that exploits the richness and flexibility of consciousness and thus avoids the pitfalls of the narrow, one-track-minded automatons. Controlled processes in higher cognition are often perceived as the quintessence of human beings, the types of processes that separate us from the rest of the animal kingdom: Making a difficult decision, flexibly pursuing a goal, willfully inhibiting one's immediate responses, and multitasking are a few examples of higher cognitive processes that are traditionally thought of as controlled.

In light of this prevalent view of automaticity and control, it is hardly surprising that the notion of nonconscious control—which appears in the title of this chapter—is widely held to be an oxymoron.[1] On the most immediate level, this widespread belief appears to rest on pure logical grounds—how can (controlled) processes be conscious and nonconscious at the same time? But a closer look reveals that the notion of nonconscious controlled processes in higher cognition is disturbing for another deep reason: It suggests that mental processes, which are central to our conception of what it is to be human, occur outside of conscious awareness and have no phenomenology.

Worries of this kind have led to a general disregard of the prospects of nonconscious controlled processes. This attitude continues to characterize the fields of cognitive psychology and social cognition despite the fact that research has started to yield evidence for nonconscious cognitive control in the area of automatic evaluation and stereotype use (see, e.g., chapters 7 and 17, this volume; Moskowitz, Gollwitzer, Wasel, & Schaal, 1999).

The main purpose of this chapter is to advance the argument for nonconscious control and nonconscious controlled processes, and it does so in three ways: First, it presents systematic data which show that WM—the mental mechanism that is perhaps most associated with controlled, conscious processing—can operate outside of conscious awareness. Second, it reviews recent findings in social cognition and shows how they suggest that motivational aspects of WM can flexibly control behavior outside of conscious awareness. Last, it presents a conceptual analysis that starts by pointing out that the notion of control is used in more than one sense. Importantly, once the meanings of *control* are un-confounded, the relations of conscious awareness and cognitive control become a matter of empirical inquiry. Hence, I argue, the notion of nonconscious control is not an oxymoron and, indeed, it cannot be one—by definition.

Overview

Due to the intimate relationships between WM and controlled processes, the arguments and evidence for implicit WM and nonconscious control are inherently interwoven—a fact that is reflected in the different sections of this chapter. The first two sections are devoted to WM. In the first, WM is succinctly described from three different perspectives: the functions that it serves, tasks that examine it, and models that describe it. A discussion of the relations of WM and conscious awareness closes the section. Next, a novel paradigm is described, and based on the conclusions of the first section it is argued that this paradigm examines cognitive components of WM. Four experiments that provide direct evidence for implicit WM—and hence nonconscious control—are subsequently discussed.

The argument for nonconscious control and implicit WM is bolstered in the third section, where it is argued that nonconscious goal pursuit (e.g., Aarts, Gollwitzer, & Hassin, in press; Bargh, 1990; Bargh, Gollwitzer, Lee-Chai, Barndollar, & Trötschel, 2001; Kruglanski et al., 2002; Shah, 2003) provides evidence for the nonconscious operation of motivational aspects of working memory. Evidence for flexible nonconscious control, via nonconscious goals, seals this section. The arguments and data are summarized in the fourth section.

Closing a circle, the epilogue reconsiders the concept of *control*. It is argued that control is used (by social and higher level cognitive psychologists alike) in two different senses, and that this confusion leads us to conceive of nonconscious control as an oxymoron. Once these two meanings are disentangled, the intimate relationships between "cognitive control" and "conscious awareness" dissolve. The notion of nonconscious control, which appears to be an oxymoron, thus turns out to be logically possible.

Working Memory

A Brief Overview

The notion of WM grew out of the literature on short-term memory (STM) in the mid-1970s (Baddeley & Hitch, 1974), and has since grown to become a major field of research in cognitive psychology and in the more recent area of cognitive neuroscience (e.g., Smith & Jonides, 1995).

Working memory, like STM, is an online mechanism that retains items in memory for short periods of time. Unlike STM, however, WM comprises multiple components, and it does more than retain information: Using its executive functions, it selectively attends to the environment (whether internal or external; see Garavan, 1998). Moreover, WM can manipulate the items retained in memory, and it can coordinate the use of these representations in complex cognitive processes.

These characteristics make WM a perfect candidate for a bridge, or gateway, between relatively simple cognitive processes (such as memorizing) and relatively complex ones (such as comprehension processes; see, e.g., Gathercole & Baddeley, 1993; Logie & Gilhooly, 1998). Findings that support this contention relate WM to problem solving and analogies (Carpenter, Just, & Shell, 1990), language comprehension (Just & Carpenter, 1992), reading comprehension (Daneman & Carpenter, 1980), reasoning (Kyllonen & Christal, 1990), general fluid intelligence (Engle, Kane, & Tuholski, 1999), and even extraversion and person perception (Lieberman & Rosenthal, 2001; Macrae, Bodenhausen, Schloerscheidt, & Milne, 1999).

Partly in light of findings of this sort, Baddeley and Logie (1999) argue that "working memory . . . allow[s] . . . humans to comprehend and mentally represent their immediate environment, to retain information about their immediate past experience, to support the acquisition of new knowledge, to solve problems, and to formulate, relate and act on current goals" (p. 28). This view of WM seems to represent the consensus among WM researchers: After reviewing major theories and findings in the WM literature, Miyake and Shah (1999) conclude that "working memory is not for 'memorizing' per se but, rather, it is in the service of complex cognitive activities such as language processing, visuospatial thinking, reasoning and problem solving, and decision making" (p. 445). To use a simple, blatantly wrong, yet illuminating metaphor, working memory seems to be the controller of controlled processes (see chapter 1).

Despite the widespread interest in WM, however, and in spite of the apparent consensus regarding its functional characterization, "it is not easy to figure out what working memory really is" (Miyake & Shah, 1999, p. 1). Since a comprehensive review of the models and tasks of working memory is beyond the scope of this chapter, I choose to describe two of the prominent models, hoping to present a relatively clear picture of working memory while emphasizing functional similarities over architectural differences (for a comprehensive review, the reader is referred to Miyake and Shah's excellent 1999 book on the subject).

Two Models of Working Memory

The following paragraphs succinctly describe two models of WM. That of Baddeley, Hitch, and their colleagues is probably most often identified as the starting point of the modern examination of WM (e.g., Baddeley & Hitch, 1974). The second model, that of Cohen and his colleagues, is probably the most biologically implemented model of WM (Cohen, Dunbar, & McClelland, 1990; O'Reilly, Braver, & Cohen, 1999).

Baddeley's classic model of WM is composed of an executive component and two slave systems (but see Baddeley, 2002, for the most recent advancement of the model). The two slave systems are the phonological loop and the visuospatial sketchpad—two specialized, temporary memory systems that actively maintain information via rehearsal. The phonological loop maintains verbally coded information, and the visuospatial sketchpad maintains visual and/or spatial information. The central executive is involved in the control and regulation of WM and WM-related tasks, and performs such tasks as coordinating the two slave systems and activating relevant representations within long-term memory. Despite its central role in WM, the central executive remains the least specified component of WM (Baddeley, 1996, p. 5).

In the model of Cohen and his colleagues (e.g., Cohen et al., 1990; O'Reilly et al., 1999), WM is defined as controlled processing involving active maintenance and/or rapid learning. The features of the model include a prefrontal cortex specialized for active maintenance of information that is dynamically updated, allowing it to bias ongoing processing; a hippocampus specialized for rapid learning of arbitrary information (that can serve, too, in the service of controlled processing), and a posterior perceptual and motor cortex that exhibits slow, long-term learning. According to this model, control—defined as biasing of relevant cognitive processes—results from the interaction of the different subsystems of WM.

Note that despite the differences in cognitive architecture, the two models are quite similar functionally: WM involves active maintenance and (rapid) learning of material, in the service of cognitive control and relatively complex cognitive processes. This view is shared by most, if not all, models of WM (see Miyake & Shah, 1999), a consensus that is also reflected in the various tasks that are used to examine WM capacities.

Measuring Working Memory

In this section, three frequently used WM tasks are described, and their similarities are outlined. Specifically, the current presentation focuses on certain mental functions and operations that are necessary for completing these tasks successfully, in the assumption that these operations reflect researchers' beliefs regarding the characteristics of WM (this list is far from being comprehensive and is meant to be illustrative; for description of more WM tasks see, e.g., Engle, Tuholski, Laughlin, & Conway, 1999).[2]

First, consider the reading span, a task developed to assess individual differences in the capacity of WM (e.g., Daneman & Carpenter, 1980, 1983). Participants engaged in this task are given increasingly long sets of sentences to read aloud. At the end of each set, they are asked to try to recall the final word of each sentence in the set. The span is defined as the maximum number of sentences the subject could read aloud while maintaining perfect recall.

What does it take to be good at this task? First, one has to be able to retain instructions in an active memory. Second, one has to be able to maintain a list of the encountered last words in memory, and to update it with each sentence one reads. Third, this retaining and updating should be somewhat resistant to interference from the words that appear in the sentences. Fourth, the information should be available to concurrent cognitive processes (that allow, e.g., verbalization of the list).

As a second example, consider the continuous performance task (CPT), which involves searching for a target stimulus in a continuous stream of stimuli (e.g., O'Reilly et al., 1999). The search in a CPT is conditional: Participants are instructed to regard a designated stimulus (e.g., H) as a target if and only if it follows another, specific, stimulus (e.g., Y). Participants are further asked to perform a certain behavior (e.g., to press a key) whenever they encounter a target. To perform well in this task, as in the reading span, one needs to successfully maintain the instructions in an active memory system. Moreover, in order to identify a target and to launch the target-related behavior, one needs to maintain—and monitor—a list of the presented letters. Last, the whole process should be somewhat resistant to interference from other letters that appear in the list.

Consider, as a last example, the N-back task, in which participants are exposed to a stream of stimuli (e.g., letters) and are asked to judge whether the stimulus that they currently see is identical (or not) to the one that they saw N trials ago (e.g., Smith & Jonides, 1999). Again, to succeed at this task, participants must be able to perform several cognitive operations successfully. First, they must keep the instructions in an active memory system. Second, they must maintain an active—and correctly ordered—list of the N last letters. Third, they must continuously compare the current letter with the one presented N trials ago, and if a match is noted they must successfully launch the target-related behavior. Last, the maintained list should be somewhat immune to interference from the letters in the list.

The above analysis, then, suggests that there is a considerable consensus regarding the characteristics examined by WM tasks like the ones discussed herein. This consensus, in turn, points to a substantial agreement regarding the functions of working memory:

1. Active maintenance of ordered information for relatively short periods of time
2. Context-relevant updating of information and goal-relevant computations involving active representations
3. Rapid biasing of (task relevant) cognitions and behaviors in the service of currently held goals
4. Some sort of resistance to interference

Conscious Awareness and Working Memory

Now that an illustrative sample of models and paradigms of WM has been presented, highlighting the intimate relationships between WM and control processes, it is time to turn to another major concern: the nature of the relations of WM and conscious awareness.

The consensus among WM and consciousness researchers seems to be that the psychological processes underlying WM, attention, and awareness are strongly related (Baars, 1997a; Kintsch, Healy, Hegarety, Pennington, & Salthouse, 1999). The nature of these relations, however, is less clear. Kintsch and colleagues (1999, p. 431) propose what might be called the subset hypothesis, according to which "a subset of the information that is actively maintained [in working memory] is also that which one is aware or conscious of."). Baars (1997b) seems to go one step further by suggesting that "consciousness is evidently involved in all WM input, output, and voluntary operations, as in explicit problem solving" (p. 369). An even stronger view of the relations is proposed by Baddeley (e.g., 1993): "conscious awareness [is] one of the functions of the central executive component of working memory" (p. 26).

These hypotheses are supported by several lines of research that relate different conscious experiences to WM processes and components. Thus, for example, Baddeley and Andrade (2000) showed that phenomenological experiences of vividness are affected by load: When WM is put under load, objects of imagery seem less vivid than when WM is not under load. Similarly, Teasdale, Dritschel, Taylor, and Proctor (1995) linked conscious-mind wandering to the central executive, by showing that stimulus-independent thoughts occurred less frequently when the central executive was put under load. In another demonstration of the causal relations obtaining between working memory and conscious awareness, a visuospatial secondary task has been shown to affect emotional experiences (e.g., Andrade, 2001; Andrade, Kavanagh, & Baddeley, 1997).

Note that the views portrayed above weave conscious awareness and components of WM closely together (cf. Kihlstrom, 1997). Some even suggest a unidirectional causal arrow, leading from WM to conscious awareness. Consequently, the main empirical inquiries into the nature of the relations between WM and conscious awareness examine the role of the former in determining the contents and qualities of conscious experience. The complementary inquiry, one that attempts to understand the role of consciousness in the functions of WM, did not receive much experimental or theoretical attention (but see Baars, 1997b). One basic form of this question concerns us here: Is conscious awareness necessary for (certain operations of) WM, or can WM operate outside of conscious awareness?

The views sketched above imply, some even explicitly, that WM cannot operate entirely outside of conscious awareness. This stance is reflected unequivocally in the nature of WM tasks: In all of the tasks presented above, and in all that we know of, participants are explicitly presented with materials that they are explicitly asked to manipulate (memorize, rehearse, add, subtract, and so on). By their very nature, then, existing WM tasks cannot systematically address questions regarding the roles of conscious awareness in WM. This is a clear indication that the field assumes—even if sometimes implicitly—that, in essence, WM is conscious.

Anecdotal evidence to the contrary comes from a neuroimaging study conducted by Jonides, Smith, Marshuetz, Koeppe, and Reuter-Lorenz (1998). In this study, four target letters were presented for storage followed, 3 seconds later, by a probe letter that either matched a target letter or did not. On some trials, when the probe did not match a target letter and therefore required a "no" response, the probe did match a target letter of the previous trial. On these trials, a "yes" response was prepotent and had to be inhibited. As hypothesized, these trials yielded brain activation in areas that are traditionally viewed as related to WM (i.e., Brodmann's area 45). Surprisingly, however, participants did not consciously remember that the targets had appeared on a previous trial, nor did they have a phenomenological experience of inhibition (Smith, personal communication, 2001).

Implicit Working Memory: The Lesson From Implicit Insights

This section presents evidence for an implicit mode of the cognitive components of WM. For the sake of brevity, I call this mode "implicit working memory" (note that by using this term, I do not suggest that there are two WMs;

it is simply a shorthand). The evidence was gathered in a novel WM paradigm that requires perceptual judgments and hence, unlike the paradigms described above, does not explicitly activate WM processes. This paradigm allows us to examine whether WM is necessarily conscious, or whether it may, under some circumstances, operate outside of conscious awareness.

This new paradigm was developed to examine one of the products of WM—insights (see Hassin & Bargh, 2004). As a cursory background, then, the first part of this section discusses the role of conscious awareness in insights and defines what implicit insights are. Then the paradigm is described, and its characteristics are compared with those of established WM paradigms. The upshot of this comparison is that this new paradigm is a WM paradigm. The results of four experiments that demonstrate implicit insights, and hence implicit WM, are presented in the last part of this section.

On Conscious Awareness and Insights

In successfully solving insight problems, one suddenly realizes that one has developed a better grasp of the underlying structure of a problem, or an improved understanding of the rules that govern a phenomenon of interest. Insights are usually conceived of as being conscious, and the associated "aha" experience is sometimes even included in the definition of *insight* (for various approaches to insights, see Sternberg & Davidson, 1995).

Unlike the insights themselves, however, it seems that the processes that yield insights do not require conscious awareness. So, for example, Metcalfe and colleagues (Metcalfe, 1986a; Metcalfe & Wiebe, 1987) have shown that when people try to solve insight problems, they do not have an accurate feeling of how far they are from finding a solution (as indicated by a "feeling thermometer"). These findings suggest that insights tend to pop up in awareness without prior conscious evidence for their formation.

In a series of studies, we (Hassin et al., 2004) further examined the role of conscious awareness in insights. More specifically, we examined whether insights can occur not only in the absence of conscious awareness of the processes that lead to them, but also in the absence of conscious awareness of the insights themselves.[3] Importantly, the insights we were interested in were those that relied on working memory processes. Thus, if implicit insights of this kind occur, they provide evidence for implicit WM.

Defining Implicit Insights In implicit insights, as in explicit ones, the mind extracts patterns, rules, or higher order invariants that relate two or more objects or events in a stimulus space. This extraction can occur even in the absence of apparent conditional probabilities between the objects/events. In other words, the processes that lead to implicit insights—like those that lead to explicit ones—do not necessarily depend on gathering specific relational facts.

Implicit insights are unconscious in that (a) they can occur without awareness of the learned rules and (b) they can be manifested in behavior without awareness. In addition, implicit insights are unintentional in that they can occur when people do not intend for them to happen, and in that they can affect behavior without a corresponding intention.

Implicit Insights and Implicit Learning Implicit insight formation is similar to implicit learning in that both processes consist of extractions of rules (or patterns) in the absence of intention and awareness (cf. Lewicki, Hill, & Bizot, 1988; Nissen & Bullemer, 1987; Reber, 1993; Stadler & Frensch, 1998). There are two major differences between these processes, though. First, implicit learning occurs only when statistical information is available, that is, when the to-be-learned patterns are abundantly repeated, thus allowing for extractions of conditioned probabilities (e.g., "stimulus H follows Y on 75% of the trials, whereas K follows Y on 25%"). Implicit insights, on the other hand, do not necessitate statistical information of this kind. Indeed, such information is often irrelevant. Finding a solution to insight problems depends on mechanisms that allow us to see underlying structures, patterns, and rules even in the absence of statistical information.

The second major difference between implicit insights and implicit learning is that the latter develops gradually over time (with the repeated presentation of the materials), whereas the former—like explicit insights—may occur very abruptly.

Implicit Insights and Working Memory

A paradigm for examining one kind of implicit insights is described below. What is crucial for the current purposes is that this paradigm examines implicit insights that occur in WM. The general characteristics of this paradigm are the following: A computer screen is divided into a matrix of 24 (columns) by 18 (lines). Small round disks that are either empty (i.e., bagel-like) or full appear in the different intersections of the matrix. The participants' task is perceptual: They are asked to indicate whether the disk is full or empty. After each response, the disk disappears and the next stimulus appears.

The stimuli appear in sets of five, which are separated from each other by a fixation point. There are three different kinds of sets, which define three conditions: rule sets (the locations of all the disks in a set follow a rule), yoked broken rule sets (the locations of the first four disks in a set follow a rule, but the location of the fifth disk does not), and yoked control sets (see an illustration in figure 8.1; examples for rules in table 8.1).[4] Importantly, in all of the experiments described below, the proportion of rule sets never exceeds 12.5%.

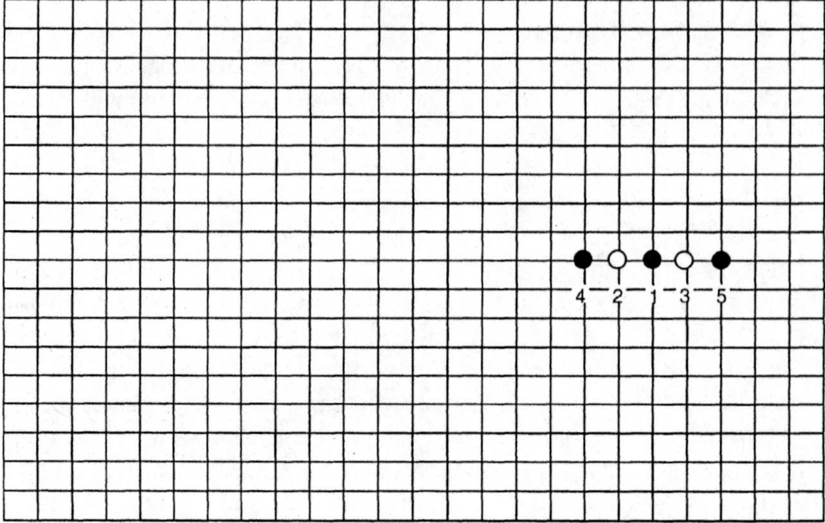

(b)

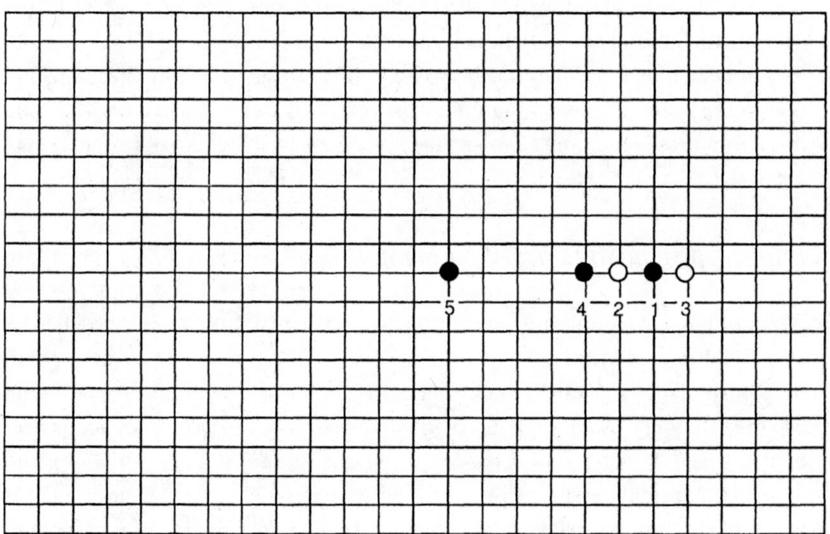

Figure 8.1 An illustration of a rule set (a) and its yoked broken rule set (b), control set (c), and scrambled set (d; adapted from Hassin et al., 2004). The numbers appearing below the locations indicate order of appearance, and did not appear in the actual experiment. The disks in the actual experiment appeared sequentially, such that subjects saw only one at a time.

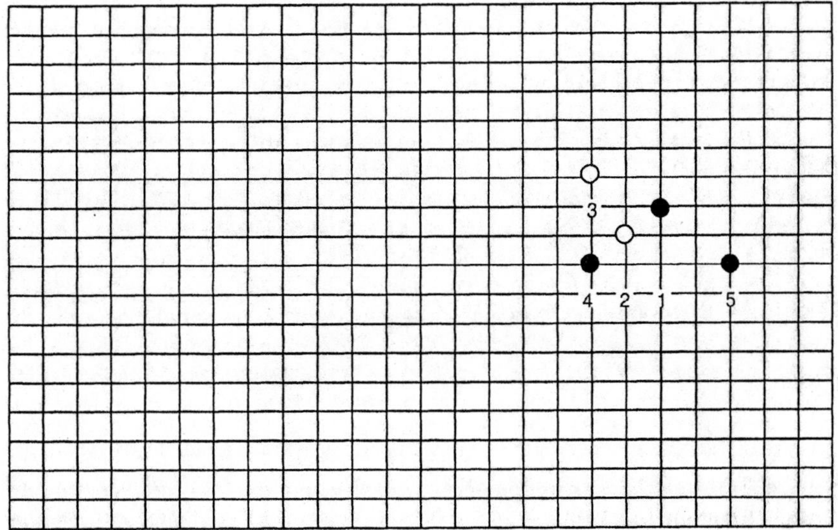

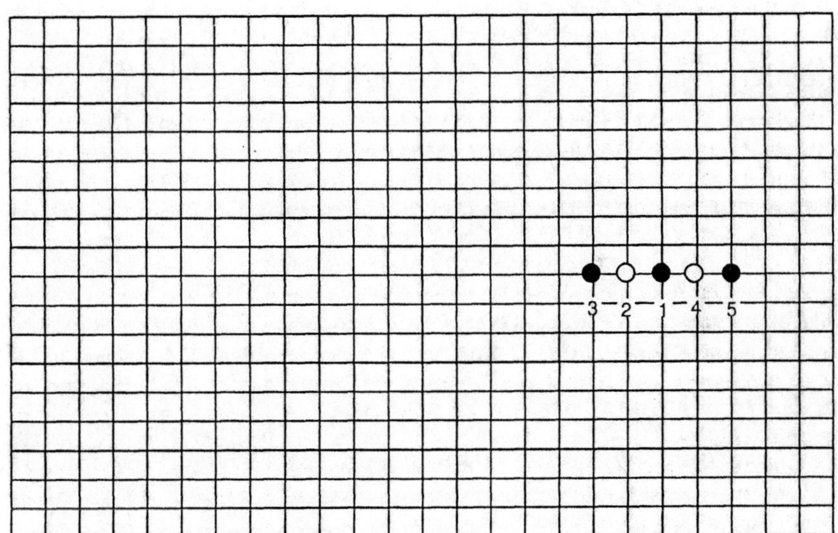

Figure 8.1 Continued.

Table 8.1 A Few Examples of Rules Used in These Experiments

	x Axis		y Axis	
Rule #	Rule	Move	Rule	Move
1	$X_{n+1} = X_n + 3$	+3, +3, +3	$Y_{n+1} = Y_n$	0, 0, 0
2	$X_{n+1} = X_n + 2$	+2, +2, +2	$Y_{n+1} + Y_n + 2 \, x \, (-1)^n$	+2, −2, +2
3	$X_{n+1} = X_n + 2^{n-1}$	+1, +2, +4	$Y_{n+1} = Y_n$	0, 0, 0
4	$X_{n+1} = X_n + 2^{n-1} \, x \, (-1)^{n+1}$	+1, −2, +4	$Y_{n+1} = Y_n$	0, 0, 0
5	$X_{n+1} = X_n + n$	1, +2, +3	$Y_{n+1} = Y_n + (n)x(-1)^n$	−1, +2, −3

Note: Numbers represent matrix units (i.e., 1 equals one cell). The + sign represents a rightward movement on the *x* axis and an upward movement on the *y* axis. There are three movements in each set before implicit insights are examined, and they are given in order from left to right.

Source: Hassin et al. (2004).

Whether the disks are full or empty is always randomly determined. Thus, the dimensions of disk type (whether they are full or empty) and disk location are orthogonal. Learning the rules that determine locations, then, cannot help participants predict the correct answers. However, if participants extract a rule during a rule set, they can correctly anticipate the location of the last disk in that particular set. This allows them to shift their eyes or attention to the right location, thus speeding up the process of identifying the disk. If they extract a rule during broken rule sets, however, their anticipations will err systematically and they will move their eyes or attention to incorrect locations, thus slowing down their responses.

Note that participants' explicit task is to judge whether the disks are empty or full. This is the only task that they are told about and—to presage later findings—the only task that they are aware of. Hence, extraction of the rules that govern the disks' locations is incidental in this paradigm. Yet it is success in this second, implicit task that may yield evidence for implicit insights.

The dependent measure of interest is the reaction time (RT) to the last disk in each rule, broken rule, and control set (this is a very easy task, and errors are minimal). Because of the hypothesized rule-driven anticipations of the disks' locations, we expected that RTs to last disks in rule sets (where rule-based anticipations are veridical) would be faster than RTs to the last disks in broken rule sets (where rule-based anticipations are systematically misleading). Importantly, by presenting each rule set and its associated broken rule set an equal number of times, we kept the conditional probabilities equal. Consequently, given four disks that follow a rule, the likelihood of a rule-following disk is identical to the likelihood of a rule-breaking disk. This measure prevents the possibility of more gradual, statistical learning in the course of the experiment.

Is this a WM paradigm? To examine the similarity between the current paradigm and the WM paradigms described previously, consider the mental operations that need to take place in order for implicit insights to occur. First, the goals of being fast and accurate need to be in place. Second, one must actively maintain and update a list of the locations of disks within each given set. Third, the locations of the disks must be maintained in order of their appearance. Fourth, mental computations that involve representations of the locations of the disks must allow for rule (or pattern) extraction. Fifth, the extracted rules must lead to anticipations regarding the locations of the last disks, such that when these anticipations are met, participants become faster than when they are not. In other words, the extracted rules bias other concurrent cognitive processes and thus control behavior.

A comparison of the above list with the list of features shared by WM tasks (in the section "Measuring Working Memory") reveals that the current paradigm is, indeed, a WM paradigm: It requires active maintenance of ordered information for relatively short periods of time; in addition, it requires updating of information (with incoming disks) and integration (rule extraction). Last, the information is processed in the service of current goals and is readily available to control behavior (i.e., responses).

Examining Implicit Working Memory

In the first experiment examining implicit WM, participants (20 New York University undergraduates) were exposed to 140 sets, 10% of which were rule, broken rule, and control sets, and 70% of which were random sets. Awareness was assessed at the debriefing: Participants were thoroughly debriefed, and the few who indicated either intention to predict locations, or any awareness of the rules, were excluded from the analysis.[5] Participants' mean RTs for rule, broken rule, and control sets were subjected to repeated measures analysis of variance, which revealed that participants were significantly faster in responding to rule sets than to broken rule sets, with responses to control sets falling in between the two. This result indicates that participants did indeed extract the rules and developed congruent expectations. When these expectations were met, participants were faster to react to the last disk than when these expectations were violated.

Examining conscious awareness at debriefing is not considered a highly sensitive measure of online awareness (e.g., Merikle & Reingold, 1992). Thus, the second experiment was designed such that the last set presented to participants was always a (randomly chosen) rule set. Immediately after the presentation of this set, participants were given a matrix and were asked to reconstruct it.[6] Only one participant successfully reconstructed the last set, thus indicating awareness, and her data were excluded from the analysis. The results of the remaining participants replicated the earlier findings: RTs for rule sets were significantly shorter than those for broken rule sets.

In another attempt to examine participants' awareness and intentions, we directly manipulated these factors. Thus, in the third experiment, half of the participants were told in advance that some of the sets would follow rules, and they were encouraged to find them (instructed condition). The other half were given the same instructions as in Experiments 1 and 2.

If participants in the first two experiments were indeed consciously looking for rules and finding them, but were nonetheless unable to report their intentions or awareness, then there should be no differences between the instructed condition and the noninstructed condition. Previous findings in the implicit learning literature, however, suggest that under certain circumstances awareness and intention interfere with rule extraction (see e.g., Reber, 1976; Berry & Broadbent, 1988). Based on these findings, we hypothesized that participants in the instructed condition would not form implicit insights, whereas participants in the noninstructed group would. Indeed, participants in the instructed condition showed no evidence for implicit insights, whereas participants in the noninstructed condition formed implicit insights. An analysis of variance corroborated: The interaction between the instruction factor and the rule factor was significant.

In the last experiment in this series, we examined whether implicit insights show one more characteristic of working memory—whether items are kept in an ordered list. To examine this question, a new condition was introduced: the scrambled sets condition. Each scrambled set was yoked to a rule set and was created by switching the locations of the third and fourth disks (see figure 8.1). If order of presentation and memorization is not important for the formation of implicit insights, then RTs to rule sets should be identical to RTs to scrambled rule sets. However, we hypothesized that the locations are kept in an ordered list and that the order is crucial for the formation of implicit insights.

No participant indicated awareness of the rules and their effects. Participants' mean RTs revealed that, as hypothesized, mean RTs to rule sets were shorter than mean RTs to scrambled rule sets. The difference between mean RTs to control and scrambled sets was not significant, however.

Summary and Conclusions

Four experiments provide evidence for implicit insights, and hence for implicit WM. That the implicit insights formed in this paradigm are nonconscious is shown both by evidence from postexperimental probing at debriefings (Experiments 1 and 3), and by evidence from immediate probing and reconstruction (Experiments 2 and 4). In addition, Experiment 3 demonstrated the implicitness of implicit insights through a direct manipulation of intent and awareness: Unlike participants who report neither intention to extract rules nor awareness of them, those who were made aware of the rules, and who were asked to look for them, did not show evidence for implicit insights.

To recap, then: Participants were certainly aware of the disks and their features, but they were not aware of the fact that they kept in active memory the ordered locations of these disks. Moreover, participants were not aware of the fact that they were using the locations to extract rules that underlie the disks' locations, and they were not aware of the fact that these extracted rules led to congruent anticipations. Last, participants were not aware of the fact that these anticipations affected their behavior and were manifested in it.

The mental operations needed for successfully forming the kind of implicit insights examined here are strikingly similar to the functions of WM and the operations examined by other WM tasks (see "Working Memory"). The current results suggest, then, that the cognitive components of WM can, at least under some circumstances, operate outside of conscious awareness.

One metatheoretical issue that is crucial for my claim has to do with the conditions that allow identification of two (or more) tasks in terms of the underlying structures that they examine. At its core, it is a question of justification; in the present case, the claim that needs to be justified is that the current paradigm examines WM. To briefly summarize the argument developed in the last two sections, I believe that there are two convincing reasons to accept this claim. First, based on a functional analysis of WM and on an analysis of tasks used to examine WM, criteria for WM tasks have been identified. The paradigm introduced here meets these criteria. Second, the claim that the implicit insight paradigm examines WM is parsimonious: If one does not accept it, then one has to postulate a cognitive mechanism that essentially does exactly what WM does, but nonconsciously.

The upshot of the research described in this section is that WM, the mental organ whose essence is cognitive control, can operate completely outside of conscious awareness. The next section examines the motivational aspects of WM in their relation to conscious awareness.

Motivational Control in Implicit Working Memory

In a series of publications, social psychologists have shown that goals can be activated and pursued without conscious awareness (Aarts et al., in press; Bargh et al., 2001; Chartrand & Bargh, 1996; Hassin & Bargh, 2004; Kruglanski et al., 2002; Moskowitz et al., 1999; chapter 2, this volume). Consider, for example, the participants in Aarts et al. (in press; see also Aarts & Hassin, in press), who took part in what allegedly was a series of short experiments. The first short experiment was bogus. The second was in actuality a priming task: Some participants read a short scenario in which an actor's behaviors implied that he was seeking a casual intimate relationship with a woman he had met earlier (casual intimacy condition), while others read a similar scenario that did not imply this goal. After the completion of this task, participants—all males—were asked to help either a female or a male experimenter by giving feedback on the first short experiment (they did not see or meet that person). Participants' wooing efforts were assessed through the amount of help they offered. As hypothesized, goals were automatically contagious: Primed participants helped the female experimenter more than nonprimed participants did, whereas help offered to the male experimenter was not affected by priming. This goal contagion effect is nonconscious in that participants were not aware of the nature of the priming episode and of their adoption of the goal.

The potential importance of goals to the issue of nonconscious control was first raised by Moskowitz and colleagues (1999). In a series of clever experiments, they looked at the differences between two populations—those who have chronic egalitarian goals and those who do not. Their findings suggest that the former population can refrain from using stereotypes at time intervals that do not allow for conscious control, a finding that they attribute to "preconscious control." Due to the inherent limitations of studies that rely on individual differences, however, these results, while highly suggestive, are not yet conclusive in regard to nonconscious control of stereotypes.

Note, though, that Moskowitz et al. (1999) share the basic intuition that in the aspects important for the current discussion, nonconscious goal pursuit goes far beyond mere priming of behaviors (cf. Dijksterhuis & Bargh, 2001; chapter 13, this volume). Whereas behavior priming may be considered as a case of mimicry, primed goals nonconsciously guide behavior in an attempt to reach a certain end state. So, for example, the results of the goal contagion study described above cannot be described as a case of behavior mimicry, because participants came up with means of wooing that were not mentioned in the priming stage. Thus, in nonconscious goal pursuit, the means that serve to reach a desired end state may be chosen nonconsciously, suggesting nonconscious control.

Implicit Working Memory and Flexible Goal Pursuit

In order to see how nonconscious goal pursuit implicates not only nonconscious control but also implicit WM, consider an example taken from one of the earliest studies examining nonconscious goal pursuit (Chartrand & Bargh, 1996, Experiment 1). In the first phase of this study, participants were primed with an information-processing or memorization goal. Priming was achieved through the scrambled sentence test, in which participants were asked to form grammatically correct four-word sentences from items containing five words presented in a scrambled order. In the impression goal condition, words related to forming an impression were embedded in some of the items, whereas in the memory condition, words related to memorizing information were embedded. Then, in an "unrelated experiment," participants were presented with behaviors of a target actor that they were later asked to recall. The results replicated those of a classic study, in which participants were explicitly instructed to either memorize behaviors of a target person or to form an impression of him: Impression formation yields more structured, better remembered mental representations (Hamilton, Katz, & Leirer, 1980).

Recall that according to the characterization presented in the previous sections, WM has a motivational aspect—it holds current goals active and biases concurrent cognitive processes in attempt to maximize goal attainment. If participants who were primed with an impression formation goal held it active in WM, this active goal might have biased the intake and integration of information in a way that is consistent with the conscious activation of this goal.

The involvement of WM in nonconscious goal pursuit was more directly examined by Hassin and Bargh (2004), who studied the effects of nonconscious goal priming on one of the most frequently used tests of WM—the Wisconsin Card Sorting Test (WCST). In a typical WCST session, participants are presented with cards that have three dimensions—color, number, and shape (e.g., one card might contain four red squares, another might contain one yellow triangle, and a third might contain three green circles). Participants are presented with one such card at a time, and their task is to sort them into piles according to one of the dimensions (e.g., shape). Participants are not told what the sorting rule is, but they are given feedback after each sorting. After 10 consecutive cards are successfully sorted, the experimenter changes the sorting rule without a warning. The participant, confronted with sudden negative feedback, has to realize that the rule has been changed, to learn a new rule (e.g., the cards are now grouped by numbers), and to sort according to it. This rule learning followed by rule change continues until all cards are sorted.

Before taking the WCST, participants in Hassin and Bargh's (2004, Experiments 1 and 2) study were either primed, or not, with an achievement goal. This was done through an "unrelated" word-search task, in which primed participants were exposed to a small number of achievement-related words (such as *win* and *achieve*), whereas the word search of the control group did not contain any achievement-related words (cf. Chartrand & Bargh, 1996). Recall that according to the received view, WM cannot be involved in nonconscious goal pursuit simply because the former is conscious while the latter is not. Our view, however, was opposite: We thought that WM is involved in nonconscious pursuit of goals. Hence, we hypothesized that primed participants should fare better on the WCST than the control group.

A thorough debriefing revealed that subjects were aware of neither the relations between the tasks nor any influence of the priming episode on their WCST performance. Moreover, there were no significant differences between the groups in terms of goal commitment. Yet participants who were primed with an achievement goal made significantly fewer mistakes than participants in the control group. These findings suggest, then, that WM may sometimes be involved in nonconscious goal pursuit, thus supporting the contention that the motivational components of WM take part in nonconsciously guiding behavior.

The WCST experiments allow us to draw another major parallel between conscious and nonconscious controlled processes. WCST measures one aspect of flexibility, namely, the ability to shift between mental sets (or tasks), an ability that allows for adaptation to sudden changes in the rules that govern the environment (Miyake, Friedman, Emerson, Witzki, & Howerter, 2000). Flexible adaptiveness is manifested in *not* committing perseverative errors—sortings that are guided by "old" rules that should no longer guide behavior. Flexibility has traditionally been exclusively ascribed to controlled processes and is perceived as one of the advantages of conscious processes over nonconscious processes (e.g., Nozick, 2001; Schneider, Dumais, & Shiffrin, 1984). Our findings show, however, that primed participants in the WCST experiment not only committed fewer errors overall, they committed significantly fewer perseverative errors. In other words, participants who nonconsciously pursued an achievement goal were better at adapting—and thus more flexible—than participants in the control group. This finding was replicated in a third experiment, in which participants were primed with the goal of being flexible. Like consciously controlled processes, then, nonconsciously controlled processes may be flexible.

Conclusion

The main argument advanced in this chapter is that controlled processes in general, and WM in particular, can operate outside of conscious awareness. These two arguments are inherently interwoven, but for the sake of clarity I have tried to disentangle them. The case for implicit WM is supported by the results of four experiments that use a novel WM paradigm and provide consistent evidence for implicit insights. In addition, recent evidence from nonconscious goal pursuit research, reviewed in the third section, strongly supports the contention that motivational aspects of WM can operate nonconsciously too.

That WM can extract rules and patterns and use them to nonconsciously guide behavior is in itself evidence for nonconscious control. The research on goal pursuit complements these findings by suggesting that WM is involved in nonconscious motivational control of behavior. Evidence from goal priming and WCST seals the argument: Nonconscious control, like its conscious counterpart, allows us to flexibly adapt our behaviors and cognitions to our environment, in the service of our goals.

Epilogue: Why "Nonconscious Control" Is Not an Oxymoron

At the outset of this chapter the prevalent view of automaticity and control was outlined: Automatic processes may be unintentional, nonconscious, ballistic, and effortless; controlled processes are intentional, conscious, stoppable, and effortful. This view entails that nonconscious control is an oxymoron, a contradiction in terms, a (psycho)logical impossibility.

Later sections provided contradicting evidence: The findings reviewed in them suggest that nonconscious control is not only logically possible, it is a psychological reality. The question that inevitably rises, then, is how can these two opposing conceptions be reconciled?

A close examination of how social psychologists and higher level cognitive psychologists use the notion of control and controlled processes holds the key to solving this apparent contradiction. The first thing that such an examination reveals is that we use these notions in more than one sense. On the one hand, we use *control* to denote cognitive processes with a certain kind of function (e.g., planning, switching, or inhibition of dominant responses). On the other hand, we use *control* relationally (as in *controlled processes*) to describe processes that are not automatic, that is, processes that are characterized as conscious, effortful, stoppable, and intentional.

To further develop the argument, consider the following working definition of control as consisting of nonperceptual manipulation of attention or information that allows the organism to overcome the habitual and to go beyond the immediately available. This is a functional definition—it anchors the meaning of *control* in a specific family of functions that capture many prevalent uses of the term. So, for example, in the Stroop literature, control is often conceived of as inhibiting or ignoring the response offered by the meaning of the word (e.g., MacDonald, Cohen, Stenger, & Carter, 2000). In the stereotype literature, control is understood to consist of refraining from succumbing to the behavioral tendencies incorporated into stereotypes (e.g., Devine & Monteith, 1999; Moskowitz et al., 1999)[7]; and the self-regulation literature assumes that control is achieved when one successfully avoids yielding to immediate temptations (e.g., Trope & Fisbach, 2000).

Note that if one adopts this functional definition of control (in actuality, *any* functional definition will do; cf. chapter 15) then there is no a priori reason to expect that controlled processes would be exclusively conscious (cf.

Kihlstrom, 1990). This is not the case with the second, relational definition of control (i.e., processes that stand in stark contradiction to automatic processes in terms of their characteristics). According to the latter, controlled processes are conscious by definition, and hence nonconscious control is a contradiction in terms.

The multiple meanings of *control* would not have created a problem had they had the exact same extensions in the world. Alas, this is not the case. The extensions of these two notions of *control* do not fully overlap, thus creating a loophole through which the appearance of contradiction may creep in: Some processes have functions that fall under functional definitions of control, but characteristics that do not fall under the second, relational definition (and vice versa). Goal pursuit, discussed in the third section, is a process of this kind: On the one hand, functional definitions of control lead us to view goal adoption and pursuit as controlled processes. On the other hand, results from the last decade show that these processes can occur nonconsciously.

The upshot of the above discussion is that the received view, according to which controlled processes are exclusively conscious, is so strongly entrenched partly due to a confusion between the two meanings of *control.* So what should we do now? For those of us who are interested in the mental processes that help us control our behavior, a functional definition seems to be the one we should stick with. The decision to stick with this type of definition carries far-reaching implications, though: Once we give up the relational definition, then all of the combinations of control and conscious awareness become logically possible and hence suitable candidates for empirical inquiry.

Bargh (1989, 1994) has convincingly argued that automatic processes (especially in the relatively complex areas studied by social cognition) need not possess all of the qualities traditionally ascribed to them (cf. Cohen et al., 1990; Kahneman & Triesman, 1984; Schneider et al., 1984). Similarly, the view developed here suggests that controlled processes need not possess all the qualities that were historically attributed to them. Controlled processes, to be sure, may be intentional and/or conscious, and/or stoppable, and/or effortful, but they do not have to be. Once we accept this, we open the way for a thorough empirical examination of the characteristics of the different psychological processes we categorize as controlled processes. Specifically, this realization calls for an experimental examination of the relations of controlled processes and conscious awareness.

Kahneman and Triesman (1984) distinguished among three levels of automaticity in perception, ranging from strong automaticity (where perceptual processing is neither facilitated by focusing attention nor impaired by diverting attention) to occasional automaticity (where perceptual processes require attention but can sometimes be completed without it). It might well be the case that the empirical examination of controlled processes in their relation to conscious awareness will reveal a similar trichotomy: (1) controlled processes that can occur both consciously and nonconsciously; (2) controlled processes that can be completed outside of conscious awareness but may be speeded, facilitated, or otherwise affected by conscious awareness; and (3) controlled processes that cannot occur nonconsciously.

In terms of this trichotomy, this chapter may be thought of as an existence proof for the first category. Still, the empirical examination of controlled processes in their relation to conscious awareness is just at its infancy, and many interesting questions—and hopefully answers—still lie ahead of us. Two such questions concern the veracity of the trichotomy (e.g., are there processes that fall under the third category?) and understanding the brain and cognitive mechanisms that underlie these different types of processes. This promises to be a difficult and complicated road, but the ramifications of this enterprise for our understanding of central notions, such as conscious awareness, control, choice, and will, may make the journey worth our while.

Acknowledgments I am grateful to John Bargh, Ed Smith, Melissa Ferguson, Alexander Todorov, Jonathan Cohen, Henk Aarts, Yaacov Trope, and Jim Uleman for stimulating discussions of the ideas presented herein. I would also like to thank Eva Walther, K. C. McCulluch, and Ravit Levy for their feedback and helpful comments. Preparation of this chapter was made possible by grant 846/03 from the Israeli Science Foundation.

Notes

1. There is an oddity in these terms that is quite striking: Every process that occurs automatically falls under the category of automatic processes (what else?). But, strangely enough, not every process that is being controlled falls under the category of controlled processes. (Aren't all processes controlled by something? Cf. Dennett, 1984.) Thus, for example, the control of routine actions such as typing does not make typing a controlled process. On the contrary, typing is widely considered an automatic process (Norman & Shallice, 1986). This imbalance taps into complex conceptual issues regarding the meaning of *control* that need to be carefully sorted out, and I start doing so in the epilogue. In the meantime, I use *control* to refer to that kind of control that results in controlled processes.

2. Needless to say, innumerous functions and operations are necessary for succeeding in tasks of this sort. These include, for example, the ability to hear and to see, to comprehend verbal information, to form intentions and to follow them, to delicately move fingers, and so forth. Here, and in similar analyses in the text, I focus on those functions that seem to characterize WM.

3. The notion of "aha-less" insights might seem odd at first. However, the identification of nonconscious correlates of prima facie conscious phenomena is far from new, and characterizes many research programs in cognitive science.

4. Defining the notion of a rule is a task that cannot be undertaken here. I concur with Marcus, Vijayan, Bandi Rao, and Vishton (1999, p. 77), who suggest that if a system learns "open ended abstract relationships for which we can substitute arbitrary items," it thereby learns a rule. These abstract relations include, among other things, equations such as $X_{x+1} = X_n + 2$ and type-token relations that allow for generalizing the characteristics of the type to new tokens.

5. The exact questions are detailed elsewhere (Hassin et al., 2004). It is important to note, however, that we asked participants about awareness of rules both in mathematical forms and in visual forms (that is, visual patterns "created" by the five disks in a given set).

6. The only other difference pertains to the rules used in the experiment. Each block of sets was composed of 10 rule sets, 10 broken rule sets, 10 control sets, and 70 random sets (instead of 7, 7, 7, and 49, respectively, in Experiment 1).

7. I use *behavior* in a wide sense that includes "real life" behaviors such as discrimination on the one hand, and laboratory behaviors such as key presses on the other.

References

Aarts, H., Gollwitzer, P., & Hassin, R. R. (in press). Goal contagion: Perceiving is for pursuing. *Journal of Personality and Social Psychology.*

Aarts, H. & Hassin, R. R. (in press). Automatic goal inferences and contagion. In J. P. Forgas, K. D. Williams, & S. Laham (Eds.), *Social motivation: Conscious and unconscious processes.* Cambridge, UK: Cambridge University Press.

Andrade, J. (2001). The contribution of working memory to conscious experience. In J. Andrade (Ed.), *Working memory in perspective* (pp. 60–78). Philadelphia: Psychology Press.

Andrade, J., Kavanagh, D., & Baddeley, A. (1997). Eye-movements and visual imagery: A working memory approach to the treatment of post-traumatic stress disorder. *British Journal of Clinical Psychology, 36*(2), 209–223.

Baars, B. (1997a). *In the theater of consciousness: The workspace of the mind.* London: Oxford University Press.

Baars, B. (1997b). Some essential differences between consciousness and attention, perception, and working memory. *Consciousness and Cognition: An International Journal, 6*(2–3), 363–371.

Baddeley, A. (1993). Working memory or working attention? In A. Baddeley & L. Weiskrantz (Eds.), *Attention: Selection, awareness, and control: A tribute to Donald Broadbent* (pp. 152–170). New York: Clarendon Press/Oxford University Press.

Baddeley, A. (1996). Exploring the central executive. *Quarterly Journal of Experimental Psychology: Human Experimental Psychology, 49A*(1), 5–28.

Baddeley, A. (2002). Fractionating the central executive. In D. T. Stuss & R. T. Knight (Eds), *Principles of frontal lobe function* (pp. 246–260). London: Oxford University Press.

Baddeley, A., & Hitch, G. (1974). Working memory. In G. Bower (Ed.), *The psychology of learning and motivation: Advances in research and theory* (Vol. 8, pp. 4789). New York: Academic Press.

Baddeley, A. D., & Andrade, J. (2000). Working memory and the vividness of imagery. *Journal of Experimental Psychology: General, 129*(1), 126–145.

Baddeley, A. D., & Logie, R. H. (1999). Working memory: The multiple-component model. In A. Miyake & P. Shah (Eds.), *Models of working memory: Mechanisms of active maintenance and executive control* (pp. 28–69). New York: Cambridge University Press.

Bargh, J. A. (1989). Conditional automaticity: Varieties of automatic influence in social perception and cognition. In J. S. Uleman & J. A. Bargh (Eds.), *Unintended Thought.* New York: Guilford.

Bargh, J. A. (1990). Goal not = intent: Goal-directed thought and behavior are often unintentional. *Psychological Inquiry, 1*(3), 248–251.

Bargh, J. A. (1994). The four horsemen of automaticity: Awareness, intention, efficiency, and control in social cognition. In R. J. Wyer & T. K. Srull (Eds.), *Handbook of social cognition* (pp. 1–40). Hillsdale, NJ: Erlbaum.

Bargh, J. A., Gollwitzer, P., Lee-Chai, A., Barndollar, K., & Trötschel, R. (2001). The automated will: Nonconscious activation and pursuit of behavioral goals. *Journal of Personality and Social Psychology, 81*(6), 1014–1027.

Berry, D. C., & Broadbent, D. E. (1988). Interactive tasks and the implicit-explicit distinction. *British Journal of Psychology, 79*, 251–272.

Carpenter, P., Just, M., & Shell, P. (1990). What one intelligence test measures: A theoretical account of the processing in the Raven Progressive Matrices Test. *Psychological Review, 97*(3), 404–431.

Chartrand, T. L., & Bargh, J. A. (1996). Automatic activation of impression formation and memorization goals: Nonconscious goal priming reproduces effects of explicit task instructions. *Journal of Personality and Social Psychology, 71*(3), 464–478.

Cohen, J., Dunbar, K., & McClelland, J. (1990). On the control of automatic processes: A parallel distributed processing model of the Stroop effect. *Psychological Review, 97*, 332–361.

Daneman, M., & Carpenter, P. (1980). Individual differences in working memory and reading. *Journal of Verbal Learning and Verbal Behavior, 19*(4), 450–466.

Daneman, M., & Carpenter, P. (1983). Individual differences in integrating information between and within sentences. *Journal of Experimental Psychology: Learning, Memory, and Cognition, 9*, 561–584.

Dennett, D. C. (1984). *Elbow room: The varieties of free will worth wanting.* Cambridge, MA: MIT Press.

Devine, P. G., & Monteith. M. J. (1999). Automaticity and control in stereotyping. In S. Chaiken & Y. Trope (Eds.), *Dual process theories in social psychology* (pp. 339–360). New York: Guilford.

Dijksterhuis, A., & Bargh, J. A. (2001). The perception-behavior expressway: Automatic effects of social perception on social behavior. In M. P. Zanna (Ed.), *Advances in experimental social psychology* (Vol. 33, pp. 1–40). San Diego, CA: Academic Press.

Engle, R., Kane, M., & Tuholski, S. (1999). Individual differences in working memory capacity and what they tell us about controlled attention, general fluid intelligence, and functions of the prefrontal cortex. In A. Miyake & P. Shah (Eds.), *Models of working memory: Mechanisms of active maintenance and executive control* (pp. 102–134). New York: Cambridge University Press.

Engle, R., Tuholski, S., Laughlin, J., & Conway, A. (1999). Working memory, short-term memory, and general fluid intelligence: A latent-variable approach. *Journal of Experimental Psychology: General, 128*(3), 309–331.

Garavan, H. (1998). Serial attention within working memory. *Memory and Cognition, 26*(2), 263–276.

Gathercole, S., & Baddeley, A. (1993). *Working memory and language.* Hove, UK: Erlbaum.

Gilbert, D. T., Pelham, B. W., & Krull, D. S. (1988). On cognitive busyness: When person perceivers meet persons perceived. *Journal of Personality and Social Psychology,* 54(5), 733–740.

Hamilton, D. L., Katz, L. B., & Leirer, V. O. (1980). Cognitive representation of personality impressions: Organizational processes in first impression formation. *Journal of Personality and Social Psychology, 39,* 1050–1063.

Hassin, R. R., & Bargh, J. A. (2004). *Flexible automaticity: Evidence from automatic goal pursuit.* Manuscript under review.

Hassin, R. R., Engell, A., Nystrom, L., McCulluch, K. C., & Bargh, J. A. (2004). *Implicit working memory.* Manuscript under review.

Jonides, J., Smith, E. E., Marshuetz, C., Koeppe, R. A., & Reuter-Lorenz, P. A. (1998). Inhibition in verbal working memory revealed by brain activation. *Proceedings of the National Academy of Sciences,* 95, 8410–8413.

Just, M., & Carpenter, P. (1992). A capacity theory of comprehension: Individual differences in working memory. *Psychological Review,* 99(1), 122–149.

Kahneman, D., & Treisman, A. (1984). Changing views of attention and automaticity. In R. Parasuraman & D. Davies (Eds.), *Varieties of attention* (pp. 29–61). New York: Academic Press.

Kihlstrom, J. (1990). The psychological unconscious. In L. Pervin (Ed.), *Handbook of personality: Theory and research* (pp. 445–464). New York: Guilford.

Kihlstrom, J. (1997). Consciousness and me-ness. In J. Cohen & J. Schooler (Eds.), *Scientific approaches to consciousness* (pp. 451–468). Hillsdale, NJ: Erlbaum.

Kintsch, W., Healy, A., Hegarety, M., Pennington, B., & Salthouse, T. (1999). Eight questions and some general issues. In A. Miyake & P. Shah (Eds.), *Models of working memory: Mechanisms of active maintenance and executive control* (pp. 412–441). New York: Cambridge University Press.

Kruglanski, A. W., Shah, J., Fishbach, A., Friedman, R., Chun, W. Y., & Sleeth-Keppler, D. (2002). A theory of goal systems. In M. P. Zanna (Ed.), *Advances in experimental social psychology* (Vol. 34, pp. 331–378). San Diego, CA: Academic Press.

Kyllonen, P., & Christal, R. (1990). Reasoning ability is (little more than) working-memory capacity? *Intelligence,* 14(4), 389–433.

Lewicki, P., Hill, T., & Bizot, E. (1988). Aquisition of procedural knowledge about a pattern of stimuli that cannot be articulated. *Cognitive Psychology, 20,* 323–337.

Lieberman, M., & Rosenthal, R. (2001). Why introverts can't always tell who likes them: Multitasking and nonverbal decoding. *Journal of Personality and Social Psychology, 80*(2), 294–310.

Logie, R., & Gilhooly, K. (1998). *Working memory and thinking.* Hove, U.K.: Psychology Press/Erlbaum.

MacDonald, A. W., Cøhen, J. D., Stenger, V. A., & Carter, C. S. (2000). Dissociating the role of dorsolateral prefrontal cortex and anterior cingulate cortex in cognitive control. *Science, 288,* 1835–1837.

Macrae, C., Bodenhausen, G., Schloerscheidt, A., & Milne, A. (1999). Tales of the unexpected: Executive function and person perception. *Journal of Personality and Social Psychology, 76*(2), 200–213.

Marcus, G. F., Vijayan, S., Bandi Rao, S., & Vishton, P. M. (1999). Rule learning by seven month old infants. *Science, 283,* 77–80.

Merikle, P., & Reingold, E. (1992). Measuring unconscious perceptual processes. In R. Bornstein & T. Pittman (Eds.), *Perception without awareness: Cognitive, clinical, and social perspectives* (pp. 55–80). New York: Guilford.

Metcalfe, J. (1986a). Feeling of knowing in memory and problem solving. *Journal of Experimental Psychology: Learning, Memory, and Cognition, 12*(2), 288–294.

Metcalfe, J. (1986b). Premonitions of insight predict impending error. *Journal of Experimental Psychology: Learning, Memory and Cognition, 12,* 623–634.

Metcalfe, J., & Wiebe, D. (1987). Intuition in insight and noninsight problem solving. *Memory and Cognition, 15*(3), 238–246.

Miyake, A., Friedman, N. P., Emerson, M. J., Witzki, A. H., & Howerter, A. (2000). The unity and diversity of executive functions and their contributions to complex "frontal lobe" tasks: A latent variable analysis. *Cognitive Psychology, 41,* 49–100.

Miyake, A., & Shah, P. (1999). *Models of working memory: Mechanisms of active maintenance and executive control.* New York: Cambridge University Press.

Moskowitz, G., Gollwitzer, P., Wasel, W., & Schaal, B. (1999). Preconscious control of stereotype activation through chronic egalitarian goals. *Journal of Personality and Social Psychology, 77*(1), 167–184.

Nissen, M. J., & Bullemer, P. (1987). Attentional requirements of learning: Evidence from performance measures. *Cognitive Psychology, 19*(1), 1–32.

Norman, D. A., & Shallice, T. (1986). Attention to action: Willed and automatic control of behaviour. In R. J. Davidson, G. E. Schwartz, & D. Shapiro (Eds.), *Consciousness and self regulation.* New York: Plenum.

Nozick, R. (2001). *Invariances: The structure of the objective world.* Cambridge, MA: Harvard University Press.

O'Reilly, R., Braver, T., & Cohen, J. (1999). A biologically based computational model of working memory. In A. Miyake & P. Shah (Eds.), *Models of working memory: Mechanisms of active maintenance and executive control* (pp. 375–411). New York: Cambridge University Press.

Reber, A. (1976). Implicit learning of synthetic languages: The role of instructional set. *Journal of Experimental Psychology: Human Learning and Memory, 2*(1), 88–94.

Reber, A. S. (1993). *Implicit learning and tacit knowledge: An essay on the cognitive unconscious.* London: Oxford University Press.

Schneider, W., Dumais, S. T., & Shiffrin, R. M. (1984). Automatic and control processing and attention. In R. Parasuraman & D. R. Davies (Eds.), *Varieties of attention* (pp. 1–27). Orlando, FL: Academic Press.

Shah, J. (2003). The motivational looking glass: How significant others implicitly affect goal appraisals. *Journal of Personality and Social Psychology, 85*(3), 424–439.

Smith, E., & Jonides, J. (1995). Working memory in humans: Neuropsychological evidence. In M. S. Gazzaniga (Ed.), *The cognitive neurosciences* (pp. 1009–1020). Cambridge, MA: MIT Press.

Smith, E., & Jonides, J. (1999). Storage and executive processes in the frontal lobes. *Science, 283,* 1657–1661.

Stadler, M. A., & Frensch, P. A. (1998). *Handbook of implicit learning.* Los Angeles: Sage.

Sternberg, R. J., & Davidson, J. E. (1995). *The nature of insight.* Cambridge, MA: MIT Press.

Teasdale, J. D., Dritschel, B. H., Taylor, M. J., & Proctor, L. (1995). Stimulus-independent thought depends on central executive resources. *Memory and Cognition, 23,* 551–559.

Trope, Y. (1986). Identification and inferential processes in dispositional attributions. *Psychological Review, 93,* 239–257.

Trope, Y., & Fishbach, A. (2000). Counteractive self-control in overcoming temptation. *Journal of Personality and Social Psychology, 79*(4), 493–506.

Tversky, A., & Kahneman, D. (1974). Judgment under uncertainty: Heuristics and biases. *Science, 185,* 1124–1131.

Wegner, D. M., & Bargh, J. A. (1998). Control and automaticity in social life. In D. Gilbert & S. Fiske (Eds.), *The handbook of social psychology* (Vol. 2, pp. 446–496). New York: McGraw-Hill.

PART III

INTENTION AND THEORY OF MIND

9

Folk Theory of Mind: Conceptual Foundations of Human Social Cognition

Bertram F. Malle

The ability to represent, conceptualize, and reason about mental states is one of the greatest achievements of human evolution. Having an appreciation for the workings of the mind is considered a prerequisite for natural language acquisition (Baldwin & Tomasello, 1998), strategic social interaction (McCabe, Smith, & LePore, 2000), reflexive thought (Bogdan, 2000), and moral development (Hoffman, 1993). The initial research on representations of mental states was sparked by the hypothesis that apes, too, have such a theory of mind (Premack & Woodruff, 1978), but more recent theories and evidence suggest that the evolutionary emergence of a genuine theory of mind occurred after the hominid split off and may thus be uniquely human (Baron-Cohen, 1999; Malle, 2002; Povinelli, 1996, 2001; Tomasello, 1998).

The ability to reason about mental states has been called a theory of mind because it shares some features with scientific theories (Gopnik & Meltzoff, 1997; Gopnik & Wellman, 1994; Wellman, 1990): It postulates unobservables, predicts them from observables, and uses them to explain other observables. This model of theoretical inference is often contrasted with a model according to which people deal with other minds by simulating, in their own minds, what is going on in the other person (Goldman, 1989, 2001; Gordon, 1986; see also Blakemore & Decety, 2001). However, the two approaches are compatible if we regard simulation as one of several processes involved in attributing mental states (another being inference) and if we recognize that both processes rely crucially on a conceptual framework of mental states and their relation to behavior. I will thus refer with the convenient phrase "theory of mind" to this conceptual framework of mind and behavior, allowing a variety of cognitive processes, such as simulation or inference, to make use of the framework (see Malle, 2001).

In social psychology, considerations of others' mental states have often been treated as a special case of dispositional inference, akin to imputing traits, or merely as a precursor to imputing traits (Jones & Davis, 1965; Shaver, 1975). Mental states are comparable to traits in that they are unobservable constructs, but they have a number of unique features. First, mental states are conceptualized in folk psychology as events that actually occur in a distinct domain—that of "minds" or subjective experience; by contrast, the location and nature of traits are left fairly unspecified and abstract. Second, perceivers expect mental states of other agents to be roughly of the same nature as their own mental states and therefore use their own minds to simulate others' mental states, whereas they do not use their own personality to simulate others' traits. Third, and most important, reasoning about mental states is part of a unique and sophisticated conceptual framework that relates different mental states to each other and links them up to behavior (D'Andrade, 1987; Malle & Knobe, 1997a). The nature and elements of this framework of mind and its central functions for social cognition are the topic of this chapter.

Theory of Mind as a Conceptual Framework

A conceptual framework can be regarded as a cognitive capacity that operates prior to any particular conscious or unconscious cognition and provides (by means of classification and process initiation) the framing or interpretation of that cognition. This framing process is unconscious in an interesting way. Most unconscious processes perform roughly the same functions as do corresponding conscious processes; they just do it more efficiently. (Therein lies the appeal of much modern research on the unconscious, which shows that plenty goes on below the awareness threshold that nevertheless is quite similar to what goes on above the threshold.) But a conceptual framework performs a function that no specific conscious or unconscious process can perform; rather, it is presupposed by these processes.

Take the case of a perceiver who notices another person pull out his wallet in front of a cashier. Without a conceptual framework of mind and behavior, the perceiver would not understand what the larger object's interaction with the smaller object means. She would also be rather ineffective at predicting the other large object's likely response. With a framework of mind and behavior, however, perceivers can parse this complex scene into fundamental categories of reaching, grasping, and exchanging (Baird & Baldwin, 2001; Woodward, Sommerville, & Guajardo, 2001), and after acquiring the pertinent cultural knowledge, they elaborate their interpretation into the script of paying (Schank & Abelson, 1977). People's theory of mind thus frames and interprets perceptions of human behavior in a particular way—as perceptions of agents who can act intentionally and who have feelings, desires, and beliefs that guide their actions (Gopnik & Meltzoff, 1997; Perner, 1991; Wellman, 1990).

When this framing and interpretation are lacking, as in the case of autism (Baron-Cohen, 1995; Frith, 2000; Leslie, 1992), the resulting social perception is strangely mechanical and raw. One autistic person (in a fascinating e-mail discussion about theory of mind) reports:

> I know people's faces down to the acne scars on the left corners of their chins and what their eyes do when they speak, and how the hairs of their eyebrows curl, and how their hairlines curve around the tops of their foreheads. . . . The best I can do is start picking up bits of data during my encounter with them because there's not much else I can do. It's pretty tiring, though, and explains something of why social situations are so draining for me. . . . That said, I'm not sure what kind of information about them I'm attempting to process. (Blackburn, Gottschewski, George, & L——, 2000)

What seems to be missing, as another autistic discussant remarks, is an "automatic processing of 'people information.'" The data come in, but they cannot be interpreted in a parsimonious way using concepts of agency and mind. "Instead, it is all processing abstract concepts and systems—much like computer programs or physical forces" (Blackburn et al., 2000). Or, as one discussant put it, "autistic people who are very intelligent may learn to model other people in a more analytical way." This mechanical, analytical mode of processing, however, is very tiresome and slow: "Given time I may be able to analyze someone in various ways, and seem to get good results, but may not pick up on certain aspects of an interaction until I am obsessing over it hours or days later" (Blackburn et al., 2000).

How is it possible that some people interpret social information so effortlessly while others struggle to find meaning in it? It has been known for some time that human cognition relies heavily on associative structures such as schemas and scripts that simplify encounters with complex stimuli (e.g., Fiske & Taylor, 1991; Schank & Abelson, 1977). But these structures are characterized as a form or process of representation that is so generally applicable that it does not constrain (or code for) the content that it represents. On the level of cognitive organization, then, the schema of a social action such as paying looks just like the schema of a rainstorm brewing.

What is then social about social cognition? The answer usually points to the type and complexity of objects that are at stake—social cognition, in short, is cognition of social objects such as people, relations, groups, and the self (Fiske & Taylor, 1991; Schneider, 1991). But the category of a social object is precisely what general cognitive structures, content-free as they are, cannot easily identify or distinguish from nonsocial objects. How does a general cognitive process "know," as it were, that it deals with another person rather than a lifeless object? (One can easily see the adaptive importance of such a discrimination.) To perform this discrimination fast and efficiently, the human mind appears to rely on a conceptual framework that classifies certain stimuli into basic social categories. Details aside, objects that are self-propelled are classified into the category of agent (Premack, 1990), the coordinated movements of an agent are classified into the category of action (Wellman & Phillips, 2001), and so forth. This category system develops early in childhood, presumably aided by an innate sensitivity to certain stimulus configurations in streams of behavior (Baldwin & Baird, 1999; Dittrich & Lea, 1994; Gergely, Nádasdy, Csibra, & Bíró, 1995; Woodward et al., 2001; see chapter 10, this volume). Once in place and well practiced, the category system can be activated very easily, as Heider and Simmel (1944) have shown with stimuli as simple as triangles that move around in space, and it can be applied to complex objects such as machines or computers (Dennett, 1987; Nass & Moon, 2000).[1]

A theory of mind is thus a framework through which certain perceptual input is interpreted or conceptualized as an agent, an intentional action, or a belief; moreover, it frames and directs further processing that is promptly performed on this input (e.g., an inference of the agent's motive for the action). People with a deficient theory of mind, by contrast, might take in all the information that is available (facial features, body movements, etc.), but they lack the network of concepts that would allow them to interpret with ease and swiftness the meaning of this information (see Baron-Cohen, 1992).

If the conceptual framework of mind and behavior, once developed to maturity, is presupposed by any specific conscious or unconscious cognition of human behavior, then this framework resembles Kantian categories of (social) perception—that is, the fundamental concepts by which people grasp social reality. Let me explore this parallel a bit further. Kant (1787/1998) postulated a number of categories that the human mind applies to the perception of objects (among them space, time, causality, and substance). These categories, Kant argued, are not just arbitrary frames of perception but the very conditions of the possibility of perception. By analogy, the concepts of a theory of mind would then be the conditions of the possibility of social cognition. This should not be taken as a logical claim (i.e., that to posit social cognition without a theory of mind would be a formal contradiction); rather, we may say that this framework provides the concepts in terms of which social cognition and interpretation have proven effective for dealing with other human beings.

This view also allows for cases in which these concepts are missing (as in autism, but also in certain forms of frontal brain damage, and in other animals) and for cases in which the concepts have not yet developed (as in very young children). Both types of cases are highly instructive as evidence for the claim that theory of mind is a domain-specific structure or module (e.g.,

Baron-Cohen, 1995; Hirschfeld & Gelman, 1994; Leslie, 1995; Wellman, 1990). For example, even though autistic children have enormous difficulties with reasoning about mental states, they show average or above-average capabilities in causal reasoning about physical events (Baron-Cohen, Leslie, & Frith, 1985; for reviews see Baron-Cohen, 2000; Leslie, 1992). However, theory of mind is not an isolated module either. Executive control appears to play a role in mental-state reasoning (Carlson, Moses, & Hicks, 1998; Hughes, 1998), and introspection may be involved in it as well (Goldman, 2001). Moreover, the capacity for language is linked to theory of mind in both development and evolution (Malle, 2002). For example, a rudimentary appreciation of others' attention focus and communicative intentions is involved in early word learning (Baldwin, 1993), but mastery of certain syntactic structures may be a prerequisite for the realization that beliefs are subjective representations of reality (De Villiers, 2000).

Unfortunately, research has focused primarily on cases in which theory of mind is either missing or not yet fully developed. It appears that the capacities to simulate and reason about mental states are taken for granted among adult social perceivers, and only the absence of this capacity attracts attention among ordinary folk or psychologists. In particular, research on the fundamental assumption that others are agents who act on the basis of mental states is not a central concern of current social psychology, even though several pioneers of the field emphasized its importance. Asch (1952), for example, argued that people "interact with each other . . . via emotions and thoughts that are capable of taking into account the emotions and thoughts of others" (p. 142). Similarly, Heider (1958) emphasized that "persons have abilities, wishes and sentiments; they can act purposefully, and can perceive or watch us" (p. 21). And Tagiuri, in the foreword to the seminal volume by Tagiuri and Petrullo (1958), proposed to use "the term person perception whenever the perceiver regards the object as having the potential of representation and intentionality" (p. x). Besides work on empathy and perspective taking (e.g., Davis, Conklin, Smith, & Luce, 1996; Ickes, 1997; Krauss, Fussell, & Chen, 1995), contemporary social psychology includes few investigations into the social perception of mental states. But perhaps this trend is reversing with the growing recognition that mental-state inference is one of the most fundamental tools of social cognition (Ames, in press; Baldwin & Tomasello, 1998; Bogdan, 2000; Graesser, Singer, & Trabasso, 1994; Malle, Moses, & Baldwin, 2001; McCabe et al., 2000; Trabasso & Stein, 1994).

Mind and Behavior

The social-cognitive function of a theory of mind is not just to paint a picture of the mental landscape but to support the understanding of and coordination with other people's behavior, which is achieved by linking behavior to mind (chapter 10). Taking into account the mental states of others helps people make sense of past behavior, permits influence on present behavior, and allows prediction of future behavior. At the same time, reasoning about the mind is grounded in behavioral evidence to maintain reliability and to permit intersubjective discourse about mental states (Bartsch & Wellman, 1995). Without this discourse, mental-state inference would be a private and haphazard endeavor, opening up radical self-other asymmetries instead of facilitating human coordination (Wittgenstein, 1953).

The specific connections between mental states and behavior are usually of two kinds: mental states finding their expression in behavior (such as anger shown in the face) and mental states guiding or influencing behavior (such as an intention to act). Significantly, behavior that is connected to mental states breaks down into two fundamentally different types (Heider, 1958): intentional action, which is caused by the agent's intention and decision; and unintentional behavior, which can be caused by internal or external events without the intervention of the agent's decision. This distinction is one of the most influential and illuminating concepts of the folk theory of mind (Malle et al., 2001).

Intentionality

Intentionality is a complex folk concept that specifies under what conditions people judge a behavior as intentional (or done on purpose).[2] This judgment relies on (at least) five conditions (Malle & Knobe, 1997a; Mele, 2001): An action is considered intentional when the agent had (1) a desire for an outcome, (2) a belief that the action would lead to that outcome, (3) an intention to perform the action, (4) the skill to perform the action, and (5) awareness of fulfilling the intention while performing the action. Of course, the cognitive process of assessing intentionality often relies on cues and heuristics rather than on a five-step decision process (e.g., Knobe, 2003). However, the folk concept sets the boundaries for any judgment of intentionality and provides the conditions that settle disputes about an action's intentionality.

Some of the individual components of the intentionality concept are themselves powerful tools for making sense of behavior. For example, people differentiate between two motivational states, desire and intention, when explaining, predicting, and influencing behavior. The two states differ in at least three respects (Malle & Knobe, 2001). First, intentions represent the intender's own action ("I intend to A," where A is an action), whereas desires can represent anything ("I want O," where O can be an object or state of affairs, including another person's actions or experiences). Second, intentions are based on a certain amount of reasoning, whereas desires are typically the input to such reasoning ("I intend to A because I want O"). Third, intentions come with a characteristic commitment to perform the intended action whereas desires do not. This distinction has clear consequences for self-regulation, interpersonal perception, and social coordination (including its breakdown in the case of misunderstandings), and future research on these relations would be highly desirable.

Another important folk distinction revealed by the intentionality concept is that between desires and beliefs. Desires are strongly embedded in a culture's shared knowledge base (Bruner, 1990) and are considered the primary motives of action (Searle, 1984, chapter 4). This is because desires represent the end toward which the agent strives, whereas beliefs represent the various aspects of the path toward that end (Dretske, 1988). Desires also seem more primitive and easier to infer for children, who learn to attribute desires before they learn to attribute beliefs (e.g., Nelson-LeGall, 1985; Wellman & Woolley, 1990; Yuill & Perner, 1988). Relatedly, most autistic children lack the ability to ascribe beliefs to other people but have less difficulty ascribing desires to them (Baron-Cohen, 1995). Among adults, too, beliefs and desires have distinct informational and impression-management functions when used in explanations of action (Malle, Knobe, O'Laughlin, Pearce, & Nelson, 2000).

The full concept of intentionality plays an important role in a number of social-cognitive phenomena. Frequently mentioned is its impact on the assignment of responsibility and blame for actions (e.g., Shaver, 1985): Agents are more likely to be held responsible or to be blamed when they performed the action in question intentionally. But even for unintentional behaviors and outcomes, the concept of intentionality is at work. Responsibility is still assigned when the outcome is considered to have been preventable (aka controllable; Weiner, 1995) by the agent and when it was his or her duty to do so (Hamilton, 1978). Both preventability and duty entail intentionality, because assigning duties to a person presumes that the person can intentionally fulfill them, and preventability presumes that the agent could have intentionally prevented the outcome.

Perhaps the most important function of the intentionality concept is to divide all behavioral events into two different domains that are subsequently manipulated in distinct ways by various cognitive tools (e.g., attention, explanation, prediction, blame). Heider (1958) was the first social psychologist to emphasize that people not only distinguish between intentional and unintentional behavior but also assume two different models of causality for them: Intentional behavior relies on agentic ("personal") causality, in which actions are based on the agent's reasons, deliberation, and formation of an intention; unintentional behavior relies on mechanical ("impersonal") causality, in which no reason or intention is involved.[3]

Observability

Another folk distinction leads to different cognitive manipulations: that between publicly observable and publicly unobservable events (Funder & Dobroth, 1987; John & Robins, 1993; Malle & Knobe, 1997b), which is really the distinction between mind and behavior. Considered jointly, the concepts of intentionality and observability generate a map of behavioral events that are relevant to social cognition—that is, events that people attend to, try to explain, predict, and evaluate (Malle & Knobe, 1997b; Malle & Pearce, 2001).

Attention to and Explanation of Behavioral Events

For convenience, we (Malle & Knobe, 1997b) adopted the following labels for the four regions of the behavioral events map: actions (observable and intentional), mere behaviors (observable and unintentional), intentional thoughts (intentional and unobservable), and experiences (unintentional and unobservable; see table 9.1). The labels themselves are of little significance, but the conceptual definitions of event types as combinations of intentionality and observability are. That is because the features of intentionality and observability allow us to predict, using a few simple postulates, the patterns of attention to and explanation of these behavioral events under various conditions (e.g., from the actor and the observer role and in communication or private thought).

Which Behaviors People Attend To To predict the allocation of attention to the four behavioral events in social interaction, we identified two factors that are known to govern attention allocation in general (e.g., Fiske & Taylor, 1991; Posner, 1980) and that are important to social interaction as well: epistemic access and motivational relevance. First, to turn one's attention to a particular behavioral event, one needs to have access to it—that is, become in some way aware of it taking place (through introspection, perception, or at least inference). Second, attention to an event increases if it is relevant (i.e., helpful) for the perceiver's processing or coordinating the current interaction (e.g., Jones & Thibaut, 1958; Wyer, Srull, Gordon, & Hartwick, 1982).

For actors, epistemic access is greater to their own unobservable events than to their own observable events, because they are constantly presented

Table 9.1 Postulated Folk Classification of Behavioral Events

	Intentional	Unintentional
Observable	Actions	Mere behaviors
Unobservable	Intentional thoughts	Experiences

with their stream of consciousness but cannot easily monitor their own facial expressions, gestures, or posture (Bull, 1987; DePaulo, 1992; Gilovich, Savitsky, & Medvec, 1998). For observers, access is greater to other people's observable events than to their unobservable (mental) events. We therefore predicted that social interactants attend to observable events more as observers than as actors, whereas they attend to unobservable events more as actors than as observers (Hypothesis 1).

In addition, for observers the perceived relevance of intentional events is greater than that of unintentional events. That is because intentional events define the main business of an encounter (Goffman, 1974), because they are directed at the other person and thereby demand a response, and because they have powerful effects on the other's emotions and moral evaluations (Shaver, 1985). By contrast, for actors the perceived relevance of unintentional events is greater than that of intentional events, because unintentional events are not controlled and therefore must be monitored and understood, whereas the execution of intentional events frequently relies on automatic programs (Norman & Shallice, 1986). We therefore predicted, second, that social interactants attend to intentional events more as observers than as actors, and they attend to unintentional events more as actors than as observers (Hypothesis 2).

We tested these predictions using an experimental paradigm in which pairs of participants had a conversation and, immediately afterward, were asked to report in writing everything "that was going on" with their partner (on one page) and with themselves (on another page), in counterbalanced order. The reports were then coded for references to behavioral events (verb phrases that referred to actions, mere behaviors, intentional thoughts, or experiences) and classified according to their intentionality and observability (for details of the coding, see http://darkwing.uoregon.edu/~interact/bevd.html).

Results across three studies confirmed both hypotheses (Malle & Pearce, 2001). In conversations among strangers, people reported overall 8 to 10 behavioral events per page (i.e., per perspective), but supporting Hypothesis 1, actors reported 2.3 more unobservable events than did observers, and observers reported 2.3 more observable events than did actors ($\eta^2 = 50–60\%$).[4] In addition, supporting Hypothesis 2, actors reported 1.1 more unintentional events than did observers, and observers reported 1.1 more intentional events than did actors ($\eta^2 = 14–19\%$). These results suggest that a social perceiver's attention to behavioral events is systematically influenced by the intentionality and observability of those events and by the psychological processes of epistemic access and motivational relevance.

Which Behaviors People Wonder About and Explain Given this effect of intentionality and observability on the events people attend to, we should expect parallel patterns in the events people wonder about and try to explain. Moreover, the principles that guided the predictions in the domain of attention should be similar to those in the domain of wondering and explaining, because the latter two processes imply a focused form of attention, guided by specific goals (Malle & Knobe, 1997b). Thus, for an event to elicit a wondering why (and, under most circumstances, an explanation), three conditions must be met: there must be access (people must be aware of the event to wonder about it), nonunderstanding (people must not already have an explanation for the event), and relevance (people must find it useful and important to generate an explanation for the event).

From these conditions, we derived two predictions about patterns of wonderings: Because of differential access, actors should wonder more often about unobservable than observable events, while observers should wonder more often about observable than unobservable events. In addition, because of differential nonunderstanding, actors should wonder more often about unintentional than intentional events, and because of relevance observers should wonder more often about intentional than unintentional events (for details, see Malle & Knobe, 1997b, pp. 289–290).

We tested these predictions in two studies, collecting wonderings from memory protocols and twentieth-century novels and systematically coding the intentionality and observability of the events explained (http://darkwing.uoregon.edu/~interact/bev.html). Confirming our predictions, actors wondered about more unobservable events (67%) than observable events (33%), whereas observers wondered about more observable events (74%) than unobservable events (26%). In addition, actors wondered about more unintentional events (63%) than intentional events (27%), whereas observers wondered about more intentional events (67%) than unintentional events (74%).

When deriving predictions about patterns of explanations (which are answers to wonderings), we drew a distinction between explanations that are directed to oneself (in private thought) and explanations that are directed to a partner (in communication). Explanations to oneself answer one's own wonderings, so they should show the same actor-observer asymmetries as wonderings do, and data collected from memory protocols and diaries strongly confirmed this prediction. Explanations to other people in communication, however, answer the others' wonderings, which come from the observer perspective, and so actors should explain behavioral events about which observers wonder, namely, intentional and observable ones. Observers, meanwhile, still explain the events that they wonder about (also intentional and observable ones), so in communication we expect no actor-observer asymmetries in the kinds of behavioral events people explain, and that was what we found (Malle & Knobe, 1997b).

The studies on attention and explanation of behavioral events suggest that one function of the folk theory of mind and behavior is to divide the diversity of human behavioral and psychological stimuli into broad classes, such as action, experience, and so on, guided by the concepts of intentionality and observability. These event classes can be more easily managed cognitively by social perceivers, and they are tied to certain assumptions, such as about epistemic access and motivational relevance. Once again, these categorizations into broad event classes and their attendant assumptions in subsequent processing are not a matter of conscious decision ("I classify this as an action"; "I will pay more attention to her actions than to my own actions"). Some of the subsequent processes can certainly be put under conscious control, such as when an empathy instruction leads social perceivers to increase their attention to the other person's thoughts and feelings (Davis et al., 1996; Klein & Hodges, 2001; Malle & Pearce, 2001). But the classificatory function of the framework of mind and behavior precedes any particular processing.

Because the conceptual presorting that is achieved by a theory of mind guides and frames subsequent processes such as attention and explanation, variations in the conceptual framework itself will have direct effects on people's attention and explanations. For example, the degree of refinement in a theory of mind will influence the balance of attention allocation to all four behavioral event types. Consider the following remark by an autistic person: "It seems impossible to try to focus on my own thoughts or feelings and consider different thoughts or feelings in another person or persons at the same time, especially if I am talking or actively listening to the other person talk" (Blackburn et al., 2000). If the process of conceptual classification comes with ease and little ambiguity along the category boundaries, then attention regulation can more easily operate on it, because a directive such as "Attend more to the other's experiences" can be readily implemented. By contrast, if the conceptual classification is onerous, unreliable, and full of vagueness, then attentional regulation will have a difficult time holding on to the correct events and letting attention, explanation, or other processes operate on it.

Folk Explanations of Behavior

After discussing the categorization of behavioral events, I now move to the question of how and for what purpose people explain behavioral events. The folk theory of mind plays a vital role in behavior explanations. Indeed, explaining behavior has sometimes been characterized as the hallmark of folk psychology, even though other processes such as prediction, control, and evaluation are of equal importance. Explanations, however, often come in verbal form and are therefore more amenable to investigation, especially if we want to learn about both their conceptual underpinnings and their role in social interaction.

Explanations and Theory of Mind

A first issue to address is the functional relation between behavior explanations and theory of mind. Is the function of a folk theory of mind to explain behavior, as most scholars assume, or is the function of explanations to rehearse and advance the theory of mind, as Gopnik (1998) suggests? Gopnik argues that explanations are like orgasm, which does not itself fulfill an evolutionary function but makes procreation, the important end, more desirable. However, the analogy becomes questionable when we consider that explanations, unlike orgasms, have many important uses beside making another end (theory advance) more desirable. That is, in addition to advancing theory of mind, explanations help in making sense of concurrent behavior, coordinating joint action, offering clarification, managing impressions, and so on. Furthermore, a theory of mind—even a very advanced one—is not really good for anything unless it improves or expands social performance and hence adaptive fitness either of the individual or the group. Behavior explanations constitute one such performance domain that is improved (or made possible) by a theory of mind, with others being prediction and influence. So the function of a theory of mind is not merely to explain behavior but to facilitate—by means of explanations and other tools—successful social cognition and social coordination (Malle, 2002). At the same time, the function of explanations is not merely to advance a theory of mind but to facilitate select social tasks, such as understanding, coordination, and impression management.

Now I can tackle in more detail the connection between the conceptual framework of mind and the social activity of offering behavior explanations. One possible position is that explanations within a theory of mind make behaviors understandable by identifying their mental causes. This is the position taken by some developmental researchers, who have traced the origin and advancement of explanations throughout the preschool years, demonstrating that children as young as 3 years systematically use "psychological" (mental state) explanations for human behavior (Wellman, Hickling, & Schult, 1997). However, these researchers group under psychological explanations statements that refer to the agent's desires and beliefs but also statements that refer to moods and lack of knowledge (Bartsch & Wellman, 1995, chapter 6; Schult & Wellman, 1997).

This global classification is problematic because it loses sight of two types of causation that people distinguish (Buss, 1978; Heider, 1958; Malle, 1999; Searle, 1983): The first type, intentional causation, refers to mental states as reasons of an agent's intentional action; the second may be called involuntary or "mechanical" causation, which refers to a variety of factors (including mental states) as causes of an agent's unintentional behavior. Current developmental studies leave open the question whether 3-year-old children who give mental-state explanations differentiate between mental states as reasons (for intentional behavior; e.g., "She bought milk because she wanted to make a cake") and mental states as mere causes (for unintentional behavior; e.g., "She was nervous because she really wanted to win the game"). Perhaps children first apply mental-state explanations broadly to human behavior and learn to distinguish between reasons and other (mental) causes only after acquiring the full-fledged concept of intentionality, around the age of 5 (Shultz & Wells, 1985). Command over this concept involves the differentiation of action-relevant mental states into the triad of belief, desire, and intention, which are partially confounded at an earlier age (chapter 10, this volume; Lyon, 1993; Moses, 2001). This emerging competence involves the understanding that beliefs and desires are combined in a reasoning process to give rise to intentions, which in turn direct action (Malle & Knobe, 1997a), and this understanding amounts to an appreciation of the scope and limits of choice, also acquired around the age of 5 (Kalish, 1998).

My goal now is to outline the fully mature system of behavior explanations among adults and its grounding in a theory of mind. This grounding entails that behavior explanations can be constructed only within the conceptual space of the folk theory of mind, and this space is broadly defined by the major distinction between intentional and unintentional behavior and by the specific concepts of reason and intention that underlie the folk notion of intentional action (Malle, 1999, 2001). To begin, I introduce a model of folk explanation that features four modes of explanation differentiated by the kinds of behaviors they explain (intentional vs. unintentional) and the specific aspects of behavior they explain. Then I discuss conditions of use for each explanation mode. I close with an emphasis on both the cognitive and interpersonal functions of explanations, which also illuminate the cognitive and interpersonal functions of the folk theory of mind.

Four Modes of Behavior Explanation

When explaining behavior, people distinguish sharply between intentional and unintentional events (Heider, 1958; Malle, 1999; White, 1991), relying on the folk concept of intentionality (discussed earlier). Unintentional events are explained by referring to mechanical causal factors (e.g., mental states, traits, others' behaviors, physical events), and we may label them *cause explanations* (top of figure 9.1). Traditional attribution models apply fairly well to these cause explanations, because people presume no other link between explanation and behavior besides causality (i.e., no components of intentionality such as awareness or intention).

Where traditional attribution theory fails is in its account of how people explain intentional behavioral events. These events are far more complex in that they are defined, according to the folk concept of intentionality, by

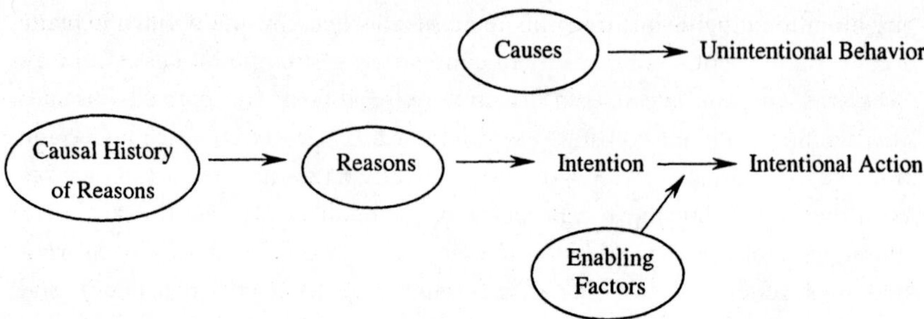

Figure 9.1 Four modes of explanation for unintentional and intentional behavior.

awareness that accompanies the behavior, an intention that precedes the behavior, and beliefs and desires that precede and rationally support the intention (Malle & Knobe, 1997a). As a result of this complex definition, explanations of intentional behavior break down into three modes, which correspond to three domains people find worth explaining (figure 9.1): *reasons, causal history of reasons*, and *enabling factors*.

Reason Explanations The first and most important mode of behavior explanation comprises the agent's reasons for acting (Audi, 1993; Buss, 1978; Davidson, 1963; Locke & Pennington, 1982; Malle, 1999). Reasons are seen as representational states (i.e., mental states that represent an object or proposition) that the agent combines in a process of reasoning that leads to an intention and, if all goes well, to the intended action.

The concept of intentionality specifies two paradigmatic types of reasons that precede the formation of an intention: the agent's desire for an outcome and a belief that the intended action leads to that outcome. For example, a student explained why she chose psychology as her major by saying, "I want to go to graduate school in counseling psychology [desire]; I think psychology is the right major to have as background for counseling psychology [belief]." In many naturally occurring explanations, other reasons are mentioned in addition to or instead of the paradigmatic ones, such as desires for avoiding alternative outcomes, beliefs about the context, beliefs about consequences, and valuings of the action itself. In all these cases, when an agent forms an intention in light of certain beliefs, desires, or valuings, these mental states constitute the reasons for which the agent forms the intention.

Reasons have two defining features, which can be labeled subjectivity and rationality (Malle, 1999, 2001; Malle et al., 2000). Subjectivity refers to the fact that reason explanations cite what explainers consider the agent's own subjective reasons for acting. That is, explainers try to reconstruct the deliberations (minimal as they may be) that the agent underwent when forming an intention to act and thus take the agent's subjective viewpoint when explaining the action. For example, the explanation "My father puts pressure on me because he wants many doors to be open to me" cites a desire in light of which (the explainer assumes) the father decided to put pressure on her. In another example, "Why did she rush off?—She thought she was late for her class," we see even more clearly the subjectivity assumption, because the explainer uses a mental verb to explicitly mark the agent's subjective belief and implies that, in reality, she probably was not late. It was that subjective belief (and not objective reality) that guided the agent's action and thus explains it.

Rationality, the second defining feature of reason explanations, refers to the fact that the contents of beliefs, desires, and valuings that are cited as reasons have to hang together so as to offer rational support for the reasonableness of the intention or action that they brought about. Philosophers often speak of a "practical reasoning argument" that has reasons as its premises and the intention to act as its conclusion (e.g., Harman, 1976; Snare, 1991). The folk concept of rational support is probably not as strict; it demands merely that the intended action is a reasonable thing to do in light of this agent's desires and beliefs about fulfilling those desires. In the example above, the agent's action of rushing off was rationally supported by her belief that she was late for class (and it would not have been rationally supported if the agent had thought there was plenty of time left or if she had had no desire to be on time). To make explicit the practical argument in this example, we would need to add (at least) her desire to be on time and her belief that rushing off may help her get to class on time. But one of the fascinating aspects of reason explanations is that the conceptual constraints that the folk theory of mind puts on reasons (particularly the assumptions of subjectivity and rationality) allow explainers to mention a single reason and to trust the audience to fill in the remaining reasons and comprehend why the agent decided to act (Malle, 1999; Slugoski, Lalljee, Lamb, & Ginsburg, 1993).

Causal History of Reason Explanations The second domain of explanation refers to factors that lie in the causal history of reasons (CHR) and thus clarify what led up to these reasons in the first place (Hirschberg, 1978; Locke & Pennington, 1982; Malle, 1994). For example, the statement "Anne invited Ben for dinner because she is friendly" attempts to explain Anne's action, but the content of the explanation ("she is friendly") refers to a factor in the causal history of her reasons, not to a reason itself. The explainer would not claim that Anne deliberated, "I am friendly—I should invite Ben for dinner"; rather, the explainer cites Anne's friendly disposition as a relevant causal history or background to whatever specific reasons Anne had for inviting Ben. Causal history explanations do not just cite traits (in fact, only about 20% of them refer to traits) but also include childhood experiences, culture, past behavior, current physiological states, and situational cues that trigger a particular belief or desire (Malle, 1999).

Even though CHR explanations help clarify intentional actions, they do not function like reasons and therefore are not subject to the constraints of subjectivity and rationality. That is, the agent need not have considered or been aware of the causal history factors cited in the explanation (Malle et al., 2000), nor do CHR factors provide rational support for an explained action.

Enabling Factor Explanations The third domain of explaining intentional action refers to factors that enabled the action to come about as intended (Malle, 1999). Such enabling factor explanations refer to the agent's skill, effort, opportunities, or facilitating circumstances (see McClure & Hilton, 1997; Turnbull, 1986). These explanations take it for granted that the agent had an intention (and reasons) to perform the behavior and clarify not what motivated the agent but how it was possible that the action was successfully performed. For example, "She hit her free throws because she had practiced them all week." There is no mention of the agent's reasons (or any causal history of those reasons); rather, the explanation clarifies how it was possible that the agent acted as she had intended.

In sum, the concept of intentionality spans four domains of explanation and their corresponding modes. When intentionality is not ascribed, people offer cause explanations. When intentionality is ascribed, people offer either reason explanations, causal history of reason explanations, or enabling factor explanations. These four explanation modes have different conceptual assumptions and linguistic features (Malle, 1999; Malle et al., 2000); they can be reliably distinguished when coding naturally occurring explanations (Malle, 1998); and together they comprise a predictively powerful model of folk behavior explanations (Malle, 1999, 2001; Malle et al., 2000; O'Laughlin & Malle, 2002).

Social-Cognitive Conditions of Explanation Modes

I now examine the conditions that determine when and for what purposes these distinct modes of explanation are used in social interaction. This exploration illustrates two tight interconnections: between conscious and unconscious processes of explanation choice and between cognitive and interpersonal functions of behavior explanations.

The conditions that distinguish between the use of cause explanations and all other explanation modes are straightforward. The primary one is conceptual: the perceived intentionality of the explained behavior. Malle (1999) showed that the rated intentionality of 20 behaviors predicted the choice between cause and reason explanations at $r \geq .90$. This choice is determined by features of the conceptual framework itself and therefore largely unconscious. The intentionality judgment itself may be difficult, requiring conscious deliberation and a search for further information; but once the perceiver arrives at a judgment of unintentionality, the decision to offer a cause explanation is conceptually bound.

The second condition that invites cause explanations is motivational in nature: the regulation of blame for socially undesirable behaviors. When an agent performs a socially undesirable behavior that could be seen as either intentional or unintentional (e.g., hitting one's opponent during racquetball), the agent will tend to offer cause explanations (e.g., "I didn't see you"), because they portray the behavior as unintentional (Malle, 1999), and thereby limit the amount of assigned blame. This decision process can be conscious (when the explainer effortfully creates a favorable impression) or unconscious (when the explainer deceives himself or herself into believing that the behavior was in fact unintentional).

More complex is the set of conditions that determine whether, given that a performed behavior is perceived as intentional, explainers offer a reason explanation (the default option for about 80% of explanations), a CHR explanation, or an enabling factor explanation. Research documents both cognitive and motivational conditions for this selection among explanation modes (see table 9.2).

Table 9.2 Conditions Determining People's Mode of Explanation for Intentional Actions

Conditions		Explanation Modes
Cognitive	Type of wondering	
	• What for? Why?	Reasons, CHRs
	• How was it possible? (difficult/obvious behaviors)	Enabling factors
	Information available	
	• Specific	Reasons
	• General	CHRs
Motivational	Impression management	
	• Appear rational	Reasons
	• Minimize blame	CHRs
	• Minimize moral implication	Enabling factors
	Audience design	
	• Listener's wondering: "Why?"	Reasons, CHRs
	"How was this possible?"	Enabling factors
	• Conversational maxims	e.g., CHRs for parsimony

CHR = causal history of reason.

Cognitive Conditions

A first cognitive condition is the type of wondering the explainer experiences when searching for an explanation. When the explainer tries to find out what motivated or instigated the behavior at hand, we may call this a "What-for?" wondering (best answered by offering reason explanations) or more generally a "Why?" wondering (best answered by offering reason or CHR explanations). By contrast, when the explainer tries to find out what made a particular intentional action possible, we may call this a "How-possible?" wondering, and it is best answered by offering enabling factor explanations.

Research shows that "How-possible?" wonderings are triggered by difficult or extreme behaviors (e.g., artistic or athletic accomplishments) and by behaviors whose motives are obvious (in the given context). In Malle et al. (2000, Study 3), for example, difficult/obvious behaviors elicited enabling factor explanations in 40% of cases, whereas easy/nonobvious behaviors elicited enabling factors in only 6% of cases. Similar results, though cast in a different terminology, were reported by McClure and Hilton (1997).

An even more powerful cognitive condition of selecting explanation modes is the type of information the explainer has available about the agent and the action (Malle, 2001; O'Laughlin & Malle, 2002). Why-questions about intentional actions typically focus on a specific agent–action unit—for example, "Why did Phil [agent] wash the dishes after the party [action]?" Reason explanations, such as, "He wanted the kitchen clean in the morning," are the default response to such questions (Malle, 1999; Malle et al., 2000). Reasons are specific to the agent (they are the presumed subjective mental states that the agent considered when forming the intention to act), and they are specific to the action (they rationally support this particular action). When explainers do not have such specific information about the particular agent performing the particular action, they try to recruit general information that is available about the type of agent or the type of action performed. General information—for example, about the agent's traits or group memberships, the situational context, or the historical background of the action—is expressed in CHR explanations. For example, Phil's washing the dishes may be explained by saying, "He is a neurotic cleaner." Or, in a conversation between two teenagers, the question "Why didn't she speak to him?" was explained by the reply "The dynamics of their relationship have always been peculiar." In such cases, explainers apparently do not know the agent's specific reasons for performing the action in question. But they have general information available about the type of agent or the type of action performed, and they use this general information to construct a CHR explanation.

In support of this role of information availability, we found that people consistently use more CHR explanations when explaining other people's behavior than when explaining their own (Malle, Knobe, & Nelson, 2004), presumably because people rarely have access to others' specific reasons. In addition, people use more CHR explanations when explaining group actions than when explaining individual actions, because people tend to have more general than specific information available about groups (O'Laughlin & Malle, 2002).

Both of these cognitive conditions—type of wondering and type of information available—are likely to engage both conscious (effortful) and unconscious (automatic) processes. On the one hand, an explainer may consciously assess the specific context of the behavior in question, the information demanded by this context, and the availability of this information. On the other hand, these assessments are automatically fed into the conceptual framework of explanations, guiding the choice between the distinct modes of reason, CHR, and enabling factor explanations. As often pointed out, such routine aspects are well executed by unconscious processes, whereas the contextually specific information assessments require some amount of effortful attention.

Motivational Conditions

The predominant motivational condition of selecting explanation modes is impression management. By crafting certain types of explanation, people are able to manage both their self-presentations and their portrayals of others. Self-presentation concerns have an obvious impact on explanations (Scott & Lyman, 1968; Tedeschi & Reiss, 1981), but this impact is not limited to a choice between "person causes" and "situation causes," as attribution researchers have suggested (e.g., Bradley, 1978; Miller & Ross, 1975).[5]

When explaining intentional behavior, people increase their use of reasons, especially belief reasons, when they want the agent (self or other) to appear rational (Malle et al., 2000, 2004), and they prefer CHR explanations to dampen the appearance of the agent's deliberation and responsibility (Nelson & Malle, 2000; Wilson, 1997). When explaining group actions, people offer reason explanations to portray a group as jointly acting (O'Laughlin & Malle, 2002) and thus perhaps as more threatening (Abelson, Dasgupta, Park, & Banaji, 1998; Malle, 2004). Finally, a number of philosophers have suggested that reasons mark an action's moral worth, whereas enabling factors, such as intelligence or skill, do not (Foot, 1978; Kant, 1785/1998). We would therefore expect that explainers who want to portray an agent as morally worthy will offer reasons, whereas explainers who want to portray the agent as capable will offer enabling factors. For example, a professor's behavior of giving especially clear lectures might either be explained with a reason (e.g., "because she wants students to really understand") and elicit moral praise, or it might be explained with an enabling factor (e.g., "because she is very intelligent"), eliciting a positive but probably not moral impression.

None of these decisions entails a conscious thought of the sort "I should offer a reason rather than a CHR factor." People do not have an explicit conception of these different explanation modes, even though they reliably distinguish between them implicitly (Malle, 1999). What people are conscious of is, again, the situationally specific demands and certain goals of dealing with them (e.g., "I should appease them"). The routinized framework of behavior explanations then provides the conceptual and linguistic tools that implement these demands and goals by means of particular modes of explanation.

Because behavior explanations are often embedded in conversation (Hilton, 1990; Kidd & Amabile, 1981; Malle & Knobe, 1997b), another important motivational condition of choosing among explanation modes is audience design—the explainer's communicative adjustment to the interest, knowledge, or expectation of the audience (Clark & Carlson, 1982; Fussell & Krauss, 1992; Higgins, McCann, & Fondacaro, 1982; Zajonc, 1960). For example, listeners can experience different types of wondering, and explainers have to choose an explanation mode that answers the listener's specific wondering. These wonderings are most clearly expressed in explicit question formulations: "Why?" "For what reason?" "How was this possible?" (Malle et al., 2000; McClure & Hilton, 1998). In one study, participants offered 95% enabling factor explanations in response to the question "How was this possible?" but only 10% in response to the question "For what reason?"[6] Once again, conversational demands are often effortfully processed if they are situationally specific and if they require fine-tuning of the message, but the implementation of the explanation in terms of particular modes and linguistic formulations will be largely automatic.

Audience design entails conformity to general conversational maxims (Grice, 1975), which are so well practiced that they are heeded automatically. When asked a why-question, people are expected to avoid giving obvious explanations, too many explanations, uninformative explanations, or no answer at all. Obeying these maxims is likely to have direct consequences for the modes of explanation people choose. For example, when they explain intentional actions of aggregate groups—whose members act independently and probably for very different reasons—explainers aim at parsimony. As a result, they prefer to offer CHR explanations, citing one or two factors that preceded and brought about the abundance of individual reasons among members of the group (O'Laughlin & Malle, 2002).

Discussion

Three general points concerning the choice among explanation modes are worth discussing. First, if folk explanations of behavior rely on key conceptual components of the folk theory of mind (e.g., the concept of intentionality, the distinction between beliefs and desires) and if a person lacks these concepts, then the person's choice of explanation should be reduced to one simple mechanical explanation mode. The following self-description of an autistic adult lends support to this hypothesis: "I assumed that everything is predetermined and that adults were taking care of us according to some sort of program, without their own decision making" (Blackburn et al., 2000; see also Baron-Cohen, 1992). Of course, systematic research on autistic children's behavior explanations is needed to test this hypothesis.

A second point concerns the microstructure of choosing between explanation modes, in which conscious representations (e.g., of the audience and its demands, of one's own curiosity) blend in gracefully with unconscious processes (e.g., reliance on conceptual assumptions and automatic choice of words when constructing a specific explanation). The division of labor between conscious and unconscious processes might appear roughly as follows: The unconscious apparatus of folk explanation is a toolbox (of conceptual assumptions and cognitive routines) whose tools are automatically assembled (e.g., put into words) before use. This toolbox represents a stable, reliable part of social cognition. By contrast, conscious representations track the moment-to-moment fluctuations in the context (and in oneself) and repeatedly converge on macro choices (e.g., to offer an explanation) that are then translated into the microelements of appropriate conceptual structure, wording, and so on. These translations are much like buttons or switches on a stereo amplifier, each of which has a broader meaning (e.g., increasing volume, selecting a source) and translates that meaning into a complex, low-level operation that reliably gets the job done.

The third point is that the conditions of choosing explanation modes depict explanations both as a cognitive tool (to answer one's own wondering) and as a social tool (to manage impressions and adapt to an audience). This duality of functions also exists at other levels of analysis (Malle, 2004). For example, reason explanations have several specific features, among them the type of reason cited (referring either to a belief state or a desire state) and the linguistic marking of that state with a mental-state verb ("I thought," "she wanted"). Knowing the agent's specific belief or desire reasons, a social perceiver can more easily understand and predict the agent's behavior, thus using explanations as a cognitive tool. But agents who explain their own behavior also use the different types of reasons for managing the audience's perception of their rationality and blameworthiness (Malle et al., 2000; Nelson & Malle, 2000). Likewise, when people explain others' behavior, they use mental-state verbs to emphasize that these are the agent's (and not some commonly accepted) reasons, thus distancing themselves from the particular reason (e.g., "Why is she not eating any dessert?" "She thinks she's been gaining weight"; Malle et al., 2000).

The fundamental duality of cognitive and social function characterizes not only modes and features of folk explanations but also the folk theory of mind as a whole, which is a conceptual apparatus that helps people solve cognitive as well as social tasks. I have pointed to several cognitive tasks, including classification of behaviors as intentional or unintentional, regulation of attention to behavioral events, and explanation as well as prediction. Among social tasks, I mentioned interpersonal influence and persuasion, impression management (of self and others), and communicative design. It should not be surprising that this diversity of tasks and functions requires far more than a system of causal reasoning or trait/situation attribution; it requires an interwoven framework of folk concepts that tie behavior to mind and thus make behavior intelligible, predictable, and socially defensible.

Conclusion

The theoretical perspective of social cognition as theory of mind has been underrepresented in recent social-psychological thinking, despite its affinity with Heider's (1958) groundbreaking investigations. Perhaps its representation will increase once sufficient data are amassed that favor, for example, a folk-theoretical model of behavior explanations over the traditional trait and causal attribution models (e.g., Malle, 1999, 2004; Malle et al., 2000; O'Laughlin & Malle, 2002). But the theory of mind perspective is more than a replacement of attribution theory. Rather, it directs the study of social cognition to the fundamental concepts by which people organize the social world, concepts that guide all other (conscious and unconscious) processing of human behavior and experience. The theory of mind perspective also makes clear what is uniquely social about social cognition: a mentalistic conceptual framework of human behavior that can evolve and develop only within a social environment (Dunn, 1999; Whiten, 1999), whose primary function is to improve social coordination (Humphrey, 1976; Malle, 2002), and whose most reliable trigger is ongoing social interaction (Ickes, 2002). While illuminating the uniqueness of human social cognition, the theory of mind perspective also links social psychology to other disciplines that are concerned with human cognition of mind and behavior, such as developmental psychology, primatology, anthropology, linguistics, and philosophy (Carruthers & Smith, 1996; Greenwood, 1991; Hurford, Studdert-Kennedy, & Knight, 1998; Malle et al., 2001; Rosen, 1995). From this perspective, then, a full understanding of the "new unconscious" includes the folk-conceptual unconscious as an essential part of social cognition, which itself ranges from the most fundamental conceptual assumptions about mind and behavior to the most sophisticated assessments of ongoing social interaction.

Acknowledgments Preparation of this chapter was supported by NSF CAREER award SBR-9703315. I am grateful to Dan Ames, John Bargh, and Jim Uleman for their comments on a previous version.

Notes

1. Heider and Simmel's (1944) findings are probably more indicative of people's sensitivity to the experimenters' intentions (to display geometric figures that move like agents) than indicative of a deep application of theory of mind to circles and triangles (Malle & Ickes, 2000). More interesting are extensions to natural phenomena (including deities) and machinery. Some scholars regard these extended uses as violating the domain specificity and modularity of a theory of mind (e.g., chapter 11). A defender of modularity might argue, however, that evolutionary and developmental primacy is critical for domain specificity, and the data do at least not speak against this primacy. Extended applications such as those to natural phenomena and machines are surely not ruled out by a domain-specific framework but may show its powerful capacity to reorganize thinking and reasoning about the world.

2. The term *intentionality* has two quite different meanings. Brentano (1874/1973) introduced it as a technical term that was henceforth used to refer to the property of all mental states as being directed toward something. Desires, for example, may be directed toward attractive objects, and beliefs toward states of affairs (Lyons, 1986; Searle, 1983). Second, intentionality is the property of actions that makes ordinary people and scholars alike call them purposeful, meant, or done intentionally. It is this second sense that I am discussing here.

3. Heider's distinction between the two modes of causality—personal (intentional) and impersonal (unintentional)—is typically misrepresented as one between person causes and situation causes for any kind of behavior (Malle, 2004; Malle & Ickes, 2000). This misunderstanding is perhaps the fundamental flaw of standard attribution theory, to which I return in more detail below.

4. The reported differences represent the actual interaction effect, computed after removing main effects (Rosnow & Rosenthal, 1989).

5. When people offer cause explanations of unintentional behaviors or outcomes (such as failure, damage, accidents, etc.), they choose between causes of various types—person versus situation, stable versus unstable, global versus specific, controllable versus uncontrollable. Theories that model these choices (e.g., Fincham, Beach, & Nelson, 1987; Weiner, 1986) are clearly of psychological significance, but they do not apply the conceptually more complex choices between modes of explanation for intentional behavior.

6. The reported numbers are for difficult behaviors. For easy behaviors, the corresponding numbers were 22% in response to "How was this possible?" and 0% in response to "For what reason?," attesting to the strong influence of the cognitive condition of explanations discussed earlier.

References

Abelson, R. P., Dasgupta, N., Park, J., & Banaji, M. R. (1998). Perceptions of the collective other. *Personality and Social Psychology Review, 2*, 243–250.

Ames, D. A. (in press). Mental state inference in person perception: Everyday solutions to the problem of other minds. *Journal of Personality and Social Psychology.*

Asch, S. E. (1952). *Social psychology.* Englewood Cliffs, NJ: Prentice-Hall.

Audi, R. (1993). *Action, intention, and reason.* Ithaca, NY: Cornell University Press.

Baird, J. A., & Baldwin, D. A. (2001). Making sense of human behavior: Action parsing and intentional inference. In B. F. Malle, L. J. Moses, & D. A. Baldwin (Eds.), *Intentions and intentionality: Foundations of social cognition* (pp. 193–206). Cambridge, MA: MIT Press.

Baldwin, D. A. (1993). Early referential understanding: Infants' ability to recognize referential acts for what they are. *Developmental Psychology, 29,* 832–843.

Baldwin, D. A., & Baird, J. A. (1999). Action analysis: A gateway to intentional inference. In P. Rochat (Ed.), *Early social cognition: Understanding others in the first months of life* (pp. 215–240). Mahwah, NJ: Erlbaum.

Baldwin, D. A., & Tomasello, M. (1998). Word learning: A window on early pragmatic understanding. In E. V. Clark (Ed.), *The proceedings of the twenty-ninth annual child language research forum* (pp. 3–23). Stanford, CA: Center for the Study of Language and Information.

Baron-Cohen, S. (1992). The girl who shouted in the church. In R. Campbell (Ed.), *Mental lives: Case studies in cognition* (pp. 11–23). Oxford: Blackwell.

Baron-Cohen, S. (1995). *Mindblindness: An essay on autism and theory of mind.* Cambridge, MA: MIT Press.

Baron-Cohen, S. (1999). The evolution of a theory of mind. In M. C. Corballis & S. E. G. Lea (Eds.), *The descent of mind: Psychological perspectives on hominid evolution* (pp. 261–277). New York: Oxford University Press.

Baron-Cohen, S. (2000). Theory of mind and autism: A fifteen year review. In S. Baron-Cohen, H. Tager-Flusberg, & D. Cohen (Eds.), *Understanding other minds: Perspectives from developmental cognitive neuroscience* (pp. 3–20). New York: Oxford University Press.

Baron-Cohen, S., Leslie, A. M., & Frith, U. (1985). Does the autistic child have a "theory of mind"? *Cognition, 21,* 37–46.

Bartsch, K., & Wellman, H. M. (1995). *Children talk about the mind.* New York: Oxford University Press.

Blackburn, J., Gottschewski, K., George, E., & L——, N. (2000, May). A discussion about theory of mind: From an autistic perspective. *Proceedings of Autism Europe's 6th International Congress, Glasgow.* Scottish Society for Autism. Downloaded from http://www.autistics.org/library/AE2000-ToM.html on May 1, 2001.

Blakemore, S., & Decety, J. (2001). From the perception of action to the understanding of intention. *Nature Reviews Neuroscience, 2,* 561–567.

Bogdan, R. J. (2000). *Minding minds: Evolving a reflexive mind by interpreting others.* Cambridge, MA: MIT Press.

Bradley, G. W. (1978). Self-serving biases in the attribution process: A reexamination of the fact or fiction question. *Journal of Personality and Social Psychology, 36,* 56–71.

Brentano, F. C. (1973). *Psychology from an empirical standpoint* (A. C. Rancurello, D. B. Terrell, & L. L. McAlister, Trans.) New York: Humanities Press. (Original work published 1874)

Bruner, J. S. (1990). *Acts of meaning.* Cambridge, MA: Harvard University Press.

Bull, P. E. (1987). *Posture and gesture.* Oxford, UK: Pergamon Press.

Buss, A. R. (1978). Causes and reasons in attribution theory: A conceptual critique. *Journal of Personality and Social Psychology, 36,* 1311–1321.

Carlson, S. M., Moses, L. J., & Hix, H. R. (1998). The role of inhibitory processes in young children's difficulties with deception and false belief. *Child Development, 69,* 672–691.

Carruthers, P. & Smith, P. K. (Eds.). (1996). *Theories of theories of mind.* New York: Cambridge University Press.

Clark, H. H., & Carlson, T. B. (1982). Speech acts and hearers' beliefs. In N. V. Smith (Ed.), *Mutual knowledge* (pp. 1–36). New York: Academic Press.

D'Andrade, R. (1987). A folk model of the mind. In D. Holand & N. Quinn (Eds.), *Cultural models in language and thought* (pp. 112–148). New York: Cambridge University Press.

Davidson, D. (1963). Actions, reasons, and causes. *Journal of Philosophy, 60,* 685–700.

Davis, M. H., Conklin, L., Smith, A., & Luce, C. (1996). Effect of perspective taking on the cognitive representation of persons: A merging of self and other. *Journal of Personality and Social Psychology, 70,* 713–726.

Dennett, D. C. (1987). *The intentional stance.* Cambridge, MA: MIT Press.

DePaulo, B. M. (1992). Nonverbal behavior and self-presentation. *Psychological Bulletin, 111,* 203–243.

De Villiers, J. (2000). Language and theory of mind: What are the developmental relationships? In S. Baron-Cohen, H. Tager-Flusberg, & D. J. Cohen (Eds.), *Understanding other minds: Perspectives from developmental cognitive neuroscience* (2nd ed., pp. 83–123). New York: Oxford University Press.

Dittrich, W. J., & Lea, S. E. G. (1994). Visual perception of intentional motion. *Perception, 23,* 253–268.

Dretske, F. (1988). *Explaining behavior: Reasons in a world of causes.* Cambridge, MA: MIT Press.

Dunn, J. (1999). Mindreading and social relationships. In M. Bennett (Ed.), *Developmental psychology: Achievements and prospects* (pp. 55–71). Philadelphia: Psychology Press.

Fincham, F. D., Beach, S. R., & Nelson, G. (1987). Attribution processes in distressed and nondistressed couples: III. Causal and responsibility attributions for spouse behavior. *Cognitive Therapy and Research, 11,* 71–86.

Fiske, S. T., & Taylor, S. E. (1991). *Social cognition* (2nd ed.). New York: McGraw-Hill.

Foot, P. (1978). Virtues and vices. In P. Foot, *Virtues and vices and other essays in moral philosophy* (pp. 1–18). Berkeley: University of California Press.

Frith, U. (2000). Cognitive explanations of autism. In K. Lee (Ed.), *Childhood cognitive development: The essential readings* (pp. 324–337). Malden, MA: Blackwell.

Funder, D. C., & Dobroth, K. M. (1987). Differences between traits: Properties associated with interjudge agreement. *Journal of Personality and Social Psychology, 52,* 409–418.

Fussell, S. R., & Krauss, R. M. (1992). Coordination of knowledge in communication: Effects of speakers' assumptions about what others know. *Journal of Personality and Social Psychology, 62,* 378–391.

Gergely, G., Nádasdy, Z., Csibra, G., & Bíró, S. (1995). Taking the intentional stance at 12 months of age. *Cognition, 56,* 165–193.

Gilovich, T., Savitsky, K., & Medvec, V. H. (1998). The illusion of transparency:

Biased assessments of others' ability to read one's emotional states. *Journal of Personality and Social Psychology, 75*, 332–346.

Goffman, E. (1974). *Frame analysis: An essay on the organization of experience.* Cambridge, MA: Harvard University Press.

Goldman, A. I. (1989). Interpretation psychologized. *Mind and Language, 4*, 161–185.

Goldman, A. I. (2001). Desire, intention, and the simulation theory. In B. F. Malle, L. J. Moses, & D. A. Baldwin (Eds.), *Intentions and intentionality: Foundations of social cognition* (pp. 207–225). Cambridge, MA: MIT Press.

Gopnik, A. (1998). Explanation as orgasm. *Minds and Machines, 8*, 101–118.

Gopnik, A., & Meltzoff, A. N. (1997). *Words, thoughts, and theories.* Cambridge: MIT Press.

Gopnik, A., & Wellman, H. M. (1994). The theory theory. In L. A. Hirschfeld & S. A. Gelman (Eds.), *Mapping the mind: Domain specificity in cognition and culture* (pp. 257–293). New York: Cambridge University Press.

Gordon, R. M. (1986). Folk psychology as simulation. *Mind and Language, 1*, 158–171.

Graesser, A. C., Singer, M., & Trabasso, T. (1994). Constructing inferences during narrative text comprehension. *Psychological Review, 101*, 371–395.

Greenwood, J. D. (Ed.). (1991). *The future of folk psychology: Intentionality and cognitive science.* Cambridge, UK: Cambridge University Press.

Grice, H. P. (1975). Logic and conversation. In P. Cole & J. L. Morgan (Eds.), *Syntax and semantics 3: Speech acts* (pp. 41–58). New York: Academic Press.

Hamilton, V. L. (1978). Who is responsible? Towards a social psychology of responsibility attribution. *Social Psychology, 41*, 316–328.

Harman, G. (1976). Practical reasoning. *Review of Metaphysics, 29*, 431–463.

Heider, F. (1958). *The psychology of interpersonal relations.* New York: Wiley.

Heider, F., & Simmel, M. (1944). An experimental study of apparent behavior. *American Journal of Psychology, 57*, 243–259.

Higgins, E. T., McCann, C. D., & Fondacaro, R. (1982). The "communication game": Goal-directed encoding and cognitive consequences. *Social Cognition, 1*, 21–37.

Hilton, D. J. (1990). Conversational processes and causal explanation. *Psychological Bulletin, 107*, 65–81.

Hirschberg, N. (1978). A correct treatment of traits. In H. London (Ed.), *Personality: A new look at metatheories* (pp. 45–68). New York: Wiley.

Hirschfeld, L. A., & Gelman, S. A. (Eds.). (1994). *Mapping the mind: Domain specificity in cognition and culture.* New York: Cambridge University Press.

Hoffman, M. L. (1993). Empathy, social cognition, and moral education. In A. Garrod (Ed.), *Approaches to moral development: New research and emerging themes* (pp. 157–179). New York: Teachers College Press.

Hughes, C. (1998). Executive function in preschoolers: Links with theory of mind and verbal ability. *British Journal of Developmental Psychology, 16*, 233–253.

Humphrey, N. K. (1976). The social function of intellect. In P. P. G. Bateson & R. Hinde (Eds.), *Growing points in ethology* (pp. 303–317). New York: Cambridge University Press.

Hurford, J. R., Studdert-Kennedy, M., & Knight, C. (Eds.). (1998). *Approaches to the evolution of language: Social and cognitive bases.* New York: Cambridge University Press.

Ickes, W. (Ed.). (1997). *Empathic accuracy.* New York: Guilford.

Ickes, W. (2002). Subjective and intersubjective paradigms for the study of social cognition. In J. P. Forgas & K. D. Williams (Eds.), *The social self: Cognitive, interpersonal, and intergroup perspectives* (pp. 205–218). Philadelphia: Psychology Press.

John, O. P., & Robins, R. W. (1993). Determinants of interjudge agreement on personality traits: The Big Five domains, observability, evaluativeness, and the unique perspective of the self. *Journal of Personality, 61*, 521–551.

Jones, E. E., & Davis, K. E. (1965). From acts to dispositions: The attribution process in person perception. In L. Berkowitz (Ed.), *Advances in experimental social psychology* (Vol. 2, pp. 219–266). New York: Academic Press.

Jones, E. E., & Thibaut, J. W. (1958). Interaction goals as bases of inference in interpersonal perception. In R. Tagiuri & L. Petrullo (Eds.), *Person perception and interpersonal behavior* (pp. 151–178). Stanford, CA: Stanford University Press.

Kalish, C. (1998). Reasons and causes: Children's understanding of conformity to social rules and physical laws. *Child Development, 69*, 706–720.

Kant, I. (1998). *Groundwork of the metaphysics of morals* (M. Gregor, Trans.). New York: Cambridge University Press. (Original work published 1785)

Kant, I. (1998). *Critique of pure reason* (P. Guyer & A. W. Wood, Ed. & Trans.). New York: Cambridge University Press. (Original work published 1787)

Kidd, R. F., & Amabile, T. M. (1981). Causal explanations in social interaction: Some dialogues on dialogue. In J. H. Harvey, W. J. Ickes, & R. F. Kidd (Eds.), *New directions in attribution research* (Vol. 3, pp. 307–328). Hillsdale, NJ: Erlbaum.

Klein, K. J. K., & Hodges, S. D. (2001). Gender differences and motivation in empathic accuracy: When it pays to care. *Personality and Social Psychology Bulletin, 27*, 720–730.

Knobe, J. (2003). Intentional action in folk psychology: An experimental investigation. *Philosophical Psychology, 16*, 309–324.

Krauss, R. M., Fussell, S. R., & Chen, Y. (1995). Coordination of perspective in dialogue: Intrapersonal and interpersonal processes. In I. Markova, C. F. Graumann, & K. Scherer (Eds.), *Mutualities in dialogue* (pp. 124–145). Cambridge, UK: Cambridge University Press.

Leslie, A. M. (1992). Autism and the "theory of mind" module. *Current Directions in Psychological Science, 1*, 18–21.

Leslie, A. M. (1995). A theory of agency. In A. J. Premack, D. Premack, & D. Sperber (Eds.), *Causal cognition: A multidisciplinary debate* (pp. 131–149). Oxford: Clarendon Press.

Locke, D., & Pennington, D. (1982). Reasons and other causes: Their role in attribution processes. *Journal of Personality and Social Psychology, 42*, 212–223.

Lyon, T. D. (1993). *Young children's understanding of desire and knowledge*. Unpublished doctoral dissertation, Stanford University, Stanford, CA.

Lyons, W. (1986). *The disappearance of introspection*. Cambridge, MA: MIT Press.

Malle, B. F. (1994). *Intentionality and explanation: A study in the folk theory of behavior*. Unpublished doctoral dissertation, Stanford University, Stanford, CA.

Malle, B. F. (1998). *F.Ex: Coding scheme for people's folk explanations of behavior*. University of Oregon. Downloaded from http://darkwing.uoregon.edu/~bfmalle/fex.html on April 1, 2004.

Malle, B. F. (1999). How people explain behavior: A new theoretical framework. *Personality and Social Psychology Review, 3*, 23–48.

Malle, B. F. (2001). Folk explanations of intentional action. In B. F. Malle, L. J.

Moses, & D. A. Baldwin (Eds.), *Intentions and intentionality: Foundations of social cognition* (pp. 265–286). Cambridge, MA: MIT Press.

Malle, B. F. (2002). The relation between language and theory of mind in development and evolution. In T. Givón & B. F. Malle (Eds.), *The evolution of language out of pre-language* (pp. 265–284). Amsterdam: Benjamins.

Malle, B. F. (2004). *How the mind explains behavior: Folk explanations, meaning, and social interaction.* Cambridge, MA: MIT Press.

Malle, B. F., & Ickes, W. (2000). Fritz Heider: Philosopher and psychologist. In G. A. Kimble & M. Wertheimer (Eds.), *Portraits of pioneers in psychology* (Vol. 4, pp. 193–214). Washington, DC and Mahwah, NJ: American Psychological Association and Erlbaum.

Malle, B. F., & Knobe, J. (1997a). The folk concept of intentionality. *Journal of Experimental Social Psychology, 33*, 101–121.

Malle, B. F., & Knobe, J. (1997b). Which behaviors do people explain? A basic actor-observer asymmetry. *Journal of Personality and Social Psychology, 72*, 288–304.

Malle, B. F., & Knobe, J. (2001). The distinction between desire and intention: A folk-conceptual analysis. In B. F. Malle, L. J. Moses, & D. A. Baldwin (Eds.), *Intentions and intentionality: Foundations of social cognition* (pp. 45–67). Cambridge, MA: MIT Press.

Malle, B. F., Knobe, J., & Nelson. S. E. (2004). *Actor-observer asymmetries in behavior explanation: New answers to an old question.* Manuscript under revision.

Malle, B. F., Knobe, J., O'Laughlin, M., Pearce, G. E., & Nelson, S. E. (2000). Conceptual structure and social functions of behavior explanations: Beyond person–situation attributions. *Journal of Personality and Social Psychology, 79*, 309–326.

Malle, B. F., Moses, L. J., & Baldwin, D. A. (Eds.). (2001). *Intentions and intentionality: Foundations of social cognition.* Cambridge, MA: MIT Press.

Malle, B. F., & Pearce, G. E. (2001). Attention to behavioral events during social interaction: Two actor-observer gaps and three attempts to close them. *Journal of Personality and Social Psychology, 81*, 278–294.

McCabe, K. A., Smith, V. L., & LePore, M. (2000). Intentionality detection and "mindreading": Why does game form matter? *Proceedings of the National Academy of Sciences, 97*, 4404–4409.

McClure, J., & Hilton, D. (1997). For you can't always get what you want: When preconditions are better explanations than goals. *British Journal of Social Psychology, 36*, 223–240.

McClure, J., & Hilton, D. (1998). Are goals or preconditions better explanations? It depends on the question. *European Journal of Social Psychology, 28*, 897–911.

Mele, A. R. (2001). Acting intentionally: Probing folk notions. In B. F. Malle, L. J. Moses, & D. A. Baldwin (Eds.), *Intentions and intentionality: Foundations of social cognition* (pp. 27–44). Cambridge, MA: MIT Press.

Miller, D. T., & Ross, M. (1975). Self-serving biases in the attribution of causality: Fact or fiction? *Psychological Bulletin, 82*, 213–225.

Moses, L. J. (2001). Some thoughts on ascribing complex intentional concepts to young children. In B. F. Malle, L. J. Moses, & D. A. Baldwin (Eds.), *Intentions and intentionality: Foundations of social cognition* (pp. 69–83). Cambridge, MA: MIT Press.

Nass, C., & Moon, Y. (2000). Machines and mindlessness: Social responses to computers. *Journal of Social Issues, 56*, 81–103.

Nelson, S. E., & Malle, B. F. (2000, April). *Explaining intentional actions in the context of social perception and judgment.* Poster presented at the annual meeting of the Western Psychological Association, Portland, OR.

Nelson-LeGall, S. A. (1985). Motive-outcome matching and outcome foreseeability: Effects on attribution of intentionality and moral judgments. *Developmental Psychology, 21,* 323–337.

Norman, D. A., & Shallice, T. (1986). Attention to action: Willed and automatic control of behavior. In G. E. Schwartz & D. Shapiro (Eds.), *Consciousness and self-regulation* (pp. 1–17). New York: Plenum Press.

O'Laughlin, M., & Malle, B. F. (2002). How people explain actions performed by groups and individuals. *Journal of Personality and Social Psychology, 82,* 33–48.

Perner, J. (1991). *Understanding the representational mind.* Cambridge, MA: MIT Press.

Posner, M. I. (1980). Orienting of attention. *Quarterly Journal of Experimental Psychology, 32,* 3–25.

Povinelli, D. J. (1996). Chimpanzee theory of mind: The long road to strong inference. In P. Carruthers & P. K. Smith (Eds.), *Theories of theories of mind* (pp. 243–329). Cambridge, UK: Cambridge University Press.

Povinelli, D. J. (2001). On the possibilities of detecting intentions prior to understanding them. In B. F. Malle, L. J. Moses, & D. A. Baldwin (Eds.), *Intentions and intentionality: Foundations of social cognition* (pp. 225–248). Cambridge, MA: MIT Press.

Premack, D. (1990). The infant's theory of self-propelled objects. *Cognition, 36,* 1–16.

Premack, D., & Woodruff, G. (1978). Does the chimpanzee have a theory of mind? *Behavioral and Brain Sciences, 1,* 515–526.

Rosen, L. (Ed.). (1995). *Other intentions: Cultural contexts and the attribution of inner states.* Santa Fe, NM: School of American Research Press.

Rosnow, R. L., & Rosenthal, R. (1989). Definition and interpretation of interaction effects. *Psychological Bulletin, 105,* 143–146.

Schank, R. C., & Abelson, R. P. (1977). *Scripts, plans, goals and understanding: An inquiry into human knowledge structures.* Hillsdale, NJ: Erlbaum.

Schneider, D. J. (1991). Social cognition. *Annual Review of Psychology, 42,* 527–561.

Schult, C. A., & Wellman, H. M. (1997). Explaining human movements and actions: Children's understanding of the limits of psychological explanation. *Cognition, 62,* 291–324.

Scott, M. B., & Lyman, S. M. (1968). Accounts. *American Sociological Review, 33,* 46–62.

Searle, J. R. (1983). *Intentionality: An essay in the philosophy of mind.* Cambridge, UK: Cambridge University Press.

Searle, J. R. (1984). *Minds, brains, and science.* Cambridge, MA: Harvard University Press.

Shaver, K. G. (1975). *An introduction to attribution processes.* Cambridge, MA: Winthrop.

Shaver, K. G. (1985). *The attribution of blame.* New York: Springer-Verlag.

Shultz, T. R., & Wells, D. (1985). Judging the intentionality of action-outcomes. *Developmental Psychology, 21,* 83–89.

Slugoski, B. R., Lalljee, M., Lamb, R., & Ginsburg, G. P. (1993). Attribution in conversational context: Effect of mutual knowledge on explanation-giving. *European Journal of Social Psychology, 23*, 219–238.

Snare, F. (1991). *Morals, motivation and convention: Hume's influential doctrines.* Cambridge, UK: Cambridge University Press.

Tagiuri, R., & Petrullo, L. (1958). *Person perception and interpersonal behavior.* Stanford, CA: Stanford University Press.

Tedeschi, J. T., & Reiss, M. (1981). Verbal strategies as impression management. In C. Antaki (Ed.), *The psychology of ordinary social behaviour* (pp. 271–309). London: Academic Press.

Tomasello, M. (1998). Uniquely primate, uniquely human. *Developmental Science, 1*, 1–16.

Trabasso, T., & Stein, N. L. (1994). Using goal-plan knowledge to merge the past with the present and the future in narrating events on line. In M. M. Haith & J. B. Benson (Eds.), *The development of future-oriented processes: The John D. and Catherine T. MacArthur Foundation series on mental health and development* (pp. 323–349). Chicago: University of Chicago Press.

Turnbull, W. (1986). Everyday explanation: The pragmatics of puzzle resolution. *Journal for the Theory of Social Behavior, 16*, 141–160.

Weiner, B. (1986). *An attributional theory of motivation and emotion.* New York: Springer-Verlag.

Weiner, B. (1995). *Judgments of responsibility: A foundation for a theory of social conduct.* New York: Guilford.

Wellman, H. (1990). *The child's theory of mind.* Cambridge, MA: MIT Press.

Wellman, H. M., Hickling, A. K., & Schult, C. A. (1997). Young children's psychological, physical, and biological explanations. In H. W. Wellman & K. Inagaki (Eds.), *The emergence of core domains of thought: Children's reasoning about physical, psychological, and biological phenomena* (pp. 7–25). San Francisco, CA: Jossey-Bass.

Wellman, H. W., & Phillips, A. T. (2001). Developing intentional understandings. In B. F. Malle, L. J. Moses, & D. A. Baldwin (Eds.), *Intentions and intentionality: Foundations of social cognition* (pp. 125–148). Cambridge, MA: MIT Press.

Wellman, H. M., & Woolley, J. D. (1990). From simple desires to ordinary beliefs: The early development of everyday psychology. *Cognition, 35*, 245–275.

White, P. A. (1991). Ambiguity in the internal/external distinction in causal attribution. *Journal of Experimental Social Psychology, 27*, 259–270.

Whiten, A. (1999). The evolution of deep social mind in humans. In M. C. Corballis & S. E. G. Lea (Eds.), *The descent of mind: Psychological perspectives on hominid evolution* (pp. 173–193). New York: Oxford University Press.

Wilson, J. Q. (1997). *Moral judgment: Does the abuse excuse threaten our legal system?* New York: HarperCollins.

Wittgenstein, L. (1953). *Philosophical investigations* (G. E. M. Anscombe, Trans.). Malden, MA: Blackwell.

Woodward, A. L., Sommerville, J. A., & Guajardo, J. J. (2001). How infants make sense of intentional action. In B. F. Malle, L. J. Moses, & D. A. Baldwin (Eds.), *Intentions and intentionality: Foundations of social cognition* (pp. 149–170). Cambridge, MA: MIT Press.

Wyer, R. S., Srull, T. K., Gordon, S. E., & Hartwick, J. (1982). Effects of processing objectives on the recall of prose material. *Journal of Personality and Social Psychology, 43*, 674–688.

Yuill, N., & Perner, J. (1988). Intentionality and knowledge in children's judgments of actor's responsibility and recipient's emotional reaction. *Developmental Psychology, 24*, 358–365.

Zajonc, R. B. (1960). The process of cognitive tuning in communication. *Journal of Abnormal and Social Psychology, 61*, 159–167.

10

The Development of the Intention Concept: From the Observable World to the Unobservable Mind

Jodie A. Baird and Janet Wilde Astington

Intentions are everywhere: in action (a lover's embrace), in conversation (an unseemly comment), even on paper (the dimpled chad of a presidential election ballot). As Premack and Woodruff (1978) remark, "It seems beyond question that purpose or intention is the state we impute most widely" (p. 515). But what does it mean to say that someone has an intention? And on what basis are attributions of intention made?

Drawing on literature from philosophy and psychology, we define intention, highlighting the complexities of this concept and pointing to features that distinguish intention from related concepts such as desire and action. We then review the literature on the development of the intention concept in infancy and early childhood. Our treatment of the literature reveals that a complete appreciation of intention is acquired only gradually and is characterized by a shift from inferences based on the observable to those based on the unobservable. In a final section, we argue that language development plays an important role in this shift in children's understanding.

The Complexities of Intention

Intentions are, at the same time, obvious and enigmatic. In their simplest form, intentions are the stuff actions are made of. Someone who is running has the intention to run; someone who is walking has the intention to walk. Intentions-in-action, as Searle (1983) calls them, arise spontaneously as an actor engages in bodily movement. They require no premeditated reasoning or forethought; rather, they emerge as a by-product of behavior. Searle distinguishes intentions-in-action from prior intentions, which are mental states that precede and motivate action. Prior intentions are formed on the basis of desires and beliefs, and provide the reasons for acting. Consider George's intention to buy a car. His intention reflects a desire for a given outcome (the freedom to go where he wants, when he wants), and a belief that the intended action will lead to that outcome (owning a car will give him that freedom). Critically, intentions specify how the desired outcome will be achieved. That is, if George's aunt bequeaths him a car, his desire for automotive freedom will be satisfied, but his intention to purchase a vehicle will remain unfulfilled.

This example points to one of the features that distinguish intention from desire. Intentions and desires are similar in that they are both "conative attitudes" (Malle & Knobe, 2001) that may launch an agent into action. Intentions and desires can also be identified as representational mental states—that is, they express an attitude toward a content, that which is intended or desired (Searle, 1983). Moreover, their satisfaction depends on changes in the world coming to match the intended or desired outcome. However, for intentions, the manner in which the outcome is achieved is relevant. As Astington and Gopnik (1991) explain, "If I want someone to be dead, my desire will be satisfied no matter how he dies. If I intend to kill someone, my intention will not be carried out unless I act on that intention and murder him" (p. 45). Searle (1983) designates this the "causal self-reference" of intention; in other words, intentions cause the actions they represent.

Malle and Knobe (2001) outline several other features that distinguish intention from desire. For one, intentions and desires differ in terms of content. Desires generally have as their content outcomes (e.g., Sarah wants to have a birthday party), whereas intentions primarily have as their content actions (e.g., she intends to make a cake) that are undertaken to achieve some outcome. In both cases, the outcomes are goal states or goals, that is, the end result that is the object of the desire or intention. Thus, both desires and intentions represent goal states, but intentions are critically different in that they also represent the means to achieving the goal. That is to say, the content of a desire is a goal, and the content of an intention is a goal-directed action. As a consequence of these differences in content, intentions and desires have different explanatory functions: Intentions usually communicate information about what an agent is going to do, whereas desires communicate information about why he or she is going to do it.

The content of intentions differs from that of desires in at least two other ways. First, one can only intend what one believes to be possible (Moses, 1993, 2001). Second, intentions are typically directed at the intender's own action; one cannot intend the uncontrollable (e.g., another person's actions or acts of nature). In contrast, there are no such constraints on the content of desires. Desires can be directed at anything, including the impossible (e.g., wanting to live forever) and uncontrollable (e.g., wanting sunny weather).

Malle and Knobe (2001) further suggest that, because of their differences in content, intentions and desires operate differently in the chain of reasoning that leads to intentional action. In particular, intentions typically represent the output of reasoning, whereas desires often are the input to reasoning. For example, a desire to help the homeless (input) may lead to an intention to volunteer at a soup kitchen (output). In line with these different roles in reasoning, intentions and desires differ with respect to their commitment to action. Intentions represent a commitment to act. For example, having formed an intention to marry Karen (and having obtained her agreement), Anthony is settled on that course of action. He need not continue to deliberate on his decision (intentions typically resist reconsideration), nor can he form an intention to marry someone else (intentions constrain other intentions; Bratman, 1987). Moreover, Anthony's reputation will likely suffer if he announces his intention to marry Karen and then jilts her at the altar (an agent may be sanctioned if intentions that are publicly expressed go unfulfilled; Malle & Knobe, 2001). Desires, in contrast, need not entail any commitment to act; Anthony could secretly yearn to marry Karen without ever acting upon that longing.

Due to their causal role in motivating action, intentions are predictive of others' behavior. That is, if people's intentions are known, their probable subsequent actions can often be inferred. Likewise, people's actions are a rich source of information about their intentions. Intentions are not, however, isomorphic with actions; rather, they stand in a many-to-many relation (Baldwin & Baird, 1999; Searle, 1984). That is, one and the same physical action (e.g., administering a drug) may be motivated by different intentions (e.g., to kill or to restore health). Likewise, one and the same intention (e.g., to kill) may engender different kinds of actions (e.g., administering a drug or shooting a firearm). As a consequence of this many-to-many relation between actions and intentions, intentions cannot be extracted directly from the behavior stream; too many possible intentions are consistent with any given action. Instead, intentions must be inferred from contextual information (e.g., time and place) and knowledge about the agent (e.g., his beliefs and desires) in addition to action information (Malle, Moses, & Baldwin, 2001).

A fully developed understanding of intention allows one to appreciate the somewhat elusive distinctions between intention and related concepts of desire, goal, and action. However, the inability to grasp such subtleties does not imply that one has no understanding of intention. As the following literature review clarifies, intention is not an all-or-nothing concept; rather, a concept as complex and multifaceted as intention has to be acquired gradually. We begin by reviewing evidence that suggests young infants may have abilities for perceiving action in ways that support an analysis of intentions, even at an age when any real understanding of intention is debatable and, in our view, unlikely. The first sign of genuine understanding is implicit, appearing in the second year of life around the same time infants' social and communicative skills begin to flourish. However, children's early concept of intention is limited to the observable world; they view intention merely as a conative attitude—a volitional state—intimately tied to acts and speech acts. It is not until later in the preschool years that children make explicit distinctions among intention, desire, goal, and action, and are capable of understanding intention as a product of the unobservable mind. Our use here of the terms *implicit* and *explicit* refers to the way children's understanding is expressed, that is, first implicitly in their actions, and later explicitly in what they say and in their responses to verbal questioning. Although this usage maps onto others' analyses of implicit/explicit understanding (e.g., Dienes & Perner, 1999; Ruffman, 2000), our purpose here is simply to refer to a distinction between behavioral versus verbal expressions of understanding.

Foundational Skills for Understanding Intentions

In order to make successful attributions of intention, one must distinguish which objects possess intentions—that is, which objects warrant intention attribution, and which portions of the behavior stream are relevant to an intentional analysis. By the end of their first year, infants are skilled at both of these discriminations.

By 12 months of age, infants can distinguish between agents—that is to say, objects possessing intentions—and inanimates, and they use this distinction to guide their inferences about and behavior toward those objects. For example, infants as young as 7 months appreciate that humans, but not inanimate blocks, can cause one another to move in the absence of direct physical contact (Woodward, Phillips, & Spelke, 1993). Moreover, infants respond differently to agents versus inanimates, even when these two classes of objects display identical patterns of motion. For example, 12-month-olds readily follow the gaze of objects perceived as agents (i.e., objects that have a face and/or respond contingently to the infant) but fail to follow the same movements performed by nonagentive objects (Johnson, Slaughter, & Carey, 1998). Furthermore, infants as young as 6 and 9 months of age assume that a human arm is goal directed when it reaches for something, but they make no such assumption when the reach is performed by an inanimate rod (Woodward, 1998).

Around the same age at which they distinguish agents and inanimates, infants also demonstrate sensitivity to the features of action that are relevant to understanding the actors' intentions. For example, Woodward (1998) demonstrated that 6- and 9-month-old infants selectively attend to the goal of an actor's reach relative to the path of the actor's reach. Infants in this study habituated to a reaching event in which a hand grasped one of two objects on display. Following habituation, Woodward reversed the positions of the objects and presented two test events: one in which the hand followed the same path of motion yet grasped a different object (new goal event), and one in which the hand took a new path of motion yet grasped the same object (new path event). If, during habituation, infants regarded the goal of the actor's reach as more significant than the path of the reach, they should show greater interest or surprise on test trials in which the goal of the reach changed. This is precisely what Woodward found: Infants showed a stronger novelty response (i.e., longer looking times) to new goal trials relative to new path trials. These findings suggest that infants selectively attend to and remember the features of action that are relevant to the actor's intention (for additional evidence, see Wellman & Phillips, 2001; Woodward, Sommerville, & Guajardo, 2001).

Woodward's (1998) findings indicate that, when faced with a discrete action (i.e., reaching for an object), infants readily attend to the intention-relevant features. However, the task of identifying others' intentions is complicated by the fact that human behavior tends to proceed in a continuous flow, lacking pauses to identify boundaries between distinct actions. Nevertheless, recent research indicates that infants as young as 10 to 11 months are sensitive to structure in behavior that coincides with the initiation and completion of intentions. Using a variant of the habituation/dishabituation paradigm, Baldwin, Baird, Saylor, and Clark (2001) showed infants digitized sequences of continuous, everyday action (e.g., a woman reaching to grasp a towel and hang it on a rack). In a familiarization phase, infants viewed the same action sequence repeatedly across several trials. In the subsequent test phase, infants viewed two different versions of the original action sequence, this time with still-frame pauses inserted at certain points in the course of action. The intention-completing test version highlighted the boundaries between intentions with a pause occurring just as the actor completed an intention (e.g., as she finished grasping the towel). The intention-interrupting test version disrupted the structure of the behavior sequence with a pause occurring prior to the completion of an intention (e.g., as the actor reached for the towel). The logic was as follows: If infants are sensitive to the structure of intentional action, they should look longer at the intention-interrupting test version (which violates this structure) than at the intention-completing test version (which preserves this structure). In fact, this is precisely what Baldwin et al. found. Following the familiarization phase, during which their interest in the unjunctured action sequence waned, infants demonstrated renewed interest (i.e., longer looking times) only in response to the intention-interrupting test version; they showed no such renewed interest in the intention-completing test version. A control study verified that, in the absence of familiarization, infants did not have a starting preference for the intention-interrupting test videos. These findings clarify that by 10 to 11 months of age, infants are sensitive to structure in behavior that coincides with the initiation and completion of intentions.[1]

In sum, by the end of their first year, infants show a variety of abilities that are relevant to the detection of intention in human action. They can distinguish between agents and inanimate objects. They are more sensitive to the goals of an action than the physical movements involved. They are also more sensitive to interruptions in action that occur before a goal is achieved than to interruptions occurring as the goal is achieved. We now turn to the issue of how to interpret these abilities.

Infant Detection of Intention: The Problem of Interpretation

The mechanisms underlying infants' abilities to detect intention-relevant structure in action are not yet understood and are the topic of much speculation and discussion (e.g., Baird & Baldwin, 2001; Povinelli, 2001). Povinelli (2001), for example, outlines three possible ways to interpret the findings from looking-time studies such as those of Woodward (1998) and Baldwin et al. (2001).

The first and most generous of these interpretations is that infants possess a genuine understanding of intention. Proponents of this viewpoint suggest that the human brain is endowed with a system or systems dedicated to the detection and interpretation of intentional action (e.g., Baron-Cohen, 1995; Premack, 1990). Such systems are innate, encapsulated, domain-specific parts of the cognitive architecture—in other words, modules. Leslie (1987, 1991), building on Fodor (1983), was the first to argue for a rich, innate endowment underlying children's understanding of other minds. His theory (e.g., Scholl & Leslie, 1999) posits a modular theory-of-mind mechanism that spontaneously computes the mental states contributing to observed behavior. Although Leslie does not focus specifically on the attribution of intention, other modular theorists do. For example, Baron-Cohen (1995) posits an intentionality detector (ID) that comes online in the first year of life and is triggered by self-propelled stimuli, interpreting such stimuli as agents that possess goals and desires. Baron-Cohen's ID is based on Premack's (1990; Premack & Premack, 1995) idea that infants are hardwired to directly perceive certain intentions—such as the intention to escape confinement or to overcome gravity—in self-propelled movement. Baron-Cohen argues, however, that ID is triggered by a broader range of motions than Premack suggests. It is a fundamental mechanism attributing (indeed sometimes over-attributing) agency and therefore, in his view, intention.

A second, more moderate view suggests not that infants are capable of attributing intentions, but that they possess skills for processing action that will ultimately lead to the construction of genuine understanding. This is the position cautiously adopted by Wellman and Phillips (2001), as well as by Woodward and colleagues (2001), who suggest that infants' attention and sensitivity to the intention-relevant features of action provide the basis for later developments in their understanding of intention.

The third alternative is that infants' ability to analyze action reflects the operation of a low-level perceptual system for detecting physical and temporal regularities in behavior (Baird & Baldwin, 2001) that is independent of an understanding of intention (Povinelli, 2001). As Povinelli explains, this interpretation "highlights the possibility that the early detection of the structural regularities of behavior are not, strictly speaking, the early manifestation of the uniquely human system for reasoning about intentions" (pp. 240–241). Rather, Povinelli argues, the system for detecting structure in behavior evolved independently of that for understanding the intentions of others. Evidence for this argument comes from the fact that, while a number of species are capable of detecting structural regularities in behavior, only humans are capable of reasoning about behavior in mentalistic terms. In human development, connections surely emerge between the low-level system for detecting structure in behavior and the high-level system for interpreting intentions (Baird & Baldwin, 2001; Povinelli, 2001). Nonetheless, the presence of structure-detection abilities in infancy does not imply that infants have embarked on genuine understanding.

However, those who are reluctant to assume that young infants' sensitivity to structure in behavior reflects an understanding of intention are convinced by the more sophisticated abilities of children in their second year of life.

Toddlers' Implicit Understanding of Intention

By 18 months of age, children demonstrate considerable social and communicative abilities. Children's rapid development in the realm of social interaction during their second year suggests that they possess real skills for perceiving others' intentions. This suggestion is confirmed by a growing number of studies in the domains of language learning, emotional understanding, and imitation, demonstrating that such young children can infer intention from the perceptual features of a person's facial, communicative, or other observable acts.

Language Learning

In any language learning context, speakers provide a number of clues to their communicative intentions. Unfortunately for infants, however, these clues are not always presented in isolation. The environment in which new object labels are offered is often cluttered with irrelevant information that may distract infants from the object of interest. In fact, for as many as 30% to 50% of labeling utterances that Western, middle-class infants hear, they are focused on an altogether different object than the one to which the speaker is actually referring (e.g., Collis, 1977). This phenomenon, termed *discrepant labeling* (Baldwin, 1991), has the potential to undermine language learning: Infants might associate the label they are hearing with the object of their own focus rather than with the object of the speaker's focus. However, research by Baldwin (1991, 1993) indicates that infants as young as 18 to 19 months tune into the direction of a speaker's gaze, and use this information to successfully infer the referent of a novel label. In her studies, infants heard novel labels for novel objects in two conditions: follow-in labeling, during which the speaker looked at and labeled the object of the infant's focus, and discrepant labeling, during which the speaker looked at and labeled an object other than that of the infant's focus. In the discrepant labeling condition, infants first checked and then followed the speaker's line of regard to the target object. When subsequently tested for comprehension of the novel label, infants correctly avoided associating the label with the object of their own focus, and instead linked the new word with its appropriate referent. These findings indicate that by 18 months of age, infants actively seek and successfully use cues to communicative intent when establishing new word-object mappings (see Baldwin & Tomasello, 1998, for a review).

Emotional Understanding

In addition to utilizing information about intentions in the domain of language learning, infants recruit similar cues to make sense of others' emotional messages. In a study by Moses, Baldwin, Rosicky, and Tidball (2001; see also Baldwin & Moses, 1994), for example, 12- and 18-month-old infants were shown two ambiguously valenced toys (e.g., a furry black spider and a moon face with sunglasses), one of which was put within infants' reach. As the infant focused on that toy and began to reach for it, the experimenter provided either a positive (e.g., "Oh! Nice!") or negative (e.g., "Iiuu! Yecch!") affective response. Similar to Baldwin's (1991, 1993) follow-in versus discrepant labeling conditions, the experimenter either looked toward the infant's toy (joint focus) or the other toy (discrepant focus) while producing the affective label. Infants' subsequent responses clearly indicated that they specifically linked the experimenter's emotion with the toy of the experimenter's focus, regardless of which toy they themselves had been focused on at the time the affective label was provided. These findings reveal infants' ability to use cues to attentional focus to discern the intended referent of an emotional display (for additional evidence, see Mumme, Fernald, & Herrera, 1996; Repacholi, 1998).

Imitation

Studies of early imitation provide yet another window on infants' understanding of intention. In a widely cited study, Meltzoff (1995) showed 18-month-old infants an adult trying and repeatedly failing to complete an action on a novel object. In one demonstration, for example, the adult made three unsuccessful attempts to pull apart a dumbbell. When subsequently given the opportunity to manipulate the object, infants immediately produced the intended action, despite having never before seen the actor achieve that goal. In fact, infants were just as likely to perform the intended action in response to viewing the adult's failed attempts as they were in response to a successful demonstration of the target action. However, infants did not reproduce the intended action if the failed attempt was modeled only once (Meltzoff, Gopnik, & Repacholi, 1999). These findings suggest that, for infants as well as adults (Heider, 1958), seeing repeated attempts at a given action is relevant for inferring the actor's intention.

Another study of early imitation similarly clarifies infants' ability to comprehend the goal directedness of others' behavior. In a study by Carpenter, Akhtar, and Tomasello (1998), 14- to 18-month-old infants watched an adult performing a sequence of two actions (e.g., pulling a handle and spinning a wheel) on a novel object. Both actions produced a salient result (e.g., a toy appeared); however, the actor linguistically marked one action as intentional ("There!"), and the other as accidental ("Whoops!"). When subsequently given the object and asked to "make it work," infants across the 14- to 18-month age span produced the action marked as intentional far more often than the accidental one. Thus, infants not only distinguished the two actions with respect to their intentional status, they apparently viewed intentional events as more informative, or perhaps as more deserving of reenactment, than accidental events (but see Meltzoff et al., 1999).

In sum, the findings reviewed in this section reveal that, by 18 months of age, infants possess an impressive ability to use information from the observable physical world (i.e., others' communications and actions) to draw inferences about intentions. However, all of the research discussed has been concerned with children's implicit understanding of intention, that is, an understanding that is revealed in children's actions and reactions. This is due, at least in part, to the methodological constraints necessarily imposed on researchers working with such young children, whose linguistic abilities are severely limited (Meltzoff et al., 1999). Once children reach 3 years of age, they can participate in experiments that require verbal skill in one or more areas, such as comprehending stories, understanding an experimenter's questions, or producing verbal responses. This research reveals children's more explicit understanding of intention.

Young Preschoolers' Explicit Understanding of Intention

Young preschoolers' understanding of intention is similar to that of older infants and toddlers insofar as it is based on observable actions and speech acts. However, it is more explicit because during the period from 18 months to 3 years of age, children's language skills develop rapidly, and they begin to refer to intention and desire. The development of talk about intention is revealed by naturalistic observations of children's conversations with parents and siblings in the home. Soon after they start to talk, children use *will* and *gonna* to refer to their own and others' future actions (Gee & Savasir, 1985; Wells, 1979). They also use *gonna*, interchangeably with *wanna*, to refer to an immediate future that expresses the child's intention or desire (Bartsch & Wellman, 1995, p. 68; Brown, 1973). In addition, between 2 and 3 years of age, children start to explain and excuse actions using intention terms (e.g., *mean, try, on purpose*; Bretherton, 1991; Dunn, 1988).

Thus, by 3 years of age, children are able to verbalize their understanding of intention, as demonstrated in a number of studies investigating preschoolers' ability to distinguish between intentional and accidental events. In a study by Shultz, Wells, and Sarda (1980), for example, children were induced to make mistakes (e.g., in trying to repeat tongue twisters) and subsequently asked whether or not their mistaken behavior was intentional (e.g., "Did you mean to do that?"). Children as young as 3 years of age could distinguish between intentional and unintentional events for their own behavior as well as for the behavior of others. However, an alternative explanation for these findings is that 3-year-olds based their judgments on the desirability of the outcome. Because mistakes are inherently undesirable, children might judge them as unintentional on this basis alone. To circumvent this possibility, Shultz and Wells (1985) presented 3-year-olds with an electronic target-shooting game in which the shooter first selected one of several targets to hit, and then fired a shot that hit either the selected target or one of the other targets. In this case, unlike the tongue twister experiment, a given target was neither inherently desirable nor undesirable. Whether or not a target was intended instead depended on the shooter's initial choice. However, unknown to the child, the apparatus was rigged so that the experimenter could control which target was actually hit. When asked to determine whether the shooter had meant to hit that target, 3-year-olds reported an intention more often when the outcome matched the shooter's stated goal than when it did not. Similarly, Yuill (1984) demonstrated that children as young as age 3 can coordinate goal and outcome information in their judgments of satisfaction. Three-year-olds in her study judged a character who wanted and achieved a certain outcome to be more pleased than a character who achieved, but did not want, the same outcome.

The findings just reviewed suggest that by 3 years of age, children have explicit knowledge of the distinction between intentional and unintentional behavior. This is perhaps not surprising given the abilities of even younger children to make this distinction implicitly (e.g., Carpenter et al., 1998). However, one concern with the aforementioned studies is that children's success could be explained by a matching strategy (e.g., Astington, 1991; Shultz & Wells, 1985). That is, rather than genuinely understanding intention, children may succeed in these tasks simply by comparing the stated desire or goal with the subsequent outcome. When the desire and outcome match, the action is labeled intentional; when they do not match, it is labeled unintentional. Children's success, however, is dependent on the desired goal state being made explicit in the experimental context (see next section).

Older Preschoolers' Understanding of Intention Based on Unobservables

In studies that preclude the use of a matching strategy by withholding desire or goal information, children do not succeed at distinguishing between intentional and unintentional behaviors until age 5. For example, Smith (1978) asked children aged 4 to 6 years to determine whether voluntary (e.g., walking), involuntary (e.g., sneezing), or object-like (e.g., being pushed by another object) movements were intentional. Four-year-olds tended to regard all types of movement as intentional, whereas 5-year-olds excluded both involuntary acts and object-like movements from the category of intentional action. Moreover, Shultz and colleagues (1980) found that 5-year-olds, but not 3- or 4-year-olds, could distinguish intended acts from reflexes or passive movements. Finally, Astington and Lee (1991) presented 3-, 4-, and 5-year-olds with pairs of stories in which one character intentionally caused an outcome and another character accidentally achieved the same outcome. However, neither story offered any explicit information about the character's desire or goal. In one story, for instance, a girl takes some bread outside, throws crumbs onto the ground, and some birds peck them up. In the paired story, another girl takes some bread outside, the crumbs just happened to drop onto the ground behind her, and some birds peck them up. When asked, "Which girl meant the birds to eat the crumbs?," 3-year-olds performed at chance levels, whereas 5-year-olds demonstrated above-chance success at identifying the intentional event.

On the basis of 3-year-olds' poor performance on tasks that preclude the use of a goal-outcome matching strategy, some researchers have suggested that young preschoolers' early concept of intention is undifferentiated from their concept of desire (e.g., Astington, 2001; Astington & Gopnik, 1991; Perner, 1991). As discussed earlier, although intentions and desires both represent goal states, intentions are critically different in that they also represent the means to achieving the goal. Thus, children must be able to think separately about the desire for an outcome and the intention to act in a manner that will bring about the outcome. A fruitful way to assess children's understanding of the distinction between desire and intention is to create scenarios in which an intention is unfulfilled but the corresponding desire is satisfied. In one such study (Schult, 2002), children heard stories in which the outcome (a) satisfied both the actor's desire and intention, (b) satisfied the desire but not the intention, (c) satisfied the intention but not the desire, or (d) satisfied neither the desire nor the intention. In one intention-unfulfilled/desire-satisfied story, for example, Becky wanted a new doll and planned to buy it at the store. Before she did so, however, her mom gave her the doll. After the story, children were asked to determine whether Becky's desire and intention were fulfilled. Specifically, children were asked, "Did Becky get what she wanted?" (desire question) and "Did Becky do what she planned to do?" (intention question). In response to the desire question, 4-, 5-, and 7-year-olds correctly stated that Becky got what she wanted. However, in response to the intention question, 4-year-olds incorrectly stated that Becky did what she had planned to do. In contrast, 5- and 7-year-olds correctly assessed that her intention had not been fulfilled. Four-year-olds also had difficulty assessing whether or not an intention was fulfilled in the other discrepant stories (intention-fulfilled/desire-unsatisfied), but evidenced no such difficulty when the fulfillment of intention coincided with the satisfaction of desire.

Interestingly, children appear to have as much difficulty distinguishing between their own desires and intentions as they do in differentiating intention from desire from a third-person perspective. Phillips, Baron-Cohen, and Rutter (1998; see also Schult, 2002) adapted the target-shooting game introduced by Shultz and Wells (1985) to create instances in which intention and desire did not coincide. Phillips et al.'s task included a row of colored cans, some of which contained prizes. Children stated which can they wanted to hit, took aim, and shot toward it. However, the game was secretly rigged so that, although children selected which color to aim for, the experimenter controlled which can actually fell and whether it contained a prize. The child's intention was to hit a particular color; the desire was to get a prize. As in the Schult (2002) study, four conditions were included: two in which the desire and intention coincided (i.e., both satisfied or neither satisfied) and two in which the desire and intention did not coincide. In the intention-fulfilled/

desire-unsatisfied condition, for example, the child hit the intended can (e.g., green) but it did not contain a prize. When subsequently asked, "Which can did you mean to shoot? The green one or the red one?," 4-year-olds were more likely to say that they meant to shoot the red one. That is, despite having hit the can they said they were aiming for, 4-year-olds reported having intended to hit a different color can when the chosen can did not contain a prize. Five-year-olds, in contrast, accurately reported their initial intention, even when its fulfillment did not coincide with the satisfaction of their desire.

Further limitations in young children's concept of intention are revealed in studies that assess their understanding of the distinction between intention and action. As discussed earlier, despite their causal role in motivating action, intentions are not isomorphic with actions. One can pursue a variety of actions to fulfill a given intention, and a given action is consistent with any number of possible intentions. In a recent study, Baird and Moses (2001) investigated children's understanding of the many-to-many relation between intentions and actions by examining 4- and 5-year-olds' ability to attribute different intentions to characters performing identical actions. Children heard stories (accompanied by pictures) in which two characters performed the same action (e.g., running), yet had different desires (e.g., to be home for dinner versus to be healthy and strong). Children were asked to determine what each character was trying to do (e.g., get somewhere fast versus get some exercise). Five-year-olds successfully assigned different intentions to the two characters, despite the fact that the characters' actions were identical. In contrast, 4-year-olds tended to attribute the same intention to both characters, even though the characters' desires clearly differed. A control condition clarified that 4-year-olds nevertheless could attribute different intentions to characters performing different actions. However, despite several task simplifications, their difficulty assigning two intentions to characters performing identical actions persisted, suggesting that young children may not appreciate the distinction between intention and action.

In sum, by the end of the preschool years, children's understanding of intention is quite sophisticated. They can distinguish between intentional and unintentional action even in cases where no information is available on which to match goal and outcome. They can correctly identify cases where desires are satisfied but intentions are not fulfilled, and corresponding cases where intentions are fulfilled but desires are not satisfied; that is, they recognize the distinction between intention and desire. They also recognize the distinction between intention and action, appreciating that the same action may be motivated by different intentions. In all of these situations, children can talk about the distinctions. Thus, by the end of the preschool years, children's understanding of intention is explicit and goes beyond inferences based on overt actions and communications.

What Have 5-Year-Olds Achieved and How Have They Achieved It?

The research reviewed in this chapter shows that children's concept of intention is gradually developed during the early years. The process begins with infants' ability to detect intention in action, which is followed by toddlers' ability to infer intention from observable actions and speech acts. Young preschoolers can make these inferences explicit in their talk about intention. However, it is not until the end of the preschool years that children understand intention as a product of the unobservable mind, distinct from the desire that precedes it and the action that ensues. Thus, over the first few years of life there is a shift from understanding expressed in behavior to verbalizable understanding, and a shift from understanding based on the observable world to one based on the unobservable mind.

How do these changes come about? In our view, language plays a crucially important role. First, and most obviously, the acquisition of intention terms by 2- and 3-year-olds allows them to refer to intention and to respond to specific questions about people's intentions. Three-year-olds can verbally distinguish between someone who meant to do something and someone who did not mean to do it. They can talk about something being done accidentally or on purpose, and about what somebody is going to do or is trying to do.

Second, and more important, it is not simply that language reveals an understanding that children already possessed, but rather it is instrumental in the development of new understanding (Astington, 1999). Obviously, as the research that we have discussed illustrates, prelinguistic infants and young toddlers have a rich understanding of intentions as they are expressed in observable actions. For example, the 18-month-olds in Meltzoff's (1995) study demonstrated some understanding of prior intention, not just intention-in-action, when they produced the action the adult meant to perform rather than the movement that they actually observed. However, as the research with 3-year-olds illustrates, young children's intention concept is still imprecise—they conceive of a motivational state that conflates intention and desire. Language significantly influences and increases children's understanding by enabling them to refine this concept. They move on from holding a generalized notion of motivation observable in behavior, to conceiving of a representational mental state that is distinct from the desire that precedes it and the action that is taken to achieve the desired outcome.

In the mature concept, then, intention occupies an intermediate place in the chain linking desire to outcome, straddling the external world of action and the internal world of the mind. Thus, 5-year-olds' achievement lies in their ability to recognize that intention and action are distinct links in the chain, mediating between desire state and outcome. Perner (1991; Perner,

Stummer, & Lang, 1999) argues that it is the development of metarepresentational ability that underlies this achievement. We agree, but, further, we would contend that language is fundamental to the development of metarepresentation. Metarepresentational ability is marked by the child's understanding that people represent the world in mind, and act on the basis of their representation of the world, even in cases where it misrepresents the actual situation in the world. Language development may be crucial to the development of metarepresentational ability because language provides a format in which the child can represent a person's misrepresentation, in the face of the conflicting actual situation that the child perceives.

Thus, the ability to metarepresent, which develops toward the end of the preschool years, allows children to think about people mentally representing the world. They then conceive of intention and other mental states, such as belief and desire, as representations that are separate from the real world of objects, events, and actions. Once a child can metarepresent, he or she recognizes that people construct the world in their minds, and that this constructed world is the world in which people act, even when their representation is a misrepresentation of reality. Research investigating the development of metarepresentational understanding has focused on children's understanding of belief, especially false belief (Wellman, Cross, & Watson, 2001). In the classic false-belief task, developed by Wimmer and Perner (1983), a story is acted out for children in which, for example, a boy places his chocolate in a drawer and goes out to play. While the boy is gone, his mother moves the chocolate to the cupboard. The boy then returns, hungry for his chocolate, and children are asked to predict where he will look for it. For the reader, the correct answer should be obvious: The boy will look in the drawer, where he thinks the chocolate is, and not in the cupboard where it actually is. For 3-year-olds, however, the correct answer is not so obvious: Most 3-year-olds predict that the boy will look in the new location—after all, he wants his chocolate and that is where it is in reality. Around 4 years of age, children begin to understand that people act not on the basis of reality, but rather on the basis of their beliefs about reality. Children who appreciate this fact clearly have metarepresentational understanding.

It may be that metarepresentational understanding also underlies the ability to distinguish between desire and intention (Astington, 2001). Three-year-olds cannot make this distinction because they do not think of a person's desires and intentions as mental representations produced by the individual. Although 3-year-olds can represent different situations, including hypothetical ones, they cannot represent themselves or another person representing the hypothetical situation. Thus, they understand intention by thinking of the goal state as a hypothetical situation and associating the person with that situation (Perner, 1991). They then can judge that the person will act to achieve the goal and will be satisfied if it is achieved (Yuill, 1984). However, in order to distinguish between desire and intention, the child must represent herself or another person representing the hypothetical desired or intended situation. That is, the child has to understand that the action to achieve a goal must be caused by some internal representation of it. In Perner's (1991, pp. 219–220) terms, in the 3-year-old's view of goal-directed action there are only goals that people have and actions that they can take to achieve those goals. There is only the goal and the action, not the separate notion of the intention to act. The child who can metarepresent can separate these two notions; that is, the intention to act can be understood as a mental state representing that one will act. The representation of the action is not a hypothetical situation but part of the same world, albeit internal, as the action itself. Intention thus connects the internal world of the mind and the external world of action, and the representational mental state can be understood as causally responsible for the action. Now it is possible to think separately of the desire for an outcome and the intention to act to achieve the outcome. Thus, Perner argues, metarepresentational ability underlies a refined concept of intention.

In support of this argument, Lang and Perner (2002) demonstrated that there is a close relation between children's understanding of false beliefs and their understanding that reflexive movements (e.g., the knee-jerk reflex) are not intentional actions. In their study, false-belief task performance and recognition that the knee jerk is unintentional were strongly correlated, even when controlling for age and verbal ability. Lang and Perner argue that the two are related because in both cases children must understand mental states as representations with causal efficacy. That is, in the false-belief task, it is the character's false belief that causes him to search in the empty location (e.g., the drawer) even though it does not satisfy his desire to find the chocolate. Similarly, one does not mean to move one's leg when it moves up in the knee-jerk reflex, because the movement is not caused by a mental state of intention. Both cases depend on the metarepresentational ability that allows the child to understand how the mind causes actions to occur.

This claim, however, leads to a further question: What promotes the development of metarepresentational ability? It is here that we would argue for the crucial role of language. It has been shown that language development precedes and promotes the metarepresentation of belief (Astington & Jenkins, 1999). In this study, 3-year-old children were tested three times over a 7-month period. At each time point, general language ability was assessed using a standardized measure of reception and production of syntax and semantics (Hresko, Reid, & Hammill, 1981). Metarepresentational ability was assessed using false-belief tasks. Earlier language abilities predicted later false-belief task performance (controlling for earlier false-belief task performance), but earlier metarepresentational ability, as measured by the false-belief tasks, did not predict later language test performance (controlling for earlier language). These findings are consistent with the argument that language is fundamental to the development of metarepresentational ability.

We do not yet know whether children's understanding of intention is as closely related to language ability as is their understanding of belief. We might suspect that it is not, because motivational states are more obvious in behavior and more closely tied to observable emotional expression. However, insofar as intentions, like beliefs, represent propositional attitudes to propositional contents, language ability may be similarly crucial to the development of the ability to metarepresent intention. In Lang and Perner's (2002) study, cited above, language ability correlates highly with both false-belief task performance and recognition that the knee jerk is unintentional. This suggests that language development is related to the ability to metarepresent both belief and intention.

In conclusion, we have argued that language is important in the development of children's concept of intention in two distinct but related ways. First, in social, communicational interaction, children acquire semantic terms to refer explicitly to intention. Second, and more speculatively, we argued that language provides the representational format for the metarepresentation of intention, which may underlie the ability to distinguish between intention and desire. That is, the development of language may enable the shift from an understanding of intention based on the observable world to one based on the unobservable mind.

Acknowledgments Preparation of this chapter was supported by a postdoctoral fellowship from the National Institute of Child Health and Human Development (#5F32 HD-08594-02) to the lead author and by a grant from the Natural Sciences and Engineering Research Council of Canada to the second author. We are grateful to Diego Fernandez-Duque, Ran Hassin, and Jim Uleman for helpful discussion and comments.

Note

1. All of the studies described in this section employ looking-time paradigms to explore infants' perceptual and cognitive abilities. Using this paradigm has a number of benefits (Haith & Benson, 1998): It is well studied, there are established indices of reliability and stability, it is relatively inexpensive and easy to use, and it requires minimal participation on the part of infant subjects. However, Haith and Benson have also outlined several drawbacks to the looking-time paradigm for studying infant cognition. First, the paradigm provides only binary (yes/no) answers to questions about infant perception (e.g., Can infants discriminate event A from event B?) and thus may not be well suited to answering more complex questions about infant cognition. Second, differential looking times reveal only that infants can discriminate between two events; they do not explain why infants look longer at one event than at another. Finally, Haith and Benson

argue that the use of a familiarization phase in looking-time studies makes it difficult to determine whether infants come to the experiment with the ability to discriminate the test events or whether they develop this ability in the process of familiarization.

References

Astington, J. W. (1991). Intention in the child's theory of mind. In D. Frye & C. Moore (Eds.), *Children's theories of mind* (pp. 157–172). Hillsdale, NJ: Erlbaum.

Astington, J. W. (1999). The language of intention: Three ways of doing it. In P. D. Zelazo, J. W. Astington, & D. R. Olson (Eds.), *Developing theories of intention: Social understanding and self control* (pp. 295–315). Mahwah, NJ: Erlbaum.

Astington, J. W. (2001). The paradox of intention: Assessing children's metarepresentational understanding. In B. F. Malle, L. J. Moses, & D. A. Baldwin (Eds.), *Intentions and intentionality: Foundations of social cognition* (pp. 85–103). Cambridge, MA: MIT Press.

Astington, J. W., & Gopnik, A. (1991). Developing understanding of desire and intention. In A. Whiten (Ed.), *Natural theories of mind: Evolution, development, and simulation of everyday mindreading* (pp. 39–50). Oxford: Blackwell.

Astington, J. W., & Jenkins, J. M. (1999). A longitudinal study of the relation between language and theory of mind development. *Developmental Psychology, 35*, 1311–1320.

Astington, J. W., & Lee, E. (1991, April). *What do children know about intentional causation?* Paper presented at the biennial meeting of the Society for Research in Child Development, Seattle, WA.

Baird, J. A., & Baldwin, D. A. (2001). Making sense of human behavior: Action parsing and intentional inference. In B. F. Malle, L. J. Moses, & D. A. Baldwin (Eds.), *Intentions and intentionality: Foundations of social cognition* (pp. 193–206). Cambridge, MA: MIT Press.

Baird, J. A., & Moses, L. J. (2001). Do preschoolers appreciate that identical actions may be motivated by different intentions? *Journal of Cognition and Development, 2*, 413–448.

Baldwin, D. A. (1991). Infants' contribution to the achievement of joint reference. *Child Development, 62*, 875–890.

Baldwin, D. A. (1993). Infants' ability to consult the speaker for clues to word reference. *Journal of Child Language, 20*, 395–418.

Baldwin, D. A., & Baird, J. A. (1999). Action analysis: A gateway to intentional inference. In P. Rochat (Ed.), *Early social cognition* (pp. 215–240). Hillsdale, NJ: Erlbaum.

Baldwin, D. A., Baird, J. A., Saylor, M. M., & Clark, M. A. (2001). Infants parse dynamic action. *Child Development, 72*, 708–717.

Baldwin, D. A., & Moses, L. J. (1994). Early understanding of referential intent and attentional focus: Evidence from language and emotion. In C. Lewis & P. Mitchell (Eds.), *Children's early understanding of mind: Origins and development* (pp. 133–156). Hove, UK: Erlbaum.

Baldwin, D. A., & Tomasello, M. (1998). Word learning: A window on early pragmatic understanding. In E. Clark (Ed.), *Proceedings of the twenty-ninth annual Child Language Research Forum* (pp. 3–23). Cambridge, UK: Cambridge University Press.

Baron-Cohen, S. (1995). *Mindblindness: An essay on autism and theory of mind.* Cambridge, MA: MIT Press.

Bartsch, K., & Wellman, H. M. (1995). *Children talk about the mind.* New York: Oxford University Press.

Bratman, M. E. (1987). *Intention, plans, and practical reason.* Cambridge, MA: Harvard University Press.

Bretherton, I. (1991). Intentional communication and the development of an understanding of mind. In D. Frye & C. Moore (Eds.), *Children's theories of mind* (pp. 49–75). Hillsdale, NJ: Erlbaum.

Brown, R. (1973). *A first language: The early stages.* Cambridge, MA: Harvard University Press.

Carpenter, M., Akhtar, N., & Tomasello, M. (1998). Fourteen- through 18-month-old infants differentially imitate intentional and accidental actions. *Infant Behavior and Development, 21,* 315–330.

Collis, G. M. (1977). Visual co-orientation and maternal speech. In H. R. Schaffer (Ed.), *Studies in mother-infant interaction* (pp. 355–375). London: Academic Press.

Dienes, Z., & Perner, J. (1999). A theory of implicit and explicit knowledge. *Behavioral and Brain Sciences, 22,* 735–808.

Dunn, J. (1988). *The beginnings of social understanding.* Cambridge, MA: Harvard University Press.

Fodor, J. A. (1983). *The modularity of mind.* Cambridge, MA: MIT Press.

Gee, J., & Savasir, I. (1985). On the use of will and gonna: Toward a description of activity-types for child language. *Discourse Processes, 8,* 143–175.

Haith, M. M., & Benson, J. B. (1998). Infant cognition. In W. Damon (Series Ed.), D. Kuhn & R. Siegler (Vol. Eds.), *Handbook of child psychology: Vol. 2. Cognition, perception, and language* (5th ed., pp. 199–254). New York: Wiley.

Heider, F. (1958). *The psychology of interpersonal relations.* New York: Wiley.

Hresko, W. P., Reid, D. K., & Hammill, D. D. (1981). *The Test of Early Language Development (TELD).* Austin, TX: Pro-Ed.

Johnson, S., Slaughter, V., & Carey, S. (1998). Whose gaze will infants follow? The elicitation of gaze-following in 12-month-olds. *Developmental Science, 1,* 233–238.

Lang, B., & Perner, J. (2002). Understanding of intention and false belief and the development of self-control. *British Journal of Developmental Psychology, 20,* 67–76.

Leslie, A. M. (1987). Pretense and representation: The origins of "theory of mind." *Psychological Review, 94,* 412–426.

Leslie, A. M. (1991). The theory of mind impairment in autism: Evidence for a modular mechanism of development? In A. Whiten (Ed.), *Natural theories of mind: Evolution, development and simulation of everyday mindreading* (pp. 63–78). Oxford: Basil Blackwell.

Malle, B. F., & Knobe, J. (2001). The distinction between desire and intention: A folk-conceptual analysis. In B. F. Malle, L. J. Moses, & D. A. Baldwin (Eds.), *Intentions and intentionality: Foundations of social cognition* (pp. 45–67). Cambridge, MA: MIT Press.

Malle, B. F., Moses, L. J., & Baldwin, D. A. (2001). The significance of intentionality. In B. F. Malle, L. J. Moses, & D. A. Baldwin (Eds.), *Intentions and intentionality: Foundations of social cognition* (pp. 1–24). Cambridge, MA: MIT Press.

Meltzoff, A. N. (1995). Understanding the intentions of others: Re-enactment of intended acts by 18-month-old children. *Developmental Psychology, 31,* 838–850.

Meltzoff, A. N., Gopnik, A., & Repacholi, B. M. (1999). Toddlers' understanding of intentions, desires, and emotions: Explorations of the dark ages. In P. D. Zelazo, J. W. Astington, & D. R. Olson (Eds.), *Developing theories of intention: Social understanding and self-control* (pp. 17–41). Mahwah, NJ: Erlbaum.

Moses, L. J. (1993). Young children's understanding of belief constraints on intention. *Cognitive Development, 8*, 1–25.

Moses, L. J. (2001). Some thoughts on ascribing complex intentional concepts to young children. In B. F. Malle, L. J. Moses, & D. A. Baldwin (Eds.), *Intentions and intentionality: Foundations of social cognition* (pp. 69–83). Cambridge, MA: MIT Press.

Moses, L. J., Baldwin, D. A., Rosicky, J., & Tidball, G. (2001). Evidence for referential understanding in the emotions domain at twelve and eighteen months. *Child Development, 72*, 718–735.

Mumme, D. L., Fernald, A., & Herrera, C. (1996). Infants' responses to facial and vocal emotional signals in a social referencing paradigm. *Child Development, 67*, 3219–3237.

Perner, J. (1991). *Understanding the representational mind.* Cambridge, MA: MIT Press.

Perner, J., Stummer, S., & Lang, B. (1999). Executive functions and theory of mind: Cognitive complexity or functional dependence? In P. D. Zelazo, J. W. Astington, & D. R. Olson (Eds.), *Developing theories of intention: Social understanding and self control* (pp. 133–152). Mahwah, NJ: Erlbaum.

Phillips, W., Baron-Cohen, S., & Rutter, M. (1998). Understanding intention in normal development and in autism. *British Journal of Developmental Psychology, 16*, 337–348.

Povinelli, D. J. (2001). On the possibilities of detecting intentions prior to understanding them. In B. F. Malle, L. J. Moses, & D. A. Baldwin (Eds.), *Intentions and intentionality: Foundations of social cognition* (pp. 225–248). Cambridge, MA: MIT Press.

Premack, D. (1990). The infant's theory of self-propelled objects. *Cognition, 36*, 1–16.

Premack, D., & Premack, A. J. (1995). Intention as psychological cause. In D. Sperber, D. Premack, & A. J. Premack (Eds.), *Causal cognition: A multidisciplinary debate* (pp. 185–199). New York: Clarendon Press.

Premack, D., & Woodruff, G. (1978). Does the chimpanzee have a theory of mind? *Behavioral and Brain Sciences, 4*, 515–526.

Repacholi, B. M. (1998). Infants' use of attentional cues to identify the referent of another person's emotional expression. *Developmental Psychology, 34*, 1017–1025.

Ruffman, T. (2000). Nonverbal theory of mind: Is it important, is it implicit, is it simulation, is it relevant to autism? In J. W. Astington (Ed.), *Minds in the making: Essays in honor of David R. Olson* (pp. 250–266). Oxford, UK: Blackwell.

Scholl, B. J., & Leslie, A. M. (1999). Modularity, development and "theory of mind." *Mind and Language, 14*, 131–153.

Schult, C. A. (2002). *Children's understanding of the distinction between intentions and desires. Child Development, 73*, 1727–1747.

Searle, J. R. (1983). *Intentionality: An essay in philosophy of mind.* Cambridge, UK: Cambridge University Press.

Searle, J. R. (1984). *Minds, brains, and science.* Cambridge, MA: Harvard University Press.

Shultz, T. R., & Wells, D. (1985). Judging the intentionality of action-outcomes. *Developmental Psychology, 21*, 83–89.

Shultz, T. R., Wells, D., & Sarda, M. (1980). Development of the ability to distinguish intended actions from mistakes, reflexes, and passive movements. *British Journal of Social and Clinical Psychology, 19*, 301–310.

Smith, M. C. (1978). Cognizing the behavior stream: The recognition of intentional action. *Child Development, 49*, 736–743.

Wellman, H. M., Cross, D., & Watson, J. (2001). Meta-analysis of theory-of-mind development: The truth about false belief. *Child Development, 72*, 655–684.

Wellman, H. M., & Phillips, A. T. (2001). Developing intentional understandings. In B. F. Malle, L. J. Moses, & D. A. Baldwin (Eds.), *Intentions and intentionality: Foundations of social cognition* (pp. 125–148). Cambridge, MA: MIT Press.

Wells, G. (1979). Learning and using the auxiliary verb in English. In V. Lee (Ed.), *Language development* (pp. 250–270). London: Croom Helm.

Wimmer, H., & Perner, J. (1983). Beliefs about beliefs: Representation and constraining function of wrong beliefs in young children's understanding of deception. *Cognition, 13*, 103–128.

Woodward, A. L. (1998). Infants selectively encode the goal object of an actor's reach. *Cognition, 69*, 1–34.

Woodward, A. L., Phillips, A. T., & Spelke, E. S. (1993). Infants' expectations about the motion of animate versus inanimate objects. In *Proceedings of the fifteenth annual conference of the Cognitive Science Society, Boulder, CO* (pp. 1087–1091). Hillsdale, NJ: Erlbaum.

Woodward, A. L., Sommerville, J. A., & Guajardo, J. J. (2001). How infants make sense of intentional action. In B. F. Malle, L. J. Moses, & D. A. Baldwin (Eds.), *Intentions and intentionality: Foundations of social cognition* (pp. 149–169). Cambridge, MA: MIT Press.

Yuill, N. (1984). Young children's coordination of motive and outcome in judgements of satisfaction and morality. *British Journal of Developmental Psychology, 2*, 73–81.

11

Theory of Mind: Conscious Attribution and Spontaneous Trait Inference

Angeline S. Lillard and Lori Skibbe

Theory of mind refers to the tendency to construe people in terms of their mental states and traits (Premack & Woodruff, 1978). If we see someone grimace, we might infer that he or she is disappointed, and if we see a man running toward a bus, we probably infer that he is trying to catch it. The word *theory* is applied to such mentalistic inferences for two reasons. First, mental states are unobservable, so their existence is merely theoretical. Second, our body of knowledge about the mind resembles a theory in several ways (Wellman, 1990). One resemblance is that knowledge about minds is causal-explanatory in nature, as are scientific theories. We explain the man running toward the bus as wanting to be on the bus and thinking it is going to pull away soon. We predict that he will be relieved if he makes it and disappointed if he does not. We also can predict that certain actions might ensue if he does not reach the bus. He may try to notify others of his late arrival by telephone, he may try to hail a taxi, or he may consult a schedule regarding the next bus. What mediates these further actions are his mental states. He will want others to know his whereabouts, he thinks that calling will accomplish that, and so on. Hence we can describe our understanding of others' mental states as a theory of mind.

The first signs of appreciation of mental states appear very early in young children. For example, Baldwin (1991) found that 18-month-olds are sensitive to an adult's focus of attention when learning words. In these experiments, a child was playing with a new toy, and an adult was nearby, looking into an opaque bucket at another new toy that the child could not see. The adult said, "It's a toma! Look at the toma!" several times. Later, the child was asked to get the toma, and was given a choice of a few toys. Children usually chose what was in the bucket (even though it had not been visible at time of naming) rather than what they themselves had been playing with. Novel words were thus mapped onto the object that an adult labeler was focused on, even when the child was playing with a different object. By 18 months, then, children are sensitive to adults' focus of attention when learning new words.

Even younger children seem cognizant about accidents, goals, and intentions. Tomasello and his colleagues found that 14- to 18-month-olds imitated adults' acts when they were followed by a confident word, "There!" but not when they were followed by "Whoops!" (Carpenter, Akhtar, & Tomasello, 1998). Gergeley, Nadasdy, Csibra, and Biro (1995) and Woodward (1998) have shown sensitivity to various aspects of goals even in the first year. In Woodward's experiments, infants were habituated to an adult repeatedly grasping one of two objects, one placed on the right and the other on the left side of a stage. For the test trial, the placement of the two objects was switched, and a new grasp was directed either at the old object in its new location or at the new object in the old location (where the hand had gone previously). In spatial terms, the latter situation was more like what had been habituated to, because the hand was moving to the same place. In intentional terms, the former was more similar, given that the hand was grasping the same object. Infants of 9 months and older recovered interest at the sight of the hand grasping the new object in the old location, suggesting they saw it as a different event. This implies that they understood something related to the actor's goals in getting the object. When the same movements were made by a pole rather than a human arm and hand, infants dishabituated in the opposite manner, apparently "interpreting" the situation in a physical, nonintentional way. Rudimentary mentalizing abilities thus appear to begin during infancy.

Theory of mind capabilities evolve throughout childhood, with simple understanding of perception and its links to knowledge emerging in the toddler years, understanding of false belief and mental representation emerging around age 4 years, and understanding of complex emotions like surprise and pride emerging somewhat later (for reviews, see Flavell & Miller, 1998; Wellman, 2002).

The very early onset and predictable developmental course of theory of mind abilities has led some to suggest that they are supported by innate processes (Baron-Cohen, 1995; Bruner, 1990; Fodor, 1992; Leslie, 1994). These theorists argue that infants are too young to infer matters as complex as mental states, and they are not explicitly taught about them. Indeed, since mental states are invisible, their existence cannot be highlighted in the ostensive manner that many elements of the world are. An adult cannot point and say, "That is a desire. See the desire?" as they do for so many early conceptual acquisitions (Scholl & Leslie, 1999). A second source of support for theory of mind stemming from an innate process is the ease with which normal adults make theory of mind attributions, at least with reference to traits. When we are told someone tripped while learning a new dance step, we automatically assume that person is clumsy (Ross & Nisbett, 1991; Uleman, Newman, & Moskowitz, 1996). Although lacking empirical evidence regarding spontaneous mental state attributions, when we see a woman running to the bus as if to get on it, it seems we cannot help but see her as wanting to get on it. Indeed, we even apply folk psychology to inanimate entities like triangles (Abell, Happe, & Frith, 2000; Heider & Simmel, 1944), a clear case of extreme overattribution. In sum, the early and automatic deployment of a theory of mind has led to speculation that it stems from an innate process. This innate process could take the form of a module (Baron-Cohen, 1995; Fodor, 1992; Leslie, 1994).

Modularity

"A module is a specialized, encapsulated mental organ that has evolved to handle specific information types of particular relevance to the species" (Elman et al., 1996, p. 36). As is apparent in this definition, which corresponds to the common usage of *module* in cognitive development today, modularity and innateness are often bedfellows, because modules are thought to have evolved in the species. Innateness is not a requirement of modules (Karmiloff-Smith, 1992)—a module could quite plausibly develop over ontogeny without being prespecified—but discussion of modules in the cognitive development literature often assumes that modules are specified a priori by a person's DNA.

The view that minds are structured a priori in a way that corresponds to the structure of knowledge can be traced to Plato's dialogue *Meno*. When the slave boy stated various geometric principles, it was agreed that he had not been taught such ideas and that the ideas must therefore be innate. Descartes (1641/1993) later conceded to innate concepts of self and of God, from which other concepts (substance, duration, number, and so on) must be derived. Gall (1835) went further, and perhaps was the first to postulate that specific brain regions are associated with specific functions. By measuring the thickness of neural tissue in specific parts or the brain (as indicated by bumps on the skull, which was soft when the tissue formed) he thought one might determine the strength of specific personality traits in the individual.

Fodor's (1983) influential monograph *The Modularity of Mind* spawned the current wave of interest in modularity. Fodor describes modules as:

1. Associated with specific brain regions
2. Showing characteristic patterns of breakdown
3. Having a specific ontogenetic course
4. Processing information very quickly

5. Concerned with specific domains of knowledge
6. Encapsulated, producing mandatory outputs from given inputs

Fodor's (1983) initial examples of modules are from perception and language, but Leslie (1992) and Fodor (1992) have presented arguments that theory of mind also functions as a module.

> The currency of our mental lives consists largely of propositional attitudes, even when we are interpreting the behaviours of others. . . . It has been suggested that this capacity—termed a "theory of mind" (ToM)—arises from an innate, encapsulated, and domain-specific part of the cognitive architecture, in short a module. (Scholl & Leslie, 1999, p. 131)

In other words, when we think about others' minds, we think about them in terms of attitudes (desire, intention, belief) toward propositions (e.g., "I eat ice cream").[1] Someone can want to eat ice cream, intend to eat ice cream, and think that he is eating ice cream. Leslie and Fodor, among others, claim that our capacity to make such mentalistic interpretations stems from a theory of mind module in the brain. Some of the six features of modules that Fodor described seem apt with reference to theory of mind. Theory of mind does appear to be associated with specific brain regions, namely the amygdala, basal ganglia, and parts of the temporal cortex and frontal cortex (Frith & Frith, 1999; Schulkin, 2000). The typical method in these studies is to have participants consider stories involving mental states, like deception, pretense, and false beliefs, as well as stories that do not involve mental states in any crucial way, and then to compare patterns of brain activation across the two types of story (Fletcher et al., 1995; Frith & Frith, 2000; Sabbagh & Taylor, 2000). These brain regions typically show elevated rates of activity when participants are asked to consider others' mental states.

There are also specific breakdowns in theory of mind, most notably in people with autism (Baron-Cohen, 1995). Although autism has many features, a persistent and notable one is an inability to decipher others' mental states in the automatic way that most of us do. Oliver Sacks (1995) describes how Professor Temple Grandin, a high-functioning autistic woman, reacted as a child on the school playground.

> Something was going on between the other kids, something swift, subtle, constantly changing—an exchange of meanings, a negotiation, a swiftness of understanding so remarkable that sometimes she wondered if they were all telepathic. She is now aware of the existence of these social signals. She can infer them, she says, but she herself cannot perceive them, cannot participate in this magical communication directly, or conceive the many-leveled kaleidoscopic states of mind behind it. Knowing this intellectually, she does her best to compensate, bringing immense intellectual effort and

computational power to bear on matters that others understand with unthinking ease. (p. 272)

Many experimental studies demonstrate that people with autism tend to fail tasks involving understanding mental states, at mental and verbal ages at which nonautistic individuals—even those with other psychological impairments like Down syndrome—easily pass (Baron-Cohen, 2000).

Theory of mind also appears to follow a specific developmental course, both within and across cultures. For example, American and Chinese children alike talk first about desires, and about 6 months later they begin to talk about beliefs, suggesting a common developmental pattern of acquisition (Bartsch & Wellman, 1995; Tardif & Wellman, 2000). Children in both developed and nondeveloped countries appear to learn around age 4 that people can have false beliefs (Avis & Harris, 1991; Wellman, Cross, & Watson, 2001).

Regarding fast processing, the bus example given earlier suggests that people process information about others' mental states rapidly and effortlessly. Experimental support for the contention that mental state information is processed quickly and automatically is lacking. There is experimental support, however, for fast processing of trait attribution. Although the theory of mind module is normally discussed with particular reference to propositional attitudes, like beliefs, desires, and pretense, theory of mind is more generally construed to include traits (Wellman, 1990). Uleman and others (reviewed in Uleman et al., 1996) have shown that when people consider another's behavior, many appear to immediately attach to the other person a personality trait that could engender that behavior. Experimental support for the fast processing of mental states is needed.

For some of Fodor's (1983) criteria, then, theory of mind abilities do seem to be modulelike. Theory of mind processing appears to be associated with specific brain regions: A particular pathology is associated with its specific breakdown; it develops in regular sequence in normal children; and, at least as regards traits, there is evidence for quick and rapid processing.

For other criteria of Fodor's, however, *module* does not seem to be a fitting descriptor for theory of mind. Somewhat problematic is the claim of domain specificity. Theory of mind attributions are sometimes made outside of the social domain, directed at inanimate entities (Abell et al., 2000; Heider & Simmel, 1944). One might even say of the sky, "It wants to rain," or of the machine on one's desk, "This computer is stupid." Either we must place triangles, weather, and computers within the social realm (which we might do), or the criterion of domain specificity is problematic.

The most major concern is the claim of encapsulation. According to this assertion, mentalistic reasoning is encapsulated from other knowledge. As Scholl and Leslie (1999) wrote, "The essence of architectural modularity is a set of restrictions on information flow . . . the modularized processes have no access to any external processing or resources" (p. 133). According to Leslie's (1994) descriptions, human behavior is input to the module, and mental state interpretations ("He wants x; he believes x; he pretends x") are output. "The theory of mind mechanism is essentially a module which spontaneously and post-perceptually attends to behaviors and infers (i.e., computes) the mental states which contributed to them" (Scholl & Leslie, 1999, p. 147). We see someone running to a bus, and we automatically infer that he believes it is a departing bus, and that he wants to get on it. Whether we should see such inferences as modular (genetically dictated) or automatic (the result of repeated use, but formed by experience) is at issue.

The parallels between modular processing and automaticity are notable. Bargh (1994) described the "four horsemen of automaticity": efficiency, lack of awareness, lack of control, and lack of intention. Modules share these same features, but the existence of the theory of mind module, according to Leslie (1994) and Baron-Cohen (1995), is due to its genetic predesignation. In contrast, automatic processes are considered habits of mind, produced by repeatedly processing certain types of information in the same manner (Bargh & Chartrand, 2000).

Cultural Variation in Conceptions of Minds

A long tradition of attribution research would seem to support the view that theory of mind is modular. For example, the tendency to attribute personality traits as explanations for behavior (Jones & Davis, 1965; Ross & Nisbett, 1991) supports the notion that a theory of mind module requires people to process others' behaviors in internal terms. Likewise, the tendency to spontaneously infer traits when considering others' behaviors (Uleman et al., 1996) supports the idea of mandatory modular output.

However, there is a great deal of other evidence against the assertion that mentalistic explanation is truly mandatory and encapsulated, as would be expected of innate modules. Anthropologists and psychologists working in different cultures around the globe have described a wealth of variation in how minds, mental states, and actions are conceived (Lillard, 1997, 1998). These differences do not necessarily indicate how the mind is spontaneously conceived, but they do beg the question of why, if our spontaneous construals all resemble European American views of the mind, there is such widespread variation in more considered (conscious) views the world over.

For example, the European American concept of mind as a self-contained, thinking entity (Geertz, 1984) contrasts with the Illongot *rinawa*, which shares some features with mind but leaves the body during sleep, is possessed by plants (but leaves when plants are processed), and is much more an organ of social context (Rosaldo, 1980). Cultures also vary greatly in the attention paid to minds, with Europeans and Americans seemingly the outliers in the world's range of cultures. We pay enormous heed to minds, as evidenced by the number of words in our languages that specify mental constructs (over 5,000 for the emotions alone), the existence of a field of psychology, the psychological nature of books about parenting (*Reviving Ophelia* is about how daughters feel), and so on. The Chewong of Malaysia are reported to have only five terms for mental processes, translated as want, want very much, know, forget, and miss or remember (Howell, 1981, 1984). Anthropologists in many cultures have commented on the people of the cultures they study claiming one cannot know others' minds, refusing to speculate about others' minds, preferring not to discuss others' minds, and simply attaching comparatively little import to minds (LeVine, 1979; Mayer, 1982; Ochs & Schieffelin, 1984; Paul, 1995; Poole, 1985). Even in terms of legal responsibility, in other courts of the world intention is often not what matters when determining retribution for a crime. Instead, what matters is the degree of harm caused by one's actions (Hamilton & Sanders, 1992; Paul, 1995). If a module automatically mandates outputting mental state concepts, these different degrees of attention seem odd. Whole cultures could not choose to ignore the output of vision modules or a language acquisition device because it would be impossible.

There is also wide variation in what some behaviors are attributed to as well, getting more squarely at the content of modular output. If all people (except those with autism) are endowed with a brain module that perceives behavior and automatically interprets it in propositional and trait terms, we would expect to see reliance on such terms to be fairly prevalent everywhere. But again, this does not seem to be the case. In one early study demonstrating this, Miller (1984) asked Hindu Indian and Chicago children and adults to think of good and bad behaviors performed by people they knew well and, for each, to explain why the people did them. Interestingly, although by adulthood Chicagoans tended to come up with personality-trait reasons for behaviors, Indians tended to come up with situational causes. One might be concerned that this was because people in the different cultures thought of different behaviors to begin with, but in a later experiment, even when provided with behaviors (for example, a case in which an attorney left the scene of a motorcycle accident he had caused), Americans tended to give trait reasons (saying that the lawyer was a villain, for example) and Indians tended to give situational ones (the lawyer had a duty to be in court). This naive dispositionalism on the part of Americans tends to be wrong—people's actions are strongly influenced by the situation—yet nevertheless it is how Americans tend to view behaviors (Ross & Nisbett, 1991). The Miller study is not an isolated case.

We revisited this result with urban and rural American and Taiwanese children (Lillard, Skibbe, Zeljo, & Harlan, 2004), reasoning that rural American children might be different from the urban ones that are most often experimental participants. Using Miller's basic procedure, we found that elementary school children from rural Pennsylvania and rural Virginia tended to use situational explanations even more so than did Taiwanese children. For example, a rural 7-year-old said the reason someone had shared a bicycle with her was because she had not brought her own bike. In contrast, 7-year-olds from a more urban area tended to explain behaviors with reference to mental states and traits of the actor, like, "Because she wanted to help me" or "Because she was nice." This pattern has held up in two different experiments drawing on different rural geographic regions. Across all groups, mental state explanations were about four times as common as trait ones. However, for rural American children, situational explanations dominated over internal ones overall.

Several other demonstrations of variations from the standard American attribution pattern have been reported. Morris and Peng (1994) presented Chinese and American high school and graduate students with nonsocial (dots) and social (fish) cartoons. For both types of cartoon, a group of entities approached a single entity, stopping at the point of contact. The single entity then moved forward. Participants were asked to rate the extent to which the movement of the single entity was caused by internal factors and the extent to which it was caused by external factors. All of the American students and the Chinese graduate students (from Taiwan) tended to claim the movement was caused more by internal factors, and less by external ones, than did the Chinese high school students (from mainland China). This effect was also noted in an everyday realm: newspaper articles. Although describing the exact same Chinese and American murderers, Chinese-language papers in the United States tended to portray the murderers as a victim of their situations ("He as a victim of the China Top Students Education policy"; "He had a bad relationship with his advisor") whereas English-language papers tended to portray the murderers in trait terms ("There was always a dark side to his character"). Lee, Hallahan, and Herzog (1996) have shown this same effect for sports articles in newspapers in Hong Kong and the United States. In line with their hypothesis, the effect was not seen in editorials, which they reasoned reflect deeper consideration of alternative viewpoints, but was seen in newspaper articles, thought to be more spontaneous (see Uleman, 1999).

Anthropologists' reports concur with these experimental findings. Lillard (1998, p. 15) reviews ethnographers' reports of people designating social causes for others' behaviors:

> If an Ifaluk person goes into a jealous rage, the person who left her or his valued possessions in plain sight of another is viewed by Ifaluk as being the cause (Lutz, 1985). In EA [European American] culture, it seems more likely that the person exhibiting the rage behavior would be seen as responsible because people are primarily in charge of their own behavior. Hamil-

ton and Sanders (1992) provide evidence for this: In assigning responsibility for unfortunate outcomes, Americans do not consider the effect of other people's influence as much as the Japanese do. For the American Cheyenne, behavior is seen as motivated by relationships more than by individual wills (Straus, 1977). One's actions are generally explained by reference to someone else's actions or to one's relationship with some other ("I hit him because he hit her . . . I drank with him because he is my cousin"; p. 33). Straus described a social worker's frustration that the Cheyenne do not take responsibility for their actions but instead make excuses. However, Straus emphasized that these are not excuses to the Cheyenne: They truly are causes. Likewise, Briggs (1970) reported that for the Utku (Northern Territories), actions are explained in terms of other people's desires, not their own. Harre (1981) also wrote that "many travelers have reported the extraordinary degree to which Eskimos seem to be influenced by their fellows. When one weeps, they all weep."

Other cultures turn more often to ethereal causes of behavior than do mainstream Americans, claiming that their actions were caused by gods or spirits. Evans-Pritchard (1976), for example, tells of a man attributing his own tripping on a stump to witchcraft. When asked whether he shouldn't take some of the blame, since of course he had not seen the stump and was clumsy, he insisted that had witchcraft not been operative, he would have seen the stump. Americans are much more prone to assume personal responsibility. There are certainly exceptions to this, however, with the recent propensity of Americans to sue others for damages that in another time would be attributed to the suer or bad luck. These reactions might be related to Americans' need for positive self-regard ("if something goes wrong, it cannot be my fault"; Heine, Lehman, Markus, & Kitayama, 1999) and high value for control (Weisz, 1984). Another exception would be when Americans invoke the hand of God to explain some if not all events (as described in Weeks & Lupfer, 2000). In both cases, intentions are ascribed to others (the person who should have foreseen and prevented the accident, or God) but not to oneself.

To summarize, in their conscious explanations of behaviors, most Americans appear to differ from many others in the world by locating explanations inside the person, in terms of theory of mind constructs like beliefs, desires, and traits. These findings are not perfectly consistent across studies, and in some cultures—those of Taiwan and Korea in particular—the difference may not be as frequently observed or as strong (Choi & Nisbett, 1998; Fiske, Kitayama, Markus, & Nisbett, 1998; Krull et al., 1999; Lillard et al., 2004; Morris & Peng, 1994). Yet certainly it has been widely noted as a cultural difference in both experimental and observational work (Markus & Kitayama, 1991). If theory of mind were mandatory and encapsulated, we think we would see much less variation in these conscious interpretations. Importantly, cultural variation in behavior interpretation extends to unconscious interpretation as well, which mandatory, encapsulated modular processing does not allow for. Automatic trait processing is particularly a feature of individualistic cultures (Duff & Newman, 1997; Newman, 1993; Triandis, 1994; Zarate, Uleman, & Voils, 2001).

Drawing on the well-replicated finding that people from more collectivist cultures use fewer trait constructs in person descriptions than do people from more individualistic ones, and the finding that trait thinking is particularly strong in middle childhood (Livesley & Bromley, 1973; Shantz, 1983), Newman (1991) examined spontaneous trait inferences in Anglo American suburban versus Hispanic urban fifth graders. He found that only the Anglo children appeared to spontaneously make trait inferences in a word recognition test. In later work, Duff and Newman (1997) gave adult participants the idiocentrism scale developed by Triandis, Bontempo, Villareal, Asai, and Lucca (1988) along with an inference task designed to reveal the extent to which participants spontaneously infer either situation or trait causes of behaviors. They found that idiocentrism was positively correlated with trait, but not with situation, cued recall (see also Newman, 1993).

In a further example of this cultural difference, Zarate and colleagues (2001) examined spontaneous trait inference with adult Hispanic and Anglo American subjects. In a first experiment, they found that Euro-American college students had significantly shorter reaction times to trait words in lexical decision-making tasks when trait words were primed by trait-implying sentences. No such difference was seen for Hispanic participants. A second experiment found a similar effect with a trait-rating task. In sum, there is strong evidence for cultural variation in the unconscious process of spontaneous trait inference.

Findings concerning cultural variation in both behavior explanations and spontaneous trait inference are at odds with a modular theory of how we interpret the behaviors of others (Lillard, 1999). If modular processing is mandatory, and if all normally functioning people have a theory of mind module that interprets behaviors, then all people should automatically infer mental states and traits in response to behaviors. Just as we cannot help, when viewing Müller-Lyer stimuli, but see one line as longer than the other, we should instinctively see behaviors as rooted in theory of mind causes (mental states and personality traits).

The Continuity of Spontaneous and Deliberate Explanations: A Study

Scholl and Leslie (1999) have taken exception to the view that variation in conscious behavior explanations is problematic for modularity theory. They pointed out that how one explains behavior after the fact, on an attribution task, and how one perceives behavior online, can be quite different: "you can't decide not to interpret lots of situations as involving intentional agents, although you can ignore the interpretation" (p. 135). (They have not responded to the spontaneous trait inference [STI] literature, but might disregard it due to its concern with traits rather than mental states, as discussed below.) According to their claim, regardless of how rural children subsequently explained the behavior, when they originally perceived the behavior, they perceived it in terms of theory of mind. Everyone who sees a man running for a train might perceive him as wanting to get to the train, although when asked why he was running, some might be more apt to say, "Because he wanted to catch the train" and others might be more apt to say, "Because the train was leaving." This is possible, and it raises an interesting issue: How does a person's style of explaining behaviors after the fact relate to a person's online encoding of those behaviors? In other words, how does spontaneous trait inference relate to deliberate attribution?

The literature suggests some divergence (Miller, Smith, & Uleman, 1981); indeed, when spontaneous trait inference works less well, it appears to be because behaviors were considered too much (Zarate et al., 2001; Zelli, Cervone, & Huesmann, 1996). "Spontaneous impressions are guided by chronically accessible constructs, whereas intentional impressions are guided more by temporarily activated goal-relevant constructs and procedures, and by implicit theories (about the meanings of actions, relationships of traits to each other, etc.)" (Uleman, 1999, p. 146).

One way to address this issue, and Scholl and Leslie's (1999) critique, is to examine the relationship between the strength of a person's tendency to make STIs (Uleman et al., 1996) and the strength of a person's tendency to explain behaviors in theory of mind terms. If automatic, unconscious theory of mind processing is modular, and after-the-fact explanations of behavior are not, there should be no consistent relationship between STI and how behavior is explained. On the other hand, if theory of mind processing is automatic, instilled through years of exposure to and practice of certain forms of inference, then the degree to which a person makes STIs and uses theory of mind constructs in conscious behavior explanation should be related.

To test for the relationship between STIs and behavior explanation styles, we gave 45 undergraduate participants both types of task. Participants were recruited from University of Virginia psychology classes and were tested in groups of up to 10 persons.

The STI task used a cued recall procedure, based on Tulving's encoding specificity principle (Tulving & Thomson, 1973). The stimuli were previously used by Duff and Newman (1997, Experiment 2). Participants were shown 10 sentences, projected one at a time for 6 seconds on the wall by an overhead projector. Prior to the projection of the first sentence, participants were told that their memory for these sentences would be important later in the experiment. The first and last sentences were filler sentences used to reduce primacy and recency effects in memory (Anderson, 1990). The 8 remaining sentences were presented in a random order, followed by two 60-second filler tasks (list as many of the U.S. states as possible, and write any thoughts you had as you were viewing the sentences). The filler tasks were intended to clear the participants' short-term memory of the sentence content, and, in the case of the second filler task, to check whether participants consciously attempted to use internal or external cues to memorize sentences.

Participants were asked to recall the sentences, using one of two recall sheets. Each recall sheet contained a list of eight cues, four of which were situational and cued half the sentences, and the other four of which were internal and cued the remaining sentences. An example of the sentences and associated cues is "The engineer/ picks up/ the papers/ from the floor." For this, the internal cue was "neat" and the external cue was "dropped them." Another example is "The accountant/ gets the day off work/ with some fellow employees/ and takes the orphans to the circus," which had an internal cue of "caring" and an external cue of "job obligation." The slashes in the sentences correspond to sentence parts for which recall was scored.

The cues were derived through extensive pretesting at other universities. When asked to explain these sentences, in pilot work, about half of undergraduates tended to spontaneously supply a situational reason, and about half tended to spontaneously supply a trait reason. The cues used in this study were the reasons most commonly given by undergraduates during pretesting (Duff & Newman, 1997). Participants were given 6 minutes to record any parts of the sentences that they could remember and were told that if one of the cues on their sheet helped them to remember any part of a sentence, then they should record that sentence part next to the relevant cue. Participants were also told that if a sentence part was recalled with no help from the cues, then they should write it on a blank line at the bottom of the recall sheet.

Following the cued recall task, three types of behavior explanation tasks were employed: forced choice, rating scale, and open-ended. Participants first answered 16 forced-choice questions concerning other people's behaviors. For each question, participants read a description of someone engaging in an action and were asked to choose which of two explanations was more likely. One of the two was judged to be internal, and the other external, according to a coding system developed for a prior study (Lillard et al., 2004). Internal explanations involved reasons internal to the actor: personality traits, beliefs, desires, emotions, and so on. External reasons were those that lay outside the actor: the situation the actor was in, another person, a relationship, a role the person had to play, and so on. Kruglanski (1975) and Ross (1978) pointed out the difficulty in making internal versus external splits, in that internal reasons are often embedded in external ones and vice versa. We take the point, yet believe that when a respondent chooses to emphasize the actor's internal qualities versus circumstances in giving explanations, important distinctions are being made (for further discussion, see Lillard et al., 2004). Opting to explain a behavior with reference to the actor rather than the situation is a nonarbitrary choice that can reflect the person's schemas and worldview. Evidence for this position would accrue if internality of behavior explanations were related to STI.

The explanation choices were selected from responses given by a different group of undergraduates who participated in a pilot study. In the pilot study, 85 undergraduate participants had been given the same actions to explain, but in an open-ended format. Their most frequent responses served as choices in the present study. Examples of items on the forced-choice tasks are: "The girl gave cookies to her neighbor," with the choices being "The neighbor just moved in" (external) or "The girl wants to be kind" (internal), and "He hit another person in the mouth," with the choices being "He disliked that person" (internal) and "They had an argument" (external).

Next, for the rating scale, participants read six sentences describing actions. Each sentence was followed by four reasonable explanations for each behavior. The sentences and the explanations were selected from responses given in the same pilot study just mentioned. Of each set of four explanations, two were internal in nature and two were external. For each explanation, participants were asked to rate how likely each explanation was on a four-point Likert scale, with 1 being not likely, and 4 being very likely. An example of an item from this task is "Sue helped Mary with her schoolwork." Participants were asked to rate how likely it was that "They are friends," and how likely it was that "Sue likes to help others."

Finally, for the open-ended task, participants answered two open-ended questions like those used in the prior study. They were asked to think of and explain a good behavior and a bad behavior, specifically, "Think of a good [bad] behavior a friend of yours engaged in during the past two weeks. What did your friend do and why did he/she do that?"

Related Individual Differences

A further goal of this study was to shed light on the kinds of person variables that are associated with arriving at more external or internal reasons for behaviors. In other work, we considered several possible contributors (Lillard et al., 2004). These speculations were based on the fact that American children from less densely populated areas tended to use internal explanations for behaviors less often than did children from more urban areas. However, the rural/urban factor was confounded in these experiments with income and education levels of the parents. The present experiment asked participants about the rural/urban nature of their childhood communities and about income and education levels in order to examine how these factors might interplay with how behaviors are explained.

In more rural communities, there are fewer people among whom to hide and perhaps a greater sense of responsibility to the group (Paul, 1995). This could lead to people in more rural communities privileging external causes of behavior. Examples include doing things because of rules or because they are the right thing to do. Yuill (1992) explained the use of fewer personality trait attributions in rural communities as being due to residents being better intuitive psychologists, because they interact more closely and frequently with the same small group of others. On the other hand, Hollos (1987) found that children in more rural communities performed much more poorly on role-taking tasks than children from urban areas, whereas performance on logical tasks, like conservation, was similar. Role-taking has been linked to theory of mind in many ways, from pretending to be other people to simulating the mental states of others to the perspective-taking studies that partially instigated theory of mind research (Astington, Harris, & Olson, 1988; Flavell, 1990; Harris, 2000; Lillard, 2002). To help us determine whether they were from more rural or urban environments, most participants filled out a brief demographic survey asking them to rate, on five-point scales, the rural versus urban nature of their childhood community.

Another factor that might be at issue with regard to behavior explanation is income level. We reasoned that the predominant income level of their community could influence the degree to which people view themselves as victims versus controllers of circumstances. People with more money tend to have more choices in America, and people with less money are more restricted (see Lillard et al., 2004). Those who are more at the mercy of their external circumstances would tend to focus more on external causes of behavior, we reasoned, whereas those with more means would tend to see behaviors more as emanating from beliefs and desires.

Similar to income, parents' education level (1 being "some high school" and 5 being "graduate degree") was also thought to be an important factor for behavior explanation because those with more education would see more possibilities and would see internal factors as leading them to choose among those possibilities. In another vein, Hollos (1987) proposed that rural children do not engage in much talking, and this could be a factor in their poor role-taking skills. Conversation could give rise to the idea that others have distinct mental perspectives that lead to their actions (Harris, 1996), and more educated parents are known to talk to children more than less educated parents. Hence, lack of conversation among rural families might also explain decreased use of theory of mind explanations.

Finally, strength of religious conviction was also examined. Weeks and Lupfer (2000) found that more religious individuals show a stronger tendency to endorse God as a cause of events. In keeping with this, we reasoned that stronger religious convictions could be associated with a tendency to place power outside the self, in the hands of God.

Commensurate with these variables was another variable that more directly assesses what several of the demographic variables were intended to get at: locus of control. Participants completed the Rotter (1966) I-E Scale and the Levenson (1981) Internality, Powerful Others and Chance Scale. Locus of control refers to whether people believe that most outcomes are the result of factors that they themselves control (an internal locus of control) or factors over which they have no control (an external locus of control) (Lefcourt, 1991). The Rotter I-E Scale is the classic measure of this construct, and was used because of its solid foundation in the literature. Levenson's scale builds on Rotter's and is particularly well suited to the specific issues addressed in this experiment. In particular, it addresses separately the respondent's beliefs about his or her own power over events, beliefs about other people's power over outcomes, and beliefs in chance or luck.

It was expected that the income and education-level variables would actually be commensurate with locus of control and that locus of control might also relate to behavior explanation choices. In particular, people who see behaviors as stemming more from inside the actor were hypothesized to have a more internal locus of control, and those who see behaviors as stemming from situations were hypothesized to have a more external locus of control. Other research has shown that locus of control varies reliably with rural or urban background as well as with other dimensions that were confounded in our sample, namely family education background and income level (Gurin, Gurin, & Morrison, 1978; but see Witt, 1989; Zimbelman, 1987).

Half the participants received the Rotter (1966) scale first, and half received the Levenson (1981) scale first. The Rotter I-E Scale is a forced-choice questionnaire. Participants read a series of pairs of statements, with each pair expressing divergent views about an issue, and then chose the situation that most closely corresponded to their own view. For example, one pair of statements reads, "Many of the unhappy things in people's lives are partly due to bad luck" (control is placed outside the person) and "People's misfortunes result from the mistakes they make" (control is seen as being inside the person). Participants circled the statement that they agreed with more. The Levenson Internality, Powerful Others, and Chance Scale also contains statements about the causes of events. However, in this case the statements systematically address internality, powerful others, and chance, and rather than asking for agreement as a forced choice, participants are asked about their level of agreement with each statement. For example, one statement reads, "Whether or not I get to be a leader depends mostly on my ability." Participants were asked whether they strongly disagree, disagree, slightly disagree, slightly agree, agree, or strongly agree with each statement. The 24 statements constitute three different subscales and are provided in a predetermined and intermingled order on the single scale.

Coding was completed as follows. For the cued recall task, each sentence was divided into four parts in accordance with criteria provided by Duff and Newman (1997) and elaborated on by Newman (personal communication, May 2000). Internal cued recall was calculated as the number of internally cued sentence parts perfectly recalled, divided by the total number of sentence parts perfectly recalled. Sentence parts were counted as internally cued when the sentence of which they were a part was cued internally on that sheet. They were counted as such even if they were not written on the same line as the cue, since recall can be cued unconsciously. Truly uncued recall could be expected to appear equally on both sheets and hence would be equivalent across the sample. Partially or imperfectly recalled sentence parts were not scored, making the scoring criteria stringent, as in Duff and Newman (1997).

For the forced-choice behavior explanation task, the total number of internal explanations selected was divided by the total number of answers provided by each participant, giving a percent internal score. For the scaled behavior explanation task, responses for each category of explanation were averaged, producing a mean likelihood score for both the external and the internal explanations. For the open-ended behavior explanation questions, the total number of internal explanations was divided by the total number of explanations given, giving a percent internal score.

The locus of control scales were coded in the standard manner. The subject's score on the Rotter (1966) I-E Scale is the total number of external statements that the subject endorsed, out of a total of 29 statements. On the Levenson (1981) Internality, Powerful Others and Chance Scale, subjects receive three separate scores, one for each subscale, ranging from 0 to 48 for each.

Findings

The demographic survey revealed that the sample was fairly homogenous. This was not expected, given that the university where testing took place draws a diverse population, from rural mountainous regions to the urban areas around Washington, DC. However, in our sample, only one participant was from a very rural community (rated as 1 on the five-point scale); most were from suburban areas ($n = 17$, 3 on the scale) or more urban ones ($n =$ 10, 4 or 5 on the scale). Education levels of their parents were also high.

Every parent had finished high school; all but 3 mothers and 1 father had some college education; and 20 fathers and 14 mothers also had postgraduate education. The mean education level was 4.2 on the five-point scale. The income levels of their communities when growing up were rated as upper-middle income, with a mean of 3.8 on the five-point scale. None were rated as lower- or middle-lower in income (1 and 2 on the scale). Religiosity was normally distributed, with a majority ($n = 15$) declaring themselves moderately religious, 11 deeply or fairly committed, and 10 barely or not at all religious. Correlational analyses revealed that these factors were not related to any of our other measures, as might be expected from the homogeneity of the sample. The homogeneity of the sample was unexpected and made the test even more stringent, since such a sample would be expected to use a preponderance of internal explanations (based on Lillard et al., 2004).

On the cued recall task, participants recalled an average of 21% of the sentence parts (6.4 of 32), comparable to results found in other research of this type (Uleman et al., 1996). The mean percentage of recalled sentence parts that were from internally cued sentences was 53 (range 0–100; $SD = 27$), indicating that, on average, participants recalled sentence parts corresponding to internal and external cues on their recall sheets about equally. This was to be expected, given that the stimuli were preselected so that undergraduates would spontaneously infer trait and situation explanations equally. The interesting issue is how recall cued by external or internal cues corresponds with how each participant consciously explained behaviors.

For the forced-choice behavior explanation questions, 51% of choices were internal (range 25–88%, $SD = 15$), indicating that, on average, participants chose internal and external explanations equally often when those explanations were provided, but they demonstrated sufficient range for possible correlation with the spontaneous trait inference task.

For the rating scale portion of the behavior explanation task, the mean rating for internal explanations was 2.99 (range 2.50–3.58; $SD = 0.27$) and the mean rating for external explanations was 3.02 (range 2.25–3.58; $SD = 0.27$), suggesting internal and external explanations were rated as about equally plausible overall. Participants found all explanations fairly likely on average when both were listed for them and they did not have to choose between them (as they had for the forced choice). Indeed, ratings on the internal and external scales were significantly correlated ($r = .38$, $p < .05$), suggesting that the ratings reflect participants' individual tendencies to use more extreme versus midpoints on the scale rather than propensity to construe others' actions in internal or external terms. As Solomon (1978) suggested, internal and external ratings are not necessarily inverse, and this correlation makes that point clearly. This aligns with prior work (Zarate et al., 2001; Zelli et al., 1996), and makes it less likely that one might find correlations between spontaneous trait inference and this task.

For the open-ended behavior explanations, the typical adult American finding was obtained. The mean percentage of internal responses was 78 (range 0–100; $SD = 26$), demonstrating that, when the participants were asked to come up with their own explanations for behaviors, they usually postulated internal ones. The range was sufficient to allow for correlations with spontaneous trait inference. One participant used no internal explanations; one used 33% internal explanations; and 23 used 100% internal explanations, with the remaining participants between 50% and 100% internal.

Cronbach's alphas were calculated for all three behavior explanation measures, and were .59, .47, and .42, for the ratings scale, forced-choice, and open-ended measures, respectively. Note that the open-ended task concerns only two items. For the other tasks, items sometimes pull for internal or external responses; hence one might not expect particularly high alphas for tasks of these sorts.

Correlations between the behavior explanation and spontaneous trait inference tasks were examined next. First, there was no significant correlation between STI and the rating scale task, as expected from the results with the rating scale, because participants tended to highly endorse both the internal and external explanation for each behavior.

A significant correlation was obtained between STI and the percentage of internal explanations for behavior for the forced choice explanation task ($r = .34$, $p < .05$). When forced to choose between an external and an internal explanation for each behavior, participants who tended to choose the internal options also tended to have spontaneously inferred traits from the brief descriptions of behaviors they read earlier in the study.

There was also a significant correlation between STI and the percentage of internal explanations participants provided on the open-ended behavior explanation task ($r = .37$, $p = .01$). Those who tended to provide more internal explanations also tended to infer traits more, as evidenced by their higher degree of trait-cued recall.

These two correlations were obtained despite the fact that the sample was not very diverse. Although the range of internal explanations provided on the open-ended task was as large as possible (0–100%), the majority of respondents provided mostly internal responses, averaging close to 80% internal. Had rural populations been better represented in the sample, perhaps even stronger correlations would have been obtained.

Interestingly, although the behavior explanation scores were both independently related to internally cued recall, they were not correlated with each other. Whereas many ($n = 23$) participants were 100% internal on the open-ended behavior explanation task, none were 100% internal on the forced-choice task. Indeed, only six participants chose internal choices on 75% or more of the forced-choice items. This makes the point that when participants are shown external options, they are apt to think them plausible, although they might not have come up with them spontaneously. Performance on the rating scale task supports this, since most participants endorsed both internal and external explanations as likely. Performance on the rating scale task was not correlated with performance on the other theory of mind tasks.

The correlation pattern suggests that some participants' internal orientations were revealed by their answers to the open-ended questions, and others' were revealed by their choices on the forced-choice questions. The reasons for this are a topic for further research. One possibility is that participants scoring high on STI come from two camps, which might be dubbed Libertarians and Psychologists. The Libertarian camp emphasizes free choice and explains behaviors internally on the forced-choice measure. Supporting this, Miller et al. (1981, Experiment 2) obtained evidence suggesting that when American respondents choose trait options on forced-choice tasks, they are not so much claiming that the trait caused the behavior as that the behavior was freely chosen. Despite their presumed idiocentrism (suggested by their choice of trait options), Libertarians might not spontaneously use internal reasons to describe those choices. The other camp, the Psychologists, use many internal explanations on the open-ended task, score high on STI, and yet do not necessarily opt for the internal options in the forced-choice task. Such people habitually consider all manner of internal constructs, including traits and mental states, in considering what causes behaviors, but when faced with the external option in the forced-choice task, their knowledge that situations often drive behavior leads them to choose the external option often.

This brings up another important refinement to the results. Internal scores on the open-ended behavior explanation measure reflect both trait and mental state explanations. The actual breakdown of the results is that participants gave mental state explanations about 64% of the time, and trait ones about 14% of the time. In other words, the vast majority of participants' open-ended explanations refer to mental states. As is pointed out by Malle (chapter 9), prior experiments have tended to focus on traits to the exclusion of mental states (e.g., Miller, 1984). Although Heider's (1958) seminal monograph considered both mental state and trait interpretations, attribution research has focused mainly on traits. Yet our participants rarely volunteered trait explanations, as compared to mental state ones. Indeed, spontaneous trait inference related strongly to mental state explanations on the open-ended task ($r = .45$, $p < .01$) and was unrelated to trait explanations alone. The lack of relation to trait explanations could be primarily due to how few trait explanations were provided overall. Still, the relation between STI and belief-desire reasons was striking.

One goal of this study was to provide evidence for what personality or demographic variables are associated with explaining behaviors in more internal or external terms. As stated, the demographic variables yielded no information on this, possibly because of insufficient variation. The personality variable of locus of control was tested to examine whether it might underlie avoidance of internal explanations in rural populations (Lillard et al., 2004). Scores on the locus of control scales were what one would expect for the population, given the results of other studies (Lefcourt, 1991). The mean score on the Rotter was 11.49, with a range of 5 to 19 and a standard deviation of 3.52; hence, the sample tended toward an internal locus of control. The mean on the Levenson Internal subscale was 32.96, with a range of 16 to 42, and a standard deviation of 4.98, suggesting the sample was rather internal overall. The Powerful Others subscale yielded a mean of 17.96, with a range of 3 to 35.0 and a standard deviation of 7.88. The Chance subscale yielded a mean of 21.44 with a range of 5.0 to 34.0 and a standard deviation of 6.31.

Scores on the Levenson Internal subscale correlated negatively with scores on the Rotter ($r = -.34$, $p < .05$), suggesting validity of these measures. Contrary to expectations, the locus of control scores did not correlate with any behavior explanation measures. It may be the case that our hypothesis is simply wrong, and that other factors, like individualism/collectivism, underlie the rural-urban findings and propensities to regard internal or external factors as responsible for behaviors (Duff & Newman, 1997; Newman, 1993; Zarate et al., 2001). Alternatively, it may be that the college sample we tested did not have sufficient variation in locus of control to allow correlations to be revealed with this size of sample.

Although significant relations with locus of control were not seen, the relationship between spontaneously inferring traits in response to behaviors and the tendency to explain behaviors in internal terms emerged clearly. Our findings come full circle with others in the literature. Miller (1984), Morris and Peng (1994), and others have found that people from more collectivist cultures tend to explain behaviors in more external, situationist terms than do Americans. Others (Duff & Newman, 1997; Newman, 1993; Zarate et al., 2001) have found that more individualistic participants, like Americans who score high on idiocentrism measures, are more apt to encode behaviors with traits, whereas collectivists are more likely to encode behaviors with situations. The present study demonstrates that within a single college sample, those who were more apt to explain behaviors with reference to internal factors like traits and mental states also were more apt to make STIs. This result was obtained both when participants were asked to come up with explanations for behaviors, and when they were asked to choose between two plausible explanations.

Conclusion

The finding that how people explain behaviors, in external or internal terms, is related to how they encode behaviors, according to situations or traits, suggests first that how one chooses to explain behavior is not an arbitrary semantic decision (Kruglanski, 1975; Ross, 1978). It relates importantly to unconscious person perception processes.

Second, it suggests that theory of mind does not arise from modular processes. Automatic person inference processes were related to more considered ones. One might object that Leslie's theory of mind module, as discussed earlier, has been proposed to explain our spontaneous and quick invocation of propositional attitudes to explain behavior, not traits. Leslie found behavior explanations irrelevant to the module because they were "after the fact." STIs, likewise, might be irrelevant because they concern traits, not mental states. Ideally, tasks similar to the STI task could be constructed, aimed at propositional attitudes. However, it is not clear how one would do this regarding beliefs and desires. Take the bus example given previously. If participants saw a sentence reading, "The man raced toward the departing bus," what would be the correct propositional-attitude cue word? *Want* for *wants to catch? Desire? Think?* How to use such cue words effectively across multiple sentences is also very problematic, since *desire* would presumably apply to several situations in a way that *clumsy* does not. Many mental states are ubiquitous; specific traits are not.

The question arises, then: Do these data address the modularity account of mind reading? If a theory of mind module is strictly limited to spontaneous propositional attitude interpretations of behaviors, then it probably does not. There is no measure, to our knowledge, of spontaneous mental state inference of the unconscious sort Leslie's theory appears to require. The open-ended behavior explanation is the closest we have to spontaneous explanations, and this task is done consciously. If theory of mind is limited to the propositional attitudes, we believe the onus is on modular theorists to come up with a task that assesses their spontaneous, encapsulated use.

Theory of mind is generally seen as more encompassing than belief-desire reasoning and includes traits. If modular processes are thought to provide social cognitive interpretations more generally, then they should be responsible for trait attributions as well as mental state ones. As pointed out previously, automatic processes are akin to modular ones in several important ways, given that they are both fast and efficient, and their output is predictable. "The essence of architectural modularity is a set of restrictions on information flow" (Scholl & Leslie, 1999, p. 133). "ToM interpretations . . . seem to be relatively . . . fast (they typically occur without lengthy and effortful reasoning), and mandatory (you can't decide not to interpret lots of situations as involving intentional agents, although you can ignore the interpretation)" (p. 135). Spontaneous trait attribution in this way looks like a modular process because one sees the behavior, and one infers the trait. However, it cannot be an innately established one, given as part of "our genetic endowment" as has been claimed for theory of mind (Scholl & Leslie, 1999, p. 134), since it is not universal but appears to vary in culturally informed ways. The information flow is not restricted; it is open to the influence of culture. The closest test we have, then, of a modular process for social interpretation processes is more supportive of an automatic than a modular account of that process. The correlations show that how one explains behavior after the fact (mostly with mental state interpretations, in the form of propositional attitudes) is clearly related to the tendency to infer traits spontaneously when reading about a behavior.

This said, it should be noted that proponents of modular theory do not always endorse a strong version of their modules. Fodor (1983) stated, "Whenever I speak of a cognitive system as modular, I . . . shall always mean to some interesting extent" (p. 37) and Scholl and Leslie (1999) stated that the restrictions on information flow are always "a matter of degree" (p. 133). Yet once one begins loosening the criteria for what constitutes a module, one loses the very essence of a module. If a module lacks restrictions on information flow, then why call it a module? Because such soft positions leave one with nothing to evaluate, in this chapter we have addressed the strong form of innate modules.

A second note is that Scholl and Leslie (1999) discussed theory of mind as having an innate basis; they were willing to concede that over development, cultural "extramodular" (p. 137) processes use the modular output in various ways. Yet "the essential character of ToM a person develops does not seem to depend on the character of their environment at all" (p. 136). We agree that the essential character of theory of mind—some concepts that map at least roughly to our concepts of belief, desire, seeing, feeling, and so on—and an understanding of individuals as having some degree of agency (although the degree and circumstances under which that agency exists may differ) is universal (Lillard, 1998). But we think the evidence favors the view that these basic universal similarities in how people construe people arise from real similarities in people, rather than a module prespecifying that people are to be interpreted in these ways. And culture influences even these basics, tipping the balance, for example, in how often we rely on mental state versus situational explanations for others' behaviors.

Why might there be a relationship between spontaneous trait inference and the use of mental constructs (beliefs and desires) in explaining behaviors? We see two possibilities. First is the possibility that idiocentric thought feeds both unconscious trait inference and conscious belief-desire reasoning. Uleman (1999) considered spontaneous inferences as part of the underground stream of unconscious thought and intentional ones as part of an above-ground aqueduct system. Taking this analogy further, both could be fed from the same source. Cultural influences could lead both to the unconscious habits of mind that are evident in spontaneous trait inference and to the more considered, but again habitual, schematic tendency to consciously think of others' behaviors as stemming from internal sources (Lillard et al., 2004; Miller, 1984). Traits occur spontaneously to people who are idiocentric, who think we act freely based on our internal proclivities rather than outside sources. Those same people, asked to reason consciously about why people do things, arrive at belief and desire explanations for those actions.

A second possibility is that both belief-desire reasoning and trait reasoning are spontaneous, unconscious processes, and that belief-desire reasoning is actually primary. The spontaneous inference task only taps trait inferences, so the automaticity of belief-desire reasoning is simply untapped. Because it is primary, belief-desire reasoning emerges most readily when people explain behaviors. These spontaneous, unconscious processes are habits of mind, with individualistic or collectivist cultures providing a "continual priming effect" (Lillard, 1998; Shweder & Bourne, 1984) leading to people's use of such constructs.

The factors that lead to these habits of mind are primarily cultural but are also rooted in our animal biology. Infants begin life with some degree of self-awareness and understanding of others' core similarity to themselves, as evidenced by infants' imitation of others' bodily movements in the first hours and weeks of life (Lillard, 1999; Meltzoff & Moore, 1995). Later, as infants become aware of their own intentions, they begin to read intentions into the actions of others (Woodward, 1998). Gallese (2000) and Rizzolatti and Arbib (1998) have found in monkeys what may be the neural analog of this process. When monkeys observe experimenters engaging in particular movements, some of the same neurons fire in the monkeys as when the monkeys themselves make those movements. Humans have been shown to have similar processes (for a superb recent review of this topic, see Dijksterhuis & Bargh, 2001). Frith and Frith (2001) as well note that the medial frontal areas of the brain that are involved in self-monitoring also are activated in interpreting others' behaviors, and several researchers have linked recent neurological evidence to theory of mind (e.g., Grezes & Decety, 2001). Although some assume that the involvement of specific brain regions suggests genetic prespecification, functional modules can arise through physical characteristics of different brain regions that come to take over types of inputs because they are more efficient at processing those inputs (Elman et al., 1996).

From this process of matching themselves with others, and perceiving some of their own mental states, young children begin to understand mental processes in others. This is the root of all cultures having some theory of mind, because all people really do operate in part from mental processes, and there is some awareness of these processes from early in ontogeny. However, cultures differ in how much those processes are emphasized and in how much they are acted upon (Lillard, 1998). Middle- and upper-middle-class educated Americans at the turn of the millennium seem to be at the extreme of thinking about inner life: witness large self-help sections in bookstores and how parents urge even very young children to make their own choices, based on their own desires. In contrast, in most other cultures (often termed collectivist) emphasis is on the society and fitting into its mores at the expense of personal desires and other internal features of the individual. In such cultures, minds are not so emphasized, although they are still understood. The habits of mind that give rise to STIs and internalistic explanations for behaviors are nurtured in individualistic cultures, and are more akin to automatic than innate-modular processes.

Acknowledgments The authors wish to thank Cara Johnson, Katie Hamm, Elizabeth Malakie, and Kimberly Patterson for their assistance with the experiment described in this chapter.

Note

1. As the reader may have inferred from the context and usage, "propositional attitudes" are not the same thing as "attitudes" in social psychology. They are mental states (thoughts, beliefs, feelings) toward particular propositions (see Churchland, 1984, pp. 63–66).

References

Abell, F., Happe, F., & Frith, U. (2000). Do triangles play tricks? Attribution of mental states to animated shapes in normal and abnormal development. *Cognitive Development, 15*, 1–16.

Anderson, J. R. (1990). *Cognitive psychology and its implications* (3rd ed.). New York: W.H. Freeman.

Astington, J. W., Harris, P. L., & Olson, D. R. (Eds.). (1988). *Developing theories of mind.* New York: Cambridge University Press.

Avis, J., & Harris, P. L. (1991). Belief-desire reasoning among Baka children: Evidence for a universal conception of mind. *Child Development, 62*, 460–467.

Baldwin, D. A. (1991). Infants' contribution to the achievement of joint reference. *Child Development, 62*, 875–890.

Bargh, J. A. (1994). The four horsemen of automaticity: Awareness, intention, efficiency, and control in social cognition. In R. S. Wyer & T. K. Srull (Eds.), *Handbook of social cognition* (Vol. 1, pp. 1–40). Hillsdale, NJ: Erlbaum.

Bargh, J. A., & Chartrand, T. L. (2000). The mind in the middle: A practical guide to priming and automaticity research. In H. T. Reis & C. M. Judd (Eds.), *Handbook of research methods in social and personality psychology* (pp. 253–285). New York: Cambridge University Press.

Baron-Cohen, S. (1995). *Mindblindness: An essay on autism and theory of mind.* Cambridge, MA: MIT Press.

Baron-Cohen, S. (2000). Theory of mind and autism: A 15-year review. In S. Baron-Cohen, H. Tager-Flusberg, & D. J. Cohen (Eds.), *Understanding other minds: Perspectives from developmental cognitive neuroscience* (2nd ed., pp. 3–21). Oxford, UK: Oxford University Press.

Bartsch, K., & Wellman, H. M. (1995). *Children talk about the mind.* Oxford, UK: Oxford University Press.

Briggs, J. (1970). *Never in anger: A portrait of an Eskimo family.* Cambridge, MA: Harvard University Press.

Bruner, J. (1990). *Acts of meaning.* Cambridge, MA: Harvard University Press.

Carpenter, M., Akhtar, N., & Tomasello, M. (1998). Fourteen- through 18-month-old infants differentially imitate intentional and accidental actions. *Infant Behavior and Development, 21,* 315–330.

Choi, I., & Nisbett, R. E. (1998). Situational salience and cultural differences in the correspondence bias and actor-observer bias. *Personality and Social Psychology Bulletin, 24,* 949–960.

Churchland, P. M. (1984). *Matter and consciousness.* Cambridge, MA: MIT Press.

Descartes, R. (1993). *Meditations on first philosophy* (D. A. Cress, Trans., 3rd ed.). Indianapolis, IN: Hackett. (Original work published 1641)

Dijksterhuis, A., & Bargh, J. A. (2001). The perception-behavior expressway: Automatic effects of social perception on social behavior. In M. P. Zanna (Ed.), *Advances in experimental social psychology* (Vol. 33, pp. 1–40). San Diego, CA: Academic Press.

Duff, K. J., & Newman, L. S. (1997). Individual differences in the spontaneous construal of behavior: Idiocentrism and the automatization of the trait inference process. *Social Cognition, 15,* 217–241.

Elman, J. L., Bates, E. A., Johnson, M. H., Karmiloff-Smith, A., Parisi, D., & Plunkett, K. (1996). *Rethinking innateness: A connectionist perspective on development.* Cambridge, MA: MIT Press.

Evans-Pritchard, E. E. (1976). *Witchcraft, oracles, and magic among the Azande.* Oxford, UK: Clarendon.

Fiske, A., Kitayama, S., Markus, H., & Nisbett, R. (1998). The cultural matrix of social psychology. In D. T. Gilbert & S. T. Fiske (Eds.), *The handbook of social psychology* (Vol. 2, pp. 915–981). Boston: McGraw-Hill.

Flavell, J. H. (1990, June). *Perspectives on perspective taking.* Paper presented at the annual meeting of the Jean Piaget Society, Philadelphia.

Flavell, J. H., & Miller, P. H. (1998). Social cognition. In D. Kuhn & R. S. Siegler (Eds.), *Handbook of child psychology: Vol. 2. Cognition, perception, and language development* (5th ed., pp. 851–898). New York: Wiley.

Fletcher, P., Happe, F., Frith, U., Baker, S., Dolan, R., Frackowiak, R., & Frith, C. D. (1995). Other minds in the brain: A functional imaging study of "theory of mind" in story comprehension. *Cognition, 57,* 109–128.

Fodor, J. (1992). A theory of the child's theory of mind. *Cognition, 44,* 283–296.

Fodor, J. A. (1983). *The modularity of mind.* Cambridge, MA: Bradford Books/MIT Press.

Frith, C., & Frith, U. (2000). The physiological basis of theory of mind: Functional neuroimaging studies. In S. Baron-Cohen, H. Tager-Flusberg, & D. J. Cohen (Eds.), *Understanding other minds: Perspectives from developmental cognitive neuroscience* (2nd ed., pp. 334–356). Oxford: Oxford University Press.

Frith, C. D., & Frith, U. (1999). Interacting minds—a biological basis. *Science, 286,* 1692–1695.

Frith, U., & Frith, C. (2001). The biological basis of social interaction. *Current Directions in Psychological Science, 10,* 151–155.

Gall, F. G. (1835). *Works: On the functions of the brain and each of its parts* (Vols. 1–6). Boston: March, Capon, and Lyon.

Gallese, V. (2000). The acting subject: Toward the neural basis of social cognition. In T. Metzinger (Ed.), *Neural correlates of consciousness: Empirical and conceptual questions* (pp. 325–333). Cambridge, MA: MIT Press.

Geertz, C. (1984). "From the native's point of view": On the nature of anthropological understanding. In R. A. Shweder & R. A. LeVine (Eds.), *Culture theory: Essays on mind, self, and emotion* (pp. 123–136). Cambridge, UK: Cambridge University Press.

Gergely, G., Nadasdy, Z., Csibra, G., & Biro, S. (1995). Taking the intentional stance at 12 months of age. *Cognition, 56,* 165–193.

Grezes, J., & Decety, J. (2001). Functional anatomy of execution, mental simulation, observation, and verb generation of actions: A meta-analysis. *Human Brain Mapping, 12,* 1–19.

Gurin, P., Gurin, G., & Morrison, B. M. (1978). Personal and ideological aspects of internal and external control. *Social Psychology, 41,* 275–296.

Hamilton, V. L., & Sanders, J. (1992). *Everyday justice.* New Haven, CT: Yale University Press.

Harre, R. (1981). Psychological variety. In P. Heelas & A. Lock (Eds.), *Indigenous psychologies* (pp. 79–104). New York: Academic Press.

Harris, P. L. (1996). Desires, beliefs, and language. In P. Carruthers & P. K. Smith (Eds.), *Theories of mind* (pp. 200–220). Cambridge, UK: Cambridge University Press.

Harris, P. L. (2000). *The work of the imagination.* Oxford: Blackwell.

Heider, F. (1958). *The psychology of interpersonal relations.* New York: Wiley.

Heider, F., & Simmel, M. (1944). An experimental study of apparent behavior. *American Journal of Psychology, 57,* 243–259.

Heine, S. H., Lehman, D. R., Markus, H. R., & Kitayama, S. (1999). Is there a universal need for positive self-regard? *Psychological Review, 106,* 766–794.

Hollos, M. (1987). Learning in rural communities: Cognitive development in Hungary and Norway. In G. D. Spindler (Ed.), *Education and cultural process: Anthropological approaches* (2nd ed., pp. 401–429). Prospect Heights, IL: Waveland Press.

Howell, S. (1981). Rules not words. In P. Heelas & A. Lock (Eds.), *Indigenous psychologies* (pp. 133–144). New York: Academic Press.

Howell, S. (1984). *Society and cosmos.* Oxford, UK: Oxford University Press.

Jones, E. E., & Davis, K. E. (1965). From acts to dispositions: The attribution process in person perception. *Advances in Experimental Social Psychology, 2,* 219–266.

Karmiloff-Smith, A. (1992). *Beyond modularity.* London: Bradford/MIT Press.

Kruglanski, A. W. (1975). The endogenous-exogenous partition in attribution theory. *Psychological Review, 82,* 387–406.

Krull, D. S., Loy, M. H.-M., Lin, J., Wang, C.-F., Chen, S., & Zhao, X. (1999). The fundamental attribution error: Correspondence bias in individualist and collectivist cultures. *Personality and Social Psychology Bulletin, 25,* 1208–1219.

Lee, F., Hallahan, M., & Herzog, T. (1996). Explaining real-life events: How culture and domain shape attributions. *Personality and Social Psychology Bulletin, 22*, 732–741.

Lefcourt, H. M. (1991). Locus of control. In J. P. Robinson, P. R. Shaver, & L. S. Wrightsman (Eds.), *Measures of personality and social psychological attitudes* (Vol. 1, pp. 413–499). San Diego, CA: Academic Press.

Leslie, A. M. (1992). Pretense, autism, and the theory-of-mind module. *Current Directions in Psychological Science, 1*, 18–21.

Leslie, A. M. (1994). ToMM, ToBy, and Agency: Core architecture and domain specificity. In L. A. Hirschfield & S. A. Gelman (Eds.), *Mapping the mind: Domain specificity in cognition and culture* (pp. 119–148). Cambridge, UK: Cambridge University Press.

Levenson, H. (1981). Differentiating among internality, powerful others, and chance. In H. M. Lefcourt (Ed.), *Research with the locus of control construct: Vol. 1. Assessment methods* (pp. 15–63). New York: Academic Press.

LeVine, S. (1979). *Mothers and wives.* Chicago: University of Chicago Press.

Lillard, A. S. (1997). Other folks' theories of mind and behavior. *Psychological Science, 8*, 268–274.

Lillard, A. S. (1998). Ethnopsychologies: Cultural variations in theory of mind. *Psychological Bulletin, 123*, 3–33.

Lillard, A. S. (1999). Developing a cultural theory of mind: The CIAO approach. *Current Directions in Psychological Science, 8*, 57–61.

Lillard, A. S. (2002). Pretend play and cognitive development. In U. Goswami (Ed.), *Handbook of cognitive development* (pp. 188–205). London: Blackwell.

Lillard, A. S., Skibbe, L., Zeljo, A., & Harlan, D. (2001). *Developing explanations for behavior in different communities and cultures.* Charlottesville: University of Virginia.

Livesley, W. J., & Bromley, D. B. (1973). *Person perception in childhood and adolescence.* London: Wiley.

Lutz, C. (1985). Cultural patterns and individual differences in the child's emotional meaning system. In M. Lewis & C. Saarni (Eds.), *The socialization of emotions* (pp. 37–51). New York: Plenum Press.

Markus, H. R., & Kitayama, S. (1991). Culture and the self: Implications for cognition, emotion, and motivation. *Psychological Review, 98*, 224–253.

Mayer, J. (1982). Body, psyche, and society: Conceptions of illness in Ommura, Eastern Highlands, Papua New Guinea. *Oceania, 52*, 240–259.

Meltzoff, A. N., & Moore, M. K. (1995). A theory of the role of imitation in the emergence of self. In P. Rochat (Ed.), *The self in infancy: Theory and research. Advances in psychology, 112* (pp. 73–93). Amsterdam, Netherlands: North-Holland/Elsevier.

Miller, F. D., Smith, E. R., & Uleman, J. (1981). Measurement and interpretation of situational and dispositional attributions. *Journal of Experimental Social Psychology, 17*, 80–95.

Miller, J. G. (1984). Culture and the development of everyday social explanation. *Journal of Personality and Social Psychology, 46*, 961–978.

Morris, M. W., & Peng, K. (1994). Culture and cause: American and Chinese attributions for social and physical events. *Journal of Personality and Social Psychology, 67*, 949–971.

Newman, L. S. (1991). Why are traits inferred spontaneously? A developmental approach. *Social Cognition, 9*, 221–253.

Newman, L. S. (1993). How individualists interpret behavior: Idiocentrism and spontaneous trait inference. *Social Cognition, 11*, 243–269.
Ochs, E., & Schieffelin, B. (1984). Language acquisition and socialization. In R. Shweder & R. LeVine (Eds.), *Culture theory: Mind, self, and emotion* (pp. 276–322). Cambridge, UK: Cambridge University Press.
Paul, R. A. (1995). Act and intention in Sherpa culture and society. In L. Rosen (Ed.), *Other intentions: Cultural contexts and the attribution of inner states* (pp. 15–45). Santa Fe, NM: School of American Research Press.
Poole, F. J. P. (1985). Coming into being: Cultural images of infants in Bimin-Kuskusmin folk psychology. In G. M. White & J. Kirkpatrick (Eds.), *Person, self, and experience* (pp. 183–244). Berkeley: University of California Press.
Premack, D., & Woodruff, G. (1978). Does the chimpanzee have a theory of mind? *Behavioral and Brain Sciences, 1*, 515–526.
Rizzolatti, G., & Arbib, M. A. (1998). Language within our grasp. *Trends in Neurosciences, 21*, 188–194.
Rosaldo, M. Z. (1980). *Knowledge and passion: Illongot notions of self and social life.* Cambridge, UK: Cambridge University Press.
Ross, L. (1978). The intuitive psychologist and his shortcomings: Distortions in the attribution process. In L. Berkowitz (Ed.), *Cognitive theories in social psychology* (pp. 337–384). New York: Academic Press.
Ross, L., & Nisbett, R. E. (1991). *The person and the situation: Perspectives of social psychology.* New York: McGraw-Hill.
Rotter, J. B. (1966). Generalized expectancies for internal versus external control of reinforcement. *Psychological Monographs, 80*(1), 1–28.
Sabbagh, M. A., & Taylor, M. (2000). Neural correlates of the theory-of-mind reasoning: An event-related potential study. *Psychological Science, 11*, 46–50.
Sacks, O. (1995). *An anthropologist on Mars.* New York: Knopf.
Scholl, B. J., & Leslie, A. M. (1999). Modularity, development, and "theory of mind." *Mind and Language, 14*, 131–153.
Schulkin, J. (2000). *Roots of social sensibility and neural function.* Cambridge, MA: MIT Press.
Shantz, C. U. (1983). Social cognition. In J. H. Flavell & E. M. Markman (Eds.), *Cognitive development* (Vol. 3, pp. 495–555). New York: Wiley.
Shweder, R. A., & Bourne, L. (1984). Does the concept of the person vary cross-culturally? In R. A. Shweder & R. A. LeVine (Eds.), *Culture theory: Essays on mind, self, and emotion* (pp. 158–199). Cambridge, UK: Cambridge University Press.
Solomon, S. (1978). Measuring dispositional and situational attributions. *Personality and Social Psychology Bulletin, 4*, 589–594.
Straus, A. (1977). Northern Cheyenne ethnopsychology. *Ethos, 5*, 326–352.
Tardif, T., & Wellman, H. M. (2000). Acquisition of mental state language in Mandarin- and Cantonese-speaking children. *Developmental Psychology, 36*, 25–43.
Triandis, H. C. (1994). *Culture and social behavior.* New York: McGraw-Hill.
Triandis, H. C., Bontempo, R., Villareal, M. J., Asai, M., & Lucca, N. (1988). Individualism and collectivism: Cross-cultural perspectives on self-group relationships. *Journal of Personality and Social Psychology, 54*, 323–338.
Tulving, E., & Thomson, D. M. (1973). Encoding specificity and retrieval processes in episodic memory. *Psychological Review, 80*, 359–380.
Uleman, J. S. (1999). Spontaneous versus intentional inferences in impression

formation. In S. T. Y. Chaiken (Ed.), *Dual-process theories in social psychology* (pp. 141–160). New York: Guilford.

Uleman, J. S., Newman, L. S., & Moskowitz, G. B. (1996). People as flexible interpreters: Evidence and issues from spontaneous trait inference. *Advances in Social Psychology, 28*, 211–279.

Weeks, M., & Lupfer, M. B. (2000). Religious attributions and proximity of influence: An investigation of direct interventions and distal explanations. *Journal for the Scientific Study of Religion, 39*, 348–362.

Weisz, J. R. (1984). Standing out and standing in: The psychology of control in America and Japan. *American Psychologist, 39*, 955–969.

Wellman, H. M. (1990). *The child's theory of mind.* Cambridge, MA: Bradford Books/MIT Press.

Wellman, H. M. (2003). Understanding the psychological world: Developing a theory of mind. In U. Goswami (Ed.), *Handbook of cognitive development* (pp. 167–187). Oxford, UK: Blackwell.

Wellman, H. M., Cross, D., & Watson, J. (2001). Meta-analysis of theory of mind development: The truth about false belief. *Child Development, 72*, 655–684.

Witt, L. A. (1989). Urban-nonurban differences in social cognition: Locus of control and perceptions of a just world. *Journal of Social Psychology, 129*, 715–717.

Woodward, A. L. (1998). Infants selectively encode the goal object of an actor's reach. *Cognition, 69*, 1–34.

Yuill, N. (1992). Children's conception of personality traits. *Human Development, 35*, 265–279.

Zarate, M. A., Uleman, J. S., & Voils, C. (2001). Effects of culture and processing goals on the activation and binding of trait concepts. *Social Cognition, 19*, 295–323.

Zelli, A., Cervone, D., & Huesmann, L. R. (1996). Behavioral experience and social inference: Individual differences in aggressive experience and spontaneous versus deliberate trait inference. *Social Cognition, 14*, 165–190.

Zimbelman, K. (1987). Locus of control and achievement orientation in rural and metropolitan youth. *Journal of Rural Community Psychology, 8*, 50–55.

PART IV

PERCEIVING AND ENGAGING OTHERS

12

The Glimpsed World: Unintended Communication and Unintended Perception

Y. Susan Choi, Heather M. Gray, and Nalini Ambady

In 1979, the sociologist Erving Goffman published *Gender Advertisements*, an examination of the ways in which images of men and women are used in advertisements. Goffman was particularly interested in how such images reflect underlying cultural values about relations between the sexes. He went on to draw a parallel between the still photographs of advertisements and the fleeting observations of strangers, gathered in the course of our lives, that comprise what he called "our glimpsed world." Just as posed photographs provide insight into sociocultural values, Goffman averred, brief glimpses of others reveal a great deal about their psychological lives. In sum, Goffman suggested that observations made in passing can be used as sources of information about the internal states, social identities, and relationships of those who make up our social worlds.

Several years after the publication of *Gender Advertisements*, Goffman's insight about the accuracy of social judgments began to receive empirical support. Psychologists have attempted to determine when and how social perceivers are correct in their judgments of others (e.g., Ambady & Rosenthal, 1992, 1993; Funder, 1987, 1995; Kenny & Albright, 1987). This work has revealed that people are often surprisingly accurate when making judgments of others based on mere glimpses. Very brief samples, or "thin slices," of others' behavior provide information about a wide range of psychological constructs, including mood states, dispositional characteristics, social relations, and job performance (for a review, see Ambady, Bernieri, & Richeson, 2000). This accuracy derives from the fact that in many situations people are quite "legible" in expressing such qualities (Ambady, Hallahan, & Rosenthal, 1995). That is, in the course of everyday social interactions, people readily give off the signals that allow others to infer a great deal about them. In particular, nonverbal channels of communication—including facial displays, gestures, and tone of voice—are extremely revealing, in that they spontaneously emit clues to the true feelings and qualities of an individual.

People's abilities to both express and interpret extremely subtle clues to internal feelings and beliefs have attracted the attention of psychologists who are interested in discovering not only what is communicated in brief social interactions but also how these communications take place. Some researchers have thus made forays into the information processing components of behavioral display, exploring the extent to which such displays are strategic or automatic (e.g., Baumeister, Hutton, & Tice, 1989; Buck, 1993; DePaulo, 1992; Pontari & Schlenker, 2000).

The purpose of this chapter is to provide an integrative review of research into the information-processing components of nonverbal displays, which we consider from the perspectives of both actors and observers. Though in the interest of clarity we discuss encoding and decoding each in turn, we adopt the integrative orientation of Patterson's (1998) parallel process model of nonverbal communication. For the purposes of this chapter, we use the convention adopted by the nonverbal communication literature and use the words *encoding* and *decoding* to denote the expression and interpretation of such cues, respectively. By bringing together work on both sides of nonverbal communication, we hope to make clear the interdependent nature of these processes, a fact that may have been obscured by empirical separation.

In keeping with the spirit of this volume, our main goal is to explore how much of these two processes—the display and interpretation of nonverbal cues to emotion, beliefs, and personalities—can be accomplished automatically. As outlined by Bargh (1994), automatic processes are characterized by unawareness, efficiency, uncontrollability (i.e., they cannot be stopped), and unintentionality (i.e., they are not begun by an act of conscious will).

We survey the nonverbal signals to a range of social psychological constructs, including emotional states, interpersonal expectations, social relationships, and personality traits. For each construct, we provide evidence that encoding and decoding result largely from automatic processes. We begin with a discussion of emotional communication. We focus first on the unintentional and uncontrollable nature of such communication, highlighting the nonverbal signals of a range of feeling states. We then discuss the processes underlying the interpretation of emotional cues. As is shown, converging lines of research suggest that emotional displays are interpreted with surprising ease. In many cases, emotional stimuli need not even reach conscious awareness to elicit evaluations and behavioral reactions. We conclude this section with an examination of emotional deception, from both the actor's and the observer's perspective. In this case, the literature suggests that strategic attempts to convey a false emotional state are seriously hindered by the uncontrollability of nonverbal displays.

We then consider the case of interpersonal expectancies. The communication of interpersonal expectancies serves as a potent reminder of people's remarkable tendencies to both understand and be influenced by the subtle, nonverbal expressions of others' beliefs regarding their abilities. Because "leaky" nonverbal channels of communication are largely responsible for the transmission of interpersonal expectancies, the process of encoding expectancies is to a great extent uncontrollable. Research has further demonstrated that the interpretation of others' expectancies also takes place even in the absence of conscious awareness.

Subtle expressions of nonverbal behavior also capture the information used in making judgments relevant to social relations, and in the third section we consider how nonverbal signals are used to convey information about relationship type and quality. In many cases, people express the cues to their social relationships without conscious awareness or intention. A lack of awareness is also common when people interpret these cues, so much so that such interpretation can also be characterized as effortless.

Finally, we discuss the communication of relatively stable personality attributes. It appears that displaying such characteristics through nonverbal behavior is largely an automatic process. In this last section, we also take the perceiver's point of view on the communication of personality traits, discussing the results of studies indicating that the interpretation of cues to others' personality traits can occur without effort, intention, or awareness.

We begin with a focus on the communication of emotion.

The Automaticity of Communicating Emotion

From the Actor's Perspective

The need to strategically control and manage emotion is a well-known fact of social life. The need is so great that from a very young age, children acquire strategies for controlling their emotional expressions (Hochschild, 1979). For instance, at just 18 months, many infants smile only when given their mothers' visual attention (Jones & Raag, 1989). Though strategically managing emotional displays is clearly a useful ability, this section focuses upon the fascinating processes by which people fail to control the expression of emotion. As is shown, emotions often spontaneously "leak" from the uncontrollable nonverbal channels of communication.

The difficulty of controlling emotion expression lies mainly in the unintentional nature of emotional displays. That is, people often do not have control over the processes that give rise to these displays because automatic mechanisms link the subjective experience of emotion to its nonverbal display (Buck,

1984; Ekman, 1972, 1977). Though many emotional states are displayed unintentionally, the nonverbal correlates of some have been particularly well studied. Here we describe just a few of these cues.

The Duchenne Smile In 1862, the French anatomist Duchenne de Boulogne (1862/1990, p. 126) wrote, "the emotion of frank joy is expressed on the face by the combined contraction of the zygomaticus major muscle and the orbicularis oculi. The first obeys the will, but the second is only put in play by the sweet emotions of the soul." This form of smiling—distinguished by the combination of activity in the muscle that orbits the eye (the orbicularis oculi) as well as the muscle that pulls up the lip corners (the zygomaticus major)—is commonly referred to as "the Duchenne smile" and it is believed to occur only during the experience of true enjoyment (Ekman, 1989).

Several lines of evidence suggest that Duchenne was correct in his belief that the smile of true enjoyment is not under conscious control. First, as demonstrated by Hager and Ekman (1985), production of the true Duchenne smile—which includes contraction of the outer strands of the eye muscle—cannot be faked. Only contraction of the inner strands of this muscle can be produced voluntarily. Second, a study by Ekman, Davidson, and Friesen (1990) demonstrates that Duchenne smiles occur spontaneously during pleasant experiences. In this study, the authors obtained measures of self-reported emotional experience while participants viewed pleasant and unpleasant films. Participants' facial expressions were surreptitiously videotaped and subsequently shown to judges who coded participants' smiles as "Duchenne smiles" or "other smiles." As predicted, Duchenne smiles occurred more often while participants viewed pleasant as opposed to unpleasant films. In addition, only Duchenne smiles occurred in combination with self-reported feelings of amusement and happiness.

Thus, it appears the Duchenne smile is an example of an unintentional emotional signal, one that occurs spontaneously upon the experience of pleasure and thus provides social perceivers a reliable and valid index of a true emotional state.

Blushing Negative emotions can also elicit unintentional nonverbal displays. Blushing, the spontaneous reddening or darkening of the face, ears, neck, and upper chest, is accompanied by the subjective experience of embarrassment, self-consciousness, and conspicuousness. It is believed to result from unwanted social attention, be it positive or negative (Leary & Meadows, 1991).

One intriguing explanation for blushing is that it represents an automatic response to the mere presence of staring eyes. Templeton and Leary (1991) tested this explanation by having participants sit on one side of a covered two-way mirror with temperature sensors attached to their cheeks. The experimenter then uncovered the mirror to reveal an audience of several people on the other side of the mirror. For half of the participants, the audience members wore dark glasses that concealed their eyes, while for the other half the audience's eyes were uncovered. In support of the "staring eyes" explanation, facial temperature was found to depend on the presence of audience members' glasses. When audience members' eyes were left uncovered, participants blushed more. These results suggest that the elevation in facial temperature that is characteristic of blushing stems, in part, from an automatic response to others' staring eyes. In this sense, blushing is clearly an unintentional process, one that is elicited by the mere presence of a stimulus in the environment.

Tone of Voice Generally considered the most leaky channel of communication, tone of voice reveals a true internal state that a speaker's words can otherwise disguise (Ekman & Friesen, 1969; DePaulo, 1992). Even very brief samples of the tone of voice are revealing about several attributes, including age and gender (Helfrich, 1979), socioeconomic status (Ellis, 1967), extroversion-introversion (Siegman & Pope, 1965), dominance (Mehrabian & Williams, 1969), and competence (Parsons & Liden, 1984). Vocal cues also provide information about a speaker's emotional state, conveying cues to depression (Pope, Blass, Siegman, & Raher, 1970), anger (Scherer, 1981), and nervousness or anxiety (Harrigan, Harrigan, Sale, & Rosenthal, 1996).

In a study examining the types of cues emitted by the tone of voice, Ambady, Hogan, and Rosenthal (2002) investigated the relationship between vocal cues of interpersonal variables and performance evaluations of a sample of business executives. Judges rated brief clips taken from audiotaped interviews of the sample on a number of dimensions. These ratings were then compared with the samples' actual performance evaluations. Business executives who were rated as "outstanding" by their supervisors were also rated by the judges as higher on interpersonal attributes such as warmth and enthusiasm. It seems plausible that, without consciously realizing it, these executives were revealing in their voice some very important information about how well they performed their jobs.

A person's level of anxiety, as spontaneously revealed through the tone of voice, is a particularly easily recognized cue that often has important interpersonal implications beyond what a speaker may intend. For instance, one study revealed that anxiety in physicians' voices was positively correlated with the success of their referrals, indicating that anxiety and nervousness in the doctor's voice may be perceived by the patient as concern (Milmoe, Rosenthal, Blane, Chafetz, & Wolf, 1967).

Duchenne smiles, the act of blushing, and tone of voice are just a few examples of nonverbal cues that provide a true window into another person's feelings. Each demonstrates that the nonverbal signals of internal states are often displayed instantaneously, unintentionally, and uncontrollably.

Why is it so difficult to strategically manage emotional displays? The answer may lie in our genetic makeup. Anthropological evidence suggests that our evolutionary ancestors needed a mechanism for quickly and easily communicating the emotions they experienced, as such communication conferred survival value in a number of ways. For instance, the display of fear—the raising and pulling together of the eyebrows—signaled submission and thus helped the actor avoid the aggression of those more powerful. Involuntary displays of emotion—such as those that signal both anger and fear—are also the manifestations of reflexlike physiological processes that guide adaptive behavior (Ekman & Davidson, 1994; Etcoff, 1986). Now, modern-day humans as well as our closest evolutionary relatives are equipped with automatic links between the experience and display of emotion (Buck, 1984; Ekman, 1972, 1977). These links are most likely responsible for the unintentional nature of the nonverbal hallmarks of emotion.

From the Perceiver's Perspective

Fortunately for the busy social perceiver, just as the expression of some emotions is governed by hardwired automatic mechanisms, the interpretation of emotion appears to be similarly preprogrammed (e.g., Dimberg, 1997). In this section, we discuss how the recognition of emotional states, a fundamental social skill, can take place without conscious awareness.

In 1980, Zajonc advanced the notion that emotion recognition can take place even in the absence of awareness. This notion has received some experimental attention at both the behavioral and neurophysiological levels. For instance, one study examined the patterning of facial muscle movements that are elicited upon the nonconscious perception of emotional stimuli (Dimberg, Thunberg, & Elmehed, 2000). Previous work had demonstrated a tendency on the part of social perceivers to spontaneously mimic the nonverbal emotional displays of others. Dimberg et al. tested the hypothesis that behavioral mimicry would take place even in the absence of conscious awareness. Participants in this study were subliminally exposed to happy, neutral, and angry facial expressions, and facial electromyographic (EMG) recordings were simultaneously obtained. EMG recordings revealed that despite the fact that they were not consciously aware of the emotional stimuli, participants reacted with facial muscle configurations that mimicked the subliminally presented faces.

Further evidence for the automatic nature of emotion recognition comes from brain imaging studies. Many studies have supported the notion that the amygdala is central to the brain's processing of emotional stimuli and is particularly responsive to the sight of fearful faces (for a review, see Whalen, 1998). Using functional magnetic resonance imaging (fMRI), Whalen and his colleagues (1998) sought to determine the role of conscious awareness in the amygdala's response to emotional stimuli. In this study, pictures of human faces bearing fearful or happy expressions were presented to participants using a backward-masking technique that rendered participants unaware of having seen the expressions. Although participants reported not seeing the expressions, amygdala activity was significantly greater during the presentation of fearful faces than during the presentation of happy faces. At the level of regional brain activation, therefore, people demonstrate a reaction to emotional stimuli even when the stimuli fail to reach conscious awareness.

These studies suggest that evaluations and behavioral reactions to emotional stimuli occur even in the absence of conscious awareness, one of the defining characteristics of automatic processes. By doing so, they have made a substantial contribution to our knowledge of the cognitive mechanisms underlying emotion recognition.

Emotion Deception From the Deceiver's Perspective

What happens when people strategically attempt to deceive others about their true feelings or beliefs? It seems reasonable to suggest that because nonverbal displays are generally conveyed in an unintentional and uncontrollable manner, people will be at a disadvantage when attempting to strategically manipulate their display. Indeed, a long line of research on the psychology of deception has suggested that several characteristics of nonverbal behavior contribute to the difficulty of successful deception. It appears that even the most skilled liars are often betrayed by uncontrollable nonverbal cues to their true feelings and beliefs. This uncontrollability arises, in part, from the fact that people are often not consciously aware of the display of some nonverbal behaviors. It also appears that when people are highly motivated to lie, the increased attention they pay to the control of their nonverbal behavior often has the paradoxical effect of generating increased skepticism about their veracity.

As discussed above, nonverbal behaviors often reveal information about a speaker's true feelings or beliefs, a phenomenon referred to as leakage (Ekman & Friesen, 1969, 1974; Rosenthal & DePaulo, 1979a, 1979b). Leakage cues are present despite people's conscious attempts to control their behavior in order to mislead others. Rosenthal and his colleagues have shown that the tone of voice is often the most revealing channel in terms of deception, followed by the body and the face (Rosenthal & DePaulo, 1979a, 1979b; Scherer, Feldstein, Bond, & Rosenthal, 1985). For example, if deceivers are seeking to disguise fear or anger, they may speak more quickly and their voices might sound higher and louder.

Paul Ekman (1985) discovered the unintended nature of emotional communication while conducting studies with nursing students who were highly motivated to hide their negative reactions to films of gory medical scenes. He found that even those students who were adept at deception unwittingly communicated their actual emotional reactions to the films through their voices and bodies. Specifically, vocal pitch increased when the students attempted to pretend that they were watching a pleasant film when, in fact, they were watching a film featuring scenes of amputations and burns. Bodily gestures were even more informative than vocal cues as to the nurses' true reactions to the films. This has been attributed to the fact that people are less aware of the body's vulnerability to leakage than they are of the potential for faces to reveal their true feelings. Feldman and White (1980) advanced an intriguing theory to explain the leakage of cues to deception through bodily channels of communication. According to this theory, the arousal that deceivers feel in the midst of a lie might be successfully kept from the face, but it will be shunted to another channel of communication, such as the body. In effect, the arousal does not just disappear but manifests itself in other, leakier channels.

DePaulo, Lanier, and Davis (1983) found that nonverbal behavior was particularly revealing when people were highly motivated to lie about their attitudes and opinions. It seems that the motivation to appear honest generates anxiety, which is manifested in the display of higher vocal pitch and fewer head movements. These behaviors are often interpreted as insincerity (Zuckerman, DePaulo, & Rosenthal, 1981). Highly motivated liars may also adopt several different strategies to convey honesty, including attempting to deliberately control all verbal and nonverbal behaviors. This, too, has the paradoxical effect of arousing suspicion, as it leads to less movement and more behavioral rigidity (Zuckerman et al., 1981).

In sum, the literature on the psychology of deception suggests that the expression of an individual's true feelings or beliefs is often not under conscious control. Even high motivation to deceive successfully cannot override the influence of instinctual and automatic behavior. Indeed, high motivation often has the paradoxical effect of alerting others to a lie.

Deception From the Lie-Detector's Perspective

People's ability to detect deception in others is only a little better than chance, as the rate of successful lie detection has been found to be approximately 60% (Zuckerman et al., 1981). One might speculate that if people were to apply all of their cognitive efforts toward accurate lie detection, their chances for success might improve. However, we suggest that this is not the case, because successful lie detection is in large part a process that naturally proceeds without our awareness. As with other types of judgments (Gilbert & Krull, 1988;

Wilson, Hodges, & LaFleur, 1995; Wilson & Schooler, 1991), increased attention may paradoxically diminish accuracy.

If lie detection can be characterized as a process whose inner workings are largely inaccessible to conscious awareness, then we can make several other hypotheses about the effects of situational constraints on its success. First, formal training should do little to improve detection accuracy. Such training may disrupt the normal ways in which we process deception cues, forcing people to rely on consciously mediated strategies when, in fact, nonconscious processing is optimal. Second, if people process cues without awareness when attempting to spot a lie, they should be unable to articulate the strategies they use in lie detection; this is, they should have no conscious awareness of the strategies they use when engaged in such processing. Therefore it also follows that there should be little to no correlation between lie detection success and confidence in lie detection. A great deal of work has investigated the success of lie detection under these conditions. The findings are consistent with the notion that lie detection is, for the most part, a nonconscious process.

In support of the first assumption, most research suggests that there are limitations and sometimes even adverse effects of formal training in lie detection. For example, Kassin and Fong (1999) found that formal training makes little difference when differentiating between true and false denials in a criminal interrogation. In fact, those who underwent training were less accurate than naive controls, though they were more confident and cited more reasons for their judgments. When left to their own devices, however, people tend to use automatic, overlearned strategies to detect untruthful statements. They are thus in large part unaware of their lie detection strategies. For this reason, lie detectors are generally unable to articulate what combination of verbal and nonverbal cues they use (Zuckerman et al., 1981). Even lie detection experts like police officers, detectives, and prison guards have been found to possess incorrect beliefs about indicators of deception (Vrij, 1993; Vrij & Semin, 1996).

In addition, there seems to be no relationship between confidence in lie detection ability and actual accuracy. DePaulo, Charlton, Cooper, Lindsay, and Muhlenbruck (1997) conducted a meta-analysis investigating this relationship and found that the accuracy–confidence correlation in the detection of deception was $r = .04$. In fact, confidence was positively correlated with the tendency to erroneously judge messages as truthful. Thus, not only are people largely unaware of their true lie detection abilities, but those who are more confident also show more false negative errors (i.e., failures to detect lying).

In sum, existing evidence suggests that the strategies used to detect deception are generally employed outside conscious awareness. Because lie detection naturally occurs in a relatively automatic fashion, attempting to exert conscious control over lie detection often results in diminished accuracy. These findings have important implications for the training of those whose jobs require accurate lie detection.

The Automaticity of Communicating Expectancies

In the previous section, we discussed how the display of emotional states can take place without intent and control, and how the interpretation of these displays can occur without conscious awareness. This is often fortunate for the busy social perceiver, who is faced with surveying an almost overwhelming amount of information at any point in time. However, the automatic communication of internal states and beliefs can often have serious and negative interpersonal consequences for the social perceiver.

This is perhaps best revealed through the pervasive presence of interpersonal expectancy effects in many settings. The work of Rosenthal and his colleagues, in particular, has revealed that privately held expectations about others' actions and abilities are often spontaneously communicated. The communication of such expectancies, even when the bases for them are false, often results in self-fulfilling prophecies (e.g., Rosenthal & Jacobson, 1968). Rosenthal's first studies revealed the tendency of participants in behavioral research to confirm the experimenter's expectations about the outcome of the study. These findings were traced to the unwitting communication of such expectancies on the part of the experimenter. Attention later turned to the communication of expectancies in real-world interactions with enormous practical importance, including those between teacher and student (Rosenthal & Jacobson, 1968), doctor and patient (e.g, Caporael, Lukaszewski, & Culbertson, 1983), and judge and jury (Blanck, 1993).

From the Actor's Perspective

How are these expectancies conveyed? A substantial body of work has addressed this question. One clear conclusion to be drawn from this work is that the expression of expectations is rather uncontrollable. To a great extent, this is because interpersonal expectations are communicated via leaky nonverbal channels of communication (Harris & Rosenthal, 1985; Rosenthal & Fode, 1963).

In the domain of teacher-student relationships, explorations of leakage hierarchies have begun to reveal the patterns of nonverbal behavior associated with expectancy communication. Babad, Bernieri, and Rosenthal (1989a) predicted that teachers who tend to be biased about their students' academic performance would display more negative affect in the leaky channels of facial and bodily movements, and less negative affect in the more controllable channel of speech content. As predicted, teachers prone to bias in their treatment of students demonstrated substantial leakage in their nonverbal display of negative affect (see also Babad, Bernieri, & Rosenthal, 1989b). Though biased teachers actively attempted to disguise their expectations for students' performance by manipulating the content of their speech, they unwittingly revealed their true beliefs through more uncontrollable channels. Thus, as demonstrated by these studies, teachers not only unintentionally expressed their negative feelings toward low-achieving students, but they also were unable to control these expressions enough to hide them completely from detection. Indeed, it is important to note that such uncontrollable leakage occurred even when teachers were aware of being videotaped and therefore presumably were on their best behavior.

Additional support for the uncontrollable nature of expectancy expression comes from a study conducted by Harris and Perkins (1995). Drawing on the work of Gilbert and his colleagues on cognitive busyness (e.g., Gilbert & Hixon, 1991; Gilbert, Pelham, & Krull, 1988), the authors speculated that if the communication of expectancies is relatively uncontrollable, then attempting to exert conscious control over this communication would be quite demanding of cognitive resources. They tested this hypothesis by examining the extent to which the partners of cognitively busy or idle participants behaved in a manner consistent with their partners' expectations. In line with the hypothesis, the partners of cognitively busy participants were more likely than the partners of cognitively idle participants to manifest expectancy effects. This finding implies that controlling the communication of expectancies is truly a cognitively demanding exercise; under conditions of strained attentional resources, privately held expectancies are more likely to elicit behavioral confirmation. This further suggests the basic efficiency of expectancy communication.

From the Perceiver's Perspective

As we have discussed some of the information processing requirements on the part of the individual who holds an expectation, it seems appropriate to consider the same issues from the point of view of the target of the expectancies. Are interpersonal expectations as automatically interpreted as they are conveyed?

Some interesting new findings in the area of stereotypes and behavioral confirmation suggest that people are influenced by others' expectations, even when they are not consciously aware that such expectancies are being communicated. Researchers in this area, recognizing that prevalent stereotypes act as expectancies in social interactions, have systematically tested whether subtly reminding people of stereotypes has any effect on behavior. For instance, Levy (1996) tested whether negative expectations about memory abilities influence the memory performance of older adults. Levy subliminally presented older adults with terms associated with the category "elderly," either negative (e.g., senile, dementia) or positive (e.g., wise, experienced). Remarkably, participants' memory performance fell in line with the subliminally presented terms. It appears that being subtly reminded of group-level expectations dramatically shapes performance.

This process appears to be at work in other performance domains and with a wide variety of stereotyped groups. Thus, Shih, Ambady, Richeson, Fujita, and Gray (2002) tested the stereotype confirmation effect among Asian American undergraduates. In this country, Asian Americans are stereotyped to have superior intellectual abilities, particularly in the domain of mathematical performance (Shih, Pittinsky, & Ambady, 1999). Consistent with this stereotype, Asian American participants who were subliminally exposed to Asian constructs demonstrated significant improvements in mathematical ability, as compared to those exposed to neutral constructs. Subliminal reminders of high performance expectations can thus produce considerable boosts to actual performance abilities.

These studies have begun to elucidate the processes underlying behavioral confirmation in social interactions. Based on these findings, it appears that group-based expectations can be automatically perceived, and this perception can in turn evoke behavioral confirmation. Without conscious awareness or intent, people are susceptible to the influence of others' beliefs about their traits and abilities.[1]

The Automaticity of Communicating Social Relations

In 1980, Zajonc advanced the notion that evaluations about others are made automatically. "One cannot be introduced to a person," Zajonc wrote, "without experiencing some immediate feeling of attraction or repulsion" (p. 153). Zajonc further claimed that nonverbal channels of communication carry the bulk of information about interpersonal attitudes. In this section, we describe research findings in support of Zajonc's view. Specifically, we present support for the claim that the transmission of information relevant to social relationships—including interpersonal attitudes, relationship type, and rapport—is transmitted and interpreted automatically, and that this information is often transmitted through fleeting displays of nonverbal behavior.

From the Actor's Perspective

As in the case of emotional states and interpersonal expectancies, the signals of relationship type and status are often found in brief expressions of nonverbal behavior. For example, Fine, Stitt, and Finch (1984) conducted a naturalistic study in which couples standing in a movie line were approached by an interviewer, who asked the woman in the couple either intimate or nonintimate questions. When the questions were intimate, the man was more likely to gaze at the woman and orient his body toward her, perhaps in an attempt to assert the connection between them. These behaviors were performed automatically by the men in response to a perceived interpersonal threat.

In a manner similar to relationship status, the quality of a social relationship is often encoded in brief nonverbal displays involving level of proximity, interactional synchrony, and touching (Gada, Bernieri, Grahe, Zuroff, & Koestner, 1997). In a clinical context, rapport is revealed through increased eye contact and body orientation (Harrigan, Oxman, & Rosenthal, 1985). Teachers and students with greater rapport have also been found to have high levels of interactional synchrony and to engage in more behavior matching (Bernieri, 1988).

Finally, people have a tendency to spontaneously reveal their attitudes toward others through nonverbal cues. Thus, in one study, Whites' tone of voice revealed their previously assessed negative attitudes toward Blacks (Weitz, 1972). Specifically, friendliness of Whites' behavior toward Blacks was positively correlated with friendliness inferred from tone of voice but negatively correlated with friendliness expressed as verbal, explicit attitudes. At the individual level, women tend to sound more approachable and sincere when talking with intimate male friends than when talking with casual male friends (Montepare & Vega, 1988). These examples demonstrate the essentially unintentional nature of many nonverbal behaviors that reveal people's true feelings about others.

In general, people convey quite naturally their feelings toward others, whether they are friends, romantic partners, members of different social groups, or strangers. These feelings are revealed by detectable cues in nonverbal behavior, and some research has shown that such cues are given off without actors' conscious awareness. For instance, one study revealed that only a quarter of participants were aware of the behaviors they use to make others like or dislike them (Palmer & Simmons, 1995). Likewise, examining social information communication from the perceiver's perspective reveals that these important signs can be decoded in a relatively automatic manner.

From the Perceiver's Perspective

How observable are the signals of relationship type? In an attempt to answer this question, Archer and Akert (1977) presented study participants with a series of video clips 30 to 60 seconds in length. These clips portrayed people interacting in a variety of contexts, and participants were asked to answer diagnostic questions regarding the true relationships between the people. Those who viewed the video clips performed significantly better on questions about the targets' kinship and relationship status than did those asked to make judgments based on a written transcript of the clips, despite the fact that the transcript contained more verbal information than the video presentation. Thus, relationship type is quite reliably inferred from very brief samples of nonverbal behavior.

The subjective experience of making judgments from brief glimpses of behavior has yet to be fully investigated, but some work indicates that these judgments are optimally made without the application of conscious resources. Ambady (2002) sought to determine whether situational constraints on information-processing strategies affected the ability to make thin-slice judgments of relationship type. Perceivers who were asked to deliberate carefully before making judgments of relationship status demonstrated diminished accuracy, as compared to those given no instructions to deliberate. In addition, cognitive load did not impact participants' accuracy. This pattern of results suggests that judgments of relationship type based on brief observations of behavior do not rely on consciously mediated strategies; in fact, it appears they are optimally made automatically (see also Patterson & Stockbridge, 1998).

Not only are observers able to differentiate between different types of relationships, they are also quite adept at judging the quality of relationships based on glimpses of behavior. Bernieri and his associates have investigated the perception of rapport in dyadic interactions. In one study (Bernieri, Davis, Rosenthal, & Knee, 1994), participants were shown brief video clips of opposite-sex strangers interacting. These video clips were created by degrading the original displays into mosaics of monocolored blocks to further reduce the amount of information available to the perceivers. Based on these glimpses, participants were able to make rapport judgments that correlated highly with the judgments of rapport made by the interactants themselves. Interestingly, participants were unable to accurately report the factors that influenced their judgments. Thus, the processes underlying judgments of rapport appear largely inaccessible to conscious reflection.

In sum, perceivers demonstrate a striking ability to detect the type and quality of others' social relationships. This ability seems to derive from a largely effortless process of detection, a process of which people are not consciously aware. This remarkable ability may be rooted in a basic need, present throughout our evolutionary history, to make quick and accurate assessments of others' group membership patterns. Indeed, the ability to categorize others' relationships has been found in nonhuman primates. After losing a fight, for instance, macaques and baboons will target their aggression toward the relatives of the monkey who defeated them (Cheney & Seyfarth, 1990). This extensive knowledge of others' social group memberships has not been found in nonprimates, and it can be viewed as a general measure of social intelligence.

The Automaticity of Communicating Personality

Cultural imperatives like "never judge a book by its cover" maintain that impressions formed on the basis of minimal information are unreliable. However, these quick judgments are inevitable features of the rapid pace and wealth of information that characterize the brief social encounters of everyday life. Fortunately for the social perceiver, research has demonstrated that such judgments can be surprisingly accurate.

This is particularly true when such judgments are made about "legible" traits that are easily observed through glimpses of nonverbal behavior, such as extroversion and agreeableness (Gifford, 1994). Clues to extroversion often lie in subtle nonverbal cues like gestures and head nods (Berry & Hansen, 2000). Other legible personality traits include dominance and submissiveness, as revealed through observations of gaze while speaking (Exline, Ellyson, & Long, 1975) and postural relaxation (Mehrabian, 1981). The following section addresses the largely automatic nature of this communication, as revealed by research on overlearned strategies of self-presentation.

From the Actor's Perspective

Self-presentation, or the ways in which people convey their identities to others, has traditionally been conceptualized as a self-conscious, strategic activity that is motivated by a desire to enhance interpersonal power (Jones & Pittman, 1982). These conceptualizations focus on self-presentation in situations like job interviews and first dates, when people have a heightened concern for and awareness of how they appear to others. However, in many situations, self-presentation may not be a salient goal. In more relaxed interactions with friends, family or coworkers, people may project and maintain their personal identities in an effortless fashion by relying on overlearned and well-practiced patterns of nonverbal display. This behavior is automatic, in that it is effortless, involuntary, and requires very little in the way of conscious monitoring.

Some studies have explored how concurrent cognitive processing affects self-presentational strategies in both formal and relaxed situations. For instance, Baumeister, Hutton, and Tice (1989) investigated the cognitive demands of self-presentation in interactions with strangers. Research has suggested that people are often motivated to present a generally positive image of themselves to strangers (e.g., Tice, Butler, Muraven, & Stillwell, 1995). Drawing on this work, Baumeister et al. assumed that in such interactions, the act of presenting a positive image would be routine and automatic, but switching from this "default" strategy into a more modest mode would be quite demanding of cognitive resources. In this study, before interacting with strangers, participants were instructed to present themselves in either a self-enhancing or a modest manner. Participants' memory for details of the interaction was later assessed. Interestingly, participants who presented themselves in a positive manner displayed greater recall for details of the interaction than did those who were instructed to present themselves more modestly. This finding suggests that self-enhancing behavior toward strangers requires relatively little cognitive effort, freeing up the resources to attend to and later recall details about other aspects of the social situation.

While interactions with strangers may call upon a self-enhancing default strategy, self-presentational displays among friends are generally more modest (Baumeister & Jones, 1978). Using the same paradigm described above, Tice et al. (1995) replicated the finding that participants who interacted with strangers in a positive manner subsequently recalled more details of the interaction than those instructed to be more modest. Further, Tice et al. discovered that participants instructed to act modestly while with friends recalled more than those instructed to act in a self-enhancing manner. Though people may have default self-presentational strategies that are routine and automatic, these strategies are specific to the type of social interaction in which they are engaged.

In addition to situationally determined goals of self-presentation, people also have default strategies that reflect their own relatively stable personality traits. Pontari and Schlenker (2000) reasoned that any "out-of-character" self-presentations (those that are incongruent with one's true dispositions) would be more demanding of cognitive resources than "in-character" displays. If this were the case, then people's abilities to portray different personality characteristics should be hindered under conditions of cognitive load. To test this hypothesis, the authors recruited self-reported extroverts and introverts. Before engaging in a mock interview with a stranger, some extroverts were instructed to appear introverted, while some introverts were instructed to appear extroverted. Other participants were simply asked to behave in a personality-congruent manner. In addition, some participants were given a cognitive load manipulation (rehearsing a digit string throughout the interview), while others were given no such instructions. Effectiveness in portraying extroversion or introversion was assessed via interview partners' ratings of the participants on these dimensions. As predicted, extroverts who were not cognitively busy during the interaction effectively portrayed themselves as introverts, whereas those who were cognitively taxed were less successful. Cognitive load made it more difficult for these individuals to effectively portray a false role. Among introverts, however, cognitive busyness actually increased the effectiveness of out-of-character presentations. Thus, the effects of cognitive busyness on the ability to project an incongruent personality are, in part, determined by degree of extroversion or introversion.

In sum, these results suggest that many cases of switching from the default self-presentational pattern to a self-incongruent or unrehearsed routine is a controlled, effortful process that is impeded by concurrent cognitive processing. In contrast, the act of portraying a self-congruent image is a process that does not demand the application of cognitive resources. Once activated, these behavioral patterns proceed autonomously, without the necessity of continual conscious monitoring. In the next section, we explore what happens when people attempt to interpret these behavioral cues to underlying personality traits, as well as more "basic" attributes like gender and age.

From the Perceiver's Perspective

At the most basic level, perceivers are often able to discern the gender of others even when presented with minimal information. Kozlowski and Cutting (1977) found that perceivers could accurately differentiate between males and females simply by viewing them in "point-light" displays. These displays were degraded such that the only things visible to observers were dots of light attached to the joints of the walkers in a black background. People express their gender through their bodily movements, and such displays happen so quickly and directly that they may be impossible to fake.

Other work has highlighted the ease with which judgments can be made about enduring personality traits. In perhaps the first study of its kind, Estes (1938) found that 2-minute film clips of people engaged in expressive movement yielded enough information for naive judges to make accurate personality assessments. Naive judges' ratings correlated highly with targets' previously administered personality assessments. Characteristics like emotionality, inhibition, and apathy were particularly well judged. Estes speculated that judges were most successful when they relied on relatively effortless decision-making strategies, and some of his findings support this contention. That is, judges who made their ratings without first analyzing their impressions were more accurate. More successful judges also completed their ratings more quickly, and they were less sure of the specific basis for their judgments. This study was one of the first to demonstrate that deliberation may have a detrimental effect on the ability to form accurate first impressions of others.

Research on spontaneous trait inference (Uleman, Newman, & Moskowitz, 1996; Winter, Uleman, & Cunniff, 1985) also suggests possible mechanisms for people's abilities to make judgments from glimpses of others. The work of Uleman and his colleagues has challenged the belief that social judgments and attributions are of necessity intentional, effortful, and conscious. This line of research has demonstrated that people can unintentionally decode personality characteristics when they perceive others. Further, people are often unaware of making these judgments (Winter & Uleman, 1984). These results suggest that people are inclined to go beyond the information provided, whether the information is in the form of written material or video displays. Thus, inferring personality traits relies to a great extent on processes that are not consciously mediated.

The inference of others' personality traits is a process of undeniable interpersonal consequence. In the workplace, important evaluations are often based solely on ratings of personality traits. For example, student evaluations of their teachers along both personality and task-relevant lines influence salary, promotion, and tenure decisions. Recognizing this, Ambady (2002) sought to determine how judgments of teachers' effectiveness, formed on the basis of thin slices of expressive behavior, are made. In this study, some participants were instructed to deliberate carefully before forming their judgments of teacher effectiveness. Accuracy in judgments of teacher effectiveness was computed by comparing naive judges' ratings with the students' end-of-semester ratings. In line with Estes's early speculation, participants who were asked to deliberate carefully demonstrated diminished judgmental accuracy compared with those in the control condition. These findings indicate that judgments in this domain rely on automatic processes of decision making.

Conclusion

Contrary to lay beliefs about the validity of impressions formed on minimal information, the research reviewed in this chapter demonstrates the remarkable accuracy of such judgments in terms of a variety of psychological constructs. This accuracy stems from two sources: people's predispositions for spontaneously expressing affective, social, and dispositional information, and the corresponding ability to perceive and interpret such information. These abilities were likely shaped by the need to act quickly and efficiently in a world teeming with social stimuli.

The unique contribution of the work presented herein arises from the attempt to understand the transmission of social information through the rich media people encounter daily, or as close an approximation as can be created in a laboratory setting. Hence the emphasis is placed on judgments of real interactions, either in real settings such as the classroom or the doctor's office, or in more contrived contexts. This drive for research that is increasingly grounded in the "real world" is consistent with a call for greater ecological validity in theories of social perception (McArthur & Baron, 1983). Because of the richness of the social world and all the messages that it conveys, researchers can selectively use elements of these displays, such as still photos, audio clips, or audiovisual clips. Though the methods might be diverse, the goal is the same: to understand the way people's behavior, intentional or unintentional, affects how they are perceived and, conversely, how they perceive others.

The need to quickly and easily process incoming social information is clearly illustrated in the following example. Imagine trying to enact and monitor all the signals that are required to convey liking of a potential mate. The need to consciously be aware of one's behavior, whether verbal or nonverbal, would require a huge amount of resources; one's abilities to do multiple things at the same time would be seriously compromised. In this example, it would be difficult to talk intelligently about the opera and also maintain eye contact while smiling and laughing at appropriate points in the conversation.

Because of the need to act quickly in social life, much of human behavior has acquired an almost reflexlike nature. This is not to say that we are automatons, completely at the mercy of processes to which we do not have access. Most social tasks are composed of components over which we can exercise a great deal of conscious control. For example, our decisions to initiate social goals can be largely conscious, though we may not be consciously aware of all the steps that are set in motion to fulfill these goals. Further, we are capable of a great deal of flexibility, possessing the ability to override automatic tendencies, integrating contextual and situational cues and modulating behavior in accordance with these cues.

Much social behavior is, therefore, the product of a trade-off between the need for quick action and the need for consciousness and control. Though we might have some conscious awareness of how our behaviors express our thoughts, feelings, and dispositions to others, we cannot always consciously monitor these expressions, because doing so would deplete precious cognitive resources. In a similar manner, though we often pay careful attention to others when attempting to interpret their behavior, doing so at all times would leave us unable to concentrate on other activities. Thus, we possess strategies for effortlessly interpreting others' subtle cues. This explains why judges in many of the studies described in this chapter were most accurate when forced to give instant reactions without deliberating and under conditions that fostered responding in a more intuitive manner.

In this chapter, we have attempted to provide an answer to the question cited by Posner and Snyder (1975) as one of the most basic and important questions of human existence: the issue of how much conscious control people have over their judgments, decisions, and behavior. Although we believe that people exert control over these components of social life, we have also shown that a great deal can be accomplished automatically. The remarkable smoothness with which people navigate their social worlds is largely due to their ability to effortlessly express their feelings, beliefs, and desires, and to just as easily interpret these experiences in those around them.

Note

1. Research is suggesting the existence of other pathways to stereotype-confirming behavior. Chief among these is the "perception-behavior expressway" model proposed by Dijksterhuis and Bargh (2001). This model posits that the activation of trait concepts directly elicits corresponding behavioral tendencies, without the involvement of expectancies or stereotypes.

References

Ambady, N. (2002). *The perils of pondering: Effects of deliberation and distraction on thin-slice judgments.* Manuscript under revision.

Ambady, N., Bernieri, F. J., & Richeson, J. A. (2000). Toward a histology of social behavior: Judgmental accuracy from thin slices of the behavioral stream. In M. P. Zanna (Ed.), *Advances in experimental social psychology* (Vol. 32, pp. 201–271). San Diego, CA: Academic Press.

Ambady, N., Hallahan, M., & Rosenthal, R. (1995). On judging and being judged accurately in zero acquaintance situations. *Journal of Personality and Social Psychology, 69*, 518–529.

Ambady, N., Hogan, D. B., & Rosenthal, R. (2002). *It only takes a minute: Evaluating organizational performance from thin slices of the voice.* Manuscript under revision.

Ambady, N., & Rosenthal, R. (1992). Thin slices of expressive behavior as predictors of interpersonal consequences: A meta-analysis. *Psychological Bulletin, 111*(2), 256–274.

Ambady, N., & Rosenthal, R. (1993). Half a minute: Predicting teacher evaluations from thin slices of nonverbal behavior and physical attractiveness. *Journal of Personality and Social Psychology, 64*(3), 431–441.

Archer, D., & Akert, R. M. (1977). Words and everything else: Verbal and nonverbal cues in social interpretation. *Journal of Personality and Social Psychology, 35*(6), 443–449.

Babad, E., Bernieri, F., & Rosenthal, R. (1989a). Nonverbal communication and leakage in the behavior of biased and unbiased teachers. *Journal of Personality and Social Psychology, 56*, 89–94.

Babad, E., Bernieri, F., & Rosenthal, R. (1989b). When less information is more informative: Diagnosing teacher expectations from brief samples of behaviour. *British Journal of Educational Psychology, 59*, 281–295.

Bargh, J. A. (1994). The four horsemen of automaticity: Awareness, intention, efficiency, and control in social cognition. In R. S. Wyer Jr. & T. K. Srull (Eds.), *Handbook of social cognition* (2nd ed., pp. 1–40). Hillsdale, NJ: Erlbaum.

Baumeister, R. F., Hutton, D. G., & Tice, D. M. (1989). Cognitive processes during deliberate self-presentation: How self-presenters alter and misinterpret the behavior of their interaction partners. *Journal of Experimental Social Psychology, 25*(1), 59–78.

Baumeister, R. F., & Jones, E. E. (1978). When self-presentation is constrained by the target's knowledge: Consistency and compensation. *Journal of Personality and Social Psychology, 36*(6), 606–618.

Bernieri, F. (1988). Coordinated movement and rapport in teacher-student interactions. *Journal of Nonverbal Behavior, 12*, 120–138.

Bernieri, F. J., Davis, J. M., Rosenthal, R., & Knee, C. R. (1994). Interactional synchrony and rapport: Measuring synchrony in displays devoid of sound and facial affect. *Personality and Social Psychology Bulletin, 20*, 303–311.

Berry, D. S., & Hansen, J. S. (2000). Personality, nonverbal behavior, and interaction quality in female dyads. *Personality and Social Psychology Bulletin, 26*, 278–292.

Blanck, P. D. (1993). Calibrating the scales of justice: Studying judges' behavior in jury and bench trials. *Indiana Law Journal, 68*, 1119–1198.

Buck, R. (1984). *The communication of emotion*. New York: Guilford.

Buck, R. (1993). The spontaneous communication of interpersonal expectancies. In P. D. Blanck (Ed.), *Interpersonal expectations: Theory, research, and applications* (pp. 227–241). New York: Cambridge University Press.

Caporael, L. R., Lukaszewski, M. P., & Culbertson, G. H. (1983). Secondary baby talk: Judgments by institutionalized elderly and their therapists. *Journal of Personality and Social Psychology, 44*, 746–754.

Cheney, D. L., & Seyfarth, R. M. (1990). *How monkeys see the world: Inside the mind of another species*. Chicago: University of Chicago Press.

DePaulo, B. M. (1992). Nonverbal behavior and self-presentation. *Psychological Bulletin, 111*(2), 203–243.

DePaulo, B. M., Charlton, K., Cooper, H., Lindsay, J. J., & Muhlenbruck, L. (1997). The accuracy-confidence correlation in the detection of deception. *Personality and Social Psychology Review, 1*(4), 346–357.

DePaulo, B. M., Lanier, K., & Davis, T. (1983). Detecting the deceit of the motivated liar. *Journal of Personality and Social Psychology, 45*, 1096–1103.

Dijksterhuis, A., & Bargh, J. A. (2001). The perception-behavior expressway: Automatic effects of social perception on social behavior. In M. P. Zanna (Ed.), *Advances in experimental social psychology* (Vol. 33, pp. 1–40). San Diego, CA: Academic Press.

Dimberg, U. (1997). Psychophysiological reactions to facial expressions. In U. Segerstrale & P. Molnar (Eds.), *Nonverbal communication: Where nature meets culture* (pp. 47–60). Mahwah, NJ: Erlbaum.

Dimberg, U., Thunberg, M., & Elmehed, K. (2000). Unconscious facial reactions to emotional facial expressions. *Psychological Science, 11*(1), 86–89.

Duchenne, G. B. (1990). *The mechanism of human facial expression or an electrophysiological analysis of the expression of the emotions* (A. Cuthbertson, Trans.). New York: Cambridge University Press. (Original work published in 1862)

Ekman, P. (1972). Universals and cultural differences in facial expressions of emotion. In J. K. Cole (Ed.), *Nebraska symposium on motivation, 1971* (pp. 207–283). Lincoln: University of Nebraska Press.

Ekman, P. (1977). Biological and cultural contributions to body and facial movement. In J. Blacking (Ed.), *The anthropology of the body* (pp. 39–84). San Diego, CA: Academic Press.

Ekman, P. (1985). *Telling lies*. New York: Norton.

Ekman, P. (1989). The argument and evidence about universals in facial expressions of emotion. In H. Wagner & A. Manstead (Eds.), *Handbook of psychophysiology: The biological psychology of emotions and social processes* (pp. 143–164). London: John Wiley.

Ekman, P., & Davidson, R. J. (Eds.). (1994). *The nature of emotion*. New York: Oxford University Press.

Ekman, P., Davidson, R. J., & Friesen, W. V. (1990). The Duchenne smile: Emotional expression and brain physiology II. *Journal of Personality and Social Psychology, 58*(2), 342–353.

Ekman, P., & Friesen, W. V. (1969). Nonverbal leakage and cues to deception. *Psychiatry, 32*, 88–106.

Ekman, P., & Friesen, W. V. (1974). Detecting deception from the face or body. *Journal of Personality and Social Psychology, 29*, 288–298.

Ellis, D. S. (1967). Speech and social status in America. *Social Forces, 45*, 431–437.

Estes, S. G. (1938). Judging personality from expressive behavior. *Journal of Abnormal and Social Psychology, 33*, 217–236.

Etcoff, N. (1986). The neuropsychology of emotional expression. In G. Goldstein & R. E. Tarter (Eds.), *Advances in clinical neuropsychology* (Vol. 3, pp. 127–179). New York: Plenum.

Exline, R. V., Ellyson, S. L., & Long, B. (1975). Visual behavior as an aspect of power role relationships. In P. Pliner, L. Krames, & T. Alloway (Eds.), *Nonverbal communication of aggression* (Vol. 2, pp. 21–51). New York: Plenum.

Feldman, R. S., & White, J. B. (1980). Detecting deception in children. *Journal of Communication, 30*, 121–128.

Fine, G. A., Stitt, J. L., & Finch, M. (1984). Couple tie-signs and interpersonal threat: A field experiment. *Social Psychology Quarterly, 47*, 282–286.

Funder, D. C. (1987). Errors and mistakes: Evaluating the accuracy of social judgment. *Psychological Bulletin, 101*, 75–90.

Funder, D. C. (1995). On the accuracy of personality judgment: A realistic approach. *Psychological Review, 102*(4), 652–670.

Gada, N. M., Bernieri, F., Grahe, J. E., Zuroff, D., & Koestner, R. (1997, May). *Love: How do observers perceive it.* Paper presented at the Midwestern Psychological Association Convention, Chicago.

Gifford, R. (1994). A lens-mapping framework for understanding the encoding and decoding of interpersonal dispositions in nonverbal behavior. *Journal of Personality and Social Psychology, 66*(2), 398–412.

Gilbert, D. T., & Hixon, J. G. (1991). The trouble of thinking: Activation and application of stereotypic beliefs. *Journal of Personality and Social Psychology, 60*(4), 509–517.

Gilbert, D. T., & Krull, D. S. (1988). Seeing less and knowing more: The benefits of perceptual ignorance. *Journal of Personality and Social Psychology, 54*, 193–202.

Gilbert, D. T., Pelham, B. W., & Krull, D. S. (1988). On cognitive busyness: When person perceivers meet persons perceived. *Journal of Personality and Social Psychology, 54*, 733–740.

Goffman, E. (1979). *Gender advertisements.* New York: Harper Colophon.

Hager, J. C., & Ekman, P. (1985). The asymmetry of facial actions is inconsistent with models of hemispheric specialization. *Psychophysiology, 22*(3), 307–318.

Harrigan, J. A., Harrigan, K. M., Sale, B. A., & Rosenthal, R. (1996). Detecting anxiety and defensiveness from visual and auditory cues. *Journal of Personality, 64*, 675–709.

Harrigan, J. A., Oxman, T. E., & Rosenthal, R. (1985). Rapport expressed through nonverbal behavior. *Journal of Nonverbal Behavior, 9*, 95–110.

Harris, M. J., & Perkins, R. (1995). Effects of distraction on interpersonal expectancy effects: A social interaction test of the cognitive busyness hypothesis. *Social Cognition, 13*, 163–182.

Harris, M. J., & Rosenthal, R. (1985). Mediation of interpersonal expectancy effects: 31 meta-analyses. *Psychological Bulletin, 97*, 363–386.

Helfrich, H. (1979). Age markers in speech. In K. R. Scherer & H. Giles (Eds.), *Social markers in speech* (pp. 63–108). Cambridge, UK: Cambridge University Press.

Hochschild, A. R. (1979). Emotion work, feeling rules, and social structure. *American Journal of Sociology, 85*, 551–575.

Jones, E. E., & Pittman, T. S. (1982). Toward a general theory of strategic self-presentation. In J. Suls (Ed.), *Psychological perspectives on the self* (Vol. 1, pp. 231–262). Hillsdale, NJ: Erlbaum.

Jones, S. S., & Raag, T. (1989). Smile production in older infants: The importance of a social recipient for the facial signal. *Child Development, 60*, 811–818.

Kassin, S. M., & Fong, C. T. (1999). "I'm innocent!": Effects of training on judgments of truth and deception in the interrogation room. *Law and Human Behavior, 23*, 499–516.

Kenny, D. A., & Albright, L. (1987). Accuracy in interpersonal perception: A social relations analysis. *Psychological Bulletin, 102*, 390–402.

Kozlowski, L. T., & Cutting, J. E. (1977). Recognizing the sex of a walker from a dynamic point-light display. *Perception and Psychophysics, 21*(6), 575–580.

Leary, M. R., & Meadows, S. (1991). Predictors, elicitors, and concomitants of social blushing. *Journal of Personality and Social Psychology, 60*(2), 254–262.

Levy, B. (1996). Improving memory in old age through implicit self-stereotyping. *Journal of Personality and Social Psychology, 71*, 1092–1107.

McArthur, L. Z., & Baron, R. M. (1983). Toward an ecological theory of social perception. *Psychological Review, 90*, 215–238.

Mehrabian, A. (1981). *Silent messages*. Belmont, CA: Wadsworth.

Mehrabian, A., & Williams, M. (1969). Nonverbal concomitants of perceived and intended persuasiveness. *Journal of Personality and Social Psychology, 13*, 37–58.

Milmoe, S., Rosenthal, R., Blane, H. T., Chafetz, M. E., & Wolf, I. (1967). The doctor's voice: Postdictor of successful referral of alcoholic patients. *Journal of Abnormal Psychology, 72*, 78–84.

Montepare, J. M., & Vega, C. (1988). Women's vocal reactions to intimate and casual male friends. *Personality and Social Psychology Bulletin, 14*, 103–113.

Palmer, M. T., & Simmons, K. B. (1995). Communicating intentions through nonverbal behaviors: Conscious and nonconscious encoding of liking. *Human Communication Research, 22*, 128–160.

Parsons, C. K., & Liden, R. C. (1984). Interviewer perceptions of applicant qualifications: A multivariate field study of demographic characteristics and nonverbal cues. *Journal of Applied Psychology, 69*, 557–568.

Patterson, M. L. (1998). Parallel processes in nonverbal communication. In M. T. Palmer & G. A. Barnett (Eds.), *Progress in communication sciences* (Vol. 14, pp. 1–18). Stamford, CT: Ablex.

Patterson, M. L., & Stockbridge, E. (1998). Effects of cognitive demand and judgment strategy on person perception accuracy. *Journal of Nonverbal Behavior, 22*, 253–263.

Pontari, B. A., & Schlenker, B. R. (2000). The influence of cognitive load on self-presentation: Can cognitive busyness help as well as harm social performance? *Journal of Personality and Social Psychology, 78*(6), 1092–1108.

Pope, B., Blass, T., Siegman, A. W., & Raher, J. (1970). Anxiety and depression in speech. *Journal of Counseling and Clinical Psychology, 35*, 128–133.

Posner, M. I., & Snyder, C. R. R. (1975). Attention and cognitive control. In R. L. Solso (Ed.), *Information processing and cognition: The Loyola symposium* (pp. 55–85). Hillsdale, NJ: Erlbaum.

Rosenthal, R., & DePaulo, B. M. (1979a). Sex differences in accommodation in nonverbal communication. In R. Rosenthal (Ed.), *Skill in nonverbal communication* (pp. 68–103). Cambridge, MA: Oelgeschlager, Gunn, and Hain.

Rosenthal, R., & DePaulo, B. M. (1979b). Sex differences in eavesdropping on nonverbal cues. *Journal of Personality and Social Psychology, 37*, 273–285.

Rosenthal, R., & Fode, K. L. (1963). The effect of experimenter bias on the performance of the albino rat. *Behavioral Science, 8*, 183–189.

Rosenthal, R., & Jacobson, L. (1968). *Pygmalion in the classroom*. New York: Holt, Rinehart, and Winston.

Scherer, K. R. (1981). Speech and emotional states. In J. K. Darby (Ed.), *Speech evaluation in psychiatry* (pp. 189–220). New York: Grune and Stratton.

Scherer, K. R., Feldstein, S., Bond, R. N., & Rosenthal, R. (1985). Vocal cues to deception: A comparative channel approach. *Journal of Psycholinguistic Research, 14*, 409–425.

Shih, M., Ambady, N., Richeson, J. A., Fujita, K., & Gray, H. M. (2002). Stereotype performance boosts: The impact of self-relevance and the manner of stereotype activation. *Journal of Personality and Social Psychology, 83*, 638–647.

Shih, M., Pittinsky, T. L., & Ambady, N. (1999). Stereotype susceptibility: Identity salience and shifts in quantitative performance. *Psychological Science, 10*(1), 80–83.

Siegman, A. W., & Pope, B. (1965). Personality variables associated with productivity and verbal fluency in the initial interview. *Proceedings of the 73rd Annual Convention of the American Psychological Association*, 273–274.

Templeton, J., & Leary, M. R. (1991, March). *Staring as a blush-inducing stimulus: Evaluation apprehension or visual threat?* Paper presented at the 37th annual meeting of the Southeastern Psychological Association, New Orleans, LA.

Tice, D. M., Butler, J. L., Muraven, M. B., & Stillwell, A. M. (1995). When modesty prevails: Differential favorability of self-presentation to friends and strangers. *Journal of Personality and Social Psychology, 69*(6), 1120–1138.

Uleman, J. S., Newman, L. S., & Moskowitz, G. B. (1996). People as flexible interpreters: Evidence and issues from spontaneous trait inference. In M. P. Zanna (Ed.), *Advances in experimental social psychology* (Vol. 28, pp. 211–279). Boston: Academic Press.

Vrij, A. (1993). Credibility judgments of detectives: The impact of nonverbal behavior, social skills, and physical characteristics on impression formation. *Journal of Social Psychology, 133*, 601–610.

Vrij, A., & Semin, G. R. (1996). Lie experts' beliefs about nonverbal indicators of deception. *Journal of Nonverbal Behavior, 20*(1), 65–80.

Weitz, S. (1972). Attitude, voice, and behavior: A repressed affect model of interracial interaction. *Journal of Personality and Social Psychology, 24*, 14–21.

Whalen, P. J. (1998). Fear, vigilance, and ambiguity: Initial neuroimaging studies of the human amygdala. *Current Directions in Psychological Science, 7*(6), 177–188.

Whalen, P. J., Rauch, S. L., Etcoff, N. L., McInerney, S. C., Lee, M. B., & Jenike, M. A. (1998). Masked presentations of emotional facial expressions modulate amygdala activity without explicit knowledge. *Journal of Neuroscience, 18*(1), 411–418.

Wilson, T. D., Hodges, S. D., & LaFleur, S. J. (1995). Effects of introspecting about reasons: Inferring attitudes from accessible thoughts. *Journal of Personality and Social Psychology, 69*, 16–28.

Wilson, T. D., & Schooler, J. W. (1991). Thinking too much: Introspection can reduce the quality of preferences and decisions. *Journal of Personality and Social Psychology, 60*, 181–192.

Winter, L., & Uleman, J. S. (1984). When are social judgments made? Evidence for the spontaneousness of trait inferences. *Journal of Personality and Social Psychology, 47*(2), 237–252.

Winter, L., Uleman, J. S., & Cunniff, C. (1985). How automatic are social judgments? *Journal of Personality and Social Psychology, 49*, 904–917.

Zajonc, R. B. (1980). Feeling and thinking: Preferences need no inferences. *American Psychologist, 35*, 151–175.

Zuckerman, M., DePaulo, B. M., & Rosenthal, R. (1981). Verbal and nonverbal communication of deception. In L. Berkowitz (Ed.), *Advances in experimental social psychology* (Vol. 14, pp. 1–59). New York: Academic Press.

13

Beyond the Perception-Behavior Link: The Ubiquitous Utility and Motivational Moderators of Nonconscious Mimicry

Tanya L. Chartrand, William W. Maddux, and Jessica L. Lakin

We live in a social world, which necessitates interacting with a wide variety of people on a regular basis. Our contact with loved ones, friends, colleagues, neighbors, and strangers often influences what we say, feel, think, and do. This is neither surprising nor controversial; one can easily visualize ways in which we emotionally, cognitively, and behaviorally respond to the presence of others in social environments. While many of these influences are obvious, less obvious is the notion that the mere act of perceiving another person can have direct, unmediated effects on our behavior. Perception and behavior are inextricably intertwined such that people automatically behave as they perceive. This "perception-behavior link" refers to the unintentional, nonconscious effects of social perception on social behavior.

Several consequences arise from the close link between perception and behavior. When we perceive the behaviors of others, we may proceed to unconsciously copy or mimic those behaviors. That is, perceiving observable aspects of others (e.g., their expressions, postures, behaviors) activates the associated representations in memory, which in turn makes us more likely to do the same. In addition to activating behavioral representations, perceiving these "observables" (Dijksterhuis & Bargh, 2001) may also lead to spontaneous trait inferences (e.g., Carlston & Skowronski, 1994; Uleman, Newman, & Moskowitz, 1996; Winter & Uleman, 1984) and the immediate activation of stereotypes (e.g., Devine, 1989). This in turn can lead to behavior in line with the activated trait constructs (Bargh, Chen, & Burrows, 1996; Carver, Ganellen, Froming, & Chambers, 1983; Epley & Gilovich, 1999; Macrae & Johnston, 1998) or stereotypes (Bargh et al., 1996; Chen & Bargh, 1997; Dijksterhuis, Bargh, & Miedema, 2000; Dijksterhuis & van Knippenberg, 1998, 2000; Levy, 1996).

Thus, the perception of observables may activate specific behavioral representations, trait constructs, or stereotypes. Once activated, these behaviors or concepts are likely to influence the subsequent behavior of the perceiver. However, an important difference exists between the mimicry of observables on the one hand, and automatic behavior resulting from spontaneous trait inferences and stereotype activation on the other. The latter involve intermediary steps between perception and behavior—people spontaneously encode abstract traits or stereotypes upon perceiving someone and then nonconsciously translate them into appropriate, concrete behavioral manifestations of these traits or stereotypes.

Mimicry, however, requires no translation of traits into behaviors, no familiarity with culturally specific stereotypes. Mimicry is a manifestation of the perception-behavior link at its most fundamental level. It is no more than copying another's observables and requires only the ability to perceive the behavior in the other person and the ability to form the behavior oneself. You smile, I smile. You rub your chin—darned if my hand doesn't gravitate toward my chin as well. There is now considerable empirical evidence that people mimic a variety of observables, including speech, facial expressions, physical mannerisms, moods, and emotions. Automatic imitation, which appears to be a result of the perception-behavior link, is the focus of this chapter.

We start by reviewing the evidence for nonconscious mimicry in the first section. We then turn our attention to the origins and utility of behavioral mimicry. In the second section, we review the arguments that the passive perception-behavior link mediates these effects (Chartrand & Bargh, 1999; Dijksterhuis & Bargh, 2001). In the third section, we explore the adaptive functions that mimicry serves and how these functions may have changed over time. Although mimicry may not be as necessary for physical survival as it was in our evolutionary past, we argue that it serves a "social survival" function today. As a result, there are factors that facilitate and inhibit mimicry, which we review in the fourth section. As part of this discussion, we also present preliminary evidence that people use mimicry to further their own goals, although they may not be cognizant of doing this. We argue that nonconscious mimicry may be an unidentified strategy in the repertoire of behaviors that help people get along with others.

Evidence for Behavioral Mimicry

Speech and Verbal Mimicry

Hermits notwithstanding, humans are social, communicative beings. Language and verbal communication are an integral part of who we are and how we are able to function in complex societies. It should come as no surprise, then, that we mimic the speech patterns, expressions, grammar, and verbal mechanisms of others. To the extent that infants are able to mimic vocally, they indeed do so. Simner (1971) has shown that 2- to 4-day-old newborns will begin crying if they hear crying from another newborn. Surprisingly, infants are able to distinguish between real cries and synthetic cries; they will not mimic the synthetic cries.

There is empirical evidence that people mimic specific words, clauses, and grammar of entire sentences (Bock, 1986, 1989; Levelt & Kelter, 1982). They also mimic the accents (Giles & Powesland, 1975), rates of speech (Webb, 1969, 1972), tones of voice (Neumann & Strack, 2000), and speech rhythms (Cappella & Panalp, 1981) of interaction partners. For instance, in a study of syntactic mimicry (Levelt & Kelter, 1982), participants were shown various drawings (e.g., of a person playing the piano). Participants were then asked one of two versions of the same question. The syntax the participants used when answering the question was primed by the phrasing of the question itself. For example, if participants were asked, "On which instrument does Paul play?" they tended to answer, "On the piano," while participants who were asked "Which instrument is Paul playing?" tended to answer "The piano." Thus, the participants mimicked the syntax used by the questioner.

People mimic other conversational variables as well. For example, Cappella and Panalp (1981) studied several dyadic conversations and found that over the course of a 20-minute conversation, partners came to match each other's conversational tendencies in a variety of ways. Partners spoke roughly the same amount, and also came to match each other's rhythm of speech, durations of pauses, and probability of breaking silences. Similarly, Webb (1969) found that the rate of speech used by interviewers elicited similar rates of speech by their interviewees.

Laughter is also contagious. If we see or hear others laugh, we tend to laugh more ourselves. In a simple and compelling demonstration, Young and Frye (1966) had participants listen to jokes and rate their level of humor. In one condition, participants performed this task alone, while in a second condition participants performed the task in groups. While the jokes were rated as equally funny in both conditions, the amount of laughter exhibited in the group condition was greater than in the alone condition. Similarly, techniques like employing canned laughter or showing visual shots of people in an audience laughing do in fact induce more laughing (Bush, Barr, McHugo, & Lanzetta, 1989; Provine, 1992). Interestingly, however, gender differences may moderate this effect, such that it is driven primarily by women (Leventhal & Mace, 1970).

While the above research was not concerned with automatic mimicking per se, the automatic nature of these effects seems likely for several reasons. First, people are much more likely to notice a lack of synchrony in conversation rather than its presence (Hatfield, Cacioppo, & Rapon, 1992). Second, in studies specifically designed to test automatic mimicking, we are unaware of a single participant ever detecting the true nature of the studies or the fact that they may have been mimicking (e.g., Chartrand & Bargh, 1999; van Baaren, Maddux, Chartrand, de Bouter, & van Knippenberg, 2003; Lakin & Chartrand, 2003; Neumann & Strack, 2000). In fact, when told the true purpose of such experiments, participants are often stunned that they may have been mimicking (e.g., Chartrand & Bargh, 1999). And because of the temporary and impersonal nature of most mimicking experiments, there seems to be little incentive to mimic others. Rather, mimicking seems to be a natural behavior that is carried out without awareness or effort.

There is, however, direct evidence that verbal mimicking is in fact automatic. A provocative set of findings from Neumann and Strack (2000, Study 2) provides evidence that individuals mimic the tone of voice of another person, even if that person is not present in the room. These researchers had participants listen to an audiotape of a person reading a philosophical text. They asked participants to shadow the text and repeat the speech out loud as they were listening to it, ostensibly to examine the way in which speech reproduction influences speech comprehension. In one condition, an actor had recorded the excerpt in a slightly happy voice, while in another condition an actor had recorded the excerpt in a slightly sad voice. Later, a separate group of judges listened to the tapes of the participants repeating the speech and rated how happy or sad each participant sounded. The results indicated that participants tended to use the same tone of voice as the person on the tape—participants who listened to the happy tone of voice repeated the speech in a happy tone, while those who listened to the sad tone of voice repeated it in a sad tone. The automatic nature of this effect is apparent in that the goal of speech comprehension prevented participants from ever becoming aware of the affective state of the speaker.

Facial Expressions

Our faces are the most noticeable parts of our bodies. As the home of most of our sensory organs, our faces are rarely covered and are usually busy perceiving the world and waiting to be perceived by others. Given the high-profile location of our faces, facial expressions should be particularly susceptible to mimicking. Indeed, we start to mimic others' facial expressions from the time we are born (Field, Woodson, Greenberg, & Cohen, 1982; Meltzoff & Moore, 1977, 1979, 1983). One-month-old infants have been shown to smile, stick out their tongues, and open their mouths when they see someone else doing the same (Meltzoff & Moore, 1977). In addition, infants as young as 9 months are able to mimic their mothers' facial expressions of joy, sadness, and anger (Termine & Izard, 1988). However, the fact that infants will mimic non–

mood-relevant expressions (sticking out the tongue, opening the mouth) suggests that facial mimicking is not mediated by mood. Infants can also elicit mimicking from their mothers. O'Toole and Dubin (1968) demonstrated that when feeding their babies, mothers often open their mouths as well, but not necessarily as a method of getting the babies to eat. Mothers usually open their mouths after the babies have already done so. Interestingly, the mothers in this study were completely unaware of having mimicked their babies.

Certain short-lived expressions that communicate specific feelings or physical states are also mimicked. The cultural myth that yawning is contagious has turned out not to be a myth at all. Empirical evidence shows that yawning does in fact elicit yawns from others (Provine, 1986). In addition, when we observe a painful injury, we may mimic the wince of the injured individual (Bavelas, Black, Lemery, & Mullett, 1986, 1987). Although this may be due in part to our imagining the same injury happening to us, the visibility of another's wince moderates the degree to which we do the same—the more visible the wince of the suffering other, the more we ourselves wince (Bavelas et al., 1986, 1987). Since intentionally mimicking laughs or winces seems to have little utility (why yawn if you're not sleepy or bored?), such effects are likely occurring automatically.

Although Bavelas and her colleagues argue that facial mimicking functions as a communication tool, there is also evidence that we mimic facial expressions even when we have no need to communicate. For example, researchers have shown that viewers mimic the facial expressions of people on television. Hsee, Hatfield, Carlson, and Chemtob (1990) had participants watch interviews in which a person described a very happy experience (i.e., a surprise birthday party thrown for him by friends) or a very sad experience (i.e., attending his grandfather's funeral at age 6). The facial expressions of these participants were surreptitiously videotaped and later coded. The results indicated that people's facial expressions matched whichever experience was being described—happy expressions were elicited when participants were watching the happy segment, while the sad segment elicited more sad expressions. Although participants may have been reliving their own similar memories, which may in turn have caused them to smile or frown, Hsee et al. also posit that nonconscious mimicry of the facial expressions may also have played a role in the congruence of expressions.

What would happen if two individuals mimicked each other's facial expressions on a regular basis, for an extended period of time? One can imagine this being the case for long-married couples. Would these shared expressions result in the couple developing similar facial features and perhaps an overall convergence in appearance? Zajonc, Adelmann, Murphy, and Niedenthal (1987) investigated just such a possibility by having participants rate the physical similarity of persons in several pairs of photographs. The pairs included couples married for 25 years, a random man and woman of similar age, and newlywed couples. Interestingly, the long-married couples were indeed rated as being more physically similar than the newlywed couples or the random couples. Thus, the couples married 25 years had actually grown to look more alike. This study is open to several causal interpretations. While Zajonc et al. focused on the possibility that shared emotions led to the increased resemblance, it is also quite plausible that long-married couples have had more chances to mimic each other and thus have developed the same facial lines and expressions.

Based on this evidence, facial mimicry seems to be quite common. Yet it may be even more common than we think. Unobservable to the naked eye, facial mimicry also occurs at a micro level, involving tiny facial muscles that are used for smiling and frowning. For example, Ulf Dimberg (1982) had participants look at pictures of people displaying happy or angry facial expressions. He then measured their subtle facial movements with electromyograph (EMG) technology. The results showed that participants moved the muscles involved in smiling upon seeing the happy expressions, and moved the muscles involved in frowning upon seeing the angry expressions. This "micromimicry" is strong evidence that we are indeed unaware of our mimicking tendencies. Moreover, the fact that the micromimicry occurs when looking at photographs—that is, in the absence of real social interaction or even the presence of another person—suggests that mimicry need not function as a communicative tool that relays the message "I like you" to others. Even when no such function can be served, and even when no person is present, it still occurs.

Behavioral Matching

Mimicking is not exclusively an "above the neck" phenomenon, limited to speech and facial expressions. We also mimic others' postures, gestures, and specific physical movements (and not just on the dance floor). As one might expect, mother-child interactions tend to be physically "in sync" with each other. Bernieri (1988) demonstrated this by recording several mother-child interactions with separate cameras. He created several versions of the interactions, all with the mother on the right side of the screen and the child on the left. One version showed the true, real-time mother-child interaction, while other versions varied the mothers and children paired together, as well as the exact timing of the interactions. As a result, participant judges were unable to tell whether mothers were interacting with their own children or different children. However, analyses indicated that even under these carefully controlled conditions, judges rated mothers as more physically in sync with their own children than with other children.

In addition, people also mimic a wide variety of commonplace and idiosyncratic movements. An experiment demonstrating the latter was carried out by Bavelas, Black, Chovil, Lemery, and Mullett (1988). An experimenter told a story to a class about attending a crowded Christmas party, and described ducking to avoid being run into by another person. As she was telling the story, she ducked to her right, demonstrating the exact movement she used. A videotape of the listeners later revealed that as this event was being described, the listeners tended to duck to their left, mirroring the exact movement of the storyteller.

Mimicking the specific posture or mannerisms of others has also received investigative attention, particularly with regard to rapport and liking (Bernieri, 1988; Charney, 1966; Dabbs, 1969; LaFrance, 1982; LaFrance & Broadbent, 1976; Maurer & Tindall, 1983; Scheflen, 1964). For example, LaFrance (1982) found that students tend to mimic their teachers' posture, and that the degree of posture mimicking was positively correlated with ratings of rapport between students and teacher. Similarly, Maurer and Tindall (1983) found that counselors who mimicked their clients were better liked than counselors who did not do so.

Thus, we mimic the behaviors of those we care about. What about strangers? Indeed, behavioral matching occurs even when strangers interact. Bernieri (1988) had dyads teach each other words and definitions for 10 minutes. When the videotapes of these interactions were analyzed, it was found that the couples whose movements were most in sync with each other also felt the most rapport. In addition, mimicry has been found to lead to more favorable evaluations on dimensions other than rapport. Dabbs (1969) found that participants rated confederates who mimicked them as having good ideas and as being well-informed. He also obtained evidence that "antimimicking," or doing the opposite of what someone else does, can have a detrimental effect on interactions. Confederates were liked less if they slouched when the participants sat erect or sat rigidly still if participants were fidgety. Interestingly, he found that participants liked confederates least when they thought they were going to be interacting with a similar other, but then were antimimicked by this person.

Most of the research thus far has focused on how rapport and behavioral matching are linked; however, could it be possible that people mimic the mannerisms of complete strangers, in situations where existing rapport or goals for future rapport are greatly minimized? In a test of this idea, Chartrand and Bargh (1999) had participants interact with two unfamiliar confederates. Several steps were taken to ensure that rapport would not develop between the participant and confederates. First, the confederates were told not to make eye contact with or smile at the participant at any point during the session. The brief sessions (approximately 5 minutes) and mundane task (describing photographs) made this fairly easy to do. Second, one of the two confederates was told to not smile at all during the experiment, and to instead have a rather negative, bored, and sullen expression throughout. It was assumed that if the default tendency was to try to affiliate with the confederate and create a sense of rapport, this tendency would be overridden or cut off by the presence of the nasty confederate. Thus, particularly with this confederate, there was little chance that rapport would develop, or that the goal to develop rapport would be present. The question then became, would mimicry occur in spite of this situation?

For half the participants, the first confederate rubbed her face and the second confederate shook her foot throughout their respective sessions. For the other half, the first confederate shook her foot and the second confederate rubbed her face. Results revealed that participants mimicked the mannerisms of the confederates—they shook their foot more when they were with the foot shaker than the face rubber, and rubbed their own face more when they were with the face rubber than the foot shaker. At the conclusion of the experiment, participants were asked about the mannerisms of the confederate, and about their own mannerisms, and none noticed either. This speaks to the nonconscious nature of the behavioral mimicry.

The fact that participants changed their own behavior to match their environment speaks to the chameleonlike nature of nonconscious mimicry. Like a chameleon that changes its colors to blend or fit in with its environment, people unwittingly change their mannerisms and behaviors to blend and fit in with their social environments. Importantly, participants even mimicked the unlikable confederates, indicating that even under minimal conditions in which there is no rapport, affiliation, or liking between interactants, nonconscious behavioral mimicry will occur.

Like facial mimicry, behavioral action tendencies may be initiated on a micro level. When watching others perform certain activities, or when listening to conversations, perceivers mimic the ongoing action so subtly that it is not noticeable to the naked eye. For example, Berger and Hadley (1975) placed a set of electrodes on participants' faces and arms, and then had them watch two videotapes. One videotape showed a person reading a list of words and constantly stuttering, while the second videotape showed an arm-wrestling match. When the participants watched the stuttering person, they exhibited tiny muscle movements around their own lips, detectable only via facial EMG. When they watched the arm-wrestling match, participants exhibited very subtle muscle activity in their own forearms and wrists. Thus, the subtle nature of this mimicking suggests that it is an unintended phenomenon of which the perceiver is unlikely to be aware.

Emotion and Mood

Up to this point, we have focused specifically on overt behavioral mimicry. Yet mimicry has implications for more internal states as well. Emotions and moods are infectious. Humans can spontaneously read how other people are feeling and naturally take on the emotional and affective states of others. In their book *Emotional Contagion*, Hatfield et al. (1994) compellingly synthesize a variety of evidence in support of this idea. In essence, emotional contagion is mimicking what others do and, subsequently, converging emotionally. Thus, happy people tend to infuse us with color and life, while sullen people can add more than a touch of gray to our days. Note that we do not intentionally pick up others' moods; otherwise a bad mood could be cut short just by desiring to be in a good mood. We pick up moods effortlessly and efficiently (and thus automatically) from our environment and the people around us. So, when heading out to social gatherings, it may be advisable to leave that melancholy mood at home.

If we define emotional mimicry as the automatic tendency to "catch" others' emotions, then two classic studies in social psychology can be reinterpreted as evidence for this phenomenon. The first is the study on cognitive labeling of emotions conducted by Schacter and Singer (1962). These researchers induced arousal in participants by injecting them with adrenalin, then had them interact with a confederate who acted either giddy and silly or angry and resentful. Following this interaction, participants were asked to describe the emotions they were feeling. Despite the fact that all participants were experiencing the same physiological arousal, they described their emotions quite differently, depending on how the confederate had acted. If he had been giddy, participants reported feeling giddy. If he had behaved angrily, participants felt angry themselves. Thus, although their physical arousal told them they were experiencing an emotion, participants looked to their environment and labeled their emotion in a way that was consistent with it. In so doing, the individuals mimicked their interaction partner, and this mimicking may have in turn actually caused the specific emotions.

A classic "self-fulfilling prophecy" study can also be understood as emotional mimicking. Snyder, Tanke, and Berscheid (1977) had male participants make telephone calls to female participants who were believed to be either attractive or unattractive. Men who had been led to believe that their telephone partners were attractive women talked in a friendly, warm manner, which in turn elicited warm reactions on the part of the women. This reaction from the women may have been at least partially due to nonconscious mimicry of the warm response from men. The opposite happened if the men believed their partners to be homely—they were more negative, and the women responded in kind, being more quiet and awkward. Again, the women seemed to catch the emotion of the men. In a similar demonstration, Siegman and Reynolds (1984) found that interviewers who behaved in a warm manner toward interviewees elicited more reciprocal warmth than interviewers who did not. Although the above studies were not specifically testing automatic mimicry, there is little reason for participants to purposely adopt angry or withdrawn moods, suggesting the moods infect us automatically.

Several experiments have shown that moods spread between people easily, quickly, and subtly. The aforementioned Neumann and Strack (2000) studies found that simply listening to happy or sad speakers went on to affect mood in a congruent manner, even though participants were not aware that the tapes had influenced their moods, nor were they aware of the affective states of the speakers. Thus, people who repeated audiotaped speeches originally spoken with a happy voice not only repeated them in the same tone of voice but also felt happier themselves. Participants who repeated a speech originally spoken with a sad voice mimicked that tone and then reported feeling more sad themselves. Notably, cognitive load exacerbated this effect, suggesting the effortlessness of this process. Similarly, Hsee et al. (1990) found that people who watched a person on television describing a happy experience later felt happy, while people who watched a person describing a sad experience later felt sad.

Just sitting quietly in a room with others can be enough to cause people to catch their mood. Friedman and Riggio (1981) asked trios of participants to sit quietly in a room together without talking, ostensibly to see how people's moods randomly fluctuate over the course of a couple of minutes. In each trio, one participant had pretested to be a highly expressive person, while the other two participants were relatively inexpressive. The results indicated that the two inexpressive participants easily picked up the mood of the expressive participant, even in the absence of any verbal communication. Similarly, Sullins (1991) found that highly expressive people are more easily able to pass along their negative moods to others than less expressive people. However, both groups are equally able to infect others with their happy moods.

Finally, there is evidence that emotional contagion has limits. We do not just indiscriminately pick up the emotions of anyone we come across; certain circumstances may inhibit their transfer. For example, when shown a videotape of then-President Ronald Reagan clearly expressing happiness and anger at different points during a news conference, Republicans reported feeling happy or angry at the same times that Reagan was expressing these emotions. However, Democrats reported feeling negative during the entire news conference (McHugo, Lanzetta, Sullivan, Masters, & Englis, 1985). Thus, although we may pick up emotions from friends, family, or even strangers, our opponents may not have such an easy time infecting us—the tendency to mimic may be overridden by general negative emotions.

Taken together, the evidence reviewed in this section suggests that mimicry is a common, multifaceted set of behaviors that we perform in a number of circumstances and in a variety of ways. We mimic people's overt, observable behaviors, including their speech patterns and syntax, facial expressions, postures, gestures, and mannerisms, as well as their internal, emotional states and moods. We engage in this mimicry with just about everybody, including strangers, family, friends, teachers, and romantic partners. Doing as others do, saying as others say, and feeling as others feel seems to be a natural part of who we are.

Why Do Humans Automatically Mimic?

Why do humans have such a robust tendency to nonconsciously mimic others? What are the causes and mediators of this process? We make four arguments in the remainder of this chapter. First, nonconscious mimicry is an automatic, default process that occurs when a person attends to and perceives another person's behavior. When this occurs, so too will nonconscious mimicry. One mechanism that attempts to account for this is the perception-behavior link, which is reviewed in detail below. Second, we also argue that automatic mimicry is quite functional and adaptive, in that it binds and bonds people together and fosters empathy, liking, and smooth interactions. Third, we present evidence that nonconscious mimicry can be facilitated and inhibited by various contextual and motivational factors. Finally, as part of the discussion of motivational facilitators of mimicry, we argue that individuals mimic others more when it has the potential to benefit them the most. Thus, individuals may use the implicit knowledge of the benefits of mimicry strategically, to their own advantage.

The Perception-Behavior Link: Minimal Conditions for Automatic Mimicry

Thinking Is for Doing

The mechanism for nonconscious mimicry that has been favored in recent years is a direct link between perception and behavior. This idea has garnered support from considerable evidence in the cognitive, social, comparative, and neuroscience literatures. It is impressive (although not surprising) that almost a century before most of this evidence accumulated, William James (1890) claimed that "thinking is for doing." He expanded upon Carpenter's (1874) principle of ideomotor action, the notion that merely thinking about doing something automatically makes one more likely to actually do it. James argued for the unintentional and unconscious nature of this effect, and further posited a passive, cognitive mechanism—the representation of an action activating or making more accessible the corresponding behavior.

Supporting James's claim of a link between thinking and doing, neurological evidence shows that thinking about doing something activates the same regions in the brain that are activated by actually doing it. For instance, Paus, Petrides, Evans, and Meyer (1993) discovered that thinking about a word or gesture activates the same area in the anterior cingulated cortex that is activated by saying the word or making that gesture. Jeannerod (1994, 1997) similarly demonstrated that the same neurons in the premotor cortex are activated by mentally simulating a behavior as by performing the same behavior. In addition, evidence exists that what goes on at the neurological level is very similar when one is imagining complex actions or actually engaging in those same actions (Decety, Jeannerod, Germain, & Pastene, 1991; Jeannerod, 1994, 1997). This supports the notion that thinking about something and doing it are neurologically similar. The two activities activate the same regions of the brain, suggesting that the two share representational systems.

Perceiving Is for Doing

Of course, thinking about engaging in a given behavior is not the only way to make that behavioral representation more accessible—perceiving another person engaging in that behavior is another way to activate the corresponding representation in memory. And once activated, it should have the same effect, leading to a tendency to engage in that behavior oneself.

As in the case of thinking, neurological data have also accumulated for a link between the perception of others' behavior and one's own behavior (see Dijksterhuis & Bargh, 2001, for a review). Specifically, there is now evidence that perceiving someone else engaging in a behavior is neurologically similar to performing that behavior. In studies with monkeys, the same area of the premotor cortex that becomes activated when a monkey perceives an experimenter performing an action also becomes activated when the monkey itself performs that same action (Di Pellegrino, Fadiga, Fogassi, Gallese, & Rizzolatti, 1992; Rizzolatti & Arbib, 1998). Studies with humans further suggest that perceiving a behavior (such as seeing an experimenter grasp an object) leads to muscular responses that are the same as those displayed while performing that same behavior.

Theories of Overlapping Representations

Although the neurological data present impressive evidence that there is in fact a link between perception and behavior, they do not offer a theoretical framework within which to understand how and why perception and behavior are mentally linked. Such theories have been put forth, however, by cognitive and social psychologists. In short, researchers positing these theories claim that perception and behavior may depend on the same representational systems.

For instance, researchers in the language acquisition domain have noted the rapid speed with which young children learn languages. Lashley (1951) attempted to account for this speed by positing that language comprehension and language production depend on the same mechanism. This became known as the common coding principle. Prinz (1990) has also argued for the common coding hypothesis in the language domain and further posited a shared representational system for perception and action more generally. That is, he argued that the coding system for perceiving behaviors in others is the same system that is used when performing those behaviors.

Similar ideas have been invoked in the social psychological domain. Berkowitz's (1984) social-cognitive account of modeling effects posits that perceiving violent acts in the media activates a representation of perceived violent acts in memory. This, then, automatically spreads to other aggressive ideas of the viewer, including aggressive behavioral representations. This makes the viewer of violence more likely to behave violently. Carver, Ganellen, Froming, and Chambers (1983) elaborated on these ideas by proposing the existence of interpretive schemas, used for perceiving and interpretating others' actions, and behavioral schemas, used for producing actions. The two types of schemas overlap with one another semantically and therefore should tend to become active at the same time. Thus, individuals perceiving an aggressive act will have their interpretive schemas for hostility activated, which will spread to increase the accessibility of their behavioral schemas for hostility, which will then make them more likely to behave aggressively.

Bidirectionality of the Perception-Behavior Link

One implication of the theory that interpretive and behavioral schemas overlap is that not only should perception lead to action, but action should lead to differential interpretation as well. That is, engaging in a certain behavior should automatically activate the corresponding behavioral representation or schema in memory, which should then spread to the overlapping interpretational schema (Berkowitz, 1984; Carver et al., 1983). This should increase the accessibility of the corresponding trait category, which should then lead the individual to use that trait when perceiving and judging others. Importantly, this would imply that one's own behavior can serve as a priming stimulus, temporarily activating the appropriate trait category, which then affects subsequent judgments of others. Chartrand, Kawada, and Bargh

(2002) provided a test of this hypothesis. In a first study, they demonstrated that the process of engaging in a certain behavior (i.e., helping to pick up pens) led to heightened accessibility (as assessed through a lexical decision task) of the corresponding trait category ("helpfulness").

In a second study, half the participants were induced to volunteer to engage in a helpful behavior (i.e., moving some heavy boxes for the experimenter). All participants then read a story that presumably another participant had written about a recent interaction with a friend. In the course of this story, the "friend" performed several ambiguously helpful acts, for which both altruistic and selfish motives could apply. The participants then rated this character on various traits, including helpfulness. If there is a bidirectional link between perception and behavior, then the participants engaging in a helpful act themselves should be more likely to rate the target person as being more helpful than participants who were not earlier helpful. This is precisely what was found. Note the passive nature of this effect, for if it were intentional, participants might be motivated to believe that others are not as helpful as they are. They might use their own helpful behavior as a standard of comparison against which they would contrast the target's ambiguously helpful behaviors.

This effect was replicated with a negative behavior prime. Participants were either induced to behave in a nosy manner (i.e., the experimenter "accidentally" left a very personal piece of paper on the participant's desk) or not. In an ostensibly separate study on body language, participants then watched a videotape of two graduate students interacting and getting to know one another. During the course of the video, one of the two people asked the other an ambiguously nosy question ("Do you believe in God?"). This could be interpreted as nosy or as being friendly and trying to succeed at the task of getting to know each other. Participants who had been nosy themselves were more likely to rate the ambiguous target as being nosy than participants who were not nosy earlier (Chartrand et al., 2002). When debriefed at the conclusion of the study, participants indicated no awareness of their own nosy behavior, or of the effect that their own behavior had on their judgment of the target.

Thus, there is substantial evidence that perception and behavior are inextricably linked; the mental activation of one automatically activates the other. This implies that attending to and perceiving another's actions are enough to activate and lead to corresponding behavior (given that one's interpretive and behavioral schema are intact). While previous work has focused on mimicry as an automatic, default tendency (Chartrand & Bargh, 1999; Dijksterhuis & Bargh, 2001), in this chapter we focus on the adaptive nature of mimicry and the ways in which it can be influenced by various contextual and motivational variables.

The Adaptive Functionality of Mimicry

That mimicry occurs nonconsciously does not preclude it from serving some higher purpose. It is not difficult to imagine how automatic mimicry might be adaptive. From an evolutionary perspective, perception is for doing: perceiving others helps us to navigate our environment and guide our own behavior accordingly. A direct link between perception and action would ensure that we are able to do this automatically, without expending unnecessary mental resources. If everyone is running away from a grizzly bear, it is not in one's best interest to find the bear, analyze the situation and determine that it is dangerous, and then run. Rather, upon seeing others run, running should come first—automatically and immediately—and analyzing the situation should come later. Natural selection ensured that it was the people with this automatic mimicking tendency who survived. While such a strategy may have caused considerable embarrassment when foolish or unimportant behaviors were mimicked, from an evolutionary and hedonic perspective, embarrassment is far preferable to a "grizzly" death. Thus, it seems likely that we inherited this nonconscious mimicry from our ancestors. And mimicry is not limited to humans; lower animals have inherited a perception-behavior link as well (see Dijksterhuis & Bargh, 2001).

Thus, automatic mimicry has its roots in the functional purpose it served in our evolutionary past. It may be, in essence, a by-product from an earlier time. Mimicry developed as an automatic, nonconscious phenomenon, and it remains that way today.

Changing Functionality: From Survival to "Social Glue"

It is usually not necessary to mimic others for survival anymore. Individuals living in modern societies do not regularly have lions or bears chasing them, or stampedes of buffalo threatening their homes (*Survivor* contestants notwithstanding). That being said, we would like to argue that mimicry still serves an adaptive function for human beings. Although physical survival may not often be at stake, social survival often is. This has probably always been true, although earlier in human history it may have been somewhat eclipsed by the importance of physical survival. The importance of social survival in modern society is quite apparent when visiting or moving to a new country with a different culture. Individuals try to fit into their new environment with different people who have different standards, norms, values, and ideals. In order to fit in and "survive" in the new social community, individuals must modify their own behaviors to acclimate to the new society. Fitting in is often crucial to gaining acceptance. If mimicking others' behaviors helps an individual to become more similar to those others, and thus more accepted by them, then this mimicry is clearly adaptive.

Mimicry is functional not only when moving to another country. Individuals within their own culture have an enormously strong need to belong and affiliate (Baumeister & Leary, 1995; Brewer, 1991). Belonging to groups and being accepted by group members is a fundamental and primary need of human beings. Individuals without this sense of belonging often have problems not only attaining happiness, but also maintaining mental, emotional, and physical health (Boer, Elving, & Seydel, 1998; Bowling, Edelmann, Leaver, & Hoekel, 1989; Heller, Thompson, Trueba, & Hogg, 1991; Kraut et al., 1998). Given the ubiquitous need to belong and be accepted, and the consequences that arise if this need is not met, mimicry is important in routine, everyday life. If I look, talk, and act similarly to someone else, that probably means we have something in common, and this will lead to greater liking, empathy, and smoother interactions. There is now substantial evidence that mimicry and affiliation are indeed related, and this evidence is reviewed below. Thus, the functionality of mimicry may have shifted from physical survival to a relatively stronger emphasis on social survival. Mimicry binds and bonds people together, and although that has been true since the beginning of our human origins (and probably before), it may be even more important now, since physical survival is less often at stake.

Facilitators and Inhibitors of Nonconscious Mimicry

The adoption of another person's speech, facial expressions, mannerisms, and emotions occurs unintentionally and effortlessly. However, that mimicry is the default tendency driven by an automatic link between perception and behavior does not preclude the possibility that contextual and motivational variables serve as facilitators and inhibitors to this tendency. In fact, the functional and adaptive nature of mimicry suggests that factors other than merely perceiving a person's behaviors will influence the degree to which mimicry occurs.

Facilitators

Rapport The review of the evidence for mimicry in the first section suggests that mimicry is linked with rapport between interaction partners. The presence of such rapport increases the likelihood of adopting the facial expressions, behaviors, and emotional states of other people. Thus, feelings of rapport and liking seem to be one class of facilitators that increase the likelihood of mimicry.

The Causal Relationship Between Mimicry and Rapport Early research on behavioral mimicry focused on posture sharing as a potential nonverbal indicator of group rapport. In 1964, Scheflen noted that body positioning in an ongoing interaction was an indicator of liking, understanding, and the relationships between group members. This foreshadowed Bavelas's later argument (e.g., Bavelas et al., 1986) that mimicry is a tool used to communicate liking for and rapport with another. Subsequent research also demonstrated that posture sharing was indicative of involvement and interest in an interaction, and feelings of togetherness. In a typical study, students were asked to report the level of rapport in their classes, and those classes were then coded for amount of posture sharing. As predicted, classes rated by students as having high rapport also manifested the greatest amount of posture sharing (La-France & Broadbent, 1976).

Because these researchers suggest that posture sharing is an indicator of rapport, they seem to be arguing that the causal path proceeds from rapport to mimicry: as rapport between interaction partners increases, people are more likely to adopt the postures and mannerisms of their interaction partners. Research examining the most extreme cases of rapport—relationships between mother and child, and between married couples—may at first glance seem consistent with this. After all, the research on the mimicry of facial expressions and behaviors between mothers and children (Bernieri, 1988; Meltzoff & Moore, 1977; O'Toole & Dubin, 1968; Termine & Izard, 1988) can be interpreted as implying that mothers and children are bound through their feelings of love and liking for one another, which leads to greater mimicry. Along these same lines, married couples are "wed" together through their ability to mimic each other. This may explain why couples who have been married for long periods of time (and who presumably have high levels of rapport) begin to eventually look alike (Zajonc et al., 1987). However, the correlational nature of these studies makes the causal direction unclear, for the posture sharing and behavioral mimicry could just as easily have led to the increased rapport in these cases, as well as in the work by LaFrance and Broadbent (1976).

Later research attempted to determine the direction of causality between posture sharing and rapport through statistical techniques. In a study using a cross-lag panel technique (LaFrance, 1979), posture sharing and rapport were each measured at two points in time. Not surprisingly, a positive correlation was found between posture sharing and rapport during each of the observational sessions. Moreover, the correlation between posture sharing at Time 1 and rapport at Time 2 ($r = .77$) was greater than the correlation between rapport at Time 1 and posture sharing at Time 2 ($r = .58$). These correlations suggest that causal priority can be given to posture sharing; however, the difference between the two correlations is not statistically significant, indicating that the causal path between posture sharing and rapport is bidirectional. Posture sharing increases rapport (LaFrance, 1979), but rapport also increases posture sharing, as earlier work suggested (LaFrance & Broadbent, 1976; Scheflen, 1964).

Although the cross-lag panel technique hints at a bidirectional causal relationship between rapport and mimicry, to truly know whether one can cause the other, one factor needs to be manipulated directly. Researchers can then see how this manipulation affects the other factor. This is precisely what Chartrand and Bargh (1999, Study 2) did. These researchers wanted to test one particular direction, from mimicry to rapport and liking. They argued that perception of another's behavior automatically causes nonconscious mimicry, which in turn creates shared feelings of empathy and rapport. In their study, participants engaged in a photo description task with a confederate. Throughout the interaction, the confederate either mimicked the behavior of the participant or had neutral, nondescript posture and mannerisms. It was expected that when the confederate mimicked the behavior of the participant, the participant would report liking the confederate more and also report that the interaction had been more smooth and harmonious. Results were as predicted, suggesting that one function that behavioral mimicry serves is to increase liking between interactants. This study also provides the first experimental demonstration that behavioral mimicry causes an increase in rapport between two interactants.

Thus, mimicry serves the adaptive function of increasing liking and rapport between the people involved in an interaction, as well as making the interaction smoother and more harmonious. One causal direction—from mimicry to rapport—has been tested and verified. The other direction—from rapport to behavioral mimicry—remains to be experimentally tested, but LaFrance's (1979) work suggests that it would be borne out as well.

Goal to Affiliate Recent work has focused on goal states as another set of contextual factors that increase the likelihood of behavioral mimicry. In fact, we would like to make an argument that may be somewhat controversial: on a nonconscious level, individuals use mimicry to their own advantage. Although individuals are usually not aware of mimicking others, they seem capable of using the implicit knowledge that mimicry and affiliation are related to further their own goals. People use mimicry to get others to like them, although they are not consciously aware of doing this or even of the adaptive function that mimicry serves. Thus, when an individual has a goal to affiliate with someone or be liked by that person, he or she will nonconsciously start to mimic the person more than usual. Thus, it is a strategy in the repertoire of behaviors that help individuals affiliate with other people. The key is that they are not aware that this is a strategy they use at all.

Consider the following scenario: two strangers meet for the first time. There is no existing rapport between them, but there is a goal to affiliate and attain rapport. Does merely having the goal to affiliate lead to more mimicry? We predicted the answer to be yes (Lakin & Chartrand, 2003). Evidence suggests that higher order goals automatically activate the respective plans of action and behavioral strategies used to achieve that goal (Aarts & Dijksterhuis, 2000). Perhaps some of these plans of action are not available to conscious awareness. We hypothesized that individuals may have an affiliation goal temporarily or chronically, and both were predicted to lead to greater nonconscious mimicry. Individuals may also have affiliation goals consciously or nonconsciously (e.g., Chartrand & Bargh, 1996), and both types of goals were also predicted to lead to greater mimicry. Thus, a first study tested whether conscious and nonconscious temporary affiliation goals increase mimicry, and a subsequent study tested whether chronic affiliation goals increase mimicry.

In a first study (Lakin & Chartrand, 2003, Experiment 1), participants performed a two-part experiment, the first part of which was a "parafoveal vigilance task" (actually a subliminal priming task; see Bargh & Chartrand, 2000). In the implicit affiliation goal condition, participants were subliminally exposed to words related to a goal to affiliate (e.g., *friend, together, affiliate*), and in the explicit goal and control conditions, participants were exposed to neutral words. In the second phase of the experiment, participants were told that they would be performing a memory task. They were instructed to watch a videotape of a person (ostensibly another participant currently in the next room, but actually a confederate videotaped earlier) performing a variety of mundane clerical tasks (e.g., filing papers, answering the phone). Participants were instructed to remember the behaviors and the order in which they were completed. This was a fairly easy task that did not put participants under a cognitive load.

For participants in the explicit goal condition, the experimenter then added that they would soon be interacting with this person next door on a cooperative task for which it was very important to get along and work together well. All participants then watched the "live feed" of the confederate, who was touching her face throughout the videotape, during and between the clerical tasks. While watching the tape, participants were surreptitiously videotaped, and the amount of face rubbing they engaged in was later measured by independent coders. The results revealed that participants with an implicit or explicit affiliation goal rubbed their face more than did participants in the control condition, but no differences were observed between the implicit and explicit goal conditions. Thus, regardless of whether the affiliation goal is consciously held and pursued or implicitly primed, individuals mimic more than those without such a temporary goal to affiliate.

In another study testing the notion that people implicitly use nonconscious mimicry as a strategy to get others to like them, we explored the effects of succeeding and failing at a nonconscious affiliation goal for mimicry

(Lakin & Chartrand, 2003, Experiment 2). We predicted that failure at a nonconscious affiliation goal would increase subsequent affiliation goal-directed behaviors, including unintentional mimicry of another's mannerisms. In this study, participants who had or had not been subliminally primed earlier with an affiliation goal conducted two interviews with other students (actually confederates). The first interview was conducted online, and the confederate (who was actually in the next room typing out scripted answers to the questions) responded in either a friendly or unfriendly way, thereby manipulating success and failure at the affiliation goal (if one existed). Participants then completed a second live interview with a confederate who gave neutral answers and shook her foot throughout the interaction.

Our main hypothesis was that participants who had an affiliation goal and experienced failure in the online interaction would be most likely to mimic the behavior of the confederate in the face-to-face interaction. Upon completion of the experiment, all participants were extensively debriefed by the experimenter, who probed for suspicions about the cover story, awareness of the affiliation goal, and awareness of the confederate's mannerisms; very few participants reported any awareness of the confederate's mannerisms, and the results are the same whether these people are included in the analysis or not. Videotapes were coded for the amount of time participants spent shaking their feet while interacting with the second confederate. A composite measure of liking for the second confederate was also created. Both measures revealed significant interactions: In the no-goal condition, percentage of time spent mimicking and liking for the confederate did not differ by success/failure condition, but in the affiliation goal condition, percentage of time spent mimicking and liking for the confederate were greater in the failure condition than in the success condition. The efforts of the participants in this condition seemed to pay off as well. Analyses of the confederate's ratings of the participants reveal a marginally significant interaction, suggesting that she liked participants in the affiliation goal/failure condition the most. Thus, the results of the current study suggest that initially failing at an affiliation goal leads to increased efforts to affiliate with a second, new interaction partner; mimicry of that person's mannerisms increases, as well as overall liking for that person. This provides further evidence that we are able to use nonconscious mimicry to our advantage.

Interdependent Self-Construals Self-construals are essentially the way in which people mentally represent the self. Extant research has identified at least two primary modes of self-representation: independent and interdependent. Those individuals who have independent self-construals tend to think of themselves as autonomous individuals separate from others, and tend to define themselves in terms of their unique personal traits. On the other hand, individuals with interdependent self-construals are more likely to think of themselves in the context of the larger social world, tending to define themselves in terms of their group memberships and relationships with others (Brewer & Gardner, 1996; Cross & Madson, 1997; Markus & Kitayama, 1991). One important consequence of an interdependent self-construal is a special concern with fostering harmonious relationships and getting along well with others; interdependent people place more importance on relationships with others and belonging to certain kinds of groups than independent people. Thus, given that mimicry seems to be facilitated when people want to facilitate positive relationships, we hypothesized that people with interdependent self-construals (chronic or temporary) would mimic the mannerisms of others more than people with independent self-construals, and we tested this prediction across several studies (van Baaren et al., 2003).

A variety of research has demonstrated that people from East Asian societies (e.g., Japan, China, Korea) tend to have chronic interdependent self-construals, while Westerners (e.g., Americans, Canadians, Western Europeans) have chronic independent self-construals. Thus, we predicted that Japanese would tend to mimic others more than Americans. To test this hypothesis, we recruited Japanese (born and lived in Japan through high school) and native-born American individuals to participate. Each participant then engaged in two separate photo-describing interactions, one with an American confederate and one with a Japanese confederate (the order was counterbalanced). The confederates engaged in constant but subtle face rubbing throughout the interactions, and the amount of face rubbing exhibited by participants was later judged by coders who watched videotapes of the interaction. The results supported our hypothesis: Japanese participants exhibited more face rubbing than American participants, even when we controlled for face rubbing that participants exhibited before the task began. Interestingly, the ethnicity of the confederates had no effect on how much mimicking Japanese people exhibited—Japanese participants mimicked the face rubbing of both the in-group member and the out-group member equally.

In another study (van Baaren et al., 2003, Experiment 2), we further demonstrated the moderating effects of self-construals. In this study, we randomly assigned Dutch participants to one of three priming conditions. In the interdependent-priming condition, participants completed a scrambled sentence task that contained 15 words related to the interdependent self-construal (e.g., *together, group, cooperate*). In the independent-priming condition, participants completed a scrambled sentence task that contained 15 words related to the independent self-construal (e.g., *unique, alone, individual*). Participants in the control condition did not receive a scrambled sentence task. Participants were then instructed to complete a separate "music rating" task while an experimenter sat nearby and played with a pen. We were interested in the extent to which participants played with their own pens (as measured in average number of seconds per minute), which was our measure of mimicry. The results indicated that, as predicted, participants primed with the interdependent self-construal played with their pen more than participants in the control condition, while participants primed with the interdependent self-construal played with their pen less than control participants. Following both of these experiments, all participants completed funnel debriefings (Bargh & Chartrand, 2000) and none guessed the actual purpose of the experiments, indicating that these mimicking effects were indeed occurring automatically. Thus, these studies provide evidence for the facilitating effect of interdependent self-construals on nonconscious mimicry.

As a whole, our most recent work suggests that while affiliation goals and interdependent self-construals are not necessary for mimicry to occur, their presence reliably increases the amount of mimicry manifested in a given situation. Moreover, recent failure at an affiliation goal results in increased efforts to satisfy that goal in a subsequent interaction. It is quite possible that other goals and individual differences also serve to facilitate or inhibit mimicry effects, and these await discovery.

Perspective Taking A study conducted by Chartrand and Bargh (1999, Study 3) suggests a final facilitating factor that could potentially increase mimicry effects: empathy. Because of the consistent relationship found between mimicry and rapport, it was hypothesized that individual differences in empathy might influence the likelihood of mimicking the behavior of an interaction partner. Perspective taking, or the ability to adopt and understand the perspective of others, is one component of empathy (Davis, 1983). Chartrand and Bargh (1999) argued that a person high in perspective taking should be more susceptible to the effects of perception on behavior because he or she spends more time perceiving the behavior of others. In line with this, they found that perspective taking reliably affected the extent of nonconscious mimicry; people who scored high on the perspective-taking subscale of Davis's (1983) empathy questionnaire were more likely than those who scored low to mimic the behavior of others. Perspective taking therefore appears to be one dispositional factor that increases the tendency to mimic. There are probably many other individual difference variables that moderate the relationship between perception and nonconscious mimicry, which introduces an additional class of variables that influence the likelihood of observing these effects.

Inhibitors

Although the research on factors that could potentially inhibit mimicry effects is quite limited, two such factors have emerged in the literature thus far: dislike for another, and self-focus. Exemplifying the first is the study reviewed in the section "Evidence for Behavioral Mimicry" suggesting that people do not adopt the moods of disliked others (McHugo et al., 1985). Democrats did not pick up the mood of Ronald Reagan while watching a videotape of him at a news conference, whereas Republicans felt happy when Reagan was happy and angry when Reagan was angry. These results indicate that dislike for another person may actually inhibit the automatic response of adopting another person's moods.

Another factor that inhibits mimicry is self-construal orientation. Just as an interdependent self-construal leads to increased mimicry, we explored the possibility that an independent self-construal might actually inhibit mimicry (van Baaren et al., 2003, Study 1). In this study, participants worked on bogus translation tasks with two different confederates. With one confederate, the words to be translated were related to the self (independent self-construal prime), whereas with the other confederate, the words to be translated were not related to the self (control prime). The confederate in each condition displayed a different type of habitual behavior (e.g., face rubbing or foot shaking), and the degree to which participants exhibited these behaviors was recorded on video. The results indicated that when participants were primed with the independent self-construal, they mimicked the confederates' specific behavior significantly less than in the control condition. Thus, having a salient independent self-construal appears to actually inhibit the natural tendency to mimic an interaction partner's behaviors. These results suggest that variables related to self-focus or self-construal are another class of factors that affect the likelihood of mimicking another person's behaviors.

Conclusion

The nonconscious mimicry of others is a continuous part of everyday existence and has become seamlessly woven into our daily lives. Because it is such a fundamental feature of our interactions with other people, we are usually not aware of the large role that mimicry plays. In our evolutionary past, such automatic mimicry was probably necessary for physical survival. If this was the case, then those who developed this capacity to automatically "do as they see"—acting first and thinking later—were the ones to survive. In this way, they may have passed on the tendency to automatically mimic to their descendants, and it became the default tendency.

Today, we still carry the torch of our ancestral heritage. Merely perceiving another person saying, feeling, or doing something makes us more likely to say, feel, and do the same thing. Even in minimal circumstances, there is substantial evidence that social perception leads to automatic social behavior. For instance, we mimic the behaviors of strangers, people with whom we have had no prior contact and have little reason to affiliate (Chartrand & Bargh, 1999). We also mimic people who are not even physically present, such as those in photographs or on television or videotapes. As a result of the link between perception and behavior, we will mimic others even under these minimal conditions.

However, in this chapter we have argued that mimicry still serves an adaptive function, that of social survival. We conceptualize mimicry as the social glue that binds and bonds humans together. Having the same facial expressions, speech patterns, moods, emotions, and behaviors of others expresses similarity, which in turn builds empathy, liking, rapport, and affiliation. Accordingly, there are variables that serve to increase or decrease the amount of mimicry engaged in at any given time, such as rapport, individual differences in perspective taking, and attentional focus.

We also have presented preliminary evidence that having a goal to affiliate with others can increase nonconscious mimicry. This occurs regardless of whether the goal is temporary or chronic, consciously pursued or nonconsciously primed. Individuals who have recently failed at an affiliative experience are also more likely to mimic a second person, presumably because the failure experience activates a goal to build rapport with someone new. In essence, then, people use nonconscious mimicry to further their own goals. This suggests that on an implicit level, individuals know of the affiliative function that mimicry serves, and that mimicking another's behaviors will help them achieve that rapport. Mimicry is an unacknowledged and unappreciated strategy in the repertoire of behaviors that people use to build rapport and increase affiliation with others. Although mimicking another person's mannerisms may be a direct result of the perception-behavior link, we believe that the existence of motivational moderators of this tendency makes this a powerful tool in a person's repertoire of affiliative behaviors.

References

Aarts, H., & Dijksterhuis, A. (2000). Habits as knowledge structures: Automaticity in goal-directed behavior. *Journal of Personality and Social Psychology, 78*, 53–63.

Bargh, J. A., & Chartrand, T. L. (2000). The mind in the middle: A practical guide to priming and automaticity research. In H. T. Reis & C. M. Judd (Eds.), *Handbook of research methods in social and personality psychology* (pp. 253–285). New York: Cambridge University Press.

Bargh, J. A., Chen, M., & Burrows, L. (1996). Automaticity of social behavior: Direct effects of trait construct and stereotype activation on action. *Journal of Personality and Social Psychology, 71*, 230–244.

Baumeister, R. F., & Leary, M. R. (1995). The need to belong: Desire for interpersonal attachments as a fundamental human motivation. *Psychological Bulletin, 117*, 497–529.

Bavelas, J. B., Black, A., Chovil, N., Lemery, C. R., & Mullett, J. (1988). Form and function in motor mimicry: Topographic evidence that the primary function is communication. *Human Communication Research, 14*, 275–299.

Bavelas, J. B., Black, A., Lemery, C. R., & Mullett, J. (1986). "I show how you feel": Motor mimicry as a communicative act. *Journal of Personality and Social Psychology, 50*, 322–329.

Bavelas, J. B., Black, A., Lemery, C. R., & Mullett, J. (1987). Motor mimicry as primitive empathy. In N. Eisenberg & J. Strayer (Eds.), *Empathy and its development* (pp. 317–338). Cambridge, UK: Cambridge University Press.

Berger, S. M., & Hadley, S. W. (1975). Some effects of a model's performance on an observer's electromyographic activity. *American Journal of Psychology, 88*, 263–276.

Berkowitz, L. (1984). Some effects of thoughts on anti- and prosocial influences of media events: A cognitive-neoassociation analysis. *Psychological Bulletin, 95*, 410–427.

Bernieri, F. J. (1988). Coordinated movement and rapport in teacher-student interactions. *Journal of Nonverbal Behavior, 12*, 120–138.

Bock, J. K. (1986). Syntactic persistence in sentence production. *Cognitive Psychology, 18*, 355–387.

Bock, J. K. (1989). Closed-class immanence in sentence production. *Cognition, 31*, 163–186.

Boer, H., Elving, W. J. L., & Seydel, E. R. (1998). Psychosocial factors and mental health in cancer patients: Opportunities for health promotion. *Psychology, Health and Medicine, 3*, 71–79.

Bowling, A. P., Edelmann, R. J., Leaver, J., & Hoekel, T. (1989). Loneliness, mobility, well-being and social support in a sample of over 85 year olds. *Personality and Individual Differences, 10*, 1189–1192.

Brewer, M. B. (1991). The social self: On being the same and different at the same time. *Personality and Social Psychology Bulletin, 17*, 475–482.

Brewer, M. B., & Gardner, W. (1996). Who is this "we"? Levels of collective identity and self-representations. *Journal of Personality and Social Psychology, 71*, 83–93.

Bush, L. K., Barr, C. L., McHugo, G. J., & Lanzetta, J. T. (1989). The effects of facial control and facial mimicry on subjective reactions to comedy routines. *Motivation and Emotion, 13*, 31–52.

Cappella, J. N., & Panalp, S. (1981). Talk and silence sequences in informal conversations: III. Interspeaker influence. *Human Communication Research, 7*, 117–132.

Carlston, D. E., & Skowronski, J. J. (1994). Savings in the relearning of trait information as evidence for spontaneous inference generation. *Journal of Personality and Social Psychology, 66*, 840–856.

Carpenter, W. B. (1874). *Principles of mental physiology*. New York: Appleton.

Carver, C. S., Ganellen, R. J., Froming, W. J., & Chambers, W. (1983). Modeling: An analysis in terms of category accessibility. *Journal of Experimental Social Psychology, 19*, 403–421.

Charney, E. J. (1966). Psychosomatic manifestations of rapport in psychotherapy. *Psychosomatic Medicine, 28*, 305–315.

Chartrand, T. L., & Bargh, J. A. (1996). Automatic activation of impression formation and memorization goals: Nonconscious goal priming reproduces effects of explicit task instructions. *Journal of Personality and Social Psychology, 71*, 464–478.

Chartrand, T. L., & Bargh, J. A. (1999). The chameleon effect: The perception-behavior link and social interaction. *Journal of Personality and Social Psychology, 76*, 893–910.

Chartrand, T. L., Kawada, C., & Bargh, J. A. (2002). *It takes one to know one: When your own behavior affects your judgments of others.* Manuscript submitted for publication, Ohio State University.

Chen, M., & Bargh, J. A. (1997). Nonconscious behavioral confirmation processes: The self-fulfilling nature of automatically-activated stereotypes. *Journal of Experimental Social Psychology, 33,* 541–560.

Cross, S. E., & Madson, L. (1997). Models of the self: Self-construals and gender. *Psychological Bulletin, 122,* 5–37.

Dabbs, J. M. (1969). Similarity of gestures and interpersonal influence. *Proceedings of the 77th Annual Convention of the American Psychological Association,* 337–339.

Davis, M. H. (1983). Measuring individual differences in empathy: Evidence for a multidimensional approach. *Journal of Personality and Social Psychology, 44,* 113–126.

Decety, J., Jeannerod, M., Germain, M., & Pastene, J. (1991). Vegetative response during imagined movement is proportional to mental effort. *Behavioural Brain Research, 42,* 1–5.

Devine, P. G. (1989). Stereotypes and prejudice: Their automatic and controlled components. *Journal of Personality and Social Psychology, 56,* 5–18.

Dijksterhuis, A., & Bargh, J. (2001). The perception-behavior expressway: Automatic effects of social perception on social behavior. *Advances in Experimental Social Psychology, 33.*

Dijksterhuis, A., Bargh, J. A., & Miedema, J. (2000). Of men and mackerels: Attention and automatic behavior. In H. Bless & J. P. Forgas (Eds.), *Subjective experience in social cognition and behavior* (pp. 36–51). Philadelphia: Psychology Press.

Dijksterhuis, A., & van Knippenberg, A. (1998). The relation between perception and behavior or how to win a game of Trivial Pursuit. *Journal of Personality and Social Psychology, 74,* 865–877.

Dijksterhuis, A., & van Knippenberg, A. (2000). Behavioral indecision: Effects of self-focus on automatic behavior. *Social Cognition, 18,* 55–74.

Dimberg, U. (1982). Facial reactions to facial expressions. *Psychophysiology, 19,* 643–647.

Di Pellegrino, G., Fadiga, L., Fogassi, L., Gallese, V., & Rizzolatti, G. (1992). Understanding motor events: A neurophysiological study. *Experimental Brain Research, 91,* 176–180.

Epley, N., & Gilovich, T. (1999). Just going along: Nonconscious priming and conformity to social pressure. *Journal of Personality and Social Psychology, 35,* 578–589.

Field, T., Woodson, R., Greenberg, R., & Cohen, D. (1982). Discrimination and imitation of facial expression by neonates. *Science, 218,* 179–181.

Friedman, H. S., & Riggio, R. E. (1981). Effect of individual differences in nonverbal expressiveness on transmission of emotion. *Journal of Nonverbal Behavior, 6,* 96–101.

Giles, H., & Powesland, P. F. (1975). *Speech style and social evaluation.* London: Academic Press.

Hatfield, E., Cacioppo, J. T., & Rapson, R. L. (1994). *Emotional contagion.* Cambridge: Cambridge University Press.

Heller, K., Thompson, M. G., Trueba, P. E., & Hogg, J. R. (1991). Peer support telephone dyads for elderly women: Was this the wrong intervention? *American Journal of Community Psychology, 19,* 53–74.

Hsee, C. K., Hatfield, E., Carlson, J. G., & Chemtob, C. (1990). The effect of power on susceptibility to emotional contagion. *Cognition and Emotion, 4*, 327–340.
James, W. (1890). *Principles of psychology*. New York: Holt.
Jeannerod, M. (1994). The representing brain: Neural correlates of motor intention and imagery. *Behavioral and Brain Sciences, 17*, 187–245.
Jeannerod, M. (1997). *The cognitive neuroscience of action*. Oxford: Blackwell.
Kraut, R., Patterson, M., Lundmark, V., Kiesler, S., Mukophadhyay, T., & Scherlis, W. (1998). Internet paradox: A social technology that reduces social involvement and psychological well-being? *American Psychologist, 53*, 1017–1031.
LaFrance, M. (1979). Nonverbal synchrony and rapport: Analysis by the cross-lag panel technique. *Social Psychology Quarterly, 42*, 66–70.
LaFrance, M. (1982). Posture mirroring and rapport. In M. Davis (Ed.), *Interaction rhythms: Periodicity in communicative behavior* (pp. 279–298). New York: Human Sciences Press.
LaFrance, M., & Broadbent, M. (1976). Group rapport: Posture sharing as a nonverbal indicator. *Group and Organization Studies, 1*, 328–333.
Lakin, J., & Chartrand, T. (2003). Using nonconscious behavioral mimicry to increase affiliation and rapport. *Psychological Science, 14*, 334–339.
Lashley, K. S. (1951). The problem of serial order in behavior. In L. A. Jeffress (Ed.), *Cerebral mechanisms in behavior: The Hixon symposium* (pp. 112–136). New York: Wiley and Sons.
Levelt, W. J. M., & Kelter, S. (1982). Surface form and memory in question answering. *Cognitive Psychology, 14*, 78–106.
Leventhal, H., & Mace, W. (1970). The effect of laughter on evaluation of a slapstick movie. *Journal of Personality, 38*, 16–30.
Levy, B. (1996). Improving memory in old age through implicit self-stereotyping. *Journal of Personality and Social Psychology, 71*, 1092–1107.
Macrae, C. N., & Johnston, L. (1998). Help, I need somebody: Automatic action and inaction. *Social Cognition, 16*, 400–417.
Markus, H. R., & Kitayama, S. (1991). Culture and the self: Implications for cognition, emotion, and motivation. *Psychological Review, 98*, 224–253.
Maurer, R. E., & Tindall, J. H. (1983). Effect of postural congruence on client's perception of counselor empathy. *Journal of Counseling Psychology, 30*, 158–163.
McHugo, G. J., Lanzetta, J. T., Sullivan, D. G., Masters, R. D., & Englis, B. G. (1985). Emotional reactions to a political leader's expressive displays. *Journal of Personality and Social Psychology, 49*, 1513–1529.
Meltzoff, A. N., & Moore, M. K. (1977). Imitation of facial and manual gestures by human neonates. *Science, 198*, 75–78.
Meltzoff, A. N., & Moore, M. K. (1979). Note responding to Anisfeld, Masters, and Jacobson and Kagan's comments on Meltzoff and Moore (1977). *Science, 205*, 217–219.
Meltzoff, A. N., & Moore, M. K. (1983). Newborn infants imitate adult facial gestures. *Child Development, 54*, 702–709.
Neumann, R., & Strack, F. (2000). "Mood contagion": The automatic transfer of mood between persons. *Journal of Personality and Social Psychology, 79*, 211–223.
O'Toole, R., & Dubin, R. (1968). Baby feeding and body sway: An experiment in George Herbert Mead's "taking the role of the other." *Journal of Personality and Social Psychology, 10*, 59–65.
Paus, T., Petrides, M., Evans, A. C., & Meyer, E. (1993). Role of human anterior

cingaluate cortex in the control of oculomotor, manual and speech responses: A positron emission tomography study. *Journal of Neurophysiology, 70*, 453–469.

Prinz, W. (1990). A common coding approach to perception and action. In O. Neumann & W. Prinz (Eds.), *Relationships between perception and action* (pp. 167–201). Berlin: Springer-Verlag.

Provine, R. R. (1986). Yawning as a stereotyped action pattern and releasing stimulus. *Ethology, 72*, 109–122.

Provine, R. R. (1992). Contagious laughter: Laughter is a sufficient stimulus for laughs and smiles. *Bulletin of the Psychonomic Society, 30*, 1–4.

Rizzolatti, G., & Arbib, M. A. (1998). Language within our grasp. *Trends in Neuroscience, 21*, 188–194.

Schacter, S., & Singer, J. E. (1962). Cognitive, social, and physiological determinants of emotional state. *Psychological Review, 69*, 379–399.

Scheflen, A. E. (1964). The significance of posture in communication systems. *Psychiatry, 27*, 316–331.

Siegman, A. W., & Reynolds, M. (1984). The facilitating effects of interviewer rapport and the paralinguistics of intimate communications. *Journal of Social and Clinical Psychology, 2*, 71–88.

Simner, M. L. (1971). Newborn's response to the cry of another infant. *Developmental Psychology, 5*, 136–150.

Snyder, M., Tanke, E. D., & Berscheid, E. (1977). Social perception and interpersonal behavior: On the self-fulfilling nature of social stereotypes. *Journal of Personality and Social Psychology, 35*, 656–666.

Sullins, E. S. (1991). Emotional contagion revisited: Effects of social comparison and expressive style on mood convergence. *Personality and Social Psychology Bulletin, 17*, 166–174.

Termine, N. T., & Izard, C. E. (1988). Infants' response to their mother's expressions of joy and sadness. *Developmental Psychology, 24*, 223–229.

Uleman, J. S., Newman, L. S., & Moskowitz, G. B. (1996). People as flexible interpreters: Evidence and issues from spontaneous trait inference. In M. P. Zanna (Ed.), *Advances in experimental social psychology* (Vol. 28, pp. 179–211). San Diego, CA: Academic Press.

van Baaren, R., Maddux, W. W., Chartrand, T. L., de Bouter, C., & van Knippenberg, A. (2003). It takes two to mimic: Behavioral consequences of self-construals. *Journal of Personality and Social Psychology, 84*, 1093–1102.

Webb, J. T. (1969). Subject speech rates as a function of interviewer behaviour. *Language and Speech, 12*, 54–67.

Webb, J. T. (1972). Interview synchrony: An investigation of two speech rate measures in an automated standardized interview. In B. Pope & A. W. Siegman (Eds.), *Studies in dyadic communication* (pp. 115–133). New York: Pergamon.

Winter, L., & Uleman, J. S. (1984). When are social judgments made? Evidence for the spontaneousness of trait inferences. *Journal of Personality and Social Psychology, 47*, 237–252.

Young, R. D., & Frye, M. (1966). Some are laughing; some are not—why? *Psychological Reports, 18*, 747–752.

Zajonc, R. B., Adelmann, K. A., Murphy, S. T., & Niedenthal, P. M. (1987). Convergence in the physical appearance of spouses. *Motivation and Emotion, 11*, 335–346.

14

Implicit Impressions

James S. Uleman, Steven L. Blader, and Alexander Todorov

Our knowledge of other people is complex and multilayered. It develops from a thousand strands: a friend's comment ("she's cool"), taste in clothing (all from The Gap), tones of voice (like a fishwife), attitudes (against the death penalty), values (pro-life), facial expressions (crooked smile with overbite), favorite haunts (jazz clubs) and foods (eggplant and garlic), what someone does with us (talk politics, gossip) and others (makes love), roles (sister-in-law), goals (stay sober), style (shy at first), and so on ad infinitum. What we know quickly extends beyond what we can say to how we feel, what we implicitly expect, and how we act toward them and with them, sometimes to everyone's surprise. Much of it is based on forgotten encounters and barely noticed events. It includes the meanings we give these events and observations, sometimes consciously with care and effort, but more often without effort or awareness.

In this chapter, we begin to develop the idea of implicit impressions of others. Implicit impressions are those impressions—or that aspect of all impressions—that do not depend on explicit memory of past encounters or the explicit meanings people have attached to them. They extend beyond verbal descriptions of others to include the intuitive basis of those descriptions that are called into play when we try to put our implicit knowledge into words for the first time. They are what is at work when we notice that someone is acting "out of character," without quite being able to say how we know this or what their character is like. They are what is behind our certainty that we "know" what someone is like without being able to say (or remember) what we know or how we know it. Implicit impressions are preverbal, nonepisodic residues in memory of our observations of, interactions with, and inferences about others. These memorial traces are linked to other people in forms that guide our explicit thoughts, our emotions, and our behavior with them, without having to emerge from the shadows and become explicit themselves.

By definition, implicit impressions are not something one can tell to others. But knowledge about others clearly passes back and forth between the implicit and explicit domain. It moves from implicit to explicit every time we first articulate it—even when it has been clear to others for years in our gestures or feelings or actions. It moves from explicit to implicit when it operates outside current awareness because we either do not remember it or cannot remember it. This explicit-turned-implicit knowledge may be about our own prior verbalizations or about their evidentiary bases that we could have described.

Distinguishing implicit from explicit impressions can be difficult. Sometimes people say one thing about someone but do another, so words and deeds are at odds. Excluding deliberate deception, such cases suggest that both explicit and implicit impressions are at work and are discrepant with each other. But when words and deeds are not in sync, the distinction depends on the memory status of the impression and the information on which it is based. Memories are implicit whenever they affect current behavior (so we know they exist) but have not been, or cannot be, deliberately retrieved. Schachter (1987) described implicit memory as "revealed when previous experiences facilitate performance on a task that does not require conscious or intentional recollections of those experiences," whereas explicit memory "requires conscious recollection of previous experiences" (p. 501). So responses to others that are affected by prior experiences with them, in the absence of explicit reference to or recollection of those prior experiences, are the result of implicit memory. We call such implicit knowledge—which affects how we think, feel, and act toward specific others—implicit impressions.

We want to make several points in this chapter. First, implicit impressions exist, and there is good experimental support for them, including Andersen's work on social-cognitive transference (see chapter 16), and Carlston and Skowronski's work on spontaneous trait inference (STI). Second, implicit impressions affect trait judgments of others. This is clear in Andersen's work and has been demonstrated in research on spontaneous trait transference (STT; Skowronski, Carlston, Mae, & Crawford, 1998), in which STIs affect trait ratings of a communicator rather than the actor. Because STTs are misattributions, they raise the question of how likely it is that STIs will be associated with the correct person, the actor, when other persons are present. New findings from our lab suggest that this is the rule and that STT errors are the exception. Third, implicit and explicit impressions of the same person can be held simultaneously, and their effects can be empirically distinguished. We illustrate how to do this with Jacoby's process dissociation procedure (PDP; see chapter 15), and new findings from our lab. Fourth, implicit impressions are potentially related to a wide range of phenomena that interest social psychologists, including errors in judging how well people know someone, stereotypes, and in-group/out-group perceptions. Speculations and evidence are offered to persuade the reader of this.

Existence Evidence

What evidence is there that implicit impressions exist? The clinical literature contains numerous anecdotes that illustrate implicit memory phenomena in social interaction. Perhaps the earliest and best known is Edouard Claparède's (1911/1951) "curious experiment" with a patient with Korsakoff's syndrome. Although she had been hospitalized for five years, she did not recognize the doctors and nurses she saw every day. "She forgot from one minute to the next what she was told, or the events that took place" (p. 68). "[T]o see whether she would better retain an intense impression involving affectivity, I stuck her hand with a pin hidden between my fingers. The light pain was as quickly forgotten as indifferent perceptions; a few minutes later she no longer remembered it. But when I again reached out for her hand, she pulled it back in a reflex fashion, not knowing why. When I asked for the reason, she said in a flurry, 'Doesn't one have the right to withdraw her hand?' and when I insisted, she said, 'Is there perhaps a pin hidden in your hand?' To the question, 'What makes you suspect me of wanting to stick you?' she would repeat her old statement, 'That was an idea that went through my mind,' or she would explain, 'Sometimes pins are hidden in people's hands.' But never would she recognize the idea of sticking as a 'memory'" (pp. 69–70). One might say that she had formed a negative but implicit impression of Dr. Claparède. But is there more systematic evidence of implicit impressions, especially with nonclinical populations?

Implicit knowledge of various kinds—attitudes, self-esteem, and stereotypes—are familiar phenomena in social psychology by now (e.g., see Fazio, 1986; http://www.harvard.edu/implicit). Greenwald and Banaji (1995) note that their defining feature "is that traces of past experience affect some performance, even though the influential earlier experience is not remembered . . . is unavailable to self-report or introspection" (pp. 4–5). Their literature survey is largely confined to implicit evaluations, including evaluations of the self and of social groups. However, the Implicit Association Test (IAT; Greenwald, McGhee, & Schwartz, 1998), which is at the empirical heart of most of this work, is not limited to assessing implicit associations between pairs of bipolar concepts and evaluative attributes. For example, Greenwald and Farnham (2000, Experiment 2) measured implicit associations with masculine and feminine attributes. Any attributes can be implicitly associated with any concept, or person.

Measuring implicit associations between concepts with the IAT requires that the concepts be explicit, so they can be presented in the test. Implicit associations are detected through their effects on speeded responses to pairs of explicit concepts on the IAT. Implicit impressions may also involve implicit associations. But impressions may be implicit because the concepts that comprise them are implicit, or events' implications are not (or cannot be) recalled. We may not know that we "know" things about other people, yet we still respond to them differently than we would have without some previous forgotten information about them. Even in the absence of explicit concepts, implicit impressions can be revealed by the classic implicit memory phenomena described by Schachter (1987; Schachter & Curran, 2000). Research summarized below demonstrates implicit impressions' impact on trait ratings. But we suspect that they also have effects on emotions, moods, expectations, nontrait descriptions, and behaviors toward others.

One might think that research with the IAT provides evidence of implicit impressions. Although we see no reason why it could not, it has not. All of the research with the IAT to date examines associations with objects, with social categories of people (often ethnic groups), or with the self. None of this work (to our knowledge) looks at implicit associations with specific individuals other than the self.

Lewicki reported a series of studies in which participants either had a brief interaction with one person (Lewicki, 1985) or observed several photos of people (Lewicki, 1986). The person and photos were associated with either positive or negative events, and each had a subtle distinctive physical feature. Participants apparently learned this association between valence and feature nonconsciously, because it affected their responses to a new person who had this feature, even though they reported no awareness of it.

Probably the most extensive body of systematic evidence for implicit impressions comes indirectly from the remarkable research by Andersen and her colleagues (e.g., see chapter 16, this volume; Andersen & Berenson, 2001; Berk & Andersen, 2000; Chen & Andersen, 1999) on social-cognitive transference. This work has shown that rich and complex representations of a significant other can affect a whole array of responses to a stranger who resembles that significant other—responses that range from mood to impressions to expectations and even to interpersonal behavior. These effects occur without any awareness that the representation from the past (which participants previously described) affects current responses to the stranger. Andersen's experimental procedures are elaborately designed to make explicit recollection of the significant other highly unlikely (see especially Glassman & Andersen, 1999). This extensive body of research demonstrates that implicit impressions exist by documenting their effects on a wide variety of reactions to strangers who resemble these significant others.

There is also extensive evidence of implicit impressions created in the laboratory by brief, incidental encounters. In this research, neither social-cognitive transference nor preexisting impressions of social categories or their members are at work. Carlston, Skowronski, and their colleagues developed their savings-in-relearning implicit memory paradigm to investigate whether memory links are established between actors and spontaneous trait inferences (Carlston & Skowronski, 1994; Carlston, Skowronski, & Sparks, 1995). STIs are trait inferences that are made in the absence of intentions to form impressions or infer traits about others. They occur in the process of comprehending trait-implying behaviors or behavior descriptions. For example, most undergraduates reading, "The secretary solved the mystery halfway through the book" spontaneously infer *clever*, even if they are simply reading the sentence as a distracter from a primary task (Winter, Uleman, & Cunniff, 1985) or for a memory test (Winter & Uleman, 1984). Evidence that STIs occur has been provided by a variety of dependent variables, including cued recall, lexical decision reaction times (RTs), and recognition probe RTs (see Uleman, Newman, & Moskowitz, 1996, for a summary). Carlston and Skowronski's work shows that STIs can also function as implicit impressions.

Carlston and Skowronski's procedure was developed to address a controversy about whether STIs are about the actors (e.g., the secretary) or merely about the behaviors. While STIs about behaviors might be interesting, the stronger traditional claim has been that they are about the actor (Winter & Uleman, 1984). If they are not about the actor, they are not implicit impressions. In Carlston and Skowronski's procedure, participants first familiarized themselves with a series of photos of people ("actors") paired with trait-implying paragraphs that described their behavior. Then after intervals as long as one week, they were asked to learn pairs of photos and traits, without any reference to their prior familiarization experience. These photo-trait pairs included the actor photos presented earlier, paired with the traits implied by the paragraphs with which they appeared. These "old photo–implied trait" pairs were easier for participants to learn than either (1) "new photo–implied trait" pairs or (2) old photos paired with other implied traits. That is, there was savings in relearning, in the sense that participants apparently learned pairings of photos and implied traits during the initial familiarization procedure, and then merely had to relearn the "old photo–implied trait" pairs later. Thus learning was easier for old photo-trait pairs. All of this occurred without any suggestion to participants that they should infer traits or form impressions, so trait inferences were spontaneous. Furthermore, the findings established that the STIs were linked to the actors rather than merely the behaviors, because savings occurred for actor-trait pairs, not for behavior-trait pairs.

This research also showed that these savings effects still occur even when learning occurs at least 2 days after the initial exposure, and even when participants show neither recognition memory for the behaviors (Carlston & Skowronski, 1994, Studies 2–4) nor recall of the inferred traits (Carlston et al., 1995, Study 5). That is, the savings occur not only with no explicit reference to the initial familiarization exposure, but also with no explicit memory for the trait-implying behaviors or the traits they implied. This "suggests an expansion of our conception of trait inference or trait knowledge to include implicit as well as explicit knowledge" (Carlston et al., 1995, p. 433). People were unaware both of making the spontaneous trait inferences and of their influence on their subsequent learning.

Evidence That Spontaneous Trait Inferences Are Linked to Actors

Carlston and Skowronski's (1994; Carlston et al., 1995) research shows that implicit impressions can be created in the laboratory and that they are "about" (i.e., linked in memory to) actors rather than merely behaviors. But it also raises the question of why prior research results with a cued-recall paradigm were so equivocal on the latter point (see Uleman et al., 1996). There are many differences between these two lines of research, including instructions (memorize vs. familiarize), the length of the trait-implying descriptions (one sentence vs. paragraph), how the actors were presented (verbally vs. visually), and dependent variables (cued recall vs. savings in relearning). A series of studies using a false recognition paradigm shows that robust actor-STI links can be created with memory instructions, one-sentence descriptions, and visual presentation of actors.

Todorov and Uleman (2002) asked participants to memorize actor photos paired with one-sentence behavior descriptions. All these descriptions implied traits, but some descriptions also made the traits explicit whereas others did not. Participants were then tested with pairs of actor photos and traits, and judged whether the trait had been explicitly presented earlier with the photo, as part of the behavior description. Six studies showed high false recognition of implied (but not presented) traits paired with target actors—higher than false recognition of implied traits paired with other familiar actors, and higher than that of other traits paired with target actors. These effects occurred even when 120 photo-behavior pairs were exposed for only 5 seconds each. And they occurred in the absence of both recognition and recall of the trait-implying behaviors. That is, implicit impressions produced explicit memory errors.

Two of these studies showed that participants went beyond the spontaneously inferred traits and exhibited less false recognition of antonyms of these inferred traits (relative to unrelated control traits) when these were paired with relevant actors. Apparently they were able to use their implicit impressions to more accurately reject traits opposite in meaning from the behaviors' implications. Furthermore, across all studies and behavior-trait pairs, the strength of explicit trait judgments about the actors from these behaviors was strongly related both to the occurrence of false recognition and to slower response times for correct rejection of implied traits. That is, these false recognition and response time effects were highly correlated with other participants' explicit trait judgments about these actor-behavior pairs. Furthermore, they were unrelated to the probability of generating the traits to the behaviors alone. This is additional evidence that the implicit impressions were about the actors rather than merely the behaviors. Additional studies (Todorov and Uleman, 2003) showed that these false recognition effects occur relatively automatically: under rapid (2 second) exposures, under shallow information processing, and in the face of a concurrent cognitive load at encoding.

This research shows that STIs from single behaviors can be bound to actors in explicit memory, even in the absence of memory for the behaviors on which they were based. These STIs have implications for judgments about other traits' (antonyms') links to actors. Thus evidence of strong, spontaneous actor-trait links is not limited to implicit memory measures such as savings in relearning. This new false recognition measure reveals them under memory instructions, with one-sentence trait-implying behaviors.[1] So there is a reassuring consistency between the robust, spontaneous actor-trait links in implicit memory revealed by the savings-in-relearning paradigm, and the strength of spontaneous actor-trait links in explicit memory revealed by the false recognition paradigm. Both implicit and explicit memory measures provide clear evidence that spontaneously inferred traits are linked to actors, relatively effortlessly and without intentions or awareness.

Thus implicit impressions not only exist, but can be created "from scratch" in the laboratory. STIs are one kind of implicit impression, created from exposure to others performing trait-implying behavior. They lead to savings in relearning (an implicit memory effect) and errors of false recognition (an explicit memory effect). The next question is, what consequences do they have, beyond those already cited to establish their existence?

Spontaneous Trait Transference

Probably the most important, ubiquitous, and apparently obvious consequence of implicit impressions is that they automatically affect intentional impressions of actors who perform the trait-implying behavior. We and several other theorists (e.g., Anderson, Krull, & Weiner, 1996; Gilbert, 1998) have assumed that STIs constitute the first stage of what may later become intentional inferences. However, this sequence has only been assumed. It has not yet been demonstrated empirically. The first empirical evidence for this is presented in the next section. As background for that evidence, it is useful to take a more detailed look at STT.

It is well established that implicit impressions can affect intentional impressions of people other than those who initially activated the trait construct. Lewicki's (1985, 1986) early work suggested this. Andersen's research on social-cognitive transference (cited above; see also chapter 16) contains many demonstrations that implicit impressions of significant others can affect a variety of responses to strangers, including trait judgments. Further, the clinical literature suggests that such effects are widespread and long-lasting, and Andersen's research shows that they occur among normal participants. This suggests that social-cognitive transference often affects our impressions of strangers.

However, neither Lewicki's nor Andersen's work demonstrates that specific trait concepts, spontaneously inferred from behavior, can affect intentional judgments of someone who is not the actor. Such evidence would be useful support for our claim that STIs and social-cognitive transference are both instances of implicit impressions. It would also provide a method for studying implicit impressions' effects, independent of the content and quality of particular long-term relationships with significant others. The best published evidence comes from Skowronski et al.'s (1998) studies of spontaneous trait transference. STT was first demonstrated by Carlston et al. (1995, Study 4) in a study of savings in relearning. Using the familiarization and savings paradigm described above, trait-implying behavior descriptions were paired not with photos of the actors, but with photos of communicators offering descriptions of other unseen people. In order to make it unmistakably clear that these were not self-descriptions, the descriptions were worded in the third person and referred to someone whose gender did not match that of the communicator in the photo. Savings in relearning showed clear evidence of STT, even though effects were about half the size of STI effects in prior savings studies. That is, familiarization with communicator-description pairs facilitated later learning of photo-trait pairs, even though these traits did not describe those in the photos.

Skowronski et al. (1998, Studies 2–4) then showed that STT affects trait ratings of the communicator. In addition, Study 2 showed that STT is trait specific, in that it does not affect ratings of unrelated traits with the same valence as the implied trait. Study 3 showed that STT occurs even when participants are told that the communicator photos and behavior descriptions have been paired randomly and that the communicators did not know the targets being described. This study was designed to undercut the possibility that STT occurs because participants believe that communicators and targets are similar because they know each other. Study 4 showed STT with more naturalistic stimuli. Participants saw videotapes of communicators telling an off-camera interviewer about either themselves or another person. Then they rated the communicators on the implied traits as well as traits of the same valence. These ratings provided clear evidence of STT, specific to the implied traits. As in Study 3, the magnitude of STT was smaller than that of STI. Study 4 also showed that STT occurs even when participants are instructed to make intentional trait inferences about the actors in the descriptive paragraphs.

The most remarkable thing about this series of studies is that it shows STIs being erroneously associated with salient others (communicators) and affecting trait ratings of them in spite of all kinds of steps taken to ensure that participants did not believe the trait-implying behaviors characterized them, and even though impression formation was not their goal. STT occurred in spite of mismatched genders and participants knowing that photos and descriptions were randomly paired. Wyer and his students showed that when participants are asked to form impressions of a target person from a conversation about the target, either between two other people (Wyer, Budesheim, & Lambert, 1990) or between another person and the target (Wyer, Budesheim, Lambert, & Swan, 1994), their impressions of the communicators are also affected. But STT occurs without any mention of impression formation and is more reminiscent of findings by Manis, Cornell, and Moore (1974) that attitude-relevant information incidentally affects impressions of the communicator. Skowronski et al. (1998) explained STT as the result of (a) spontaneous trait activation during the familiarization task, followed by (b) erroneous association of the trait with the communicator photo, and then (c) the associated traits' influence on subsequent ratings of the communicator. They contrasted this associative process with the more deliberate processes of intentional impression formation, in which inferences are accurately made about actors from the outset.

This series of studies was not primarily designed to show that implicit impressions affect trait ratings of actors. But one study (Skowronski et al., 1998, Study 3) suggests they might. As noted above, in this study participants learned that communicator photos and behavior descriptions were actually randomly paired. Half the behavior descriptions were worded in the first person, so that participants who forgot about the random pairing might have interpreted these descriptions as self-descriptions and produced STIs. Then on the judgment test, these participants might have unwittingly "read traits into faces" (Hassin & Trope, 2000) without explicitly recalling the randomly paired behavior descriptions. Results showed that the effects of first-person descriptions on trait ratings were comparable to the effects of third-person descriptions, and both effect sizes were similar to other STT effects. So these first-person descriptions may have produced STIs that affected trait ratings. But it is also possible that the trait ratings were based on recalling behavior descriptions. Unfortunately, participants' recall of descriptions and whether they were first or third person were not assessed. Carlston and Skowronski (1994; Carlston et al., 1995) have shown savings in relearning in the absence of both recognition and recall of the behaviors, suggesting this effect may not have depended on behavior recall.

Thus STI effects on trait ratings of actors in the absence of explicit memory for, or reference to, the behaviors are certainly plausible. One study (Skowronski et al., 1998, Study 3) is at least consistent with this idea. In the next major section of this chapter, we describe a new method of examining this issue, and results consistent with our speculations. These studies show that implicit impressions (specifically STIs) do have automatic (uncontrollable) effects on trait ratings.

A Probable Boundary Condition on Spontaneous Trait Transference

Before we consider that work, it is worth taking a closer look at what may be a boundary condition on STT. In all the STT studies, the only photos presented were photos of communicators. Does STT depend on the presence of only the communicator's photo? Would STIs become associated with communicators if photos of both actors and communicators were present during familiarization with or memorization of the trait-implying materials? Although we have no direct evidence on this question, new findings from our lab suggest that STT would disappear or be attenuated.

Todorov and Uleman (in press) used the false recognition paradigm described above to see whether STIs would become associated with any facial photo or are uniquely associated with the actor's face. In three studies, single trait-implying sentences were presented simultaneously with the faces of two people of the same age and gender, and participants were asked to study them for a subsequent memory test. The actors were named, and one photo was identified with the actor's name and the other (control face) with a different name. In the subsequent false recognition test, the actor's face produced significant false recognition of implied traits compared to the control face. This suggests that STIs are more strongly associated with actors' faces, if they are presented, than with other faces or persons present. However, this result could have occurred because the second face received less attention. So in Study 4, two trait-implying sentences and two facial photos were presented simultaneously, with each sentence's actor identified with a different face. This ensured that both faces (as well as both sentences) would be attended to equally. In the subsequent false recognition test, actors' faces produced more false recognition of implied traits than control faces, even though the same faces represented actors and controls for different traits.

This suggests that STT might disappear or be attenuated if actors' faces were presented along with the communicators' faces, using the familiarization instruction and savings-in-relearning paradigm of Carlston and Skowronski (1994; Carlston et al., 1995). STT may only occur when there is no visual representation (e.g., a photo) of the actor. However, the necessary research—with savings in relearning and trait ratings as dependent variables—remains to be done.

Overall, research on STT strongly suggests that STIs can have implicit effects, that is, effects that make no reference to and do not depend on recalling the behavioral evidence on which they are based. The work by Todorov and Uleman (2002, 2003, in press) provides good evidence that STIs based on single behaviors are linked to appropriate actors' faces, even when they are present at the same time as others' faces. So it is clear that single behaviors spontaneously produce implicit impressions of actors, in the form of STIs. These impressions, made without awareness and without explicit memory of their behavioral bases, may then have automatic effects on subsequent explicit judgments of the actors. In the next section, we describe evidence that directly supports this idea.

Implicit Impressions' Automatic Effects on Trait Judgments

Cognitive processes can be automatic in a variety of ways, as Bargh (1994) pointed out so clearly. Perhaps the most important sense of "automatic" is being uncontrollable (rather than taking place without awareness, being unintentional, or being extremely efficient). Cognitive control is central to a host of social judgment and self-regulatory phenomena (e.g., Wegner & Pennebaker, 1993). Having an implicit impression of someone should affect explicit judgments, as the STT research (above) suggests. The central question we address here is, how controllable are these effects? Of course, if one is not aware of the implicit impression, its influence is necessarily (and perhaps uninterestingly) uncontrollable. But what if one is made aware of implicit impressions and their potential effects? Can these effects be controlled? If so, how much control is possible?

The last two decades have seen an explosion of research in social psychology on automaticity, where the dominant question has been, "Is it automatic or controlled?" Wegner and Bargh (1998) even argued that most of the classic studies in social psychology, beginning with Festinger and Carlsmith's (1959) dissonance studies, are classics in part because they demonstrate how little control people have over their own social behavior. The list of social phenomena—cognitions, evaluations, and behaviors—that are wholly or partly a function of automatic processes continues to grow, to the point that the very existence of freely acting agents seems to be in doubt (e.g., Bargh & Ferguson, 2000).

Yet even as the domain of automatic social behavior has grown and that of controlled processes has shrunk, it has become clear that the basic question of whether particular social behaviors are automatic or controlled poses a misleading dichotomy. Most phenomena of interest to social psychologists are governed by a combination of automatic and controlled processes. One more demonstration that phenomena we used to believe were controlled (or intentional or volitional) are also affected by automatic processes will not change that. Nor will it demonstrate that these phenomena are entirely automatic, or that volition plays no role. Furthermore, as long as we think of automaticity and control as dichotomous and mutually exclusive, and seek more and more evidence of automaticity, control is in danger of being defined by default as merely whatever is not automatic, however automatic is defined. In such a framework, the amount of control depends on the kind of automaticity being considered. Therefore it is important to adopt a more affirmative definition of control and a theoretical framework that includes both automatic and controlled processes, operating at the same time.

Wegner and Bargh (1998, pp. 464–465) offer a typology of the ways automatic and controlled processes can combine, including operating in parallel, one launching the other, one overriding the other, and one transforming into the other. When governance of a phenomenon is not passing back and forth between automatic and controlled processes sequentially, it is shared by both of them. Automatic and controlled processes operate in parallel, or in tandem (when brief enough sequences can be isolated). In both of these cases, the appropriate question is not whether something is automatic or controlled, but how much is automatic and how much controlled? Therefore, we need ways of estimating the relative contributions of automatic and controlled processes to social phenomena. Then we can begin to ask about the conditions that affect the size of the simultaneous automatic and controlled contributions, and move beyond the simple but relatively uninformative question of whether something is automatic at all.

The Process Dissociation Procedure

Fortunately, when mental phenomena depend on the effects of observable prior events, there is a model and a method that can disentangle the automatic from the controllable processes that are based on those events: Jacoby's PDP (see Jacoby, 1991; Jacoby, Toth, & Yonelinas, 1993; Jacoby, Yonelinas, & Jennings, 1997; chapter 15, this volume). The PDP seems to us ideally suited to get at controlled processes because, in a remarkably clear and straightforward operationalization of the idea of personal control, it simply asks participants to control the influence of prior events on their current responses.

To be more precise, the PDP asks participants to include the influence of prior events on their responses on some trials (the inclusion trials) and to exclude those influences on other trials (the exclusion trials). The difference between performance on inclusion and exclusion trials provides the estimate of control. Then (if it can be assumed or demonstrated that controlled and automatic processes operate independently of each other) a few simple equations allow calculation of the influence of automatic processes. The only other requirement for using this method is that there be some criterion of performance accuracy, that is, a way to distinguish between right and wrong answers. The basic ideas are simple and straightforward, but operationalizing them is more complex. Perhaps the best way to understand them is to work through a concrete example.

Word stem completions (e.g., tri_ _ _) require finding words in semantic memory that fit the cues presented. It is well known that a recent exposure to a word that can complete the stem makes that completion more likely, even in the absence of any explicit memory for that exposure. Two processes are at work here. A word stem may be completed by explicitly recalling recently seen words or by just waiting for the word (e.g., *trials*) to pop into one's mind when one looks at the stem. How much can people control the processes involved in word stem completion? More generally, can we assume that an explicit memory task such as recall is completely controlled because it is deliberate? Or might explicit recall be influenced by automatic processes, such as those that bring a word to mind without effort? Likewise, can we assume that asking people to simply let words come freely to mind will tap only automatic processes and prevent them from occasionally trying deliberate recall? Jacoby (1991) argues that there are few process-pure tasks, tasks that tap purely controlled or purely automatic processes. Most tasks depend on a combination of controlled and automatic processes. The way to separate these processes within any task (such as word stem completion) that depends on prior exposure is to (a) define controlled processes as those that people can control and automatic processes as those they cannot; (b) estimate control by examining the performance difference between conditions when people perform the task by intentionally including that prior information versus intentionally excluding it; and (c) use a set of simple assumptions to estimate the importance of automatic processes, once controlled processing has been estimated.

Jacoby et al. (1993, Experiment 1b) examined the effect of divided attention at exposure on subsequent word stem completions. In the first phase of the study, half the participants (in the full attention condition) read 32 words out loud, presented on a computer screen, and tried to memorize them for a subsequent memory test. The other half of the participants (in the divided attention condition) did two tasks at once, reading and listening. They listened to a tape-recorded list of digits and pressed a key whenever they heard three odd digits in a row (e.g., 1, 7, 3). At the same time, they read words out loud on the computer screen, but tried to not let this reading interfere with their digit-monitoring task. In the second phase of the study, all participants completed word stems created from the words they had read earlier. If the word stem "appeared in green, they were to use it as a cue to help them remember a word that was presented earlier. . . . If they could not think of an old word, they were to complete the stem with the first word that came to mind." If the word stem appeared in red, they were to use it "as a cue for remembering words presented earlier but . . . complete those stems with a word that was not presented earlier" (p. 145). So the green trials were inclusion trials, and red trials were exclusion trials.

Without any concurrent cognitive load at encoding, the probabilities of completing the word stems with an old word in the inclusion condition and the exclusion condition were .61 and .36, respectively. With the concurrent digit detection task, these probabilities in both conditions were .46 (see Jacoby et al., 1993, table 1). Under no load, subtracting the exclusion probability from the inclusion probability gives .25 (= .61 – .36) as the estimate of controlled influences (*C*) of prior exposure to the words. That is, controlled processes increased the probability of word stem completions by .25. The maximum possible control for any task is 1.00, so this represents 25% of the theoretical maximum. Thus under no load, participants had some control but not a lot, relative to the maximum theoretical possibility.

Under load, this estimate of control is 0.00 (= .46 – .46). That is, the concurrent load at encoding completely eliminated controlled processes' contribution to word stem completions. (The fact that load reduced controlled processes to 0.00 is not particularly significant. Less load would simply have reduced control less.)

What about the influence of automatic processes (*A*)? Based on the assumption that *C* and *A* are independent, one can calculate *A* as the exclusion probability divided by (1 – *C*). Under no load, this was .47 (= .36/.75); under load, it was .46 (= .46/1.00; see Jacoby et al., 1993, table 2). That is, the influence of automatic processes was not affected by concurrent load. This result is as we would expect, if *A* truly reflects automatic processes, because automatic processes should be unaffected by cognitive load.

Using the Process Dissociation Procedure to Estimate Implicit Impressions' Automatic Effects

How can the PDP be used to estimate implicit impressions' automatic effects? Several methods are conceivable, but we (Uleman & Blader, 2001) adapted the procedures of Skowronski et al. (1998) to illustrate one possibility. Recall that Skowronski et al. asked participants to rate the personality traits of people shown in photos that they had previously seen paired with trait-implying behaviors. So memory of prior exposures (both explicit and implicit) is clearly involved. But unlike effects of exposure to words on word stem completions (as in Jacoby et al., 1993), these are effects of exposure to behavior-photo pairs and the spontaneous inferences that are drawn from them, all of which can affect subsequent trait ratings of these photos. These effects might be completely mediated by implicit impressions (STIs), as suggested by Carlston and Skowronski (1994; Carlston et al., 1995) and Skowronski et al. (1998). They showed that STI occurs, and its effects do not depend on explicit memory for the behaviors. On the other hand, under other conditions, these effects might also be mediated by explicit recall of the behaviors and any trait implications intentionally drawn from them, in response to the trait-rating scale. The PDP model describes how to estimate the effect of both automatic and controlled processes on trait ratings. The automatic processes are the consequence of implicit impressions because, as prior research shows (Uleman et al., 1996), participants are unaware of making STIs. Being unaware of them, they cannot control their effects.

In order to apply the PDP to this phenomenon, two problems had to be solved. First, we had to work out how to obtain trait ratings of the photos under inclusion and exclusion conditions. Second, because there are no objectively correct or incorrect trait ratings of photos of strangers, a way of defining the proportion of correct responses had to be developed. We (Uleman & Blader, 2001) tried the following solutions, in two studies. Participants studied behavior-photo pairs for a subsequent memory test (rather than under Skowronski et al.'s, 1998, familiarization instructions, to maximize the parallels with Jacoby et al., 1993). Just as in the Carlston and Skowronski studies described earlier, participants viewed photos paired with behaviors. Then they got another booklet containing only photos, some of which had been paired with behaviors in the first part of the study and some of which were new. They were asked to examine the photos in this second booklet to form impressions of the pictured people and to rate each one on three traits.

However, the instructions for the rating task were varied to create the inclusion and exclusion conditions. In the inclusion condition, participants were told,

> In the earlier memory task, the pictures were paired with descriptions of behaviors. In every case, those behavior descriptions were about the person in the photo. They were provided by that person. Since the behaviors are about the person in the photo, they're informative and will make it easier to form an accurate impression of him or her. So try to remember the behaviors and then use them as you form your impressions from the photo.

In the exclusion condition, they were told,

> In the earlier memory task, the pictures were paired with descriptions of behaviors. In every case, those behavior descriptions were NOT about the person in the photo. They describe someone else, and do not describe the person in the photo. (We checked with the people to be sure.) We paired them with photos randomly. Since the behaviors are NOT about the person in the photo, they're potentially misleading and may make it harder to form an accurate impression of him or her. So try to remember the behaviors and then ignore them, so you're not influenced by them as you form your impressions from the photo.

In other words, in the inclusion condition participants were asked to remember and use the information they received earlier to form an impression of the person (if the person was among those paired with a behavior in the first part of the study). In the exclusion condition, participants were asked to remember the prior information but then intentionally avoid using it in impression formation, just as participants in the Jacoby et al. (1993) study were asked to remember the words presented earlier and avoid using them to complete the stems.

These instructions were designed to produce an intention to use the earlier trait inference in the inclusion condition and an intention to not use the trait inference in the exclusion condition (rather than simply producing no intention in the exclusion condition). Thus, trait judgments in the inclusion condition should be a result of both controlled (recollection) and automatic processes. However, in the exclusion condition, any influence of prior exposure to the photo-behavior pairs should be the result of uncontrollable (i.e., automatic) processes, because participants exclude the influence of prior exposure as completely as they can.

The proportion of correct responses for "old" (previously seen) photos was defined for trait ratings relative to how the photos were rated in the absence of any prior exposure to them. That is, ratings of those photos on the traits by participants who had never seen the photo before served as the baseline. In the trait-rating phase of each study, 12 of the photos were new to half of the participants, and 12 were old. Participants rated each photo on the same three trait types: the one implied by the behavior, a trait of congruent valence, and a trait of incongruent valence (as in Carlston & Skowronski, 1994). Ratings were averaged among participants for whom the photos were new, creating unique base-rate estimates for each photo of how it would be rated without prior exposure to behavioral information. Among participants for whom the photo was old, a score of 1 was assigned if their rating was above this base rate, and a score of 0 otherwise. Averaged across old photos, this score gives the proportion of photos rated above the base rates, that is, the proportion correct in the sense that prior exposure to behavior-photo pairs increased trait ratings—just as prior exposure to words increased word stem completions.

In both studies (Uleman & Blader, 2001), we varied the delay between exposure to behavior-photo pairs and trait ratings of the photos. A third of participants had no delay; a third had a 20-minute delay; and a third had a 2-day delay. We predicted that delay would significantly decrease the influence of controlled processes on the trait ratings, but not affect the influence of automatic processes as much (just as cognitive load did not affect automatic processes in the Jacoby et al., 1993, study). The larger objective of these studies was to show that this adaptation of the PDP and Skowronski et al.'s (1998) procedures produces results that are theoretically reasonable and useful for studying the duality of automatic and controlled processes in implicit impressions.

In the first study, we were concerned that it would be difficult for participants to switch back and forth between inclusion and exclusion instructions, as they rated the 12 old photos. So they were given either inclusion or exclusion instructions for all the ratings. This made it impossible to calculate *C* or *A* for each participant, because we did not have both inclusion and exclusion performance for each one. But we were able to calculate *C* and *A* for each critical trait, performing analyses with stimuli as the unit of analysis.

Figure 14.1 shows the values of *C* and *A* as a function of delay. (Values of *A* were adjusted by subtracting the chance probability of .5 that would result if prior exposure had had no influence; see Jacoby et al., 1993, for a discus-

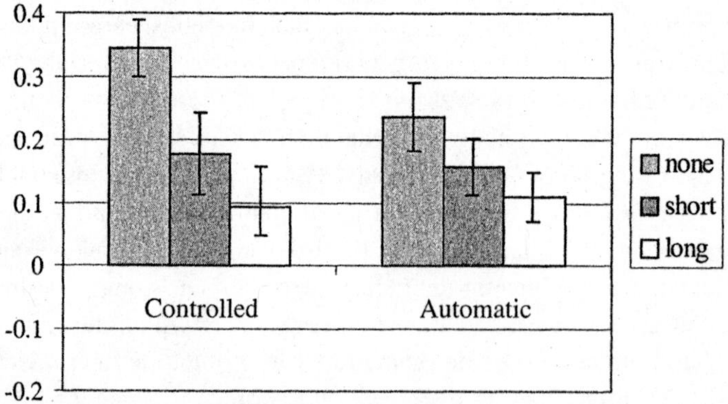

Figure 14.1 Estimates of the magnitude of controlled (left) and automatic (right) effects of prior exposure to behavior-photo pairs on subsequent trait ratings of those photos, under no delay, 20-minute delay, and 2-day delay. Inclusion-exclusion instructions between-Ss; traits as unit.

sion of how to treat neutral base rates.) Estimates of *C* were significantly above chance when there was no delay ($p < .001$) and a short, 20-minute delay ($p < .05$). But there was no evidence of significant controlled processing at the long, 2-day delay. On the other hand, estimates of *A* were significantly above chance levels at no delay ($p < .001$), at the short delay ($p < .01$), and at the long delay ($p < .05$).[2] Both *C* and *A* showed significant linear trends over delay ($ps < .01$).

These estimates of *C* and *A* fit our expectations. First, at brief delays, prior exposure to pairs of trait-implying behaviors and photos do influence trait ratings through both controlled and automatic processes. (It may seem surprising that automatic processes play any role at all after no delay. But with many pairs and the resulting delay between initially seeing a photo and rating it on traits later, some delay and imperfect explicit memory are inevitable.) Second, after 2 days' delay, only automatic processes continued to affect trait ratings. This is consistent with results noted above (Carlston & Skowronski, 1994; Carlston et al., 1995) showing that after 2 days' delay, participants showed neither recognition nor recall of the trait-implying behaviors, yet implicit impressions still had effects.

In Study 2, we directly addressed the question of whether participants could switch between inclusion and exclusion instructions. This study was similar to Study 1 except that participants rated a block of six old photos under inclusion instructions and another block of six old photos under exclusion instructions. Blocks and instructions were counterbalanced, so that some participants had inclusion instructions first and others had exclusion instructions first. Then they were told that the other instruction applied to the next block of trials. Block and order had no effects. Figure 14.2 shows the values of *C* and *A* as a function of delay, again using stimuli as the unit of analysis (for comparability). Estimates of *C* were significantly above chance for the two shortest delays ($ps < .05$), but not at the 2-day delay. On the other hand, automatic processes had effects at the two shortest delays ($ps < .001$) and also at the 2-day delay ($p < .01$). Although *C* showed a main effect and linear trend for delay ($ps < .03$), *A* showed neither ($ps > .15$). Analyses with participants as the unit of analysis showed the same pattern. Thus, essentially the same effects occurred when inclusion-exclusion instructions were varied between subjects and within subjects (although delay no longer affected *A*). This suggests that participants were able to switch decision processes between blocks with different instructions.

More important, both studies (Uleman & Blader, 2001) showed that a 2-day delay had the predicted effect of reducing controlled processing to insignificance, while the automatic effects of implicit impressions on trait ratings persisted. Thus implicit impressions have automatic effects on impressions that people deliberately form of others. And at least with this paradigm, these automatic effects of implicit impressions persist longer than the controlled

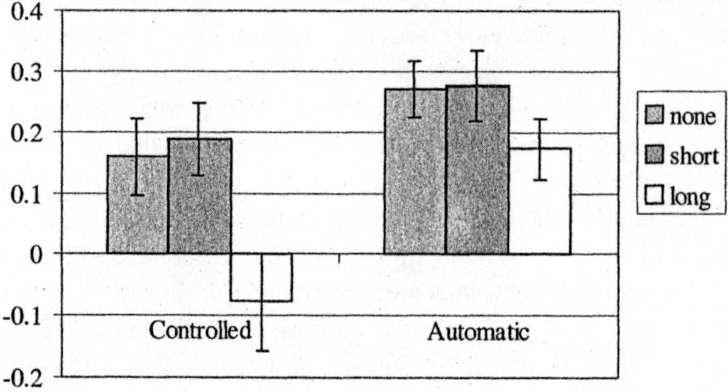

Figure 14.2 Estimates of the magnitude of controlled (left) and automatic (right) effects of prior exposure to behavior-photo pairs on subsequent trait ratings of those photos, under no delay, 20-minute delay, and 2-day delay. Inclusion-exclusion instructions within-Ss; traits as unit.

effects do. At short delays, both implicit impressions and controlled processes had significant effects.

Without something like the PDP and its ability to separately estimate automatic and controlled processing in tasks that engage both, we could not have demonstrated any of this. These results provide another example of why tasks or behaviors should not be called automatic simply because they are influenced by automatic processes—controlled processes may also be operating at the same time. Participants could control effects of prior exposure to the photo-behavior pairs, at least to some degree for shorter delays. Likewise, demonstrating control does not rule out the influence of automatic processes. Prior exposure had automatic effects—the effects of implicit impressions—in all conditions. It takes something like the PDP to let us estimate the contribution of each process type when they both contribute to performance at the same time.

Our adaptation of Jacoby's PDP to study implicit impressions separates their effects from controlled effects. It also takes us beyond the simple question, "Are effects of prior exposures to photo-behavior pairs automatic or controlled?" and allows us to ask, "How automatic and how controlled are they, and under what conditions?" It seems to us that at this point in the development of our knowledge of social cognitive processes, these are the really interesting questions. Even without the present demonstration, we would have guessed that, at short delays, the automatic effects of implicit impressions are accompanied by controlled effects. The challenge was to find a way to demonstrate this and generate estimates of both. Now that we have done this, we can move on to more interesting questions. How do the various encoding, storage, and retrieval conditions that arise in social life affect the automatic and controllable impact of incidental exposure to actors behaving diagnostically? How do individual and cultural differences—which clearly influence the encoding, storage, and retrieval of information about others—affect these automatic and controllable processes? How much can the automatic effects of implicit impressions be brought under control, by telling participants about them and their likely effects? Or would such instructions do nothing more than engage participants' theories about these effects, leading not to control but to correction of automatic effects (as in Wegener and Petty's, 1997, flexible correction model)? This is the kind of research agenda that will move us into the next generation of research on automaticity and control in social cognition.

Other Features of Implicit Impressions

Years of research on STIs have taught us a great deal about implicit impressions, because STIs are a kind of implicit impression. So a brief review of more recent research on STIs is in order here, because it adds to our understanding of implicit impressions.

Implicit impressions should arise not only from printed verbal descriptions of behavior, but also from observing behavior. Skowronski et al. (1998, Study 4) demonstrated STT with videotaped rather than printed stimuli. But the videotaped communicators verbally described behaviors, so the trait-implying behaviors were not enacted. More recently, Fiedler and Schenck (2001) reported evidence for STI from single-frame silhouettes of action. This is an important finding because it provides the first direct evidence that observed behaviors can prompt STI and, by implication, implicit impressions.

Implicit impressions include more than trait inferences. For example, Winter et al. (1985) and Uleman and Moskowitz (1994) showed that "gist cues" (that summarize the action without implying traits) are just as effective as trait cues in the cued recall STI paradigm. That is, people spontaneously encode other aspects of behavior, in addition to their trait implications. Uleman and Moskowitz found the effectiveness of trait cues and gist cues was positively correlated across participants, suggesting that drawing these implications are not mutually exclusive, and that those who infer traits also infer gists. Fiedler and Schenck (2001, Study 2) used the linguistic category model to further explore these processes. They asked participants to verify "whether the indicated behavior could be seen in the preceding picture" (p. 1541). These behavior descriptions were either direct action verbs (DAVs, e.g., *to feed, to hit*), interpretive action verbs (IAVs, e.g., *to nourish, to chastise*), or nontrait adjectives (ADJs, e.g., *sacrificial, severe*). IAVs (which specify goals) were verified most quickly, suggesting that goals are spontaneously inferred most readily. In addition, subsequent trait identifications (e.g., *caring, merciless*, in a task that gradually revealed perceptually degraded trait terms) were quickest when they were preceded by DAVs, suggesting that DAV verification mediates STIs more than the other linguistic categories. All of this indicates that STIs are not the only spontaneous inferences prompted by descriptions or observations of behavior. Future research should examine the breadth and abstractness of these inferences and how they contribute to the implicit impressions that people form.

Implicit impressions are affected by priming, and can act as primes themselves. When behaviors have ambiguous trait implications, prior activations of trait concepts affect STIs. Newman and Uleman (1990) had participants read such sentences for a subsequent memory test. For example, "Molly would not take 'No' for an answer" can imply that she is either persistent (+) or stubborn (–). Priming with synonyms of these traits (as well as memory for the primes) affected which trait cues were more effective for cued recall. Ferguson and Bargh (2001) found that affective priming, in which the primes have no semantic relationship to the traits or behaviors, produces assimilative STIs. They used the same behaviors and trait cues as Newman and Uleman, but their primes consisted of positively and negatively valenced nouns, such as *sunshine* and *disease*. Finally, implicit impressions can be primes. Moskowitz and Roman (1992) showed this, as did Stapel, Koomen, and van der Pligt (1996). Stapel et al. demonstrated that STIs, as primes, can produce either assimilation or contrast effects, depending on whether the STIs refer to the abstract trait concepts (assimilation) or to particular actors (contrast).

Errors and Biases in Implicit Impressions

At least three decades of research have documented the errors and biases that affect intentional impressions (e.g., Gilbert, 1998), and there is no reason to believe that implicit impressions are immune from these errors and biases. But there may be some errors that are unique to implicit impressions.

Spontaneous Trait Transference

Carlston et al. (1995, Study 4) and Skowronski et al. (1998) have identified one error that implicit impressions can produce: STT. As previously described, STT occurs when particularly vivid communicators (pictured in photos or videotape) describe an absent (not pictured) person in trait-implying terms. Under such circumstances, the descriptions' trait implications are transferred to or associated with the communicator. Carlston et al. (1995) found that

STT did not occur in the savings paradigm when participants deliberately formed impressions of the communicator or target; it only occurred under familiarization (spontaneous) instructions.

However, Skowronski et al. (1998) uncovered a more complex picture. They found (in Study 1) comparable trait transference under familiarization instructions and instructions to avoid STT by forming intentional impressions, when savings were measured after a brief delay. However, after a 2-day delay, trait transfer was evident only under familiarization instructions, but not among participants forming intentional impressions. In Study 4, with trait ratings rather than savings the dependent variable, they found that STT was unaffected by familiarization versus intentional impression formation instructions.

These findings suggest that trait transference—misattributing implied traits to the wrong person—is more likely under spontaneous than intentional inference conditions. They also suggest that STTs have longer-lasting effects than intentional inferences under otherwise comparable conditions. Finally, it is important to remember the boundary condition for STT suggested above. STT may only occur when there is no visual representation (e.g., a photo) of the actor.

Repetition and Apparent Truth

If we hear something false presented often enough, are we more likely to believe it? There is good evidence that we are (Begg, Anas, & Farinacci, 1992; Hasher, Goldstein, & Toppino, 1977), whether these things are presented as facts or opinions (Arkes, Hackett, & Boehm, 1989) or are presented in a visual or an auditory mode (Bacon, 1979), even when we are told that some items are repeated (Bacon, 1979). This frequency-validity effect can persist for weeks (Bacon, 1979; Hasher et al., 1977). Similarly, making the same decision repeatedly increases confidence in that decision (Einhorn & Hogarth, 1978). Expressing the same attitude repeatedly increases its accessibility—one of the components of attitude strength—and hence increases our confidence in it and the likelihood that we will act on it (Fazio, 1995).

One basis for these effects is that explicit thoughts or events that are repeated are also more familiar, and a familiarity-validity heuristic tells us (arguably with some basis in reality) that what is familiar is more likely to be true. However, Whittlesea (1993) has shown that more frequent prior exposure is not the only basis for greater feelings of familiarity, and that other sources of perceptual or conceptual fluency can affect perceived familiarity, often without participants' awareness. Thus, although prior frequency of exposure can be a reliable guide to truth value, using perceived familiarity to judge truth value can also lead to systematic errors. In the domain of impression formation, Gill, Swann, and Silvera (1998) examined the "representational richness" of people's impressions of others, as one basis for people's widely documented overconfidence in impressions. They showed that representational richness (the extensiveness and integration of person information) is one determinant of judgment fluency, and that judgment fluency increases confidence. Furthermore, other events unrelated to richness (e.g., priming in Study 3) can affect confidence, presumably by affecting judgment fluency.

All of this research (and more) that shows repeated exposure increasing confidence and judged validity uses repetitions of explicit information. But it raises the interesting possibility that the same effects might occur with implicit information. Imagine someone forming an implicit impression of a person (face) on one exposure to a face-behavior pair, and then seeing that face repeatedly without any trait-implying behavior. If the face has become associated with the implicit impression, mere repetition of the face without any explicit repetition of the behavior or its implications should produce greater confidence in trait ratings of the person, in much the same way that repeated exposure to an attitude object increases the accessibility of the attitude toward it. Thus, simple repeated exposure to others about whom we really know very little should lead to increasing confidence that we know them well. Research is needed to test this basic prediction. If it were supported, one could then go on to investigate what conditions promote or impede people's control of this effect, once they are informed of it. Such research would be most informative if it used the PDP adaptation outlined above.

Implicit Impressions, Stereotypes, and In-Groups and Out-Groups

Implicit impressions are about individuals; implicit stereotypes are about groups. Now that we know how to create implicit impressions, it should be possible to create implicit stereotypes—about novel groups with novel content—rather than relying exclusively on existing stereotypes to discover how stereotypes are acquired, change, and function. Crawford, Sherman, and Hamilton (2002) have laid a solid foundation for such research with three impressive studies of implicit stereotype formation, using STT. Participants familiarized themselves with behaviors paired with photos of people from two groups. Results showed more STT (savings in relearning) between members of high-entitativity (e.g., high similarity or coherence) groups than between members of low-entitativity groups or unrelated individuals. In addition, reading times in Study 3 provided evidence of online formation of stereotypes of the high- but not the low-entitativity group. Thus these results demonstrate the development and operation of implicit stereotypes of groups.

At least four other interesting stereotypes and in-group/out-group phenomena are associated with implicit impressions. First, descriptions of actors with ethnic names, who perform behaviors that imply stereotype-consistent traits, spontaneously activate those traits more readily than either the names or behaviors. Howard (2000, Experiments 1 and 2) used a lexical decision task in a series of studies of STIs among Euro-American undergraduates. Participants read sentences and responded to a lexical decision probe immediately afterward. Some of the behaviors implied traits consistent with stereotypes of African Americans (e.g., athletic) or Asian Americans (e.g., shy), and some implied traits consistent with stereotypes of Euro-Americans (e.g., analytical). Some of the actors had typical African American names (e.g., Jamal), while others had typical Asian American or Euro-American names. Lexical decisions for relevant traits were fastest when the actor's ethnicity was consistent with the stereotype-implying behavior. There was no evidence that mismatched names or behaviors activated stereotype traits.

These studies suggest two conditions in which stereotype activation may be less inevitable than many think (e.g., Bargh, 1999). If the eliciting stimulus is weak (e.g., ethnic names rather than faces), spontaneous stereotype activation might not occur. And if it is accompanied by inconsistent information, spontaneous stereotype activation might be blocked. Both of these possibilities need to be examined by further research.

A second phenomenon was uncovered by Todorov, Gonzalez, Uleman, and Thaden (2004). Mismatches between actors and behaviors in terms of gender stereotypes seemed to inhibit implicit impression formation. Using the false recognition paradigm described above, they looked at false recognition of implied traits (in photo-trait pairs) as a function of the trait's gender stereotype and the actor's gender. Relative to pairs with randomly chosen actors, there was higher false recognition of implied traits when they were paired with the actual actor than otherwise, replicating the basic finding described above. But within this result, the false recognition effect was smaller for gender-stereotyped (vs. neutral) traits when the actor was of the other gender. It is not clear from these results whether the mismatch between actors' and traits' genders led to weaker trait activation, weakened actor-trait binding, affected recognition judgments directly through the plausibility of the pairs, or all three. Perhaps the most interesting possibility is that mismatched actors and behaviors prompted spontaneous situation inferences rather than trait inferences. But more research is needed to clarify this phenomenon, the conditions under which it occurs, and the processes that underlie it.

Banaji, Hardin, and Rothman (1993) demonstrated implicit gender stereotyping with a very different paradigm. They showed that the activation of a gender-stereotyped trait (dependence or aggression) primed participants' intentional impressions, formed from ambiguous behaviors of Donald or

Donna, but only when the genders of trait and actor matched. They called this effect

> a previously undocumented effect of implicit stereotyping which . . . we have labeled social category applicability. Social category markers such as race, gender, age, social class, and disability may function like magnetic fields to attract and repel previously encountered stereotyped information['s impact] on judgment (a) when such information is extraneous to the judgment, and (b) without awareness that the stereotyped information is a source of influence on judgment. (p. 278)

The findings by Todorov et al. (2004) provide another instance of social category applicability and extend its generality to the formation of implicit impressions.

Third, there is good evidence that characteristics of actors, including their social group memberships, influence the kinds of spontaneous inferences that occur. Dunning and Sherman (1997, Study 3) showed this with occupational stereotypes. Participants read sentences with ambiguous trait-implying behaviors, and rated how "readable" they were. Actor occupations were chosen that would disambiguate the behaviors in particular ways. Participants were then tested on their recognition memory for the sentences, with critical foils containing unambiguous variants of the sentences. False alarms were higher for sentence variants that were stereotype consistent than stereotype inconsistent. That is, stereotypes seemed to disambiguate the behaviors' meanings. These disambiguated meanings were stored in long-term memory and later led to accepting the unambiguous foils. Somewhat similarly, Delmas (1992; described in Uleman et al., 1996, p. 246) reported that actors' occupations facilitated occupational stereotype-related STIs, as seen in cued recall for the trait-implying sentences.

These studies, along with our speculations about the familiarity-validity heuristic described above, raise an interesting possible mechanism for the persistence of stereotypes. Once a stereotype is established, it can disambiguate ambiguous behaviors in a way that is consistent with the stereotype, serving to confirm it for particular individuals, as in Dunning and Sherman (1997). Then the mere repetition of that individual's face, with which the stereotype trait has become implicitly associated, should increase the perceived validity of a stereotyped perception of that person. All of this should occur without any explicit inference about the person or any awareness of the process. Of course, further research is needed to test this speculation directly.

The studies described above all concern the ways that particular stereotypes can affect implicit impressions of individuals, conditions that affect activation and/or binding of stereotype traits to actors. One other study concerns not particular stereotypes per se, but in-group/out-group effects. It illustrates an additional way that social group membership may affect implicit impressions. Otten and Moskowitz (2000) examined whether membership in minimal groups would bias STIs. Participants read trait-implying sentences that described either in-group or out-group members—with membership established through a standard minimal group manipulation. Sentences were read in a recognition probe reaction time paradigm, in which participants had to judge whether a probe word appearing after each sentence had been explicitly present in the sentence. When the sentences implied the trait and described in-group members and the trait was positive, response times were longer. (In this paradigm, longer times to correctly decide that the implied trait had not been explicit in the sentence are evidence that the trait was inferred.) That is, in-group favoritism (but not out-group derogation) occurred, as evidenced by this spontaneous facilitation of positive in-group trait inferences. It is remarkable that this effect emerged without any explicit comparisons of in-group and out-group, on a measure that virtually assured participants' lack of awareness of what they were responding to and how.

So there is good research on the formation of implicit stereotypes and evidence that stereotypes and group membership affect implicit impressions in a variety of ways consistent with other research. More interestingly, these studies suggest that some of the methods used to study implicit impressions are also useful for increasing our understanding of the processes behind stereotyping and in-group/out-group phenomena.

Conclusion

The idea that we have implicit impressions of others—knowledge that we do not or cannot make explict, which nonetheless affects how we view and interact with others—is not new. It is captured in everyday speech about interpersonal "chemistry," "vibes," and intuition. Some of these intuitions come from social-cognitive transference, when the person resembles a significant other and, without realizing it, we assimilate the new person to the old one (e.g., chapter 16). And some of these intuitions come from past encounters with and inferences about that very person, but which we do not or cannot recall. These are the intuitions that this chapter is about.

STIs are implicit impressions because they are formed without intentions or awareness. There is now good evidence that they are inferences about people, not merely about behaviors. Carlston and Skowronski (1994; Carlston et al., 1995) showed this with their savings-in-relearning paradigm, and Todorov and Uleman (2002, 2003) showed it with their false recognition paradigm. Although STIs are occasionally associated with the "wrong" person—someone such as a communicator telling about the actor, as in Skowronski et al.'s (1998) STT—evidence from Todorov and Uleman (in press) suggests that this is relatively rare. STT probably requires a much more vivid presentation of the communicator than the actor, such as a photo of the communicator but none of the actor.

The STT research provides the first rigorous demonstrations that incidental encounters with others leave impressions that persist long after the details of the encounter have faded from memory. (Hastie and Park's, 1986, now-classic distinction between online and memory-based impressions refers exclusively to intentionally formed impressions.) Participants in these studies spontaneously formed impressions from the behaviors they read about, and these impressions affected later behavior (relearning), even when memory for the behaviors was gone (Carlston & Skowronski, 1994; Carlston et al., 1995). Although Skowronski et al. (1998) emphasized that these implicit impressions were about the wrong person, the important points here are that they were formed without awareness (spontaneously), and they presumably became the sole basis for subsequent trait ratings because (on the evidence of Carlston et al.) the behaviors had been forgotten.

All of this suggests that whenever people encounter others they have seen before, their responses and reactions depend both on whatever they remember and on implicit impressions. Our adaptation of Jacoby's (1991) PDP provided a direct test and confirmed this suggestion. Right after an encounter, trait ratings of actors were based on both explicitly remembered (controlled) and implied (automatic) impressions. Two days later, only implicit impressions had any effect.

The spontaneity of STIs is a description of encoding processes: without intention or awareness. The implicitness of implicit impressions is a description of retrieval limitations: without explicit reference or memory. Presumably, implicit impressions can arise under many conditions. What makes them implicit is their memorial status at the moment. In PDP terms, they are the uncontrollable (automatic) effects of past encounters that affect current performance.

This formulation and set of paradigms suggest many questions for future research. What kinds of responses are particularly sensitive or insensitive to the impact of implicit impressions? What encoding and/or retrieval conditions affect this impact? The same questions can be, and have been, asked about explicit impressions (e.g., Wyer & Srull, 1989), but we cannot assume the answers are the same. In fact, the PDP model assumes A and C processes operate independently of each other. So reducing the impact of controlled processes need not increase the impact of implicit impressions.

More substantively, this formulation suggests directions for future research not only on implicit impressions, but also on STT, the bases for people's feelings that they know someone very well, stereotypes, in-group/out-group phenomena, and more.

Acknowledgments This research was conducted while Steven L. Blader was supported by the National Institute of Mental Health Grant T32-MH19890. The authors wish to thank Larry Jacoby and John Skowronski for their helpful comments on an earlier draft. We also thank Bianca Acevedo, Craig Herman, Lauren Pagano, Tarika Singh, Emily Thaden, and Kevin Young for their assistance in conducting some of the studies described here.

Notes

1. Part of the advantage of this false recognition measure over the cued recall measure used in prior research to detect actor-trait links may lie in the fact that false recognition is affected by both trait → actor links and actor → trait links (which also operate in savings in relearning). Prior research with trait-cued recall of actors tapped only the trait → actor links. It may be that actor → trait links are even stronger and formed more readily.

2. We did not test to see whether there was an interaction between delay and process type because it is not clear that the two process types are estimated on comparable scales.

References

Andersen, S. M., & Berenson, K. R. (2001). Perceiving, feeling, and wanting: Experiencing prior relationships in present-day interpersonal relations. In J. P. Forgas & K. D. Williams (Eds.), *The social mind: Cognitive and motivational aspects of interpersonal behavior* (pp. 231–256). New York: Cambridge University Press.

Anderson, C. A., Krull, D. S., & Weiner, B. (1996). Explanations: Processes and consequences. In E. T. Higgins & A. W. Kruglanski (Eds.), *Social psychology: Handbook of basic principles* (pp. 271–296). New York: Guilford.

Arkes, H. R., Hackett, C., & Boehm, L. (1989). The generality of the relation between familiarity and judged validity. *Journal of Behavioral Decision Making, 2,* 81–94.

Bacon, F. T. (1979). Credibility of repeated statements: Memory for trivia. *Journal of Experimental Psychology: Human Learning and Memory, 5,* 241–252.

Banaji, M. R., Hardin, C., & Rothman, A. J. (1993). Implicit stereotyping in person judgment. *Journal of Personality and Social Psychology, 65,* 272–281.

Bargh, J. A. (1994). The four horsemen of automaticity: Awareness, intention, efficiency, and control in social cognition. In R. S. Wyer, Jr., & T. K. Srull (Eds.), *Handbook of social cognition: Vol. 1. Basic processes* (pp. 1–40). Hillsdale, NJ: Erlbaum.

Bargh, J. A. (1999). The cognitive monster: The case against the controllability of automatic stereotype effects. In S. Chaiken & Y. Trope (Eds.), *Dual-process theories in social psychology* (pp. 361–382). New York: Guilford.

Bargh, J. A., & Ferguson, M. J. (2000). Beyond behaviorism: On the automaticity of higher mental processes. *Psychological Bulletin, 126,* 925–945.

Begg, I. M., Anas, A., & Farinacci, S. (1992). Dissociation of process in belief: Source recollection, statement familiarity, and the illusion of truth. *Journal of Experimental Psychology: General, 121,* 446–458.

Berk, M. S., & Andersen, S. M. (2000). The impact of past relationships on interpersonal behavior: Behavioral confirmation in the social-cognitive process of transference. *Journal of Personality and Social Psychology, 79*, 546–562.

Carlston, D. E., & Skowronski, J. J. (1994). Saving in the relearning of trait information as evidence for spontaneous inference generation. *Journal of Personality and Social Psychology, 66*, 840–856.

Carlston, D. E., Skowronski, J. J., & Sparks, C. (1995). Savings in relearning: II. On the formation of behavior-based trait associations and inferences. *Journal of Personality and Social Psychology, 69*, 420–436.

Chen, S., & Andersen, S. M. (1999). Relationships from the past in the present: Significant-other representations and transference in interpersonal life. In M. P. Zanna (Ed.), *Advances in experimental social psychology* (Vol. 31, pp. 123–190). San Diego, CA: Academic Press.

Claparède, E. (1951). Recognition and "me-ness." In D. Rapaport (Ed. & Trans.), *Organization and pathology of thought* (pp. 58–75). New York: Columbia University Press. (Original work published 1911)

Crawford, M. T., Sherman, S. J., & Hamilton, D. L. (2002). Perceived entitativity, stereotype formation, and the interchangeability of group members. *Journal of Personality and Social Psychology, 83*, 1076–1094.

Delmas, F. (1992, July). *Impact of target's category membership on spontaneous trait inference.* Poster presented at the XXV International Congress of Psychology, Brussels, Belgium.

Dunning, D., & Sherman, D. A. (1997). Stereotypes and tacit inference. *Journal of Personality and Social Psychology, 73*, 459–471.

Einhorn, H. J., & Hogarth, R. M. (1978). Confidence in judgment: Persistence of the illusion of validity. *Psychological Review, 85*, 395–416.

Fazio, R. H. (1986). How do attitudes guide behavior? In R. M. Sorrentino & E. T. Higgins (Eds.), *Handbook of motivation and cognition: Foundations of social behavior* (Vol. 1, pp. 204–243). New York: Guilford.

Fazio, R. H. (1995). Attitudes as object-evaluation associations: Determinants, consequences, and correlates of attitude accessibility. In R. E. Petty & J. A. Krosnick (Eds.), *Attitude strength: Antecedents and consequences* (pp. 247–282). Mahwah, NJ: Erlbaum.

Ferguson, M. J., & Bargh, J. A. (2001). *Beyond response time: Consequences of automatic evaluative processes for the interpretation of subsequent stimuli.* Manuscript under review, New York University.

Festinger, L., & Carlsmith, J. M. (1959). Cognitive consequences of forced compliance. *Journal of Abnormal and Social Psychology, 58*, 203–210.

Fiedler, K., & Schenck, W. (2001). Spontaneous inferences from pictorially presented behaviors. *Personality and Social Psychology Bulletin, 27*, 1533–1546.

Gilbert, D. T. (1998). Ordinary personology. In D. T. Gilbert, S. T. Fiske, & G. Lindzey (Eds.), *The handbook of social psychology* (Vol. 2, 4th ed., pp. 89–150). Boston: McGraw-Hill.

Gill, M. J., Swann, W. B., Jr., & Silvera, D. H. (1998). On the genesis of confidence. *Journal of Personality and Social Psychology, 75*, 1101–1114.

Glassman, N. S., & Andersen, S. M. (1999). Activating transference without consciousness: Using significant-other representations to go beyond what is subliminally given. *Journal of Personality and Social Psychology, 77*, 1146–1162.

Greenwald, A. G., & Banaji, M. (1995). Implicit social cognition: Attitudes, self-esteem, and stereotypes. *Psychological Review, 102*, 4–27.

Greenwald, A. G., & Farnham, S. D. (2000). Using the Implicit Association Test to measure self-esteem and self-concept. *Journal of Personality and Social Psychology, 79*, 1022–1038.

Greenwald, A. G., McGhee, D. E., & Schwartz, J. L. K. (1998). Measuring individual differences in implicit cognition: The implicit association test. *Journal of Personality and Social Psychology, 74*, 1464–1480.

Hasher, L., Goldenstein, D., & Toppino, T. (1977). Frequency and the conference of referential validity. *Journal of Verbal Learning and Verbal Behavior, 16*, 107–112.

Hassin, R., & Trope, Y. (2000). Facing faces: Studies on the cognitive aspects of physiognomy. *Journal of Personality and Social Psychology, 78*, 837–852.

Hastie, R., & Park, B. (1986). The relationship between memory and judgment depends on whether the judgment task is memory-based or on-line. *Psychological Review, 93*, 258–268.

Howard, P. (2000). *Racial knowledge effects on minorities: How stereotypic knowledge biases African-Americans' inferences.* Unpublished doctoral dissertation, New York University.

Jacoby, L. L. (1991). A process dissociation framework: Separating automatic from intentional uses of memory. *Journal of Memory and Language, 30*, 513–541.

Jacoby, L. L., Toth, J. P., & Yonelinas, A. P. (1993). Separating conscious and unconscious influences of memory: Attention, awareness, and control. *Journal of Experimental Psychology: General, 122*, 139–154.

Jacoby, L. L., Yonelinas, A. P., & Jennings, J. M. (1997). The relation between conscious and unconscious (automatic) influences: A declaration of independence. In J. D. Cohen & J. W. Schooler (Eds.), *Scientific approaches to consciousness* (pp. 13–47). Mahwah, NJ: Erlbaum.

Lewicki, P. (1985). Nonconscious biasing effects of single instances on subsequent judgments. *Journal of Personality and Social Psychology, 48*, 563–574.

Lewicki, P. (1986). Processing information about covariations that cannot be articulated. *Journal of Experimental Psychology: Learning, Memory, and Cognition, 12*, 135–146.

Manis, M., Cornell, S. D., & Moore, J. C. (1974). Transmission of attitude-relevant information through a communication chain. *Journal of Personality and Social Psychology, 30*, 81–94.

Moskowitz, G. B., & Roman, R. J. (1992). Spontaneous trait inferences as self-generated primes: Implications for conscious social judgment. *Journal of Personality and Social Psychology, 62*, 728–738.

Newman, L. S., & Uleman, J. S. (1990). Assimilation and contrast effects in spontaneous trait inferences. *Personality and Social Psychology Bulletin, 16*, 224–240.

Otten, S., & Moskowitz, G. B. (2000). Evidence for implicit evaluative in-group bias: Affect-biased spontaneous trait inference in a minimal group paradigm. *Journal of Experimental Social Psychology, 36*, 77–89.

Schachter, D. L. (1987). Implicit memory: History and current status. *Journal of Experimental Psychology: Learning, Memory, and Cognition, 13*, 501–518.

Schachter, D. L., & Curran, T. (2000). Memory without remembering and remembering without memory: Implicit and false memories. In M. S. Gazzaniga (Ed.), *The new cognitive neurosciences* (2nd edition, pp. 829–840). Cambridge, MA: MIT Press.

Skowronski, J. J., Carlston, D. E., Mae, L., & Crawford, M. T. (1998). Spontaneous trait transference: Communicators take on the qualities they describe in others. *Journal of Personality and Social Psychology, 74,* 837–848.

Stapel, D. A., Koomen, W., & van der Pligt, J. (1996). The referents of trait inferences: The impact of trait concepts versus actor-trait links on subsequent judgments. *Journal of Personality and Social Psychology, 70,* 437–450.

Todorov, A., & Uleman, J. S. (2002). Spontaneous trait inferences are bound to actors' faces: Evidence from a false recognition paradigm. *Journal of Personality and Social Psychology, 83,* 1051–1065.

Todorov, A., & Uleman, J. S. (2003). The automaticity of binding spontaneous trait inferences to actors' faces. *Journal of Experimental Social Psychology, 39,* 549–562.

Todorov, A., & Uleman, J. S. (in press). The person reference process in spontaneous trait inferences. *Journal of Personality and Social Psychology.*

Todorov, A., Gonzalez, C., Uleman, J. S., & Thaden, E. P. (2004). *A dissociation between spontaneous and intentional stereotyped trait inferences.* Unpublished manuscript, New York University.

Uleman, J. S., & Blader, S. (2001). *A process dissociation analysis of using spontaneous trait inferences.* Unpublished data, New York University.

Uleman, J. S., & Moskowitz, G. B. (1994). Unintended effects of goals on unintended inferences. *Journal of Personality and Social Psychology, 66,* 490–501.

Uleman, J. S., Newman, L. S., & Moskowitz, G. B. (1996). People as flexible interpreters: Evidence and issues from spontaneous trait inference. In M. P. Zanna (Ed.), *Advances in experimental social psychology* (Vol. 28, pp. 211–279). San Diego, CA: Academic Press.

Wegener, D. T., & Petty, R. E. (1997). The flexible correction model: The role of naïve theories of bias in bias correction. In M. P. Zanna (Ed.), *Advances in experimental social psychology* (Vol. 29, pp. 141–208). Mahwah, NJ: Erlbaum.

Wegner, D. M., & Bargh, J. A. (1998). Control and automaticity in social life. In D. T. Gilbert, S. T. Fiske, & G. Lindzey (Eds.), *The handbook of social psychology* (Vol. 1, 4th ed., pp. 446–496). Boston: McGraw-Hill.

Wegner, D. M., & Pennebaker, J. W. (Eds.). (1993). *Handbook of mental control.* Englewood Cliffs, NJ: Prentice Hall.

Whittlesea, B. W. A. (1993). Illusions of familiarity. *Journal of Experimental Psychology: Learning, Memory, and Cognition, 19,* 1235–1253.

Winter, L., & Uleman, J. S. (1984). When are social judgments made? Evidence for the spontaneousness of trait inferences. *Journal of Personality and Social Psychology, 47,* 237–252.

Winter, L., Uleman, J. S., & Cunniff, C. (1985). How automatic are social judgments? *Journal of Personality and Social Psychology, 49,* 904–917.

Wyer, R. S., Budesheim, T. L., & Lambert, A. J. (1990). Cognitive representation of conversations about persons. *Journal of Personality and Social Psychology, 58,* 218–238.

Wyer, R. S., Budesheim, T., L., Lambert, A. J., & Swan, S. (1994). Person memory and judgment: Pragmatic influences on impressions formed in a social context. *Journal of Personality and Social Psychology, 66,* 254–267.

Wyer, R. S., Jr., & Srull, T. K. (1989). *Memory and cognition in its social context.* Hillsdale, NJ: Erlbaum.

15

Attitudes as Accessibility Bias: Dissociating Automatic and Controlled Processes

B. Keith Payne, Larry L. Jacoby, and Alan J. Lambert

In February 1999, four New York Police Department officers ordered West African immigrant Amadou Diallo to freeze as he stood in his apartment's darkened alcove. Diallo raised his wallet in the air, and 41 bullets later, he was dead. Somewhere between the time Diallo pulled out his wallet and the first officer drew his gun, one of the officers made a judgment that their lives were in danger. The incident caused local protests and national controversy, as the public and the courts debated whether that judgment depended on the fact that Amadou Diallo was Black.

We will not speculate on what actually took place in the Diallo case—a question that is unlikely ever to be answered definitively. But the incident provides a compelling way to frame some broader psychological questions we have been studying. For example, can racial prejudice influence the decisions people make in such high-pressure situations? If so, what is the mechanism by which this influence occurs?

We highlight an important distinction that has been made in social cognition research between automatic or implicit attitudes and more controlled, explicit processes as distinct influences on judgments. We describe an experiment in this tradition in which we used separate direct and indirect tests to measure how explicit and implicit attitudes contribute to a social judgment.

Next, we describe a process dissociation approach (Jacoby, 1991) that treats implicit attitudes as a source of "guessing" or "accessibility bias." Our emphasis on accessibility effects builds on the "New Look" movement in perception (e.g., Bruner, 1957; Greenwald 1992, along with accompanying commentaries). The New Look movement held that perception is strongly influenced by expectancies, values, attitudes, and needs. According to Bruner, perception involves categorization, as do other cognitive activities, and thus reflects differences in the accessibility of categories. As we discuss, subsequent research questioned whether such accessibility effects reflect an influence on people's ability to discriminate real-world, objective differences or, instead, have their effect through an influence on bias, reflected by people's guesses.

In the Diallo case, the question is whether prejudice resulted in a lessened ability to discriminate between the visual features of a gun versus a wallet or, alternatively, had its effect through an automatic influence on guessing. By the latter alternative, prejudice did not change "true" perception but, rather, because of an inability to distinguish between a gun and a wallet, police relied on their "guess," which may have been, perhaps unconsciously, influenced by Diallo's race. In this chapter, we separately measure the contributions of controlled and automatic processes within a task (e.g., judging whether a gun was present) and treat a measure of accessibility bias as reflecting an automatic, implicit attitude. Note that the contrast we draw between controlled and automatic uses of information is not between explicit versus implicit attitudes. Rather, we identify cognitive control with the ability to respond in a manner consistent with a goal (e.g., task instructions) based on appropriate information in the task at hand (e.g., distinguishing between a gun and a wallet). We end by showing the generality of our approach as a means of analyzing a wide range of accessibility effects of the sort that have been prominent in social psychology.

Automatic and Controlled Processes in Social Cognition

One of the important findings to emerge from the contemporary social cognition literature is that the use of category-based knowledge can be guided by both automatic and controlled processes (e.g., Devine, 1989). Noticing a person's race, for example, has the potential to trigger both a spontaneous stereotype and efforts to control that stereotype (e.g., Dunton & Fazio, 1997). In their efforts to study how automatic and controlled processes guide behavior, researchers have developed several innovative techniques to isolate the two types of processes. One popular approach in recent social cognition research identifies automatic processes with performance on indirect tests, and controlled processes with performance on direct tests.

Implicit attitude studies build on implicit memory studies, in which indirect tests have been used to measure the effects of past experience in the absence of conscious memory for an event (e.g., Jacoby & Dallas, 1981; Roediger & McDermott, 1993). Memory researchers have used tasks such as word fragment and stem completion, lexical decision, and other indirect tests as measures of automatic memory influences. Direct tests, such as recall and recognition, are used to assess explicit memory.

Evidence to support the distinction between implicit (automatic) and controlled (explicit) uses of memory has been gained by showing dissociations between performances on the two types of test. As an example, amnesiacs show striking memory dissociations. Because of neurological damage, these patients show severe deficits on direct memory tests and may claim no conscious memory for material they have studied. However, on indirect tests such as word stem completions, amnesiac patients perform very similar to the neurologically healthy (see Shimamura, 1986). Similar dissociations between direct and indirect test performance have been shown by people with normally functioning memory (for a review, see Roediger & McDermott, 1993). Finding situations in which direct and indirect test performance can be dissociated provides evidence that processes underlying the two types of test are distinct.

Social psychologists have used indirect methods including word completions (Gilbert & Hixon, 1991), priming tasks (Devine, 1989; Fazio, Jackson, Dunton, & Williams, 1995), and implicit association tasks (Greenwald, McGhee, & Schwartz, 1998) to measure automatic influences of stereotypes and attitudes (see Bargh & Chartrand, 2000). Self-report scales have been used to measure explicit attitudes. Correlational studies have sometimes shown that direct test performance is dissociated from (uncorrelated with) indirect test performance (e.g., Devine, 1989; Fazio et al., 1995). However, other studies have shown that direct and indirect measures of stereotypes or attitudes covary with one another (Lepore & Brown, 1997; Wittenbrink, Judd, & Park, 1997). In the next section, we describe an experiment in which we used separate tasks to measure explicit and implicit attitudes. We show that even when they are uncorrelated with each other, implicit and explicit attitudes can have independent roles in predicting prejudiced responses to stereotyped people.

Identifying Processes With Tasks

The contrasting of direct and indirect measures has led to important theoretical advances in models of stereotyping and prejudice. Social cognition researchers have focused in part on developing indirect tests as measures of individual differences in automatic processing. In this way, automatic and controlled processes are identified with different tasks, which relate to different behaviors. The question addressed by this approach is whether, and under what conditions, each kind of process is active in guiding people's overt responses. A pioneering study by Fazio and colleagues (1995) showed that explicit racial attitudes—as measured by a traditional attitude scale—predicted blatantly race-related judgments such as satisfaction with the verdict in the case of Rodney King. This judgment was considered easily controllable and clearly related to race. Implicit racial attitudes, as measured by an indirect priming task, did not correlate with opinions about the Rodney King verdict. However, indirect test performance predicted subtler behavior, such as participants' friendliness during an interaction with an African American experimenter (for a similar conceptual and methodological approach, see Dovidio, Kawakami, Johnson, Johnson, & Howard, 1997).

However, it would be a mistake to generalize from these unambiguous examples to all social behaviors. Both automatic and controlled processes simultaneously contribute to most social behaviors, although it may be easier to detect one in some situations than others (see also Wilson, Lindsey, & Schooler, 2000). A study in our laboratory provides a case in point (Lambert, Payne, Ramsey, & Shaffer, in press). In this research, we investigated the joint contribution of implicit and explicit racial attitudes to impressions of a single individual. Participants' explicit racial attitudes were assessed using a number of self-report measures (e.g., the Modern Racism Scale [MRS]; McConahay, Hardee, & Batts, 1981). Implicit attitudes were measured using a lexical decision task as an indirect measure. The direct and indirect measures were used to predict participants' subsequent judgments of the target person.

In the indirect measure, participants decided whether various letter strings were words after being primed (200 ms duration) with either the words *Whites* or *Blacks* or a row of Xs used as a control prime. The words in this study included personality adjectives that varied in whether they were favorable and whether they were related to the Black or White stereotype. The interval between primes and target words (stimulus onset asynchrony, SOA) in this task was 200 ms, well within the range typically used to prevent participants from intentional control of their responses (cf. Fazio et al., 1995; Neely, 1977). As the dependent variable, participants read a short story about a character whose behaviors were ambiguous. They could be interpreted as high or low in hostility and in intelligence. Information participants received was identical except for the race of the target person (Black or White). Although participants' evaluations were subject to strategic control, the race of the target was manipulated subtly, in the context of other demographic information. As a result, there was no clear norm for the appropriate or socially desirable response.

Results showed that, while the indirect (lexical decision performance) and direct (MRS) attitude measures were uncorrelated with one another, each measure independently predicted impressions of the Black target. In other words, participants' overall impressions of the Black target appeared to be driven by two distinct types of attitudes: one measured by the indirect test and the other by the direct test. Neither measure predicted judgments of the White target. These data are provocative in that they suggest a somewhat different view of explicit versus implicit measures compared to that offered by Fazio et al. (1995) and Dovidio et al. (1997). That research suggests that explicit and implicit tasks should be predictive of different classes of behaviors. In contrast, our findings suggest that any given judgment (e.g., the extent to which a Black person is perceived to be intelligent) can be influenced by both explicit and implicit processes.

However, the contrasting of direct and indirect measures has limitations. When a dissociation between direct and indirect tests is found, questions can arise about whether the lack of a relationship reflects differences in the processes they are intended to measure, or low reliability in the indirect measure (Cunningham, Preacher, & Banaji, 2001; Kawakami & Dovidio, 2001). Second, neither indirect nor direct tests are likely to represent a process-pure measure. On one hand, controlled processes may "contaminate" performance on indirect tests, so that people's strategies can distort the measurement of the memories, attitudes, or stereotypes that researchers are trying to capture. For example, a word completion task may require participants to complete a stem with whatever first comes to mind. If nothing springs to mind, a participant may intentionally search for a word to use from memory. On the other hand, automatic processes may bias responses to self-report measures (Jacoby, 1991). If participants do not know how to respond to a question, they may answer with whatever comes to mind most readily, which can reflect their implicit attitude.

Finally, using different tests to measure separate processes leaves the underlying process confounded with the properties of the test used to measure it. For example, if the results of a self-report measure are sensitive to a manipulation while the results of a word completion task are not, does that dissociation reflect a difference in explicit versus implicit processes, or does it reflect a difference in the sensitivity of the measures?

Attitudes as Accessibility Bias

A complementary approach to teasing apart automatic and controlled processes is to arrange experimental conditions such that the contributions of the two types of processes can be estimated within the same task. Our approach does this by measuring automaticity as a systematic bias in the way people respond. We treat bias or guessing as reflecting attitudes. To illustrate how guessing patterns can be informative about implicit processes, consider the following example of an early indirect attitude test.

Hammond (1948): Guessing as a Measure of Implicit Attitudes

Guessing, by definition, does not fully reflect judgments that are based on objective knowledge about the world. Nevertheless, systematic biases in guessing can be a rich source of information about the ways that people think, as well as the ways they respond. In a classic work, Sherif (1935) noted that there are cases in which "objective determination is lacking, thus allowing internal factors such as attitudes, subjective norms, and values to play the dominant role in organization of the perceptual field" (p. 60).

An early and clever study by Hammond (1948) showed how a systematic bias in guesses can reveal those internal factors. This article anticipated so closely issues currently being debated in social cognition research that it is worth considering in some detail. Hammond was concerned with measuring unintentional effects of attitudes, even labeling the technique an indirect test. Much like our focus, his method aimed at dissociating the unintentional influence of attitudes from other bases for responding to questions. Finally, Hammond was concerned with the reliability of indirect tests compared to direct tests of attitudes, foreshadowing present efforts to measure and correct for the reliability of indirect measures (Cunningham et al., 2001; Kawakami & Dovidio, 2001).

Fascinated with projective tests such as the Rorschach (1942) inkblot being used to diagnose personality disorders, social psychologists had begun searching for indirect methods for measuring attitudes that could penetrate people's concerns with self-presentation. But being disenchanted with the interpretability of projective tests, Hammond designed a bogus "information test" to reveal unexpressed attitudes. "Much of the difficulty with present methods of attitude measurement," wrote Hammond (1948, p. 38), "lies in the trouble authors have in deciding just what it is they are trying to measure."

In one test, questions about Russia and organized labor were used to measure attitudes toward Communism. In these questions, there was either no factual answer (e.g., "Russia's removal of heavy industry from Austria was (a) legal (b) illegal") or the alternatives were both incorrect (e.g., "Man-days lost because of strikes from January to June, 1946, were (a) 35 million (b) 99 million"). In the latter example, the true answer is 67 million days, midway between the two alternatives provided. The response alternatives provided one favorable choice and one choice unfavorable toward socialist policies (e.g., making union activity appear very costly).

By making no answer factually correct, Hammond attempted to eliminate objective knowledge as a basis for responding, so participants had to guess. Those guesses were not random, but were informed by participants' attitudes toward socialist policies. Hammond compared the responses of American business owners with the responses of union workers. During that historical period, businesspeople were strongly opposed to organized labor and collectivist policies because they feared that such policies would undermine the free market system on which they depended. Union workers were, understandably, expected to be more sympathetic toward collectivist policies. The businesspeople tended to choose antilabor test alternatives to a greater extent than did union members (55% versus 9%). Not only were responses systematically related to the two groups' political leanings, but the responses showed high consistency, producing reliability coefficients from .78 to .87.

Hammond's article is striking in the extent to which it anticipated many of the theoretical and methodological questions that psychologists are grappling with today. He was interested in the contrast between direct and indirect measures of attitudes and the different processes they revealed. Although Hammond's work is an excellent example of how guesses can reflect implicit processes, we are now in a position to go far beyond the possibilities raised by this early indirect method. We use Hammond's test as an example to illustrate how distinct bases for responding can be measured within the same task.

Separating Knowledge and Attitude

A weakness of the approach introduced by Hammond is that it does not allow for the possibility that some subjects in his experiments knew the correct answer to his questions. As an example, suppose that someone knew how many man-days were lost because of strikes. How would such knowledge influence responding? Differences in knowledge could be measured by adding a condition in which one of the alternatives was the correct one. The importance of separating these two sources of information is evidenced by the different kinds of reactions people have to decisions based on each. When people are concerned with fairness and social justice, responses stemming from prejudice rather than from knowledge trigger outrage. That outrage is based on the assumption that prejudice (attitudes) and knowledge serve as alternative bases for responding. How can the contribution of the two bases for responding be separated?

To do this, suppose we constructed two types of test items. Each test item includes the correct response paired with an incorrect response that is either larger or smaller than the correct response. First, we have an item in which the alternatives are 67 million (correct) versus 35 million (incorrect). From the perspective of the businessperson, the correct alternative can be chosen either because of knowledge or, in the absence of knowledge, because of prejudice (it is the alternative least favorable toward socialism). In the other form of the question, the alternatives might be 67 million (correct) versus 99 million. For the businessperson, the larger, incorrect answer will be chosen because of his or her attitude in the absence of knowledge. In this case, knowledge opposes prejudice.

To illustrate how knowledge and prejudice can be disentangled, we present some idealized data from a fictional test in which businesspeople and union members from 1948 have answered questions of the sort we just described. Anti-Communist items are those on which the correct answer is the anti-

Communist answer. Pro-Communist items are those on which the correct answer is pro-Communist. Table 15.1 shows the hypothetical data.

Look first at the column of pro-Communist items (second column). Notice that the businesspeople made more errors than the union members, showing a tendency to err on the side against Communism, just as Hammond (1948) found. However, these overall performance measures do not allow us to separate knowledge from bias. To do so, consider the processes by which these errors could be made. An anti-Communist error will be made if a person does not know the answer ($1 - K$), and relies on anti-Communist attitudes (A). The probability of an error in the pro-Communist condition can be written as $p(\text{error} \mid \text{pro-Communist item}) = A(1 - K)$.

Next look at the column of anti-Communist items. Both knowledge and anti-Communist attitudes would lead to a correct answer on these items. For these items, the probability of scoring a correct answer can be written as the probability of using knowledge (K) plus the probability of using attitudes (A) in the absence of knowledge ($1 - K$). So, $p(\text{correct} \mid \text{anti-Communist item}) = K + A(1 - K)$.

With these two equations, we can estimate knowledge and attitudes by solving for K and A algebraically. Knowledge can be solved as $p(\text{correct} \mid \text{anti-Communist item}) - p(\text{error} \mid \text{pro-Communist item})$. That amounts to this simple "proof" equation: $K = K + A(1 - K) - A(1 - K)$. Consulting our table, we see that for the businesspeople, $K = .90 - .40 = .50$. For the union workers, $K = .60 - .10 = .50$. This shows that the businesspeople and union members know the same amount about the facts in question.

To measure the respondents' attitude-based biases, we begin with the errors in the pro-Communist condition. Recall that the probability of producing an error here is $p(\text{error} \mid \text{pro-Communist item}) = A(1 - K)$. To solve for A, we need to divide the term $A(1 - K)$ by $(1 - K)$. Because we have solved for K already, we know that $(1 - K)$ for both the businesspeople and the union members is $1 - .50 = .50$. Consulting table 15.1, we see that the attitude bias for businesspeople is $.40 \div .50 = .80$. The attitude bias for union members is $.10 \div .50 = .20$. A bias value of .50 represents unbiased responding, whereas scores greater than .50 represent an anti-Communist bias, and scores below

Table 15.1 Hypothetical Responses to an Adapted Version of Hammond's Indirect Attitude Test

Social Group	Correct on Anti-Communist Items $K + A(1 - K)$	Errors on Pro-Communist Items $A(1 - K)$	Estimates	
			Knowledge	Attitude
Businesspeople	.90	.40	.50	.80
Union	.60	.10	.50	.20

that point represent pro-Communist bias. The businesspeople have a much stronger bias against Communism than the union members, who actually have a pro-Communist bias.

Use of our equations shows that the businesspeople and union workers differed not in their knowledge but in their biases. Some readers will have recognized the above equation for measuring knowledge as being the same equations commonly used to "correct for guessing" on a multiple-choice test. Interest has typically been in "true" scores, with guessing treated as being largely random and of little interest. In contrast, our approach treats guesses as revealing unintended influences of memory, attitudes, needs, and so on. Our example thus far has shown how guessing bias can reflect attitudes, and how bias can be separated from knowledge. However, there is nothing in what we have done to guarantee that the attitude bias is automatic or that the use of knowledge is controlled. Next, we consider how our approach defines automaticity and control, and how these assumptions are tested.

Defining Automaticity: Processes versus Tasks

Automatic processing has typically been defined as unintentional, unconscious, uncontrollable, and highly efficient, in the sense that an automatic process operates rapidly and does not demand attentional effort (Shiffrin & Schneider, 1977). Several theorists have argued that no task meets all the criteria to be considered automatic in an unqualified way (Bargh, 1989; Logan & Cowan, 1984). We agree that tasks do not meet the criteria of automaticity. However, our interest is in processes, not tasks. We hold that some processes or components of task performance are automatic.

What about the automatic versus strategic qualities in our measure of attitude toward Communism defined as bias? In our approach, we make the qualities traditionally associated with automatic processing independent variables and predict dissociations between the two processes. For instance, by placing intentional and unintentional processes both in opposition to one another and in concert with one another, we demonstrate one process that is sensitive to intentions, and one that is invariant with respect to intentions. By manipulations such as divided attention and speeded responding, we show that controlled processes require attention, and automatic processes operate with little attention.

In the case of Hammond's indirect attitude test, we could test whether the attitude bias was automatic by manipulating factors traditionally associated with automaticity and predicting dissociations. If responses based on conscious knowledge were controlled but prejudice were automatic, then manipulations of fast responding or divided attention would influence knowledge but not bias.

Discriminability and Accessibility Bias in Perception

The above thought experiment serves to introduce the process dissociation procedure (Jacoby, 1991). In this section, we begin by further illustrating that procedure by describing its use to examine effects of expectancy on word identification. Next, we return to the Diallo example and use the process dissociation procedure to analyze how prejudice has its effects.

The words of Sherif (1935) quoted earlier reflect the Gestalt emphasis on internal factors that help construct people's perceptions. Later those ideas were incorporated into the New Look movement (Bruner, 1957), which emphasized the role of expectations in perceptions. Much of the research done to support the New Look movement showed that expectations serve to resolve ambiguity in ways relied upon when projective tests are used. The notion of perceptual defense (McGinnes, 1949) serves as an example. In that research, it was claimed was that the perceptual system protects against noxious stimuli such as obscene words. Ambiguity was created by flashing words for a duration that was so short as to not reliably allow their full identification. Results showed that words that were obscene had to be flashed for a longer duration to be identified than did words that were not obscene, and this disadvantage of obscene words was said to reflect perceptual defense. However, later research sought to explain such "defense" in more mundane ways by appealing to effects of factors such as frequency in the language. It was noted that obscene words occur less frequently in the written language than do words that are similar but not obscene, and the poor perception of obscene words was explained as produced by their low frequency (for a review, see Erdelyi, 1974).

How do expectations that reflect frequency in a person's prior experience have their effect? One possibility is that expectations based on experience serve to truly influence what is perceived so that reality is constructed. Alternatively, such expectations might serve as a source of accessibility bias. For example, suppose that when a four-letter word was flashed, only three of its four letters were identified (e.g., sh_t). The partial information does not allow the word to be identified, so the viewer must guess. The ambiguous stimulus might be interpreted as the word that fits the fragment and is most readily accessible due to prior experience. An experiment by Jacoby (reported by Jacoby, McElree, & Trainham, 1999) examined effects of expectations in identifying ambiguous words.

In Jacoby's experiment, expectations were created by means of training. During training, participants were presented with context cues paired with word fragments that could be plausibly completed in two ways (e.g., knee-b_n_). Participants guessed the completion, and then were given feedback from the computer as to the "correct" completion. In one condition, a typical completion (e.g., bend) was created by presenting that completion on two thirds of the trials, and an atypical response (e.g., bone) on the remaining one third of the trials. This training phase created expectancies of different strength for how the ambiguous stimulus, the word fragment, would be completed. Frequent and recent pairings between the cue and certain targets made those typical targets highly accessible completions for the fragment.

Following training, participants were again asked to complete fragments. However, this time they were asked to complete the fragments with a masked word that was flashed briefly just before the fragment was shown. The duration of the flash was either 20 or 40 ms. Those trials in which the typical word from training was also the flashed word can be considered congruent trials, because both the typical, accessible response from training and perception of the flashed word would lead to the same correct response. On incongruent trials, the atypical word from training was flashed. On those trials, perception of the flashed word would lead to a correct response, but relying on the accessible response from training would cause an error.

On congruent trials, the correct response might be given either by perceptually identifying the flashed word (P) or by relying on accessibility bias (A), created during training, in the absence of perceptual identification ($1 - P$). Thus, the probability of a hit in the congruent condition is $P + A(1 - P)$. On incongruent trials, accessibility bias is pitted against perception, so that participants are expected to make errors when they rely on accessible information in the absence of perception. If a participant successfully perceives the word completion based on the objective information flashed, then the accessibility of a habitual response is not expected to influence responses. The probability of a false alarm in the incongruent condition is $A(1 - P)$, reflecting that a false alarm is likely to the extent that accessibility bias is active (A) but perception is not ($1 - P$).

Perceptual identification can be estimated by subtracting hits in the congruent condition from false alarms in the incongruent condition: $P = p(\text{Hit} \mid \text{congruent}) - p(FA \mid \text{incongruent})$. Mathematically, this can be seen by the fact that subtracting the term $A(1 - P)$ from the term $P + A(1 - P)$ yields P. Given an estimate of perception, accessibility bias can be estimated as $A = p(FA \mid \text{incongruent})/(1 - P)$. It should be noted that this estimation procedure is the same as illustrated in our thought experiment based on Hammond's (1948) study.

Results from Jacoby's experiment (table 15.2) show that flash duration influenced perception but had no influence on estimated accessibility bias. That is, accessibility bias was nearly identical in the short and long flash-duration conditions. This is important in showing that differences in perception did not influence accessibility bias ("guessing") but, rather, only influenced the opportunity for guessing to drive responses. Again, consider the equation for correct responses in the congruent condition: $P + A(1 - P)$. By that equation, A has an effect only when perception fails, which happens

Table 15.2 Probability of Fragment Completions on Congruent and Incongruent Trials With Estimates of Perception and Habit

Duration (ms)	Correct on Congruent Trials $P + A(1 - P)$	Errors on Incongruent Trials $A(1 - P)$	Estimates	
			Perception	Habit
20	.60	.60	.01	.60
40	.78	.35	.44	.62

Note: Data from Jacoby, McElree, and Trainham (1999).

more often in the short-duration condition. We emphasize this point because we later argue that it is an important one for theories about how prejudice has its effects.

The dissociation displayed in table 15.2 shows an influence on perception with accessibility bias left unchanged, whereas the dissociation in table 15.1 shows an influence on accessibility bias with knowledge left unchanged. We have found dissociations of both sorts in memory and perception experiments. Estimates of accessibility bias can be influenced by manipulating expectancies or typicality in training. Doing so produced differences in estimated accessibility bias that approximated the difference in training probabilities (i.e., probability matching), but left the estimated contribution of controlled processing (recollection in their experiments) unchanged (e.g., Hay & Jacoby, 1996). Note that in the experiment described above, the estimate of accessibility bias is near the training probability (.61 vs. .67). Jacoby and colleagues have found probability matching of this sort in several experiments (e.g., Hay & Jacoby, 1996). Manipulating the amount of time allowed for responding reduced controlled processing but left estimated accessibility bias unchanged, just as would be expected if accessibility bias was a more automatic basis for responding. Results from these and other experiments (e.g., Jacoby, Debner, & Hay, 2001) justify treating accessibility bias as an automatic basis for responding.

One of the assumptions underlying the process dissociation procedure is that the processes of discrimination and bias are independent of one another. This assumption has generated some controversy (see Hintzman & Curran, 1997; Jacoby, Begg, & Toth, 1997, for a discussion of these assumptions). Finding variables such as those reported here that selectively affect the estimated contribution of the two types of processes provides support for the validity of the independence assumption. For example, findings that presentation duration and amount of time required for responding selectively influence perception while prior expectations selectively influence accessibility bias suggest that the two bases for responding operate independently.

Discriminability and Accessibility Bias in Stereotypical Inferences

The experiments described above showed that expectations can bias perceptual judgments and that the influence of expectations can be separated from perception itself. We have been concerned with stereotypes as one source of expectations that may create a similar accessibility bias. Consider the case alluded to earlier, of a police officer in a confrontation with a suspect who is holding an object. The judgment of whether that object is a weapon is urgent, and it must be made quickly. Unfortunately, such a fast decision is the type that is most likely to be influenced by the social category of the suspect (Macrae, Milne, & Bodenhausen, 1994).

Specifically, the fact that African Americans are stereotypically expected to be more violent and criminal than White Americans creates the worry that people might let their stereotypical expectations influence their perceptual identification of weapons. Can race affect people to the point that they claim to see guns where there are none? Under some conditions, it can. Payne (2001) conducted a study with the aim of dissociating automatic bias and controlled responding when racial prejudice influences perceptual judgments. Participants saw pictures of handguns and hand tools on a computer monitor. Their task was to classify each item as either a gun or a tool. Immediately before each target item, faces of White and Black men were flashed briefly, but visibly (200 ms). Some participants were required to respond quickly (in under 500 ms), while others were allowed to respond at their own pace.

Participants under time pressure showed a stereotypical pattern of errors. In addition to making more errors overall, participants mistakenly classified a tool as a gun more often when it was paired with a Black face than when paired with a White face. There was no actual correlation between the color of the face and the identity of the target within the experiment. However, because of people's preexisting stereotypes, a Black face paired randomly with an object was sufficient to cause that object to be misclassified as a gun.

As table 15.3 shows, participants' performance was separated into estimates of accessibility bias and discriminability using the process dissociation equations. Congruent conditions were those in which a Black face preceded

Table 15.3 Process Estimates in Each Prime and Deadline Condition

	Accessibility Bias		Discriminability	
	Black Prime	White Prime	Black Prime	White Prime
Deadline	.57	.49	.40	.44
No deadline	.61	.48	.86	.88

Source: From Payne (2001).

a gun, or a White face preceded a tool. The Black-tool and White-gun pairs provided the incongruent conditions. Accessibility bias was coded so that higher scores indicate a tendency to respond "gun." Process estimates showed that requiring participants to respond quickly cut their discriminability by more than half, but left their bias estimate unchanged. In contrast, the race of the face influenced the accessibility bias estimate, but did not change discriminability. Black faces led to a greater bias toward classifying an object as a gun, compared to the White faces.

We regard the accessibility bias as an automatic influence for several reasons. First, the bias occurred whether or not it was consistent with the goals required for the task. The instructions were to respond "gun" if and only if a gun is present; respond "tool" if and only if a tool is present. The face primes influenced performance regardless of which response was appropriate to the task goal. Second, the bias took place within a very short time period (200 ms SOA), and the response deadline did not affect it. The magnitude of participants' accessibility bias was the same whether or not their processing time was restricted. Together, this evidence suggests that the racial bias caused by the faces of different races may, under some circumstances, be an unintentional and efficient use of information akin to implicit memory.

In addition to showing a double dissociation between accessibility bias and discriminability within the priming task, we tested the relationship between this automatic bias and participants' racial attitudes as measured by a direct test. We measured participants' racial attitudes with the MRS (McConahay et al., 1981) and the Motivation to Control Prejudice Scale (MCP; Dunton & Fazio, 1997). The MCP measures the extent to which people are willing to express any negative attitudes toward other racial groups. We found a positive correlation between the automatic bias estimate and attitudes expressed via the MRS ($\beta = +.51$), but only for participants who were unmotivated to avoid racial prejudice, as measured by the MCP scale. For those who found it inappropriate to express unfavorable attitudes about Blacks, the bias estimate did not correlate with MRS scores ($\beta = -.23$, nonsignificant). These findings converge with other research using different procedures that shows participants' automatic biases correlated positively with their directly expressed attitudes only when they were not motivated to appear unprejudiced (Fazio et al., 1995).

To summarize, in the studies reviewed here, stereotypes and habits created an accessibility bias. Several lines of research suggest that accessibility biases and discriminability often operate simultaneously and independently to jointly determine people's actions. The experiments described above show why process dissociation is useful for breaking down complex effects into separate, quantifiable processes. Those processes can each then be studied individually. When factors traditionally identified with automatic processing are either built into an experimental design (e.g., using the logic of opposition) or manipulated, it is possible to draw conclusions about underlying processes.

Consciousness and Control

In many of the domains we have described, cognitive control as modeled by discriminability estimates is closely related to conscious subjective experiences. In an explicit test of the relationships between objectively estimated memory processes and subjective experience, Jacoby et al. (2001) had participants describe the phenomenology of each response on a memory test as something they consciously "remembered," just "knew," or "guessed." Those experiments showed a very strong association between estimates of memory discriminability (recollection) and the conscious experience of remembering. Some provocative work has been interested in the possibility of nonconscious control (chapters 7 and 8, this volume; Moskowitz, Gollwitzer, Wasal, & Shaal, 1999). As our approach shows, we see the relationship between consciousness and cognitive control as an empirical question. Having a means for estimating cognitive control independent of participants' reports allows the two to be empirically compared.

Just as the consciousness of control mechanisms may be put to direct test, so can the relationships between consciousness and accessibility biases of different sorts. In some situations, for example, people may be able to become aware of a process that is initially unconscious. As suggested by the psychodynamic tradition, achieving awareness of a mental process can provide a basis for controlling it. An experiment has shown that people can harness their biases strategically if they are made aware of them.

Dolan and Jacoby (2000) conducted a memory study in which the colors of words carried biasing information. During a recognition test, words were tested in either red or green. Two thirds of the old words were tested in green, and one third of the old words were tested in red. Thus, if a word was tested in green, it was more likely to be old than new. Results showed that participants had learned this pattern, in that they made more hits and false alarms for green words than for red words. That is, they were more likely to respond "old" to green words whether they were actually studied or not. However, postexperiment questioning revealed that participants were not aware that there was a relationship between color and the status of the word.

A second experiment avoided relying on participants' self-reports of awareness. In this experiment, participants were either allowed to remain unaware of the color relationship or they were forced to notice it. The unaware condition was the same as described above. In the aware condition, however, participants had to use different response keys, depending on the color of the word. This arrangement forced participants to attend to the word color. In this experiment, participants were allowed to respond both at their own pace and at a speeded pace in a separate phase of the experiment.

Results showed that neither the color of the words nor awareness of the color relationship affected discriminability. The speeded response condition, in contrast, did reduce discriminability. Expectancies based on word colors affected the bias estimate—participants were biased toward calling green words "old." When participants responded at their own pace, the color bias was the same for aware and unaware conditions. Critically, when they were required to respond rapidly, participants who were aware of the color relationship relied on it heavily, creating a color bias much larger than that of the unaware participants. The point to note is that the bias was in place in all conditions, but awareness of the bias allowed participants to use it strategically. Under difficult speeded conditions, aware participants informed their judgments with the bias, using it to accomplish the task goal. Unaware participants had no such flexible control over their biases. In the next section, we describe additional subtle and even ironic effects that may arise from biases created by accessible attitudes.

A New Look at Some Old Constructs: Habits and Dominant Responses

The construct of habit is one of the oldest in experimental psychology, as it lies at the core of many classic theories of motivation and learning (e.g., Hull, 1951; Spence, 1956). More recently, the importance of habit emerged in the context of the social facilitation literature. Habitual behaviors (or "dominant responses" as they are called in this area) may become more likely when organisms perform a task with, or while being observed by, members of the same species (Zajonc, 1965). The notions of "habit" and "dominant response" have historically been construed in behavioral terms. The well-learned response typically includes some behavior that the organism (be it a rat or a college sophomore) has acquired through repetition, such as successfully negotiating a maze or solving an anagram. However, there is no reason why such constructs could not be usefully extended to domains more familiar to the "cognitive" domain (see James, 1890).

Indeed, a theme running tacitly through many of the experiments reported here is that certain stimuli (or situations) may stimulate well-learned, habitual bases for responding. These habits may be fairly mundane, such as the tendency to automatically think of *bend* when presented with the word *knee*. Other habits carry more immediate consequences, such as the tendency for mere presentation of a Black face to automatically activate images of guns or other stereotypical associations. This raises the more general point that the construct of attitudes (perhaps the most ubiquitous construct in social psychology) fits quite well within the habit framework, in that attitudes are often defined as a well-learned association between an object and one's positive or negative appraisal of it (Fazio, 1986).

On one hand, framing attitudes as habits or dominant responses does not represent a startling theoretical advance per se. Nevertheless, if this conceptualization is used to make new connections between recent social-cognitive work on attitudes and a long tradition of investigating dominant or habitual responses, then the notion may prove quite useful. In particular, research in the social facilitation literature has shown that the presence of other people facilitates dominant responses, while interfering with subordinate responses (Zajonc, 1965; see also Spence, 1956).

Somewhat surprisingly, our review of this literature shows that researchers have focused almost exclusively on the effects of audiences on performance. Although we are not aware of any previous efforts to make this connection, it seems reasonable that attitudes, like other well-learned responses, may be facilitated by the presence of an audience. If attitudes are construed as dominant evaluative responses, then one would expect the relationship between people's attitudes on one hand and their judgments and behaviors on the other to be strengthened when they are in the presence of others, or are generally aroused.

When applied to racial attitudes, this rationale makes an extremely counterintuitive prediction. Both research and intuition suggest that people are motivated to appear unprejudiced in public settings (e.g., Gaertner & Dovidio, 1986; Plant & Devine, 1998). Thus, it would seem natural that evaluations of stereotyped individuals would be more positive in public than in private settings, and that such evaluations would be more consistent with the perceiver's attitudes in private settings. However, if attitudes are understood as dominant or habitual responses, then one would predict precisely the opposite results: assuming that most people have some level of prejudice, this framework suggests that evaluations of a stereotyped person should be more negative and more closely related to racial attitudes in public settings. In fact, this is exactly what was found in a series of experiments reported by Lambert, Cronen, Chasteen, and Lickel (1996). These researchers found that there was greater "attitude-behavior consistency" in public compared to a private setting, insofar as participants' stereotypical attitudes toward Blacks (as measured by an explicit measure prior to the main study) were more strongly related to judgments of a single Black individual in the former compared to the latter condition.

One ambiguity of these findings is that they can be interpreted in one of two ways. On one hand, the "public expression effect" could reflect heightened accessibility bias. This interpretation is more or less consistent with a Hullian/Zajonc model of social facilitation, which emphasizes the energizing or drivelike effects of audiences on habitual responses. Another interpretation, however, is that the findings by Lambert et al. (1996) reflect reduced cognitive control, an interpretation that might be predicted by attentional conflict models of social facilitation (Groff, Baron, & Moore, 1983). One way of distinguishing between these accounts is that they presume either that something is being added (increased stereotypical bias) or that something is being taken away (control). It is worth emphasizing that this ambiguity applies not only to the Lambert et al. (1996) investigation but to the social facilitation area as a whole, as theorists in this area have not yet resolved whether drive-based versus control-based accounts provide viable accounts of social facilitation. Nor has a methodology been proposed that can successfully tease these models apart.

We have gained some important leverage in these matters (Lambert et al., 2003). In one study, we followed up on the findings reported by Lambert et al. (1996), showing that the public expression effect was moderated by dispositional levels of anxiety. Highly anxious participants showed strong facilitation of racial attitudes in public compared to private, whereas less anxious participants did not. (Low-anxiety participants showed a nonsignificant reversal of this pattern.) These data are useful insofar as they further demonstrate the important parallelism between our line of work and the social facilitation area, which typically shows these sorts of moderation effects as well.

Even more important, a second study was able to provide a direct test of the two theoretical accounts described above. In this study, participants were randomly assigned to perform the gun versus tool identification task used by Payne (2001) in either a private or anticipated public context. Results revealed significantly more stereotypical errors in public compared to private—especially among participants experiencing high levels of anxiety—conceptually replicating and extending our earlier work in the impression-formation domain. Moreover, use of the process dissociation procedure offered strong leverage in testing the viability of a drive-based account (which would predict heightened bias) versus a control-based account (which would predict lower discriminability). Results showed much stronger support for the latter, as the increase in stereotypical errors was due entirely to lower discriminability in the public condition. These and other current efforts in our laboratory may thus hold potential for clarifying issues in both the stereotyping and the social facilitation areas.

Toward Choosing Among Models: The Tyranny of Automaticity?

Social psychologists have explained a broad range of judgmental biases by the accessibility of mental categories. For example, Bruner (1957) described perceptual distortions as a result of categorization, which is influenced by the relative accessibility of different categories. Recent use of a trait category can make it more accessible and therefore more likely to be used when forming an impression of a new person (Higgins, Rholes, & Jones, 1977). Even without a recent priming, chronically used attitudes and trait categories can influence the way that social information is processed (Fazio, 1986; Higgins, King, & Mavin, 1982; Wyer & Srull, 1989). Such accessibility effects have typically been revealed by using ambiguous stimuli or by showing errors that result from reliance on accessibility.

Studies of social perception have placed a heavy emphasis on ambiguous situations (e.g., Higgins et al., 1977). The conclusions of research using ambiguous situations are applicable to the extent that everyday judgments are made under ambiguity. No doubt, situations can be ambiguous. However, unambiguous information is frequently available to use as a basis for controlled responding. A problem with using truly ambiguous stimuli, in which there is no "correct" response, is that ambiguous stimuli tell us little about the basis for accessibility effects. In those cases, accessibility effects could arise either from an influence on perception or from accessibility bias. With ambiguous materials, it is impossible to choose between mechanisms. In contrast, we use situations in which there is a "correct" answer and arrange conditions such that bias is either congruent or incongruent with the objective basis for obtaining that correct answer. By doing so, we can separate effects of accessibility on perception and bias.

In some ways, our approach is similar to that of Banaji and Greenwald (1995). As did we, they used a measure of bias to index implicit attitudes. For example, they used signal-detection theory (SDT) to separate effects of discriminability and bias in people's ability to distinguish between famous and nonfamous names. Finding a bias against judging female names as famous was used as a measure of implicit sexism. However, an important difference between their approach and ours is the meaning of the term *bias*. By SDT, a single-process model, bias refers to a quantitative difference in the amount of information needed to make a decision. In contrast, by our dual-process model, accessibility bias reflects a basis for judgments that is qualitatively different from that used for a consciously controlled judgment (e.g., discriminating between a tool and a gun) with regard to the type of information used. Jacoby, McElree, and Trainham (1999) discuss the relation between single- and dual-process models of bias effects (see also Jacoby, Kelley, & McElree, 1999).

Several models of stereotyping take the form of dual-process models (e.g., Brewer, 1988; Devine, 1989; Fiske & Neuberg, 1990). However, research testing these models does not typically measure both processes within the same task. As a result, the operation of each process and the relationships between processes cannot be directly examined. Separate estimates of control and accessibility bias provide a means to test the relationships between processes, and so provide a basis for choosing between competing models.

This ability represents an important strength, because as Gilbert (1999) noted, dual-process models can take many forms, with separate processes combining in any number of ways to determine behavior. A productive way to proceed is to identify plausible competing theories and test them against one another (Popper, 1994). In the next section, we describe an approach we have taken that exploits the estimates derived from our approach to test which of two plausible dual-process models best accounts for the data we gathered in the weapon identification experiment described earlier.

A Test of Two Models: Accessibility Bias or Attitude Inhibition?

The basic process dissociation model spells out how controlled and automatic processes interact, with automatic processing, accessibility bias, serving as a basis for responses only in the event that control fails. Controlled processes have clear priority, constraining the likelihood that a bias will have the opportunity to affect behavior. This arrangement contrasts with "inhibition" models that are common in current social psychology research. These models assume that when people enter into a social situation, automatic processing constitutes a first stage, which must then be suppressed or inhibited for a person to make a controlled response (Bodenhausen & Macrae, 1998; Devine, 1989; Wegner, 1994).

Lindsay and Jacoby (1994) found that an inhibition model of this sort provides a good description of performance in the Stroop task. In the Stroop task, participants are asked to name the color of the pigment in which words are printed. The critical words are the names of colors themselves. The typical finding is that people have more difficulty naming the color in which a word is printed if the word is the name of some other color. It is believed that in this task, word reading is an automatic process that operates so readily that it must be suppressed if one is to perform well by naming the color of the word rather than the word itself.

Are stereotypes the sort of things that leap out at us with such force that we must struggle to inhibit them if we are to relate objectively to another person? Is our hypothetical officer likely to "read" an object in the hand of a Black person as a gun as spontaneously as one reads words for meaning? Or do stereotypes operate more subtly, so that they have an opportunity to shape judgments primarily when more controlled processes fail?

We have used a multinomial processing tree (MPT) approach to empirically test which kind of model best fits the data generated in our weapon identification paradigm (see Batchelder & Riefer, 1999, for a discussion of

MPT modeling). In an MPT model, mental processes are represented as a series of branches. Figure 15.1 shows the tree diagrams for an accessibility bias (top panel) and an inhibition model (bottom panel). As with a traditional flowchart, a process can operate or not operate at each step. What distinguishes this approach from a traditional flowchart is that the likelihood that each process is active is represented by a probability. On the right hand side of the figure are the responses expected as a result of each processing path. The number of correct and incorrect responses in each condition from an experiment can be used to test whether each model fits the pattern of actual data.

Look first at the accessibility bias model. This model represents the same equations used in the process dissociation procedure described throughout. In this model, controlled discriminability of the target either succeeds with probability *C*, or it fails with probability $(1 - C)$. If control fails, then an accessibility bias may occur with probability *A*, or fail to occur with probability

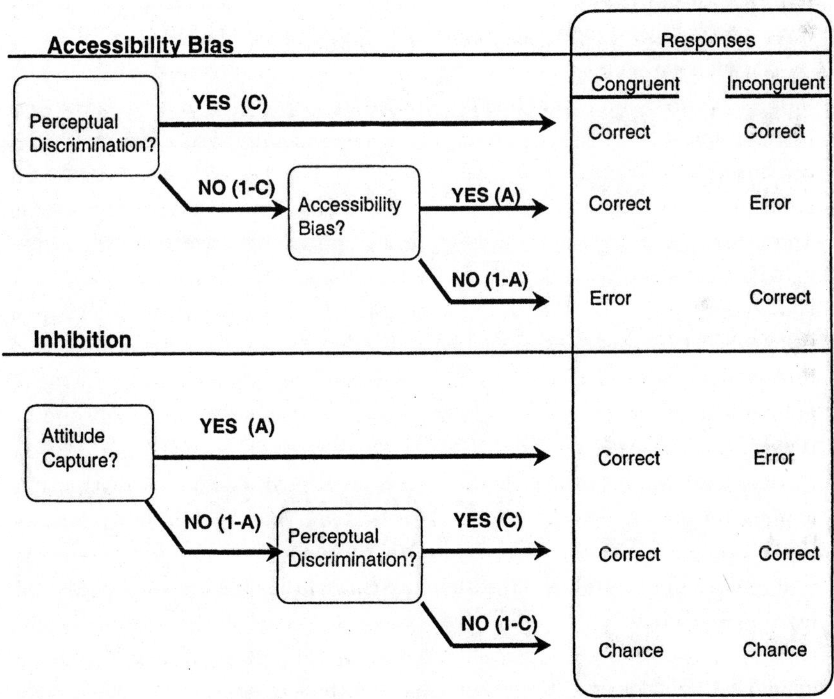

Figure 15.1 A comparison of two models of the relationships between controlled and automatic processes. Note that the order of processes depicted does not refer to temporal stages, but to the relative dominance of each process. In the event that both processes occur, the process in the first position determines the response.

$(1 - A)$. Rather than operating only when able to inhibit an automatic response, controlled processing begins very early. However, it may take longer to complete than automatic processing. Psychologically, this sequence would describe a process in which an officer encountering a suspect attempts to discern whether the object is a gun or not, based on the physical characteristics of the object. If controlled processing is successful, then racial stereotypes do not influence the weapon identification.

In contrast, when control is impaired (e.g., by rushed responding due to the intense pressure of the situation), the automatic processing of the suspect's race may cause a stereotypical judgment to be made. This is a case of an accessibility bias left unopposed by controlled processing. To see the relationship between the equations used in the process dissociation procedure and the probabilities represented in the diagram, notice the paths denoted by the arrows. As shown in figure 15.1, a respondent can give a correct answer in the congruent condition either by control of the response (C) or by an accessibility bias in the absence of control: $A(1 - C)$. The fact that accessibility bias can only drive responses when control fails amounts to the equation used in process dissociation, where an error in the incongruent condition occurs when accessibility bias operates in the absence of control: $A(1 - C)$.

The alternative inhibition model reverses the positions of these processes (and so changes the equations used). The influence of attitude (A) is given priority, and controlled discrimination is allowed only when the attitude is inhibited, with probability $(1 - A)$. By this account, an officer encountering a suspect experiences an automatic effect of attitude that drives the response unless the officer is able to inhibit that impulse. Reliance on attitude expressed as a stereotype will produce correct responding only in the congruent condition, just as relying on accessibility bias produces correct responding for the congruent condition. The primary difference between the two models is that in the first model, accessibility bias can only drive responses if control fails. In the inhibition model, one can exert control only if the effect of attitude is inhibited.

Note that the order depicted in this model refers to logical priority, not temporal ordering. The model is not sequential. We assume both processes begin at the same time and can proceed simultaneously and independently. The priority of one process over the other means that the second process can drive the behavior only in the absence of the first. If both processes occur, then the first one dominates and determines the response. In effect, the priority of one process over the other expresses which one "wins" when both processes are active.

Once the branches of the multinomial tree model are filled out using equations based on the probabilities just described, the model can be statistically tested against experimental data. Rather than solving for the estimates algebraically, the control and accessibility parameters are estimated using a solver algorithm. The data from Payne (2001) were used to test the models. The pattern of errors and correct responses predicted by the different models was compared to experimental data, and a statistical goodness-of-fit test was used. In testing the fit of multinomial models, a G^2 statistic is used, which is similar to a chi-square statistic. For this particular model, with a significance level of .01, the critical value for G^2 is 13.28. Values below that limit are considered an acceptable fit, and values above that limit indicate that the model is rejected.

The accessibility bias model fit the data well ($G^2 = 3.64$), but the inhibition model did not ($G^2 = 27.23$). The estimates yielded by the accessibility bias model converged nicely with the process dissociation estimates calculated originally on this data set. The controlled parameter was held constant across both prime races, and was different for short ($C = .42$) and long ($C = .87$) response deadlines. The accessibility bias parameter was held constant across deadlines, and varied between the Black ($A = .59$) and White ($A = .53$) prime conditions. Our results suggest that participants were not "blinded" by race so that they could only discriminate between weapons and tools when they inhibited the race bias. Instead, the actual objects and racial bias served as separate bases for responding, with decisions based on perceptual discrimination requiring cognitive control. When that control failed, the automatic race bias had its effect.

Taken in combination, these findings emerging from our laboratory challenge contemporary models of stereotyping in several ways. First, most models assume a two-stage mechanism in which the automatic activation of the stereotype can be subsequently overridden by controlled processes, but only if perceivers have the motivation and ability to do so (e.g., Devine, 1989; see also Bodenhausen & Macrae, 1998; Gilbert & Hixon, 1991). Second, the fact that stereotypes have greater impact on social judgment under cognitive load—or other manipulations that compromise careful processing—is typically interpreted as a consequence of "knocking out" perceivers' ability to implement the secondary correction process. The research on weapon misidentifications discussed above suggests that these rarely tested assumptions may not always be correct. Particularly important is the idea that constraints on controlled processing affect discriminability but not accessibility bias. Thus, the notion that prejudice plays a greater role in social perception under situational duress—such as might have occurred in the Diallo case—may reflect compromised ability to respond based on objective properties rather than a failure to successfully override the stereotype.

Our argument is not that inhibition models are never applicable. As alluded to earlier, Lindsay and Jacoby (1994) found that a similar model was a good description of the way that interference occurs in the Stroop task. However, different models are useful to describe different psychological effects. It is important to have a means of choosing between different models of the processes underlying different kinds of behaviors. The choice of models used to explain the effects of prejudice has important consequences for attempts to control prejudice.

An inhibition model suggests that if objective information is to guide judgments, automatic impulses must be inhibited. If they are not, then the more controlled basis for responding does not matter. Inhibition-related assumptions lead to an emphasis on suppressing prejudiced reactions. Research has focused on attempts to suppress stereotypical thoughts from initially entering consciousness (Wegner, 1994), to replace stereotypical thoughts with egalitarian ones (Monteith, 1993), and to adjust judgments once stereotypical thoughts have already come to mind (Wilson & Brekke, 1994).

Attempts to reduce prejudice by these routes have left some theorists pessimistic. It is argued that in order to correct stereotypical thinking by "thinking twice," people must be aware of their bias as well as being motivated and able to override it (Bargh, 1999; Wilson & Brekke, 1994). They may not be aware of the bias because it has operated automatically, and thus it may be unconscious. This pessimism is supported by studies showing that attempts to suppress stereotypes sometimes fail, causing an ironic increase in stereotype use (Macrae, Bodenhausen, Milne, & Jetten, 1994; Monteith, Spicer, & Toomen, 1998; Payne, Lambert, & Jacoby, 2002). In addition, the demands of constantly second-guessing oneself may be overwhelming.

An alternative approach suggested by the accessibility bias model emphasizes maximizing cognitive control rather than overriding the effect of accessible information. By this approach, it is not necessary to be aware of any bias, and there is no need to suppress automatic thoughts so long as objective grounds provide a basis for responding. According to this model, accessibility bias only influences responses when controlled processes fail. As an example, consider the word-perception experiments described earlier. The habitual response only influenced behavior when perception failed. If the situation had been structured to maximize perception, then even the strongest accessibility bias would have no impact on responses.

In fact, this is precisely what happened in Payne's (2001) weapon identification study. When participants were allowed unlimited time to respond, their accessibility bias was just as strong as in the speeded condition. However, this accessibility bias only translated into significantly more stereotypical errors in the speeded condition. When participants were allowed cognitive control by responding slowly, the accessibility bias was unable to cause actual errors. Situations structured so that people can use objective information as a basis for control reduce the consequences of accessible information. And they do so without (often futile) attempts to suppress automatic thoughts. The choice between theoretical models can inform choices about interventions. Thus, we believe the approach described here is as relevant to pragmatics as it is to processes.

References

Banaji, M. R., & Greenwald, A. G. (1995). Implicit gender stereotyping in judgments of fame. *Journal of Personality and Social Psychology, 68*, 181–198.

Bargh, J. A. (1989). Conditional automaticity: Varieties of automatic influence in social perception and cognition. In J. S. Uleman & J. A. Bargh (Eds.), *Unintended thought* (pp. 3–51). New York: Guilford.

Bargh, J. A. (1999). The cognitive monster: The case against the controllability of automatic stereotype effects. In S. Chaiken & Y. Trope (Eds.), *Dual-process theories in social psychology* (pp. 361–382). New York: Guilford.

Bargh, J. A., & Chartrand, T. L. (2000). The mind in the middle: A practical guide to priming and automaticity research. In H. T. Reis & C. M. Judd (Eds.), *Handbook of research methods in social and personality psychology* (pp. 253–285). New York: Cambridge University Press.

Batchelder, W. H., & Riefer, D. M. (1999). Theoretical and empirical review of multinomial process tree modeling. *Psychonomic Bulletin and Review, 6*, 57–86.

Bodenhausen, G. V., & Macrae, C. N. (1998). Stereotype activation and inhibition. In R. S. Wyer, Jr. (Ed.), *Advances in social cognition* (Vol. 11, pp. 1–52). Mahwah, NJ: Erlbaum.

Brewer, M. B. (1988). A dual process model of impression formation. In R. S. Wyer, Jr., & T. K. Srull (Eds.), *Advances in social cognition* (Vol. 1, pp. 1–36). Hillsdale, NJ: Erlbaum.

Bruner, J. S. (1957). On perceptual readiness. *Psychological Review, 64*, 123–152.

Cunningham, W. A., Preacher, K. J., & Banaji, M. R. (2001). Implicit attitude measures: Consistency, stability, and convergent validity. *Psychological Science, 121*, 163–170.

Devine, P. G. (1989). Stereotypes and prejudice: Their automatic and controlled components. *Journal of Personality and Social Psychology, 56*, 5–18.

Dolan, P. O., & Jacoby, L. L. (2000). *Response biases, implicit learning, and the effects of age*. Unpublished manuscript, New York University.

Dovidio, J. F., Kawakami, K., Johnson, C., Johnson, B., & Howard, A. (1997). On the nature of prejudice: Automatic and controlled processes. *Journal of Experimental Social Psychology, 33*, 510–540.

Dunton, B. C., & Fazio, R. H. (1997). An individual difference measure of motivation to control prejudiced reactions. *Personality and Social Psychology Bulletin, 23*, 316–326.

Erdelyi, M. H. (1974). A new look at the new look: Perceptual defense and vigilance. *Psychological Review, 81*, 1–25.

Fazio, R. H. (1986). How do attitudes guide behavior? In R. M. Sorrentino & E. T. Higgins (Eds.), *Handbook of motivation and cognition: Foundations of social behavior* (pp. 204–243). New York: Guilford.

Fazio, R. H., Jackson, J. R., Dunton, B. C, & Williams, C. J. (1995). Variability in automatic activation as an unobtrusive measure of racial attitudes: A bona fide pipeline? *Journal of Personality and Social Psychology, 69*, 1013–1027.

Fiske, S. T., & Neuberg, S. L. (1990). A continuum model of impression formation, from category-based to individuating processes: Influences of information and motivation on attention and interpretation. *Advances in Experimental Social Psychology, 23*, 1–74.

Gaertner, S. L., & Dovidio, J. F. (1986). The aversive form of racism. In J. F. Dovidio & S. L. Gaertner (Eds.), *Prejudice, discrimination, and racism* (pp. 61–89). Orlando, FL: Academic Press.

Gilbert, D. T. (1999). What the mind's not. In S. Chaiken & Y. Trope (Eds.), *Dual process models in social psychology* (pp. 3–11). New York: Guilford.

Gilbert, D. T., & Hixon, J. G. (1991). The trouble of thinking: Activation and application of stereotypic beliefs. *Journal of Personality and Social Psychology, 60*, 509–517.

Greenwald, A. G. (1992). New Look 3: Unconscious cognition reclaimed. *American Psychologist, 47*, 766–779.

Greenwald, A. G., McGhee, D. E., & Schwartz, J. L. K. (1998). Measuring individual differences in implicit cognition: The implicit association test. *Journal of Personality and Social Psychology, 74*, 1464–1480.

Groff, B. D., Baron, R. S., & Moore, D. L. (1983). Distraction, attentional conflict, and drivelike behavior. *Journal of Experimental Social Psychology, 19*, 359–380.

Hammond, K. R. (1948). Measuring attitudes by error choice: An indirect method. *Journal of Abnormal and Social Psychology, 43*, 38–48.

Hay, J. F., & Jacoby, L. L. (1999). Separating habit and recollection in young and elderly adults: Effects of elaborative processing and distinctiveness. *Psychology and Aging, 14*, 122–134.

Higgins, E. T., King, G. A., & Mavin, G. H. (1982). Individual construct accessibility and subjective impressions and memory. *Journal of Personality and Social Psychology, 43*, 35–47.

Higgins, E. T., Rholes, W. S., & Jones, C. R. (1977). Category accessibility and impression formation. *Journal of Experimental Social Psychology, 13*, 141–154.

Hintzman, D. L., & Curran, T. (1997). More than one way to violate independence: Reply to Jacoby and Shrout (1997). *Journal of Experimental Psychology: Learning, Memory, and Cognition, 23*, 511–513.

Hull, C. L. (1951). *Essentials of behavior*. New Haven, CT: Yale University Press.

Jacoby, L. L. (1991). A process dissociation framework: Separating automatic from intentional uses of memory. *Journal of Memory and Language, 30*, 513–541.

Jacoby, L. L., Begg, I. M., & Toth, J. P. (1997). In defense of functional independence: Violations of assumptions underlying the process-dissociation procedure? *Journal of Experimental Psychology: Learning, Memory, and Cognition, 23*, 484–495.

Jacoby, L. L., & Dallas, M. (1981). On the relationships between autobiographical memory and perceptual learning. *Journal of Experimental Psychology: General, 110*, 306–340.

Jacoby, L. L., Debner, J. A., & Hay, J. F. (2001). Proactive interference, accessibility bias, and process dissociations: Valid subjective reports of memory. *Journal of Experimental Psychology: Learning, Memory, and Cognition, 27*, 686–700.

Jacoby, L. L., Kelley, C. M., & McElree, B. D. (1999). The role of cognitive control: Early selection vs. late correction. In S. Chaiken & Y. Trope (Eds.), *Dual-process theories in social psychology* (pp. 383–400). New York: Guilford.

Jacoby, L. L., McElree, B., & Trainham, T. N. (1999). Automatic influences as accessibility bias in memory and Stroop tasks: Toward a formal model. In D. Gopher & A. Koriat (Eds.), *Attention and performance XVII* (pp. 461–486). Cambridge, MA: Bradford, MIT Press.

James, W. (1890). *Principles of psychology* (Vol. 1). New York: Henry Holt.

Kawakami, K., & Dovidio, J. F. (2001). The reliability of implicit stereotyping. *Personality and Social Psychology Bulletin, 27*, 212–225.

Lambert, A. J., Cronen, S., Chasteen, A. L., & Lickel, B. (1996). Private vs. public expressions of racial prejudice. *Journal of Experimental Social Psychology, 32*, 437–459.

Lambert, A. J., Payne, B. K., Ramsey, S., & Shaffer, L. (in press). On the predictive validity of implicit attitude measures: The moderating effect of perceived group variability. *Journal of Experimental Social Psychology*.

Lambert, A. J., Payne, B. K., Shaffer, L. M., Jacoby, L. L., Chasteen, A., & Khan, S. (2003). Attitudes as dominant responses: On the "social facilitation" of prejudice in anticipated public contexts. *Journal of Personality and Social Psychology, 84*, 277–295.

Lepore, L., & Brown, R. (1997). Category and stereotype activation: Is prejudice inevitable? *Journal of Personality and Social Psychology, 72*, 275–287.

Lindsay, D. S., & Jacoby, L. L. (1994). Stroop process dissociations: The relationship between facilitation and interference. *Journal of Experimental Psychology: Human Perception and Performance, 20*, 219–234.

Logan, G. D., & Cowan, W. B. (1984). On the ability to inhibit thought and action: A theory of an act of control. *Psychological Review, 91*, 295–327.

Macrae, C. N., Bodenhausen, G. V., Milne, A. B., & Jetten, J. (1994). Out of mind but back in sight: Stereotypes on the rebound. *Journal of Personality and Social Psychology, 67*, 808–817.

Macrae, C. N., Milne, A. B., & Bodenhausen, G. V. (1994). Stereotypes as energy-saving devices: A peek inside the cognitive toolbox. *Journal of Personality and Social Psychology, 66*, 37–47.

McConahay, J. B., Hardee, B. B., & Batts, V. (1981). Has racism declined in America? It depends on who is asking and what is asked. *Journal of Conflict Resolution, 25*, 563–579.

McGinnes, E. (1949). Emotionality and perceptual defense. *Psychological Review, 56*, 244–251.

Monteith, M. J. (1993). Self-regulation of prejudiced responses: Implications for progress in prejudice reduction efforts. *Journal of Personality and Social Psychology, 65*, 469–485.

Monteith, M. J., Spicer, C. V., & Toomen, G. D. (1998). Consequences of stereotype suppression: Stereotypes on AND not on the rebound. *Journal of Experimental Social Psychology, 34*, 355–377.

Moskowitz, G. B., Gollwitzer, P. M., Wasel, W., & Schaal, B. (1999). Preconscious control over stereotype activation through chronic egalitarian goals. *Journal of Personality and Social Psychology, 77*, 167–184.

Neely, J. H. (1977). Semantic priming and retrieval from lexical memory: Roles of inhibitionless spreading activation and limited capacity attention. *Journal of Experimental Psychology: General, 106*, 226–254.

Payne, B. K. (2001). Prejudice and perception: The role of automatic and controlled processes in misperceiving a weapon. *Journal of Personality and Social Psychology, 81*, 181–192.

Payne, B. K., Lambert, A. J., & Jacoby, L. L. (2002). Best laid plans: Effects of goals on accessibility bias and cognitive control in race-based misperceptions of weapons. *Journal of Experimental Social Psychology, 38*, 384–396.

Plant, E. A., & Devine, P. G. (1998). Internal and external motivation to respond without prejudice. *Journal of Personality and Social Psychology, 75*, 811–832.

Popper, K. R. (1994). *The myth of the framework*. London: Routledge.

Roediger, H. L., & McDermott, K. B. (1993). Implicit memory in normal human subjects. In H. Spinnler & F. Boller (Eds.), *Handbook of neuropsychology* (Vol. 8, pp. 63–131). Amsterdam: Elsevier.

Rorschach, H. (1942). *Psychodiagnostics: A diagnostic test based on perceptions.* Bern, Switzerland: Hans Huber.

Sherif, M. (1935). A study of some social factors in perception. *Archives of Psychology, 187*, 60.

Shiffrin, R., & Schneider, W. (1977). Controlled and automatic human information processing: II. Perceptual learning, automatic attending, and a general theory. *Psychological Review, 84*, 127–190.

Shimamura, A. P. (1986). Priming effects in amnesia: Evidence for a dissociable memory function. *Quarterly Journal of Experimental Psychology: Human Experimental Psychology, 38*, 619–644.

Spence, K. W. (1956). *Behavior theory and conditioning.* New Haven, CT: Yale University Press.

Wegner, D. M. (1994). Ironic processes of mental control. *Psychological Review, 101*, 34–52.

Wilson, T. D., & Brekke, N. (1994). Mental contamination and mental correction: Unwanted influences on judgments and evaluations. *Psychological Review, 116*, 117–142.

Wilson, T. D., Lindsey, S., & Schooler, T. Y. (2000). A model of dual attitudes. *Psychological Review, 107*, 101–126.

Wittenbrink, B., Judd, C., & Park, B. (1997). Evidence for racial prejudice at the implicit level and its relationship with questionnaire measures. *Journal of Personality and Social Psychology, 72*, 262–274.

Wyer, R. S., Jr., & Srull, T. K. (1989). *Memory and cognition in its social context.* Hillsdale, NJ: Erlbaum.

Zajonc, R. B. (1965). Social facilitation. *Science, 149*, 269–274.

16

The Unconscious Relational Self

Susan M. Andersen, Inga Reznik, and Noah S. Glassman

The notion that previous knowledge is brought to bear in extracting and constructing meaning is fundamental in social cognition. This process can be understood in terms of mental representations of self and of others that give both idiosyncratic and shared meaning to experience. The relational self, or the self one experiences in relation to another person, thus reflects the personal as well as the interpersonal. We characterize the relational self as social-cognitive and draw on personality and clinical theory in making the assumption that significant others play a critical role in both self-definition and self-regulation (Andersen & Chen, 2002). According to our model, each individual has an overall repertoire of selves, each of which stems from a relationship with a significant other. The repertoire is a repository for, and later a source of, interpersonal patterns the individual experiences. In short, each relational self is tied to a mental representation of a significant other. When activated, the representation of this significant other and the aspects of the self linked to it end up imbuing current experiences with different meaning, depending on the content of the relationship and the context in which this is evoked. People may, we assume, have nearly as many selves as they have significant interpersonal relationships (Sullivan, 1953; see also Kelly, 1955), and this provides for both contextual variability in the self and for the chronic influence of long-standing patterns.

In our research, we assess idiosyncratic knowledge representations in memory and trace their influence in affect and motivation. We also examine how self-regulatory processes modulate people's responses. Our conceptualization focuses on the ways the self is linked to other people who are significant—who have had an impact on one's life and in whom one is emotionally invested. This includes parents, siblings, extended family members, lovers, spouses, best friends, mentors, close colleagues, and the like. Mental representations of individual significant others and their relational linkages to the self are central in the model, and the assumption is that one's emotional investment in significant others is partly why they shape one's responses. One has a relatively unique relationship with each significant other in one's life and a relatively unique way of experiencing the self in relation to this person (see Allport, 1937; Kelly, 1955).

When referring to knowledge structures denoting self and other, we mean to imply whatever bundles of knowledge one wishes to assume people hold in memory about significant others, as well as the linkages to the self encapsulating the self-other relationship. These are activated in everyday social encounters in response to new people. In this social-cognitive process, "entangled" selves (or aspects of the self that are unique to the relationship with the significant other) are called to the fore in new situations, and we have identified this phenomenon—as it arises in everyday social relations—as transference (Andersen & Chen, 2002; Andersen & Glassman, 1996).

The transference process is at the heart of our notion of the relational self. This social-cognitive model involves mental representations of significant others that operate in accord with basic processes of transient and chronic accessibility governing the operation of social constructs (e.g., see Higgins, 1996a). Such processes require little attention or volition, which is the case for many cognitive processes, as well as many involving motivation, affect, and the self, as refinements of social-cognitive models suggest (e.g., Bargh & Barndollar, 1996; Higgins, 1996c). Hence, the processes by which the relational self operates can be considered largely unconscious.

The New Unconscious in Our Framework

In our view, research in the realm of the "new unconscious" has demonstrated that unconscious processes occur in everyday life. Normal cognitive processes often occur outside of awareness and require little in the way of attention or effort, even as they influence perception, judgment, emotion, and motivation (e.g., Bargh, 1994, 1997; Greenwald, 1992; Greenwald & Banaji, 1995; Monahan, Murphy, & Zajonc, 2000; Niedenthal, Halberstadt, & Innes-Ker, 1999). Moreover, "cold" cognitive processes can be distinguished from "hot" ones involving emotion, motivation, and self-regulation (e.g., Metcalfe & Mischel, 1999). We highlight the relational self in conceiving the new unconscious, and argue that most of our evidence on significant-other representations and the relational self can be seen as arising on the basis of relatively automatic processes. Exactly which elements of the process of transference—based on activation of significant-other representations and also the relational self—are literally unconscious and which are not is complex to determine, and we suggest a multilayered answer.

Overall, we present a wide array of findings that address this issue and support four main conclusions about the unconscious and the relational self:

1. Significant-other representations are activated automatically in transference.
2. Affect arises relatively automatically in transference when the significant-other representation is activated.
3. The relational self is activated relatively automatically when the significant-other representation is activated.
4. Some self-regulatory processes in the relational self are evoked in response to "threat" (e.g., negative cues) in transference and may be automatic.

Our model is supported by experimental research in social cognition that has demonstrated the activation of significant-other representations in person perception and their use in making sense of newly encountered individuals (Andersen & Baum, 1994; Andersen & Cole, 1990; Andersen, Glassman, Chen, & Cole, 1995; Andersen, Reznik, & Manzella, 1996; Hinkley & Andersen, 1996). In the process, the past comes to the fore in the present. Past relationships reemerge in current ones through patterns of responding relevant to the self and to personality (Andersen & Chen, 2002; Mischel & Shoda, 1995; Sullivan, 1953). Specifically, as bundles of knowledge, significant-other representations are used to interpret and respond to new people, and in the process the chronic tendency to have particular kinds of relationships as linked with these significant others comes into play, much as relational schemas do (e.g., Baldwin, 1992). This enables both stability in the self over time and variability as a function of triggering cues in a new person that activate previously stored knowledge (Andersen & Chen, 2002).

The research bearing on the model demonstrates that transient contextual cues in a new person activate a given significant-other representation and the relevant relational self. Social-cognitive processes transpiring when a mental representation is activated are known to operate largely automatically, and hence the mechanisms we examine in our work are not likely to be dependent on systematic or strategic processing (e.g., see Bargh, 1989, 1994, 1997). Beyond this supposition, we have direct evidence that significant-other representations can be activated unconsciously and without effort, and we present this evidence in some detail. We also present evidence on the relative immediacy with which affect is elicited based on activation of a significant other representation, which suggests that this affect may be triggered relatively automatically in transference rather than arising later, downstream in the processing sequence when effortful thought is more likely. In addition, we describe evidence that tends to offer some support for an automatic spread of activation from the significant other to the self in the context of transference and, likewise, of the triggering of self-regulation. In this way, both the transference process and the functioning of the relational self reveal phenomena relevant to the "new unconscious."

The associative processes presumed to underlie transference require neither the "intention" to think about a significant other nor any concerted effort to use a significant-other representation in responding to a particular new person. Hence, we assume the transference process is largely in the domain of unintended thought, and while we have not yet systematically examined exactly how effortful and intentional each aspect of transference is or how readily each can be corrected through strategic effort, we assume that mental representations of significant others are subject to automatic activation and use. Indeed, affect and motivation in transference should also arise relatively effortlessly, without any special strategic thought or conscious awareness, consistent with the broader literature showing that motivations can be activated unconsciously by contextual cues (Bargh, Gollwitzer, Lee-Chai, Barndollar, & Troetschel, 2001; Fitzsimons & Bargh, 2003). We assume, as well, that under some circumstances one should be able to correct for transference processes (Chaiken & Trope, 1999) and also discuss this in detail.

Research on unconscious processes in social cognition suggests that lack of awareness in processing is only one of several dimensions of automatic social information processing (Bargh, 1994). Automaticity can be defined in terms of multiple cognitive characteristics that do not always co-occur. Along with the lack of conscious awareness, other dimensions include effortlessness, lack of intentionality, and an inability to control the process. In some work we present, we focus on effortlessness or processing efficiency in transference, while in other research we focus on the unconscious nature of transference. Overall, there is now little doubt that associative processes are influenced by stimuli presented and perceived outside of awareness (e.g., Bornstein & Pittman, 1992; Kihlstrom, 1987; chapter 4, this volume;but see Holender, 1986). As such, unconscious influences affect social perception, in part by biasing interpretations of otherwise ambiguous behavior in a new person (e.g., Bargh, Bond, Lombardi, & Tota, 1986; Bargh & Pietromonaco, 1982; Devine, 1989). Both chronic accessibility, based on long-term patterns of activation, and transient accessibility, based on local, particular experience, are profoundly important in construct use and interpretation (e.g., Bargh, 1989; Bargh et al., 1986; Higgins & Brendl, 1995; see also Andersen et al., 1995). Our focus is on triggering cues that need not be consciously perceived and on representations that are chronically accessible. Indeed, research on categorization processes shows that the way one assesses the similarity between a new stimulus and stored mental representations is not necessarily active and intentional (chapter 5, this volume).

Contemporary research in social cognition has contributed greatly to our understanding of automaticity and of the new unconscious, and this literature is crucial to locating our work in a broader scholarly context. In the interest of getting to our central points now, however, we turn to our theory and evidence, only later in the chapter addressing in more detail the broader literature to ask what questions it raises concerning our work. At that point, we briefly address literatures on automatic evaluation, familiarity effects, perceptual fluency, implicit stereotyping, dual-process models, stereotype inhibition, and automaticity in self-regulation or self-correction. In advance of this, we begin by saying more about our model and methods. We then present the evidence from our research program, and finally consider the implications of our findings and some of the provocative concerns they raise.

As a preview of our evidence showing the unconscious relational self, we first tap the outside-of-awareness element of automaticity (see Bargh, 1989, 1994) by examining the impact of contextual triggers presented subliminally (Glassman & Andersen, 1999a). These procedures tap the efficiency and lack-of-control elements of initial activation (when control is defined in terms of whether or not the process requires control to proceed effectively rather than whether or not it can be controlled). Subliminal priming procedures can directly address unconscious activation of significant-other representations (see also Baldwin, Carrell, & Lopez, 1990), and our evidence shows that this occurs in transference. Our work is also suggestive of effortless processes of activation and use in transference because of the clear evidence it provides for the chronic accessibility and transient contextual cueing or transient activation of significant-other representations in transference (Andersen et al., 1995; Chen, Andersen, & Hinkley, 1999; Glassman & Andersen, 1999b). Next, we present evidence that automatic affect may arise when significant-other representations are activated in transference. The affect associated with the representation emerges in facial expressions evoked rather immediately in transference, verifying this key element of our model. Following this, we show facilitated latencies in responding to relevant aspects of the self in transference, and to corresponding shifts in self-evaluation, which are suggestive of a relatively automatic spread of activation from the significant other to the self in transference. These aspects should be used with more ease or efficiency in transference when the relevant significant-other representations are activated. Finally, we show that some self-regulatory processes in transference appear to transpire automatically, while others may not, again using this ease of processing measure as well as our measure of the expressions of facial affect. Overall, we argue that these measures provide evidence for the unconscious relational self, and we turn now to a more in-depth presentation of our model.

Our Theory of the Relational Self

Our Social-Cognitive Model

As noted, significant-other representations are linked to knowledge about the self as experienced with the other, and transient activation of a significant-other representation by immediate contextual cues spreads to aspects of the relational self-with-this-other (Andersen & Chen, 2002; Andersen, Reznik, & Chen, 1997). This notion is based on a widely held assumption that all knowledge about the self cannot be activated in its entirety, and that only a subset is active in working memory at any given moment (e.g., Linville & Carlston, 1994). When contextual cues activate a significant-other representation, the subset of self-aspects experienced when with the significant other is then recruited into the working self-concept and becomes available in working memory. This process leads to shifts in the phenomenal self toward the self one is when in the presence of this significant other. Thus, the self may be essentially newly constructed in each interpersonal context, as contextual cues trigger particular self-attributes that are then recruited into the working self-concept. In fact, our research has demonstrated that when a significant-other representation is activated in an encounter with a new person, one tends to become the version of oneself one typically is with this significant other (Hinkley & Andersen, 1996). This shift in the contents of the working self-concept also prompts other self-relevant processes.

An approach consistent with ours is that focusing on relational schemas (Baldwin, 1992), which also assumes the memory linkages between significant others and the self that contain self-other relationship patterns. This line of work has been valuable and evocative and has contributed significantly to the literature. On the other hand, whereas we have focused more on the idiographic nature of significant-other representations, and the unique version of the self one is in relation to each significant other in one's life (Hinkley & Andersen, 1995; see Chen & Andersen, 1999), much of that research has focused on generic relational patterns (e.g., Baldwin, Fehr, Keedian, Seidel, & Thompson, 1993) and aspects of self (e.g., Baldwin & Sinclair, 1996). Of course, we also trace the activation and use of significant-other representations in transference and the relational self and in our recent work have begun to extend our thinking to normative representations of self and the self-other relationship (e.g., Andersen & Chen, 2002; Baum & Andersen, 1999).

Contextual Activation, the Self, and Personality

As noted, our research has shown that even in the absence of transient, contextual cues, significant-other representations have a high activation readiness, that is, they are chronically accessible (e.g., Andersen et al., 1995). At the same time, research has shown that cues emanating from a new person that overlap to some extent with stored knowledge about a significant other provide additional contextual activation (Chen et al., 1999). In our experimental work, we rely on cues about a new person to transiently activate transference. Our experiments are usually conducted in two sessions. In the first, participants provide descriptions of their significant others. In the second (held a couple of weeks later), we manipulate the interpersonal context that participants are faced with, in that participants usually anticipate meeting a new person who is or is not characterized by descriptors participants themselves provided at pretest about a significant other.

Contextual variability in the self depends in part on whether or not transference is set into motion by the presence of contextual cues. Just as a professional setting is associated with the self one is at work, a new person may constitute a "context" which activates a relevant significant-other representation and, accordingly, the associated self-with-significant-other (Andersen & Chen, 2002). These assumptions are compatible with conceptualizing personality in if-then terms, with ifs representing situations and thens representing particular behaviors elicited in them (Mischel & Shoda, 1995). Accordingly, personality reflects an individual's overall pattern of if-then relations. Our theory parallels this model in the idea that variability across different situations is fundamental (see also Higgins, 1990; Mischel, 1999). However, our focus is specific in its emphasis on interpersonal ifs—newly encountered individuals who, by virtue of their resemblance to a significant other, serve as contexts that activate significant-other representations and thus bring to the fore relevant changes in the self. An individual's overall repertoire of relational selves—aspects of the self tied to a significant other—thus represents a major source of the interpersonal patterns that characterize his or her personality across contexts (Andersen & Chen, 2002).

The Uniqueness of Significant-Other Representations and Their Activation

How are significant-other representations different from various other representations? We have proposed (e.g., Andersen & Glassman, 1996) that each mental representation of a significant other designates a specific, unique individual, rather than a shared notion of a social category, type, or group (e.g., Andersen & Klatzky, 1987; Brewer, 1988; Cantor & Mischel, 1979; Fiske & Taylor, 1991; Higgins & King, 1981). Representations of significant others are n-of-one representations or exemplars (Linville & Fischer, 1993; Smith & Zarate, 1992). While they contain generic knowledge about the significant person, as well as unique knowledge and experience, it is the representation of the person that accounts for the coherence of these associations in memory. No generic label referring to more than one person can quite serve this function. Thus, significant-other representations contain descriptive knowledge generalized from experiences with the individual as well as specific memories (Brooks, 1987; Gilovich, 1981), and both should be brought to bear in interpreting new people in transference.

Evidence supports the distinction between exemplars and generic constructs by showing that memory is far more specific than would be expected if only generic knowledge were retained (e.g., Smith, 1998; Smith & Zarate, 1990, 1992; chapter 5, this volume; see also Macrae et al., 1998). Although both exemplars and generic knowledge are connected in memory, can activate each other, and are used in social perception, exemplar-based processing is readily distinguishable from category-based processing (e.g., Karylowski, Konarzewski, & Motes, 1999; Smith, Stewart, & Buttram, 1992). Our research has shown that significant-other representations are a type of exemplar that is more chronically accessible than are generic social constructs (e.g., Andersen et al., 1995; Andersen, Lambert, & Dick, 2001; Chen et al., 1999; see also Karylowski et al., 1999). Moreover, consistent with exemplar notions, our work has emphasized the uniqueness of each significant other in a person's life. Assorted idiographic knowledge is contained in representations of significant others, such as physical characteristics, ways of relating, interests, habits, and other personality attributes (e.g., Andersen & Cole, 1990; Prentice, 1990), including the other's interpersonal behaviors, inner feelings, and motivations (e.g., Andersen, Glassman, & Gold, 1998; Chen, 2001; Johnson & Boyd, 1995). Such individualized knowledge is activated as part of the significant-other representation when a new person is similar to the significant other (a process akin to that in analogy-based models; see Gilovich, 1981; Gentner & Markman, 1997; Read & Cessa, 1991; Spellman & Holyoak, 1992).

When attributes of a significant other are encountered in a new target person, the internal organization of the significant-other representation should facilitate the spread of association within the representation from encountered attributes to those not encountered and yet relevant to the significant other. This should result in inferences about the target person that go beyond what was learned (Collins & Loftus, 1975). And this structural property of inner organization (see also chapter 5), combined with the chronic accessibility of significant-other representations, makes these representations likely to be activated outside of awareness.

It is important to note, however, that although we characterize our model of transference and the activation of significant-other representations in terms of spread of activation—which assumes an associative network model of knowledge activation (e.g., Collins & Loftus, 1975; Wyer & Carlston, 1979)—alternative models exist. For example, in connectionist models (e.g.,

Smith, 1996), conjoint activation takes place simultaneously based on connection weights. We have no investment in the relative accuracy of these models, and to a large extent they make the same predictions. Our theoretical investment is in the linkages within the significant-other representations that are modeled either as connection weights or as spread of activation, and in the linkages between the significant other and the self. We argue that there is an automatic tendency to use significant-other representations in social perception and interpersonal relations, such that the relational self is called into play automatically as well. The notion that similarity-based activation transpires without need of active processing in everyday cognition supports this assumption in our work (chapter 5).

Activation of Generic Relational Knowledge Linked to the Significant Other

Because knowledge about each significant other is linked in memory with unique aspects of the self and unique relational patterns, we highlight idiographic elements of significant-other representations and relational selves. Activating significant-other representations also activates generic, socially shared constructs, such as social categories or social identities associated with the significant other. In support of this assumption, research has shown that when significant-other representations are primed, the gender category to which the person belongs is automatically activated, providing evidence for a link in memory between significant-other representations and generic social categories (Karylowski et al., 1999). This evidence also supports the relative ease with which activation spreads from significant-other representations to categorical social knowledge.

In transference, then, activation of a significant-other representation should also spread to generic constructs that have normative implications. One form of such knowledge is one's interpersonal role with the significant other. This hypothesis is important, given increasing interest in relational roles (e.g., Berscheid, 1994; Fiske, 1992; Mills & Clark, 1994; see also Bugental, 2000). Such a role relationship with a significant other should thus be invoked when the significant-other representation is activated. As a result, role-based expectations and goals, along with their affective consequences if, for example, a role-violation is experienced, should also emerge (Baum & Andersen, 1999). While much theoretical work on roles defines them in terms of the broad survival goals they serve (e.g., Bugental, 2000; Kenrick, Maner, Butner, Li, & Becker, 2003) or the taxonomies into which they are nested (e.g., Fiske, 1992; Mills & Clark, 1994), our work focuses specifically on a single, actual relationship and the self-other role in that relationship. In the case of a significant other, the role relationship is often, but not always, communal—based on mutuality and needs for connection and belonging.

Generic, socially shared elements of one's relational selves should also include notions about the significant other's standards for the self, such as the significant other's hopes and wishes (ideal standards) or notions about the qualities it is one's duty or obligation to possess (ought standards). In self-discrepancy theory (Higgins, 1987, 1996b), standards for the self are defined in normative, categorical terms (although they are idiographically assessed), and they may be inconsistent with perceptions of the actual self, resulting in emotional distress (Higgins, 1997). Such normative elements of self-other relationships, moreover, may become activated in transference in the form of self-standards and self-discrepancies, along with the corresponding negative affective experience arising from one's perceived failure to meet these standards (Reznik & Andersen, 2004a).

In sum, while not all aspects of self are linked with significant others, and knowledge of self involves many other elements, such as abilities, values, goals, opinions, and standards, the profound emotional-motivational importance of significant others combined with the chronic accessibility of significant-other representations suggests a strong baseline influence of significant-other representations on day-to-day functioning. Moreover, while representations of anyone one knows or has known, whether significant or not, are likely to exert some influence on social perception by means of this kind of process (e.g., Karylowski et al., 1999), the depth, extensiveness, and detail of the knowledge represented about significant others (Andersen & Cole, 1990), encompassing both the mundane and the sublime, make significant-other representations particularly likely to be activated in response to new people.

Evidence on Significant Others and Transference

We now turn to the evidence that supports our theoretical model, highlighting findings that most directly address the new unconscious in transference. The evidence obtained speaks to the nature of the unconscious in transference even when it does not contain explicit measures of unconscious processes. This is so because our model and methods rely entirely on the activation and use of social constructs or exemplars, which are known to operate outside of awareness in well-specified ways. In reviewing this body of work, we emphasize findings concerning automatic activation of significant-other representations, their related affect, the spread of activation to the relational self (and self-evaluation) from the significant-other representation, and the elicitation of self-regulation.

Ease of Processing and Chronic Accessibility

At the outset, it should be noted that a wide body of evidence suggests that it is with a special ease of processing that people use mental representations of significant others in various cognitive operations. Qualities of significant others are called to mind more rapidly as people complete sentences about these individuals than are the features of less significant others or of generic categories like stereotypes (Andersen & Cole, 1990; Andersen et al., 1998; Chen, 2001). Likewise, people are able to indicate especially rapidly whether or not a significant other would (or would not) have particular experiences—as compared with how quickly they can make such judgments for a nonsignificant other (Andersen, Lambert, & Dick, 2001; in a paradigm adapted from Andersen, Klatzky, & Murray, 1990; see also Karylowski et al., 1999). Overall, people also, it turns out, make faster judgments about whether or not features of significant others are self-descriptive (Aron, Aron, Tudor, & Nelson, 1991) or are descriptive of the other (Prentice, 1990). Indeed, they in fact make faster decisions about any familiar conceptual structure than about any unfamiliar one, such as their own home or car (Keenan & Baillet, 1980; see also Andersen & Glassman, 1996). In a related vein, significant-other primes facilitate judgments about gender categories far more than do nonsignificant-other primes, and even do so more than gender itself (the words *male* or *female*; Karylowski et al., 1999). In another paradigm, in a Stroop task, people take longer to name the color in which a sentence-stem describing a significant other is written than to name the color in which a nonsignificant-other sentence-stem is written or that in which a sentence-stem about another person's significant other is written (Andersen & Prasad, 2000). These data clearly indicate a special processing ease associated with significant-other representations.

Inference and Memory Effects

Turning to the transference paradigm, our early research on transference measured primarily inference and memory effects that could be traced to the activation of a significant-other representation and its use in interpreting a new person (Andersen & Cole, 1990). The evidence shows that knowledge about significant others is used to go beyond the information given (Bruner, 1957) about new people. In our experimental paradigm, participants encounter a new person who resembles a significant other—in terms of sentences read about this person that were derived from descriptions of a significant other. Later, when completing a memory task about the new person, participants tend to be especially confident about having seen descriptions of this new person that were not in fact presented about him or her, but that are characteristic of the significant other.

In particular, after learning about various fictional characters, people's inferences and memory about these characters show they are more likely to go beyond what they learned for the character resembling a significant other than for one resembling a nonsignificant other or a stereotype (Andersen et al., 1995; Andersen & Cole, 1990; Chen et al., 1999; Glassman & Andersen, 1999b). They are more likely to use the particular activated representation to make inferences about the fictional character when it is a significant-other representation. This suggests that significant-other representations are even more ubiquitous in social judgment than stereotyping or other kinds of social-construct-based processing (see also Karylowski et al., 1999). We have obtained our memory effects repeatedly, and they are not accounted for either by the self-generated nature of the descriptors (self-generation effects; see Greenwald & Banaji, 1989) or, as noted, by reliance on generic stereotypes (Andersen et al., 1995).

In a similar paradigm, after learning about a new person allegedly seated next door, people's inferences and memory are more likely to go beyond what they learned when this person resembles a significant other from their own life rather than resembling a significant other from another participant's life (e.g., Andersen & Baum, 1994). To assess this, we yoke each participant in the control group on a one-to-one basis (without replacement) with a participant in the significant-other-resemblance condition so that the yoked participant is exposed to exactly the same triggering features as is the experimental participant. The inference and memory measure also makes use of the experimental participant's significant-other features. Hence, across conditions, not only is stimulus content identical, but so is inference/memory content (as tested). Such contents are perfectly controlled, and this means that the effects cannot be attributed, for example, to semantic associations among just anyone's significant-other features that would lead to heightened inference and memory during the test phase when the test also involves this same person's significant-other features (as encountered in the learning phase). We conclude, using this design, that when a new person has some minimal resemblance to one's own significant other, one will have a specific readiness to use the representation to make sense of the new person. The effect holds for both positive and negative significant others, and cannot be accounted for by significant-other valence (Andersen et al., 1996; Berenson & Andersen, 2004; Berk & Andersen, 2000; Hinkley & Andersen, 1996; Reznik & Andersen, 2004a). Moreover, the effect also holds even when a thorough debriefing procedure is used in which participants are given the opportunity to indicate any suspicions they may have, and they reveal little or no suspicion. It holds as well when participants are in fact excluded from the study if they do happen to correctly guess the connection between the features of the target person in the experiment and the prior session in which they listed features of their significant other (e.g., Berenson & Andersen, 2004; Reznik & Andersen, 2004b).

Of course, because representations of significant others are so highly familiar (among other reasons), they are chronically accessible; that is, they are likely to be used willy-nilly even when not contextually triggered (Bargh et al., 1986; Higgins, 1996a; Higgins & Brendl, 1995; Higgins & King, 1981; Prentice, 1990). No priming is required for their use (as is the case with other chronically accessible constructs), nor is any special applicability to the new person required (Andersen et al., 1995, Study 1; Chen et al., 1999). Significant-other representations are so readily accessed and used that no contextual cues—in the new person—are necessary for the representation to be activated and used. Still, significant-other-based memory is greater when relevant contextual cues are present in the new person than when not, and contextual sources of activation appear to combine additively with chronic accessibility to increase the likelihood that these representations will be used (Andersen et al., 1995, Study 2; see also Bargh et al., 1986). Consistent with this notion, evidence in the area of object categorization has shown that, even in the domain of objects, people will map the internal, functional structure of an object category onto a new stimulus and will infer new features not observed on this basis, in what is termed *structure mapping* (Gentner & Markman, 1997; chapter 5, this volume). Hence, the phenomenon of filling in the blanks about a new stimulus based on an existing category obviously occurs for object categories, and relational elements within a given category are also relevant to what is inferred about a new stimulus. Indeed, relational elements within a significant-other representation have been shown to be very strongly linked in memory, such that triggering, for example, a particular inner experience a significant other may have (such as "when she feels angry") will trigger the significant other's response to that inner experience ("she is withdrawn and won't speak to me"), suggesting an internal structure of significant other representations that may be relevant to what is assumed about a new person when a given significant other representation is activated (Chen, 2001, 2003).

None of these results can easily be explained by the intention to use one's knowledge of a particular significant other in social perception. In all of our work in the transference paradigm, we instruct participants to be accurate in their inferences and memory, and such an accuracy goal should work against any strategy to show bias toward the significant other. On the other hand, participants in this paradigm have some intention to think about the new person in order to respond to questions about him or her, in that we later ask them to indicate what they think and how they feel about the person, so we cannot rule out all intentionality in our effects. Of course, it should be possible to activate a significant-other representation outside of conscious awareness altogether, and we assume this should lead to the same pattern of transference-based inferences. We describe research addressing this issue below. Evidence of this kind provides further support for the argument that conscious strategies are not necessary for the effect to occur (Glassman & Andersen, 1999a).

Unconscious Activation of Transference

As the preceding discussion implies, contextual triggering of significant-other representations may arise through exposure to consciously perceived triggering cues in the new person. We also argue that transference is likely to have an unconscious basis—that is, that a significant-other representation may become activated without awareness based on the attributes of a new person perceived only unconsciously (Glassman & Andersen, 1999a). Similarly, changes in the self may involve conscious experience of the self in the context of significant-other activation and transference in addition to less conscious effects.

Because significant-other representations should not require effort to be activated, they should readily be activated subliminally, which would support the potentially ubiquitous role of significant-other representations in social perception and social relations. The question of the extent to which transference can take place outside of conscious awareness is also noteworthy because of its long-standing historical interest. Freud (1912/1958), along with most psychoanalysts, believed that transference is unconscious. Hence, empirical demonstration of the unconscious nature of transference would lend important support to long-standing clinical assumptions (e.g., Ehrenreich, 1989; Luborsky & Crits-Christoph, 1990). It would rule out the necessity of being consciously reminded of a significant other as a precondition for the process to occur.

In short, one need not "try" to think of or to be influenced by significant-other representations in the course of everyday relations. Hence, we argue that transference does not need to be evoked consciously and can be activated subliminally. The evidence of unconscious activation of transference is also important because it provides a basis for the possibility that most of the basic processes of transference—emotional, motivational, and cognitive—emerge without the need for conscious awareness or effortful processing.

Studying the Unconscious Although research on subliminal perception has a controversial history in the cognitive and social-psychological literatures (e.g., Bowers, 1984; Greenwald & Banaji, 1995; Holender, 1986; Kihlstrom, Barnhardt, & Tataryn, 1992), our work is informed by a growing body of evidence showing that subliminally presented stimuli can be processed outside of awareness, influencing lexical decision tasks (Blair & Banaji, 1996; Greenwald, Klinger, & Schuh, 1995; Marcel, 1983), self-evaluation (Baldwin, 1994; Baldwin, Carell, & Lopez, 1990), impressions and recall of otherwise ambiguous target persons (Bargh et al., 1986; Devine, 1989; Erdley & D'Agostino, 1988; Lewicki, 1986; Macrae, Bodenhausen, & Milne, 1995), and even social behavior (e.g., Chen & Bargh, 1997; Fitzsimons & Bargh, 2003; Neuberg, 1988).

Subliminal methodologies are "high-tech" and may seem disconnected from normal experience, yet there are analogies to subliminal activation in real life (cf. Bargh, 1992). For instance, the most important attribute or feature that triggers transference may not be the one we know we have seen, possibly because our attention was elsewhere at the time, or because the feature was exhibited or expressed by a target person so briefly that we were not aware of perceiving it. The subliminal method provides a way to ensure that the activation process is literally taking place without the participant's knowledge.

Ways of Being Unconscious In our framework, we assume that transference can be unconscious in several ways (Glassman & Andersen, 1999c). For example, the content of what is transferred in transference may not be available to consciousness or, by contrast, one may be aware of the content but not aware of the cues that end up triggering the effect (Kihlstrom, 1987; Luborsky, Crits-Christoph, Friedman, Mark, & Schaffler, 1991; Singer & Salovey, 1991; for definitions of awareness, see also Bargh, 1994, 1997; Uleman, 1987). On another level, one may not be conscious of making a significant-other-based interpretation about a new person. We know of no other empirical evidence that has examined the unconscious nature of transference, though the subliminal activation of significant-other representations has been shown in other research (e.g., Baldwin, 1994; Baldwin et al., 1990). In our work, we examined unconscious activation of transference using cues presented subliminally.

Subliminal Paradigm In the experiment, participants sat at a computer terminal to play a "computer game" with a partner seated elsewhere. They were told to focus their attention on a white dot in the center of a computer screen in order to read supraliminal stimuli presented there, while simultaneously responding to random flashes on the left and right sides of the screen by pressing "left" or "right" on a response box. The flashes were subliminal descriptors consisting of four or fewer words, flashed for less than 100 ms in parafoveal vision and then pattern masked (as in Bargh et al., 1986). They were derived either from the participant's own significant-other descriptors (generated in a pretest session; i.e., in the experimental condition); a yoked participant's significant-other descriptors (i.e., in the yoked control condition); or the participant's own descriptors generated earlier that constituted no particular category or mental representation (i.e., in the no-representation control condition; cf. Greenwald, 1981; Greenwald & Banaji, 1989). The supraliminal stimuli were irrelevant to the significant other.

After completing the computer game, participants offered their impression of their game partner by rating the descriptiveness of several statements. Participants exposed to subliminal presentations derived from their own significant other (experimental condition) performed the inference task by assessing the new person based on descriptors derived from their own significant other. Similarly, participants in the yoked control condition, even though they were exposed subliminally to a yoked participant's significant-other features, also performed the inference task by assessing the new person using the features of their own significant other, thus equating the chronic accessibility of the significant-other features appearing in the inference task across these conditions. Finally, participants in the no-representation control condition, having been exposed subliminally to their own no-representation features, later performed the inference task using these same kinds of no-representation features, so that we could control for self-generation effects in both the subliminal stimuli and test items. In all conditions, we focused in data analyses on inferences indexed by descriptors that were not subliminally presented to participants.[1] Importantly, the results of a subliminality check performed at the end of the experiment indicated that participants were not able to guess at better than chance levels the content of the subliminal exposures. Hence, the data suggest they were unaware of the content of the subliminal triggering cues.

Subliminal Results Of greatest interest, and as figure 16.1 shows, participants in the experimental condition—that is, those for whom their game partner subliminally resembled their own significant other—made stronger significant-other–derived inferences than did those in both control conditions. Specifically, as predicted, participants in the significant-other condition rated not-presented items from their own significant other as describing the new person more than did participants in the yoked control condition.

These data support our hypothesis about the unconscious activation of transference. From a methodological standpoint, it is important to note that each control participant was exposed subliminally to the exact same features to which one participant in the experimental condition was exposed. That is, he or she was yoked on a one-to-one basis (without replacement) with a participant in the experimental condition, which perfectly controlled for subliminal content across the experimental and control conditions, even while assessing each participant's own significant-other–derived inferences about the new person. On the other hand, because the subliminal cues presented in the own-significant-other condition were self-generated, the factor of self-

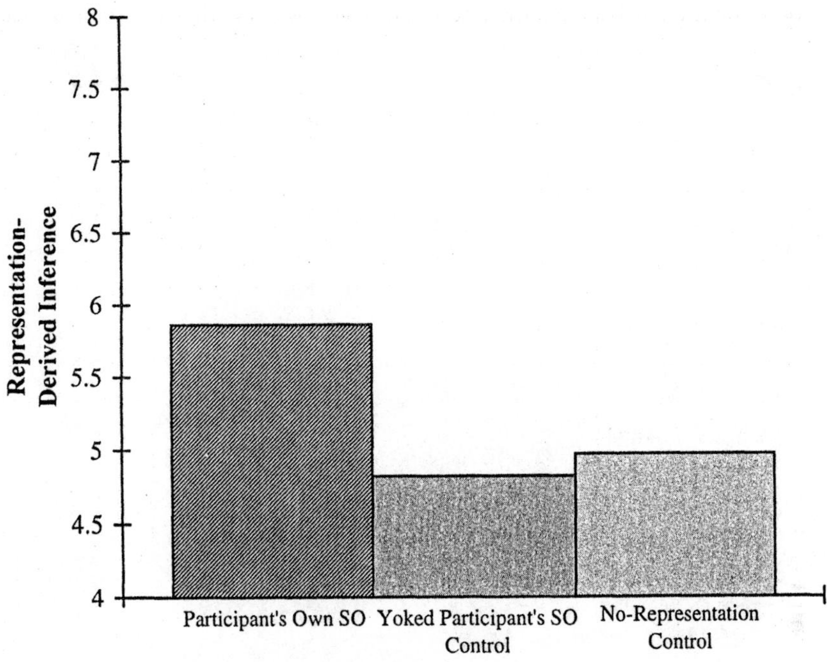

Figure 16.1 Automatic activation, Study 1: Significant-other-derived inference as a function of subliminal exposure condition (adapted from Glassman & Andersen, 1999a).

generation alone could perhaps have accounted for the apparent effect. That is, the subliminal significant-other condition involved self-generated cues, and the yoked-control condition did not. As figure 16.1 shows, however, our additional control condition was able to rule out self-generation effects (Greenwald & Banaji, 1989) because inference ratings in the own-significant-other condition were greater than those in the no-representation condition.

Subliminal Replication In another study (Glassman & Andersen, 1999a) that conceptually replicated this work, we included both the experimental and the yoked control conditions, and we also controlled for the valence of the significant-other representation. In Study 1, the affect associated with the significant other was unspecified. In Study 2, the significant-other representations were explicitly positive. As shown in figure 16.2, the results of the study indicated that participants went beyond the subliminally given information to a greater extent when their game partner subliminally resembled their own rather than a yoked participant's significant other. This evidence clearly shows that transference can be triggered unconsciously, and that the phe-

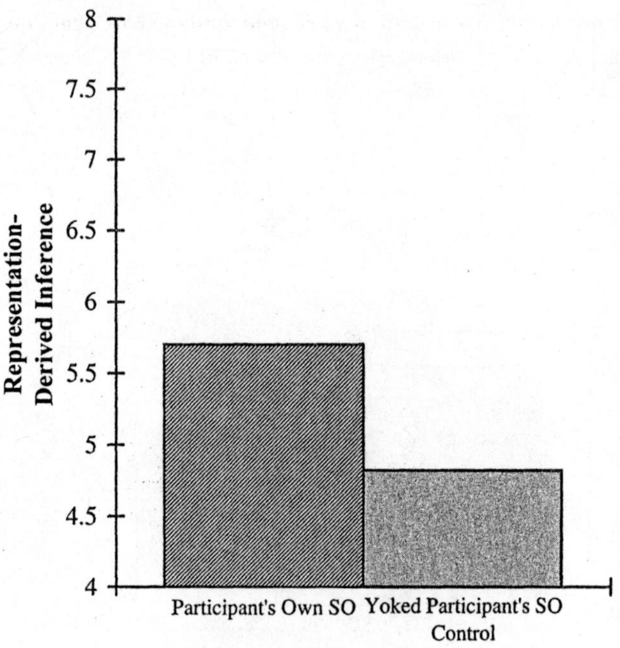

Figure 16.2 Subliminal activation, Study 2: Significant-other-derived inference as a function of subliminal exposure condition (adapted from Glassman & Andersen, 1999a).

nomenon does not appear to depend on perceivers being consciously reminded of a significant other. Our data also support the argument that well-established or overlearned constructs, that is, those based on frequently rehearsed experiences, acquire a special readiness to be activated unconsciously (Logan, 1988; Meichenbaum & Gilmore, 1984; Singer & Bonanno, 1990; Smith & Lerner, 1986).

We now turn to a wider review of a variety of findings concerning transference and the relational self, emphasizing affect and self-regulation with relevance to unconscious or automatic processes.

Evoking Positive Evaluation

The simplest affective finding emerging from our work is that the activation of a significant-other representation elicits the affect typically experienced in relation to the significant other, as in the theory of schema-triggered affect, characterizing how category-based evaluation is ascribed to a new person

(Fiske & Pavelchak, 1986). In a paradigm designed to examine such responses, participants learn about a new individual who resembles either their own positive significant other or their own negative significant other, or, in a control condition, learn about a new person who resembles someone else's positive or negative significant other. In such a design, participants are also more likely to evaluate the new person positively, that is, to express liking for him or her, when he or she resembles their positive rather than negative significant other, an effect that does not occur in the no-resemblance condition (e.g., Andersen & Baum, 1994). We have repeatedly demonstrated more liking of a new person in a positive transference, even though an equal number of positive and negative features are encountered about the new person in both the positive and the negative transference conditions. We argue that this process takes place in the "real" world. One comes to like or dislike the new person by virtue of some minimal resemblance he or she has to a significant other—based on the overall affect associated with the significant other (Andersen & Baum, 1994; Andersen et al., 1996; Baum & Andersen, 1999; Berk & Andersen, 2000; Reznik & Andersen, 2004a).

Eliciting Automatic Positive Facial Affect

We assume that evaluation is evoked when the significant-other representation is activated, which involves activation of the affect associated with the representation. Because significant-other representations can be activated outside of conscious awareness and without effort, the affect linked to these representations should in fact be triggered with little cognitive effort or consciousness. Although self-report measures of evaluation do not permit conclusions about potential effortlessness of schema-triggered evaluation, effects obtained in nonverbal behavior are more compelling. Indeed, our data on people's relatively immediate facial expressions provide converging evidence for the automatic elicitation of affect in transference. We have shown that when people encounter significant-other-resemblance cues while reading each descriptive sentence about the new person, their immediate facial affect reflects the affect associated with the significant other (Andersen et al., 1996; Berenson & Andersen, 2004). Participants' relatively immediate affect in the transference context—in the few moments during which each cue was encountered—reflects the positive or negative regard they have for the significant other. As shown in figure 16.3, participants in transference expressed more positive facial affect when the new person resembled their positive rather than negative significant other, a pattern that did not occur in the no-resemblance control condition.

Because of the relative immediacy of this measure, the observed changes in facial displays of affect can be conceptualized as involving little deliberation

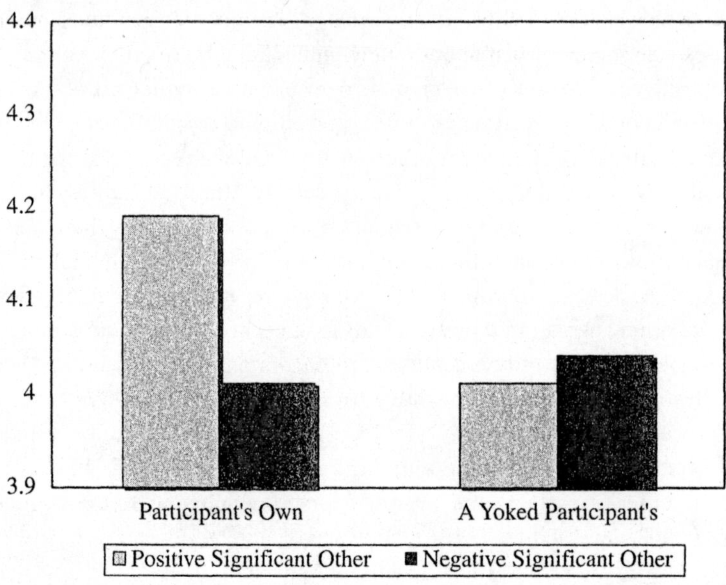

Figure 16.3 Automatic evaluation: Judges' average rating of positivity in facial affect at encoding as a function of significant-other resemblance and overall evaluative tone (adapted from Andersen, Reznik, & Manzella, 1996).

or effort. The data thus imply that schema-triggered affect in transference may arise relatively automatically, though these methods do not permit entirely unequivocal conclusions (for more on unconscious vs. conscious emotions, see Oehman, 1999). The data do, however, provide grist for the notion that, as with affect, the evaluation of a new person in transference arises relatively automatically. In a later section, we present more nuanced findings with regard to immediate expressions of facial affect, addressing the issues of self-regulation in transference.

Evoking Motivation for Interpersonal Closeness

Along the same lines of affectively charged responses, self-reported approach motivation with significant others has also been observed in transference. Specifically, people want to be emotionally intimate and close with new others, rather than withdrawing from them and being closed and distant, when the new person resembles a positive significant other, that is, someone with whom there is or was such closeness (Andersen et al., 1996; Berk & Andersen, 2000; Reznik & Andersen, 2004a). This is provocative given other evidence on the automatic activation of goal states and related behavior (Bargh & Barndollar, 1996; Bargh & Chartrand, 1999; Bargh et al., 2001;

see also Aarts & Dijksterhuis, 2000), and in fact automatic motives based on activated significant-other representations (Shah, 2003).

Triggering Expectancies for Acceptance versus Rejection

Beyond motivation, we have demonstrated that participants' expectations for acceptance by or rejection from significant others come into play with new people in the context of transference, again as a function of the affect associated with the significant other (e.g., Andersen et al., 1996; Berk & Andersen, 2000; Reznik & Andersen, 2004a). When the new person resembles a positive significant other, people report expecting to be accepted rather than rejected by the new person. The growing literature on rejection sensitivity and the ease with which it can be triggered supports the possible automaticity of such processes (Downey & Feldman, 1996; see also Baldwin & Meunier, 1999), although we have yet to explicitly examine this in our research. In particular, this related work suggests that people who are especially sensitive to rejection have a vigilance system for approval or disapproval by others that is readily activated and which involves automatic negative expectations. When such automatic processes are set in motion, it is only "strategic" attention deployment (to non–rejection-related information) that counteracts negative interpersonal consequences (Ayduk et al., 2000).

Eliciting Interpersonal Behavior: Positive Affect Expressed in Conversation

Another line of research extends this evidence to overt behavior, more specifically, dyadic interpersonal behavior in an unstructured telephone conversation. When a new person activates a significant-other representation, interpersonal behavior comes to reflect the affect associated with the significant other (Berk & Andersen, 2000). That is, using a classic paradigm (Snyder, Tanke, & Berscheid, 1977), conversational behavior of two people was assessed, in this case focusing on the "target" person in an interaction with a perceiver who was or was not experiencing a positive or a negative transference. As predicted, behavioral confirmation arose in the target person's conversational behavior in the context of transference. That is, the target's conversational behavior came to reflect the affect associated with the significant other, as coded by independent judges who could not hear the perceiver's contributions to the conversation. Although these data are silent on automatic elicitation of behavior, the behavioral confirmation process is not thought to require a conscious intention to lure the other person into becoming what one anticipates. The affect triggered virtually instantaneously in perceivers appears to unfold sequentially in the interaction such that it is ultimately reciprocated by the new person's behavior. Because behavioral confirmation has been shown to occur nonconsciously (Chen & Bargh, 1997), we assume that the process occurred without perceivers being consciously aware of it.

Evidence on the Relational Self

Activating Idiographic Self-With-Other Knowledge

Of importance in our thinking about the relational self is research showing that encounters with people who bear some resemblance to a significant other lead one to become the self one typically is when with this significant other (Hinkley & Andersen, 1996). When a new person activates a significant-other representation, this activation should spread to elements of the self linked with the significant other, resulting in an influx of these self-with-significant-other features into the working self-concept. This process should take place relatively automatically. In addition, changes in self-evaluation should also occur in transference. That is, the activated relational self should be associated with a positive self-evaluation in a positive transference and with a negative self-evaluation in a negative transference. This influx of positivity or negativity into the self should occur without particular effort.

In our working self-concept paradigm, participants generated sentences to characterize the self at the moment—an idiographic measure of the working self-concept. They also classified each sentence they listed as either positive or negative, as an idiographic measure of self-evaluation. They completed this task both in a preliminary session and in the experiment itself after learning about a new person. Importantly, in the preliminary session only, participants also listed sentences that described aspects of the self they experienced when with the significant other. The number of overlapping sentences between participants' working self-concept in the experiment and the self with the significant other was computed. This overlap was then examined, controlling for overlap at pretest. As predicted, the evidence supported the predicted transference-based change in self-concept by showing more self-with-other features in the working self-concept when the new person resembled participants' own significant other (relative to the no-resemblance control condition). In transference, participants' self-concepts came to reflect the self-aspects they tended to experience with the significant other. This occurred for both positive and negative significant others.

In terms of self-evaluation, we calculated the self-evaluation associated with the working self-concept in transference by summing the valence ascriptions participants gave to the particular aspects of their working self-concept that changed to reflect the relational self—that is, the self with the other. As

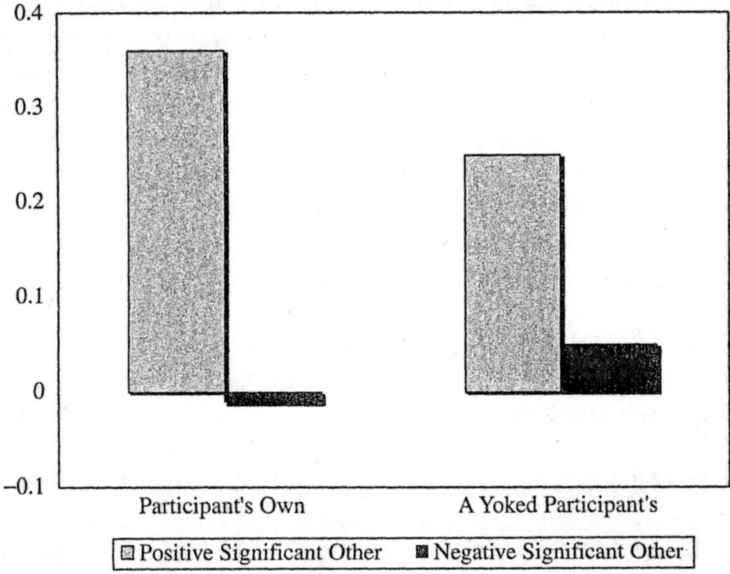

Figure 16.4 Changes in self-evaluation deriving from the relationship: Valence of working self-descriptors overlapping with the relevant self-with-significant-other, corrected for pretest valence, as a function of significant-other resemblance and overall evaluative tone (adapted from Hinkley & Andersen, 1996).

shown in figure 16.4, participants' self-evaluation associated with the change in the working self-concept—for those features that overlapped with the self-with-significant-other in the working self-concept—was more positive (covarying out the same scores at pretest) when the new person resembled the participants' positive, rather than negative, significant other. This pattern did not occur in the no-resemblance control condition (Hinkley & Andersen, 1996; Reznik & Andersen, 2004b). Put differently, self-evaluation was less positive (and somewhat more negative) in the negative rather than positive transference, which did not occur in the comparable conditions without significant-other resemblance.

We now turn to evidence on activation of various self-aspects in transference, showing that activation of a significant-other representation activates shared relational-self constructs that are normative and prescriptive.

Activating Interpersonal Roles and Associated Affect

As one example, the interpersonal role one occupies with a significant other should be activated in transference, that is, when a significant-other representation is activated. When a role is activated, violated expectations of the new person should lead to negative or dysphoric mood, and our research shows this occurs in transference (Baum & Andersen, 1999). When a significant other is an authority figure, activation of the significant-other representation activates the authority-novice role, and violations of this role become problematic. These findings are noteworthy given the increasing importance of roles (along with associated motives and expectancies) in contemporary personality and social psychology (e.g., Fiske, 1992; Mills & Clark, 1994; see also Bugental, 2000; Kenrick et al., 2003), even if they do not speak explicitly to aspects of automaticity.

Activating Standards and Self-Discrepancies

Another example of shared relational constructs that are linked to significant others can be found in the standards a significant other holds for the self. According to self-discrepancy theory (e.g., Higgins, 1996b), such self-standards should be linked to the significant other in memory. Our evidence shows that activating a significant-other representation in fact activates (indirectly) the standards and self-discrepancies held from the standpoint of this significant other, and, thus, any discrepancy between the significant other's wishes or "shoulds" and one's actual self. Hence, significant-other activation results in the kind of affective consequences, as indexed by self-report mood measures, that self-discrepancy theory predicts. Specifically, ideal-discrepant participants manifest dejection-related affect, while ought-discrepant participants manifest agitation-related affect (hostility and resentment) when the new person resembles the significant other with whose standards they are discrepant (Reznik & Andersen, 2004a).

In addition to influencing mood states, standards should also determine self-regulatory processes. A self-regulatory focus on obtaining (or not losing) positive outcomes originates from ideal self-standards, while a self-regulatory focus on avoidance or prevention of negative outcomes stems from ought self-standards (e.g., Higgins, 1997, 1998). Our evidence largely supports the notion that self-regulatory focus is activated in transference, yielding a pattern consistent with self-discrepancy and self-regulatory focus theories. Ideal-discrepant individuals are more eager to engage with the new person while anticipating the interaction with him or her than when no longer expecting it. By contrast, ought-discrepant individuals are more likely to wish to avoid the other while expecting the interaction with him or her than when no longer expecting it (Reznik & Andersen, 2004a). In short, the tendency of ideal-discrepant individuals to strive toward positive outcomes with the other and the tendency of ought-discrepant individuals to avoid negative outcomes with the other are manifested in transference.

Overall, the evidence shows spread of activation from significant-other representations to normative self-aspects such as roles and standards, and extends prior work on idiographic aspects of the relational self (Hinkley & Andersen, 1996), by linking these significant-other representations to shared social constructs (see Karylowski et al., 1999; Smith & Zarate, 1992). The data support the activation of relevant aspects of the self—on the basis of significant-other activation—and we assume that the basic underlying mechanisms are likely to occur automatically.

Evidence on Self-Regulation and the Relational Self

Self-regulatory responses occur in transference, we argue, because significant others and relationships with these individuals are imbued with special emotional resonance. Significant others are uniquely positioned both to provide comfort and to disrupt affective equilibrium because one deeply cares about how they perceive things, how they feel, and what they do. For these reasons, the transference context may provide not only familiarity, a sense of closeness and ease, but also vulnerability and the need for self-regulation (Andersen, Chen, & Miranda, 2002).

One way to think about self-regulation is that when a threat to the self is experienced in transference, a kind of compensatory self-enhancement arises in response to it—to protect the self. Self-enhancement, positive illusions, and ego-defensive biases have commonly been observed (e.g., Greenberg & Pyszczynski, 1985; Showers, 1992; Steele, 1988; Taylor & Brown, 1988). The familiarity and closeness activated in transference make such processes especially likely when threat to the self is experienced because of considerable relevance to the self. One context in which this may occur is when a significant-other representation laden with negative affect is activated. The negativity associated with the person poses a threat to the self, such that compensatory self-enhancement should occur, assuming that capacity for such self-regulatory responses is not compromised by factors like low self-esteem.

Indeed, beyond self-enhancement in response to a threat to the self, in transference people should engage in other-enhancing or relationship-enhancing processes (Andersen & Chen, 2002). When a threat to the regard one has for the significant other is experienced, compensatory processes should arise. The need to remain close with significant others, to see them as friend not foe, holds sway. This kind of compensatory enhancement of the other should thus be observed in transference. Both self-protective and relationship-protective self-regulation should arise.

Evoking Self-Protective Self-Regulation

In terms of self-protective self-regulation, the research on the working self-concept described earlier (Hinkley & Andersen, 1996) involved shifts in the content of the working self-concept—in the direction of the self with the significant other. In the negative transference condition, the shift in self-evaluation was negative, and hence threatening. We thus assumed that self-protective self-regulation would be activated in this condition. The negative shift in self-evaluation for these features ought to be accompanied by a counteracting shift in self-evaluation directed against this negative blow to the self, and we found support for this assumption (Hinkley & Andersen, 1996).

In support of this self-regulatory hypothesis, participants' evaluations of those aspects of their working self-concept that did not change in the direction of the negative relationship with the significant other were actually more positive in this negative transference condition (controlling for pretest evaluation) than in any other condition. As shown in figure 16.5, when the new person resembled participants' own negatively regarded significant other, the aspects of their self-evaluation that did not change to reflect the content of the self-with-other reversed the blow to self-evaluation that occurred in that condition. In the negative transference, an overwhelming number of positively evaluated self-descriptors entered into the working self-concept, contrasting against the average valence of the descriptors associated with the self-with-other (Hinkley & Andersen, 1996). We argue that such self-enhance-

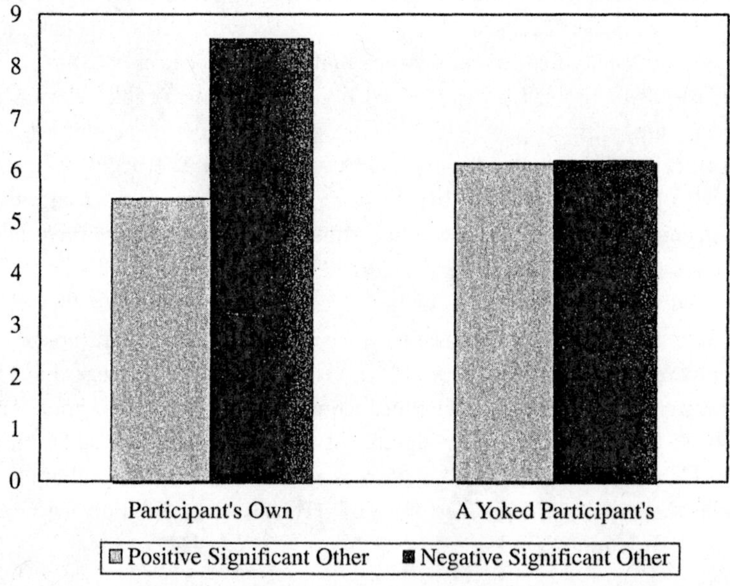

Figure 16.5 Self-protective self-regulation: Valence of working self-descriptors nonoverlapping with the relevant self-with-significant-other, corrected for pretest valence, as a function of significant-other resemblance and overall evaluative tone (adapted from Hinkley & Andersen, 1996).

ment reflects a self-protective, self-regulatory response to the influx of negative self-aspects into the working self-concept, much as observed in self-affirmation theory (e.g., Steele, 1988) or in terror management theory (e.g., Greenberg, Pyszczynski, Solomon, & Chatel, 1992)—to repair self-esteem (Greenberg & Pyszczynski, 1985) and perhaps regulate affect (Tice & Bratslavsky, 2000).

This evidence verifies that the relational self with the significant other is activated in transference, leading to changes in self-evaluation consistent with the affect that defines the relationship, and leading as well to changes in self-evaluation entirely inconsistent with this affect—when the transference is negative. The spread of activation to the relevant relational self activates negative self-evaluations, which presumably provokes self-protective self-regulation. Such self-regulation should promote feeling better and may well be relatively effortful and intentional, as it counteracts what is likely to be an unintended associative process, although this warrants investigation.

Evoking the Dreaded Self

Research along the same lines focuses on dreaded and desired relational selves, and addresses the question of whether or not transference-based changes and the self-regulatory processes that such changes set in motion occur relatively automatically or more effortfully (Reznik & Andersen, 2004b). It conceptually replicates prior work (Hinkley & Andersen, 1996) and focuses exclusively on positive significant others (rather than on comparing positive with negative). In particular, since dreaded selves are among the multiple selves an individual possesses, in some cases linked to a positive significant other, activating such significant-other representations should activate the dreaded self. One may love someone and yet frequently find oneself having dreaded feelings about him or her, or about the self, or both, and behaving dreadfully around that person as well. Hence, when a positive significant-other representation linked to a dreaded self is activated, it may activate this dreaded self, leading to similar consequences.

In particular, we studied this not by focusing on individual differences in desired and dreaded selves, but rather by assuming that all people can think of a significant other they love with whom they behave badly and another with whom they are at their best. Participants in the research had no trouble doing so, and we assessed changes in their self-evaluation in transference using our working self-concept paradigm (Hinkley & Andersen, 1996). Extending beyond this paradigm, we also adopted a reactive measure that examined response latencies as participants judged positive and negative adjectives. Overall, participants learned about a new person who resembled a positive significant other from their own life (from their family of origin)—a significant other associated with either a dreaded or a desired self—or they learned about a new person who resembled a significant other from the life of a yoked control participant (as usual).

Freely Listed Working Self-Concept As in prior research (Hinkley & Andersen, 1996), when the new person resembled a significant other, the contents of participants' working self-concept shifted in the direction of the self-when-with-the-significant-other. This shift occurred whether the significant other was associated with a dreaded self or with a desired self, and was indexed by the influx of features of the self-with-other into the working self-concept (controlling for the same score at pretest). When the new person resembled participants' own significant other with whom participants tend to be at their best, the contents of their working self-concept shifted in the direction of their desired self. When the new person resembled participants' own significant other with whom they tend to be at their worst, their self-concept features shifted in the direction of their dreaded self.

In terms of self-evaluation, when the significant other associated with the participant's dreaded self was activated, the self-descriptors shifting toward the self-with-other were significantly more negative, a pattern that did not occur in the no-resemblance control condition. Hence, when the dreaded or desired self is activated in transference, corresponding self-evaluation arises, and yet self-regulation also arises, findings that lend support to prior work. Participants recruit more positive self-attributes into the overall working self-concept. Self evaluation thus shifted not only in accord with the valence of the relational self, but also in a counteracting direction, suggesting self-protective self-regulation based on this dreaded relational self.

Response Latency and the Working Self-Concept As noted, the free-response data, as provocative as they are, do not address the issue of cognitive accessibility or ease of processing. Likewise, simple endorsement rates, much like free-response measures, tap the availability of desired and undesired self-attributes in one's self-conception, but not necessarily accessibility (Higgins, 1996a). On the other hand, response latency can be seen as an index of accessibility. Although it, too, may at times be subject to intentional, strategic influence, this is not always so. Using such a measure, participants did in fact say yes far more quickly to items descriptive of the dreaded self when the new person resembled participants' own significant other associated with the dreaded self rather than their desired self. Such self-descriptions and evaluations were presumably activated automatically, with shorter latencies reflecting increased cognitive accessibility for these aspects of self (see also Baldwin, 1994; Baldwin et al., 1990). Thus, in transference, dreaded self-attributes were not only more likely to be freely listed among other working self-concept descriptors but were also more cognitively accessible. The inverse was also true in the desired self condition, in which participants made slower yes decisions for dreaded-self adjectives. When the new person resembled a significant other associated with participants' desired self rather than the dreaded self, the dreaded self was apparently inhibited.

In terms of self-protective self-regulation, the data provided no support for faster latencies in judging desired-self items or other especially positive self-attributes in the dreaded-self condition of transference—which might have been expected if it were assumed that compensatory self-aspects are triggered relatively automatically to counteract the threat to the self in this condition. However, no such effect emerged.

Overall, we assume that the faster response latency to judge dreaded-self items in the dreaded-self condition occurred by means of the spread of activation from the significant other to the relational self, which should occur without investment of effort. We assume this heightened accessibility arose in a way that was unintended rather than being dependent on a concerted effort by participants to speed up their responses to negative self-descriptors. Our use of random assignment ruled out individual differences across the desired and dreaded self conditions and hence, although we cannot rule out effortful processing deriving from self-presentational concerns or other intentions altogether, we can think of no likely reason why participants would have taken up the strategy of responding particularly quickly to dreaded-self items in one of the four conditions. Moreover, no similar effect emerged for desired-self items in the desired-self condition, implying that the experiment provoked no general intention to respond quickly to items consistent with the activated self. The lack of such an effect in the desired-self condition may have been due to a rather small shift from any baseline accessibility of the desired self among these undergraduate participants.

It is instructive as well to consider whether participants said yes or no to these descriptors. In the context of the significant-other resemblance (vs. no-resemblance) associated with a dreaded self, participants endorsed significantly more dreaded-self items, as expected. However, they also endorsed just as many desired-self items as did participants in the desired-self condition in transference. Maintaining the desired self at the same level can be interpreted as having self-regulatory utility, even while the dreaded self is activated. This may buffer, to a degree, the influx of negativity into the working self-concept to preserve self-integrity and equilibrium (Andersen & Chen, 2002; Hinkley & Andersen, 1996; see also Showers, Abramson, & Hogan, 1998; Steele, 1988; Steele, Spencer, & Lynch, 1993). Because no heightened accessibility of positive self-attributes arose in the dreaded-self condition, however, these self-regulatory effects do not appear to operate automatically (Reznik & Andersen, 2004b). Still, imprecision in this particular measure leaves open the question of exactly how much consciousness, effort, or intention is needed or is at work in these effects.

Relationship-Protective Self-Regulation

As indicated, another form of self-regulation involves protecting the other person. And another means of assessing potentially automatic responding can be found in the virtually immediate expressions of facial affect, as described above. Such measures provide evidence for schema-triggered affect in transference—in accord with the overall tone of the significant-other representation. Facial expressions of positive affect arise relatively immediately based on the activation of a positive significant-other representation rather than a negative one (Andersen et al., 1996). We now turn to self-regulation with a relationship-protective function using this same measure. In research already described (Andersen et al., 1996), the features one learns about a new person derived from a significant other are both positive and negative regardless of the overall positivity or negativity of the representation. When one encounters a negative descriptor of a new person that is characteristic of a positively regarded significant other, this negative aspect of the new person may pose a threat as it runs counter to the overall positivity of the significant other and the relationship. A positive transference involves the motivation for emotional closeness and connection, even while the negative aspects of a person evoke negative responses. Hence, a compensatory process in transference should occur that somehow softens the negative implications of these threatening cues.

As shown in figure 16.6, participants experiencing a positive transference showed significantly more pleasant facial affect in response to learning about the negative characteristics of this positive significant other—as features of a new person—than they did in learning about the positive characteristics derived from this same significant other or indeed about the negative characteristics derived from a negative transference or any positive or negative feature in the no-resemblance condition. Thus, the overall positive evaluation associated with the significant other, and not the valence of the characteristic, determines facial affect in this condition. Despite participants' own classifications of these characteristics as negative (in a preliminary session), this affect was reversed in the positive facial affect they expressed in the positive transference condition of the experiment.

This heightened positivity of facial affect to negative cues in positive transference occurs relatively immediately and appears to constitute a self-regulatory response that serves to protect the other. The effect presumably arises from people's need for connection with positive significant others despite their flaws. Being reminded (consciously or unconsciously) of negative attributes of a positive significant other in transference may pose a threat to these connection needs. Finding ways to perceive such negative attributes positively may be critical in maintaining close relationships and may thus be very well

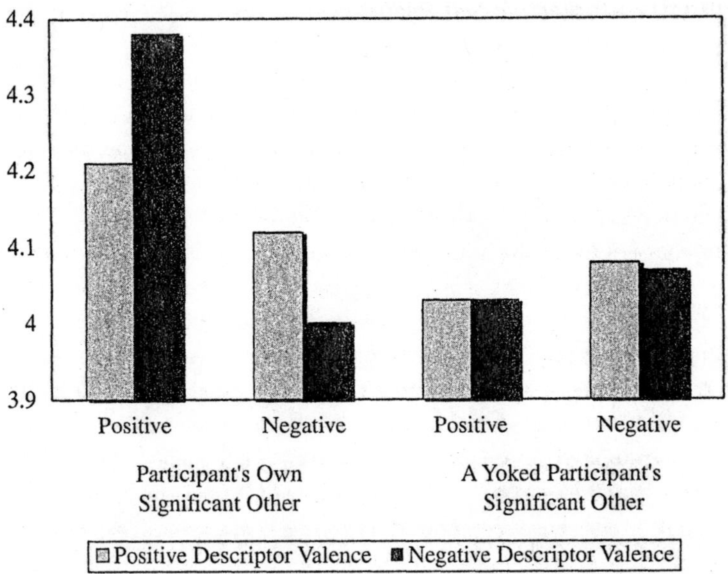

Figure 16.6 Automatic relationship-protective self-regulation: Judges' average rating of positivity in facial affect in response to positive and negative characteristics at encoding as a function of significant-other resemblance and overall regard for the significant other (adapted from Andersen, Reznik, & Manzella, 1996).

practiced. Consistent with our transference-based findings, research on romantic relationships has shown that people neutralize the negative attributes of their romantic partners. Indeed, recalling a negative event from a current romantic relationship actually results in a heightened positive evaluation of the partner (e.g., Holmes & Rempel, 1989; Murray, 1999; Murray & Holmes, 1993, 1994).

Furthermore, because people should be well practiced in this form of self-regulation, it may take place relatively automatically. Although we found no direct support for automaticity in self-protective self-regulation in transference (even while such evidence exists outside of transference; e.g., Fein & Spencer, 1997; Spencer, Fein, Wolfe, Fong, & Dunn, 1998), the evidence suggests that relationship-protective self-regulation may occur relatively automatically or at least immediately. Of course, differences in assessment methods preclude simple comparison and prevent definitive conclusions on differential automaticity. Nonetheless, the data suggest that one can protect one's relationship in transference through affect regulation in ways that may require little effort.

Relationship-Protective Self-Regulation in Potentially Dangerous Relationships

Another line of research making use of the same measure of facial affect conceptually replicates and extends these general conclusions (Berenson & Andersen, 2004). This research addressed whether or not the relationship-protective process in a positive transference extends to somewhat ambiguous danger cues—even among individuals exposed to violence from the significant other. To the degree that a similar pattern in facial affect arises, presumably to protect the positivity of the transference relationship, this could be quite maladaptive, especially if the perception of similarity (unconscious or otherwise) that provokes the transference is valid. Even though we regard transference as a normal process that generalizes across people and across various significant others, this particular phenomenon might have different implications for a dangerous relationship with someone who is loved; for example, with a physically abusive parent. Moreover, if these processes are relatively automatic, questions about their potential intractability or at least challenges that might arise in attempting remediation become more intricate (if remediation is warranted by problematic consequences). If the process of positively transforming the negative features of a positive significant other were to emerge for painful, negative material linked to prior abuse history with an otherwise loved parent, it would highlight important clinical implications of this work.

In a study focused on the role of child abuse on interpersonal patterns in young adults, we examined the activation of mental representations of parents who had previously been physically violent (e.g., threatened the participant, while growing up, with a gun or knife; Berenson & Andersen, 2004). Female college students exposed to physical and psychological abuse by a parent they loved, along with nonabused students, participated in a study in which they learned about a new person who did or did not resemble this parent and was or was not said to be getting increasingly irritable at that moment. That is, after reading the descriptors of the new person, participants, in one condition, were presented with an additional descriptive statement that allegedly reflected a trained interviewer's summary assessment of how the new person seemed "right now," and indicated that he or she was getting increasingly tense and irritable. This contextual cue was clearly regarded as negative by all participants.

Overall, the results showed that regardless of abuse history, all participants expressed more positive facial affect at the moment of encoding the features of the new person who resembled their own parent—that is, a highly positive significant other—rather than resembling someone else's parent. This shows that the overall positive tone of the parental representation was evoked in transference at the level of immediate, automatic, nonverbal responding. As predicted, participants abused by their parent while growing up also showed this response, even though in their later self-reports they indicated more mistrust of the new person in transference than did nonabused participants. They also reported significantly higher expectancies for rejection, as well as greater indifference to being liked by the new person in transference than did nonabused participants. This evidence suggests that the transference experience was aversive for previously abused participants, and, in spite of this, their immediate schema-triggered facial affect was just as positive as that of nonabused participants.

Moreover, both previously abused and nonabused participants showed especially positive facial affect in response to the statement indicating that the new person was in an irritable mood—when in the context of transference relative to the control condition. Both groups of participants transformed the negative irritability cue into positive affect in the transference involving a well-loved parent. This finding conceptually replicates our previous work on relationship-protective self-regulation (Andersen et al., 1996) and does so with especially problematic relationships. The work again suggests that this well-practiced phenomenon of transforming negative features in positively valued relationships by construing these features as endearing (Holmes & Rempel, 1989; Murray, 1999; Murray & Holmes, 1993, 1994) may arise automatically in transference (Berenson & Andersen, 2004). On the other hand, although abused individuals may have even more extensive practice than their nonabused peers with enhancing negative qualities of parents, or of working harder to do so and doing so under duress, we found the effect to be no greater among abused participants than among those who were not abused. Still, in the case of transference involving an abusive parent, the response of transforming a negative into a positive could conceivably be equivalent to responding positively to a danger cue that should be heeded.

We argue that these data provide suggestive evidence that there may be some forms of self-regulation in transference that transpire relatively automatically, and they offer evidence that relationship-protective self-regulation can sometimes proceed automatically, although we have no evidence that self-protective self-regulation can also proceed in an automatic fashion. On the other hand, findings from other research indicate that there are circumstances under which compensatory self-enhancement occurs rather efficiently (e.g., Fein & Spencer, 1997; Harmon-Jones, Simon, Greenberg, & Pysczcynski, 1997; Showers, 2001; Spencer et al., 1998), suggesting that more research is needed to draw definitive conclusions on this important issue, especially since the methods employed to assess these two forms of self-regulation in our research cannot be compared directly.

Summarizing Our Evidence and Implications for the Unconscious

To summarize our evidence, we believe we have shown that the relational self arises according to basic principles of social cognition, such as transient and chronic accessibility, priming, and applicability—processes known to transpire with little cognitive effort, attention, consciousness, or necessity for effortful control. Therefore, we assume that most of our evidence on significant-other representations and the self in transference can be seen as arising on the basis of automatic processes, leading to contextual variation in the relational self across interpersonal situations. Our work highlights the interpersonal nature of the new unconscious and its relevance for the self, as the processes we examine would seem to arise largely unconsciously and without effort.

Our evidence supports four main conclusions. First, automatic activation of significant-other representations in transference occurs in the form of subliminal triggering of significant-other representations. Second, the affect linked to the significant other can be automatically activated in transference when the significant-other representation is activated. Third, there is an automatic spread of activation from the significant-other representation to the self in transference, specifically, to the relational self as experienced with this other and to the self-evaluation (positive or negative) that goes along with it (see also Baldwin, 1994; Baldwin & Sinclair, 1996; Baldwin et al., 1990). Fourth, self-regulation may arise in transference to protect the self or to protect the significant-other relationship in response to some infringement, and the data suggest that such self-regulation may not always be effortful, even though it may typically be.

Self-Regulation and the Relational Self

Our data demonstrate self-regulatory phenomena in the relational self, making it interesting to ask how far downstream in the transference process such self-regulation occurs. Given the importance of self-regulation in understanding the self and its proposed sovereignty (Higgins, 1997; Higgins & May, 2001), the degree of consciousness or effort or control required in its operation is of considerable importance. When a relationship with a significant other is laden with negative affect, its activation evokes this affect relatively automatically and thus threatens the self, as any insult is likely to do. Moreover, this evokes compensatory self-enhancement. Even though such processes may not always occur (Erber & Erber, 2000), they are observed quite frequently when self-regulatory responses are not compromised by factors such as depression or low self-esteem (e.g., Greenberg & Pyszczynski, 1985; Greenberg et al., 1992; Steele et al., 1993). In our work, we have shown that chronically accessible negative significant-other representations, triggered by relevant contextual cues in transference, set self-enhancement processes in motion. We have no evidence that this occurs without strategic, cognitive effort per se, although we suspect there may be conditions under which self-enhancement processes with significant others—and hence those in transference and in the relational self—end up transpiring relatively effortlessly.

Individuals also engage in relationship enhancement (as contrasted with self-enhancement) in response to threatening cues relevant to the significant other. The evidence indicates that when a person's overall regard for a positive significant other is threatened, such as when presented with cues reflecting negative aspects of this person, compensatory enhancement of the other occurs. Highly positive affect is expressed facially in response to these relationship-threatening cues, and this happens relatively immediately in the transference context (Andersen et al., 1996). In a positive transference, people appear to respond to negative cues with positive affect, even when a very problematic relationship is evoked in the transference, that is, the relationship with an abusive parent. In our research, participants experiencing a positive parental transference showed more positive affect than did control participants when learning that the new person was in an increasingly irritable mood. This finding occurred regardless of participants' abuse history with this parent, and the finding thus highlights the fact that relationship-protective responses are quite general across differing backgrounds (see also Murray & Holmes, 1993).

The relative immediacy of the facial affect observed in this research suggests that it is not likely to have arisen deliberatively or effortfully and may thus have been automatic. Hence, not only does there appear to be a relatively automatic elicitation of affect consistent with the overall tone of the significant-other representation in transference, but there also appears to be a relatively automatic self-regulatory response that protects the other in a positive transference in the face of negative cues. Although affect regulation may sometimes occur further downstream in the processing sequence, the effect observed in this work does not.

Overall, other-protective self-regulation, indexed by facial affect, arose in a way that suggests its automaticity. Although it is tempting to conclude on this basis that other-protective self-regulation is automatic whereas self-protective self-regulation is not, such a conclusion would be too simplistic. In transference, automaticity in both self-protective and other-protective self-regulation is likely to be feasible but to depend on various person variables and the exact context. Likewise, it is clear that significant-other activation evokes self-regulatory processes, and those that have frequently been practiced in the past may come to transpire automatically later.

In short, it is plausible that both self-regulation that protects others and that which protects the self can conceivably occur in ways that do not depend on deliberation or effort. Some forms of self-regulation for some people under some circumstances should occur automatically, while others require virtually herculean effort. We consider these issues a bit more below, along with a range of related issues that are among the implications of our findings. We then turn to a consideration of the overall literature on the nature of the unconscious, evaluating our findings in this scholarly context and considering unanswered questions.

Implications of Unconscious Relational Selves for Vulnerability and Resilience

We believe the relatively automatic aspects of transference and of the relational self that we have demonstrated speak to the new unconscious. Along with the automatic activation of transference and the relational self, there is the automaticity of some self-regulatory mechanisms in the process through which people repair automatically elicited negativity. While such regulation may most typically arise at a point further downstream in the processing sequence and with effort, some may occur with relative immediacy and little thought or deliberation. Presumably, strategies that are well-practiced can become automatic in their own right, no longer requiring attentional resources and motivation, and such automaticity in transference, the relational self, and corresponding self-regulation has implications for both resilience and vulnerability (Andersen et al., 2002).

In terms of resilience, one may be willing to give a new person the benefit of the doubt in a positive transference involving a significant other who is much liked or loved. One may assume mutual positive regard at the outset and be motivated to be emotionally connected and open with the person, treating him or her as friend not foe—possibly even as "family." Having at least one positive relationship with a significant other in one's background may offer a model on the basis of which to form a new positive relationship. It may become the basis of positive assumptions about a new person, facilitating the formation of a new positive relationship characterized by trust and mutual respect. Hence, we view significant others and the relational self as a potential source of resilience.

Positive relationships contribute to an individual's resilience by providing positive self-other relationship templates and capacities for protective self-regulation. The self-protective self-regulatory efforts we observe in normal college students may be associated with effective and resilient functioning in challenging interpersonal situations—when negative significant-other relationships are evoked and are potentially disruptive. The observed recruitment of positive self-aspects into working memory in a negative transference, or in a transference evoking a dreaded relational self (even with a positive significant other), serves a self-protective function that may be of value in resilience (Hinkley & Andersen, 1996; Reznik & Andersen, 2004b). Supporting this view, self-enhancement is less likely among people low in self-esteem than among those high in self-esteem (e.g., Baumeister & Vohs, 2001; Taylor & Brown, 1988), presumably due to insufficient cognitive, emotional, or social resources. If self-protective self-regulation were to be compromised in a negative transference, the increased accessibility of negative self-aspects may lead to problematic responses beyond contextual drops in self-esteem (e.g., Crocker & Wolfe, 2001). Indeed, using traditional measures of self-esteem, compensatory self-enhancement when the dreaded self is evoked in transference does not actually appear to fully ward off contextual decreases in self-esteem (Reznik & Andersen, 2004b). Hence, even self-protective self-regulation is not necessarily an effective buffer against blows to self-esteem, and the effect of such processes over the long term thus warrants examination.

At the same time, self-enhancement in its many forms can become problematic, if taken to extremes. It can become destructive, as may be the case with narcissistic individuals (Baumeister & Vohs, 2001; Morf & Rhodewalt, 2001). Highly narcissistic people are so self-protective and self-enhancing in response to threat that it is likely to be problematic for their relationships, as they give more benefit of the doubt to themselves than they give to others (Andersen, Miranda, & Edwards, 2001). Thus, compensatory responding is not always healthful, although it is certainly associated with resilience among those with less extreme responses (e.g., Taylor & Brown, 1988).

Of course, it is not simply the positivity or negativity of one's significant-other representations that brings about resilience or vulnerability in transference, but rather how the self is experienced in the relationship. A positive transference can lead to suffering in its own right by being linked to standards that disrupt positive affect (Reznik & Andersen, 2004a). It can also lead to suffering by involving content that is painful, destructive, or dangerous (Berenson & Andersen, 2004; Reznik & Andersen, 2004a, 2004b). Ultimately, most significant-other relationships are probably neither entirely negative nor entirely positive, and we suspect most, if not all, significant-other relationships begin positively and may become negative or more likely ambivalent, while emotional relevance remains high.

In our research, we identify social-cognitive mechanisms by which past interpersonal patterns reemerge in new relationships. We believe that it is the content of the significant-other representation, the dynamics of the relationship, the nature of the relational self, and the particular self-regulatory patterns triggered in transference that determine whether transference becomes problematic (Andersen et al., 2002). As with self-protective self-regulation, it is likely that the severity and extremity of relationship-protective self-regulation determines whether or not it promotes resilience or vulnerability. If one employs extreme relationship-protective efforts in transference that lead negative evidence about a new person to be discounted, one may not be aware of potential interpersonal cues suggesting danger. Indeed, our evidence on young adults who were physically abused as children by a loved parent provides some support for this assumption (Berenson & Andersen, 2004). Transforming a significant other's neglectful, rejecting, or abusive qualities into positive ones through relationship-protective self-regulation could promote the formation and/or maintenance of maladaptive relationships. On average, however, the maintenance of relationships is of value to the human organism, as is the capacity to do what is needed to accomplish this task, skills likely to be relevant to resilience (see also Kenrick et al., 2003).

Just as positive transference may facilitate development of positive relationships, negative transference may lead to negative perceptions and mistrust. Moreover, negative relationships with significant others can lead to self-fulfilling prophecies (just as positive ones can), and this process can conceivably make negative transference self-defeating—by superimposing the old negative relationship onto the new one and ultimately eliciting the very behaviors expected from the other person. Put differently, a negative transference may involve automatic negative responses that impact interpersonal perceptions and relations negatively with little intention or effort. Indeed, self-protective self-regulation and the self-enhancement inherent in it may at times be off-putting and even designed to shut others out, perhaps interfering with developing new relationships that might not be problematic.

Importantly, if negative transference is veridical (i.e., is based on a relatively accurate perception of problematic characteristics in a new person), reliance on prior knowledge of the negative significant-other relationship can of course serve an adaptive (even possibly an alerting) function. The question of veridicality in transference is extremely important because of the utility of veridical perceptions—whether positive or negative—in better enabling people to navigate their lives, through effective use of prior knowledge. Our data suggest that the activation and use of significant-other representations in transference has a veridicality component (Andersen & Cole, 1990), in addition to inferences that go beyond the information given about the new person. This suggests appropriate and effective utilization of different elements of the self in different contexts (e.g., Banaji & Prentice, 1994) and in different relationships (e.g., Chen & Andersen, 1999). Of course, more work remains to be done on the place and function of veridical cueing and inference in the context of research on transference and the relational self.

Beyond the question of when elements of transference and the relational self operate automatically versus in an effortful way, there is the issue of when automaticity itself becomes maladaptive. Automatic transference processes are likely to become maladaptive when they involve "mindless" or rigid activation and application of significant-other representations in new contexts (Langer, 1989), preventing the individual from accurately perceiving reality and from correcting for misperceptions. When the content of transference is problematic for a new relationship, it will result in interpersonal difficulties, perhaps repeatedly (Andersen & Berk, 1998). Hence, being mindful and taking control of the transference process may be important, especially if its content or consequences are otherwise problematic, painful, or dangerous.

Can people control the transference process and their relational selves? Under the right circumstances, they presumably can. That is, activation of the significant-other representation may take place automatically, but the consequences stemming from this activation can perhaps be interrupted. Just as with the use of stereotypes in social perception, if problematic transference patterns are noticed, based on activation of a significant-other representation, they may then be critically examined and corrected—when cognitive capacity is available and there is a desire to respond differently. With practice, such correction processes may then become relatively effortless or automatic themselves (see also Moskowitz, Gollwitzer, Wasel, & Schaal, 1999; Moskowitz, Salomon, & Taylor, 2000) and integrated into one's sense of identity (Devine & Monteith, 1999). On the other hand, it is plausible that the affect and motivation associated with the activation of significant-other representations may at times compromise attentional capacity, and in so doing make it difficult and perhaps even impossible to intervene in the consequences of transference, so as to redirect one's responses. In this case, new patterns will not even be tried, let alone become well practiced.

One way to begin to control problematic transference processes, nonetheless, may be to become increasingly aware of what goes through one's mind in interpersonal contexts, what one does, the consequences, and the cues that trigger such patterns, particularly if they are habitual and self-defeating (Andersen & Berk, 1998). Attention and monitoring may help to reveal problematic interpersonal patterns that are based on past relationships with significant others, and may provide the motivation necessary to be inspired to try out and practice new, more adaptive ways of being and relating. Attention to one's stream of associations, thoughts, feelings, sensations, and emergent self-aspects triggered in transference may even be an essential first step in being able to disrupt a cycle of self-defeating or self-destructive relationship patterns (Glassman & Andersen, 1999a, 1999c; see also Bonanno & Singer, 1993).

Under conditions of relative mindfulness, moreover, if one is presented with an opportunity to develop a more trusting and positive relationship with another person (relative to one's repertoire of significant-other relationships), one may in fact select this option. In so doing, one may begin to break the cycle of negative relationships by forming a new significant-other representation in the context of a loving, caring, mutually respectful self-other relationship. New relationship templates may thus develop and become the basis for new and positive transference experiences, breaking the self-defeating cycle

(Andersen et al., 2002). Even though significant-other representations produce automatic associations when cued, the formation of new representations is still possible.

The Relational Self in Light of the Broader Literature on the Unconscious

Multiple literatures on unconscious processes are informative about the nature of transference and the relational self. These various literatures involve affect and evaluation, and also automatic versus controlled processes.

Automatic Evaluation

The notion that the affect associated with significant others is evoked automatically appears to parallel what is known about automatic evaluation in the domain of attitude objects (e.g., Bargh, Chaiken, Govender, & Pratto, 1992; Bargh, Chaiken, Raymond, & Hymes, 1996; Chen & Bargh, 1999; Fazio, Sanbonmatsu, Powell, & Kardes, 1986; Giner-Sorolla, Garcia, & Bargh, 1999). The literature shows that all people, places, and things evoke an immediate positive or negative response (e.g., Bargh et al., 1992, 1996; Fazio, 1986; see also Russell, 2003), an automatic evaluation that does not appear to depend on having strongly held attitudes in a domain; weak attitudes will do. Indeed, automatic evaluation occurs even for stimuli that are entirely unfamiliar and cannot be readily categorized using preexisting knowledge (Duckworth, Bargh, Garcia, & Chaiken, 2002).

Implicit Stereotyping

Likewise, research on implicit memory and stereotyping has shown that stimuli associated with social stereotypes (clearly a category in memory) also evoke an automatic positive or negative evaluation as predicted by the stereotype (Banaji & Greenwald, 1995; Banaji, Hardin, & Rothman, 1993; Greenwald & Banaji, 1995). Differences in automatic positive and negative evaluations arise based on both race and gender (e.g., Banaji & Hardin, 1996; Banaji & Dasgupta, 1998) in ways that people do not intend and that are outside of awareness and difficult to control (Banaji & Dasgupta, 1998). Alternative interpretations of implicit stereotyping based on differential familiarity of judged stimuli have been ruled out (Dasgupta, McGhee, Greenwald, & Banaji, 2000), and the various measures of implicit stereotyping have been shown to be substantially intercorrelated (Cunningham, Preacher, & Banaji, 2001).

Implicit processes parallel both the automatic evaluation effect writ large and the implicit stereotyping literature in that the elicitation of affect based on the affect associated with significant-other representations appears to arise automatically.

Still, more systematic investigation of the parallel is warranted in each case using procedures honed in these literatures to enable a more thorough understanding of the role each process plays in the relational self.

Positive Evaluation Based on Mere Exposure

Automatic affect has also been shown to occur based on mere exposure to a stimulus, which subtly increases its familiarity and processing fluency, even when this is not consciously perceived. Given the tremendous familiarity of significant others, these effects would appear to be relevant to those we have observed. In the mere exposure effect (Zajonc, 1968), encountering a stimulus, especially repeatedly, increases liking (Bornstein, 1992; Bornstein & D'Agostino, 1992; Kunst-Wilson & Zajonc, 1980). This has consistently been demonstrated, even when the stimuli are presented subliminally (e.g., Murphy, Monahan, & Zajonc, 1995). In fact, the magnitude of the effect increases with the relative unconsciousness of the stimuli (Bornstein, 1992), showing that when undetected consciously, familiarity profoundly impacts evaluation (Monahan et al., 2000).

Conceptions of automatic affect based on mere exposure (Zajonc, 1998) predict that previously encountered stimuli will be easier to encode and process than will novel stimuli, and this ease of processing or perceptual fluency will be experienced as liking (Bornstein & D'Agostino, 1992; Smith, 1998). Clearly, repeated practice in doing virtually anything increases procedural efficiency in doing that thing in the domain in question and even in other domains (e.g., Smith, 1989; Smith & Lerner, 1986; Smith, Branscombe, & Bormann, 1988), or, for example, the accessibility of the cognitive mapping of a given memory representation which may be the basis of inferences made about another stimulus (Bowdle & Gentner, 1997; Gentner & Bowdle, 2001; chapter 5, this volume). Moreover, such ease of processing can in principle be misattributed, for example, to liking. Repeated exposure, whether conscious or subliminal, also enhances overall positive affect in ways that are rather diffuse. That is, the positive affect attaches not only to original "source" stimuli, but also to novel, similar stimuli. The affect arising from mere exposure also extends to unfamiliar, distinct stimuli (Monahan et al., 2000), in that the positive affect generated from subliminal repeated exposure "spills over" to unrelated objects. A related effect also occurs in transference when significant-other representations are used to make extended inferences about a new person who is similar to the significant other in only minor ways or to a new person who is entirely unrelated. Although this particular evidence involves inferences and mere exposure involves evaluation, the generalization process is parallel, and given how affectively laden significant-other representations are and how readily such affect is reexperienced with a new person, the process may be relevant to affect, linking to it in some as yet unspecified manner.

On another level, the diffuse nature of affect based on mere exposure indicates that a portion of automatic affect is "undedicated"—that is, independent of cognition (see Monahan et al., 2000; Zajonc, 2000), defined as any cognitive process or mental representation. That is, the mere exposure effect is independent of the unconscious priming of affect using affectively loaded stimuli (Zajonc, 1998, 2000). Of course, this does not mean we ought to assume that cognition plays no role in affect, in that cognitive representations and meaning clearly seem to matter in the affect one experiences (Lazarus, 1982; see also, e.g., Higgins, 1987; Keltner, Ellsworth, & Edwards, 1993; Smith, Haynes, Lazarus, & Pope, 1993). In our work, in fact, we focus on the cognitive mediation of affect by significant-other representations.[2] Yet we also concur that affect elicited in the process of transference or by any other means may well facilitate, combine with, or inhibit the cognitive-mediational effects we observe, depending on how consistent the affect is with the overall tone of the significant-other representation (see Niedenthal, Halberstadt, & Setterlund, 1997; Niedenthal et al., 1999).

Moreover, since one is repeatedly exposed to significant others, it is self-evident that part of the phenomena observed in our work involves familiarity with these others (i.e., mere exposure to them) and the spilling over of this affect onto a new person, whether or not the person is similar to the significant other. The profound nature of the role of familiarity in automatic affect may even help "explain how infants across species bond not only with their caregivers, but also with their surroundings and are extremely hesitant to separate from either" (Monahan et al., 2000, p. 466; see also Zajonc, 1971).[3] The special familiarity of significant others (e.g., Keenan & Bailett, 1980; Prentice, 1990) should also make it more likely that these representations are used. Familiar domains, which are typically better structured, are more likely to be used as points of comparison in judging less familiar domains (chapter 5, this volume; see also Karylowski et al., 1999). Moreover, the high degree of co-occurrence of significant others with the self in people's phenomenal experience suggests a well-established significant-other/self association in memory (e.g., Andersen & Chen, 2002; Baldwin, 1992; Wisniewski & Bassok, 1999) that should be associated with contextual activation of the relational self. Unpacking the elements of familiarity in contextual shifts in the relational self would be helpful.

Emotional/Motivational Relevance of Significant Others

The emotional and motivational relevance of significant others vests them with their significance. The corner grocer is quite familiar, and this is not irrelevant. But a parent, sibling, spouse, child, best friend, close colleague, mentor, or mentee matter more. There is something more emotionally laden about the latter individuals. One's emotional well-being is to a degree contingent on them. As other researchers have argued (e.g., Holmes & Murray, 1996), we assume as well that most significant others start out as positive representations, at least in expectancy and hope. Some of our evidence hints at this, that is, that there may be a general ease and comfort with all significant others, even those who have quite negative or problematic qualities (Berenson & Andersen, 2004; see also McGowan, 2002). This would imply that whether or not one's hopes and needs in relation to a significant other are satisfied, having experienced them with another other, along with some sense of interdependence, may to a degree "stick" with the representation.

This suggests there is far more to significant others than familiarity-induced positive affect. Indeed, not all significant others are positive, nor is the relatively automatic affect that is elicited always positive. It depends on the overall positivity or negativity of the affect associated with the significant other, and this evidence rules out mere exposure in positive affect as the sole basis of the evidence about affect we have obtained. Indeed, when triggered, negative and positive significant-other relationships function quite differently in their impact on the relational self. Indeed, motives also appear to be especially relevant in the relational self. Motivational material is clearly activated when a significant-other representation is activated. The motivation to be personally close with a new person arises in a positive transference and the motivation to be distant in a negative transference, and there is now abundant evidence that motives can be automatically activated, just as other social constructs can be (e.g., Bargh & Barndollar, 1996; Bargh & Chartrand, 1999; Bargh et al., 2001). A similar automatic activation of motives by contextual cues has also been shown to occur based on activation of a significant-other representation (Fitzsimons & Bargh, 2003; Shah, 2003). It is thus clear that motives arise and operate without effort in the relational self.

Feelings as Information

To the degree that affect automatically arises when a significant-other representation is activated, this affect should also be used as a basis for making a whole variety of other inferences about the self (Schwarz, 1990) and others. That is, people use their feelings as a basis for inferring their own qualities (e.g., Andersen, 1984; Andersen & Williams, 1985) and also their overall well-being (Levine, Wyer, & Schwarz, 1994; Schwarz, 1990). For example, people's affects often vary in accord with extraneous factors such as the weather, and they thus may feel cheerier on sunny days and gloomier on cloudy ones, while misattributing their affective fluctuations to their satisfaction with their own lives. Likewise, people also use positive affect as a cue that they are safe and are proceeding unimpeded toward their goals, while using negative affect as a cue that something is awry and that a course correction may be needed. In this sense, the automatic affect one experiences in conjunction with transference and the relational self is likely to have a wide variety of "unintended" consequences, as it is used as input in subsequent inference processes about the self and about the texture of one's interpersonal relations.

Intention and Effort in Countering Unconscious Responses

Whether the focus is affect, motivation, or cognition, unconscious processes can also be considered in terms of the degree to which they can be controlled through effortful cognitive processes, a matter that takes center stage in dual-process models within social cognition (e.g., Chaiken & Trope, 1999; see also Brewer, 1988; Neuberg & Fiske, 1987). These models typically focus on stereotypes, attitudes, or other social categories that are activated automatically, and on the kinds of self-regulatory processes that might be undertaken to correct an activated response after the fact (e.g., Glaser & Banaji, 1999; Macrae, Bodenhausen, Schloerscheidt, & Milne, 1999; Martin, 1986).

With respect to our work, these literatures pose the question of whether or not transference can be controlled. One way of considering this is in terms of the degree to which someone has the attentional capacity available with which to try to counteract habitual, routinized responses, a question which researchers have often examined using dual-task paradigms (Macrae et al., 1999; see also Andersen, Spielman, & Bargh, 1992; Bargh & Tota, 1988). In such paradigms, one task is designed to require so much attention and strategic effort that little remains for the other task, for which the assessment of automaticity is being undertaken. The latter task should no longer proceed efficiently if it does require attention and effort, whereas it should proceed just fine if it does not require them. Of course, compromised attentional capacity is hardly the only question here because, even if capacity is available, the crucial variable of motivation must still be taken into account. The motivation to use executive functions to regulate and correct one's own path-of-least-resistance responses is fundamental (Devine & Monteith, 1999; Devine, Monteith, Zuwerink, & Elliot, 1991; Macrae, Bodenhausen, Milne, Thorn, & Castelli, 1997; Neuberg & Fiske, 1987). For example, a stereotype may be activated and yet not applied to a target person, based on the motivation not to think stereotypically (Kunda, 1990). Hence, when it is in people's interests to do so, they can perhaps inhibit stereotyping (Sinclair & Kunda, 1999). Such inhibition appears to depend on a variety of factors, including the experience of outcome dependency with the target person (Depret & Fiske, 1999; Neuberg & Fiske, 1987), accountability to others by having to justify one's judgments to them (Pendry & Macrae, 1996; see also Lerner & Tetlock, 1999), and motivation to be accurate (Kunda & Sinclair, 1999), as well as the degree of extremity and contrast of any stereotype prime encountered (Glaser & Banaji, 1999), one's mood (Park & Banaji, 2000), and the internalization of standards suggesting one should not be prejudiced (Devine & Monteith, 1999).

In short, having a counterstereotypical intention (or goal) and having the cognitive capacity to use it may conceivably enable one to regulate the use of stereotypes—and presumably the enactment of prejudice—through intention and effort (e.g., Blair & Banaji, 1996), although these processes are the subject of some controversy (Bargh, 1999; Higgins, 1996c; Mischel, Cantor, & Feldman, 1996). Early work on stereotyping indicated that even people who are not prejudiced will automatically activate disparaging assumptions about stigmatized groups and will apply such inferences to group members if their attentional resources are depleted. The notion that strategic effort is needed to remediate stereotyping and prejudice thus has some support (e.g., Devine, 1989). Yet research has challenged this position as well by showing that nonprejudiced responses may sometimes be so well learned as to operate relatively automatically (Moskowitz et al., 1999). That is, it appears that stereotype activation can be controlled through intent, even at a preconscious level, without requiring resources. In this sense, the person may be complicit in what is thus a kind of strategic automaticity (Bargh, 1999). As an example, chronic egalitarian goals and perspective taking can control activation of stereotypes at both preconscious and conscious levels (Galinksy & Moskowitz, 2000; Moskowitz et al., 1999, 2000). It is thus becoming increasingly clear that prejudice is not inevitable and that correction processes can themselves become automatic (Lepore & Brown, 1997). On the other hand, rebound effects (e.g., Wegner, 1994) also occur in stereotyping, such that after consciously trying not to think about someone in stereotyped ways, the stereotypical thoughts come flooding back (e.g., Macrae, Bodenhausen, Milne, & Jetten, 1994; Monteith, Sherman, & Devine, 1998), suggesting that the process of learning to resist habitual modes of response is hardly uncomplicated.

Process Dissociation

In terms of transference and the relational self, in spite of the relative precision of our experimental social-cognitive research, a precise estimate of conscious and unconscious influences, respectively, has eluded us thus far in our work. As indicated, implicit memory effects should occur not only without conscious awareness, but also without control or intent. Although "process pure" measures of the unconscious relative to conscious experience (Jacoby, Toth, Lindsay, & Debner, 1992) may not exist—and requiring such purity can define most unconscious experience out of existence (Bowers, 1984; Merikle & Reingold, 1992)—the process-dissociation paradigm offers a means of separating the respective contribution of conscious and unconscious influence by placing the two in opposition experimentally (Jacoby & Kelley, 1987; Jacoby et al., 1992; see also Greenwald et al., 1995). Under conditions of opposition, people hold the conscious intention not to engage in the process in question, and this can have an impact on responses when people have cognitive capacity available (e.g., Jacoby, Woloshyn, & Kelley, 1989; see also Merikle, 1992; Merikle & Reingold, 1992) and presumably motivation.

Qualitative differences in conscious relative to unconscious processes can thus be observed and their relative influence estimated by comparing opposition and nonopposition conditions when people are and are not under attentional load. An example of a domain in which these procedures have been used is one in which people are exposed to names of both famous and nonfamous people, and later are asked to identify famous names among those in another list. In this paradigm, they are more likely to say that the nonfamous names they just saw are famous (relative to those they did not just see), because they misattribute the perceptual fluency experienced with the nonfamous names to the fame of the person named (e.g., Jacoby, Kelley, Brown, & Jasechko, 1989). The conscious and unconscious elements of the process can be decomposed and estimated when people are randomly assigned to a condition in which they are or not under cognitive load at retrieval (when deciding whether or not the names are "famous") and also to one in which they are or are not informed about the misattribution process and are asked not to do it.

In our work, this process dissociation paradigm would involve explicitly asking people to try not to engage in transference when they have (or do not have) the attentional capacity available to make this feasible. Such research would enable estimation of the conscious and unconscious elements of the processes underlying the emergence of transference and the relational self. We assume that both conscious and unconscious components of these phenomena are likely to coexist and hence that some control may often be feasible when attentional capacity is available—at least with respect to consequences likely to follow on the heels of activation, such as the use of the representation (vs. its activation per se). Moreover, we assume rebound effects after suppression (trying not to engage in transference) may also be also likely, and yet that with effective practice, a different response may become capable of transpiring with a kind of strategic automaticity (Bargh, 1999). It is worth noting that the affect associated with significant-other representations and evoked in transference may sometimes dampen cognitive capacity in its own right or otherwise drive processing in such a way that taking control of consequences of transference becomes more difficult, as occurs for other highly affective processes (e.g., see Esses & Zanna, 1995). Research designed to illuminate each of these matters further as it pertains to the unconscious relational self would be of value to the field.

Conclusion

In sum, we argue that the nature of the self is fundamentally interpersonal and relational, providing all people with a repertoire of relational selves grounded in the web of their important interpersonal relationships. It is a contextual model based in social-cognitive processes that are known to transpire outside of awareness and without effort, though they may also be corrected for under some conditions, either effortfully or in well-practiced, routinized ways. Many questions remain to be examined more explicitly about the relational self and self-regulation, and the degree to which they transpire automatically or in a way that demands attention and effortful processing, but our evidence leaves little doubt that contextual, relational selves play a profound role in shaping our interpersonal lives. The evidence suggests that self-regulation is central in transference, in that activation of a significant-other representation has important self-regulatory consequences that may be triggered outside of awareness. The role of the unconscious in the relational self is thus quite clear, as is perhaps the promise of mindfulness and its cultivation through practice, if one acquires some openness to change and to the unexpected, and of course some discernment.

Acknowledgments This research was funded in part by a grant from the National Institute of Mental Health (R01-MH48789).

Notes

1. Our research has repeatedly shown that when a new person resembles someone else's significant other (in terms of features presented in conscious awareness) and when the inference/memory assessment also involves features of this same person's significant other (i.e., still testing with someone else's features), these control participants show far less representation-consistent inference/memory than do experimental participants for whom the new person actually resembles their own significant other (and they are tested with their own significant-other features). From our research, then, which has repeatedly controlled both stimulus content and test content in this way, it is clear that there is no special

semantic association among the features listed for any given significant other that would produce representation-consistent inferences just by being exposed to test items that are descriptive of another person's significant other, even when some "relevant" cues derived from the same person's significant other are presented as cues about the new person. Given that no such association exists, it seemed unhelpful and unnecessary to demonstrate this again in the context of cues about the new person that were presented subliminally.

Instead, in the present study, it was crucial to show that when cues derived from one's own significant other are presented subliminally, they do in fact activate the significant-other representation and lead to significant-other–based inferences (using features that were not actually subliminally presented) at a level over and above what occurs based on chronic accessibility in significant-other representations alone. This necessitated that we measure the degree to which control participants made use of their own significant-other representation to make inferences about the new person, even though the subliminal cues they encountered did not involve their own significant other. In other prior work of ours, we have shown such a difference over and above chronic activation and use based on whether or not the new person slightly resembles one's own significant other, based on consciously presented cues (Andersen et al., 1995, Study 1). The effect size is smaller, requiring a larger *n* to reach statistical significance, but the evidence is clear, and to obtain it one must hold constant chronic accessibility (in one's own significant-other features) across conditions by including an inference/memory measure in each condition that involves the participant's own significant-other features, varying only the presence or absence of own-significant-other triggering cues (Andersen et al., 1995). This is what we did in the present paradigm. Participants in the yoked control condition completed an inference measure (in awareness) containing their own significant-other descriptors, just as experimental participants did, but they were presented subliminally with cues that would not trigger their own significant-other representation (i.e., were derived from the experimental participant's significant other). Only when the subliminal triggering cues to which participants were subliminally exposed resembled their own significant other should subliminal triggering occur and should heightened significant-other-based inferences be especially likely. In a third condition, we controlled for self-generation effects by exposing participants to self-generated descriptors subliminally and testing them using an inference measure (within awareness) using comparable self-generated features.

2. While precise debates about the cognitive mediation of affect are not well addressed by our data, we show that the activation of mental representations of significant others, cognitively defined, evoke affect.

3. It is worth noting, however, that our various effects, and specifically our subliminal activation effect, cannot be reduced to mere exposure. Participants were in fact exposed to equal numbers of stimulus repetitions subliminally. Even when stimuli were self-generated but not about the significant other, and thus quite familiar, they were still subliminally repeated at an equal rate, and nonetheless the effect was significantly less pronounced in this condition. Hence, familiarity alone is insufficient to account for the effects.

References

Aarts, H., & Dijksterhuis, A. (2000). Habits as knowledge structures: Automaticity in goal-directed behavior. *Journal of Personality and Social Psychology, 78*, 53–63.

Allport, G. (1937). *Personality: A psychology interpretation*. New York: Holt, Rinehart and Winston.

Andersen, S. M. (1984). Self-knowledge and social inference: II. The diagnosticity of cognitive/affective and behavioral data. *Journal of Personality and Social Psychology, 46*, 294–307.

Andersen, S. M., & Baum, A. (1994). Transference in interpersonal relations: Inferences and affect based on significant-other representations. *Journal of Personality, 62*, 459–498.

Andersen, S. M., & Berk, M. S. (1998). Transference in everyday experience: Implications of experimental research for relevant clinical phenomena. *Review of General Psychology, 2*, 81–120.

Andersen, S. M., & Chen, S. (2002). The relational self: An interpersonal social-cognitive theory. *Psychological Review, 109*, 619–645.

Andersen, S. M., Chen, S., & Miranda, R. (2002). Significant others and the self. *Self and Identity, 1*, 159–168.

Andersen, S. M., & Cole, S. W. (1990). "Do I know you?": The role of significant others in general social perception. *Journal of Personality and Social Psychology, 59*, 383–399.

Andersen, S. M., & Glassman, N. S. (1996). Responding to significant others when they are not there: Effects on interpersonal inference, motivation, and affect. In R. M. Sorrentino & E. T. Higgins (Eds.), *Handbook of motivation and cognition* (Vol. 3, pp. 262–321). New York: Guilford.

Andersen, S. M., Glassman, N. S., Chen, S., & Cole, S. W. (1995). Transference in social perception: The role of chronic accessibility in significant-other representations. *Journal of Personality and Social Psychology, 69*, 41–57.

Andersen, S. M., Glassman, N. S., & Gold, D. (1998). Mental representations of the self, significant others, and nonsignificant other: Structure and processing of private and public aspects. *Journal of Personality and Social Psychology, 75*, 845–861.

Andersen, S. M., & Klatzky, R. L. (1987). Traits and social stereotypes: Levels of categorization in person perception. *Journal of Personality and Social Psychology, 53*, 235–246.

Andersen, S. M., Klatzky, R. L., & Murray, J. (1990). Traits and social stereotypes: Efficiency differences in social information processing. *Journal of Personality and Social Psychology, 59*, 192–201.

Andersen, S. M., Lambert, L., & Dick, W. (2001). *Significant-other exemplars: Processing efficiency in instance-based judgments*. Unpublished manuscript, New York University.

Andersen, S. M., Miranda, R., & Edwards, T. (2001). When self-enhancement knows no bounds: Are past relationships with significant others at the heart of narcissism? *Psychological Inquiry, 12*, 197–202.

Andersen, S. M., & Prasad, A. (2000). Chronic accessibility and schematicity: The structure and function of significant-other representations. Unpublished manuscript, New York University.

Andersen, S. M., Reznik, I., & Chen, S. (1997). The self in relation to others: Motivational and cognitive underpinnings. In J. G. Snodgrass & R. L. Thompson (Eds.), *The self across psychology: Self-recognition, self awareness, and the self-concept* (pp. 233–275). New York: New York Academy of Science.

Andersen, S. M., Reznik, I., & Manzella, L. M. (1996). Eliciting facial affect, motivation, and expectancies in transference: Significant-other representations in social relations. *Journal of Personality and Social Psychology, 71*, 1108–1129.

Andersen, S. M., Spielman, L. A., & Bargh, J. A. (1992). Future-event schemas and certainty about the future: Automaticity in depressives' future-event predictions. *Journal of Personality and Social Psychology, 63*, 711–723.

Andersen, S. M., & Williams, M. (1985). Cognitive/affective reactions in the improvement of self-esteem: When thoughts and feelings make a difference. *Journal of Personality and Social Psychology, 49*, 1086–1097.

Aron, A., Aron, E. N., Tudor, M., & Nelson, G. (1991). Close relationships as including other in the self. *Journal of Personality and Social Psychology, 60*, 241–253.

Ayduk, O., Mendoza-Denton, R., Mischel, W., Downey, G., Peake, P. K., & Rodriguez, M. (2000). Regulating the interpersonal self: Strategic self-regulation for coping with rejection sensitivity. *Journal of Personality and Social Psychology, 79*, 776–792.

Baldwin, M. W. (1992). Relational schemas and the processing of information. *Psychological Bulletin, 112*, 461–484.

Baldwin, M. W. (1994). Primed relational schemas as a source of self-evaluative reactions. *Journal of Social and Clinical Psychology, 13*, 380–403.

Baldwin, M. W., Carrell, S. E., & Lopez, D. F. (1990). Priming relationship schemas: My advisor and the Pope are watching me from the back of my mind. *Journal of Experimental Social Psychology, 26*, 435–454.

Baldwin, M. W., Fehr, B., Keedian, E., Seidel, M., & Thompson, D. W. (1993). An exploration of the relational schemata underlying attachment styles: Self-report and lexical decision approaches. *Personality and Social Psychology Bulletin, 19*, 746–754.

Baldwin, M. W., & Meunier, J. (1999). The cued activation of attachment relational schemas. *Social-Cognition, 17*, 209–227.

Baldwin, M. W., & Sinclair, L. (1996). Self-esteem and "if . . . then" contingencies of interpersonal acceptance. *Journal of Personality and Social Psychology, 71*, 1130–1141.

Banaji, M. R., & Dasgupta, N. (1998). The consciousness of social beliefs: A program of reearch on stereotyping and prejudice. In V. Y. Yzerbyt & G. Lories (Eds.), *Metacognition: Cognitive and social dimensions* (pp. 157–170). Thousand Oaks, CA: Sage.

Banaji, M. R., & Greenwald, A. G. (1995) Implicit gender stereotyping in judgments of fame. *Journal of Personality and Social Psychology, 68*, 181–198.

Banaji, M. R., & Hardin, C. D. (1996). Automatic stereotyping. *Psychological Science, 7*, 136–141.

Banaji, M. R., Hardin, C., & Rothman, A. (1993). Implicit stereotyping in person judgment. *Journal of Personality and Social Psychology, 65*(2), 272–281.

Banaji, M. R., & Prentice, D. A. (1994). The self in social contexts. *Annual Review of Psychology, 45*, 297–332.

Bargh, J. A. (1989). Conditional automaticity: Varieties of automatic influence in social perception and cognition. In J. S. Uleman & J. A. Bargh (Eds.), *Unintended thought* (pp. 3–51). New York: Guilford.

Bargh, J. A. (1992). Does subliminality matter to social psychology? Awareness of the stimulus versus awareness of its influence. In R. F. Bornstein & T. S. Pittman (Eds.), *Perception without awareness* (pp. 236–255). New York: Guilford.

Bargh, J. A. (1994). The four horsemen of automaticity: Awareness, intention, efficiency, and control in social cognition. In R. S. Wyer, Jr., & T. K. Srull (Eds.), *Handbook of social cognition* (Vol. 1, pp. 1–40). Hillsdale, NJ: Erlbaum.

Bargh, J. A. (1997). The automaticity of everyday life. In R. S. Wyer, Jr. (Ed.), *Advances in social cognition* (Vol. 10, pp. 1–61). Mahwah, NJ: Erlbaum.

Bargh, J. A. (1999). The cognitive monster: The case against the controllability of automatic stereotype effects. In S. Chaiken & Y. Trope (Eds.), *Dual-process theories in social psychology* (pp. 361–382). New York: Guilford.

Bargh, J. A., & Barndollar, K. (1996). Automaticity in action: The unconscious as repository of chronic goals and motives. In P. M. Gollwitzer & J. A. Bargh (Eds.), *The psychology of action: Linking cognition and motivation to behavior* (pp. 457–481). New York: Guilford.

Bargh, J. A., Bond, R. N., Lombardi, W. J., & Tota, M. E. (1986). The additive nature of chronic and temporary sources of construct accessibility. *Journal of Personality and Social Psychology, 50*, 869–878.

Bargh, J. A., Chaiken, S., Govender, R., & Pratto, F. (1992). The generality of the automatic attitude activation effect. *Journal of Personality and Social Psychology, 62*, 893–912.

Bargh, J. A., Chaiken, S., Raymond, P., & Hymes, C. (1996). The automatic evaluation effect: Unconditionally automatic attitude activation with a pronunciation task. *Journal of Experimental Social Psychology, 32*, 185–210.

Bargh, J. A., & Chartrand, T. (1999). The unbearable automaticity of being. *American Psychologist, 54*, 462–479.

Bargh, J. A., & Gollwitzer, P. M. (1994). Environmental control of goal-directed action: Automatic and strategic contingencies between situations and behavior. *Nebraska Symposium on Motivation, 41*, 71–124.

Bargh, J. A., Gollwitzer, P. M., Lee-Chai, A., Barndollar, K., & Troetschel, R. (2001). The automated will: Nonconscious activation and pursuit of behavioral goals. *Journal of Personality and Social Psychology, 81*, 1014–1027.

Bargh, J. A., & Pietromonaco, P. (1982). Automatic information processing and social perception: The influence of trait information presented outside of conscious awareness on impression formation. *Journal of Personality and Social Psychology, 43*, 437–449.

Bargh, J. A., & Tota, M. E. (1988). Context-dependent automatic processing in depression: Accessibility of negative constructs with regard to self but not others. *Journal of Personality and Social Psychology, 54*, 925–939.

Baum, A., & Andersen, S. M. (1999). Interpersonal roles in transference: Transient mood states under the condition of significant-other activation. *Social Cognition, 17*, 161–185.

Baumeister, R. F., & Vohs, K. D. (2001). Narcissism as addiction to esteem. *Psychological Inquiry, 12*, 206–210.

Berenson, K., & Andersen, S. M. (2004). *Emotional numbing in transference: Triggering a parental representation linked with childhood physical abuse.* Unpublished manuscript, New York University.

Berk, M. S., & Andersen, S. M. (2000). The impact of past relationships on interpersonal behavior: Behavioral confirmation in the social-cognitive process of transference. *Journal of Personality and Social Psychology, 79*, 546–562.

Berscheid, E. (1994). Interpersonal relationships. *Annual Review of Psychology, 45*, 79–129.

Blair, I. V., & Banaji, M. R. (1996). Automatic and controlled processes in stereotype priming. *Journal of Personality and Social Psychology, 70*, 1142–1163.

Bonanno, G. A., & Singer, J. L. (1993). Controlling one's stream of thought through perceptual and reflective processing. In D. M. Wegner & J. W. Pennebaker (Eds.), *Handbook of mental control* (pp. 149–170). Englewood Cliffs, NJ: Prentice-Hall.

Bornstein, R. F. (1992). Subliminal mere exposure effects. In R. F. Bornstein & T. S. Pittman (Eds.), *Perception without awareness* (pp. 191–210). New York: Guilford.

Bornstein, R. F., & D'Agostino, P. R. (1992). Stimulus recognition and the mere exposure effect. *Journal of Personality and Social Psychology, 63*, 545–552.

Bornstein, R. F, & Pittman, T. S. (Eds.). (1992). *Perception without awareness.* New York: Guilford.

Bowdle, B. F., & Gentner, D. (1997). Informativity and asymmetry in comparisons. *Cognitive Psychology, 34*, 244–286.

Bowers, K. S. (1984). On being unconsciously influenced and informed. In K. S. Bowers & D. Miechenbaum (Eds.), *The unconscious reconsidered* (pp. 227–272). New York: Wiley.

Brewer, M. B. (1988). A dual process model of impression formation. In T. K. Srull & R. S. Wyer, Jr. (Eds.), *A dual process model of impression formation* (pp. 1–36). Hillsdale, NJ: Erlbaum.

Brooks, L. R. (1987). Decentralized control of categorization: The role of prior processing episodes. In U. Neisser (Ed.), *Categories reconsidered: The ecological and intellectual bases of categories* (pp. 141–174). Cambridge, UK: Cambridge University Press.

Bruner, J. S. (1957). Going beyond the information given. In H. E. Gruber, K. R. Hammond, & R. Jessor (Eds.), *Contemporary approaches to cognition* (pp. 41–69). Cambridge, MA: Harvard University Press.

Bugental, D. B. (2000). Acquisition of algorithms of social life: A domain-based approach. *Psychological Bulletin, 126*, 187–219.

Cantor, N., & Mischel, W. (1979). Prototypes in person perception. In L. Berkowitz (Ed.), *Advances in experimental social psychology* (Vol. 12, pp. 3–52). New York: Academic Press.

Chaiken, S., & Trope, Y. (Eds.). (1999). *Dual-process theories in social psychology.* New York: Guilford.

Chen, M., & Bargh, J. A. (1997). Nonconscious behavioral confirmation processes: The self-fulfilling consequences of automatic stereotype activation. *Journal of Experimental Social Psychology, 33*, 541–560.

Chen, M., & Bargh, J. A. (1999). Consequences of automatic evaluation: Immediate behavioral predispositions to approach or avoid the stimulus. *Personality and Social Psychology Bulletin, 25*, 215–224.

Chen, S. (2001). The role of theories in mental representations and their use in social perception: A theory-based approach to significant-other representations and transference. In G. B. Moskowitz (Ed.), *Cognitive social psychology: The Princeton symposium on the legacy and future of social cognition* (pp. 125–142). Mahwah, NJ: Erlbaum.

Chen, S. (2003). Psychological state theories about significant others: Implications for the content and structure of significant-other representations. *Personality and Social Psychology Bulletin, 29*, 1285–1302.

Chen, S., & Andersen, S. M. (1999). Relationships from the past in the present: Significant-other representations and transference in interpersonal life. In M. P. Zanna (Ed.), *Advances in experimental social psychology* (Vol. 31, pp. 123–190). San Diego, CA: Academic Press.

Chen, S., Andersen, S. M., & Hinkley, K. (1999). Triggering transference: Examining the role of applicability and use of significant-other representations in social perception. *Social Cognition, 17*, 332–365.

Collins, A. M., & Loftus, E. F. (1975). A spreading-activation theory of semantic processing. *Psychological Review, 82*, 407–428.

Crocker, J., & Wolfe, C. T. (2001). Contingencies of worth. *Psychological Review, 108*, 593–623.

Cunningham, W. A., Preacher, K. J., & Banaji, M. R. (2001). Implicit attitude measures: Consistency, stability, and convergent validity. *Psychological Science, 12*, 163–201.

Dasgupta, N., McGhee, D. E., Greenwald, A. G., & Banaji, M. R. (2000). Automatic preference for White Americans: Eliminating the familiarity explanation. *Journal of Experimental Social Psychology, 36*, 316–328.

Depret, E., & Fiske, S. T. (1999). Perceiving the powerful: Intriguing individuals versus threatening groups. *Journal of Experimental Social Psychology, 35*, 461–480.

Devine, P. G. (1989). Stereotypes and prejudice: Their automatic and controlled components. *Journal of Personality and Social Psychology, 56*, 5–18.

Devine, P. G., & Monteith, M. J. (1999). Automaticity and control in stereotyping. In S. Chaiken & Y. Trope (Eds.), *Dual-process theories in social psychology* (pp. 339–360). New York: Guilford.

Devine, P. G., Monteith, M. J., Zuwerink, J. R., & Elliot, A. J. (1991). Prejudice without compunction. *Journal of Personality and Social Psychology, 60*, 817–830.

Downey, G., & Feldman., S. I. (1996). Implications of rejection sensitivity for intimate relationships. *Journal of Personality and Social Psychology, 70*, 1327–1343.

Duckworth, K. L., Bargh, J. A., Garcia, M., & Chaiken, S. (2002). The automatic evaluation of novel stimuli. *Psychological Science, 13*, 513–519.

Ehrenreich, J. H. (1989). Transference: One concept or many? *Psychoanalytic Review, 76*, 37–65.

Erber, R., & Erber, M. W. (2000). The self-regulation of moods: Second thoughts on the importance of happiness in everyday life. *Psychological Inquiry, 51*, 360–392.

Erdley, C. A., & D'Agostino, P. R. (1988). Cognitive and affective components of automatic priming effects. *Journal of Personality and Social Psychology, 54*, 741–747.

Esses, V., & Zanna, M. P. (1995). Mood and the expression of ethnic stereotypes. *Journal of Personality and Social Psychology, 69*, 1052–1068.

Fazio, R. H. (1986). How do attitudes guide behavior? In R. M. Sorrentino & E. T. Higgins (Eds.), *Handbook of motivation and cognition: Foundations of social behavior* (pp. 204–243). New York: Guilford.

Fazio, R. H., Sanbonmatsu, D. M., Powell, M. C., & Kardes, F. R. (1986). On the automatic activation of attitudes. *Journal of Personality and Social Psychology, 50*, 229–238.

Fein, S., & Spencer, S. J. (1997). Prejudice as self-image maintenance: Affirming the self through derogating others. *Journal of Personality and Social Psychology, 73*, 31–44.

Fiske, A. P. (1992). The four elementary forms of sociality: Framework for a unified theory of social relations. *Psychological Review, 99*, 689–723.

Fiske, S. T., & Pavelchak, M. (1986). Category-based versus piecemeal-based affective responses: Developments in schema-triggered affect. In R. M. Sorrentino & E. T. Higgins (Eds.), *Handbook of motivation and cognition* (pp. 167–203). New York: Guilford.

Fiske, S. T., & Taylor, S. E. (1991). *Social cognition* (2nd ed.). New York: McGraw-Hill.

Fitzsimons, G. M., & Bargh, J. A. (2003). Thinking of you: Nonconscious pursuit of interpersonal goals associated with relationship partners. *Journal of Personality and Social Psychology, 84*, 148–163.

Freud, S. (1958). The dynamics of transference. In J. Strachey (Ed. & Trans.), *The standard edition of the complete psychological works of Sigmund Freud* (Vol. 12, pp. 99–108). London: Hogarth Press. (Original work published 1912)

Galinsky, A. D., & Moskowitz, G. B. (2000). Perspective-taking: Decreasing stereotype expression, stereotype accessibility, and in-group evaluation. *Journal of Personality and Social Psychology, 78*(4), 708–724.

Gentner, D., & Bowdle, B. F. (2001). Convention, form, and figurative language processing. *Metaphor and Symbol, 16*, 223–247.

Gentner, D., & Markman, A. B. (1997). Structural alignment in analogy and similarity. *American Psychologist, 52*, 45–56.

Gilovich, T. (1981). Seeing the past in the present: The effect of associations to familiar events on judgments and decisions. *Journal of Personality and Social Psychology, 40*, 797–808.

Giner-Sorolla, R., Garcia, M. T., & Bargh, J. A. (1999). The automatic evaluation of pictures. *Social Cognition, 17*, 76–96.

Glaser, J., & Banaji, M. R. (1999). When fair is foul and foul is fair: Reverse priming in automatic evaluation. *Journal of Personality and Social Psychology, 77*, 669–687.

Glassman, N. S., & Andersen, S. M. (1999a). Activating transference without consciousness: Using significant-other representations to go beyond what is subliminally given. *Journal of Personality and Social Psychology, 77*, 1146–1162.

Glassman, N. S., & Andersen, S. M. (1999b). Transference in social cognition: Persistence and exacerbation of significant-other based inferences over time. *Cognitive Therapy and Research, 23*, 75–91.

Glassman, N. S., & Andersen, S. M. (1999c). Streams of thought about the self and significant others: Transference as the construction of interpersonal meaning. In J. A. Singer & P. Salovey (Eds.), *At play in the fields of consciousness* (pp. 103–140). Mahwah, NJ: Erlbaum.

Greenberg, J., & Pyszczynski, T. (1985). Compensatory self-inflation: A response to the threat to self-regard of public failure. *Journal of Personality and Social Psychology, 49*, 273–280.

Greenberg, J., Pyszczynski, T., Solomon, S., & Chatel, D. (1992). Terror management and tolerance: Does mortality salience always intensify negative reac-

tions to others who threaten one's world view? *Journal of Personality and Social Psychology, 58*, 308–318.
Greenwald, A. G. (1981). Self and memory. In G. H. Bower (Ed.), *Psychology of learning and motivation* (Vol. 15, pp. 201–236). New York: Academic Press.
Greenwald, A. G. (1992). New Look 3: Unconscious cognition reclaimed. *American Psychologist, 47*, 766–779.
Greenwald, A. G., & Banaji, M. R. (1989). The self as a memory system: Powerful, but ordinary. *Journal of Personality and Social Psychology, 57*, 41–54.
Greenwald, A. G., & Banaji, M. R. (1995). Implicit social cognition: Attitudes, self-esteem, and stereotypes. *Psychological Review, 102*, 4–27.
Greenwald, A. G., Klinger, M. R., & Schuh, E. S. (1995). Activation by marginally perceptible ("subliminal") stimuli: Dissociation of unconscious from conscious cognition. *Journal of Experimental Psychology: General, 124*, 22–42.
Harmon-Jones, E., Simon, L., Greenberg, J., & Pyszczynski, T. (1997). Terror management theory and self-esteem: Evidence that increased self-esteem reduced mortality salience effects. *Journal of Personality and Social Psychology, 72*, 24–36.
Higgins, E. T. (1987). Self discrepancy: A theory relating self and affect. *Psychological Review, 94*, 319–340.
Higgins, E. T. (1990). Personality, social psychology, and person-situation relations: Standards and knowledge activation as a common language. In L. A. Pervin (Ed.), *Handbook of personality* (pp. 301–338). New York: Guilford.
Higgins, E. T. (1996a). Knowledge: Accessibility, applicability, and salience. In E. T. Higgins & A. W. Kruglanski (Eds.), *Social psychology: Handbook of basic principles* (pp. 133–168). New York: Guilford.
Higgins, E. T. (1996b). Ideals, oughts, and regulatory focus: Affect and motivation from distinct pains and pleasures. In P. M. Gollwitzer & J. A. Bargh (Eds.), *The psychology of action* (pp. 91–114). New York: Guilford.
Higgins, E. T. (1996c). The self-digest: Self-knowledge serving self-regulatory functions. *Journal of Personality and Social Psychology, 71*, 1062–1083.
Higgins, E. T. (1997). Beyond pleasure and pain. *American Psychologist, 52*, 1280–1300.
Higgins, E. T. (1998). Promotion and prevention: Regulatory focus as a motivational principle. In M. P. Zanna (Ed.), *Advances in experimental social psychology* (Vol. 30, pp. 1–46). New York: Academic Press.
Higgins, E. T., & Brendl, C. M. (1995). Accessibility and applicability: Some "activation rules" influencing judgment. *Journal of Experimental Social Psychology, 31*, 218–243.
Higgins, E. T., & King, G. (1981). Accessibility of social constructs: Information processing consequences of individual and contextual variability. In N. Cantor & J. F. Kihlstrom (Eds.), *Personality, cognition and social interaction* (pp. 69–121). Hillsdale, NJ: Erlbaum.
Higgins, E. T., & May, D. (2001). Individual self-regulatory functions: It's not "we" regulation, but it's still social. In C. Sedikides & M. Brewer (Eds.), *Individual self, relational self, collective self* (pp. 47–67). Philadelphia: Psychology Press/Taylor and Francis.
Hinkley, K., & Andersen, S. M. (1996). The working self-concept in transference: Significant-other activation and self change. *Journal of Personality and Social Psychology, 71*, 1279–1295.
Holender, D. (1986). Semantic activation without conscious identification in dich-

otic listening, parafoveal vision, and visual masking: A survey and appraisal. *Behavioral and Brain Sciences, 9,* 1–23.

Holmes, J. G., & Murray, S. L. (1996). Conflict in close relationships. In E. T. Higgins & A. W. Kruglanski (Eds.), *Social psychology: Handbook of basic principles* (pp. 622–654). New York: Guilford.

Holmes, J. G., & Rempel, J. K. (1989). Trust in close relationships. *Review of Personality and Social Psychology, 10,* 187–219.

Jacoby, L. L., & Kelley, C. M. (1987). Unconscious influences of memory for a prior event. *Personality and Social Psychology Bulletin, 13,* 314–326.

Jacoby, L. L., Kelley, C. M., Brown, J., & Jasechko, J. (1989). Becoming famous overnight: Limits on the ability to avoid unconscious influences of the past. *Journal of Personality and Social Psychology, 56,* 326–338.

Jacoby, L. L., Toth, J. P., Lindsay, D. S., & Debner, J. A. (1992). Lectures for a layperson: Methods for revealing unconscious processes. In R. F. Bornstein & T. S. Pittman (Eds.), *Perception without awareness* (pp. 81–120). New York: Guilford.

Jacoby, L. L., Woloshyn, V., & Kelley, C. M. (1989). Becoming famous without being recognized: Unconscious influences of memory produced by dividing attention. *Journal of Experimental Psychology: General, 118,* 115–125.

Johnson, J. T., & Boyd, K. R. (1995). Dispositional traits versus the content of experience: Actor/observer differences in judgments of the "authentic self." *Personality and Social Psychology Bulletin, 21,* 375–383.

Karylowski, J. J., Konarzewski, K., & Motes, M. (1999). Recruitment of exemplars as reference points in social judgments. *Journal of Experimental Social Psychology, 36,* 275–303.

Keenan, J. M., & Baillet, S. D. (1980). Memory for personally and socially significant events. In R. S. Nickerson (Ed.), *Attention and performance* (Vol. 8, pp. 651–669). Hillsdale, NJ: Erlbaum.

Kelly, G. A. (1955). *The psychology of personal constructs.* New York: Norton.

Keltner, D., Ellsworth, P. C., & Edwards, K. (1993). Beyond simple pessimism: Effects of sadness and anger on social perception. *Journal of Personality and Social Psychology, 64,* 740–752.

Kenrick, D. T., Maner, J. K., Butner, J., Li, N. P., & Becker, D. V. (2003). Dynamical evolutionary psychology: Individual decision rules and emergent social norms. *Psychological Review, 110,* 3–28.

Kihlstrom, J. F. (1987). The cognitive unconscious. *Science, 237,* 1445–1452.

Kihlstrom, J. F., Barnhardt, T. M., & Tataryn, D. J. (1992). The psychological unconscious: Found, lost, and regained. *American Psychologist, 47,* 788–791.

Kunda, Z. (1990). The case for motivated reasoning. *Psychological Bulletin, 108*(3), 480–498.

Kunda, Z., & Sinclair, L. (1999). Motivated reasoning with stereotypes: Activation, application, and inhibition. *Psychological Inquiry, 10*(1), 12–22.

Kunst-Wilson, W. R., & Zajonc, R. B. (1980). Affective discrimination of stimuli that cannot be recognized. *Science, 207,* 557–558.

Langer, E. J. (1989). *Mindfulness.* Reading, MA: Addison-Wesley.

Lazarus, R. S. (1982). Thoughts and relations between emotion and cognition. *American Psychologist, 37*(9), 1019–1024.

Lepore, L., & Brown, R. (1997). Category and stereotype activation: Is prejudice inevitable? *Journal of Personality and Social Psychology, 72,* 275–287.

Lerner, J. S., & Tetlock, P. E. (1999). Accounting for the effects of accountability. *Psychological Bulletin, 125*, 255–275.

Levine, S. R., Wyer, R. S., & Schwarz, N. (1994). Are you what you feel? The affective and cognitive determinants of self-judgments. *European Journal of Social Psychology, 24*, 63–77.

Lewicki, P. (1986). *Nonconscious social information processing*. San Diego, CA: Academic Press.

Linville, P. W., & Carlston, D. E. (1994). Social cognition of the self. In P. G. Devine, D. C. Hamilton, & T. M. Ostrom (Eds.), *Social cognition: Impact on social psychology* (pp. 143–193). New York: Academic Press.

Linville, P. W., & Fischer, G. W. (1993). Exemplar and abstraction models of perceived group variability and stereotypicality. *Social Cognition, 11*, 92–125.

Logan, G. D. (1988). Toward an instance theory of automatization. *Psychological Review, 95*, 492–527.

Logan, G. D. (1989). Automaticity and cognitive control. In J. L. Uleman & J. A. Bargh (Eds.), *Unintended thought* (pp. 52–74). New York: Guilford.

Luborsky, L., & Crits-Christoph, P. (1990). *Understanding transference: The CCRT method.* New York: Basic Books.

Luborsky, L., Crits-Christoph, P., Friedman, S. H., Mark, D., & Schaffler, P. (1991). Freud's transference template compared with the core conflictual relationship theme (CCRT): Illustrations by the two specimen cases. In M. J. Horowitz (Ed.), *Person schemas and maladaptive interpersonal patterns* (pp. 167–195). Chicago: University of Chicago Press.

Macrae, C. N., Bodenhausen, G. V., & Milne, A. B. (1995). The dissection of selection in person perception: Inhibitory processes in social stereotyping. *Journal of Personality and Social Psychology, 69*, 397–407.

Macrae, C. N., Bodenhausen, G. V., Milne, A. B., Castelli, L., Schloerscheidt, A. M., & Greco, S. (1998). On activating exemplars. *Journal of Experimental Social Psychology, 34*, 330–354.

Macrae, C. N., Bodenhausen, G. V., Milne, A. B., & Jetten, J. (1994). Out of mind but back in sight: Stereotypes on the rebound. *Journal of Personality and Social Psychology, 67*, 808–817.

Macrae, C. N., Bodenhausen, G. V., Milne, A. B., Thorn, T. M.-J., & Castelli, L. (1997). On the activation of social stereotypes: The moderating role of processing objectives. *Journal of Experimental Social Psychology, 33*, 471–489.

Macrae, C. N., Bodenhausen, G. V., Schloerscheidt, A. M., & Milne, A. B. (1999). Tales of the unexpected: Executive function and person perception. *Journal of Personality and Social Psychology, 76*, 200–213.

Marcel, A. J. (1983). Conscious and unconscious perception: Experiments on visual masking and word recognition. *Cognitive Psychology, 15*, 197–237.

Martin, L. L. (1986). Set/reset: Use and disuse of concepts in impression formation. *Journal of Personality and Social Psychology, 51*, 493–504.

McGowan, S. (2002). Mental representations in stressful situations: The calming and distressing effects of significant others. *Journal of Experimental Social Psychology, 38*, 152–161.

Meichenbaum, D., & Gilmore, J. B. (1984). The nature of unconscious processes: A cognitive-behavioral perspective. In K. Bowers & D. Meichenbaum (Eds.), *The unconscious reconsidered.* New York: Wiley.

Merikle, P. M. (1992). Perception without awareness: Critical issues. *American Psychologist, 47*, 792–795.

Merikle, P. M., & Reingold, E. M. (1992). Measuring unconscious perceptual processes. In R. F. Bornstein & T. S. Pittman (Eds.), *Perception without awareness* (pp. 55–80). New York: Guilford.

Metcalfe, J., & Mischel, W. (1999). A hot/cool-system analysis of delay of gratification: Dynamics of will power. *Psychological Review, 106*, 3–19.

Mills, J., & Clark, M. S. (1994). Communal and exchange relationships: Controversies and research. In R. Erber & R. Gilmour (Eds.), *Theoretical frameworks for personal relationships* (pp. 29–42). Hillsdale, NJ: Erlbaum.

Mischel, W. (1999). Personality coherence and dispositions in a cognitive-affective personality (CAPS) approach. In D. Cervone & Y. Shoda (Eds.), *The coherence of personality: Social-cognitive bases of consistency, variability, and organization* (pp. 37–60). New York: Guilford.

Mischel, W., Cantor, N., & Feldman, S. (1996). Principles of self-regulation: The nature of willpower and self-control. In E. T. Higgins & A. W. Kruglanski (Eds.), *Social psychology: Handbook of basic principles* (pp. 329–360). New York: Guilford.

Mischel, W., & Shoda, Y. (1995). A cognitive-affective system theory of personality: Reconceptualizing situations, dispositions, dynamics, and invariance in personality structure. *Psychological Review, 102*, 246–268.

Monahan, L. M., Murphy, S. T., & Zajonc, R. B. (2000). Subliminal mere exposure: Specific, general, and diffuse effects. *Psychological Science, 11*(6), 462–466.

Monteith, M. J., Sherman, J. W., & Devine, P. G. (1998). Suppression as a stereotype control strategy. *Personality and Social Psychology Review, 2*, 63–82.

Morf, C. C., & Rhodewalt, F. (2001). Unraveling the paradoxes of narcissism: A dynamic self-regulatory processing model. *Psychological Inquiry, 12*, 177–196.

Moskowitz, G. B., Gollwitzer, P. M., Wasel, W., & Schaal, B. (1999). Preconscious control of stereotype activation through chronic egalitarian goals. *Journal of Personality and Social Psychology, 77*(1), 167–184.

Moskowitz, G. B., Salomon, A. R., & Taylor, C. M. (2000). Preconsciously controlling stereotyping: Implicitly activated egalitarian goals prevent the activation of stereotypes. *Social Cognition, 18*(2), 151–177.

Murphy, S. T., Monahan, J. L., & Zajonc, R. B. (1995). Additivity of nonconscious affect: Combined effects of priming and exposure. *Journal of Personality and Social Psychology, 69*(4), 589–602.

Murray, S. L. (1999). The quest for conviction: Motivated cognition in romantic relationships. *Psychological Inquiry, 10*, 23–34.

Murray, S. L., & Holmes, J. G. (1993). Seeing virtues in faults: Negativity and the transformation of interpersonal narratives in close relationships. *Journal of Personality and Social Psychology, 65*, 707–722.

Murray, S. L., & Holmes, J. G. (1994). Storytelling in close relationships: The construction of confidence. *Personality and Social Psychology Bulletin, 20*, 650–663.

Neuberg, S. L. (1988). Behavioral implications of information presented outside of conscious awareness: The effect of subliminal presentation of trait information on behavior in the Prisoner's Dilemma Game. *Social Cognition, 6*, 207–230.

Neuberg, S. L., & Fiske, S. T. (1987). Motivational influences on impression formation: Outcome dependency, accuracy-driven attention, and individuating processes. *Journal of Personality and Social Psychology, 53*, 431–444.

Niedenthal, P. M., Halberstadt, J. B., & Setterlund, M. D. (1997). Being happy and seeing "happy": Emotional state mediates visual word recognition. *Cognition and Emotion, 11*, 403–432.

Niedenthal, P. M., Halberstadt, J. B., & Innes-Ker, A. H. (1999). Emotional response categorization. *Psychological Science, 11*, 179–182.

Oehman, A. (1999). Distinguishing unconscious from conscious emotional processes: Methodological considerations and theoretical implications. In T. Dalgleish & M. J. Power (Eds.), *Handbook of cognition and emotion* (pp. 321–352). Chichester, UK: Wiley.

Park, J., & Banaji, M. (2000). Mood and heuristics: The influence of happy and sad states on sensitivity and bias in stereotyping. *Journal of Personality and Social Psychology, 78*, 1005–1023.

Pendry, L. F., & Macrae, C. N. (1996). What the disinterested perceiver overlooks: Goal-directed categorization. *Personality and Social Psychology Bulletin, 22*, 249–256.

Prentice, D. (1990). Familiarity and differences inn self- and other-representations. *Journal of Personality and Social Psychology, 59*, 369–383.

Read, S. J., & Cessa, I. L. (1991). This reminds me of the time when . . . : Expectation failures in reminding and explaining. *Journal of Experimental Social Psychology, 27*, 1–25.

Reznik, I., & Andersen, S. M. (2004a). *Individual differences and transference: Implications of self-discrepancy theory for affect and motivation.* Unpublished manuscript, New York University.

Reznik, I., & Andersen, S. M. (2004b). *Being one's dreaded self: Painful self-experience concerning positive significant others in transference.* Unpublished manuscript, New York University.

Russell, J. A. (2003). Core affect and the psychological construction of emotion. *Psychological Review, 110*, 145–172.

Schwarz, N. (1990). Feelings as information: Informational and motivational functions of affective states. In E. T. Higgins & R. M. Sorrentino (Eds.), *Handbook of motivation and cognition* (Vol. 2, pp. 527–561). New York: Guilford.

Shah, J. Y. (2003). Automatic for the people: How representations of significant others affect goal pursuit. *Journal of Personality and Social Psychology, 84*, 661–681.

Showers, C. (1992). Compartmentalization of positive and negative self-knowledge: Keeping bad apples out of the bunch. *Journal of Personality and Social Psychology, 62*, 1036–1049.

Showers, C. J. (2001). Self-organization in emotional contexts. In J. P. Forgas (Ed.), *Feeling and thinking: The role of affect in social cognition* (pp. 283–307). New York: Cambridge University Press.

Showers, C. J., Abramson, L. Y., & Hogan, M. E. (1998). The dynamic self-concept: How the content and structure of self-concept change with mood. *Journal of Personality and Social Psychology, 75*, 478–493.

Sinclair, L., & Kunda, Z. (1999). Reactions to a black professional: Motivated inhibition and activation of conflicting stereotypes. *Journal of Personality and Social Psychology, 77*, 885–904.

Singer, J. L., & Bonanno, G. (1990). Personality and private experience: Individual variations in consciousness and in attention to subjective phenomena. In L. A. Pervin (Ed.), *Handbook of personality: Theory and research* (pp. 419–444). New York: Guilford.

Singer, J. L., & Salovey, P. (1991). Organized knowledge structures and personality: Person schemas, self schemas, prototypes and scripts. In M. J. Horowitz (Ed.), *Person schemas and maladaptive interpersonal patterns* (pp. 33–79). Chicago: University of Chicago Press.

Smith, C. A., Haynes, K. N., Lazarus, R. S., & Pope, L. K. (1993). In search of the "hot" cognitions: Attributions, appraisals, and their relation to emotion. *Journal of Personality and Social Psychology, 65*, 916–929.

Smith, E. R. (1989). Procedural efficiency: General and specific components and effects on social judgment. *Journal of Experimental Social Psychology, 25*, 500–523.

Smith, E. R. (1996). What do connectionism and psychology have to offer each other? *Journal of Personality and Social Psychology, 70*, 893–912.

Smith, E. R. (1998). Mental representation and memory. In D. T. Gilbert, S. T. Fiske, & G. Lindzay (Eds.), *The handbook of social psychology* (Vol. 1, 4th ed., pp. 391–445). New York: McGraw-Hill.

Smith, E. R., Branscombe, N., & Bormann, C. (1988). Generality of the effects of practice on social judgment tasks. *Journal of Personality and Social Psychology, 54*, 385–395.

Smith, E. R., & Lerner, M. (1986). Development of automatism of social judgments. *Journal of Personality and Social Psychology, 50*, 246–259.

Smith, E. R., Stewart, T. L., & Buttram, R. T. (1992). Inferring a trait from a behavior has long-term, specific effects. *Journal of Personality and Social Psychology, 62*, 753–759.

Smith, E. R., & Zarate, M. A. (1990). Exemplar and prototype use in social categorization. *Social Cognition, 8*, 243–262.

Smith, E. R., & Zarate, M. A. (1992). Exemplar-based model of social judgment. *Psychological Review, 99*, 3–21.

Snyder, M., Tanke, E. D., & Berscheid, E. (1977). Social perception and interpersonal behavior: On the self-fulfilling nature of social stereotypes. *Journal of Personality and Social Psychology, 35*, 656–666.

Spellman, B. A., & Holyoak, B. A. (1992). If Saddam is Hitler then who is George Bush? Analogical mapping between systems of social roles. *Journal of Personality and Social Psychology, 62*, 913–933.

Spencer, S. J., Fein, S., Wolfe, C. T., Fong, C., & Dunn, M. A. (1998). Automatic activation of stereotypes: The role of self-image threat. *Personality and Social Psychology Bulletin, 24*, 1139–1152.

Steele, C. M. (1988). The psychology of self-affirmation: Sustaining the integrity of the self. In L. Berkowitz (Ed.), *Advances in experimental social psychology* (Vol. 21, pp. 261–302). New York: Academic Press.

Steele, C. M., Spencer, S. J., & Lynch, M. (1993). Self-image resilience and dissonance: The role of affirmation resources. *Journal of Personality and Social Psychology, 64*, 885–896.

Sullivan, H. S. (1953). *The interpersonal theory of psychiatry*. New York: Norton.

Taylor, S. E., & Brown, J. D. (1988). Illusion and well-being: A social psychological perspective on mental health. *Psychological Bulletin, 103*, 193–210.

Tice, D. M., & Bratslavsky, E. (2000). Giving in to feel good: The place of emotion regulation in the context of general self-control. *Psychological Inquiry, 11*, 149–159.

Uleman, J. S. (1987). Consciousness and control: The case of spontaneous trait inferences. *Personality and Social Psychology Bulletin, 13*, 337–354.

Wegner, D. M. (1994). Ironic processes of mental control. *Psychological Review, 101*, 34–52.

Wisniewski, E. J., & Bassok, M. (1999). What makes a man similar to a tie? Stimulus compatibility with comparison and integration. *Cognitive Psychology, 39*, 208–238.

Wyer, R. S., & Carlston, D. E. (1979). *Social cognition, inference and attribution.* Hillsdale, NJ: Erlbaum.

Zajonc, R. (1968). Attitudinal effects of mere exposure. *Journal of Personality and Social Psychology, 9*, 1–27.

Zajonc, R. B. (1971). Attraction, affiliation, and attachment. In J. E. Eisenberg & W. S. Dillon (Eds.), *Man and beast: Comparative social behavior* (pp. 141–179). Washington, DC: Smithsonian Institution Press.

Zajonc, R. (1998). Emotions. In D. T. Gilbert, S. T. Fiske, & G. Lindzey (Eds.), *The handbook of social psychology* (Vol. 1, 4th ed., pp. 591–632). New York: McGraw-Hill.

Zajonc, R. B. (2000). Feeling and thinking: Closing the debate over the independence of affect. In J. P. Forgas (Ed.), *Feeling and thinking: The role of affect in social cognition* (pp. 31–58). New York: Cambridge University Press.

PART V

SELF-REGULATION

17

The Control of the Unwanted

Peter M. Gollwitzer, Ute C. Bayer, and Kathleen C. McCulloch

> How often does the will have to peek through the window, before the deed walks out of the door?
>
> —Erasmus von Rotterdam (1466–1536)

Intentions to do more good and less bad are reliably associated with actual efforts in the intended directions (Ajzen, 1991; Godin & Kok, 1996; Sheeran, 2002). However, intention-behavior relations are modest, largely due to the fact that people, despite having formed strong intentions, fail to act on them (Orbell & Sheeran, 1998). Given this predicament, one wonders what people can do to facilitate the translation of intentions into behavior. In this chapter, it is suggested that people should engage in a second act of willing by making if-then plans (i.e., implementation intentions) that specify how the (goal) intention is to be realized. We argue that such plans produce automatic action control by intentionally delegating the control of one's goal-directed thoughts, feelings, and behaviors to specific situational cues. Thus, by forming implementation intentions, people can strategically switch from conscious and effortful control of their goal-directed behaviors to being automatically controlled by selected situational cues. We understand this type of automatic action control as strategic automaticity or instant habits (Gollwitzer, 1999), as it originates from a single act of will rather than being produced by repeated and consistent selection of a certain course of action in the same situation (i.e., principles of routinization; Anderson, 1987; Fitts & Posner, 1967; Newell & Rosenbloom, 1981).

The first part of the chapter discusses research that explores how implementation intentions can help people to promote getting started on their goals. In the second part, we discuss findings on how people can use implementation intentions in an attempt to prevent straying off-course from goal attainment.

Implementation Intentions: A Strategic Attempt to Instill Automatic Self-Regulation

The concept of intention is central in human goal striving (e.g., Bandura, 1991; Fishbein & Ajzen, 1975; Gollwitzer & Moskowitz, 1996; Kuhl, 1984; Locke & Latham, 1990; Wicklund & Gollwitzer, 1982). In traditional theories on goal striving, the intention to achieve a certain goal is seen as an immediate determinant (or at least predictor) of goal-directed action. Accordingly, for decades research has dealt with the factors that make for strong intentions (Ajzen & Fishbein, 1980), and little attention was paid to mechanisms mediating the effects of intentions on behavior. Over time, evidence accumulated showing that forming strong intentions was only a prerequisite for goal attainment. To translate intentions into action, problems associated with the implementation of intentions need to be solved (Gollwitzer, 1996).

For instance, after having set a goal, people may procrastinate in acting on their intentions and thus fail to initiate goal-directed behavior. Moreover, in everyday life people normally strive for multiple, often even competing, goals, many of which are not simple short-term but long-term projects that require repeated efforts (e.g., starting a new business). Goal pursuit may come to an early halt because competing projects have temporarily gained priority and the individual fails to successfully resume the original project. Also, in order to meet their goals, people have to seize viable opportunities to act, a task that becomes particularly difficult when attention is directed elsewhere (e.g., one is absorbed by competing goal pursuits, wrapped up in ruminations, gripped by intense emotional experiences, or simply tired) and when these opportunities are not obvious at first sight or only present themselves briefly.

In all of these cases, automatic action control comes in handy as established routines linked to a relevant context release the critical goal-directed behavior immediately, efficiently, and without a conscious intent. Often, however, such routines are not established and the goal-directed behavior is not part of an everyday routine. As a substitute, people can resort to forming implementation intentions that strategically place the intended goal-directed behavior under direct situational control.

Goal Intentions versus Implementation Intentions

Gollwitzer (1993, 1999) suggested that automatic action control can be achieved strategically by forming implementation intentions that take the format, "If Situation X is encountered, then I will perform Behavior Y!" In an implementation intention, a mental link is created between a specified future situation and the anticipated goal-directed response. Holding an implementation intention commits the individual to perform a certain goal-directed behavior once the critical situation is encountered.

Implementation intentions are to be distinguished from goals. Goals have the structure of "I intend to reach Z!" whereby Z may relate to a certain outcome or behavior to which the individual feels committed. Gollwitzer (1993, 1999) refers to goals as *goal intentions* to make a strong distinction between goals and plans (i.e., implementation intentions). Both are acts of willing, whereby the first specifies an intention to meet a goal and the second refers to an intention to perform a plan. Commonly, implementation intentions are formed in the service of goal intentions as they specify the when, where, and how of goal-directed responses. For instance, a possible implementation intention in the service of the goal intention to eat healthy food would link a suitable situational context (e.g., one's order is taken at a restaurant) to an appropriate behavior (e.g., ask for a vegetarian meal). As a consequence, a strong mental link is created between the critical situation of the waiter taking an order and the goal-directed response of asking for a vegetarian meal.

The mental links created by implementation intentions are expected to facilitate goal attainment on the basis of psychological processes that relate to both the anticipated situation and the specified behavior. Because forming implementation intentions implies the selection of a critical future situation (i.e., a viable opportunity), it is assumed that the mental representation of this situation becomes highly activated, hence more accessible (Gollwitzer, 1999). This heightened accessibility should make it easier to detect the critical situation in the surrounding environment and readily attend to it even when one is busy with other things. Moreover, this heightened accessibility should facilitate the recall of the critical situation.

The Specified Situation

This accessibility hypothesis (i.e., the mental representation of the situation specified in the if-part of the implementation intention becomes highly activated) was tested in studies measuring how well participants holding implementation intentions attended to, detected, and recalled the critical situation (Gollwitzer, Bayer, Steller, & Bargh, 2002) as compared to participants who had only formed goal intentions. In a study using a dichotic-listening paradigm, it was observed that words describing the anticipated critical situation were highly disruptive to focused attention in implementation intention participants as compared to goal intention participants (i.e., the shadowing performance of the attended material decreased). This finding implies that opportunities to act, as specified in implementation intentions, will not easily escape people's attention, even when people focus on other things (e.g., a stimulating conversation).

Also supporting the hypothesis that implementation intentions lead to high accessibility of the critical situation are the results of a study using the embedded figures test (Gottschaldt, 1926), where smaller a-figures were hidden within larger b-figures. Enhanced detection of the hidden a-figures was observed when participants had specified the a-figure in the if-part of an implementation intention (i.e., had made plans on how to create a traffic sign from the a-figure). In addition, the heightened accessibility hypothesis was tested via a cued recall procedure. Research participants had to form implementation intentions specifying when, where, and how they wanted to play prepared games from numerous predesigned options. Immediately, or 48 hours later, participants were given a surprise task to recall all of the options provided cued by where, when, and how. Options specified in implementation intentions were recalled better than nonspecified options, no matter whether recall was tested immediately or at a later point.

Further support for the accessibility notion comes from Aarts, Dijksterhuis, and Midden (1999) using a lexical decision task. Shorter lexical decision time was observed for those words that described critical cues specified in implementation intentions. As well, the faster lexical responses to these critical words (i.e., their heightened accessibility) mediated the beneficial effects of implementation intentions on goal attainment. These results imply that the goal-promoting effects of implementation intentions are based on the heightened accessibility of selected critical situational cues.

The Specified Goal-Directed Behavior

Forming implementation intentions involves first the selection of an effective goal-directed behavior, which is then linked to the selected critical situation. The mental act of linking a critical situation to an intended behavior in the form of an if-then plan leads to automatic action initiation in the sense that action initiation becomes swift, efficient, and does not require conscious intent once the critical situation is encountered. By forming implementation intentions, people can strategically switch from conscious and effortful action initiation (guided by goal intentions) to having their goal-directed actions effortlessly elicited by the specified situational cues. This postulated automatization of action initiation (also described as strategic "delegation of control to situational cues") has been supported by the results of various experiments that tested immediacy, efficiency, and the presence or absence of conscious intent.

Gollwitzer and Brandstätter (1997, Study 3) demonstrated the immediacy of action initiation in a study wherein participants had been induced to form implementation intentions that specified viable opportunities for presenting counterarguments to a series of racist remarks made by a confederate. Participants with implementation intentions initiated the counterargument more quickly than the participants who had formed the mere goal intention to counterargue.

In further experiments (Brandtstätter, Lengfelder, & Gollwitzer, 2001, Studies 3 and 4), the efficiency of action initiation was explored. Participants formed the goal intention to press a button as fast as possible if numbers appeared on the computer screen, but not if letters were presented (Go/No-Go task). Participants in the implementation intention condition also made the plan to press the response button particularly fast if the number 3 was presented. This Go/No-Go task was then embedded as a secondary task in a dual-task paradigm. Implementation intention participants showed a substantial increase in speed of responding to the number 3 compared to the control group, regardless of whether the simultaneously demanded primary task (a memorization task in Study 3 and a tracking task in Study 4) was either easy or difficult to perform. Apparently, the immediacy of responding induced by implementation intentions is also efficient in the sense that it does not require much in the way of cognitive resources (i.e., can be performed even when dual tasks have to be performed at the same time).

A final set of two experiments (Bayer, Moskowitz, & Gollwitzer, 2002) tested whether implementation intentions lead to action initiation without conscious intent once the critical situation is encountered. In these experiments, the critical situation was presented subliminally, and its facilitating influences on preparing (Study 1) or performing (Study 2) the respective goal-directed behavior were assessed. In Study 1, the goal of asserting oneself against a rude experimenter was analyzed. Half of the participants were encouraged to set the goal of "telling her off" by pointing to her rude behavior (goal intention condition), while the other half was in addition asked to plan to do this as soon as they met her in person (implementation intention condition). Afterward, faces of either the rude experimenter or a neutral person were presented subliminally (primes), and the activation of knowledge relevant to rudeness (target words such as *offensive, mean, conceited*) was measured via reading latencies. Results indicated that after the subliminal presentation of the critical primes, implementation intention participants, but not participants who only had formed goals, showed faster reading times for words related to rudeness.

In Study 2, participants were asked to classify a series of geometric figures (e.g., circles, ellipses, triangles, squares) as rounded or angular objects by left or right button-press responses. All participants formed the goal intention to classify the figures as fast and accurately as possible. Implementation intention participants were in addition asked to make the following plan: "And if I see a triangle, then I press the respective button particularly fast!" Participants worked on a set of 240 figures, presented in succession on a computer screen. Some of the figures were preceded by the subliminal presentation of the critical figure (i.e., a triangle), whereas others were preceded by a control prime (i.e., a percent sign: %). In accord with the results of Study 1, participants in the implementation intention condition had faster classification responses for angular figures when the triangle instead of the percent sign was presented as a subliminal prime; no such effect was observed with goal intention participants. The subliminal priming effects observed in the experiments reported by Bayer, Moskowitz, et al. (2002) suggest that when planned via implementation intentions, the initiation of goal-directed behavior becomes triggered by the anticipated situational cue, without the need for further conscious intent.

One might wonder whether in addition to or even instead of the stimulus perception and response initiation processes described above, an increase of commitment may also promote implementation intention effects on goal attainment. However, this possible alternative process mechanism has not received any empirical support. For instance, when Brandstätter et al. (2001, Study 1) analyzed whether heroin addicts under withdrawal benefit from forming implementation intentions in handing in a newly composed curriculum vitae before the end of the day, they also measured participants' commitment to do so. While the majority of the implementation intention participants succeeded in handing in the curriculum vitae in time, none of the goal intention participants succeeded in this task. These two groups, however, did not differ in terms of their goal commitment ("I feel committed to compose a curriculum vitae," and "I have to complete this task") measured after the goal intention and implementation intention instructions had been administered. This finding was replicated with young adults who participated in a professional development workshop (Oettingen, Hönig, & Gollwitzer, 2000, Study 2), and analogous results are reported in research on the effects of implementation intentions on meeting health promotion and disease prevention goals (e.g., Orbell, Hodgkins, & Sheeran, 1997).

Implementation Intentions and Their Effects on Wanted Behavior

Given that implementation intentions facilitate attending to, detecting, and recalling viable opportunities to act toward goal attainment and, in addition, automate action initiation in the presence of such opportunities, people who form implementation intentions should show higher goal attainment rates compared to people who do not furnish their goal intentions with implementation intentions. This hypothesis is supported by the results of a host of studies examining the attainment of various types of goal intentions.

Types of Goals

As a general research strategy, goal intentions are selected for study that are not easily attained for reasons specified above (e.g., distractions, unpleasantness). Gollwitzer and Brandstätter (1997) analyzed a goal intention that had to be performed at a bad time (e.g., writing a report about Christmas Eve during the subsequent Christmas holiday). Other studies have examined the effects of implementation intentions on goal attainment rates with goal intentions that are somewhat unpleasant to perform. For instance, the goal intentions to perform regular breast self-examinations (Orbell et al., 1997), have cervical cancer screenings (Sheeran & Orbell, 2000), resume functional activity after joint replacement surgery (Orbell & Sheeran, 2000), and engage in physical exercise (Milne, Orbell, & Sheeran, 2002) were all more frequently acted upon when people had furnished these goals with implementation intentions. Moreover, implementation intentions were found to facilitate the attainment of goal intentions where it is easy to forget to act on them (e.g., regular intake of vitamin pills, Sheeran & Orbell, 1999; the signing of work sheets with the elderly, Chasteen, Park, & Schwarz, 2001).

Potential Moderators

The strength of the beneficial effects of implementation intentions depends on the presence or absence of several moderators. First, the more difficult it is to initiate the goal-directed behavior, the more apparent implementation intention effects are. For instance, implementation intentions were more effective in completing difficult as compared to easy goals (Gollwitzer & Brandstätter, 1997, Study 1). Moreover, forming implementation intentions was more beneficial to frontal lobe patients, who typically have problems with executive control, than to college students (Lengfelder & Gollwitzer, 2001, Study 2).

Second, the strength of commitment to the respective goal intention also matters. Orbell et al. (1997) reported that the beneficial effects of implementation intentions on compliance in performing a breast self-examination were observed only in those women who strongly intended to perform a breast self-examination. This finding suggests that implementation intentions do not work when the respective goal intention is weak. In line with this conclusion, the beneficial effects of implementation intentions on a person's recall of the specified situations (Gollwitzer, Bayer, et al., 2002, Study 3) can no longer be observed when the respective goal intention has been abandoned (i.e., the research participants were told that the assigned goal intention need no longer be reached, as it had been performed by some other person).

Third, Sheeran, Webb, and Gollwitzer (2002) conducted two experiments that suggest that implementation intentions facilitate the initiation of goal-directed behavior only if the superordinate goal intention is activated. Experiment 1 showed that combining a goal-setting intervention with the formation of an implementation intention produced the greatest increase in study behavior compared to the goal-setting and implementation intention interventions on their own, and a no-intervention control condition. In Experiment 2, either a relevant or an irrelevant superordinate goal was activated outside of participants' conscious awareness. Implementation intentions affected the accessibility of respective behavior (as assessed in a lexical decision task) only when the relevant but not when the irrelevant goal had been activated.

An experiment (Bayer, Jaudas, & Gollwitzer, 2002) using the Roger and Monsell (1995) task switch paradigm also makes the point that implementation intention effects depend on the activation of the superordinate goal. In this study, we varied whether the task goal was related or unrelated to the stimulus specified in the if-part of the implementation intention (i.e., to respond to the critical stimulus particularly fast). Implementation intention effects were only observed when the activated goal was speaking to the formed implementation intention.

Fourth, the strength of the commitment to the formed implementation intention matters. In Gollwitzer, Bayer, et al.'s (2002) Study 3, the strength of the commitment to the implementation intention was varied by telling the participants (after an extensive personality testing session) that they were the kind of people who would benefit from either rigidly adhering to their plans (i.e., high commitment) or staying flexible (i.e., low commitment). The latter group showed lower implementation intention effects (i.e., cued recall performance for selected opportunities) than the former.

Fifth, the strength of the mental link between the if-part and the then-part of an implementation intention should also affect how beneficial forming implementation intentions turns out to be. For example, if a person takes much time and concentration encoding the if-then plan, or keeps repeating a formed if-then plan by using inner speech, stronger mental links should emerge, which in turn should produce stronger implementation intention effects.

Implementation Intentions and Their Effects on Unwanted Behavior

Research on implementation intentions conducted thus far has almost exclusively focused on the self-regulatory issue of getting started with goals that one wants to achieve. Certainly, goal attainment becomes more likely if the critical problem of getting started has been tackled successfully. However, once a person has initiated goal pursuit, it still needs to be brought to a successful ending. People need to protect an ongoing goal from being thwarted by attending to attractive distractions or falling prey to conflicting bad habits (e.g., the goal of being fair with others may conflict with the habit of stereotyping and prejudging certain groups of people). In the following section, we describe the numerous ways in which implementation intentions can be used to help people to control the "unwanted" that could hamper successfully pursuing wanted goals.

Responding to Critical Situations With the Suppression of Unwanted Responses

In principle, implementation intentions can suppress the unwanted by using different strategies. For instance, if a person wants to be friendly and not unfriendly to a friend who is known to frequently make outrageous requests, she can protect herself from showing the unwanted unfriendly response by forming any of the following three implementation intentions, each of which has a particular strategy. The first type of implementation intention is geared toward controlling the unwanted by focusing on suppressing the unwanted response: "And if my friend approaches me with an outrageous request, then I will not respond in an unfriendly manner!" This implementation intention specifies the critical situation in the if-part of the implementation intention and not performing the unwanted response in the then-part. The second type of implementation intention focuses on facilitating the initiation of the respective wanted response: "And if my friend approaches me with an outrageous request, then I will respond in a friendly manner!" In this case, the critical situation is specified in the if-part, and the then-part entails performing the wanted response that is threatened by disruptive unwanted responses. Finally, the third type of implementation intention takes focus away from the critical situation: "And if my friend approaches me with an outrageous request, then I'll ignore it!" In this variant, the critical situation is specified in the if-part of the implementation intention, and the then-part suggests showing no response (i.e., to ignore it). We have conducted various experiments that used these three types of implementation intentions to control unwanted spontaneous responding to distractions, as well as the activation of unwanted stereotypical beliefs and prejudicial feelings.

Suppressing Unwanted Spontaneous Attentional Responses

When concentrating on pursuing a current goal becomes threatened by attractive distractions, shielding one's goal-directed behaviors from derailment becomes an issue. Such shielding should be particularly hard when the distractive stimuli are so pronounced and attractive that attention is spontaneously directed toward them (e.g., beautiful objects and people). Being that the responses specified in implementation intentions are initiated in an automatic manner (i.e., are immediate and efficient, and do not require conscious intent), they should have a good chance in winning the horse race with spontaneous attentional responses toward distracting stimuli.

In research on the resistance to tempting distractions, participants are commonly asked to perform a task that is somewhat boring but demands much concentration. In the process of performing the task, participants are then distracted at random intervals by being presented with attractive attention-grabbing stimuli. For instance, Patterson and Mischel (1976) had children stick numerous pegs into a large pegboard placed on a desk, while attractive toys were shown in a nearby box dressed as a clown. Similarly, Gollwitzer and Schaal (1998) asked college students to perform a series of self-paced arithmetic problems presented on a computer screen, while distracting clips of award-winning commercials were interspersed at random intervals on a video screen mounted on top of the computer terminal.

Implementation intentions turned out to be more effective in protecting participants from these distractions (measured as level of performance on the task at hand) than mere goal intentions ("I will not let myself get distracted!"). However, it mattered whether implementation intentions were phrased as distraction-inhibiting ("And if a distraction arises, then I will ignore it!") or as task-facilitating ("And if a distraction arises, then I will increase my effort at the task at hand!"). Distraction-inhibiting implementation intentions always helped to ward off the distraction, no matter whether the motivation to perform the tedious task was low or high. Task-facilitating implementation intentions, on the other hand, could only achieve this when motivation to perform the tedious task was low. When motivation was high to begin with, task-facilitating implementation intentions did not help to escape distractions. Apparently, forming task-facilitating implementation intentions creates some kind of overmotivation under such circumstances and thus undermines performance.

The different effects of task-facilitating versus distraction-inhibiting implementation intentions suggest that effective willing appears (i.e., when motivation is high to begin with) more closely associated with "cold" cognitive strategies of guiding attention than with the "hot" determined mobilization of effort. It seems appropriate, therefore, to advise motivated individuals who suffer from being distracted (e.g., ambitious students doing their homework) to resort to forming implementation intentions that focus on the ignoring of distractions, rather than on the strengthening of efforts.

Suppressing Habitual Stereotypical and Prejudicial Responses

The use of stereotypes in impression formation can be controlled effectively by effortful correctional strategies (Bodenhausen & Macrae, 1998; Brewer, 1988; Devine, 1989; Fiske & Neuberg, 1990). However, the activation of stereotypes carries features of automaticity due to a long history of being repeatedly activated in the presence of members of the particular group (Bargh, 1999; Devine, 1989). Accordingly, stereotype activation should be more difficult to control than stereotype use, and the question arises as to whether people who have the goal to judge others in a fair manner can protect themselves from the automatic activation of stereotypes by forming implementation intentions focused on the suppression of the "bad habit" of stereotyping others. Again, if one applies the horse race metaphor, it seems possible that the response specified in the then-part of a fairness-oriented implementation intention can win out over the activation of stereotypical beliefs.

Findings of priming studies using short stimulus onset asynchronies (less than 300 ms) suggest that forming implementation intentions indeed inhibit the automatic activation of stereotypical beliefs (Gollwitzer, Achtziger, Schaal, & Hammelbeck, 2002). When participants had furnished their goal intentions of judging the elderly in a nonstereotypical manner with the respective implementation intention ("If I see an old person, then I tell myself: Don't stereotype!"), the typical automatic activation of stereotypical beliefs (assessed through pronunciation speed in a semantic priming paradigm) was even reversed. Implementation intentions were also found to effectively suppress the automatic activation of gender stereotypes in a study where participants had to play the role of a personal manager in a simulated hiring situation. When participants had formed the goal intention to judge women applicants in a nonstereotypical way and furnished this goal intention with the implementation intention to ignore the gender of a certain applicant ("If I see this person, then I will ignore her gender!"), no automatic activation of stereotypical beliefs about this woman (assessed through response latencies in a Stroop task using stereotypical words) was observed.

Finally, implementation intentions were also observed to suppress the automatic activation of prejudicial feelings in a study on homeless people. When participants' goal intentions to judge the homeless in a nonprejudicial manner were furnished with respective implementation intentions ("And if I see a homeless person, then I will tell myself: No prejudice!" or "And if I see a homeless person, then I will ignore that he is homeless!"), the automatic negative evaluation of the homeless (assessed in an affect priming paradigm) vanished.

Work by Achtziger (2002) on prejudicial feelings toward soccer fans indicates that implementation intentions ("And if I see a soccer fan, then I won't evaluate him negatively!") can control such negative feelings in a very flexible manner. In this study, a sequential priming paradigm was used where pictures of soccer fans served as primes and relevant negative versus positive person attributes as targets (e.g., rowdy, comradely) that had to be read as fast as possible. Half of the depicted soccer fans (primes) were cued with a signal tone, and the participants were told that the formed implementation intention would only apply to those presentations of soccer fans cued with the signal tone. Implementation intention effects (i.e., positive attributes are read faster than negative attributes) were only observed when the depiction of soccer fans was accompanied with a signal tone.

In sum, it seems that stereotypical beliefs and prejudicial feelings can be controlled via implementation intentions in a very effective manner, no matter whether the then-part specifies a don't response or an ignore response. Whether a response of "then I will be particularly fair" also produces strong effects remains to be explored in future research. Nevertheless, our research on resistance to distractions suggests that, at least with individuals who are highly motivated to be fair to others, an overmotivation effect might occur that undermines the effectiveness of this type of implementation intention. Finally, the research reported here suggests that people may strategically form implementation intentions to protect themselves from stereotyping and prejudice. People may form these plans on the spot whenever they are needed to promote goal attainment, and they still can rely on the automatic initiation of the specified responses. In other words, no extensive consistent and repeated practice is needed, as is the case with automaticity stemming from habit formation. Moreover, people can strategically limit the applicability of their implementation intentions to select certain situational contexts, but not others. No extensive discriminative learning is needed that separates critical situational contexts from noncritical ones.

Blocking Detrimental Self-States

In the research presented above, implementation intentions specified a critical situation or problem in the if-part, which was linked to a then-part that described an attempt at suppressing the unwanted response. This type of self-regulation by implementation intentions implies that the person must not only be aware of what makes the desired goal difficult to attain, but also needs to anticipate the occurrence of potential hindrances and what kind of unwanted responses these hindrances commonly elicit.

Implementation intentions can also be used to protect the self from the "unwanted" by taking a completely different approach. Instead of gearing implementation intentions toward anticipated potential hindrances and the unwanted responses triggered thereby, the person may form implementation intentions geared at stabilizing the goal pursuit at hand. For instance, if a person is tired and a friend approaches her with an outrageous request, chances are high that she will respond in an unfriendly manner. However, if she has stipulated in advance in an implementation intention how she will respond to outrageous requests by her friend, being tired should not play a role. The critical interaction should simply proceed as planned, and the self-state of being tired should fail to affect the person's responding to outrageous requests in a negative, unwanted direction. As is evident from this example, the present self-regulatory strategy should be of special value whenever the influence of detrimental self-states (e.g., being upset) on one's goal-directed behavior has to be controlled. This should be true no matter whether such self-states and/or their influence on behavior reside in the person's consciousness or not.

We tested these assumptions in a series of experiments (Gollwitzer & Bayer, 2000) by asking participants to make plans regarding their performance on an assigned task (via implementation intentions) or not. Prior to beginning the task, participants' self-states were manipulated in such a way that performing the task became more difficult. We predicted that these manipulations of the critical self-state should affect task performance only for those participants who had not planned out working on the task via implementation intentions. In order to construct a critical test of our hypothesis, we asked participants in the no-implementation-intention control condition to perform well on the task (i.e., assigned the goal intention to do well).

The Incomplete Self and Social Insensitivity

The first study was a self-completion experiment (patterned after Gollwitzer & Wicklund, 1985) that tested whether the negative effects of self-definitional incompleteness on social sensitivity in a subsequent getting-to-know-another-person situation can be attenuated by forming implementation intentions. Participants were law students highly committed to becoming successful lawyers. Participants were told that the study was designed to analyze the effects of goals on how people get to know each other. For this purpose, participants would be given a chance to get to know another person, and all participants were assigned the goal to take the perspective of this other person during the conversation. Half of the participants were, in addition, asked to furnish this goal with the following implementation intention: "And if my partner expresses a preference for a specific conversation topic, then I will turn the conversation around to it!" Then, participants had to fill out either a questionnaire on how they studied law or the same questionnaire with three additional questions pointing to shortcomings with respect to being a successful lawyer (e.g., Do you have courtroom experience as a judge or district attorney?), thus creating a sense of self-definitional incompleteness.

Finally, all participants were informed that the conversation partner with the name of Nadja had already indicated her preferences with respect to potential conversation topics. When participants were handed a sheet of paper describing her preferences, it became absolutely clear that Nadja did not want to talk about law but rather about her last vacation and popular movies. To assess whether self-definitional concerns would increase participants' readiness to still push law as the conversation topic, and whether implementation intentions could eliminate this effect, we asked all participants to indicate their own conversation topic preferences to Nadja.

In the control condition in which no implementation intentions were formed, participants' preferences for law as a potential conversation topic clearly demonstrated a self-completion effect (i.e., participants with an incomplete self-definition preferred law more as a conversation topic than participants with a complete self-definition, even though Nadja had expressed her disinterest). Interestingly, implementation intention participants were protected against this effect (i.e., participants with complete and incomplete self-definition showed the same low preference for law as a potential conversation topic). Therefore, we posit that implementation intentions disconnect the absorbing self-state of self-definitional incompleteness from its negative effects on interacting sensitively with others.

Being in a Good Mood and Stereotyping

In a third study, we explored a further self-state, this time an affective state of the self. More specifically, we wanted to know whether the good-mood effect on increased stereotyping (Bless, 1997; Bless & Fiedler, 1995) can be eliminated by forming implementation intentions. In this experiment, participants were first either put in a positive mood by watching a humorous movie presenting stand-up comedians, or put in a less positive, neutral mood by watching a documentary film on the training of apprentices in German vocational schools. In a presumed second study, participants were told that the German language allows describing people at different levels of abstraction and that we would show them illustrations of people and then ask them to describe the depicted people by the use of prepared statements worded at different levels of abstraction. The alleged purpose of the study was to explore whether the individual goals of the perceiver would lead to distinct preferences for different types of descriptions. Participants in the positive mood condition were then split up into three further groups. One group was assigned the goal of forming a nonstereotypical impression of the depicted characters (goal intention group). The implementation intention group was not only assigned the goal to form a nonstereotypical impression, but also asked to make the respective plan: "If I start to evaluate a character, then I will ignore the character's gender!" The third group neither set a fairness goal nor made respective plans.

Finally, two scenarios were presented, one depicting a character called Sabine who looked at herself in a mirror, and another depicting a character called Gerda who shouted at a child attempting to walk on a tightrope. Each scenario was accompanied with four descriptions of the events, and participants were asked to mark the one that they thought matched best. These descriptions varied in terms of their stereotypicality (Semin & Fielder, 1988, 1991; Maass, Salvi, Arcuri, & Semin, 1989). When participants' description choices were analyzed, results showed that positive mood indeed facilitated gender-stereotypical descriptions (e.g., "Sabine is vain" vs. "Sabine combs her hair" and "Gerda is caring" vs. "Gerda hollers at a child") as compared to neutral-mood participants, thus replicating the standard effect. Importantly, the mere goal of forming nonstereotypical impressions failed to attenuate this effect. However, if this goal was furnished with respective implementation intentions, the positive mood effect on increased stereotyping was eliminated.

Ego-Depletion and Self-Control Failure

According to ego-depletion theory as suggested by Baumeister (2000; Muraven, Tice, & Baumeister, 1998), performing an initial task that demands much self-regulation makes performance on a second task that also demands self-regulation less optimal. We therefore wondered if ego-depletion's influence on self-regulatory performance can be blocked by implementation intentions.

We tested this hypothesis by using a classic ego-depletion paradigm. Participants first had to watch a humorous movie with the instruction to either express their emotions or show no emotions at all. For the subsequent task of solving difficult anagrams, all participants formed the goal intention to solve as many anagrams as possible. Half of the ego-depleted participants also formed an implementation intention on how to meet this goal intention: "And if I have solved one anagram, then I will immediately start to work on the next!"

When we compared anagram performance in the three groups, we first observed the classic ego-depletion effect (i.e., controlling one's emotion on the first task hampered performance on the subsequent anagram task). However, this ego-depletion effect was completely eliminated when participants had furnished the goal to perform well on the subsequent task with a respective implementation intention.

Further support for the hypothesis that implementation intentions block ego-depletion effects comes from an experiment by Webb and Sheeran (2003, Study 2). First, half of the participants were given an ego-depletion manipulation (i.e., standing on one's weaker leg and counting down in 7s from 1,000), while the other half were given a control task (i.e., stand normally and count to 1,000 in 5s). Then, all participants were given the goal intention to read as quickly as possible the ink color of words presented in one of four different colors. In addition, a subset of the participants were also asked to make the following plan: "As soon as I see the word, then I will ignore its meaning [e.g., by concentrating on the second letter only] and name the ink color it is printed in!" Among participants who had been ego depleted in the initial task, forming implementation intentions improved subsequent performance in the Stroop task to a level exhibited by nondepleted controls.

In summary, by forming implementation intentions, people can protect themselves from the negative effects of ego depletion on performing tasks that put some strain on a person's self-regulatory resources. People only need to furnish their goals to perform well with relevant plans that spell out in an if-then manner how the task at hand is to be performed.

Summary: Becoming a Better Person Without Changing the Self

The presented research provides a new perspective on the psychology of self-regulation. Commonly, effective self-regulation is understood in terms of strengthening the self, so that the self can meet the challenge of being a powerful executive agent (Baumeister, Heatherton, & Tice, 1994). It is emphasized that the self may fail to fulfill its executive function of setting goals and monitoring their attainment. Therefore, most research on goal-directed self-regulation focuses on strengthening the self in such a way that threats and irritations become less likely, or on restoring an already threatened or irritated self. For example, personal self-esteem threats may be dealt with by becoming more competent or reducing one's aspirations, and social self-esteem threats may be attenuated by relating to different social groups. Finally, irritations can be reduced by reinterpreting the stressing stimuli or calming the physiological and experiential aspects of irritations and strong emotions.

It is important to recognize that all of these maneuvers focus on changing the self so that the self becomes a better executive. In this line of research, we introduce a perspective on goal-directed self-regulation that focuses on facilitating action control without changing the self. We start with the assumption that action control becomes easy if a person's behavior is directly controlled by situational cues, and that forming implementation intentions achieves such direct action control. As this mode of action control circumvents the self, it does not matter if the self is threatened or secure, agitated or calm, because the self is effectively disconnected from its influence on behavior. Our findings support this line of reasoning by demonstrating that task performance (e.g., getting to know another person, judging women in a nonstereotypical manner, solving difficult anagrams, or performing the Stroop task) does not suffer any impairment from various detrimental self-states (e.g., self-definitional incompleteness, mood, and ego-depletion) if performing these tasks has been planned out via implementation intentions.

Blocking Adverse Contextual Influences

People's goal pursuits are threatened not only by detrimental self-states, but also by adverse situational contexts. Many situations have negative effects on goal attainment unbeknownst to the person who is striving for the goal. A prime example is the social loafing phenomenon, in which people show reduced effort in the face of work settings that produce a reduction of accountability (i.e., performance outcomes can no longer be checked at an individual level). As people are commonly not aware of this phenomenon, they cannot form implementation intentions that specify a social loafing situation as a critical situation, thereby rendering an implementation intention that focuses on suppressing the social loafing response as an unviable self-regulatory strategy. As an alternative, people may resort to forming implementation intentions that stipulate how the intended task is to be performed and thus effectively block any negative situational influences.

Deindividuated Work Settings and Social Loafing

When people are asked to work in groups, where individual performances cannot be checked, they are known to show reduced effort and performance (Karau & Williams, 1993; Latané, Williams, & Harkins, 1979). This social loafing effect is particularly strong when very simple tasks are to be performed. To explore the effect of plans on the phenomenon of social loafing, we ran the following experiment. We asked participants to think of a common knife and generate as many uses as possible. This task had to be performed under either of the two following assumptions. The first is that the uses generated will be pooled with those of seven other participants so that no individual contribution can be determined by the experimenter. The second is that the task had to be performed under the assumption that individual solutions will not be pooled, but linked to each individual participant so that the experimenter can measure each participant's performance.

Before participants started the task of generating different uses for a common knife, all participants were given the goal to generate as many uses as possible (goal condition). Half of the participants furnished this goal with an implementation intention stating, "And if I have generated a certain use, then I will immediately turn to generating a further possible use!" When we counted how many uses participants had generated in 12 minutes, we observed that goal-intention participants reported 21 uses if participants' performances were individually identified, but only 17 uses if participants' performances were pooled. This finding replicates the classic social loafing effect. However, the decrement in the performances of participants in the pooled condition completely disappeared when participants had formed implementation intentions, demonstrating that the negative effect of a work setting with pooled performance outcomes can be eliminated by forming implementation intentions.

Loss-Framed Negotiation Settings and Suboptimal Negotiation Outcomes

People may frame desired outcomes in terms of gains or losses (Kahneman & Tversky, 1979). Research on dispute resolution suggests that cognitive processes resulting from the loss or gain framing of the negotiation situation at hand have a strong impact on negotiation processes and outcomes (De Dreu, Carnevale, Emans, & van de Vliert, 1995; Neale & Bazerman, 1985). Cognitive loss frames lead to comparatively unfair agreements and hinder integrative solutions. Thus, one might question whether the cognitive barriers arising from loss framing of the negotiation situation can be successfully overcome if prosocial goals, such as being fair and integrative, are furnished with respective implementation intentions.

We tested these possibilities in two experiments (Trötschel & Gollwitzer, 2002). In the first experiment, pairs of participants were each assigned the role of two neighboring countries and asked to negotiate the distribution of a disputed island. The island consisted of 25 regions, each representing one of four different types of landscapes: mountains, cornfields, pastures, and forests. Within each pair of negotiators, one participant was subjected to a loss frame by showing him or her an issue chart that listed the four different kinds of regions with a corresponding negative number indicating the losses for giving it away. Gain-framed participants were shown an issue chart with positive numbers indicating the gains for receiving it. Both negotiators were told that they had to agree on the ownership of the 25 regions during a 15-minute session.

To instill a fairness goal, participants of each pair were handed a sheet of paper informing them that fair negotiation outcomes are often hard to achieve. Therefore, right before participants entered the negotiation, they were told that they should set themselves the following goal: "I want to find a fair solution!" Half of the participants were in addition asked to make a plan on how to implement the goal: "And if I receive a proposal on how to share the island, then I will offer a fair counterproposal!" Finally, participants in the control condition received neither the fairness goal nor the implementation intention instructions.

Negotiation behavior was assessed in terms of individual profits within each pair of negotiators. We tested for each group whether the difference in profits between loss- and gain-framed participants was significantly different from zero. For the goal intention group and the control group, we observed significant differences indicating that loss-framed participants showed significantly higher profits than gain-framed participants. This unfair outcome in favor of loss-framed participants was no longer observed in the implementation intention group, in that profits were equally distributed.

In a subsequent second experiment, pairs of negotiators were both either loss or gain framed. In this experiment, the payoff charts were constructed in such a way that integrative solutions were also possible (i.e., cornfields and pastures were equally valuable for both negotiation partners, whereas forests were valuable for one negotiation partner but not for the other, and the reverse was true for mountains). Outcome frames were again manipulated by expressing each region's value with either positive value points (gain-frame group) or negative value points (loss-frame group). The loss-framed participants were then separated into three groups, one in which a mere goal intention instruction was assigned ("I want to cooperate with my counterpart!"), another in which participants were asked in addition to form an implementation intention ("And if I receive a proposal on how to share the island, then I will offer a cooperative counterproposal!"), and a final group that was asked neither to set a goal nor to make a plan.

When the 10-minute period allowed for island-sharing negotiations was over, negotiation behavior was assessed in terms of profits and the number of integrative solutions. Gain-framed pairs of negotiators achieved significantly more integrative solutions than loss-framed pairs, no matter whether the loss-framed pairs had formed a prosocial goal or not. However, the highest number of integrated solutions was found among the loss-framed pairs of negotiators who furnished the prosocial goal with a respective implementation intention. The profits that the pairs of negotiators made in the four different groups closely paralleled the pattern of results found for the number of integrative solutions. Interestingly, mediation analyses revealed that the effects of implementation intentions on alleviating the negative effect of loss framing on making profits was completely mediated by finding integrative solutions.

Situational Contexts That Prime Chronic Goal Orientations

Auto-motive theories hold that if a goal is activated and acted on repeatedly and consistently in a given situation, this situation acquires the potential to trigger the critical goal pursuit without conscious intent (Bargh, 1990). If, for instance, a person has repeatedly and consistently chosen to discuss work problems at social gatherings (e.g., parties), the contextual cues associated with parties should directly (i.e., outside of awareness) trigger behavior serving this goal. Given that the person enters a party with the assigned or newly set goal to simply socialize, such direct and nonconscious activation of the chronic goal to discuss work problems is a hindrance. Overcoming this hindrance by forming an implementation intention that specifies this hindrance in its if-part requires that the individual is aware of the possibility that a work goal becomes activated when entering the party, but this cannot be assumed with chronic goals (or auto-motives) that are triggered outside of awareness by a respective situational context. Can forming implementation intentions, which lay down in advance how the new goal is to be attained, protect a person's goal pursuit from auto-motive effects?

To test whether forming implementation intentions can protect ongoing goal pursuit from becoming derailed by a directly (situationally) activated competing goal pursuit, two experiments were conducted (Gollwitzer, 1998). In the first study, a driving simulator was used in which participants had to drive a race car through a racecourse. In two baseline rounds, participants' driving speed and driving mistakes were assessed. Then all participants were given instructions on how to drive the final two test rounds. In the goal intention condition, participants were asked to set the goal to reach the finishing post as fast as possible without making a mistake (i.e., running off the road). The implementation intention group was also asked to plan how to achieve this goal (i.e., "And if I enter a straight section of the race course, then I will drive as fast as possible!" and "And if I enter a curve, then I will reduce my speed!").

Before participants were allowed to drive the final two test rounds, the following auto-motive manipulations were used. For half of the participants, the auto-motive "moving fast" was activated by asking participants to draw in 5 minutes as many figures (e.g., flowers, animals, objects) as possible by simply connecting numbered dots on different sheets of paper. For the other half, the auto-motive "moving slowly" was activated by asking participants to draw these figures as carefully and neatly as possible, taking as much time for each figure as needed.

When we looked at the participants' driving speed and driving mistakes in the final two rounds, the auto-motive priming had strong assimilative effects for the participants who had been assigned only the goal intention to be fast without making mistakes (i.e., priming to move fast led to higher speed and significantly more mistakes than priming to move slowly). For participants who also had formed implementation intentions on how to reach this goal, no such priming effect was observed (i.e., participants in both priming conditions showed moderate speed and made hardly any mistakes). These findings suggest that goal pursuits carefully planned by implementation intentions are no longer affected by auto-motives (chronic goals) directly activated by situational cues.

In a follow-up study, goal intention participants were assigned the goal of solving two sets of arithmetic problems as correctly as possible. Implementation intention participants were also asked to plan for potential distractions: "If my mind gets sidetracked, then I will respond by concentrating on the task at hand!" Between the first and the second set of arithmetic problems, participants were subjected to a priming procedure that activated either the chronic goal of achievement or the chronic goal of helping others (i.e., participants had to find typographical errors in a biographical essay on Margaret Thatcher or Mother Theresa, respectively). In the middle of working on the second set of arithmetic problems, participants were disrupted by a confederate of the experimenter, who was asking for help by following a predesigned script (e.g., "Do you know where the experimenter is?" "Do you know when she is coming back?").

Our critical measure was the length of time it took participants to terminate their conversation with the confederate. In the implementation intention condition, participants managed to end the conversation in a very short amount of time (i.e., 12 seconds), no matter whether an achievement or a prosocial goal had been primed by editing the biographical essays. Participants who formed only a goal intention, with respect to working on the arithmetic task, took significantly longer to terminate the disruption. Goal intention participants with the primed prosocial goal took significantly longer than goal intention participants with the primed achievement goal. We concluded from these results that the goal of solving arithmetic problems as correctly as possible was not affected by the activation of chronic goals that facilitate or hinder task performance (i.e., an achievement goal vs. a prosocial goal) if attaining this task goal had been planned out via implementation intentions.

Taken together, the findings of the two auto-motive studies reported demonstrate again that goal pursuits planned out via implementation intentions are protected from adverse situational influences (in the present case, situationally activated chronic goals or auto-motives). The implications for effective self-regulation of unwanted auto-motives are obvious. Returning to a previous example, a person who habitually submits to the goal of using parties to discuss work problems can fight this bad habit by furnishing the ad hoc goal to socialize with respective implementation intentions. As a consequence, the critical situational cue of being at a party should fail to trigger the habitual goal of talking about work.

Summary: Becoming a Better Person Without Changing the World

In the previous section, we described experiments demonstrating that goal pursuits planned by forming implementation intentions become invulnerable to adverse situational influences. This is true for situations that negatively affect a person's achievement (e.g., deindividuated work settings and their negative effects on intellectual performances; loss-framed negotiation settings and their negative effects on fair and cooperative negotiation outcomes) and also for situations that activate competing chronic goal pursuits. It appears then that the self-regulatory strategy of planning goal pursuit places a person in a position to reap positive outcomes without having to change the environment from an adverse to a facilitative one. Such change is often very cumbersome (e.g., it takes the costly interventions of mediators to change the loss frames of conflicting parties into gain frames) and hard to achieve. The main problem seems to be that often people are not aware of the adverse influences of the current environment (e.g., a deindividuated work setting or a loss-framed negotiation setting), or they do not know what alternative kind of setting is actually facilitative (e.g., an individualized work setting or a gain-framed negotiation setting). Finally, with respect to the activation of unwanted auto-motives, people are not aware that the given situation is triggering chronic goals, and of the operation of these goals once they have been activated (Bargh, Gollwitzer, Lee-Chai, Barndollar, & Troetschel, 2001). Accordingly, the self-regulatory strategy of specifying critical situations in the if-part of an implementation intention and linking them to a coping response in the then-part does not qualify as a viable alternative self-regulatory strategy. Rather, people need to resort to the strategy of planning goal pursuit via implementation intentions, thereby protecting it from adverse situational influences.

Costs of Using Implementation Intentions

Given the benefits of forming implementation intentions, one wonders about the possible costs, if any. Three issues come to mind when considering this possibility. First, action control by implementation intentions may be characterized by rigidity and thus may hurt performance that requires flexibility. Second, forming implementation intentions may be a very costly self-regulatory strategy in terms of producing a high degree of ego depletion and consequently handicap needed self-regulatory resources. Third, even though implementation intentions successfully suppress unwanted thoughts, feelings, and actions in a given context, these very thoughts, feelings, and actions may rebound in a subsequent different context.

Using Implementation Intentions Does Not Produce Rigidity

The social loafing study reported above addressed the issue of rigidity. One could argue that implementation intention participants might have shown rigidity in the sense of creating very repetitive solutions for the knife-use task, in that the higher quantity of solutions generated in the implementation intention group should have had costs in terms of a lack of variety or creativity. However, when we grouped the listed uses into different conceptual categories, implementation intention participants gathered their solutions from a higher number of different categories than mere goal intention participants. These findings suggest that the higher quantity of uses generated in the implementation intention group did not compromise their quality.

Using Implementation Intentions Does Not Produce Ego Depletion

According to ego-depletion theory (Muraven et al., 1998), any self-regulatory strategy is assumed to have costs with respect to depleting a person's general resources for self-regulation. As forming implementation intentions produces impressive self-regulatory outcomes, how much ego depletion is associated with using this strategy? According to our assumption that implementation intentions delegate the control of behavior to situational cues, the self is not implicated when behavior is controlled via implementation intentions. As a consequence, the self should not become depleted when task performance is regulated by implementation intentions.

We tested this hypothesis by using the aforementioned classic ego-depletion paradigm (Gollwitzer & Bayer, 2000). Participants were asked to watch a humorous movie while heeding one of three directions: One group was asked to yield to their emotions; another group was asked to control their emotions; and a third group was asked to try to control their emotions and to furnish this goal with the implementation intention "If an amusing scene is presented, then I will tell myself: These are just stupid, silly jokes!"

After participants had watched the movie for 12 minutes, they were asked to solve as many of a series of difficult anagrams as possible in 10 minutes. Participants had worked on similar anagrams prior to the start of the experiment; and this performance was taken as a baseline. Baseline corrected final anagram performance indicated that control participants (expression of emotions) performed better than self-regulation participants (control of emotions); however, this difference vanished when self-regulation participants used implementation intentions to control their emotions while watching the humorous video.

Further support for the hypothesis that self-regulation based on implementation intentions does not lead to ego depletion, comes from an experiment by Webb and Sheeran (2003, Study 1). Participants who had formed implementation intentions to perform well on an initial task (i.e., a Stroop task; implementation intention instructions as described above), showed significantly greater persistence on a subsequent unsolvable puzzle task compared to participants who performed the task without implementation intentions. These results, in conjunction with our own, suggest that self-regulation that is based on implementation intentions is not costly in terms of using self-regulatory resources.

Using Implementation Intentions Does Not Produce Rebound Effects

A third cost issue relates to the well-known rebound effects in mental control. Wegner (1994; Wenzlaff & Wegner, 2000) postulated and observed that conscious attempts to control one's thoughts lead to rebound in the sense that the thoughts to be controlled become more readily accessible and thus surface in subsequent thoughts and behavior. To see whether the control of stereotyping via implementation intentions leads to a rebound in stereotyping, we devised the following experiments.

We (Gollwitzer, Trötschel, & Sumner, 2002) ran two rebound experiments following research paradigms developed by Macrae, Bodenhausen, Milne, and Jetten (1994). In the first study, participants had to read a story about a homeless person. One group of participants was assigned the goal of forming a nonstereotypical impression of this person ("I want to suppress my stereotypical thoughts about homeless people!"). A second group was asked to furnish this goal with the additional implementation intention "And if I describe a given homeless person, then I will avoid stereotypical statements!" A third group was asked to study the story without further instructions. All participants were then asked to provide a written statement capturing their impression of this homeless person. After a 5-minute filler task, all participants were asked to evaluate homeless people in general (i.e., a group of homeless people). For this purpose, they were handed a semantic differential–type questionnaire that presented numerous bipolar adjectives in five pairs related to stereotypes, such as drunk/sober, well groomed/sloppy, busy/lazy.

First, regarding the written statement, goal intention as well as implementation intention participants described the person in a less stereotypical manner than control participants. But who showed the stronger rebound? In the final task, the participants who had performed the prior task of providing a written statement about the homeless person with the mere goal to form a nonstereotypical impression were more stereotypical in their judgments than control participants. Participants who had in addition furnished this lofty goal with simple implementation intentions, however, were protected against such rebound.

In a second experiment, rebound was assessed differently. Again, the study started with reading a story about a homeless person and then forming an impression of that person under different instructions (see above). After the subsequent filler task, however, participants had to perform a lexical decision task in which nonwords, critical words (stereotypes), and neutral words (matched for length and valence) were presented. The results showed that participants who had been assigned the goal of controlling stereotypical thoughts while forming an impression of the described person in the first part of the experiment were faster in identifying stereotypes as words as compared to irrelevant words, indicating that stereotype concepts were more activated. No such effect was observed with participants who had been asked to furnish this goal with a relevant if-then plan.

Therefore, it appears that implementation intentions may serve to insulate an individual's goals from these ironic processes by subverting the systems that allow rebound effects. Specifically, Wegner proposed that two systems contribute to people's control of their mental states, one being conscious and one being nonconscious. While the conscious operating system actively "looks" for mental contents consistent with the given goal or task, the nonconscious monitoring system keeps the former system in check by identifying the contents incompatible with the goal. These incompatible elements, in turn, pop into awareness when cognitive resources are taxed. We suggest that implementation intentions shield one's conscious mental state from rebound effects in the following manner. As the link between the critical situation and the response serves to isolate the plan from present internal states or external conditions, the plan runs off in an effortless, efficient manner, and does not tax cognitive resources (of the conscious operating system).

Summary: Is Forming Implementation Intentions a Foolproof Self-Regulatory Strategy?

Even though the implementation intentions used in the presented experimental research were always highly effective, without costs in terms of rigidity, rebound, or ego depletion, this does not mean that all implementation intentions are highly effective in terms of meeting one's goals. In everyday life, people may not succeed in forming effective implementation intentions for various reasons. For instance, a person may link a critical situation to a behavior or outcome that turns out to be outside of the person's control (e.g., if a person who has the goal to eat healthy food plans to ask for a vegetarian meal, but the restaurant she frequents does not offer such meals). The same is true for implementation intentions that specify opportunities that hardly ever arise (e.g., if a person who plans to ask for a vegetarian meal when the waiter in a restaurant takes her order mostly cooks for herself at home) or implementation intentions that specify behaviors that have zero instrumentality with respect to reaching the goal (e.g., if a person with the goal of eating healthy food plans to ask for a vegetarian meal not knowing that most restaurants add fatty cheese to make it tasty).

Finally, there is the question of how concretely people should specify the if-parts and then-parts of their implementation intentions. If the goal is to eat healthy food, one can form an implementation intention that holds either this behavior in the then-part or a more concrete operationalization of it. The latter seems appropriate whenever a whole array of specific operationalizations is possible, as planning in advance which type of goal-directed behavior is to be executed, once the critical situation is encountered, prevents disruptive deliberation in situ (with respect to choosing one behavior over another). An analogous argument applies to the specification of situations in the if-part of an implementation intention. People should specify the situation in the if-part to such a degree that a given situation will no longer raise the question of whether it qualifies as the critical situation or not.

Conclusion

People can use implementation intentions not only to promote the initiation of goal pursuits, but also to protect their goal pursuits (i.e., to be fair to others) from being thwarted. The latter can be achieved in two ways. As long as we are in a position to anticipate what could potentially make us stray off course (the relevant hindrances, barriers, distractions, and temptations), we can specify these critical situations in the if-part of an implementation intention and link it to a response that facilitates goal attainment. The response specified in the then-part of an implementation intention can then be geared toward either ignoring disruptive stimuli, suppressing the impeding responses to them, or blocking obstructions to goal pursuit by engaging in it all the more.

This way of using implementation intentions to protect goal pursuit from straying off course necessitates that we know what kind of obstacles and distractions need to be watched for. Moreover, we need to know what kind of unwanted responses are potentially triggered (so that we can attempt to suppress them), or what kind of goal-directed responses are particularly effective in blocking these unwanted responses (so that we can engage in these goal-directed activities). Consequently, much social, clinical, and cognitive psychological knowledge is required to be in a position to come up with effective if- and then-components of such implementation intentions.

However, an easier solution is available. Instead of concentrating on potential obstacles and various ways of effectively dealing with them, people may concern themselves exclusively with the intricacies of implementing the goal pursuit at hand. People can plan how to pursue a goal by forming implementation intentions that determine how the various steps toward goal attainment are to be executed. Such careful planning encapsulates goal pursuit, protecting it from the adverse influence of potential obstacles and distractions, whether internal or external. This self-regulatory strategy of goal pursuit permits attaining goals without having to change a noncooperative self or an unfavorable environment. Crucially, one does not need to possess any psychological knowledge of how to effectively deal with adverse self-states or situational contexts. It completely suffices if the person is simply aware of the demands of the current goal being pursued.

Once these demands have been incorporated into a plan, however, one no longer needs to be aware of them to bring goals to fruition. Further, while these plans can be formed instantly by an act of will, no such conscious effort is needed to carry out the planned goal-directed action. As goals are mentally represented as knowledge structures, these encapsulated plans too have a specific structure. Implementation intentions create cognitive links between select situational cues and intended goal-directed behaviors. The effectiveness of implementation intentions lies in the fact that after generation, the mental representation of the specified situational cue becomes highly activated. Once this cue is actually encountered, the planned behavior runs off automatically, overriding and defying any habits or divisive spontaneous attentional responses. Given our limited resources for conscious self-regulation, delegating control to situational cues by one express act of fiat is an effective way to bridge the gap that exists between our best intentions and the successful attainment of our goals.

References

Aarts, H., Dijksterhuis, A., & Midden, C. (1999). To plan or not to plan? Goal achievement or interrupting the performance of mundane behaviors. *European Journal of Social Psychology, 29*, 971–979.

Achtziger, A. (2002). *Sozial-, kognitions- und motivationspsychologische Determinaten des Eindrucksbildungsprozesses unter besonderer Berücksichtigung der Stereotypisierung.* (Social-cognitive and motivational determinants of evaluating and judging others). Unpublished doctoral dissertation. University of Konstanz, Germany.

Ajzen, I. (1991). The theory of planned behavior. *Organizational Behavior and Human Decision Processes, 50*, 179–211.

Ajzen, I., & Fishbein, M. (1980). *Understanding attitudes and predicting social behavior.* Englewood Cliffs, NJ: Prentice-Hall.

Anderson, J. R. (1987). Skill acquisition: Compilation of weak-method problem solutions. *Psychological Review, 94*, 192–210.

Bandura, A. (1991). Self-regulation of motivation through anticipatory and self-reactive mechanisms. In R. A. Dienstbier (Ed.), *Nebraska symposium on motivation: Perspectives on motivation* (Vol. 38, pp. 69–164). Lincoln, NE: University of Nebraska Press.

Bargh, J. A. (1990). Auto-motives: Preconscious determinants of social interaction. In E. T. Higgins & R. M. Sorrentino (Eds.), *Handbook of motivation and cognition: Foundations of social behavior* (Vol. 2, pp. 93–130). New York: Guilford.

Bargh, J. A. (1999). The cognitive monster: The case against the controllability of automatic stereotype effects. In S. Chaiken & Y. Trope (Eds.), *Dual-process theories in social psychology* (pp. 361–382). New York: Guilford.

Bargh, J. A., Gollwitzer, P. M., Lee-Chai, A., Barndollar, K., & Troetschel, R. (2001). The automated will: Nonconscious activation and pursuit of behavioral goals. *Journal of Personality and Social Psychology, 81*, 1014–1027.

Baumeister, R. F. (2000). Ego-depletion and the self's executive function. In A. Tesser, R. B. Felson, & J. M. Suls (Eds.), *Psychological perspectives on self and identity* (pp. 9–33). Washington, DC: American Psychological Association.

Baumeister, R. F., Heatherton, T. F., & Tice, D. M. (1994). *Losing control: How and why people fail at self-regulation.* San Diego, CA: Academic Press.

Bayer, U. C., Jaudas, A., & Gollwitzer, P. M. (2002). *Do implementation intentions facilitate switching between tasks?* Poster presented at the International Symposium on Executive Functions, Konstanz, Germany.

Bayer, U. C., Moskowitz, G. B., & Gollwitzer, P. M. (2002). *Implementation intentions and action initiation without conscious intent.* Unpublished manuscript, University of Konstanz, Germany.

Bless, H. (1997). *Stimmung und Denken: Ein Modell zum Einfluss von Stimmung auf Denkprozesse* (Mood and reasoning: A model on the impact of mood on cognitive processes). Bern: Hans Huber.

Bless, H., & Fiedler, K. (1995). Affective states and the influence of activated general knowledge. *Personality and Social Psychology Bulletin, 21*, 766–778.

Bodenhausen, G. V., & Macrae, C. N. (1998). Stereotype activation and inhibition. In R. S. Wyer, Jr. (Ed.), *Advances in social cognition* (Vol. 11, pp. 1–52). Mahwah, NJ: Erlbaum.

Brandstätter, V., Lengfelder, A., & Gollwitzer, P. M. (2001). Implementation intentions and efficient action initiation. *Journal of Personality and Social Psychology, 81*, 946–960.

Brewer, M. (1988). A dual process theory of impression formation. In T. K. Srull & R. S. Wyer (Eds.), *Advances in social cognition* (Vol. 1, pp. 1–36). Hillsdale, NJ: Erlbaum.

Chasteen, A. L., Park, D. C., & Schwarz, N. (2001). Implementation intentions and facilitation of prospective memory. *Psychological Science, 12*, 457–461.

De Dreu, C. K. W., Carnevale, P. J. D., Emans, B. J. M., & van de Vliert, E. (1995). Outcome frames in bilateral negotiation: Resistance to concession making and frame adoption. In W. Stroebe & M. Hewstone (Eds.), *European review of social psychology* (Vol. 6, pp. 97–125). Chichester, UK: Wiley.

Devine, P. G. (1989). Stereotypes and prejudice: Their automatic and controlled components. *Journal of Personality and Social Psychology, 56*, 5–18.

Fishbein, M., & Ajzen, I. (1975). *Belief, attitude, intention, and behavior: An introduction to theory and research.* Reading, MA: Addison-Wesley.

Fiske, S. T., & Neuberg, S. L. (1990). A continuum of impression formation, from category-based to individuating processes: Influences of information and motivation on attention and interpretation. In M. P. Zanna (Ed.), *Advances in experimental social psychology* (Vol. 23, pp. 1–74). San Diego, CA: Academic Press.

Fitts, P. M., & Posner, M. I. (1967). *Human performance.* Monterey, CA: Brooks-Cole.

Godin, G., & Kok, G. (1996). The theory of planned behavior: A review of its applications in health-related behaviors. *American Journal of Health Promotion, 11*, 87–98.

Gollwitzer, P. M. (1993). Goal achievement: The role of intentions. *European Review of Social Psychology, 4*, 141–185.

Gollwitzer, P. M. (1996). The volitional benefits of planning. In P. M. Gollwitzer & J. A. Bargh (Eds.), *The psychology of action: Linking cognition and motivation to behavior* (pp. 287–312). New York: Guilford.

Gollwitzer, P. M. (1998). *Implicit and explicit processes in goal pursuit.* Paper presented at the symposium "Implicit vs. Explicit Processes" at the annual meeting of the Society of Experimental Social Psychology, Atlanta, Georgia.

Gollwitzer, P. M. (1999). Implementation intentions: Strong effects of simple plans. *American Psychologist, 54*, 493–503.

Gollwitzer, P. M., Achtziger, A., Schaal, B., & Hammelbeck, J. P. (2002). *Intentional control of stereotypical beliefs and prejudicial feelings.* Unpublished manuscript. University of Konstanz, Germany.

Gollwitzer, P. M., & Bayer, U. C. (2000). *Becoming a better person without changing the self.* Paper presented at the Self and Identity Preconference of the annual meeting of the Society of Experimental Social Psychology, Atlanta, Georgia.

Gollwitzer, P. M., Bayer, U. C., Steller, B., & Bargh, J. A. (2002). *Delegating control to the environment: Perception, attention, and memory for pre-selected behavioral cues.* Unpublished manuscript. University of Konstanz, Germany.

Gollwitzer, P. M., & Brandstätter, V. (1997). Implementation intentions and effective goal pursuit. *Journal of Personality and Social Psychology, 73*, 186–199.

Gollwitzer, P. M., & Moskowitz, G. B. (1996). Goal effects on action and cognition. In E. T. Higgins & A. W. Kruglanski (Eds.), *Social psychology: Handbook of basic principles* (pp. 361–399). New York: Guilford.

Gollwitzer, P. M., & Schaal, B. (1998). Metacognition in action: The importance of implementation intentions. *Personality and Social Psychology Review, 2*, 124–136.

Gollwitzer, P. M., Trötschel, R., & Sumner, M. (2002). *Mental control via implementation intentions is void of rebound effects.* Unpublished manuscript. University of Konstanz, Germany.

Gollwitzer, P. M., & Wicklund, R. A. (1985). Self-symbolizing and the neglect of others' perspectives. *Journal of Personality and Social Psychology, 56*, 531–715.

Gottschaldt, K. (1926). Über den Einfluss der Erfahrung auf die Wahrnehmung von Figuren (On the effects of familiarity on the perception of figures). *Psychologische Forschung, 8*, 261–317.

Kahneman, D., & Tversky, A. (1979). Prospect theory: An analysis of decision under risk. *Econometrica, 47*, 263–291.

Karau, S. J., & Williams, K. D. (1993). Social loafing: A meta-analytic review and theoretical integration. *Journal of Personality and Social Psychology, 65*, 681–706.

Kuhl, J. (1984). Volitional aspects of achievement motivation and learned helplessness: Toward a comprehensive theory of action control. In B. A. Maher & W. A. Maher (Eds.), *Progress in experimental personality research* (Vol. 13, pp. 99–171). New York: Academic Press.

Latané, B., Williams, K., & Harkins, S. (1979). Many hands make light the work: The causes and consequences of social loafing. *Journal of Personality and Social Psychology, 37*, 822–832.

Lengfelder, A., & Gollwitzer, P. M. (2001). Reflective and reflexive action control in patients with frontal brain lesions. *Neuropsychology, 15*, 80–100.

Locke, E. A., & Latham, G. P. (1990). *A theory of goal setting and task performance.* Englewood Cliffs, NJ: Prentice-Hall.

Maass, A., Salvi, D., Arcuri, L., & Semin, G. (1989). Language use in intergroup contexts: The linguistic intergoup biases. *Journal of Personality and Social Psychology, 57*, 981–993.

Macrae, C. N., Bodenhausen, G. V., Milne, A. B., & Jetten, J. (1994). Out of mind but back in sight: Stereotypes on the rebound. *Journal of Personality and Social Psychology, 67*, 808–817.

Milne, S., Orbell, S., & Sheeran, P. (2002). Combining motivational and volitional interventions to promote exercise participation: Protection motivation theory and implementation intentions. *British Journal of Health Psychology, 7*, 163–184.

Muraven, M., Tice, D. M., & Baumeister, R. F. (1998). Self-control as a limited resource: Regulatory depletion pattern. *Journal of Personality and Social Psychology, 74*, 774–789.

Neale, M. A., & Bazerman, M. H. (1985). The effects of framing and negotiator overconfidence on bargaining behaviors and outcomes. *Academy of Management Journal, 28*, 34–49.

Newell, A., & Rosenbloom, P. S. (1981). Mechanisms of skill acquisition and the law of practice. In J. R. Anderson (Ed.), *Cognitive skills and their acquisition* (pp. 1–55). Hillsdale, NJ: Erlbaum.

Oettingen, G., Hönig, G., & Gollwitzer, P. M. (2000). Effective self-regulation of goal attainment. *International Journal of Educational Research, 33*, 705–732.

Orbell, S., Hodgkins, S., & Sheeran, P. (1997). Implementation intentions and the theory of planned behavior. *Personality and Social Psychology Bulletin, 23*, 945–954.

Orbell, S., & Sheeran, P. (1998). "Inclined abstainers": A problem for predicting health-related behavior. *British Journal of Social Psychology, 37*, 151–165.

Orbell, S., & Sheeran, P. (2000). Motivational and volitional processes in action initiation: A field study of the role of implementation intentions. *Journal of Applied Social Psychology, 30*, 780–797.

Patterson, C., & Mischel, W. (1976). Effects of temptation-inhibiting and task-facilitating plans on self-control. *Journal of Personality and Social Psychology, 33*, 209–217.

Roger, D., & Monsell, S. (1995). Costs of a predictable switch between simple cognitive tasks. *Journal of Experimental Psychology: General, 124*, 207–231.

Semin, G. R., & Fiedler, K. (1988). The cognitive functions of linguistic categories in describing persons. *Journal of Personality and Social Psychology, 54*, 558–568.

Semin, G. R., & Fiedler, K. (1991). The linguistic category model, its bases, applications, and range. In W. Strobe & M. Hewstone (Eds.), *European review of social psychology* (Vol. 2, pp. 1–30). Chichester, UK: Wiley.

Sheeran, P. (2002). Intention-behavior relations: A conceptual and empirical review. *European Review of Social Psychology, 12*, 1–30.

Sheeran, P., & Orbell, S. (1999). Implementation intentions and repeated behavior: Augmenting the predictive validity of the theory of planned behavior. *European Journal of Social Psychology, 29*, 349–369.

Sheeran, P., & Orbell, S. (2000). Using implementation intentions to increase attendance for cervical cancer screening. *Health Psychology, 19*, 283–289.
Sheeran, P., Webb, T. L., & Gollwitzer, P. M. (2002). *The interplay between goals and implementation intentions.* Manuscript under review.
Trötschel, R., & Gollwitzer, P. M. (2002). *Implementation intentions and the control of framing effects in negotiations.* Manuscript under review.
Webb, T. L., & Sheeran, P. (2003). Can implementation intentions help to overcome ego-depletion? *Journal of Experimental Social Psychology, 39*, 279–286.
Wegner, D. M. (1994). Ironic processes in mental control. *Psychological Review, 101*, 34–52.
Wenzlaff, R. M., & Wegner, D. M. (2000). Thought suppression. *Annual Review of Psychology, 51*, 59–91.
Wicklund, R. A., & Gollwitzer, P. M. (1982). *Symbolic self-completion.* Hillsdale, NJ: Erlbaum.

18

Motivational Sources of Unintended Thought: Irrational Intrusions or Side Effects of Rational Strategies?

E. Tory Higgins

For over a century, psychologists have been fascinated with unconscious mechanisms that influence people's thought processes. In the early twentieth century, the mechanisms that received the most attention were motivational, especially psychodynamic mechanisms. Attention shifted in the late twentieth century to cognitive mechanisms, especially those associated with automaticity. The purpose of this chapter is to return attention to the role of motivational mechanisms in unintended thought, but with a different perspective on the nature of the underlying mechanisms.

The classic psychodynamic perspective was that unconscious forces (drives, instincts, defense mechanisms, etc.) disrupted and distorted thought processes to serve basic needs (e.g., A. Freud, 1937; S. Freud, 1920/1952; Jung, 1954). Although many classic social psychological models were inspired by Gestalt rather than psychodynamic ideas, they too postulated mechanisms that served basic needs, such as the need for consistency (e.g., Festinger, 1957; Heider, 1958), and produced irrational thought distortions. The notion that motivational needs can disrupt and distort thought processes continues to be the predominant perspective on the role of motivation in unintended thought. The central idea of this classic motivational perspective is that motivational needs disrupt rational thought processes.

I propose an alternative motivational perspective that does not explain unintended thought in terms of irrational and disruptive motivational forces. Instead, motivation is related to distinct types of self-regulatory orientation that each have their own strategic rationality. Within each self-regulatory orientation, the use of a specific strategy is both rational and effective rather than irrational and disruptive. Despite the thought processes being rational and effective, however, there are unintended side effects of strategies that occur without people's awareness. Indeed, the consequences for thought of these unintended side effects can be, if anything, more significant than simply disrupting or distorting thought processes, because they can alter the basic nature of problem solving and decision making.

What I mean by saying that the thought processes are rational and effective is that the strategies suit or fit the self-regulatory state involved in the goal pursuit. For example, if people are motivated to attain a goal that is represented as an aspiration or an accomplishment, it makes sense that they would pursue the goal eagerly, seeking all means of advancement. If they are motivated to attain a goal that is represented as safety or as a responsibility, it makes sense that they would pursue the goal in a vigilant way, being careful to do what is necessary. It is beneficial to pursue accomplishments with eagerness and to pursue safety with vigilance, and people want these benefits. In this sense at least, the strategies are rational and intentional. To some extent, people are also aware of the strategies they use. It is not likely that people are aware of them fully, because the specific strategic processes can be quite complex. However, during goal pursuit, people are aware of feeling eager (enthusiastic) or feeling vigilant (careful). In addition, people are aware of the emotions that are produced by the success or failure of their goal-pursuit strategies. For example, people are aware of feeling happy when eager pursuit of accomplishments succeeds, and they are aware of feeling relieved and relaxed when vigilant pursuit of safety succeeds.

At least to some extent, then, people intend to use and are aware of using the strategic processes by which they derive benefits in goal pursuit. However, the strategies people use have additional side effects that they do not intend and of which they are unaware. In this chapter, I discuss two sources of strategic side effects that have unintended consequences for thought—*trade-offs* and *value transfer*.

The first unintended negative side effect of strategic rationality derives from the trade-offs of strategic self-regulation. Consider strategic eagerness and strategic vigilance, for example. As I discuss in more detail later, one benefit of strategic eagerness (a "risky" bias) is a reduction in errors of omission, but this reduction typically comes at the cost of an increase in errors of commission. The opposite is true of strategic vigilance (a "conservative" bias). People are typically unaware of the trade-offs in their use of goal-pursuit strategies. Because of these trade-offs, the costs of strategic rationality can have unintended side effects that influence thought.

In addition to the unintended side effects of the costs of strategic rationality, the benefits of strategic rationality can themselves have unintended side effects that influence thought. One of the benefits of using strategies that are suitable to or fit the self-regulatory state involved in goal pursuit is that the goal-pursuit activity itself increases in value—one "feels right" about what one is doing (Higgins, 2000). According to rational models of decision making, this value from the manner of goal pursuit should not be confused with the value from the outcome of goal pursuit. It would not be "rational" to value an outcome more simply because one valued the manner of decision making more. Nonetheless, as I discuss more fully later, such value transfer does occur. Value transfer is another unintended side effect of strategic rationality that influences thought. To illustrate both of these kinds of unintended side effects of strategic rationality (i.e., trade-offs and value transfer), I review research that has examined the effects of eagerness versus vigilance strategies on basic thought processes. Because this research derives from regulatory focus theory (Higgins, 1997, 1998), I begin by describing this theory.

Promotion Eagerness and Prevention Vigilance

Regulatory focus theory assumes that self-regulation operates differently when serving fundamentally different needs, such as the distinct survival needs of nurturance (e.g., nourishment) and security (e.g., protection). Parents' social regulatory style, for example, can emphasize either nurturance or security. It can emphasize nurturance by encouraging desired end states and by withdrawing love when desired end states are not met. It can emphasize security by safeguarding desired end states and by criticizing when desired end states are not met. These different social regulatory styles communicate distinct concerns about getting along in the world. Nurturant social regulation engenders a promotion focus, in which self-regulation is concerned with the presence and absence of positive outcomes. Security social regulation engenders a prevention focus, in which self-regulation is concerned with the absence and presence of negative outcomes (see Higgins & Silberman, 1998).

Earlier work on self-discrepancy theory (e.g., Higgins, 1987, 1989, 1991) describes how certain modes of caretaker–child interaction increase the likelihood that children will acquire strong promotion concerns reflecting hopes, wishes, and aspirations for them (strong ideals) or strong prevention concerns reflecting beliefs about their duties, obligations, and responsibilities (strong oughts). The hopes, wishes, and aspirations represented in ideals function like maximal goals. Actual self-congruencies to ideals represent the presence of positive outcomes, and discrepancies represent the absence of positive outcomes. With its emphasis on ensuring the presence of positive outcomes and ensuring against the absence of positive outcomes, ideal self-regulation involves promotion focus concerns with advancement, aspirations, and accomplishments.

The duties, obligations, and responsibilities represented in oughts function more like minimal goals that a person must attain (see Brendl & Higgins, 1996). Actual self-congruencies to oughts represent the absence of negative outcomes, and discrepancies represent the presence of negative outcomes (see Gould, 1939; Rotter, 1982). With its emphasis on ensuring the absence of negative outcomes and on ensuring against the presence of negative outcomes, ought self-regulation involves prevention focus concerns with protection, safety, and responsibilities.

Momentary situations are also capable of temporarily inducing either promotion focus concerns or prevention focus concerns. Just as the responses of caretakers to their children's actions communicate to them about how to attain desired end states, current feedback from a boss to an employee or from a teacher to a student is a situation that can communicate gain/nongain concerns with the presence and absence of positive outcomes (promotion concerns) or nonloss/loss concerns with the absence or presence of negative outcomes (prevention concerns). Task instructions that frame outcome contingencies in terms of gains/nongains versus losses/nonlosses can also induce promotion or prevention concerns, respectively. Thus, the distinction between promotion focus concerns and prevention focus concerns does not apply only to individual differences. Situations and tasks can also vary in regulatory focus concerns.

Regulatory focus theory also distinguishes between different strategic means of goal attainment. It distinguishes between eagerness means and vigilance means (see Crowe & Higgins, 1997; Higgins, 1997, 1998). In signal detection terms (e.g., Tanner & Swets, 1954; see also Trope & Liberman, 1996), eagerness involves ensuring "hits" and ensuring against errors of omission or "misses," and vigilance involves ensuring "correct rejections" and ensuring against errors of commission or "false alarms." Regulatory focus theory (Crowe & Higgins, 1997; Higgins, 1997, 1998) proposes that there is a natural fit between promotion focus concerns and the use of eagerness means because eagerness means ensure the presence of positive outcomes (ensure hits; look for means of advancement) and ensure against the absence of positive outcomes (ensure against errors of omission; do not close off possibilities). There is also a natural fit between prevention focus concerns and the use of vigilance means because vigilance means ensure the absence of negative outcomes (ensure correct rejections; be careful) and ensure against the presence of negative outcomes (ensure against errors of commission; avoid mistakes).

In sum, a promotion orientation is concerned with advancement and accomplishment, with the presence and absence of positive outcomes. When individuals are in a promotion orientation, they are inclined to use eagerness means in goal pursuit. In contrast, a prevention orientation is concerned with safety and responsibility, with the absence and presence of negative outcomes. When individuals are in a prevention orientation, they are inclined to use vigilance means in goal pursuit.

Trade-Offs of Eagerness and Vigilance

It is rational for people to use either eagerness means or vigilance means in goal pursuit. As reflected in signal detection theory, each strategy contributes to accuracy. However, each strategy alone contributes to a unique bias in decision making. Eagerness has the benefit of reducing errors of omission, but the "risky" emphasis on ensuring hits increases the likelihood of errors of commission. Vigilance has the benefit of reducing errors of commission, but the "conservative" emphasis on ensuring correct rejections increases the likelihood of errors of omission. When making a choice, such as choosing between a coffee mug and a pen offered as gifts, it would be reasonable either to think of what you would gain by selecting the mug or the pen (eagerness strategy) or to think of what you would lose by not selecting the mug or the pen (vigilance strategy). Although beneficial and reasonable, these different self-regulatory strategies have consequences of which people are not aware, including costs. The next sections review the results of studies that illustrate the pervasive impact on thought from eagerness and vigilance as two kinds of strategic rationality.

Risky and Conservative Biases

Decision makers in a promotion focus prefer to use eagerness means more than vigilance means to make their decision, whereas the reverse is true for decision makers in a prevention focus. As discussed above, eagerness in signal detection terms (e.g., Tanner & Swets, 1954; see also Trope & Liberman, 1996) involves ensuring hits and ensuring against errors of omission or misses, and vigilance involves ensuring correct rejections and ensuring against errors of commission or false alarms. From a signal detection perspective, using the eagerness means of ensuring hits and ensuring against errors of omission would produce a risky bias, whereas using the vigilance means of ensuring correct rejections and ensuring against errors of commission would produce a conservative bias. Decision makers in a promotion focus should prefer to use eagerness means more than vigilance means to make their decision, thus producing a risky bias. Decision makers in a prevention focus should prefer to use vigilance means more than eagerness means to make their decision, thus producing a conservative bias.

These predictions were tested in a recognition memory study by Crowe and Higgins (1997). The participants were first shown a list of target items. Following a delay, they were then given test items that included both old target items from the original list and new distractor items not from the original list. The participants were asked to respond "Yes" if they believed the test item was an old target item, and to respond "No" if they believed the test item was a new distractor item. In this task, "Yes" responses reflect a risky bias of ensuring hits and ensuring against errors of omission, and "No" responses reflect a conservative bias of ensuring correct rejections and ensuring against errors of commission. The participants were told that they would first perform a recognition memory task and then would be assigned a second, final task. A liked and a disliked activity had been selected earlier for each participant to serve as the final task. The participants were told that which of the alternative final tasks they would work on at the end of the session depended on their performance on the initial recognition memory task.

The relation between performance on the initial memory task and which of the final tasks they would do was described as contingent for everyone, but the framing varied as a function of both regulatory focus (promotion versus prevention) and outcome valence (success versus failure). The promotion framing of the contingency stated that by doing well on the initial memory task, the participant would get to do the liked task (or by not doing well, they would not get to do the liked task). The prevention framing of the contingency stated that by not doing poorly on the initial memory task, the participant would not have to do the disliked task (or by doing poorly, they would have to do the disliked task). The study found that, independent of success versus failure framing (which itself had no effect), participants with a promotion orientation had a risky bias of saying "Yes" in the recognition memory task, whereas participants with a prevention orientation had a conservative bias of saying "No" (see also Friedman & Forster, 2001).

Generating Alternatives

A fundamental process in decision making, and in hypothesis testing more generally, is the generation of alternatives. Another study by Crowe and Higgins (1997) examined the impact of promotion and prevention orientations on generating alternatives when deciding how to classify and characterize objects in the world. Some decision tasks allow people to produce either few or many alternatives without penalty. On a sorting task, for example, individuals can choose to use the same criterion, such as color, to sort a set of fruits and to sort a set of vegetables, or they can choose to use different criteria, such as color for the fruits and shape for the vegetables. Either means of doing the task is considered correct. The requirement is only that within each category the sorting criterion be consistent across all members of that category. Thus, individuals can reduce the likelihood of making a mistake and still be correct by simplifying the task, such as sticking to one criterion for both categories.

If decision makers in a prevention focus prefer to use vigilance means more than eagerness means, they should be inclined to be repetitive in this task. In contrast, decision makers in a promotion focus should not be inclined to be repetitive if they prefer to use eagerness means more than vigilance means. By sticking to one category, alternative dimensions or criteria would be omitted during the sorting task, and the use of eagerness means ensures against such omissions. Decision makers in a promotion focus should eagerly pursue hits and thus should be inclined to generate different alternatives.

These predictions were tested by Crowe and Higgins (1997) with two tasks previously used by Mikulincer, Kedem, and Paz (1990) to study creativity. One of these tasks was a sorting task like the one just described. The other task was a characteristic listing task. Participants were presented with the names of furniture objects, such as "desk," "couch," or "bed," and were asked to write down all of the characteristics they could think of for each object. Promotion and prevention focus was induced through an experimental framing technique like that used in the recognition memory study. The study found that, compared to prevention focus participants, promotion focus participants were more fluent in choosing different category dimensions and in listing unique characteristics for different category members. In contrast, prevention focus participants were more repetitive in employing sorting criteria across categories and in using specific descriptive terms or words across category members (controlling for fluency).

Studies by Friedman and Forster (2001) have examined the effects of regulatory focus on creativity more directly. In one set of studies, the participants worked on an ostensibly unrelated task in which they had to complete a paper-and-pencil maze before they were given measures of creativity. The maze had a cartoon mouse trapped inside and the participants' task was to "find the way for the mouse." Different versions of the maze manipulated the regulatory focus of the participants. In the promotion version, a piece of cheese was depicted as lying outside the maze, and thus the participants would be moving the mouse toward nurturance. In the prevention version, an owl was depicted as hovering above the maze, and thus the participants would be moving the mouse toward safety. After completing the maze, the participants did the Snowy Pictures Test (Ekstrom, French, Harman, & Dermen, 1976), in which participants are given a series of images of simple objects that are hidden within complex patterns of visual noise. The participants need to disembed and name each object under conditions that meet the criteria for creative insight (see Friedman & Forster, 2001). The study found that the promotion focus participants performed better than the prevention focus participants. This same result was replicated in another study that used the generation of creative uses for a brick as the measure of creativity.

The sorting and characteristic listing tasks used by Crowe and Higgins (1997) are a special case of people generating alternatives. As Bruner, Goodnow, and Austin (1956) pointed out years ago, the basic process of people deciding what they are perceiving involves generating hypotheses. A central issue for self-regulation is how many hypotheses to generate. Generating more hypotheses increases the likelihood of finding a correct hypothesis (i.e., more hits) and decreases the likelihood of leaving out a correct hypothesis (i.e., fewer misses). If decision makers in a promotion focus prefer to use eagerness means more than vigilance means, then they should be inclined to generate more hypotheses. In contrast, if decision makers in a prevention focus prefer to use vigilance means more than eagerness means, then they should not be inclined to generate more hypotheses. This is because generating more hypotheses also increases the likelihood of including a wrong hypothesis (i.e., more false alarms) and decreases the likelihood of rejecting a wrong hypothesis (i.e., fewer correct rejections).

These predictions were tested in a couple of studies by Liberman, Molden, Idson, and Higgins (2001). The participants varied chronically in the strength of their promotion focus and in the strength of their prevention focus. Consistent with previous work on attitude accessibility (see Bassili, 1995, 1996; Fazio, 1986, 1995), promotion focus strength was operationalized in terms of the chronic accessibility of a person's hopes and aspirations (ideal strength), and prevention focus strength was operationalized in terms of the chronic accessibility of a person's beliefs about his or her responsibilities and obligations (ought strength). Chronic accessibility of a person's ideals and oughts was measured via response times to inquiries about his or her ideal attributes and ought attributes. Accessibility is activation potential, and knowledge units with higher activation potentials should produce faster responses to knowledge-related inputs (see Higgins, 1996). Ideal (or ought) strength was measured by response latencies in listing ideal (or ought) attributes, with stronger ideals (or oughts) being operationalized by shorter response latencies (for more details about this strength measure, see Higgins, Shah, & Friedman, 1997).

Promotion and prevention strength were measured in a first session. In the second session, held weeks later, the participants were introduced to an object-naming task in which they received a booklet with four pictures, each on a separate page. Each picture showed a familiar object from an unusual angle, making it difficult to recognize (see Mayseless & Kruglanski, 1987). The task was to guess what the object was in each picture. The participants were told that they could list as many or as few answers as they wanted. As predicted, participants with greater promotion strength (controlling for prevention strength) generated more hypotheses about what the object was in each picture, and, independently, participants with greater prevention strength (controlling for promotion strength) generated fewer hypotheses.

The results of this study were replicated in another study by Liberman et al. (2001), in which participants' regulatory focus was experimentally manipulated by framing success on the task, either in terms of adding points and gaining a dollar (promotion focus) or in terms of not subtracting points and not losing a dollar (prevention focus). The participants in the promotion focus condition generated approximately 30% more hypotheses than those in the prevention focus condition.

Because generation of hypotheses is a fundamental part of causal attribution processes, Liberman et al. (2001) hypothesized that regulatory focus might also influence such processes. When observing an event that has multiple possible causes, individuals with a vigilant prevention focus should attempt to find a necessary cause and reject the rest, as postulated by standard attribution models. On the other hand, individuals with an eager promotion focus should keep all causal possibilities alive in order not to omit a hit, thereby discounting less than would be predicted by standard attribution models. These hypotheses were supported in two studies in which regulatory focus varied as both a chronic personality variable (promotion strength versus prevention strength) and as a situationally manipulated variable (by priming ideals versus oughts).

Would the influence of promotion eagerness and prevention vigilance influence even basic categorization processes? This question was addressed in studies by Molden and Higgins (in press). In one set of conditions, participants were given a vague behavioral description of a target person and were asked to form an impression of the person. Consistent with the results of the previous studies just described, individuals with a vigilant prevention focus formed a clear impression of the person (rejecting alternatives) whereas individuals with an eager promotion focus maintained the vagueness by considering multiple possibilities.

Counterfactual Thinking

Generating alternatives also occurs in counterfactual thinking. As part of decision making, people imagine or simulate what would happen under different conditions (e.g., Kahneman & Tversky, 1982), for example, if they were to do X or they were not to do X, and what might have happened under different conditions, for example, if they had also done X (action/addition) or if they had refrained from doing X (inaction/subtraction) (see Kahneman & Miller, 1986; Roese & Olson, 1993). Thoughts of alternatives to past events—what might have happened "if"—are counterfactual thoughts, and such thoughts contribute to future decision making (see Roese, 1997).

Roese, Hur, and Pennington (1999; see also chapter 6, this volume) have proposed two sets of interrelations involving regulatory focus and counterfactuals. First, there is the relation between a promotion focus, the absence of positive outcomes, additive (action) counterfactuals, and causal sufficiency. Second, there is the relation between a prevention focus, the presence of negative outcomes, subtractive (inaction) counterfactuals, and causal necessity. These proposed relations are consistent with the notion that decision makers in a promotion focus will prefer to use eagerness means more than vigilance means to make their decision, whereas the reverse will be true for decision makers in a prevention focus. As discussed earlier, eagerness means involve an inclination toward hits (i.e., addition) as a goal-pursuit strategy, whereas vigilance means involve an inclination toward correct rejections (i.e., subtraction). Eagerness means would be used to correct a past error of omission (i.e., addition), whereas vigilance means would be used to correct a past error of commission (i.e., subtraction). As noted earlier, Liberman et al. (2001) found in their studies of causal attributions that eagerness means relate to causal sufficiency, whereas vigilance means relate to causal necessity.

In one of the studies testing their proposed interrelations, Roese et al. (1999) had participants read equivalently negative scenarios involving failure situations, with half of the scenarios involving promotion failure (e.g., failure to attain an accomplishment goal) and the other half involving prevention failure (e.g., failure to attain a safety goal). Immediately after each scenario, there was a measure of counterfactual thinking adapted from Kahneman and Tversky (1982) in which participants completed a counterfactual sentence, "If only . . . " As predicted, participants were more likely to complete the sentence with additive counterfactuals for promotion than prevention scenarios, and to complete it with subtractive counterfactuals for prevention than promotion scenarios.

Another study by Roese et al. (1999) used regulatory focus-related mood to induce regulatory focus. All participants were asked to think of a negative event they experienced sometime during the past year. Participants in the promotion focus condition were told to think of an event that made them feel dejected. Participants in the prevention focus condition were told to think of an event that made them feel agitated. As in the other study, the participants were then asked to give "if only" thoughts about their negative experience. As predicted, participants were more likely to complete the sentence with additive counterfactuals for promotion-negative experiences than prevention-negative experiences, and to complete it with subtractive counterfactuals for prevention-negative experiences than promotion-negative experiences.

Combining Value and Expectancy

Expectancy-value (or subjective utility) models historically have been the most influential models regarding the evaluative processes underlying decision making. A basic assumption shared by these models is that in addition to there being main effects of expectancy and value on goal commitment, there is also an effect from their multiplicative combination (Lewin, Dembo, Festinger, & Sears, 1944; Tolman, 1955; Vroom, 1964; for a review, see Feather, 1982). The multiplicative assumption is that as either expectancy or value increases, the impact of the other variable on commitment increases. For example, it is assumed that the effect on goal commitment of a high versus a low likelihood of attaining the goal is greater when the goal has high value than when the goal has little value. This assumption reflects the notion that the goal commitment involves a motivation to maximize the product of value and expectancy.

Not all studies have found the predicted positive interactive effect of value and expectancy, however. One possible explanation for the inconsistencies in the literature is variability across individuals and/or situations in the regulatory focus of participants during decision making (see Shah & Higgins, 1997). Decision makers in a promotion focus prefer to use eagerness means more than vigilance means to make their decision, whereas the reverse is true for decision makers in a prevention focus. What would the use of eagerness means versus vigilance means imply about the multiplicative relation between expectancy and value? Goal pursuit with eagerness means involves ensuring hits and advancement. This implies trying to maximize outcomes, which is consistent with promotion focus ideals that function like maximal goals (see Brendl & Higgins, 1996). Goal pursuit with vigilance means involves being careful not to make mistakes. This implies doing only what is necessary, which is consistent with prevention focus oughts that function like minimal goals (see Brendl & Higgins, 1996). How would this difference in strategic approach influence the multiplicative relation between expectancy and value?

Shah and Higgins (1997) suggested that making a decision with a promotion focus is more likely to involve the motivation to maximize the product of value and expectancy; that is, the motivation that is assumed by most models in the literature. Goal pursuit with eagerness means would involve pursuing highly valued goals with the highest expected utility, which maximizes value X expectancy. Thus, Shah and Higgins (1997) predicted that the positive interactive effect of value and expectancy assumed by classic expectancy-value models would be greater when decision makers have a stronger promotion focus.

In contrast, goal pursuit with vigilance means would involve avoiding all unnecessary risks by striving to meet only responsibilities that are either clearly necessary (i.e., high value prevention goals) or safely attainable (i.e., high expectancy of attainment). This strategic inclination would create a different interactive relation between value and expectancy. When goal pursuit becomes a necessity, such as ensuring the safety of one's child, one must do whatever one can to succeed regardless of the ease or likelihood of goal attainment. That is, although expectancy information would always be relevant, it would become relatively *less* relevant as goal pursuit becomes more like a necessity. Thus, Shah and Higgins (1997) predicted that as strength of prevention focus increased, the interactive effect of value and expectancy would become negative.

To summarize, Shah and Higgins (1997) hypothesized that as strength of promotion focus increased, the positive interactive effect of value and expectancy would increase, but as strength of prevention focus increased, the interactive effect of value and expectancy would decrease. It should be emphasized that these predictions concern the weight given to a higher expectancy as value increases (and vice versa). Goal commitment would generally be stronger for high versus low expectancy and for high versus low value. The predictions concern the relation between these two main effects. For a strong promotion focus, consistent with classic models, it is predicted that the stronger goal commitment from a higher expectancy would be greater for high- than low-value goals. For a strong prevention focus, it is predicted that the stronger goal commitment from a higher expectancy would be less for high-value than low-value goals, because a high-value goal is experienced as a necessity that has to be pursued no matter what. (It should be noted, with respect to the main effects, that there is also some evidence that the main effect for higher value tends to be stronger for a promotion focus than a prevention focus, and the main effect for higher expectancy tends to be stronger for a prevention focus than a promotion focus. The interaction preditions, however, are independent of these regulatory focus differences in the main effects.)

The above predictions were tested in a set of studies in which participants were asked to make decisions about taking a class in their major or taking an entrance exam for graduate school. One study obtained measures of the participants' subjective estimates of value and expectancy, and the other two studies experimentally manipulated high and low levels of value and expectancy. One study involved comparing individuals who differed chronically in promotion and prevention strength, and the other two studies experimentally manipulated regulatory focus using a framing procedure that induced a promotion focus or a prevention focus. Together these studies found, as predicted, that the interactive effect of value and expectancy was more positive when promotion focus was stronger but was more negative when prevention focus was stronger.

In one study, for example, participants were asked to evaluate the likelihood that they would take a course in their major for which the value of doing well and the expectancy of doing well in the course were experimentally manipulated, and participants' promotion strength and prevention strength were measured. High versus low value was established in terms of 95% versus 51% of previous majors being accepted into their honor society when they received a grade of B or higher in the course. High versus low expectancy was established in terms of 75% versus 25% of previous majors receiving a grade of B or higher in the course. The study found that, as predicted, the contrast representing the expectancy × value effect on the decision to take the course was positive for individuals with a strong promotion focus (i.e., high ideal strength) but was negative for individuals with a strong prevention focus (i.e., high ought strength).

The Speed/Accuracy (or Quantity/Quality) Trade-Off

One of the fundamental questions since the beginning of experimental psychology has been when and why people are fast or accurate (Woodworth, 1899). Across psychological areas, the so-called speed/accuracy trade-off or quantity/quality conflict has been of major concern (e.g., Dickman & Meyer, 1988; Fitts & Peterson, 1964; Meyer, Abrams, Kornblum, & Wright, 1988). Given the extensive interest in speed/accuracy decisions, it is surprising that the basic processes underlying these decisions are still poorly understood. Why are some people fast and why are some accurate?

Forster, Higgins, and Bianco (2003) proposed that one answer concerns the regulatory focus of the performer. People in a promotion focus are eager for hits, and this strategic eagerness would incline them toward speed and quantity of output. In contrast, people in a prevention focus are vigilant against making mistakes (errors of commission), and this strategic vigilance would incline them toward accuracy and quality of output. Forster et al. (2003) further proposed that each of these strategic inclinations would increase in intensity as people move closer to completing a task, resulting in stronger speed/accuracy effects of regulatory focus toward the end of a task than at the beginning of a task. They based this prediction on earlier research relating regulatory focus to the "goal looms larger" effect. This effect refers to the fact that motivation increases as the distance to the goal decreases (see Lewin, 1935; Miller, 1944). Forster, Higgins, and Idson (1998) found that as the participants in their studies moved closer to completing the task, the eagerness of people in a promotion focus increased and the vigilance of people in a prevention focus increased.

Forster et al. (2003) predicted that speed and accuracy would follow the same motivational "goal looms larger" principle. In promotion-focus eagerness, speed in speed/accuracy tasks should increase the closer one is to completing the task, whereas accuracy should not. In prevention-focus vigilance, accuracy should increase the closer one is to task completion, whereas speed should not. The task involved four pictures taken from a children's drawing book. For each picture, a participant had to connect sequentially numbered dots in order to draw the picture within a given time period. When correctly completed, all pictures depicted cartoon animals. The number of the dot for each picture where a participant ended after the time period was added across the four pictures. This sum score was the dependent measure of speed. Considering for each picture only those dots up to the dot where a participant ended after the time period, the number of dots that a participant missed (i.e., that were not connected) was added across the four pictures. This sum score was the dependent measure of inaccuracy (mistakes).

Regulatory focus varied both as a chronic individual difference (promotion versus prevention strength) and as an experimentally manipulated variable (through gain/nongain versus nonloss/loss framing). Forster et al. (2003) found that speed increased as promotion-eager participants moved closer to task completion, whereas there was no increase in speed for prevention-vigilant participants. In contrast, accuracy increased (mistakes decreased) as prevention-vigilant participants moved closer to task completion, whereas accuracy decreased for promotion-eager participants. These speed and accuracy effects were independent of one another.

In sum, studies on risky versus conservative biases in decision making, generating alternative hypotheses, attributions, and categorizations about objects and events in the world, additive (action) versus subtractive (inaction) counterfactual thinking, combining value and expectancy, and the speed/accuracy trade-off all have found that promotion-focus eagerness and prevention-focus vigilance produce profoundly different thought processes. Moreover, from a normative perspective in which thought processes are optimal, each strategic inclination is rational and beneficial on the one hand, but has clear costs on the other hand. When people are in a promotion focus, they want to use eagerness means of goal pursuit, and such means are beneficial. Likewise, when people are in a prevention focus, they want to use beneficial vigilance means. In both cases, the choice of means is rational. However, each strategy has costs as well as benefits. At any point in time, one cannot have both a strong risky bias and a strong conservative bias, optimize speed and optimize accuracy, weight a higher expectancy more as value increases and weight it less, and so on. Across different situations or tasks, or even across phases of a single goal pursuit, it would be possible to switch from one strategy to another, and such switching could be highly adaptive. But the utility of such switching is precisely because one cannot strongly emphasize both eagerness and vigilance simultaneously.

The next section considers another unintended side effect of strategic rationality that influences thought. This time, the side effect derives from a benefit rather than a cost of using a rational strategy. What recent research has shown is that making decisions in a manner that suits a regulatory focus produces the benefit of increasing the value of the decision process itself. However, an unintended side effect is that this value from decision means is transferred to the value of the decision outcome, thereby confusing means value and outcome value. This kind of confusion would be considered irrational according to most standard models of decision making, not only in psychology but in other disciplines such as economics.

Value Transfer

I proposed (Higgins, 2000) that another factor beyond outcomes or consequences that makes a decision good is value from fit. The fit concerned the relation between an individual's orientation to a goal pursuit and the means used to pursue that goal. Individuals can pursue the same goal with different orientations and different means. Consider, for example, students in the same course who are working to attain an A grade. Some students are oriented toward an A as an accomplishment (promotion focus), whereas others are oriented toward an A as a responsibility (prevention focus). Some students read material beyond the assigned readings as a means to attain an A (strategic eagerness), whereas others are careful to fulfill all course requirements (strategic vigilance). The fit between these different goal orientations and goal-pursuit means varies. Reading extra, nonassigned material fits an accomplishment promotion orientation better than a responsibility orientation, whereas fulfilling course requirements fits a responsibility orientation better than an accomplishment orientation. For all students, receiving an A in the course will have outcome benefits regardless of their goal orientation and goal means. Independent of this value from worth, however, there is an additional value from fit.

I proposed that, independent of outcomes, people experience a regulatory fit when they use goal-pursuit means that fit their goal orientation, and this regulatory fit increases the value of what they are doing (i.e., they "feel right"). Once a decision has been made, the value of the consequences of the decision should be separate from how the decision was made. That is, postdecisional value from the outcomes of a decision should be independent of predecisional value from the manner in which the decision was made. But if people experience value as they experience other objects and events in their lives, then they could confuse their experiences of different kinds of value. It is well known, for example, that people confuse the sources of episodic experience (Johnson & Raye, 1981), accessibility experience (Tversky & Kahneman, 1973), and excitation experience (Schachter & Singer, 1962; Schwarz & Clore, 1983; Zillman, 1978). What if people confuse the sources of different value experiences? What if people confuse the experience of value from fit with the experience of outcome value? If they do, then the fit experience could influence outcome value.

If goal pursuits with regulatory fit "feel right," then people's retrospective evaluations of past decisions or goal pursuits will be more positive when there was regulatory fit, and people will assign higher value to a positive object that was chosen with regulatory fit. If this is the case, then strategic rationality would produce value transfer such that, independent of actual outcomes, a final decision would be assigned greater value simply because there was a fit between the decision maker's regulatory focus and the process of making the decision. This would be strong evidence of an unintended negative side effect of strategic rationality. Let us now consider some evidence that supports this conclusion.

As part of a larger battery of measures, participants' ideal strength (chronic promotion orientation) and ought strength (chronic prevention orientation) were measured in a study by Higgins, Idson, Freitas, Spiegel, and Molden (2003). After completing the battery, the participants were told that, over and above their usual payment for participating, they would receive a gift. They could choose between a coffee mug and a pen as their gift. (The coffee mug cost more, and pretesting had shown that it was clearly preferred to the pen.) The means of making the decision was manipulated through framing of the choice strategy. Half of the participants were told to think about what they would gain by choosing A and what they would gain by choosing B (gain-related eagerness framing), where A and B alternated between being the mug or the pen. The other half were told to think about what they would lose by not choosing A, and what they would lose by not choosing B (loss-related vigilance framing).

As expected, almost all of the participants chose the coffee mug. These participants were then asked to assess the price of the mug they had chosen (in one study) or were given the chance to buy it (in another study). Predominant promotion-focus individuals assigned or offered a higher price for the mug when they had chosen it using eagerness means than vigilance means, and predominant prevention-focus individuals assigned or offered a higher price for the mug when they had chosen it using vigilance means than eagerness means. The price did not vary as a function of either the predominant focus of the decision maker or the type of means used to make the decision. Differences in price were a function of only the interaction of predominant focus and type of means used—regulatory fit. Indeed, when using their own money, the participants in the regulatory fit conditions offered almost 70% more money to buy the mug compared to participants in the non-fit conditions. The results of these studies support the conclusion that strategic rationality has costly unintended consequences.

Conclusion

Both promotion-focus eagerness and prevention-focus vigilance are adaptive. For example, promotion-focus eagerness has the benefit of generating hits that underly creativity, and prevention-focus vigilance has the benefit of correct rejections that underly accuracy. On the other hand, promotion-focus eagerness can sacrifice quality for quantity, and prevention focus can sacrifice creativity for the status quo. A risky bias has both benefits and costs, as does a conservative bias. When people are in a promotion focus, whether from a chronic disposition or experimentally induced, they are not aware of the trade-offs of their strategic eagerness in decision making or problem solving. The same is true for the strategic vigilance of people in a prevention focus. Individuals experience their strategic eagerness or vigilance and they want the benefits of the strategy they use, but they are unlikely to intend or be aware of the costs of the strategy they use. These costs occur nonetheless and are an unintended side effect of the trade-offs of using a strategy that also has benefits.

Strategic rationality has another unintended side effect that derives from the benefits rather than the costs of strategic use. The motivational strength and enjoyment of goal pursuit is increased by using a strategy that fits one's regulatory state. The fit has the benefit of increasing the value of the goal-pursuit activity itself. But the fit experience can affect outcome value, thereby confusing means value and outcome value. Such value confusion is clearly not intended, and people are not aware of it.

The take-away message is that rational use of beneficial strategies to pursue goals has unintended side effects on decision making, problem solving, and other forms of thought. The side effects discussed in this chapter would be considered negative from most traditional perspectives. For example, prevention-focus vigilance that reduces creativity would be considered negative, as would paying more to buy a coffee cup simply because your decision means happened to fit your current state. It is not always clear, however, that the unintended side effects of strategic rationality are negative. For example, is it negative when prevention-focus vigilance reduces the weight given to a higher expectancy for goals that are very highly valued? Standard maximization models of subjective utility would say yes. However, it not clear that maximization is always adaptive. Maximization makes sense when one is choosing among alternatives. But for parents, there is no alternative to the life of their child. For some religious people, there is no alternative to the Ten Commandments. For such perceived *necessities*, the impact on commitment from a higher expectancy *should be less* than for goals that have alternatives.

Thus, whether the side effects of prevention vigilance on expectancy–value integration should be considered negative or positive could vary across goals. This is also true of the fit experience affecting outcome value. People could possess the same object either by receiving it as a gift or by working for it in a way that fits their regulatory orientation. In the latter but not the former case, the fit experience could affect outcome value. If people valued the object more when they worked for it because of value transfer, would this be negative? Not only might the object be appreciated longer, but it might receive better care and last longer. Future research needs to examine more critically whether a side effect is truly negative or positive. Psychologists tend to equate unintended consequences with negative consequences. We need to consider more seriously the possibility that unintended side effects can be adaptive as well as maladaptive.

Historically, the dominant way of thinking about how motivation produces unintended thought has been in terms of irrational motivational forces disrupting and distorting thought. This chapter has considered an alternative motivational source of unintended thought. I have presented evidence for the conclusion that unintended thought is also a product of the rational use of basic self-regulatory strategies. Motivational strategies like eagerness and vigilance have critical benefits that people would not want to give up. However, our use of motivational strategies has unintended side effects of which we are unaware. It is not possible to take advantage of just the benefits of these strategies by using both strategies simultaneously, such as being risky and conservative at the same time. Nevertheless, it is possible that across time there might be ways to optimize the benefits and reduce the costs. One strategy may be relatively better for some tasks, situations, or goal phases than others, and learning when to switch strategies could be very useful. Learning how people could do so is a major challenge for motivational science.

References

Bassili, J. N. (1995). Response latency and the accessibility of voting intentions: What contributes to accessibility and how it affects vote choice. *Personality and Social Psychology Bulletin, 21,* 686–695.

Bassili, J. N. (1996). Meta-judgmental versus operative indexes of psychological attributes: The case of measures of attitude strength. *Journal of Personality and Social Psychology, 71,* 637–653.

Brendl, C. M., & Higgins, E. T. (1996). Principles of judging valence: What makes events positive or negative? In M. P. Zanna (Ed.), *Advances in experimental social psychology* (Vol. 28, pp. 95–160). New York: Academic Press.

Bruner, J. S., Goodnow, J. J., & Austin, G. A. (1956). *A study of thinking.* New York: Wiley.

Crowe, E., & Higgins, E. T. (1997). Regulatory focus and strategic inclinations: Promotion and prevention in decision-making. *Organizational Behavior and Human Decision Processes, 69,* 117–132.

Dickman, S. J., & Meyer, D. E. (1988). Impulsivity and speed-accuracy tradeoffs in information processing. *Journal of Personality and Social Psychology, 54,* 274–290.

Ekstrom, R. B., French, J. W., Harman, H. H., & Dermen, D. (1976). *Manual for kit of factor-referenced cognitive tests.* Princeton, NJ: ETS.

Fazio, R. H. (1986). How do attitudes guide behavior? In R. M. Sorrentino & E. T. Higgins (Eds.), *Handbook of motivation and cognition: Foundations of social behavior* (pp. 204–243). New York: Guilford.

Fazio, R. H. (1995). Attitudes as object-evaluation associations: Determinants, consequences, and correlates of attitude accessibility. In R. E. Petty & J. A. Krosnick (Eds.), *Attitude strength: Antecedents and consequences* (pp. 247–282). Mahwah, NJ: Erlbaum.

Feather, N. T. (1982). Actions in relation to expected consequences: An overview of a research program. In N. T. Feather (Ed.), *Expectations and actions: Expectancy-value models in psychology* (pp. 53–95). Hillsdale, NJ: Erlbaum.

Festinger, L. (1957). *A theory of cognitive dissonance.* Evanston, IL: Row, Peterson.

Fitts, P. M., & Peterson, J. R. (1964). Information capacity of descrete motor responses. *Journal of Experimental Psychology, 67,* 103–112.

Forster, J., Higgins, E. T., & Idson, L. C. (1998). Approach and avoidance strength during goal attainment: Regulatory focus and the "goal loom larger" effect. *Journal of Personality and Social Psychology, 75,* 1115–1131.

Forster, J., Higgins, E. T., & Bianco, A. T. (2003). Speed/accuracy decisions in task performance: Built-in trade-off or separate strategic concerns? *Organizational Behavior and Human Decision Processes,* 90, 148–164.

Freud, A. (1937). *The ego and the mechanisms of defense.* New York: International Universities Press.

Freud, S. (1952). *A general introduction to psychoanalysis.* New York: Washington Square Press. (Original work published 1920)

Friedman, R. S., & Forster, J. (2001). The effects of promotion and prevention cues on creativity. *Journal of Personality and Social Psychology, 81,* 1001–1013.

Gould, R. (1939). An experimental analysis of "level of aspiration." *Genetic Psychology Monographs, 21,* 3–115.

Heider, F. (1958). *The psychology of interpersonal relations.* New York: Wiley.

Higgins, E. T. (1987). Self-discrepancy: A theory relating self and affect. *Psychological Review, 94,* 319–340.

Higgins, E. T. (1989). Self-discrepancy theory: What patterns of self-beliefs cause people to suffer? In L. Berkowitz (Ed.), *Advances in experimental social psychology* (Vol. 22, pp. 93–136). New York: Academic Press.

Higgins, E. T. (1991). Development of self-regulatory and self-evaluative processes: Costs, benefits, and tradeoffs. In M. R. Gunnar & L. A. Sroufe (Eds.), *Self processes and development: The Minnesota symposia on child psychology* (Vol. 23, pp. 125–165). Hillsdale, NJ: Erlbaum.

Higgins, E. T. (1996). Knowledge activation: Accessibility, applicability, and salience. In E. T. Higgins & A. W. Kruglanski (Eds.), *Social psychology: Handbook of basic principles* (pp. 133–168). New York: Guilford.

Higgins, E. T. (1997). Beyond pleasure and pain. *American Psychologist, 52,* 1280–1300.

Higgins, E. T. (1998). Promotion and prevention: Regulatory focus as a motivational principle. In M. P. Zanna (Ed.), *Advances in experimental social psychology* (Vol. 30, pp. 1–46). New York: Academic Press.

Higgins, E. T. (2000). Making a good decision: Value from "fit." *American Psychologist, 55,* 1217–1230.

Higgins, E. T., Idson, L. C., Freitas, A. L., Spiegel, S., & Molden, D. C. (2003). Transfer of value from fit. *Journal of Personality and Social Psychology, 84,* 1140–1153.

Higgins, E. T., Shah, J., & Friedman, R. (1997). Emotional responses to goal attainment: Strength of regulatory focus as moderator. *Journal of Personality and Social Psychology, 72,* 515–525.

Higgins, E. T., & Silberman, I. (1998). Development of regulatory focus: Promotion and prevention as ways of living. In J. Heckhausen & C. S. Dweck (Eds.), *Motivation and self-regulation across the life span* (pp. 78–113). New York: Cambridge University Press.

Johnson, M. K., & Raye, C. L. (1981). Reality monitoring. *Psychological Review, 88,* 67–85.

Jung, C. G. (1954). *The practice of psychotherapy: Volume 16 of the collected works of C. G. Jung*. New York: Bollingen Series.

Kahneman, D., & Miller, D. T. (1986). Norm theory: Comparing reality to its alternatives. *Psychological Review, 93,* 136–153.

Kahneman, D., & Tversky, A. (1982). The simulation heuristic. In D. Kahneman, P. Slovic, & A. Tversky (Eds.), *Judgment under uncertainty: Heuristics and biases* (pp. 201–208). New York: Cambridge University Press.

Lewin, K. (1935). *A dynamic theory of personality*. New York: McGraw-Hill.

Lewin, K., Dembo, T., Festinger, L., & Sears, P. S. (1944). Level of aspiration. In J. McHunt (Ed.), *Personality and the behavior disorders* (Vol. 1, pp. 333–378). New York: Ronald Press.

Liberman, N., Molden, D. C., Idson, L. C., & Higgins, E. T. (2001). Promotion and prevention focus on alternative hypotheses: Implications for attributional functions. *Journal of Personality and Social Psychology, 80,* 5–18.

Mayseless, O., & Kruglanski, A. W. (1987). What makes you so sure? Effects of epistemic motivations on judgmental confidence. *Organizational Behavior and Human Decision Processes, 39,* 162–183.

Meyer, D. E., Abrams, R. A., Kornblum, S., & Wright, C. E. (1988). Optimality in human motor performance: Ideal control of rapid aimed movements. *Psychological Review, 95,* 340–370.

Mikulincer, M., Kedem, P., & Paz, D. (1990). The impact of trait anxiety and situational stress on the categorization of natural objects. *Anxiety Research, 2,* 85–101.

Miller, N. E. (1944). Experimental studies of conflict. In J. M. Hunt (Ed.), *Personality and the behavior disorders* (Vol. 1, pp. 431–465). New York: Ronald Press.

Molden, D. C., & Higgins, E. T. (in press). Categorization under uncertainty: Resolving vagueness and ambiguity with eager versus vigilant strategies. *Social Cognition.*

Roese, N. J. (1997). Counterfactual thinking. *Psychological Bulletin, 121,* 133–148.

Roese, N. J., Hur, T., & Pennington, G. L. (1999). Counterfactual thinking and regulatory focus: Implications for action versus inaction and sufficiency versus necessity. *Journal of Personality and Social Psychology, 77,* 1109–1120.

Roese, N. J., & Olson, J. M. (1993). The structure of counterfactual thought. *Personality and Social Psychology Bulletin, 19,* 312–319.

Rotter, J. B. (1982). Some implications of a social learning theory for the practice of psychotherapy. In J. B. Rotter (Ed.), *The development and applications of social learning theory* (pp. 237–262). New York: CBS Educational and Professional Publishing.

Schachter, S., & Singer, J. E. (1962). Cognitive, social and physiological determinants of emotional state. *Psychological Review, 69,* 379–399.

Schwarz, N., & Clore, G. L. (1983). Mood, misattribution, and judgments of well-being: Informative and directive functions of affective states. *Journal of Personality and Social Psychology, 45,* 513–523.

Shah, J., & Higgins, E. T. (1997). Expectancy X value effects: Regulatory focus

as a determinant of magnitude and direction. *Journal of Personality and Social Psychology, 73*, 447–458.
Tanner, W. P., Jr., & Swets, J. A. (1954). A decision-making theory of visual detection. *Psychological Review, 61*, 401–409.
Tolman, E. C. (1955). Principles of performance. *Psychological Review, 62*, 315–326.
Trope, Y., & Liberman, A. (1996). Social hypothesis testing: Cognitive and motivational mechanisms. In E. T. Higgins & A. W. Kruglanski (Eds.), *Social psychology: Handbook of basic principles* (pp. 239–270). New York: Guilford.
Tversky, A., & Kahneman, D. (1973). Availability: A heuristic for judging frequency and probability. *Cognitive Psychology, 5*, 207–232.
Vroom, V. H. (1964). *Work and motivation.* New York: Wiley.
Woodworth, R. S. (1899). Accuracy of voluntary movements. *Psychological Review, 3*, 1–101.
Zillmann, D. (1978). Attribution and misattribution of excitatory reactions. In J. H. Harvey, W. J. Ickes, & R. F. Kidd (Eds.), *New directions in attribution research* (Vol. 2, pp. 335–368). Hillsdale, NJ: Erlbaum.

19

Going Beyond the Motivation Given: Self-Control and Situational Control Over Behavior

Yaacov Trope and Ayelet Fishbach

A basic theme running through much of the social psychological literature is the idea that the immediate situation is a powerful determinant of human behavior. Inspired by Kurt Lewin's (1935) field theory, social psychologists have sought to demonstrate that a wide range of human behavior, socially desirable as well as undesirable, is under the control of immediate situational forces (Asch, 1952; Cartwright, 1959; Milgram, 1963). Indeed, the field of social psychology has been defined as the study of situational determinants of thought, feeling, and action (Ross & Nisbett, 1991). Research on automaticity has provided a new impetus to the study of situational control over behavior (Bargh, 1990, 1994; Bargh & Chartrand, 1999; Wegner & Bargh, 1998). This research suggests that situational cues can govern behavior without being consciously processed and without making a deliberate choice of an appropriate course of action. Situational cues that have been consistently and frequently associated with certain goals acquire the capacity to directly elicit these goals and thus directly control action.

The strong influence an immediate situation can exert over behavior poses a self-control problem when this influence is in conflict with long-term goals (Ainslie, 1992; Loewenstein, 1996; Metcalfe & Mischel, 1999; Mischel, 1974; Mischel, Shoda, & Peake, 1988; Rachlin, 1995, 1996, 1997; Shoda, Mischel, & Peak, 1990). People may want to act according to their long-term goals. They may also have the prerequisite knowledge, skill, and opportunity. Nevertheless, short-term motives, especially those that are automatically triggered by the immediate stimulus situation, may prevent people from pursuing their long-term goals. For example, a student may want to study for an important exam, know how to study for the exam, and possess the required materials. Nevertheless, a television show may be sufficiently tempting to prevent the student from studying for the exam and achieving his long-term academic goals.

Our question in this chapter is how people protect their long-term goals against temporary, situationally elicited motives. We propose that when short-term motives threaten the attainment of long-term goals, people proactively employ counteractive self-control strategies—strategies that are designed to offset the influence of short-term motives on behavior. Counteractive control is often an intentional process of committing to long-term goals and eliminating tempting alternatives. For example, before an exam, a student may deliberately decide to study in the library rather than at home to avoid the temptation to view her favorite television show. Counteractive control may also be an unconscious process. The temptation to watch television may automatically bring to mind thoughts about the student's goal to do well on the exam and associated achievement and self-fulfillment values, which in turn may boost her motivation to study.

This chapter describes a program of research on these counteractive control strategies. We start with a general characterization of the counteractive control process. Next, we describe research on specific counteractive control strategies, what activates them, and how they help overcome immediate temptations. Finally, we describe research bearing on the goal-directedness, flexibility, and implicitness of counteractive self-control.

Counteractive Self-Control

People face a self-control problem when they perceive a conflict between the short-term and long-term outcomes of an action (Loewenstein, 1996; Mischel, 1974; Mischel, Shoda, & Rodriguez, 1989; Rachlin, 1996). For example, the discomfort that is often associated with dieting, physical exercise, or undergoing a medical test is a price people have to pay to attain their long-term health goals. Similarly, suppressing a desire to retaliate may be necessary to prevent an interpersonal conflict from escalating, and foregoing immediate social and material gains may be necessary for achieving long-term academic aspirations. In general, unfulfilled immediate wishes and desires are the short-term costs of pursuing long-term goals. Short-term costs may thus pose a threat to long-term goals. Counteractive control theory (CCT) posits that self-control efforts serve to overcome such threats. According to this theory, short-term costs affect action via two paths (see figure 19.1). Directly, these costs act to decrease the likelihood of acting according to long-term goals. Indirectly, however, short-term costs elicit counteractive control efforts, which, in turn, act to increase the likelihood of this action. As a result, the actual choice of a preferred action may remain unaffected by its short-term costs.

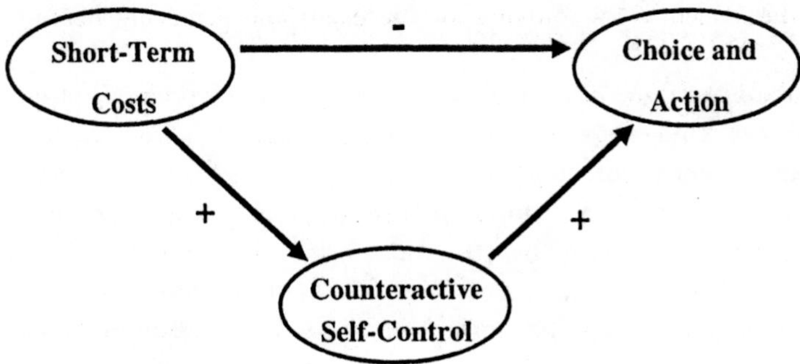

Figure 19.1 The influence of short-term outcomes on choice and action.

For example, the possibility of being tempted to watch television before an exam may lead students to bolster the value of the exam or even impose on themselves various penalties for failing to study for the exam. When uninteresting television shows are expected, the perceived threat to studying will be small, and little or no counteractive control will be exercised. However, when one's favorite television show is expected, the greater threat to studying may elicit more intensive counteractive control efforts. As a result, a student expecting a favorite television show may study as much as a student who does not expect such a show. In itself, the attractiveness of a television show acts to diminish the motivation to study. However, the counteractive control efforts elicited by the anticipated pleasure of watching one's favorite show may prevent this anticipated pleasure from actually affecting the time one devotes to studying.

CCT assumes that people exert counteractive control efforts as means to the end of achieving their long-term goals. Three hypotheses follow from this means-end assumption: First, counteractive control is goal dependent. People will exert more counteractive control when short-term motives threaten important rather than unimportant long-term goals. Furthermore, once a long-term goal is achieved, counteractive control will cease. Second, counteractive control is flexible. Counteractive control will be exercised when it determines whether or not long-term goals will be achieved. Little or no counteractive control will be exerted when short-term motives are weak and thus easy to resist or very strong and thus impossible to resist. Greater counteractive control will be exerted when the strength of short-term motives is at an intermediate level, because at this level counteractive control determines whether long-term goals will be achieved. Third, counteractive control is substitutable. Counteractive control will be exerted when it is necessary for achieving one's long term goals. When other, external means of control are in place, counteractive self-control will cease.

Counteractive Self-Control Strategies

A wide range of self-control strategies have been proposed in the literature on delay of gratification (Mischel, 1984; Mischel, Cantor, & Feldman, 1996), implementation of intentions (Gollwitzer, 1990, 1999; Gollwitzer & Bayer, 1999; Gollwitzer & Brandstatter, 1997; Kuhl, 1982, 1986; Kuhl & Beckmann, 1985), and control over impulsive behavior (Baumeister, Bratslavsky, Muraven, & Tice, 1998; Baumeister & Heatherton, 1996). We distinguish between strategies that change the choice situation and those that change the subjective meaning of the situation. People may change the choice situation in several ways: They may impose on themselves penalties ("side bets") for failing to act according to their long-term goals (Ainslie, 1975; Becker, 1960). These self-imposed penalties may then serve as external deterrents against failure to pursue long-term goals. For example, one may be willing to pay a relatively large cancellation fee for missing a painful medical test. By itself, the expected pain increases the likelihood of failing to actually take the test and having to pay the cancellation fee. Simple economic considerations (minimizing expected monetary penalties) should therefore lead people to impose on themselves a relatively small fee to the extent that the medical test is more painful. CCT predicts, however, that the more painful a test is expected to be, the higher the cancellation fee people will be willing to pay.

Another way in which people may change future choice situations is by making rewards contingent upon acting according to their long-term interests. Instead of receiving a reward unconditionally, people may prefer to receive it only if they act according to their long-term interests. For example, people may prefer to receive a bonus for actually completing a painful but subjectively important medical test rather than for merely agreeing to do it. By making penalties and rewards contingent on performing an activity, people precommit themselves to the activity (Brickman, 1987). People may precommit themselves more directly by eliminating action alternatives and thus making a decision to act according to their long-term interests irreversible (Ainslie, 1975; Green & Rachlin, 1996; Rachlin & Green, 1972; Schelling, 1978, 1984; Strotz, 1956; Thaler, 1994; Thaler & Shefrin, 1981). For example, people may eliminate opportunities to cancel an appointment for a painful medical test to ensure that they actually take the test.

Other counteractive control strategies change the psychological meaning of future choice situations. People may selectively attend to, encode, and interpret information about future situations so as to bolster the value of long-term goals and discount the aversiveness of short-term costs (Mischel, 1984). The value of long-term goals may be enhanced by linking the attainment of these goals to self-standards. Failure to pursue long-term outcomes is then construed as a violation of one's values and a threat to one's sense of self-worth and determination (Bandura, 1989). In addition, people may bolster the value of attaining long-term goals by elaborating upon what makes attainment of these goals important (Beckmann & Kuhl, 1984; Kuhl, 1984). For example, in trying to decide whether to undertake a medical test, people may think of how undertaking the test may help them detect and prevent potential health problems. Counteractive control may also aim to discount short-term costs. People may try to attenuate the anticipated aversiveness of short-term costs by focusing on the abstract, "cool" properties of these costs rather than on their concrete, "hot" properties (Metcalf & Mischel, 1999). People may also try to regulate their mood so as to improve their ability to cope with short-term costs (Trope & Neter, 1994). For example, people may seek mood-enhancing experiences to buffer the anticipated unpleasantness of a medical procedure.

We conducted a series of studies to demonstrate some of these counteractive control strategies and their influence on behavior (Trope & Fishbach, 2000). Several of these studies are described below.

Self-Imposed Penalties

One study (Trope & Fishbach, 2000, Study 1) examined the monetary penalties participants imposed on themselves for possible failure to undertake an activity that had long-term benefits but short-term costs. The short-term costs were either small or large, and the question was how these costs affected the magnitude of self-imposed penalties. Participants were offered an opportunity to take a test of the influence of glucose intake on their cognitive functioning. The feedback from the test was described as very useful, but as requiring abstinence from food containing glucose (e.g., candy, bread) for either a short period of time (6 hours) or a long period of time (3 days). Before deciding whether to take the test, participants were asked to indicate the amount of money they would be willing to pay (if any) as a penalty for failing to complete the test. This payment was said to cover expenses caused by canceling the test session.

Consistent with CCT, the results showed that participants set higher penalties for failure to complete a long period of abstinence than a short period of abstinence. In itself, a long period of abstinence increases the likelihood of failure and thus the likelihood of having to pay the monetary penalty. Economic considerations should have led participants to impose on themselves a smaller penalty when a longer abstinence period is required. The reverse pattern of preferences we found is indicative of counteractive control. Participants apparently used the penalties to ensure that the abstinence did not prevent them from obtaining the useful feedback regarding their eating habits. A long period of abstinence threatened participants' ability to complete the test, and it was in an attempt to counteract this threat that participants imposed on themselves relatively high monetary penalties. This finding thus provided the first experimental evidence for what economists call side bets (Becker, 1960), namely, the voluntary attachment of a monetary fine for failure to act according to long-term preferences.

Self-Imposed Contingencies for Receiving a Bonus

The study described above examined participants' willingness to make a penalty contingent on completing an unpleasant medical test. Another study (Trope & Fishbach, 2000, Study 2) examined participants' willingness to make a bonus contingent upon completing such a test. Participants were offered an opportunity to take part in a study on the risk of heart disease that included a cardiovascular test. Participants were told that the test was highly diagnostic and that they would receive an explanation of the results. The test was described as involving either a low or high degree of physical discomfort. The high-discomfort test required an hour of arduous exercise during which several hormone samples would be taken by a nurse. The hormone sampling was described as "rather painful" and the overall test procedure as strenuous and unpleasant. The low-discomfort test required an hour of relaxation (reading a paper or book while lying on a bed) during which a number of hormone samples would be taken by a nurse. The hormone sampling was said to be unpainful and the overall test procedure easy and comfortable.

Participants were told that they would be able to receive a bonus (extra credit hours) for taking part in the study. They were further told that the bonus would be available before and after taking the test, but for administrative purposes were asked to indicate exactly when they preferred to receive it. Choosing to receive the bonus before the test meant no obligation to actually take it, whereas choosing to receive the bonus after the test made the bonus contingent on completing the test. We assumed that imposing such a contingency would reflect a self-control strategy designed to ensure that the test was actually completed. We therefore predicted that participants would prefer the bonus to be contingent on completing the test when the test involved a high (rather than low) level of discomfort.

The results confirmed this prediction. Participants could earn the bonus without having to take the cardiovascular test. Nevertheless, they preferred to make the bonus contingent on performing the test, particularly when the test was expected to be highly unpleasant. In imposing on themselves this contingency, participants risked losing the bonus, but at the same time they also motivated themselves to complete the arduous cardiovascular test. Like self-imposed penalties, self-imposed contingencies for receiving a reward changed the choice situation so as to counteract the influence of short-term costs and, thus, maintain a high probability of acting according to long-term goals.

Bolstering the Subjective Value of an Activity

The preceding two studies demonstrate that people sometimes change the immediate situation to ensure that it does not prevent them from pursuing their long-term interests. We now turn to a different form of counteractive control, namely, bolstering the value of acting according to one's long-term interests. People may bolster the value of an activity by thinking about it as important, interesting, and likely to yield useful outcomes. CCT predicts that the greater the temporary unpleasantness of an activity, the more likely people are to bolster its value. Moreover, unlike dissonance theory, CCT predicts that people will bolster the value of an activity before engaging in it. Two studies tested this prediction.

Evaluative Bolstering of an Unpleasant Test To test this prediction, participants were offered an opportunity to take a test of the influence of glucose intake on their cognitive functioning (Trope & Fishbach, 2000, Study 3). As before, the test was described as requiring abstinence from glucose-containing food for either a short period (6 hours) or a long period (3 days). After receiving a description of the test, but before indicating their decision, participants rated the usefulness of the test results, the importance of taking the test, the importance of the study, the importance of participating in scientific research, and the extent to which the study was interesting. These ratings were designed to assess bolstering of the subjective value of the test.

Across these different ratings, participants evaluated the test more positively when the test required 3 days of glucose abstinence than when it required only 6 hours of glucose abstinence. Consistent with CCT, then, participants bolstered the value of the offered test when it was expected to cause high rather than low levels of physical discomfort.

This study also assessed participants' intention to actually take the test. A path analysis tested the hypothesis that counteractive control prevented the physical discomfort of the test from diminishing participants' willingness to actually undertake the test. Consistent with this hypothesis, the analysis revealed opposite direct and indirect effects of abstinence duration on participants' intention to take the test (see figure 19.2). Specifically, in itself, a long versus short period of abstinence acted to decrease participants' willingness to take the test. This negative direct effect of abstinence duration on intention was offset by its positive indirect effect via bolstering of the value of the test. Specifically, a long versus short period of abstinence elicited bolstering of the value of the test. Bolstering the value of the test, in turn, increased participants' willingness to actually undertake the test. Thus, via counteractive bolstering, a long versus short period of abstinence acted to increase willingness to undertake the test. As a result, the overall (unmediated) effect of abstinence duration on intention to take the test was negligible ($\beta = -.05$), indicating

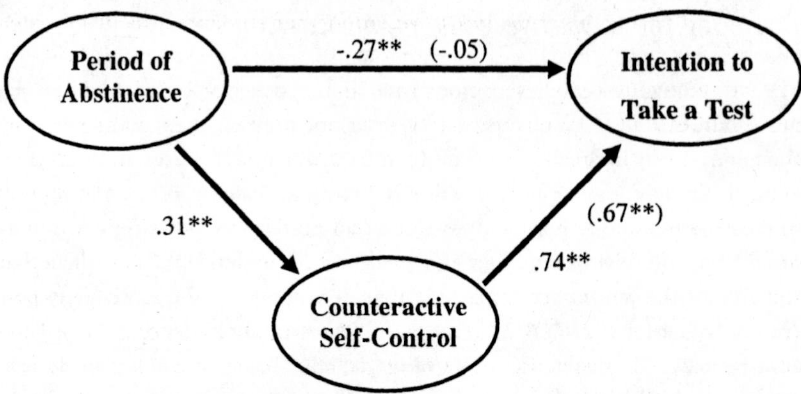

Figure 19.2 Path model of the influence of period of abstinence on intention to take a test. Numbers in parentheses are zero-order standardized betas. $**p < .05$ (Trope & Fishbach, 2000, Study 3).

that the longer abstinence requirement did not weaken participants' intentions to take the test.

Evaluative Bolstering of Studying When Social Motives Are Primed A potential obstacle to acting according to long-term interests is thinking about tempting alternatives. A student may want to focus on her studies, but thoughts about the pleasure of spending time with friends might somehow be primed and undermine her motivation to study. However, to the extent that the exam is important, the priming of competing social motives may intensify self-control efforts and thus help the student maintain a high level of motivation to study. Instead of reducing the motivation to study, priming of competing social motives may enhance the motivation to study and thus enable the student to prepare for the exam and even perform well on it.

These predictions were tested in a real-life setting (Trope & Fishbach, 2000, Study 5). Our participants were students taking a midterm exam in an introductory psychology course. Social motives were primed by asking the students to answer a series of open-ended questions regarding their social life 1 week before the exam. These questions were followed by questions regarding the value and importance of the exam. We examined how priming of social motives affected the students' evaluation of the importance of studying and the students' grades on the midterm exam. It was hypothesized that the priming of social motives before the exam would lead students to boost the subjective value of studying for the exam, which should, in turn, act to prevent the priming of social motives from lowering the students' grades on the midterm exam.

Consistent with this hypothesis, we found that students attached greater importance to the exam when social motives were primed than when social motives were not primed. Moreover, path analysis indicated that this evaluative bolstering helped students' performance on the exam. As can be seen in figure 19.3, social priming produced a negative direct effect on grades. Thus, in itself, social priming impaired performance on the exam. However, this negative direct effect of social priming was counteracted by its positive indirect effect. Specifically, social priming led participants to bolster the value of studying. Bolstering the value of studying, in turn, predicted relatively high grades on the exam. Thus, social priming acted to increase participants' grades on the exam via counteractive bolstering of the value of studying. This positive indirect effect of social priming cancelled its negative direct effect, so that, overall, social priming did not impair participants' performance on the exam.

The results of this study suggest that it is necessary to take into account self-control processes in predicting the motivational and behavioral consequences of priming a motive. When the primed motive threatens the attainment of long-term goals, people may engage in counteractive control that shields these goals against the primed motive. In the present study, the priming of social motives before an exam threatened participants' ability to study for an exam. In response to this threat, participants boosted the value of studying. Instead of weakening the motivation to study, the priming of social motives strengthened the motivation to study. This, in turn, prevented the priming of social motives from impairing participants' performance on the exam.

Together, these studies provide initial evidence for some of the counteractive control strategies people employ when they anticipate situations that pit

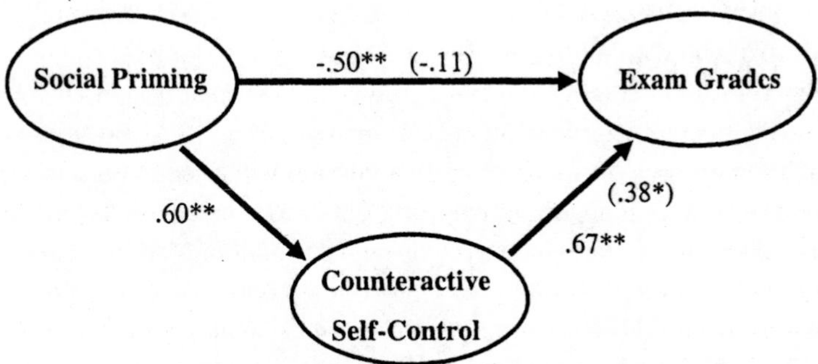

Figure 19.3 Path model of the influence of social priming before an exam on grades. Numbers in parentheses are zero-order standardized betas. $^*p < .07$; $^{**}p < .05$ (Trope & Fishbach, 2000, Study 5).

short-term outcomes against long-term goals. These strategies proactively change the motivational givens of the situation so that it does not threaten the attainment of long-term goals. The greater the short-term costs and the resulting temptation to abandon long-term goals, the more likely people are to exercise counteractive control and, as a result, remain committed to pursuing their goals. Self-imposing incentives for pursuing long-term goals is an example of how people proactively change future situations. Our studies suggest that such proactive changes enable people to be under situational control without having to relinquish their long-term goals. Moreover, our studies show that counteractive control annulled but did not reverse the effect of short-term cost on behavior. In other words, counteractive control did not produce overcorrection, a greater likelihood of engaging in the more unpleasant activities. It seems that participants exerted the amount of self-control that was just sufficient to offset the influence of short-term costs on their decisions. As discussed below, this is consistent with the present view that counteractive control is a goal-directed process—a means to the end of ensuring the attainment of long-term goals.

The Goal-Directedness of Counteractive Control

CCT assumes that counteractive control efforts are means to the end of attaining long-term goals. An alternative view is that these efforts have intrinsic value. According to this alternative view, encountering short-term costs creates a challenge for the individual—a challenge that invigorates attempts to overcome the influence of short-term costs, regardless of one's long-term goals (Atkinson & Birch, 1978; Brehm & Self, 1989; Brehm, Wright, Solomon, Silka, & Greenberg, 1983; Wright & Brehm, 1984). CCT differs from this interpretation in positing that counteractive control efforts have no inherent value, that the motivation to exert such efforts derives entirely from their instrumental value in ensuring the attainment of long-term goals. Our findings that counteractive control actually helps people attain their long-term goals is consistent with the present means-end analysis. But more critical to this analysis is the assumption that counteractive control efforts depend on people's long-term goals and whether they can be achieved. Several implications follow from this goal-directedness assumption: First, counteractive control will be exercised when long-term goals are important rather than unimportant. Second, counteractive control will be exercised before rather than after achieving long-term goals. Third, counteractive control efforts will be exercised when they are necessary for achieving long-term goals. The research described below tests these implications of the goal-directedness assumption.

Goal-Dependent Counteractive Control

According to CCT, the temporary unpleasantness of an activity will elicit self-control efforts only when failure to perform the activity threatens the attainment of an important long-term goal. The study on the self-imposed contingencies for receiving a reward tested this hypothesis (Trope & Fishbach, 2000, Study 2). Recall that in that study participants were offered an opportunity to take a cardiovascular test that was described as involving either a low or high degree of physical discomfort. Participants could receive a bonus for taking part in the study, and the question was whether participants would make the bonus contingent on completing the cardiovascular test.

The importance participants placed on good health was assessed before they received the information about the cardiovascular test. As described earlier, participants were generally more interested in making the bonus contingent on completing the test when the test was more unpleasant. However, this was true only for participants to whom health was important. Participants to whom health was not very important tended to choose according to what simple economic considerations would prescribe, namely, accepting the bonus before rather than after completing the test, particularly when the test was expected to be very unpleasant. This finding demonstrates the goal dependence of counteractive control. Short-term costs do not elicit counteractive control unless they threaten important long-term goals.

Goal Completion and Counteractive Control

The CCT goal-directedness assumption states that counteractive control serves the purpose of enabling people to pursue their long-term goals. Hence, short-term costs should elicit counteractive control before rather than after an opportunity to pursue their long-term goals. This prediction was tested in the study on counteractive bolstering of the value of studying for an exam in response to priming of competing social motives (Trope & Fishbach, 2000, Study 5). Before an exam, bolstering the value of studying may help students better prepare for the exam. After the exam, studying is no longer a goal, and bolstering its value can only reduce the dissonance created by what students had to sacrifice in order to prepare for the exam (Aronson, 1997; Cooper & Fazio, 1984; Festinger, 1957; Shultz & Lepper, 1996). According to CCT, then, the priming of social motives should lead students to bolster the importance of studying before performing the exam, but not after performing it.

As described above, the subjective value of studying before the exam was more positive when social motives were primed than when these motives were not primed. After the exam, however, the subjective value of studying was low regardless of whether or not social motives were primed. Thus, participants bolstered the value of studying before the exam, when studying served participants' goals; but they did not bolster the value of studying after the exam, when studying no longer served participants' goals. Consistent with the CCT goal-directedness assumption, these findings suggest that counteractive control is exercised only when it is instrumental for achieving long-term goals.

Nonmonotonic Effects of Short-Term Costs on Counteractive Control

CCT predicts that the effect of short-term costs on counteractive control is nonmonotonic. As short-term costs increase, counteractive control efforts would also increase. However, the short-term costs might reach a level beyond which people may feel unable to resist their influence, and counteractive control efforts will accordingly decrease. Thus, when the short-term costs of an activity are very low, people may feel capable of undertaking an activity without exerting self-control efforts. When short-term costs are extremely high, people may feel incapable of undertaking the activity even if they exert self-control efforts. It is only when the short-term costs of an activity are moderate that counteractive control efforts determine whether or not the activity would be undertaken. Moderate costs should, therefore, elicit a relatively high level of counteractive control efforts. For example, bolstering of the value of a medical test should be an inverted U-shaped function of the anticipated discomfort of the test. Initially, increasing levels of expected discomfort should intensify counteractive bolstering. However, beyond a certain point, such self-control efforts should diminish (see Atkinson & Feather, 1966; Brehm & Self, 1989; Kukla, 1974, for similar predictions regarding effort exertion in skill-related tasks).

To test these predictions, participants were offered an opportunity to take a diagnostic test of their cognitive functioning at night (Trope & Fishbach, 2000, Study 4). Participants were informed that the test consisted of several parts, all of which would be administered over the telephone on one of the following two nights. To vary the level of discomfort of performing the test, participants were told that the test would take place at either a convenient time (9:30 p.m.), a moderately inconvenient time (12:30 a.m.), or an extremely inconvenient time (3:30 a.m.). Two forms of self-control were assessed: One was bolstering the value of the test. The other was attaching emotional significance to performing the test. This form of self-control reflected the emotional gratification participants expected to experience if they perform the test.

As predicted, both the subjective value of the test and its emotional significance increased from 9:30 p.m. to 12:30 a.m., but then decreased from

12:30 a.m. to 3:30 a.m. (see figure 19.4). On both indices of counteractive control, the 12:30 a.m. test received higher scores than either the 9:30 p.m. or the 3:30 a.m. tests, which were not different from each other. Counteractive control was thus a nonmonotonic, inverted U-function of lateness of testing hour.

This study also assessed participants' performance of the test at the three different hours of the night. In itself, lateness should impair test performance. Indeed, performance was worst at 3:30 a.m. However, performance at 12:30 a.m. was as good as performance at 9:30 p.m., suggesting that the greater counteractive control in anticipation of the 12:30 a.m. testing prevented the lateness of the testing hour from impairing performance.

Together, these counteractive control and performance data support the goal-directedness assumption of CCT. Performing a test at midnight is much less convenient than performing it in the early evening. This, however, did not diminish interest in the midnight test. On the contrary, participants attached greater importance and emotional value to performing the midnight test than the early evening test. These self-control efforts prevented the midnight testing hour from impairing participants' performance. However, when the test was scheduled at an extremely inconvenient hour (3:30 a.m.), the attempts to boost the value of the test weakened, and performance drastically dropped. As predicted by the CCT goal-directedness assumption, then, self-control efforts were an inverted U-shaped function of the unpleasantness of the test. Initially, higher levels of unpleasantness intensified self-control efforts. Such efforts were apparently perceived as instrumental for test performance. However, when the unpleasantness of the test became too extreme to be compensated for by self-control efforts, these efforts lost their instrumental value and were no longer employed.

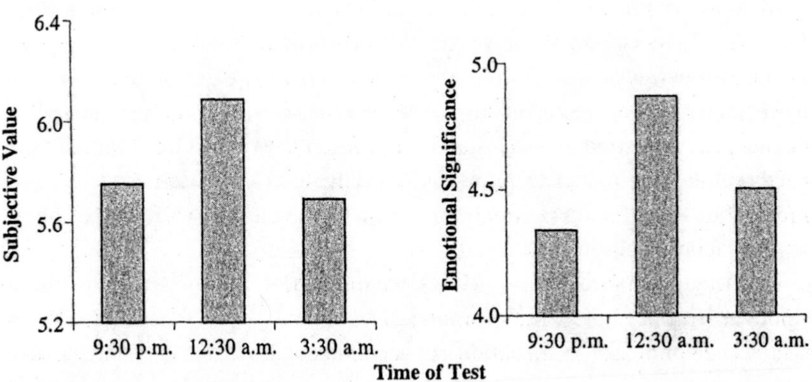

Figure 19.4 Subjective value and emotional significance of test by time of test (Trope & Fishbach, 2000, Study 4).

Positive Mood as a Resource

The preceding findings regarding nonmonotonic counteractive control are related to those obtained in research on the mood-as-a-resource hypothesis (see Trope, Ferguson, & Raghunathan, 2001; Trope & Neter, 1994; Trope & Pomerantz, 1998; see also Aspinwall, 1998; Aspinwall & Taylor, 1997; Reed & Aspinwall, 1998). According to this hypothesis, positive mood serves as a buffer against the immediate emotional cost of negative but diagnostic feedback and thereby facilitates the seeking and processing of such feedback. In our terms, the use of mood as a resource is a counteractive control strategy designed to overcome the immediate short-term costs of processing negative feedback. Most relevant here, one of Trope and Neter's studies examined the extent to which participants attend to positive information about themselves (and thus boost their mood) before receiving new feedback about themselves. This study found that when positive feedback was expected, participants made little effort to self-induce a positive mood. Attempts to self-induce a positive mood intensified when more negative feedback was anticipated. However, when the offered feedback was very negative and, therefore, too hard to accept, attempts to self-induce a positive mood declined. Consistent with the nonmonotonic counteractive control effect found by Trope and Fishbach (2000), these results demonstrate that attempts to self-induce a positive mood were most intense when they could determine one's feedback-seeking decision, namely, when the offered feedback was moderately negative.

Trope and Neter (1994) and Trope and Pomerantz (1998) also found that positive mood indeed increases people's interest in receiving feedback about their weaknesses in important performance domains. Importantly, Trope, Gervey, and Bolger (2003) found that this mood-incongruent information search was conditional on the usefulness of the offered feedback. When the feedback was diagnostic of an important ability, participants who were in a positive mood preferentially solicited and extensively processed feedback regarding their weaknesses. However, when the offered feedback was nondiagnostic or when it pertained to an unimportant ability, participants who were in a positive mood preferred to receive feedback regarding their strengths rather than their weaknesses. Apparently, when the offered feedback was not very useful, participants were primarily motivated to maintain their positive mood and, therefore, preferred to hear positively valenced rather than negatively valenced information.

Raghunathan and Trope (2002) extended the test of the mood-as-a-resource hypothesis to the processing of health-related persuasive messages (see also Aspinwall, 1998). Their studies assessed how mood (positive, neutral, or negative) influenced people's recall and acceptance of information regarding the health risks and benefits associated with their caffeine consumption habits. These studies found that people in a positive mood, compared to people in a neutral or negative mood, not only selectively seek but also better remember and accept negatively valenced information—information that specifies the health risks associated with their caffeine consumption habits. This processing strategy dampened participants' positive mood, but at the same time enhanced their willingness to give up unhealthy habits.

In sum, the studies reviewed in this section provide consistent support for the goal-directedness assumption of counteractive control. People exert counteractive control efforts when the attainment of important long-term goals is threatened, when attaining long-term goals is difficult but not impossible, and when counteractive control can contribute to attainment of these goals. Counteractive control thus seems to be a goal-directed process that serves to shield long-term goals from the influence of the immediate stimulus situation.

The Substitutability of Counteractive Control

Self-control is not the only means for overcoming the influence of the immediate situation. Sometimes an individual's long-term goals coincide with those of other persons, groups, or organizations. Employers may want their employees to undergo medical tests, parents may want their children to eat healthy food, and team members may expect each other to act cooperatively. Under such circumstances, social agents may use social control to ensure that individuals pursue their long-term goals. Social control may take various forms, including social monitoring, explicit requests, and social and material incentives. The question, then, is how these various forms of social control affect counteractive self-control. For example, we found that people self-impose higher penalties for failure to take an aversive test than a nonaversive test. Will the aversiveness of the test have the same effect on self-imposed penalties when taking the test is socially rewarded? Will higher temporary costs lead people to value an activity more positively when the activity is socially prescribed?

According to the CCT means-end analysis, counteractive control is an active process that helps individuals pursue long-term interests. The implications regarding the effect of social control are straightforward: In the absence of social control, counteractive self-control will be exercised because it determines the likelihood of pursuing long-term goals. In the presence of social control, counteractive self-control may become superfluous, as social control may be sufficient to maintain a high probability of acting according to long-term goals. Social control may thus substitute for self-control.

Consider, for example, the effects of social control on self-imposed penalties. In the absence of social control, people will self-impose higher penalties for failure to choose an activity with long-term value to the extent that the activity has short-term costs. Such penalties, in turn, will increase the likelihood of choosing the activity and will thus offset the impact of short-term costs. In contrast, when social control is exercised, self-imposed penalties will no longer be used as a counteractive self-control measure. That is, people will not set higher penalties for failure to perform an activity that has high short-term costs.

To test these substitutability predictions, Fishbach and Trope (in press) offered participants an opportunity to take a "cognitive test" and receive detailed feedback regarding their cognitive abilities. Participants were told that the test would be administered over the telephone the following night. The short-term cost of taking the test was varied by scheduling the test at either a convenient time (9 p.m.) or an inconvenient time (1 a.m.). Social control was varied by either offering or not offering a payment ($20) for taking the test. To assess self-imposed fines, participants were asked to indicate the amount of money they were prepared to pay as a cancellation fee if they failed to complete the test. To participants who were offered a payment, it was also made clear that, in addition to the cancellation fee, they would not receive the $20 payment if they failed to complete the test. Evaluative bolstering was assessed by asking participants to rate the importance of the test, its informativeness, the extent to which they expected to benefit personally from taking the test, and the extent to which they expected taking the test to be unpleasant. Finally, participants were asked to decide whether they actually intended to take the test.

Analysis of the self-imposed fines yielded the expected effect of payment for the test and inconvenience of the test. Replicating our earlier findings, the fines unpaid participants imposed on themselves were higher when the time of the test was inconvenient than when it was convenient. The higher penalty for failure to complete the inconveniently scheduled test indicates a counteractive attempt to overcome the influence of the temporary inconvenience of the test. In contrast, the fines paid participants imposed on themselves were unaffected by the inconvenience of the test. This finding suggests that payment eliminated the need to use the fines as a self-control strategy. In this respect, social control substituted for counteractive self-imposed penalties.

Analysis of participants' evaluations of the offered test also yielded the expected effect of the payment for the test and the convenience of the test. Unpaid participants evaluated the inconvenient test more positively than the convenient test, indicating counteractive evaluative bolstering of the value of the inconvenient test. In contrast, the evaluations by paid participants showed a more conventional effect of the inconvenience of the test, that is, a less positive evaluation of the inconvenient test than the convenient test. These participants apparently allowed the inconvenience of the test to diminish their evaluation of the test. Again, the promised payment substituted for evaluative bolstering of the inconvenient test.

Turning to the behavioral intention data, we found that, overall, payment significantly increased participants' interest in taking the test. This finding suggests that payment was an effective means of control over participants' decisions. More important, participants were no less interested in performing the 1 a.m. test than the 9 p.m. test. This finding, in conjunction with the finding that paid participants evaluated the 1 a.m. test more negatively, suggests that the payment prevented the negative evaluation of the 1 a.m. test from diminishing interest in the test. External control thus enabled the participants to maintain their interest in taking the test despite its temporary unpleasantness. In the absence of external control, the unpaid participants were apparently able to overcome the influence of the temporary unpleasantness of the 1 a.m. test by exercising counteractive self-control.

Path analyses of the behavioral intention data support this assumption (see figure 19.5). In these analyses, counteractive control (indexed by the self-imposed penalty and evaluative bolstering combined) served as a mediator. Considering first the unpaid participants, a negative direct path from lateness of the test to intention to take the test indicated that, in itself, lateness of the test acted to diminish these participants' willingness to take the test. However, the analysis also yielded a positive indirect path from lateness to counteractive control and from counteractive control to willingness to take the test. This path indicated that participants exercised greater counteractive control when considering the 1 a.m. test, which, in turn, offset the influence of the lateness of the test on participants' willingness to take the test. The path diagram for paid participants showed a marginal negative indirect path from lateness of the test to counteractive control and from counteractive control to willingness to take the test. This indirect path indicated that the lower evaluation of the 1 a.m. test acted to reduce the motivation to take the test. However, a null direct path from lateness to intention indicated that this reduced motivation did not affect participants' willingness to take this test. The payment was apparently sufficient to overcome the negative impact of lateness on participants' motivation.

Fishbach and Trope (in press) obtained similar results when the short-term costs of taking a test were the amount of time it required and its expected dullness and when social control was instituted by presenting the test as mandatory (rather than optional) or by monitoring whether the test was actually performed. The results of these studies are consistent with the CCT substitutability assumption. The temporary unpleasantness of an activity is an immediate cost that tempts people to avoid activities that have long-term value. In the absence of socially instituted means for overcoming this temptation, people try to ensure that they undertake the unpleasant activity by exercising counteractive self-control. Social controls help guarantee that an activity with long-term value is undertaken despite its temporary unpleasantness. Counteractive control efforts under these circumstances are superfluous, and

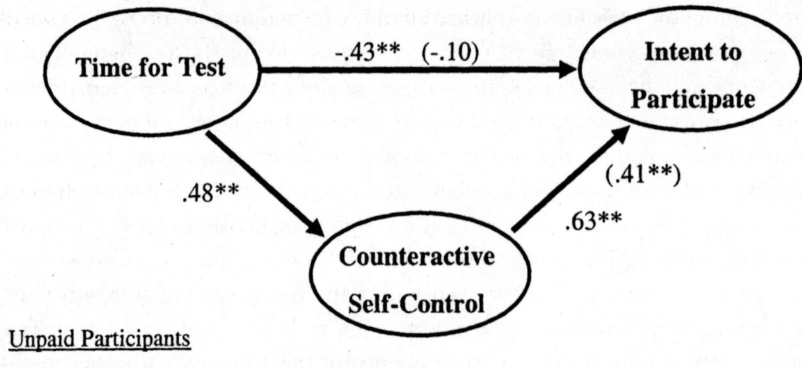

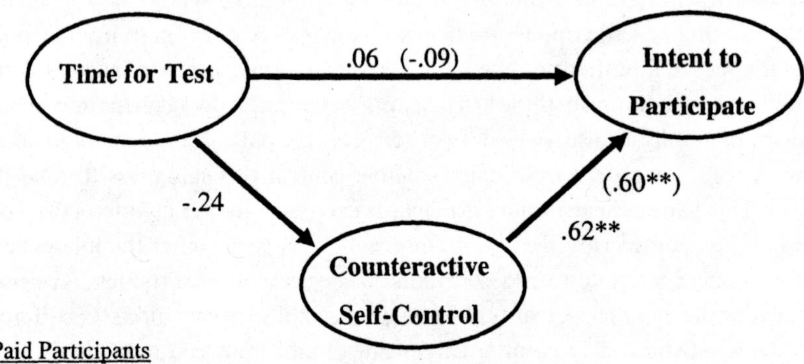

Figure 19.5. Path model of the influence of lateness on intention to take a test. Numbers in parentheses are zero-order standardized betas. $^{**}p < .05$ (Fishbach & Trope, in press).

people can allow the short-term costs of an activity to reduce their evaluation of the activity without reducing the likelihood of undertaking the activity. Self-control and social control are thus substitutable in that self-control is exercised only in the absence of social control.

Resource-Dependent Counteractive Control

Our research shows that people do not engage in counteractive control unless it is necessary for protecting their long-term interests. Counteractive control is exercised only when there is a threat to important long-term goals, when these goals are achievable, before rather than after the achievement of these goals, and when social controls are absent. One possible reason for this selectivity is that counteractive control is an effortful process. By definition, the immediate unpleasantness of an activity makes it unattractive. The counteractive control strategies needed to overcome this immediate tendency—convincing oneself that the activity is worthwhile and precommitting oneself to undertaking it—may require considerable cognitive and emotional resources. People are therefore unlikely to use such resources unless they are necessary for attaining their long-term goals.

Consistent with this analysis, research on ego depletion by Baumeister, Muraven, and their colleagues found that exercising self-control in one task depletes a person's ability to exercise self-control in a subsequent task (Baumeister et al., 1998; Baumeister, Heatherton, & Tice, 1994; Leith & Baumeister, 1996; Muraven, Tice, & Baumeister, 1998). Self-control in these studies apparently came at the expense of participants' emotional resources. It is possible, however, that ego depletion occurs only as a result of actual exposure to temptation. The question, then, is whether counteractive control exercised proactively—before exposure to temptation—is also resource dependent. A related question is whether counteractive control depends on cognitive resources, not only emotional resources. We conducted two studies to address these questions (Fishbach & Trope, 2002).

One study examined counteractive control by high school students before or after an important matriculation exam. Our earlier research shows that people exert more counteractive control before rather than after an academic exam (Trope & Fishbach, 2000). We predicted, however, that this should depend on students' cognitive resources. To test this prediction, we administered to students a questionnaire assessing evaluative bolstering of the value of studying either 1 week before or 1 week after the exam. Students responded to the questionnaire under either cognitive load (holding in memory a seven-digit number) or no cognitive load. The questionnaire included a variety of questions regarding the importance of studying and getting high grades.

Participants' answers to these questions were combined into an overall index of evaluative bolstering. Under no load, we found greater evaluative bolstering of studying before the exam than after the exam. However, under load, evaluative bolstering before and after the exam did not significantly differ. It seems, then, that cognitive load interfered with students' ability to bolster the value of studying before an exam. Under cognitive load, students were unable to motivate themselves to study when studying could determine their performance.

More relevant to the question of resource-dependent counteractive control is how cognitive load affects people's responses to increasing short-term costs of an activity with long-term benefits. The signature of counteractive control is that when an activity serves long-term goals, it is valued more positively when it has high rather than low short-term costs. If counteractive control is a resource-dependent process, then cognitive load should eliminate this positive relationship between short-term costs of an activity and the tendency to evaluate the activity more positively. Moreover, our earlier research shows that counteractive control actually helps offset the influence of short-term costs on people's decisions (Trope & Fishbach, 2000). Cognitive load should therefore diminish people's ability to resist the influence of short-term costs on their decisions.

We used the late-night testing paradigm (Trope & Fishbach, 2000, Study 4) to test these predictions. Participants were offered an opportunity to take a cognitive ability test, to be administered over the telephone, at either a convenient time (8 p.m.) or an inconvenient time (1 a.m.). The lateness of testing is a temporary inconvenience that should elicit evaluative bolstering of taking the test. Evaluative bolstering was assessed by asking participants to respond to a questionnaire regarding the importance of taking the test, the importance of feedback from the test, and a variety of study-related self-standards. The questions were answered either under cognitive load (silently counting even numbers) or under no cognitive load. After responding to this questionnaire, participants indicated their interest in actually taking the test.

As before, we combined participants' responses into an overall index of evaluative bolstering. The results from the no-load condition replicated our earlier findings; that is, the test was evaluated more positively when it was scheduled for 1 a.m. than for 8 p.m. This positive relationship between lateness of the test and the subjective value of taking it is indicative of counteractive control. The opposite pattern of results emerged under cognitive load; that is, the 8 p.m. test was evaluated more positively than the 1 a.m. test. Here, inconvenience reduced the attractiveness of taking the test. This standard effect of inconvenience indicates that cognitive load eliminated counteractive control. Under load, participants seemed unable to convince themselves that taking a very late night test was highly valuable.

Turning to the intention data (see figure 19.6), the results for the no-load condition showed that lateness of testing did not reduce participants' willingness to take the test. Path analysis showed that this null effect reflected the operation of counteractive control. Specifically, in itself the lateness of the test acted to reduce willingness to take it, as indicated by the negative direct path from lateness to intention to take the test (controlling for evaluative bolstering). However, this negative direct effect was offset by a positive indirect path from lateness to evaluative bolstering and from evaluative bolstering to intention to take the test. As in our earlier research, then, counteractive control prevented inconvenience from affecting intentions to take a diagnostic test.

A different pattern of results was obtained for the cognitive-load condition. Here, lateness of testing did reduce participants' willingness to take the test.

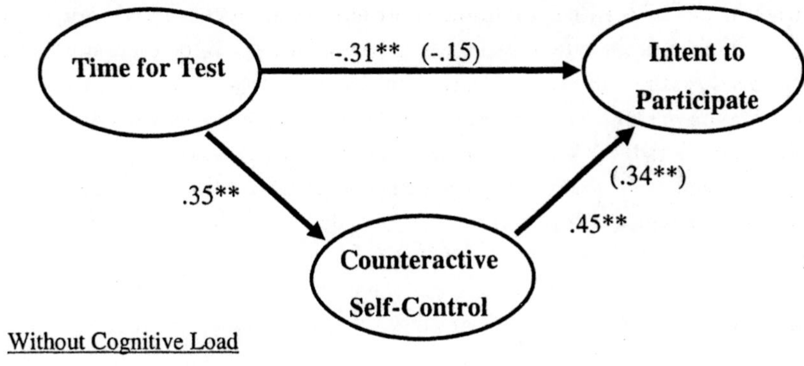

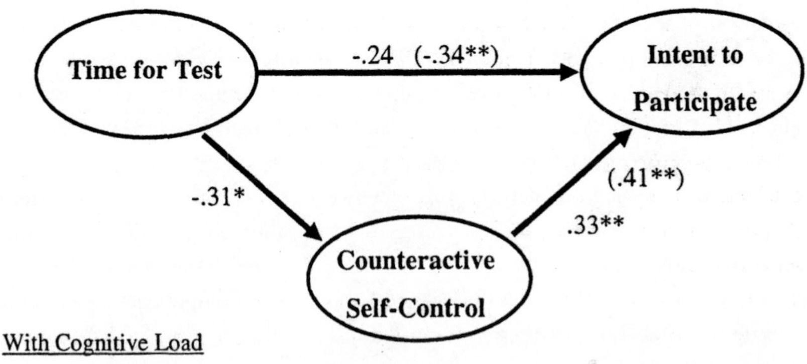

Figure 19.6 Path model of the influence of lateness on intention to take a test, in the absence and in the presence of cognitive load. Numbers in parentheses are zero-order standardized betas. $*p < .07$; $**p < .05$ (Fishbach & Trope, 2002).

Path analysis showed that this effect was partially mediated by the evaluation of the test. Specifically, lateness decreased test evaluation, which in turn diminished willingness to take the test. Controlling for this negative indirect effect of lateness on intention, the negative effect of lateness on intention became insignificant. Thus, under cognitive load, participants evaluated the inconvenient test more negatively, and this negative evaluation undermined their willingness to actually take the test.

Together, the results of these studies demonstrate the dependence of counteractive control on cognitive resources. Temporary unpleasantness of an activity naturally deters people from undertaking it even when it serves their long-term interests. When people possess cognitive resources, people are able to convince themselves that this activity is particularly valuable. The more unpleasant the activity, the harder they try to reach such conviction. This, in turn, enables them to actually undertake the activity. However, when processing resources are limited, people seem less capable of exercising such counteractive control strategies. Instead, temporary unpleasantness of an activity simply reduces its attractiveness. People's ability to resist the influence of short-term costs is reduced, and their willingness to actually undertake the activity is undermined.

Implicit Counteractive Self-Control

The preceding research suggests that at least some forms of self-control involve deliberate reasoning. People may consciously consider their long-term goals, assess the threat short-term costs pose for these goals, evaluate alternative counteractive self-control strategies, and implement the one that seems the most effective. Evaluative bolstering, for example, would reflect, then, a conscious attempt to overcome the influence of short-term costs by selectively attending to information that emphasizes long-term goals. It is possible, however, that intentional self-control is sometimes supplemented and even supplanted by more implicit forms of self-control. Long-term goals are often in conflict with immediate, situationally elicited motives. Over time, people may acquire effective counteractive strategies for resolving such conflicts (Metcalfe & Mischel, 1999; Mischel, 1974; Mischel et al., 1988; Rachlin, 1995, 1997; Shoda et al., 1990). With frequent and successful applications of counteractive control strategies, people may develop efficient ways of anticipating certain self-control problems, accessing appropriate counteractive control strategies, and applying them proactively. Counteractive control may thus become a well-practiced skill, and at least some forms of counteractive control may require very little conscious intention.

In the simplest form of counteractive control, exposure to short-term costs may automatically activate one's long-term goals and thus prevent these costs from affecting one's behavior. For example, exposure to tempting food may activate a restrained eater's weight-watching goals, which in turn may enable the restrained eater to overcome the temptation. Some, if not all, of the steps in this process may be performed without conscious intention. Importantly, subliminal exposure to food may be sufficient to activate weight-watching goals. Exposure to tempting food may thus unconsciously boost rather than undermine the restrained eaters' resolve. Moreover, the enhanced accessibility of weight-watching goals may persist over time. As a result, initial subliminal exposure to tempting food may improve the restrained eaters' resistance to subsequent temptations. The logic here is similar to that of the priming effect in Trope and Fishbach (2000, Study 5). As described above, this study found that priming social goals before a midterm exam enhanced students' evaluation of the importance of the exam, which in turn improved the students' performance on the exam. In general, by activating an individual's long-term goals, exposure to immediate temptation may produce implicit inoculation, making the individual more resistant to subsequent temptation.

Initial evidence for implicit counteractive self-control has been obtained by Fishbach, Friedman, and Kruglanski (2003). These studies suggest that subliminal presentation of a construct representing a potentially obstructive temptation facilitates the activation level of a construct representing a potentially obstructed goal. For example, one of these studies (Fishbach et al., Study 1) used participants' self-reported goals and temptations to obtain goal-temptation pairs such as "study-basketball." This study found that goal-related keywords (e.g., *study*) were more quickly recognized following subliminal presentation of temptation-related keywords (e.g., *basketball*) than following subliminal presentation of temptation-unrelated primes (e.g., *chocolate*). Interestingly, this effect was asymmetrical; that is, whereas goal recognition was facilitated by temptation primes (e.g., academic targets were facilitated by procrastination primes), temptation recognition was inhibited by goal primes (e.g., procrastination targets were inhibited by academic primes). Subsequent studies found that temptation-goal activation was independent of available cognitive resources (Fishbach et al., Study 2), more pronounced for successful self-regulators (Studies 3–4), and increasing with subjective importance of a goal (Study 4). It seems, then, that implicit self-control develops over the course of successful implementation of self-control and, like explicit counteractive control, depends on the subjective importance of the overriding goal.

In still another study, temptation-related cues were supraliminal but incidental aspects of the situation (Fishbach et al., 2003, Study 5). In this study, restrained eaters were observed in three situations: a room with popular fatty foods (temptation prime), a room with weight-watching magazines (dieting prime), and a room with general interest magazines (neutral prime). These priming stimuli were allegedly irrelevant to the purpose of the experiment. It was found that priming the temptation to consume fattening food, like priming the goal of dieting, facilitated recognition of *diet* in a subsequent lexical decision task. Moreover, when offered a gift, participants in the fattening food and in the diet prime conditions preferred to get an apple rather than a chocolate bar, whereas participants in the neutral condition preferred chocolate. Finally, participants in the fattening food prime condition expressed greater willingness to avoid tempting food than participants in the dieting and the neutral prime conditions.

These findings suggest that counteractive boosting of long-term goals (e.g., dieting) and the resulting resistance to temptation (e.g., fatty food) may be implicit processes. It is possible, then, that counteractive self-control is a dual-process mechanism. This mechanism may be operate in an explicit mode—intentionally, consciously, and effortfully—but it may also operate in an implicit mode—unintentionally, unconsciously, and uneffortfully. How are the two modes of counteractive control related? Does the implicit mode precede the explicit mode? Does the implicit mode substitute for the explicit mode? Do the two modes of counteractive control occur simultaneously? These are important questions for future research on self-control.

Conclusion

Self-control problems arise when the immediate situation elicits short-term wishes and desires that are in conflict with long-term goals. People may prefer to pursue their long-term goals and may possess the prerequisite skills and freedom of choice. Nevertheless, they may be uncertain that this is what they will actually do. People may suspect that in the actual situation they will be unable to resist the temptation posed by the immediate outcomes. Counteractive control strategies are designed to enable people to act according to their long-term goals despite the short-term costs of such action.

This chapter reviewed research on the antecedents, consequences, and process of counteractive control. Some counteractive control strategies change the choice alternatives, whereas others change the subjective evaluation of the alternatives. People may change the choice alternatives by attaching a punishment or reward to their choices or by precommitting themselves to the preferable alternative and thus eliminating others. The subjective value of the choice alternatives may be changed by bolstering the value of acting according to long-term goals and linking such action to emotional gratification and central self-standards. Counteractive control thus proactively changes the motivational givens of the situation in favor of pursuing long-term goals. With counteractive controls in place, the situation can exert strong and even automatic influence over behavior without jeopardizing individuals' long-term interests.

The signature of counteractive control is that it increases the value of acting according to long-term goals to the extent that such action has high short-term costs. Without counteractive control, an action becomes less attractive when it is associated with high short-term costs. The sacrifices that are required by dieting, exercising, or studying ordinarily reduce the attractiveness of engaging in these activities. Our research shows that counteractive control acts to increase the attractiveness of such activities in direct proportion to their temporary unpleasantness. As a result, counteractive control helps maintain a high probability of pursuing long-term goals despite the short-term costs this may entail. This enables people to set long-term goals and formulate plans for achieving them with a sense of assurance that they will not be tempted to deviate from their plans in a way they will later regret.

Our research also shows that counteractive control is a flexible, goal-directed process. First, people seem to exercise counteractive control when short-term costs threaten their ability to pursue important rather than unimportant long-term goals. Second, counteractive control is exercised before but not after performing the preferred activity. Before performing an activity, counteractive control could help participants choose and carry out the activity, whereas after performing the activity, counteractive control ceases to have instrumental value and could only reduce dissonance and regret (Aronson, 1997; Cooper & Fazio, 1984; Festinger, 1957). Third, counteractive control efforts are an inverted U-shaped function of short-term costs. When short-term costs are very low, counteractive control is unnecessary. When these costs are very high, counteractive control is insufficient. It is only at intermediate levels of short-term costs that counteractive control determines whether long-term goals will be pursued. It is therefore at this level that counteractive control efforts are maximally exerted. Finally, counteractive control is substitutable. People's exposure to short-term outcomes does not occur in a social vacuum. Social interactants, groups, and organizations may institute incentives, sanctions, and rules that are designed to help individuals overcome temptations. People seem sensitive to such alternative means of control. Counteractive control is exercised when it is necessary for achieving long-term goals. When other, external means of control are in place, counteractive control ceases.

The flexibility and goal directedness of counteractive control strategies does not necessarily mean that the use of these strategies is always based on conscious deliberation. Like any knowledge, counteractive control strategies may be automatized after being repeatedly and successfully employed in resolving previous self-control problems. As a result, people may exercise very little conscious control in carrying out some or all of the steps in counteractive control. People may identify the threat to their long-term goals, use a self-control strategy (e.g., evaluative boosting of long-term goals), and consequently pursue their long-term goals more vigorously without being aware of the relationships among these steps or consciously intending to carry them out. People may be aware of the threat to their long-term goals and aware of their self-control efforts, without realizing that it is the threat that caused the self-control efforts. A student may attribute his preoccupation with an upcoming exam to the importance of the exam itself rather than to situational temptations not to study for the exam. In general, people may see their biased evaluations and precommitments as reflecting the inherent value of the available options rather than as means to the end of overcoming the threat posed by short-term outcomes. Our research has been primarily concerned with the conscious and deliberate aspects of counteractive control. Examining the less conscious aspects of counteractive control and how they relate to conscious aspects of counteractive control remains an interesting topic for future research.

Acknowledgments The research reported in this chapter was supported by National Institutes of Mental Health Grant 1R01MH59030-01A1 and National Science Foundation Grant SBR-9808675 to the first author.

References

Ainslie, G. (1975). Specious reward: A behavioral theory of impulsiveness and impulse control. *Psychological Bulletin, 82*, 463–496.

Ainslie, G. (1992). *Picoeconomics: The strategic interaction of successive motivational states within the person.* Cambridge, UK: Cambridge University Press.

Aronson, E. (1997). The theory of cognitive dissonance: The evolution and vicissitude of an idea. In: C. McGarty & A. Halsam (Eds.), *The message of social psychology: Perspective on mind in society* (pp. 20–35). Cambridge, MA: Blackwell.

Asch, S. E. (1952). Effects of group pressure on the modification and distortion of judgments. In G. E. Swanson, T. M. Newcomb, & E. L. Hartley (Eds.), *Readings in social psychology* (2nd ed., pp. 2–11). New York: Holt.

Aspinwall, L. G. (1998). Rethinking the role of positive affect in self-regulation. *Motivation and Emotion, 22*, 1–32.

Aspinwall, L. G., & Taylor, S. E. (1997). A stitch in time: Self-regulation and proactive coping. *Psychological Bulletin, 121*, 417–436.

Atkinson, J. W., & Birch, D. (1978). *An introduction to motivation.* New York: Van Nostrand.

Atkinson, J. W., & Feather, N. T. (Eds.). (1966). *A theory of achievement motivation.* New York: Wiley.

Bandura, A. (1989). Self-regulation of motivation and action through internal standards and goal systems. In L. A. Pervin (Ed.), *Goal concept in personality and social psychology* (pp. 19–85). Hillsdale, NJ: Erlbaum.

Bargh, J. A. (1990). Auto-motives: Preconscious determinants of social interaction. In E. T. Higgins & R. M. Sorrentino (Eds.), *Handbook of motivation and cognition* (Vol. 2, pp. 93–130). New York: Guilford.

Bargh, J. A. (1994). The four horsemen of automaticity: Awareness, intention, efficiency and control in social cognition. In R. S. Wyer & T. K. Srull (Eds.), *Handbook of social cognition* (Vol. 1, 2nd ed., pp. 1–40). Hillsdale, NJ: Erlbaum.

Bargh, J. A., & Chartrand, T. L. (1999). The unbearable automaticity of being. *American Psychologist, 54*, 462–479.

Baumeister, R. F., Bratslavsky, E., Muraven, M., & Tice, D. M. (1998). Ego depletion: Is the active self a limited resource? *Journal of Personality and Social Psychology, 74*, 1252–1265.

Baumeister, R. F., & Heatherton, T. F. (1996). Self-regulation failure: An overview. *Psychological Inquiry, 7*, 1–15.

Baumeister, R. F., Heatherton, T. F., & Tice, D. M. (1994). *Losing control: How and why people fail at self-regulation.* San Diego: Academic Press.

Becker, H. S. (1960). Notes on the concept of commitment. *American Journal of Sociology, 66*, 32–40.

Beckmann, J., & Kuhl, J. (1984). Altering information to gain action control: Functional aspects of human information processing in decision making. *Journal of Research in Personality, 18*, 224–237.

Brehm, J. W., & Self, E. A. (1989). The intensity of motivation. *Annual Review of Psychology, 40*, 109–131.

Brehm, J. W., Wright, R. A., Solomon, S., Silka, L., & Greenberg, J. (1983). Perceived difficulty, energization, and the magnitude of goal valence. *Journal of Experimental Social Psychology, 19*, 21–48.

Brickman, P. (1987). *Commitment, conflict, and caring*. Englewood Cliffs, NJ: Prentice-Hall.

Cartwright, D. (1959). *Studies in social power*. Ann Arbor, MI: Institute for Social Research.

Cooper, J., & Fazio, R. H. (1984). A new look at dissonance theory. In L. Berkowitz (Ed.), *Advances in experimental social psychology* (Vol. 17, pp. 229–264). Orlando, FL: Academic Press.

Festinger, L. (1957). *A theory of cognitive dissonance*. Evanston, IL: Row, Peterson.

Fishbach, A., Friedman, R. S., & Kruglanski, A. W. (2003). Leading us not into temptation: Momentary allurements elicit overriding goal activation. *Journal of Personality and Social Psychology, 84*(2), 296–309.

Fishbach, A., & Trope, Y. (in press). *The substitutability of external control and self-control*.

Fishbach, A., & Trope, Y. (2002). *Resource-dependent counteractive self-control*. Unpublished manuscript.

Gollwitzer, P. M. (1990). Action phases and mind-sets. In R. M. Sorrentino & E. T. Higgins (Eds.), *Handbook of motivation and cognition: Foundations of social behavior* (Vol. 2, pp. 53–92). New York: Guilford.

Gollwitzer, P. M. (1999). Implementation intentions: Strong effects of simple plans. *American Psychologist, 54*, 493–503.

Gollwitzer, P. M., & Bayer, U. (1999). Deliberative versus implemental mindsets in the control of action. In S. Chaiken & Y. Trope (Eds.), *Dual process theories in social psychology* (pp. 403–422). New York: Guilford.

Gollwitzer, P. M., & Brandstatter, V. (1997). Implementation intentions and effective goal pursuit. *Journal of Personality and Social Psychology, 73*, 186–199.

Green, L., & Rachlin, H. (1996). Commitment using punishment. *Journal of the Experimental Analysis of Behavior, 65*, 593–601.

Kuhl, J. (1982). Action vs. state-orientation as a mediator between motivation and action. In W. Hacker, W. Volpert, & M. Von Cranach (Eds.), *Cognitive and motivational aspects of action* (pp. 67–85). Berlin: VEB.

Kuhl, J. (1984). Volitional aspects of achievement motivation and learned helplessness: Toward a comprehensive theory of action control. In: B. A. Maher (Ed.), *Progress in experimental personality research* (Vol. 13, pp. 99–171). New York: Academic Press.

Kuhl, J. (1986). Motivation and information processing: A new look at decision making, dynamic change and action control. In: R. M. Sorrentino & E. T. Higgins (Eds.), *Handbook of motivation and cognition: Foundations of social behavior* (pp. 404–434). New York: Guilford.

Kuhl, J., & Beckmann, J. (1985). *Action control from cognition to behavior*. New York: Springer-Verlag.

Kukla, A. (1974). Performance as a function of resultant achievement motivation (perceived ability) and perceived difficulty. *Journal of Research in Personality, 7*, 374–383.

Leith, K. P., & Baumeister, R. (1996). Why do bad moods increase self-defeating behavior? Emotion, risk taking, and self-regulation. *Journal of Personality and Social Psychology, 71*, 1250–1267.

Lewin, K. (1935). *The dynamic theory of personality*. New York: McGraw-Hill.

Loewenstein, G. (1996). Out of control: Visceral influences on behavior. *Organizational Behavior and Human Decision Process, 65*, 272–292.

Metcalfe, J., & Mischel, W. (1999). A hot/cool-system analysis of delay of gratification: Dynamics and willpower. *Psychological Review, 106*, 3–19.

Milgram, S. (1963). Behavioral study of obedience. *Journal of Abnormal and Social Psychology, 67*, 371–378.

Mischel, W. (1974). Processes in delay of gratification. In L. Berkowits (Ed.), *Advances in experimental social psychology* (Vol. 7, pp. 249–292). San Diego, CA: Academic Press.

Mischel, W. (1984). Convergences and challenges in the search for consistency. *American Psychologist, 39*, 351–364.

Mischel, W., Cantor, N., & Feldman, S. (1996). Principles of self-regulation: The nature of willpower and self-control. In E. T. Higgins & A. W. Kruglanski (Eds.), *Social psychology: Handbook of basic principles* (pp. 329–360). New York: Guilford.

Mischel, W., Shoda, Y., & Peake, P. K. (1988). The nature of adolescent competencies predicted by preschool delay of gratification. *Journal of Personality and Social Psychology, 54*, 687–696.

Mischel, W., Shoda, Y., & Rodriguez, M. L. (1989). Delay of gratification in children. *Science, 244*, 933–938.

Muraven, M., Tice, D. M., & Baumeister, R. F. (1998) Self-control as limited resource: Regulatory depletion patterns. *Journal of Personality and Social Psychology, 74*, 774–789.

Rachlin, H. (1995). Self-control: Beyond commitment. *Behavioral and Brain Sciences, 18*, 109–159.

Rachlin, H. (1996). Can we leave cognition to cognitive psychologists? Comment on an article by George Loewenstein. *Organizational Behavior and Human Decision Process, 65*, 296–299.

Rachlin, H. (1997). Self and self-control. *Annals of the New York Academy of Sciences, 818*, 85–97.

Rachlin, H., & Green, L. (1972). Commitment, choice and self-control. *Journal of the Experimental Analysis of Behavior, 17*, 15–22.

Raghunathan, R., & Trope, Y. (2002). Walking the tightrope between feeling good and being accurate: Mood as a resource in processing persuasive messages. *Journal of Personality and Social Psychology, 83*(3), 510–525.

Reed, M. B., & Aspinwall, L. G. (1998). Self-affirmation reduces biased processing of health-risk information. *Motivation and Emotion, 22*, 99–132.

Ross, L., & Nisbett, R. E. (1991). *The person and the situation: Perspectives of social psychology*. New York: McGraw-Hill.

Schelling, T. (1984). Self command in practice, in theory and in a theory of rational choice. *American Economic Review, 74*, 1–11.

Schelling, T. C. (1978). Egonomics, or the art of self-management. *American Economic Review, 68*, 290–294.

Shoda, Y., Mischel, W., & Peake, P. K. (1990). Predicting adolescent cognitive and self-regulatory competencies from preschool delay of gratification: Identifying diagnostic conditions. *Developmental Psychology, 26*, 978–986.

Shultz, T. R., & Lepper, M. R. (1996). Cognitive dissonance reduction as constraint satisfaction. *Psychological Review, 103*, 219–240.

Strotz, R. H. (1956). Myopia and inconsistency in dynamic utility maximization. *Review of Economic Studies, 23*, 166–180.

Thaler, R. H. (1994). *Quasi rational economics*. New York: Russel Sage Foundation.

Thaler, R. H., & Shefrin, H. M. (1981). An economic theory of self-control. *Journal of Political Economy, 89*, 392–406.

Trope, Y., Ferguson, M., & Raghunathan, R. (2001). Mood as a resource in processing self-relevant information. In J. P. Forgas (Ed.), *Handbook of affect and social cognition* (pp. 256–274). Hillsdale, NJ: Erlbaum.

Trope, Y., & Fishbach, A. (2000). Counteractive self-control in overcoming temptation. *Journal of Personality and Social Psychology, 79*, 493–506.

Trope, Y., Gervey, B., & Bolger, N. (2003). The role of perceived control in overcoming defensive self-evaluation. *Journal of Experimental Social Psychology, 39*, 407–419.

Trope, Y., & Neter, E. (1994). Reconciling competing motives in self-evaluation: The role of self-control in feedback seeking. *Journal of Personality and Social Psychology, 66*, 646–657.

Trope, Y., & Pomerantz, E. M. (1998). Resolving conflicts among self-evaluative motives: Positive experiences as a resource for overcoming defensiveness. *Motivation and Emotion, 22*, 53–72.

Wegner, D. M., & Bargh, J. A. (1998). Control and automaticity in social life. In: D. T. Gilbert & S. T. Fiske (Eds.), *The handbook of social psychology* (Vol. 2, 4th ed., pp. 446–496). Boston: McGraw-Hill.

Wright, R. A., & Brehm, J. W. (1984). The impact of task difficulty upon perception of arousal and goal attractiveness in an avoidance paradigm. *Motivation and Emotion, 8*, 171–181.

Author Index

Subject Index